The Proceedings of the Thirteenth West Coast Conference on Formal Linguistics

The Proceedings of the Thirteenth West Coast Conference on Formal Linguistics

edited by Raul Aranovich, William Byrne,
Susanne Preuss, & Martha Senturia

Published for the
Stanford Linguistics Association
by the
Center for the Study of Language and Information

Printed in the United States

ISBN 1–881526–76–3
ISSN 1042–1068

∞The recycled, acid-free paper used in this book meets the minimum requirements of the American National Standard for Information Sciences—Permanence of Paper for Printed Library Materials, ANSI Z39.48-1984.

Contents

Phonology

Syntax

Preface

This volume is organized into four sections: phonology, syntax, syntax/semantics, and semantics. As always, this should not be taken as a strict division since some papers could be appropriately placed in more than one category. Within each section, papers are arranged in alphabetical order. The volume begins with S.-Y. Kuroda's welcoming speech given the morning of the first day of the conference. We believe the themes and tone of the conference are reflected in his opening remarks. We would like to thank the contributors and participants of WCCFL XIII for making it a successful conference.

The editors

Raúl Aranovich, William Byrne, Susanne Preuss, Martha Senturia

Introduction

S.-Y. KURODA
University of California, San Diego

I would like to welcome you to the Thirteenth WCCFL. The notorious Southern California weather seems to be welcoming you, too. Let me start with a personal note. For some time now, when I attend a meeting like NELS or WCCFL, I find that I am one of the oldest, or perhaps *the* oldest, among the attendees. (LSA is different; I feel very young at LSA; in fact, I may be on the job market at next year's LSA.) It's now over 30 years since I started my graduate work in the United States. If you project 30 years or so back from then, you reach the year Bloomfield's *Language* was published. The publication of Bloomfield's *Language* must have looked like ancient history to beginning graduate students at MIT 30 years ago. No wonder, then, if I look like ancient history to you. Thirty years is in fact a long time for a vigorously active science like linguistics. You may feel that a generation is passing, and we seem to be again at a crossroads, with a sense of uncertainty as well as of expectation. Is the sudden sweep of optimality theory across the field of phonology the sure sign of a coming era, or does it remind us of the rise and fall of generative semantics? Where is the minimalist program leading us? or leading them? How will the younger attendees here look back on this meeting of WCCFL 30 years hence? We can only speculate.

In a recent issue of *The New York Times Book Review*, a passage from a book by the physicist Michio Katu is quoted. Discussing string theory, he states: "we are able to turn a few dials and press a few buttons with the theory, and out pops the supergravity theory, ... But we are at a loss to explain why it works..." (does it not sound somewhat familiar?) "...while 21st century physics fell accidentally into the 20th century, 21st century mathematics hasn't been invented yet."

Linguistic theory is not as closely tied to mathematics as physics is. Nonetheless, there certainly is an underlying bass note, from Bloomfieldian and post-Bloomfieldian structuralism through generative grammar, that has echoed with contemporary mathematical thought. Certain trends in mathematics have influenced the development of linguistic thought in an indirect but fairly substantial manner: the spirit of abstract and finite mathematics has made a mark on structuralism[1], and formal logic or the theory of formal systems on generative grammar. But now we connect strings minimally and arrange constraints optimally and out pop universalist accounts of syntax and phonology. We seem also to be at a loss to explain why it works. Perhaps we might also wonder if 21st century mathematics hasn't yet been invented for formal linguistics, either.

Changing perspectives, we note that both in syntax and phonology, research has been developing in neurolinguistics and phonetics that relates the results of formal studies to concrete physical measurements. We seem to be ready to ground formal constructs on empirical bases.

We are assembled here at an exciting time. I wish you an enjoyable and productive three days; I hope you will long remember this conference for the number of small steps, if not a giant leap forward, that you will have taken, toward the formal linguistics of the 21st century.

---

[1] It may be worthwhile to mention that a hint of reverse influence is also found. André Weil, one of the founding members of Bourbaki, testifies that notable progess was made in Bourbaki's enterprise when the notion of structure was adopted and, believes that it is not a mere coincidence that this word had already been in the vocabulary of linguists, as he had had contacts with the linguists' circle, in particular, with Emile Benveniste. See Weil, A. (1991). *Souvenirs d'appretissage*, Birkhaeuser, Boston.

Phonology

Barra Gaelic Vowel Copy and (non-)Constituent Spreading

MÁIRE NÍ CHIOSÁIN
University College Dublin

1. Introduction

An underlying assumption of Feature Geometry accounts of assimilation processes is that spreading processes involve constituents - single features or class nodes. Spreading of more than one feature in a single process is generally taken to argue for grouping such features together as dependents of a single node which is then the target of the spreading process, e.g. Clements (1985), McCarthy (1988). Thus Nasal Place Assimilation in which, for example, N + b, N + g and N + gb become mb, ŋg and ŋmgb, respectively, is typically represented as spreading of the Place node as in (1). Spreading of the Place node involves spreading of all dependent place features.

[1]I would like to thank Jaye Padgett for valuable discussion. I would also like to thank an audience at UC Santa Cruz for helpful comments on an earlier version of this paper.

(1)

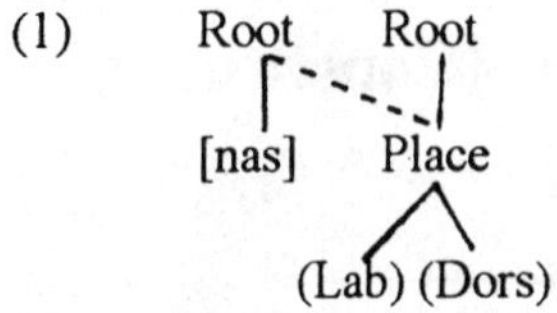

Such processes have also been represented as spreading of individual features (to varying degrees and with varying assumptions), by e.g. Selkirk (1988, 1991), Padgett (1991, 1994), Halle (1993) and Halle & Vaux (1994), (see also Steriade 1987, Goldsmith 1990:296). Under this view, the same Nasal Place Assimilation process is represented by spreading the individual place features, as in (2); (2)a after Padgett (1991, 1994) (where class nodes are omitted from the representation), (2)b after Halle (1993), Halle & Vaux (1994) (where class nodes are retained in the representation).

(2) (a) Root Root [nas] (Lab) (Dors) (b) Root Root [nas] Place Place (Lab) (Dors)

Within these approaches, we might expect that spreading processes need not in every case be restricted to constituents (all members of a class), as in the first approach outlined and illustrated in (1) above. Rather, with individual feature spreading, we might expect that spreading processes could also involve NON-CONSTITUENTS, that is less than all members of a class or all features dominated by the same class node[2]. However, non-constituent spreading would arguably occur only when individual features within a class targeted by a particular spreading process were prevented from spreading (e.g. by the Line Crossing Prohibition).

Non-constituent spreading has been argued for by e.g. Sagey (1988), Halle (1993), Halle & Vaux (1994) and Padgett (1994). Barra Gaelic Vowel Copy has been argued by the former three researchers to involve such spreading, (see also Clements 1986). The relevant argument made in these works can be summarized as follows: In Barra Gaelic what looks like spreading of all vowel features to an epenthetic vowel is blocked only by a [back] specification on an intervening consonant. In that case, the height features and [round] (which is contrastive in the back vowels) spread from the first vowel to the epenthetic vowel. Since these features do not form a natural grouping, the spreading process is argued to be

---

[2]The targets of a single spreading process are, however, restricted to membership of a class in the works cited above.

non-constituent spreading, with the vowel features spreading individually, as in (3).

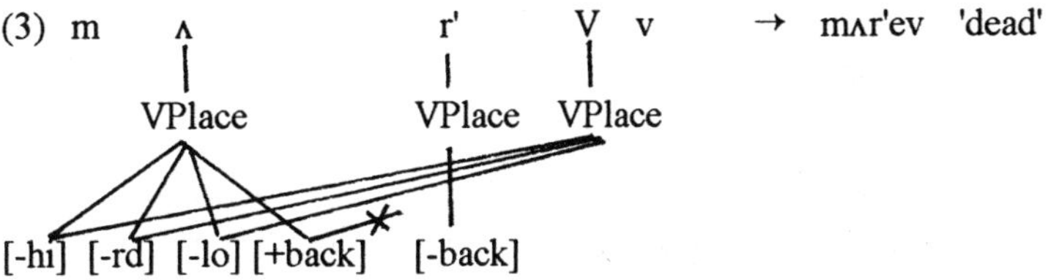

This paper presents a reevaluation of the data from Barra Gaelic used to argue for non-constituent spreading, and concludes that it involves Height spreading only, with other vowel features independently determined. Only data involving low vowels may actually require spreading of the non-constituent Height and [round]. However, these facts require further investigation.

2. Barra Gaelic Epenthesis

The short vowel and consonant inventories of Barra Gaelic are given in (4) and (5). The data discussed are taken from the traditional descriptions of Borgstrøm (1937, 1940). The vowel inventory in (4) was adapted by Clements (1986) from Borgstrøm; C' = palatalized consonant.

(4)			
	i	ɨ	u
	e	ʌ	o
	æ	a	O

(5)			
	p	t t'	k k'
	b	d d'	g g'
	f	s s'	x x'
	v		ɣ
	m	n N N'	ŋ ŋ'
		l' L L'	
		r r' R	
			j

Barra Gaelic epenthesis, illustrated in (6) and (7), involves vowel insertion between a sonorant consonant and a following non-homorganic obstruent. In (6), the intervening consonant shares a [back] specification with the stem vowel ((6)a is an apparent exception to which I return), and the epenthetic vowel, which is underlined, is a copy of the preceding vowel.

(6)
a. t'imix'aL 'round about'
b. mer'ek' 'rust'
c. ær'æk'at 'money'
d. Luruka 'a leg'
e. marav 'dead'
f. gOrOm 'blue'

In (7), the consonant following the stem vowel disagrees in backness, and the epenthesized vowel shares the backness specification of both the preceding and the following consonant. (7)e and g are apparent exceptions in this respect. Other vowel features agree with the preceding vowel.

(7)
a. inixiN'ə 'brain'
b. bul'ik' 'bellows' gen sg
c. dil'ix' 'sorry'
d. s'enaxəs 'lore'
e. mʌr'ev 'the dead'
f. færak 'anger'
g. karæt' 'friend'

In what follows I outline an account - essentially that pursued by Clements and Sagey and adopted by Halle - of the forms in (6) and (7) in which it is assumed that all vowel features spread from the preceding vowel unless blocked. It is clear from this account that some non-constituent spreading seems to be entailed. However, I then argue that a broader look at the distribution of the vowel features in Barra Gaelic points to an alternative account in which only the height of the epenthesized vowel is determined by the preceding vowel. I assume here a geometry in which the vowel features are organized together as dependents of VPlace (e.g. Clements 1991, Ní Chiosáin 1991).

In *t'imix'aL*, (6)a, spreading involves all vowel features, assuming labials, represented in (5) without a backness contrast, are unspecified for [back].

(8)

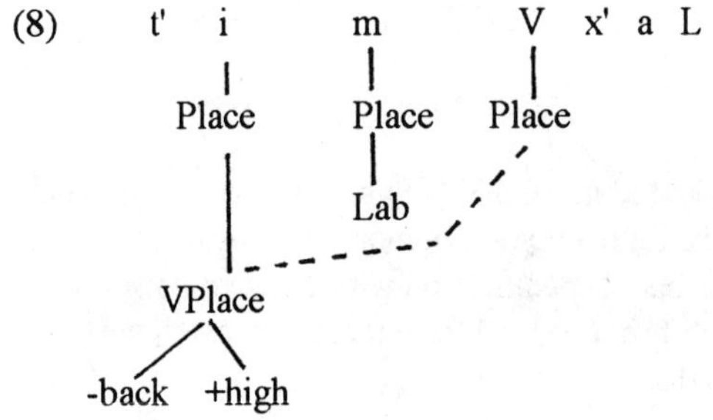

If [back] is specified for nonpalatalized consonants (see Ní Chiosáin forthcoming, on (related) Irish), spreading of VPlace in *Luru̱kə*, (6)d, is blocked. In this case, [back] must spread from the consonant to the vowel.[3] Since [round] is argued to be contrastive for back vowels, it must spread from the first vowel, along with Height. Hence, spreading involves a non-constituent.

(9)

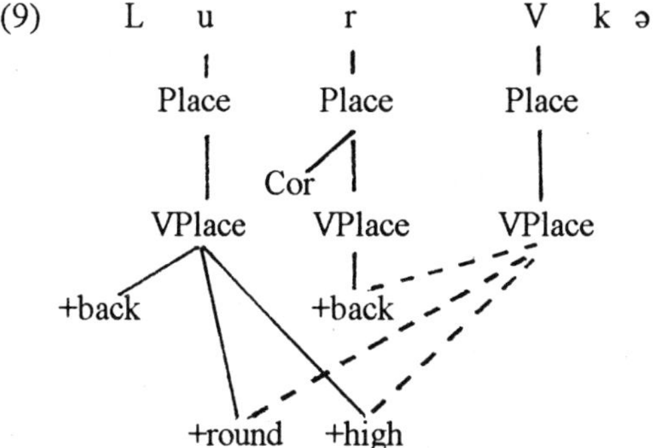

However, if nonpalatalized consonants are unspecified for [back], spreading in (9) can clearly be represented as spreading of VPlace, just as in (8). This is not possible in *bul'ik'* (7)b, on the other hand, where the intervening consonant is palatalized and thus specified for [-back]. The epenthetic vowel acquires its backness specification from this consonant and [+high] from the preceding vowel, assuming *[-back, +round].

(10)

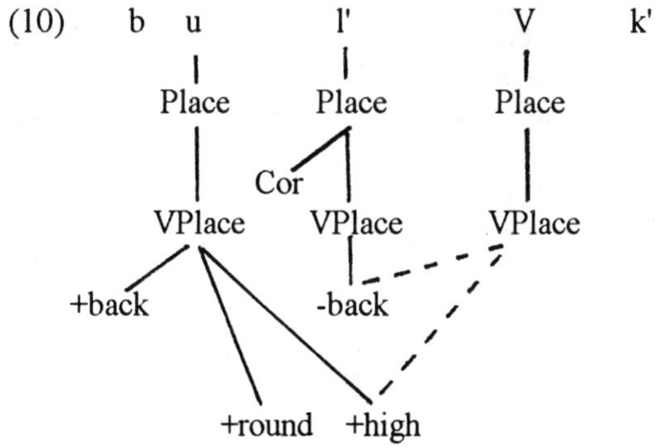

[3]Note that one would have to ask whether in this respect the Sagey/Halle account also involves more than one process, i.e. Spread VPlace features (V-to-V), Spread [back] (C-toV).

Clearly, if Barra Gaelic Vowel Copy is represented as in (9) and (10) above, some non-constituent spreading seems to be entailed.

However, this process should not in the first place be seen as spreading of all VPlace features from the stem vowel to the epenthetic vowel. It can be shown that the [back] specification of (all) short vowels and the [round] specification of non-low short vowels in Barra Gaelic are independently determined by adjacent consonants. Therefore, only the height features obviously spread from the preceding vowel. [round] **might** spread in the epenthesised forms of low vowels - I return to this issue below. Therefore the lexical vowel inventory of Barra Gaelic is greatly simplified, involving a height distinction (three heights) and a (possible) rounding contrast in the low vowels only. The spreading rules that determine the quality of the epenthetic vowel in Barra Gaelic are then the following:

(i) Rightward Height spread (from V to V)

(ii) Rightward [back] spread (from C to V) - affects **all** Gaelic short vowels.

(iii) ??Rightward [round] spread (from V to V) - unclear and affects low vowels only. [round] is independently determined for non-low vowels.

The following sections are concerned with showing that both the backness and roundness specifications of short vowels are determined by adjacent consonants.

3. Backness in Barra Gaelic short vowels

There is independent evidence that the backness specification of short vowels is determined by adjacent consonants: front in a palatalized environment and back in a nonpalatalized environment. (For comparable Irish data, see Ó Siadhail 1989, Ní Chiosáin 1991, forthcoming). The distribution of the short high front vowel [i] and the short high back rounded vowel [u] is given in (11) and (12), respectively. The A. groups (highlighted) in these examples are the most relevant ones. I return to the short high back unrounded vowel [ɨ] in the following section.

(11) Distribution of [i]:

A. Palatalized environment: C' __ C'

a. s'il'əɣ 'to rain'
b. hik' (<t'ik') 'will come'
c.[4] mil'is' 'sweet'

B. Mixed environment: C' __ C; [i] retracted to 'mixed-position'.

d. bir 'a pin'
e. fiɣ 'wood'

C. # __ C (L, N); [i] retracted to 'mixed position'

f. iLir'ə 'an eagle'
g.[5] iNəN 'same'

(11)C can be analyzed as having an initial empty palatalized consonant - see Ní Chiosáin 1991 on such V-initial stems in Irish, where the evidence in favour of positing partially specified onsets involves a series of prothetic consonants with unpredictable secondary articulations. The retraction to a 'mixed position' in a mixed environment in (11)B can be viewed as phonetic. It follows that short vowels are front following palatalized consonants.

(12) Distribution of [u]:

A. Non-palatalized environment: C __ C

a. bun 'bottom'
b. duh 'black'
c. Luxak 'a mouse'
d. furəstə 'easy'
e. muxk 'a pig'

---

[4]The initial labial in (11)c, d, and e can be shown to be phonologically palatalized, see discussion following (13) below.

[5]Borgstrøm (1937:83): "in slow pronunciation nearly iiNəN".

B. Mixed environment: $C_{Lab/Dors}$ ___ C'

f.	kuN'	'when?'
g.[6]	mur'	'sea'
h.	ful'	'blood'

C. # ___ C'

i.	us'ak	'a lark'
j.	us'k'ə	'water'

As in (11)C, (12)C can be viewed as having an initial empty consonant, a non-palatalised consonant. Thus, short vowels are back after non-palatalized consonants.

Of immediate relevance in the present context is the fact that consonant clusters in Gaelic are uniformly palatalized or nonpalatalized. Therefore the consonants flanking the epenthetic vowel share a specification for [back], and thus fall under (11)A and (12)A above: the epenthetic vowel is front between palatalized consonants and back between nonpalatalized consonants. Epenthesis into a palatalized cluster is illustrated in (13).

(13)

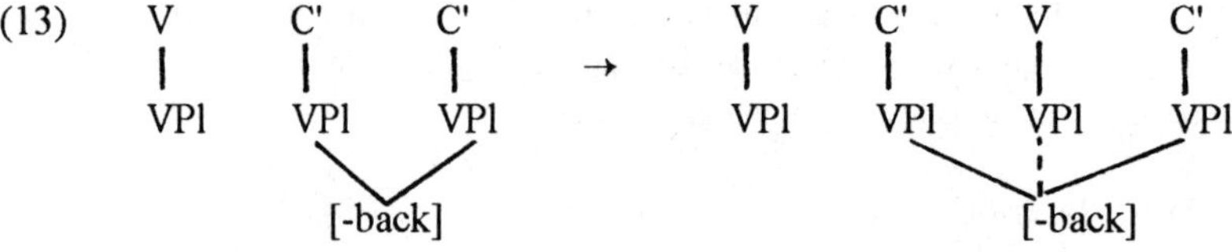

Clusters that contain labial consonants are only apparent exceptions to the generalization that clusters are uniformly specified for [back]. Since labials do not contrast phonetically in backness, they have been argued to be unspecified for [back]. Forms like t'imix'aL and æmæs'ir' have been taken to indicate that **all** vowel features spread from the first vowel to the epenthetic vowel: since labials are unspecified for [back], they were considered transparent to spreading of the vowel features. However, labial segments can be argued to have phonological specification for [back]:

- since the [back] specification of short vowels is determined by adjacent consonants, the contrast between e and ʌ is eliminated - except after labials.

---

[6]According to Borgstrøm (1937:86), the vowel in (12)g-i (near a 'mixed position') is more forward, less narrow and less rounded than in the other examples in (12).

If labials are not specified for [back], we need this contrast only here, in forms like mer'ek' 'rust' (6)c, mʌr'ev 'the dead' (7)e. (This holds also for other short vowels). Indeed, historically, labials were palatalized and the distinction is still encoded in spelling, e.g. *meirg* 'rust', *mairbh* 'the dead'.

- diminishment/neutralization of back contrast in labials is common, also occurring to various degrees in Irish (e.g. Ó Siadhail 1989:83) and in Slavic (e.g. Polish, Czaykowska-Higgins 1988:137).
- a phonetic off-glide of a palatalized labial in fact appears preceding long back vowels (Borgstrøm 1940:18).

Therefore, we can conclude that a palatalized/nonpalatalized distinction is lexically encoded for labial consonants, even if later neutralized. Clusters containing labial consonants are thus no longer exceptional and spreading in *t'imix'aL* (6)a, for example, is represented as in (14).

(14)
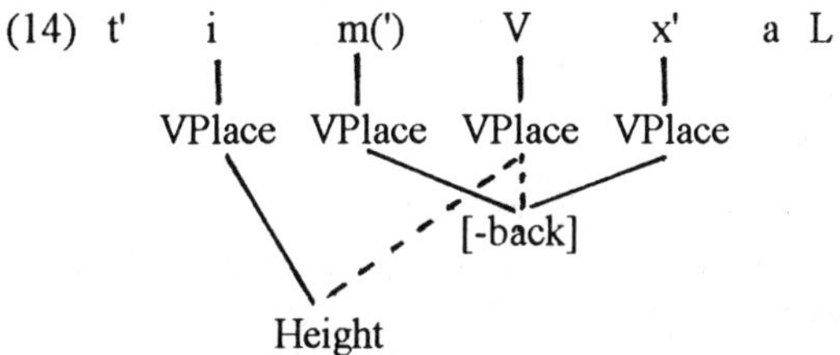

4. [round] in Barra Gaelic back vowels

As seen in the vowel inventory in (4), repeated below in (15), Barra Gaelic back vowels contrast in rounding. This has been interpreted as phonemic rounding, with the roundness specification considered unpredictable.

(15)

i	ɨ	u
e	ʌ	o
æ	a	O

If this contrast were phonemic, we would indeed appear to require two independent V-to-V spreading rules: (i) V-to-V Height spreading and (ii) V-to-V [round] spreading, as illustrated in (16) for *Lur̲ukə*.

(16)

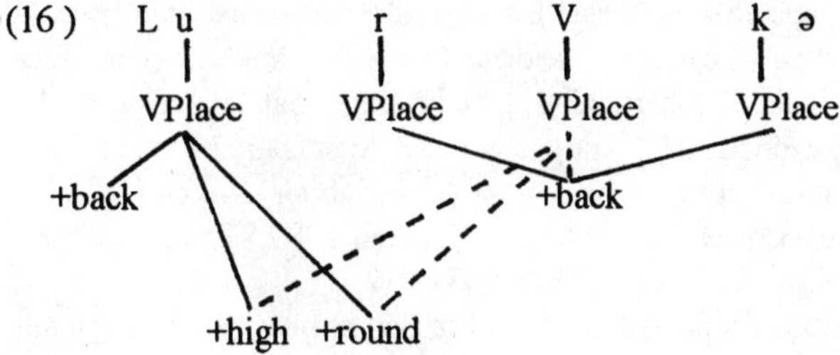

Since these two spreading rules occur together, it would follow that these data indeed provide a case of nonconstituent spreading. However, contrary to assumptions made in earlier accounts, rounding is not phonemically contrastive in Barra Gaelic. As shown below, the occurence of unround non-low short back vowels is predictable. As noted earlier, this results in a lexical distinction of height only in non-low short vowels, and height and (possibly) round in the low vowels.

4.1 Unround non-low back vowels

According to Borgstrøm (1940:139), the distinction between high back unrounded [u] and high back unrounded [ɨ] 'has next to no phonological value' and [ɨ] 'is used nearly only between dentals (except L, N, R)'. Scrutiny of the data in Borgstrøm allows the following generalizations about the distribution of high back unrounded [ɨ] to be ascertained:

(17) Distribution of [ɨ]

C_{Cor} ___ $C(')_{Cor}$

a.	drɨt'	'to close'
b.	dɨl'ix'	'sorry'
c.	trɨstər	'bad fellow/woman'
d.	tɨrəs	'a journey'

C_{Cor} ___ . (i.e. before hiatus)

e.	brɨ.iN'	'to talk'
f.	nas Lɨ.ə	'smaller'

[ɨ] occurs between coronal consonants in (17)a-d, and following a coronal consonant in hiatus position in (17)e and f. We can conclude that [+round] is the default value for back vowels, with [-round] assigned in circumscribed environments. Here derounding can be seen as a concomitant effect of fronting around coronal consonants.

This conclusion can also be extended to the mid back vowels. The distribution of the mid back unrounded vowel [ʌ] is given in (18).

(18) Distribution of [ʌ][7]

C_{Cor} ___ ɣ

a.	drʌɣ	'trouble'
b.	kLʌɣ	'burying place'

\# or C_{Cor} ___ .[8]

c.	kLʌ.əx	'to dig'
d.	ʌ.ir'k'	'a horn'

$C_{Cor/Dors}$ ___ C'_{Cor}

e.	gʌl'	'to boil'
f.	kʌr'əx	'guilty'
g.	Lʌs'k'i	'will burn/shoot'
h.	tʌj	'house'(dat)

[ʌ] occurs following a coronal consonant and preceding the voiced velar fricative in (18)a and b; in hiatus position, following a coronal consonant in (18)c or word-initially in (18)d; and preceded by either a coronal or a dorsal consonant and followed by a palatalized coronal consonant in (18)e-h.

The above environments, like those in (17), have a strong coronal bias and are notable for the absence of labial consonants. Thus, the rounding specification of the epenthetic vowel is clearly determined by the adjacent consonants and is not the result of spreading from the preceding vowel.

4.2 Unround low back vowels

Unlike the non-low back vowels, it appears that rounding is not predictable for the low back vowels (if the contrast between a and O is in fact one of rounding

---

[7]Exceptions to the generalizations set out in (18) are: *fʌl'ʌm* 'helm in a boat', which also violates CV-[back] sharing since we would expect the epenthetic vowel to be front, and *mʌr'ev* 'the dead', which is derived by morphological palatalization from *marav*, thus ʌ < a by raising.

[8]In these forms, ɣ, which in (18)a, c and d (also (17)a) was a lenited voiced coronal, was (historically) dropped intervocalically resulting in hiatus.

in the first instance - see Borgstrøm who describes O as being 'as a rule very badly rounded'). Both sounds occur in near identical environments, though this is not quite true of the epenthesized forms where the following patterns of occurrence are found:

(19)a. Stem and epenthetic vowels = low back unrounded [a]:

C_1 __ r,R,L,n __ C_2
where C_1, C_2 = voiceless non-labial consonant, or labial consonant

b. Stem and epenthetic vowels = low back rounded [O]:

C_1 __ r __ C_2
where C_1 = voiced non-coronal stop, or coronal stop; C_2 = velar fricative or labial nasal

If we assume that 'rounding' is not predictable in the low vowels, then it must spread, along with height, from the stem vowel to the epenthetic vowel. This spreading would then constitute non-constituent spreading. However, the facts require further investigation.

5. Conclusion

The focus of this paper was the data used in the literature to argue for non-constituent spreading, a spreading type predicted to occur assuming individual feature spreading. A closer look at the phonology of vowel features in Barra Gaelic reveals the process in question to be spreading of the height features only in the case of non-low short vowels, rather than spreading of VPlace or the non-constituent Height and [round]. In the case of the low short vowels, on the other hand, it appears that non-constituent spreading of Height and [round] may occur.

References

Borgstrøm, Carl Hj. 1937. The dialect of Barra in the Outer Hebrides. *NorskTidsskrift forSprogvidenskap*, VIII. Oslo: Norwegian Universities Press. 71-242.

Borgstrøm, Carl Hj. 1940. A linguistic survey of the Gaelic dialects of Scotland, Vol. I: The dialects of the Outer Hebrides. *Norsk Tidsskrift for Sprogvidenskap*, Suppl. Bind I. Oslo: Norwegian Universities Press.

Clements, G.N. 1985. 'The geometry of phonological features. *Phonology Yearbook* 2. 223-250.

Clements, G.N. 1986. 'Syllabification and epenthesis in the Barra dialect of Gaelic'. In K. Bogers, H. van der Hulst & M. Mous (eds.) *The Phonological Representation of Supra-segmentals*. Dordrecht: Foris.

Czaykowska-Higgins, Eva. 1988. Investigations into Polish morphology and phonology. PhD. dissertation, MIT.

Goldsmith, John. 1990. Autosegmental and Metrical Phonology. Basil Blackwell, Cambridge MA.

Halle, Morris. 1993. Feature geometry and feature spreading. Ms. MIT

Halle, Morris & Bert Vaux. 1994. Feature spreading and vocalic place. Ms. MIT and Harvard University.

Jackson, Kenneth. 1967. 'Palatalisation of labials in the Gaelic languages. In W. Meid (ed.) *Beiträge zur Indogermanistik und Keltologie*. Innsbruck: Innsbrucker Beiträge zur Kulturwissenschaft 13. 179-92.

MacAuley, Donald. 1966. 'Palatalisation of labials in Scottish Gaelic and some related problems in phonology'. *Scottish Gaelic Studies* 11. 72-84.

Ní Chiosáin, Máire. 1991. Topics in the phonology of Irish. PhD dissertation, University of Massachusetts, Amherst.

Ní Chiosáin, Máire. forthcoming. 'Vowel features and underspecification: evidence from Irish. In *Phonologica 1992*. Proceedings of the 7th International Phonology Meeting, Krems, Austria.

Oftedal, Magne. 1963. 'On 'palatalised' labials in Scottish Gaelic'. *Scottish Gaelic Studies*, 10. 71-81.

Ó Siadhail, Micheál. 1989. *Modern Irish: grammatical structure and dialect variation*. Cambridge University Press.

Padgett, Jaye. 1991. Stricture in Feature Geometry. PhD dissertation, University of Massachusetts, Amherst.

Padgett, Jaye. 1994. 'On the bases of interaction'. Talk presented at the Tri-lateral Phonology Weekend, Stanford University and UCLA.

Sagey, Elizabeth. 1986. The representation of features and relations in non-linear phonology. PhD dissertation, MIT.

Sagey, Elizabeth. 1988. 'Non-constituent spreading in Barra Gaelic'. Ms. UC Irvine.

Selkirk, Elisabeth O. 1988. 'Dependency, place and the notion 'tier''. Unpublished ms. University of Massachusetts, Amherst.

Selkirk, Elisabeth O. 1991. 'A two-root theory of length', in E. Dunlap and J. Padgett, eds. University of Massachusetts Occasional Papers in Linguistics 14: Papers in Phonology. GLSA, UMass, Amherst.

Steriade, Donca. 1987. 'On class nodes'. Unpublished ms. MIT.

Ternes, Elmer. 1973. *The phonemic analysis of Scottish Gaelic, based on the dialect of Applecross, Ross-shire*. Hamburg: Helmut Buske Verlag.

Prosodic Alignment and Misalignment in Diyari, Dyirbal, & Gooniyandi: An Optimizing Approach

MEGAN J. CROWHURST
Yale University

1. Introduction

Diyari (Austin 1981, Poser 1989), Dyirbal (Dixon 1972), and Gooniyandi (McGregor 1990), languages of Australia, are metrically similar in assigning stress initially in all morphemes containing at least two syllables.[1] In Diyari and Gooniyandi, the third syllable of a quadrisyllabic morpheme is also stressed. Examples are shown in (1).[2]

(1)a. *Diyari* (Austin 1981:31)

pínadu	'old man'	káṇa-wàṛa	'man-pl.'
ŋándawàlka	'to close'	pínadu-wàṛa	'old man-pl.'

---

* This paper has benefitted from useful comments by Stanley Insler and Donca Steriade, and from extensive discussion of the analysis with Scott Myers. I am grateful in addition to R.M.W. Dixon for providing additional information and forms by electronic communication (these forms are followed by "p.c." below). Any flaws are, as always, the sole responsibility of the author.

1 Diyari and Dyirbal are Pama-Nyungan languages while Gooniyandi is a member of the distantly related Bunaban family (Ruhlen 1987). I have followed the transcriptions of Austin (1981) and Dixon (1972) for Diyari and Dyirbal. McGregor's orthography for Gooniyandi has been modified to include IPA symbols, where this would result in greater clarity. For example, the vowel given by McGregor as *oo* is really a short /u/ (see McGregor 1990:58), and the orthographic sequences *dd* and *ng* have the phonemic values /ɾ, ŋ/.

2 Stress in Gooniyandi is complicated by vowel length in trisyllabic and quinquesyllabic morphemes. However, within morphemes containing an even number of syllables, regardless of vowel length, and in most trisyllabic morphemes, the facts are as described here.

b. *Dyirbal* (Dixon 1972:275,230 and Dixon, personal communication)

ɖúgumbil	'woman'	búnɖul-múŋa	'spank-part.'
múlumíyan	'whale' (p.c.)	búrbula-gára	'Burbula-1 of a pr'

c. *Gooniyandi* (McGregor 1990:120-125)

wáɾamba	'flood'	bírla-bíɲi	'yams-per.'
ŋíɾiwárndi	'across'	ŋáɾagi-ní̱ŋi	'my-abl.'

The pattern illustrated in (1) suggests that in these languages, (i) left edges of morphemes and stress feet ideally coincide, and (ii) morpheme-internal footing is iterative to the limits of enforced binarity. A ban on monosyllabic feet is indicated by the absence of stress on monosyllabic sequences in word-final and pre-stress positions. The feet required, quantity-insensitive disyllabic trochees, are exemplified in (2) with forms from Dyirbal and Gooniyandi.

(2)	*Dyirbal*	*Gooniyandi*
	(ɖúgum)bil	(ŋíɾi)(wárndi)
	*(ɖúgum)(bíl)	*(ŋíɾi)warndi
	(búrbu)la-(gára)	(wáɾam)ba
	*(búrbu)(lá)-(gára)	*(wáɾam)(bá)
	*(búrbu)(lá-ga)ra	

Language-specific differences begin to emerge in the treatment of strings containing monosyllabic suffixes, which by themselves cannot accommodate a disyllabic foot. In Diyari, no monosyllabic morpheme is assigned stress, even when two or more occur adjacently, as in (3) (forms followed by a reference with *P* are from Poser 1989).

(3) *Diyari*

a. yáṯa-yi	(yáṯa)-yi	'speak-pres.' A42
b. púdi-ya-ni-wu	(púdi)-ya-ni-wu	'aux.-imp.-number marker-distort.' A86
c. máɖa-l̠a-n̠i	(máɖa)-l̠a-n̠i	'hill-char-locative' A40
d. wáɖaɽu-ɲʈa	(wáɖa)ɽu-ɲʈa	'how-number' A43
e. ṯúraɽa-yi-l̠a	(ṯúra)ɽa-yi-l̠a	'lie-pres-NI' A83
f. ṇánda-na-màṯa	(ṇánda)-na-(màṯa)	'hit-part-ident.' P119
g. púlʸudu-n̠i-màṯa	(púlʸu)du-n̠i-(màṯa)	'mud-loc.-ident.' P119
h. páɖaka-yìrpa-ṇa	(páɖa)ka-(yìrpa)-ṇa	'carry-be.-rel.' A78

Like Diyari, Dyirbal (i) avoids stress on a sole monosyllabic suffix after a disyllabic or trisyllabic root, (4a,b). In a sequence of monosyllabic suffixes, however, Dyirbal assigns stress to the first of each pair, proceeding from left to right, (4c,d,e,f). More striking is the fact that when a monosyllabic suffix is flanked by a root and a following disyllabic suffix, as in (4g,h), the monosyllable is stressed and the initial syllable of the following suffix is not.[3] (*P/p* in (4) is the present/past inflection.)

(4) *Dyirbal* (Dixon 1972:274,275,280,284; Dixon, personal communication)

a. wáyɲɖi-ŋu	(wáyɲɖi)-ŋu	'motion uphill-rel.cl.'
b. búrguɽum-bu	(búrgu)ɽum-bu	'jumping ant-erg.'
c. búyba-rí-ɲu	(búyba)-(rí-ɲu)	'hide-refl.-pres/past'
d. wáyɲɖi-ŋú-gu	(wáyɲɖi)-(ŋú-gu)	'motion uphill-rel.cl.-dat.'
e. núdil-mál-ɖa-ɲu	(núdil)-(mál-ɖa)-ɲu	'cut-com.-loc.-p/p'
f. bánagay-mbá-ri-ɲu	(bána)gay-(mbá-ri)-ɲu	'return-refl.-comit.-p/p'
g. ɖáŋga-ná-mbila	(ɖáŋga)-(ná-mbi)la	'eat-pron.-with'
h. mándalay-mbál-bila	(mánda)lay-(mbál-bi)la	'play-comit.-lest' p.c.

In Gooniyandi, quite simply, sequences of a root followed by a string of monosyllabic suffixes (a prosodic word; see §5) display a straightforwardly iterative stress pattern. Prominence is assigned to odd-numbered syllables counted from the left, (5b-e), but never to a final syllable, (5a,e). The significant difference from Dyirbal is that when a monosyllabic suffix follows a trisyllabic root, the root-final syllable is stressed, whether or not a second monosyllabic suffix follows, (5d,e) (cf. DY *(búrgu) ɽum-bu, (bána)gay-(mbá-ri)-ɲu*).

(5) *Gooniyandi*

a. níyi-ya	$[\text{(níyi)-ya}]_{PW}$	'that-loc.' M124
b. ŋábu-wá-ŋga	$[\text{(ŋábu)-(wá-ŋga)}]_{PW}$	'father-his-erg.' M125
c. míla-jíɾ-iɲ-bíɾ-a	$[\text{(míla)-(jíɾ-iɲ)-(bíɾ-a)}]_{PW}$	'we'll see you' M127
d. márlamí-ya	$[\text{(márla)(mí-ya)}]_{PW}$	'nothing-loc.' M124
e. ŋáɾaɲú-wa-ŋga	$[\text{(ŋáɾa)(ɲú-wa)-ŋga}]_{PW}$	'mother-his-erg. M125

Intuitively, the differences illustrated in (3)-(5) can be summed up as follows. In Diyari, syllables may not be grouped into feet across a morpheme boundary. Here, the licensing of syllables by feet is sacrificed to a requirement of morphological integrity imposed on foot structures. The existence of forms like *(búyba)-(rí-ɲu)* in Dyirbal demonstrates the opposite case: in this language, it is apparently better to assign foot structure than for feet to respect morphological integrity. Grouping *forward* across a morpheme boundary in forms like *(bána)gay-(mbá-ri)-ɲu* suggests that in Dyirbal, heteromorphemic footing is possible only when the left boundary of the resulting foot is aligned with that of a morpheme. The opposite pattern, footing *backwards* across a morpheme boundary, does not occur in

---

[3] I have been unable to find forms which are marked for stress and which contain a sequence of four monosyllabic suffixes. However, Dixon's (1972:274-5) description clearly indicates that an alternating stress pattern would be expected. The form in (4h) was provided by Dixon (personal communication).

Dyirbal: The final syllable of a trisyllabic root is never parsed into a foot with a following, heteromorphemic syllable (e.g. DY *(búrgu) ɲum-bu*, **(búrgu)(ɲúm-bu)*). However, this pattern does occur in Gooniyandi when a trisyllabic root is followed by a monosyllabic suffix (e.g. GO *[(márla)(mí-ya)]$_{PW}$*, **[(márla)mí-ya]$_{PW}$*), suggesting that the left-alignment requirement is relaxed in Gooniyandi if by so doing, the monosyllable could be licensed by a foot. That the attested form in (5e) is *[(ŋáɾ a)(ɲ ú-wa)- ŋga]$_{PW}$* and not *[(ŋáɾ a) ɲ u-(wá- ŋ ga)]$_{PW}$* shows that syllable licensing is not the only important factor: the second foot also occurs as close as possible to the left edge of the prosodic word.

This paper proposes an optimizing analysis of the similarities and differences between Diyari, Dyirbal, and Gooniyandi discussed above. Before proceeding to the analysis, I provide a working introduction to the principles and assumptions of Optimality Theory (Prince & Smolensky 1991, 1993; McCarthy & Prince 1993a,b) most important for this study.

2. Optimality Theory

The central claim of OPTIMALITY THEORY (OT) is that cross-linguistic variation along specific phonological dimensions follows from interactions among a set of universally available constraints whose relative priorities are language-specifically determined. In shifting the burden of explanation from derivation to constraint systems, OT abolishes phonological rules and other derivational notions, replacing them with the functions in (6a) and (6b) (Prince & Smolensky 1993:4, McCarthy & Prince 1993a:4). GEN is a generative function which takes an input representation and returns an infinitely large set of possible output forms, or CANDIDATES. The candidate set returned by GEN for some input *i* expresses the complete set of inter-elemental relationships that would result from applying phonological rules in a general and unconstrained manner (or alternatively, which would occur under a system of free coindexation).

(6)a. GEN: $\text{Gen}(\text{in}_i) \rightarrow \{\text{cand}_1, \text{cand}_2, \ldots\}$
b. EVAL: $\text{Eval}(\{\text{cand}_1, \text{cand}_2, \ldots\}) = \text{out}_{real}$

The task of EVAL is to evaluate the harmony of candidates as measured in terms of a hierarchy of constraints whose relative priorities are determined by the language. The OPTIMAL, most harmonic candidate (by hypothesis, the true output) is that which best satisfies the constraint hierarchy. OT eschews the notion of grammaticality in favour of harmony or optimality because *grammatical* implies that all relevant constraints have been satisfied, whereas the central goal of OT is to account for the observation that constraints are in fact often violated. In this context, *best satisfaction* entails minimal constraint violation. In other words, the optimal candidate is the one that does the least damage, given relevant constraint rankings and the limitations of the input representation.

Constraint violation is inevitable when the properties of an input form are such that it can satisfy either, but not both of two competing constraints. To illustrate, consider the widely attested observation that feet ideally consist of exactly two elements, morae or syllables (Prince 1980; McCarthy & Prince 1986, 1993a,b; Kager 1989; Hayes 1994), expressed in (7) as the constraint FOOT BINARITY (FtBin; Prince & Smolensky 1993:47).

(7) *Foot Binarity:* Feet are binary under some level of analysis (μ, σ).

Under FtBin, feet with the structure (σ σ) count as optimal (for the languages in question), while (σ) is disfavoured. A second well-accepted generalisation is that syllables are ideally dominated by foot structure. McCarthy & Prince (1993b:11) state this requirement as PARSE-σ in (8).[4]

(8) *Parse-σ:* All syllables must be parsed by feet.

Under (8), every syllable not dominated by foot structure in a candidate will incur a violation of Parse-σ.

In a hypothetical grammar consisting of only these constraints, candidates based on a trisyllabic input must violate either FtBin or Parse-σ. Crucial ranking among constraints is determined by examining exactly such cases of conflict. Tableau 1 shows that when Parse-σ has higher priority than FtBin, FtBin may be violated by the optimal candidate to gain success on Parse-σ.[5] By contrast, if FtBin outranks Parse-σ (Tableau 2), then the candidate incurring no FtBin violations wins, at the expense of Parse-σ:

Tableau 1: Parse-σ » FtBin

Candidate	Parse-σ	FtBin
(σ́ σ) σ	*!	
✓ (σ́ σ)(σ́)		*

Tableau 2: FtBin » Parse-σ

Candidate	FtBin	Parse-σ
✓ (σ́ σ) σ		*
(σ́ σ)(σ́)	*!	

4 When syllables cannot be parsed by F due to conflict with higher ranking constraints, I assume they are dominated by PrWd in output representations. This relaxation of the Strict Layer Requirement (Selkirk 1984:26), which imposes strict dominance relations on prosodic representations, has been discussed insightfully by Hewitt (1992) and Itô & Mester (1992).

5 The following conventions are used in this paper: a constraint to the left of the symbol "»" receives higher priority than the symbol to its right (e.g. FtBin » Strict Layer). A colon (e.g. Ft Bin : Strict Layer) indicates equal priority. In tableaux, crucially ranked constraints are separated by a solid vertical line, with the highest ranking constraint in the left. Unranked constraints are separated by a dotted line. A fatal constraint violation is followed by "!", optimal candidates are checked "✓", and shading obscures cells whose contents play no crucial role in determining the relative harmony of a candidate.

When all candidates pass the highest ranking constraint, illustrated in Tableau 3 with a quadrisyllabic input, then the decision is passed to the constraint next in priority.

Tableau 3: Ft Bin » Parse-σ

Candidate	FtBin	Parse-σ
✓ (σ́ σ)(σ́ σ)		
(σ́ σ) σ σ		*! *

Similarly, if all candidates fail the highest ranking constraint, the deciding role is still performed by the next constraint in the hierarchy. A final possibility is that if FtBin and Parse-σ are unranked with respect to one another, then a violation of either counts equally, predicting the existence of alternative optimal candidates, other factors being equal. In general, I adopt the OT assumption that interacting constraints are in fact ranked, except in the case of undominated constraints, and when the absence of ranking is crucial for the analysis (see §4).

3. Diyari

Recall from the first section that Diyari stresses the first syllable of all morphemes of at least two syllables, but never monosyllabic morphemes or the third syllable of a trisyllabic morpheme (e.g. *(pá ḍa)ka-(yìrpa)-ṇa, (púdi)-ya-ni-wu*). The analysis proposed here requires the constraints FtBin and Parse-σ introduced in (7) and (8). In addition, it must be explained why the single foot assigned to a trisyllabic morpheme abuts the left and not the right edge, as indicated by initial, trochaic stress.

The stress-attracting property of morpheme-initial syllables in general can be expressed in terms of the constraint MORPHEME-FOOT-LEFT (MFL) in (9).

(9) *Morpheme-Foot-Left:* Align(Morpheme, L, Foot, L)

MFL states that the left boundary of every morpheme must coincide with the left boundary of a foot. A single violation is assessed for every morpheme which does not meet this requirement.

Tableau 4 illustrates the interaction of FtBin, Parse-σ, and MFL in selecting optimal candidates based on monomorphemic trisyllabic and quadrisyllabic inputs /pinadu/ and /ŋandawalka/, respectively. FtBin is unviolated in Diyari, and hence, we may assume, undominated in the constraint hierarchy. Candidates violating FtBin in tableau 4-1a,b (henceforth T4-1, etc.) are excluded immediately, since non-violating candidates exist. Next to FtBin in priority is MFL. Only one candidate, T4-1e, passes MFL and is selected as optimal, even though it contains a single parse violation.

Tableau 4: Trisyllabic inputs /pinadu/ and / ŋandawalka/.

Candidates		FtBin	MFL	Parse-σ
1a.	(pína)(dù)	*!		
b.	(pí)(nàdu)	*!		
c.	pinadu		*!	***
d.	pi(nádu)		*!	*
e. ✓	(pína)du			*
2a. ✓	(ŋánda)(wàlka)			
b.	(ŋánda)walka			*! *
c.	ŋan(dáwal)ka		*!	**
d.	ŋanda(wálka)		*!	**

As discussed earlier, failure to parse a single syllable to foot structure is a consequence of the dominant status of FtBin. When the input is a quadrisyllabic morpheme, as with /ŋandawalka/ in T4-2, FtBin and Parse-σ are not in conflict. Thus, of the two candidates which pass MFL (T4-2a,b), the optimal candidate, T4-2a, is the one which contains two disyllabic feet and no unparsed syllables. Thus, the optimal *(ŋánda)(wàlka)* violates none of the constraints in the hierarchy established so far. (Note that there is no evidence for crucial ranking between Parse-σ and MFL. The attested forms *pínadu* and *ŋándawàlka* will also be correctly selected as optimal if the two constraints are unranked, or under an alternative in which Parse-σ dominates MFL.)

Sequences of a disyllabic root plus a monosyllabic or disyllabic suffix display the same stress patterns respectively as the monomorphemic *pínadu* and *ŋándawàlka.* Tableau 5, based on the inputs /yata-yi/ and /kaṇa-waṛa/, shows that these results, too, are predicted by our constraints. The absence of stress on the monosyllabic suffix in T5-1 shows that MFL, like Parse-σ, is crucially dominated by FtBin.

Tableau 5: Inputs /yata-yi/, /kaṇa-waṛa/

Candidates		FtBin	MFL	Parse-σ
1a.	(yáṯa)-(yì)	*!		
c.	ya(ṯá-yi)		**!	*
b. ✓	(yáṯa)-yi		*	*
2a. ✓	(káṇa)-(wàṛa)			
b.	(káṇa)-waṛa		*!	**
c.	kaṇa-(wáṛa)		*!	**

The striking property of Diyari is that even though footing is iterative in morphemes longer than three syllables, stress is never assigned to any of a sequence of adjacent monosyllabic suffixes. The constraints

FtBin, MFL, and Parse-σ alone cannot determine the attested outcome in the latter cases. As before, FtBin rules out candidates in which monosyllabic suffixes are analysed as degenerate feet. However, relying on Parse-σ and MFL for adjudication when the input is a disyllabic or trisyllabic root followed by a string of monosyllabic suffixes (e.g. /pudi-ya-ni-wu/, /t̠uraṛa-yi-l̠a/) incorrectly predicts that as many syllables as possible will be parsed as long as the resulting feet are left-aligned with morphemes, as in *(púdi)-(yà-ni)-wu, *(t̠úra)ṛa-(yì-l̠a). The true victors, (púdi)-ya-ni-wu and (t̠úra)ṛa-yi-l̠a, differ from their rivals in failing to parse syllables into feet across morpheme boundaries. This generalisation is captured by assigning high priority to the constraint TAUTOMORPHEMIC-FOOT (or Tauto-F), which requires that foot parsing be faithful to morphological structure.

(10) *Tautomorphemic-Foot:* $*_{F}[\sigma\ _{M}[\ \sigma]$

Under Tauto-F, any foot whose syllables straddle a morpheme boundary incurs a violation. When Tauto-F is dominant, it is better to leave syllables unparsed than to endure a heteromorphemic foot. Like FtBin, Tauto-F is unviolated in Diyari and therefore, we assume, undominated. The correct outcome is ensured if Tauto-F dominates Parse-σ. Using as an illustration the polymorphemic input /pudi-ya-ni-wu/, Tableau 6 shows that a single violation of Tauto-F triumphs over two or three violations each of MFL and Parse-σ.

Tableau 6: Input /pudi-ya-ni-wu/.

Candidates		FtBin	Tauto-F	MFL	Parse-σ
1a. ✓	(púdi)-ya-ni-wu			***	***
b.	(púdi)-(yà-ni)-wu		*!	**	*
c.	(púdi)-ya-(nì-wu)		*!	**	*
d.	(púdi)-(yà)-(nì)-(wù)	*! **			

Tableau 7 shows that the high ranking assigned to Tauto-F also precludes the assignment of stress to the third syllable of a suffixed trisyllabic root.

Tableau 7: Inputs /waḍaṛu-ɲä u/, /t̠uraṛa-yi-l̠a/, /puly udu-ni-mata/.

Candidates		FtBin	Tauto-F	MFL	Parse-σ
1a. ✓	(wáḍa)ṛu-ɲäa			*	**
c.	(wáḍa)(ṛù-ɲäa)		*!	*	
b.	(wáḍa)ṛu-(ɲäà)	*!			*

Tableau 7, continued

Candidates		FtBin	Tauto-F	MFL	Parse-σ
2a. ✓	(ṯúra)ṛa-yi-ḻa			**	***
b.	(ṯúra)ṛa-(yì-ḻa)		*!	*	*
c.	(ṯúra)(ṛà-yi)-ḻa		*!	**	*
d.	(ṯúra)ṛa-(yì)-(ḻà)	*! *			*
3a. ✓	(púl^{y}u)du-ṉi-(màta)			*	**
b.	(púl^{y}u)(dù-ṉi)-(màta)		*!	*	
c.	(púl^{y}u)du-(ṉì)-(màta)	*!			*

To summarise, stress in Diyari is assigned (i) initially in morphemes of at least two syllables, but never to monosyllables, and (ii) to the third syllable of a quadrisyllabic, but never a trisyllabic morpheme. This array of facts submits to an analysis in which four interacting constraints, Foot Binarity in (7), Parse-σ in (8), Morpheme-Foot-Left in (9) and Tautomorphemic-Foot are assigned the language-specific priorities in the constraint subhierarchy in (11). (The relationship of dominance between MFL and Parse-σ is not crucial. What is important is that these constraints are outranked by FtBin and Tauto-F.)

(11) *Diyari:* FtBin : Tauto-F » MFL » Parse-σ

The treatment of Diyari presented here has emphasised the roles of the constraints MFL and Tauto-F. MFL ensures the presence of a foot at the left edge of every morpheme large enough to support it under FtBin dominance, while Tauto-F insists that syllable-to-foot parsing be faithful to morphological structure.

4. Dyirbal

Dyirbal differs most significantly from Diyari in permitting the construction of feet across morpheme boundaries as long as the left edge of every foot occurs at the left edge of a morpheme. In Dyirbal, then, it is often better to parse syllables even if feet unfaithful to morphological structure result, leading to Tauto-F violations. In terms of the hierarchy, this difference is expressed by demoting Tauto-F from undominated status (in Diyari) to a position below Parse-σ in Dyirbal.

Tableau 8 presents analyses of the input /buyba-ri-ɲu/, a disyllabic root followed by two monosyllabic suffixes, with the constraints employed in §3. Like Diyari, Dyirbal imposes an absolute ban on monosyllabic feet (cf. *ɖúgumbil*, **ɖúgumbìl*), and is therefore again assigned undominated status. Due to its revised status, Tauto-F is routinely violated in surface forms like *búyba-rí-ɲu* , its effect suppressed by the dominant constraints MFL and Parse-σ. In Tableau 8 the candidate with FtBin violations is ruled out, leaving three contenders, all containing MFL violations. The optimal candidate is *(búyba)-(rí-ɲu)*, the minimal violator of MFL.

Tableau 8: Input /buyba-ri-ɲu/.

Candidates		FtBin	MFL	Parse-σ	Tauto-F
a.	(búyba)-(rí)-(ɲú)	*! *			
b.	buy(bá-ri)-ɲu		**! *	**	*
c.	(búyba)-ri-ɲu		**!	**	
d. ✓	(búyba)-(rí-ɲu)		*		*

(So far we have seen no evidence for ranking MFL and Parse-σ; any of the rankings MFL » Parse-σ, Parse-σ » MFL, or Parse-σ : MFL will yield the attested output. Evidence for the ranking MFL » Parse-σ, another difference between Diyari and Dyirbal, is provided below.)

Unmodified, the constraint hierarchy established so far does not select an optimal candidate when the input is a disyllabic or trisyllabic root followed by two monosyllabic suffixes, such as /nudil-mal-ɖa-ɲu/ or /banagay-mba-ri-ɲu/; the constraints in Tableau 8 fail to decide between *(núdil)-(mál-ɖa)-ɲu* and its rival **(núdil)-(mál-ɖa)-ɲu* which violate Parse-σ and MFL equally. The generalisation so far eluded is that in the attested output *(núdil)-(mál-ɖa)-ɲu*, the second foot lies as close to the left edge of the stem as possible without violating MFL (cf. *(bána)gay-(mbá-ri)-ɲu*, **(bána)gay-mba-(rí-ɲu)*). Assuming the stem to be coextensive with the category prosodic word (PrWd), this generalisation can be captured by introducing the constraint ALIGN FOOT-PRWD (or F-PrWd) in (12).

(12) *Align Foot-PrWd:* Align(F, L, PrWd, L)

F-PrWd states that for every left foot boundary, there exists a corresponding left PrWd boundary. Violation is evaluated gradiently, one infrigement assessed for every syllable separating a foot from the left edge of the PrWd.

Tableau 9 analyses the polysyllabic input /nudil-mal-ɖa-ɲu/ under the new constraint hierarchy. We see that when the root contains an even number of syllables and candidates are tied with equal numbers of MFL (and parse) violations (e.g. T9-a,b), the decision falls to F-PrWd.

Tableau 9: Input /nudil-mal-ɖa-ɲu/.

Candidates		FtBin	MFL	Par-σ	F-PrWd	Taut-F
a.✓	[(núdil)-(mál-ɖa)-ɲu]		**	*	**	*
b.	[(núdil)-mal-(ɖá-ɲu)]		**	*	***!	*
c.	[(núdil)-mal-ɖa-ɲu]		***!	***		
d.	[(núdil)-(mál-ɖa)-(ɲú)]	*!			** ****	*

Tableau 9 shows, at least, that F-PrWd must not be ranked more highly than MFL and Parse-σ since in that case, **núdil-mal-ɖa-ɲu* should be optimal. (Some prioritisation among the three constraints will be crucial, as T9-a and the unattested T9-c are tied with six violations across MFL, Parse-σ, and F-PrWd.)

Evidence for finer ranking distinctions emerges in Tableau 10. Here, the optimal form T10-e is correctly selected if MFL dominates F-PrWd and Parse-σ, and if F-PrWd and Parse-σ are not ranked with each other. Excluding candidates with FtBin and excessive MFL violations, we are left with T10-d,e,f, tied with two MFL violations. In this case, T10-e, with fewest violations across F-PrWd and Parse-σ as a block triumphs. (Parse-σ must not dominate F-PrWd since in that case, T10-d should be optimal.) It is interesting to note that while the rightmost foot in *núdil-mál-ɖa-ɲu*, Tableau 9, lies as close as possible to the left edge of the PrWd, this is not true in *bánagay-mbá-ri-ɲu.* The generalisation is that when competitors violate MFL equally, the candidate in which the second foot is shifted one syllable to the right wins, as this forestalls F-PrWd violations that would be incurred by a third foot (compare T10d,e).[6]

Tableau 10: Input /banagay-mba-ri-ɲu/.

Candidates		FtBin	MFL	Par-σ	F-PrWd	Taut-F
a.	[(bána)gay-(mbá-ri)-(ɲú)]	*!	*	*	*** *****	*
b.	[ba(nágay)-(mbá-ri)-ɲu]		***!	**	* ***	*
c.	[(bána)gay-mba-ri-ɲu]		***!	****		
d.	[(bána)(gáy-mba)-(rí-ɲu)]		**		** ****!	**
e.✓	[(bána)gay-(mbá-ri)-ɲu]		**	**	***	*
f.	[(bána)gay-mba-(rí-ɲu)]		**	**	****!	*

6 A similar rightward shift with an input consisting of a disyllabic root plus four monosyllabic suffixes (e.g. σ σ-σ-σ-σ-σ) would yield an extra MFL violation, and thus should not occur. The predicted optimal output, (σ σ)-(σ-σ)-(σ-σ), is consistent with Dixon's (1972) description of Dyirbal stress. However, a search of Dixon (1972) yielded no forms which might be used to test this prediction.

Candidates		FtBin	MFL	Par-σ	F-PrWd	Taut-F
a.	[(σ σ)-σ-(σ-σ)-(σ)]	*!	**	*	*** *****	*
b.✓	[(σ σ)-(σ-σ)-(σ-σ)]		**		** ****	**
c.	[(σ σ)-σ-σ-(σ-σ)]		***!	**	****	
d.	[(σ σ)-σ-(σ-σ)-σ]		***!	**	***	*
e.	(σ σ)-σ-σ-σ-σ		***!*	****		

Tableau 10 also shows that MFL domination over Parse-σ and F-PrWd is crucial. If these constraints were unranked, then T10-c should be optimal: since candidates T10-c and T10-e are tied with an equal number of violations across the three constraints, the deciding role should fall to Tauto-F.

So far, it has been assumed that F-PrWd and Parse-σ are unranked. In fact, the absence of ranking between these constraints is crucial to correctly determine optimal candidates based on quadrisyllabic inputs such as /burguṭum-bu/ and /mulumiyan/. Tableau 11 is based on the input /burguṭum-bu/, a trisyllabic root plus a single monosyllabic suffix. Doubly and singly-footed candidates, T11-b and T11-a, contain equal numbers of MFL violations. Furthermore, T11-a contains two parse violations, T11-b two F-PrWd violations. The tie between these otherwise equally harmonic candidates is broken by Tauto-F, which rules out T11-b.

Tableau 11: Input /burguṭum-bu/.

Candidates		FtBin	MFL	Par-σ	F-PrWd	Taut-F
a.✓	[(búrgu)ṭum-bu]		*	**		
b.	[(búrgu)(ṭúm-bu)]		*		**	*!
c.	[(búrgu)(ṭúm)-(bú)]	*! *			** ***	

Note that *(búrgu) ṭum-bu* in T11-a would still be selected as optimal under the ranking F-PrWd » Parse-σ. Evidence that this ranking cannot be correct is provided by an analysis of the monomorphemic /mulumiyan/. In this case, the doubly-footed candidate *(múlu)(míyan)*, with two F-PrWd violations, and not the singly-footed *(múlu)miyan* with two parse violations, is optimal--the scenario opposite to that in Tableau 11. Tauto-F is irrelevant for monomorphemic inputs, however, and cannot break the tie between the two main contenders. The correct result is obtained if we invoke MORPHEME-FOOT-RIGHT (MFR; the right-edge counterpart of MFL), stated in (13), and rank this final constraint at the bottom of the hierarchy below Tauto-F.

(13) *Morpheme-Foot-Right:* Align(M, R, F, R)

Analyses of quadrisyllabic /mulumiyan/ and the trisyllabic /ḍugumbil/ are presented in Tableau 12.

Tableau 12: Input /mulumiyan/.

Candidates		FtBin	MFL	Par-σ	F-PW	Taut-F	MFR
1a.✓	[(múlu)(míyan)]				**		
b.	[(múlu)miyan]			**			*!
c.	[mulu(míyan)]		*!	**	**		
d.	mulumiyan		*!	****			*

Tableau 12, continued.

Candidates		FtBin	MFL	Par-σ	F-PW	Taut-F	MFR
2a.✓	[(ɖúgum)bil]			*			*
b.	[ɖu(gúmbil)]		*!	*	*		
c.	ɖugumbil		*!	***			*
d.	[(ɖúgum)(bíl)]	*!			**		

Evidence for the ranking Tauto-F » MFR is provided by the analysis of the input form /burguɽum-bu/ in Tableau 11. As discussed above, the tie between T11-a,b is settled by excluding the candidate with a Tauto-F violation, even though this leads to two MFR violations in the optimal candidate *(búrgu) ɽum-bu.*

Another distinctive property of Dyirbal is that a monosyllabic suffix may be footed with the initial syllable of a disyllabic suffix across a morpheme boundary, showing that even though MFR is active in the hierarchy, it does not assert itself when F-PrWd is at stake.

Tableau 13: Input / ɖaŋga-na-mbila/.

Candidates		FtBin	MFL	Par-σ	F-PW	Taut-F	MFR
a.✓	[(ɖáŋga)-(ná-mbi)la]		*	*	**	*	**
b.	[(ɖáŋga)-na-(mbíla)]		*	*	***!		*
c.	[(ɖáŋga)-(ná)-(mbíla)]	*!			** ***		

In this section, I have argued that the facts of stress assignment in Dyirbal can be accommodated under the constraint hierarchy in (14).

(14) *Dyirbal:* FtBin » MFL » Parse-σ : F-PrWd » Tauto-F » MFR

Comparing the metrical systems of Diyari and Dyirbal in OT terms, we see that FtBin is unviolated in both languages. Important differences between the two languages are the low ranking assigned to Tauto-F, and the crucial roles played by F-PrWd and MFR in Dyirbal. Finally, MFL must outrank Parse-σ in Dyirbal, but not in Diyari. In §5 we turn to an examination of stress in Gooniyandi.

5. Gooniyandi

Gooniyandi demonstrates the cross-linguistically unmarked pattern of iterative footing from left to right within a PrWd. McGregor (1990:125) states that "[a]ll but a couple of disyllabic and polysyllabic morphemes bear initial stress, and constitute separate phonological words from the words to which they are attached."[7] That is, the PrWd consists of a minimally disyllabic morpheme and any following monosyllabic suffixes. To maximise the contrast with Diyari and Dyirbal, the analysis presented in this section is limited to the PrWd, the domain of stress in the three languages of this paper.[8]

The absence of stress on final odd-numbered syllables in forms like *wáɾamba* and *ŋáɾaɲú-wa-ŋga* shows that FtBin is once again undominated in Gooniyandi. That as many syllables as possible are parsed and that the resulting feet occur as close as possible to the left edge of the PrWd shows that Parse-σ and F-PrWd are active, with the former dominating the latter constraint to account for iterative footing. Tableau 14 presents analyses for the monomorphemic inputs /waɾamba/ and /ŋiɾiwarndi/ under the rankings FtBin » Parse-σ » F-PrWd » MFL.

Tableau 14: Unaffixed roots, inputs /waɾamba/, /ŋiɾiwarndi/.

Candidates		FtBin	Parse-σ	MFL	F-PrWd
1a. ✓	[(wáɾam)ba]		*		
b.	[wa(ɾámba)]		*	*!	*
c.	waɾamba		**!*	*	
d.	[(wáɾam)(bá)]	*!			**
2a. ✓	[(ŋíɾi)(wárndi)]				**
b.	[(ŋíɾi)warndi]		*! *		
c.	[ŋiɾi(wárndi)]		*! *	*	**
d.	[ŋi(ɾíwarn)di]		*! *	*	*

The significant difference between Gooniyandi and Dyirbal is that the final syllable of a trisyllabic root is footed with a following suffixed syllable in Gooniyandi, but not in Dyirbal (cf. GO *márlamí-ya*, DY *búrguɽum-bu*). The Dyirbal pattern was accounted for by positing crucial nonranking between Parse-σ and F-PrWd. The change in the constraint hierarchy of Gooniyandi which accounts for the metrical contrast is that Parse-σ dominates F-PrWd. As in Dyirbal, Tauto-F is routinely violated (cf. *ŋáɾaɲú-wa-ŋga*), suggesting that Tauto-F is again subordinated to Parse-σ and MFL. Tableau 15 shows that for the polymorphemic inputs /marlami-ya/, /ŋaɾaɲu-wa-ŋga/, /mila-jiɾ-iɲ-biɾ-a/, iterative footing across morpheme boundaries is driven by Parse-σ and F-PrWd, with MFL and Tauto-F having no effect.

---

[7] Another Australian language with this property is Yidin^y (Dixon 1977a,b).

[8] The emergence of multiple PrWds could be accounted for with a constraint Align(Morpheme, L, PrWd, L) (MORPH-PRWD), which requires that the left edge of every morpheme be aligned with the left edge of a PrWd. Under the ranking FtBin » Morph-PrWd, only suffixes of at least two syllables will be properly aligned with respect to Morph-PrWd.

Tableau 15: Inputs /marlami-ya/, / ŋaɾaɲu-wa- ŋga/, /mila-jiɾ-iɲ-biɾ-a/.

Candidates		FtBin	Pars-σ	F-PrWd	MFL	Taut-F
1a.	[(márla)mi-(yá)]	*!	*	***		
b.	[mar(lamí)-ya]		*! *	*	**	
c.	[(márla)mi-ya]		*! *		*	
d.✓	[(márla)(mí-ya)]			**	*	*
2a.	[(ŋáɾa)(ɲú-wa)-(ŋgá)]	*!		** ****	*	*
b.✓	[(ŋáɾa)(ɲú-wa)-ŋga]		*	**	**	*
c.	[(ŋáɾa)ɲu-(wá-ŋga)]		*	***!	*	*
3a.✓	[(míla)-(jíɾ-iɲ)-(bíɾ-a)]			** ****	**	**
b.	[(míla)-jiɾ-iɲ-(bíɾ-a)]		*! *	****	***	*
c.	[(míla)-jí(ɾ-iɲ-bíɾ)-a]		*! *	***	****	*
d.	[(míla)-jiɾ-iɲ-biɾ-a]		*! ***		****	

Dominance of Parse-σ is crucial for each of the inputs /marlami-ya/ and /mila-jiɾ-iɲ-biɾ-a/ in Tableau 15. Under the alternative, F-PrWd » Parse-σ, T15-1c should be optimal instead of T15-1d for /marlami-ya/, and T15-3d should be optimal instead of T15-3a for /mila-jiɾ-iɲ-biɾ-a/. (Equal ranking, Parse-σ : F-PrWd, would be equally unsuccessful.) Evidence that F-PrWd must outrank MFL is that under the opposite or equal ranking, T15-2c and not T15-2b should be optimal. There is no evidence that MFL and Tauto-F are crucially ranked with respect to one another.

To sum up, the left-to-right iterative stress pattern of Gooniyandi is captured in an OT analysis under the constraint hierarchy in (15).

(15) *Gooniyandi:* FtBin » Parse-σ » F-PrWd » MFL » Tauto-F

Only the undominated position of FtBin and the rankings Parse-σ » F-PrWd and F-PrWd » MFL are crucial. Relevant differences between Gooniyandi and Diyari, Dyirbal are that in Gooniyandi, Parse-σ dominates all constraints but FtBin, followed in the hierarchy by F-PrWd.

6. Conclusion

This paper has shown that variations in the assignment of stress in Diyari, Dyirbal, and Gooniyandi can be analysed in optimality-theoretic terms by differently prioritising six constraints, Foot Binarity, (7); Parse-σ, (8); Tautomorphemic-Foot, (10); Morpheme-Foot-Left, (9); Foot-PrWd, (12); and Morpheme-Foot-Right, (13). The constraint subhierarchies in (16) were posited to account for metrical differences across the three languages.

(16)

Diyari:	FtBin : Tauto-F » MFL » Parse-σ
Dyirbal:	FtBin » MFL » Parse-σ : F-PrWd » Tauto-F » MFR
Gooniyandi:	FtBin » Parse-σ » F-PrWd » MFL » Tauto-F

Of the constraints in (16), only Foot Binarity is surface-true of the three languages discussed. Beyond this, the following significant differences between Diyari, Dyirbal, and Gooniyandi are observed. Diyari places an absolute ban on foot structures incorporating syllables from different morphemes. The constraint which plays a crucial role in enforcing this is Tauto-F. Dyirbal permits heteromorphemic footing, but insists that the left edge of every foot be aligned with the left edge of a morpheme. Surprisingly, this result emerged as an effect of crucial nonranking between Parse-σ and F-PrWd, not as a product of MFL. In Gooniyandi, morphological faithfulness in foot parsing and left-edge foot/morpheme alignment are sacrificed to parsing requirements and the requirement that feet must occur as close as possible to the left edge of the prosodic word.

References

Austin, P. 1981. *A grammar of Diyari, South Australia.* NY and London: Cambridge University Press.

Dixon, R.M.W. 1972. *The Dyirbal Language of North Queensland.* NY & London: Cambridge University Press.

Hayes, B. 1994. *Metrical Stress Theory: Principles & Case Studies.* Chicago: The University of Chicago Press.

Hewitt, M. 1992. *Vertical Maximization & Metrical Theory.* PhD dissertation, Brandeis University.

Itô & Mester. 1992. Weak Layering & Word Binarity. UCSC unpublished ms.

Kager, R. 1989. *A Metrical Theory of Stress & Destressing in English & Dutch.* Dordrecht: Foris.

McGregor, D. 1990. *A functional grammar of Gooniyandi.* Amsterdam: John Benjamins.

McCarthy, J. & A. Prince 1986. Prosodic Morphology. UMass/Rutgers unpublished ms.

McCarthy, J. & A. Prince 1993a. *Prosodic Morphology I.* UMass/Rutgers unpublished ms. (forthcoming, MIT Press).

McCarthy, J. & A. Prince 1993b. Generalized Alignment. UMass/Rutgers unpublished ms.

Poser, W. 1989. The metrical foot in Diyari. *Phonology* 6.117-148.

Prince, A. 1980. A Metrical Theory of Estonian Quanity. *LI* 11.511-562.

Prince, A. & P. Smolensky. 1991. Optimality. Paper given at the *Arizona Phonology Conference* (Tucson).

Prince, A. & P. Smolensky. 1993. *Optimality Theory: Constraint Interaction in Generative Grammar.* Rutgers/Univ. of Colorado unpublished ms. (forthcoming, MIT Press).

Ruhlen, M. 1987. *A Guide to the World's Languages. Volume 1: Classification.* Stanford, CA: Stanford University Press.

Selkirk, E.O. 1984. *Phonology & Syntax: The Relation Between Sound & Structure.* Cambridge, MA & London, Eng.: The MIT Press.

Geminate Consonants in Moraic Phonology

STUART DAVIS
Indiana University

1. Introduction

In Hayes's (1989) theory of moraic phonology, a short vowel underlyingly consists of one mora while a long vowel underlyingly consists of two moras. With respect to consonants, a geminate consonant is represented as being underlyingly moraic while other consonants are nonmoraic. Nonmoraic consonants that are syllabified as part of the coda may become moraic by a language-specific rule of Weight-by-Position, shown in (1).

```
(1)     σ               σ
        |               |\
        μ      --->     μ μ
        |               | |
        V C             V C    (Condition: σ dominates only one mora)
```

Given Hayes's theory of moraification, there are two types of syllables that are bimoraic in languages that lack the rule of Weight-by-Postion): CVV syllables and CVG syllables (where CVG represents a syllable that is closed by the first part of a geminate consonant). These are shown in (2).

b. CVG syllable

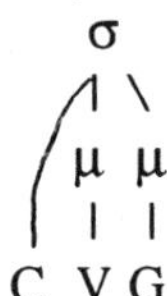

On the other hand, CV and CVC syllables (where a CVC syllable is a syllable closed by a nongeminate) would be monomoraic, as seen in (3).

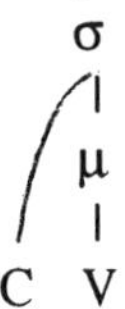

b. CVC syllable

Selkirk (1990) and Tranel (1991) independently make the observation that Hayes's moraification theory predicts the existence of languages where the syllable types in (2) pattern together as bimoraic with respect to stress and other phonological and morphophonological phenomena while the syllable types in (3) would pattern as monomoraic. This follows from Hayes's theory, since in languages where Weight-by-Position does not apply and where there are geminate consonants, the two syllable types in (2) would be the only bimoraic syllables. It would then be expected that processes like stress would distinguish the bimoraic types in (2) from the monomoraic ones in (3). Both Selkirk and Tranel are critical of this possibility. Neither of these researchers are able to find cases where the two syllable types in (2) pattern together. They each refer to problematic cases for the prediction. Most problematic are languages with geminates that possess rules stressing syllables containing long vowels but ignoring all closed syllables including those closed by a geminate. If syllable weight is determined by moraic structure, then Hayes's theory makes a clear prediction that CVG syllables should not be ignored by such stress rules since they are bimoraic.

There are several languages that can be cited to show that Hayes's theory makes an incorrect prediction. The specifc example cited by Tranel (1991) is the Paleo-Siberian language Selkup based on the data in Halle and Clements (1983). In Selkup, stress falls on the rightmost heavy syllable, or if there are no heavy syllables, stress falls on the initial syllable. The relevant data from Halle & Clements are shown in (4).

(4) Selkup (Halle & Clements 1983)

a.	kɨpɔ́	'tiny'
b.	qumó:qi	'two human beings'
c.	ú:cɨqo	'to work'
d.	qumo:qlɪlí:	'your two friends'
e.	ú:cɨkkak	'I am working'
f.	u:cɔ́:mɨt	'we work'
g.	qúmɨnɨk	'human being (dat.)'
h.	ámɨrna	'eats'

The key data are in (4e) and (4f). In (4e) the first syllable has a long vowel and the second syllable is closed by the first part of a geminate. In (4f) the first two syllables contain long vowels. In the right-to-left scansion of the stress rule the seemingly bimoraic CVG second syllable of (4e) is passed over whereas the bimoraic CVV second syllable of (4f) receives the stress. Under the assumption that the Selkup stress rule picks out heavy (or bimoraic) syllables, the lack of second syllable stress in (4e) is unexpected given Hayes's theory since the supposed bimoraic second syllable of (4e) fails to act as such.

To show that Selkup is not an isolated example, one can point to the same phenomena in Chuvash, an Altaic language of the Turkic group. According to the description of stress in Krueger (1961), primary stress falls on the rightmost syllable with a full vowel or else on the initial syllable. (I follow Hayes 1981 in assuming that the difference between a full vs. reduced vowel is equivalent to long vs. short.) Chuvash has geminates, but a CVG syllable is not treated as heavy by the stress rule. As in Selkup, they are skipped in the determination of stress. Some relevant examples are given in (5).

(5) Chuvash (Krueger 1961)

a.	lăšá	'horse'
b.	ĕné	'cow'
c.	kămaká	'stove'
d.	sarlaká	'window'
e.	álăk	'door'
f.	yĕnérčĕk	'saddle'
g.	kálăttămăr	'we would say'

The key piece of data is (5g), where stress falls on the first syllable of the word even though the second syllable is closed by a geminate. Thus in both Chuvash and Selkup CVG syllables do not seem to function like bimoraic

CVV syllables but rather like monomoraic CV and CVC syllables.

Based on evidence like that seen in Chuvash and Selkup, Tranel (1991) and Selkirk (1990) contend that geminate consonants are not underlyingly moraic. However, they each make a different proposal on how to account for this. Tranel proposes that the reason why stress rules do not distinguish CVG syllables from CVC syllables derives from the Principle of Equal Weight for Codas. Under this principle, geminates are not special; a syllable closed by a geminate is treated like any other closed syllable in the language. If a language treats closed syllables as heavy then CVG syllables are heavy, but if a language treats closed syllables as light then CVG syllables are light. Thus, on Tranel's account, in languages like Selkup and Chuvash all coda consonants are weightless, even if they are part of a geminate; neither CVC nor CVG syllables are heavy.

On the other hand, Selkirk (1990) argues that geminates are represented underlyingly as having two root nodes that share stricture and place features as shown in (6). (RN = root node)

```
(6)     RN RN
          \/
       [±cont]
           |
         Place
```

On Selkirk's account, a geminate is not underlyingly moraic. The implication of this is that if Weight-by-Position applies in a language assigning a mora to a coda consonant it would assign a mora to the initial root node of a geminate. But since in Selkup and Chuvash, Weight-by-Position does not apply, a geminate does not make a syllable heavy.

Given the work of Selkirk (1990) and Tranel (1991), it seems that Hayes's theory makes wrong predictions in treating the syllable types in (2) as patterning together as bimoraic. In this paper, though, I present evidence from Hindi and Korean that supports the view that CVV and CVG syllables can pattern together as bimoraic as opposed to CV and CVC syllables which pattern as monomoraic and thus supports Hayes's moraification algorithm. In Section 2, I show that stress in the Hindi dialect described by Gupta (1987, 1988) treats CVV and CVG syllables as heavy as opposed to CV and CVC syllables which are treated as light. In Section 3, I consider data from Korean umlaut that supports a view of moraification in Korean in which CVG syllables are bimoraic whereas CVC syllables are monomoraic. In Section 4, I conclude by discussing the implications for moraic theory of the patterning of CVV and CVG syllables as heavy and by discussing why in some languages geminates seem to be underlyingly bimoraic while in other languages they seem not to be.

2. Hindi

If Hayes's (1989) algorithm for moraification is correct, one might expect to find a language in which long vowels could normally occur in closed syllables (CVVC) but not in a syllable closed by a geminate (CVVG), given the strong cross-linguistic tendency for syllables to be maximally bimoraic. In such a language, a potential CVVG syllable would have three moras and should be disallowed, while CVVC syllables would just have two moras and so should occur. The existence of such languages would provide strong support for geminates being underlyingly moraic. One such language reported in the literature is Hindi. Consider M. Ohala's (1983) discussion on syllables and phonotactics in Hindi. Ohala specifically gives the template in (7) for (native) Hindi syllables.

(7) Template for Hindi syllables (Ohala 1983)
CCVVCC

Ohala further observes that a geminate consonant cannot immediately follow a long vowel. She states this as an if-then type sequential constraint, given in (8).

(8) Sequential constraint on the co-occurrence of long vowels and geminates (Ohala 1983:57)

"If a consonant is [+long] then the preceding segment must be a vowel and [-long]."

A similar observation is made by Gupta (1988) and is consistent with the data and discussion on Hindi syllable weight and stress found in such works as Sharma (1969), M. Ohala (1977), Gupta (1987), Pandey (1989), and Shukla (1990). Words such as that in (9) with CVVC syllables are common in Hindi, but there are no words with CVVG syllables.

(9) a.máan.viiy.taa 'inhuman'

The observation that Hindi allows for long vowels in closed syllables but not in syllables closed by a geminate can be accounted for if in Hindi syllables are maximally bimoraic, if Weight-by-Position does not apply, and if geminates are underlyingly moraic. In this way, a potential syllable with a long vowel closed by a geminate is disallowed since it would be trimoraic, but a syllable with a long vowel closed by a nongeminate is allowed since it would only be bimoraic. This is shown in (10).

(10) a. Ill-formed trimoraic CVVG syllable   b. Well-formed bimoraic CVVC syllable

The difference of the syllable types in (10) is unexpected given Tranel's Principle of Equal Weight for Codas, but it is consistent with Hayes's view.

Additional support that geminates are underlyingly moraic in Hindi comes from the dialectal stress pattern described by Gupta (1987, 1988) and analyzed by Davis (1989). Gupta describes a dialect of Hindi where stress is sensitive to multiple degrees of syllable weight. In her description, CVG syllables pattern with CVV syllables in functioning as heavy or bimoraic in attracting stress, while CV and CVC syllables behave as light or monomoraic. The data in (11) reflect primary stress in words without superheavy (CVVC) syllables.[1]

(11)

a.	rí.pu	'enemy'	j.	bée.čaa.raa	'pitiable'
b.	lí.pi	'script'	k.	bá.ra.sa.naa	'to shower'
c.	sú.ru.či	'good taste'	l.	pá.ri.či.taa	'female acquaintance'
d.	á.nu.ma.ti	'permission'	m.	sil.váa.ne	'to stitch'
e.	kú.la.pa.ti	'patriarch'	n.	bah.láa.ne	'to entice'
f.	da.káa.rẽ	'belches'	o.	sú.bak.naa	'to sob'
g.	ka.yáa.mat	'catastrophe'	p.	mu.hál.la	'locality'
h.	ni.šáa.nii	'clue'	q.	át.taa.li.kaa.ye	'attics'
i.	áa.vaa.raa	'vagabond'	r.	ni.hát.taa	'without arms'

In the data in (11), primary stress falls on the leftmost heavy syllable. If there are no heavy syllables then stress falls on the initial syllable. Specifically, in examining the data, (11a-e) show that in words with only CV syllables the first one receives primary stress. The data in (11f-g) show that if there is only one (nonfinal) syllable in the word with a long vowel then that syllable receives stress. The data in (11h-j) show that if there is more than one CVV syllable in the word then the leftmost one receives stress. The data in (11k-l) show that a word final syllable is normally considered extrametrical. The data in (11m-o) show that a CVC syllable is not normally considered as heavy; it does not attract stress even if it is in position to do so. The data in (11p-r), however, show that CVG syllables are treated as heavy with respect to assignment of primary stress. Thus the Hindi stress pattern provides a telling example where CVV and CVG syllables are treated by stress assignment as heavy or bimoraic as opposed to CV and CVC syllables which are treated as light or monomoraic.

The heaviness of CVV and CVG syllables in Hindi as opposed to CVC syllables can be accounted for under Hayes's theory of moraification if Weight-by-Position does not apply in Hindi. On this view only CVV and CVG syllables are bimoraic, as illustrated in (12) where the moraification and syllable structure of the words in (11h), (11r), and (11o) are provided, respectively.

(12) a. σ σ σ b. σ σ σ c. σ σ σ

μ μμ μμ μ μμ μμ μ μ μμ

a. n i š a n i [nišáanii]

b. n i h a t a [nihάttaa]

c. s u b a k n a [súbaknaa]

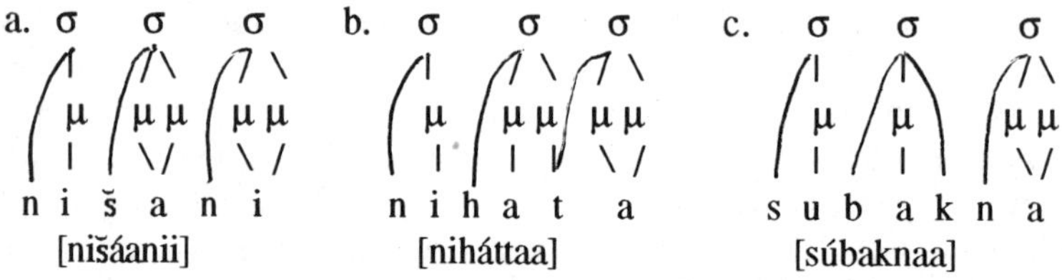

The Hindi stress rule puts stress on the leftmost bimoraic syllable (CVV or CVG) or else the first syllable. Thus, Hindi constitutes a clear case where CVG syllables are distinguished from CVC syllable in functioning as bimoraic along with CVV syllables.

3. Korean

Another language in which CVG syllables behave as bimoraic whereas other closed syllables behave as monomoraic is Korean. The evidence that Korean CVG syllables are bimoraic does not come from the accent system (which traditionally is assumed to be an initial accenting language, though this is not completely accepted) nor from shortening in closed syllables since Korean allows for long vowels to occur in all types of closed syllables. Rather, the evidence comes from the umlaut process.

Korean has an umlaut process that fronts a vowel when the vowel /i/ is in the following syllable. Sample data are shown in (13) and come from Lee (1993).

(13) a. /aki/ ---> [agi] or [ægi] 'baby'
b. /əmi/ ---> [əmi] or [emi] 'mother'
c. /tatɨmi/ ---> [tadɨmi] or [tadimi] 'fulling block'
d. /soncapi/ --> [sonjabi] or [sonjæbi] 'handle'
e. /s'ɨli/ ---> [s'ɨri] or [s'iri] 'to be sick'
f. /tani/ ---> [tani] or [tæni] 'to go to and from'
g. /mati/ ---> [madi] or [mædi] 'knot'
h. /ak'i/ ---> [ak'i] or [æk'i] 'to hold dear'

Umlaut is subject to a number of morphological and phonological conditions. Some of these conditions have been previously discussed by Hume (1990) and Lee (1993). With respect to morphological conditions, certain suffixes do not trigger umlaut such as the nominative marker /-i/ as shown in (14). This should be compared with the nominalizer suffix /-i/ in (15) which does trigger umlaut.

(14) Nominative /-i/
a. /salam + i/ ---> [sarami] *[saræmi] 'a man (nominative)'
b. /cam + i/ ---> [cami] *[cæmi] 'sleep (nominative)'

(15) Nominalizer /-i/
a. /mək + i/ ---> [məki] or [meki] 'food'
b. /soncap + i/ ---> [sonjabi] or [sonjæbi] 'handle'

With respect to phonological conditions on umlaut, it is well known that palatal consonants block the spread of umlaut as seen by the data in (16).

(16) a. /kac^{h}i/ ---> [kac^{h}i] *[kæc^{h}i] 'value'
b. /taci/ ---> [taji] *[tæji] 'to mince'
c. /p^{h}əci/ ---> [p^{h}əji] *[p^{h}eji] 'to spread out'

The observation that the palatal coronals block umlaut but that the anterior coronals /t/, /l/, and /n/ do not (as seen by data like that in (13e-g)) motivates Hume's (1990) analysis of umlaut as involving the regressive spreading of the V-Place Coronal Node of /i/ to the preceding vowel. Hume's umlaut rule is shown in (17).

(17) Korean Umlaut (Hume 1990)

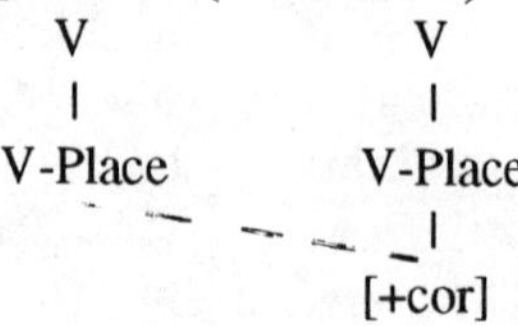

On Hume's account, palatal consonants block umlaut because they are specified for the V-Place Coronal Node. The blocking behavior of palatals is shown in (18) where the V-Place [+coronal] cannot spread regressively to the preceding vowel because of the V-Place coronal specification of the intervening palatal consonant.

(18) Palatal Blocking

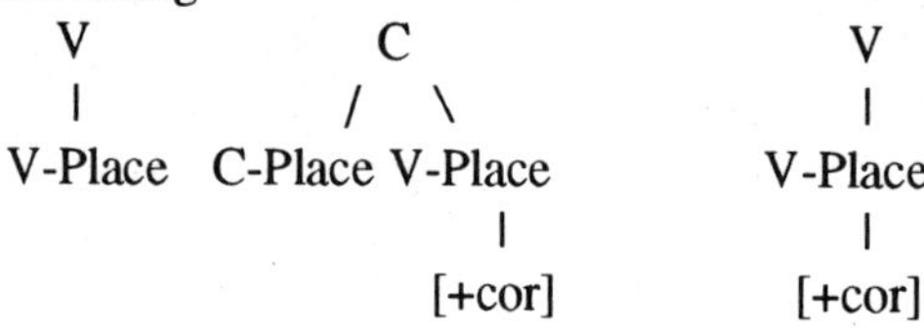

Lee (1993) observes other phonological conditions on umlaut in addition to palatal blocking. For example, Lee observes that long vowels fail to undergo umlaut as seen by the data in (19).

(19)	a. /sa:lm + ki/	--->	[sa:mgi] *[sæ:mgi]	'to be boiled'
	b. /pə:li/	--->	[pə:ri] *[pe:ri]	'earning'

Based on this observation one can posit a revision of the umlaut rule as in (20).

(20) Umlaut Rule (revised)

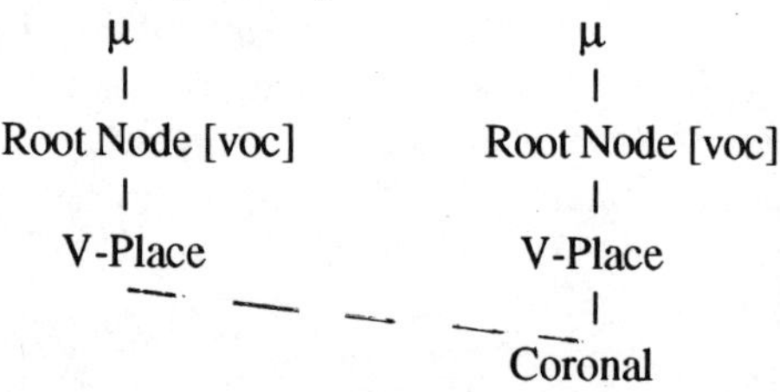

Given the rule in (20), the lack of application of umlaut to long vowels as in (19) can be accounted for by the Linking Constraint of Hayes (1986) so that umlaut only applies if both the target and trigger vowels are linked to a single mora. That is, under the revised rule in (20), umlaut applies between two vowels that are short and moraically adjacent.

Lee (1993) further discusses the effect of an intervening consonant cluster on the application of umlaut. Normally, umlaut applies over an intervening consonant cluster as shown by the data in (21).

(21) Umlaut occurring over an intervening consonant cluster

a. /nampi/	--->	[nambi] or [næmbi]	'kettle'
b. /əŋki/	--->	[əŋgi] or [eŋgi]	'to be curdled'
c. /namki/	--->	[naŋgi] or [næŋgi]	'to leave behind'
d. /anki/	--->	[aŋgi] or [æŋgi]	'to be embraced'
e. /palk + hi/	-->	[palk^{h}i] or [pælk^{h}i]	'to brighten'

Given that in the data in (21) the target vowel for umlaut is in a closed syllable, the data show that the presence of a coda consonant does not block umlaut. However, Lee (1993) makes the interesting observation that umlaut does not apply over an intervening geminate consonant, whether derived or underlying. Relevant data are provided in (22).

(22) Umlaut does not occur over an intervening geminate

a. /ənni/	--->	[ənni]	*[enni]	'sister'
b. /al+li/	--->	[alli]	*[ælli]	'to inform'
c. /kəl+li/	--->	[kəlli]	*[kelli]	'to be hung'
d. /p'al+li/	--->	[p'alli]	*[pælli]	'to be sucked'
e. /mal+li/	--->	[malli]	*[mælli]	'to dry'
f. /ak+ki/	--->	[akk'i]	*[ækk'i]	'instrument'
g. /kammi (lop-ta)/	-->	[kammi]	*[kæmmi]	'to be sweet'

The relevant factor in the blocking of umlaut in (22) does seem to be the occurrence of a geminate consonant. The presence of an intervening cluster does not normally block umlaut as seen in (21), and, moreover, the singleton counterparts of these geminate consonants do not block umlaut as seen by the data in (23).

(23)

a. /tani/	--->	[tani] or [tæni]	'to go to and from'
b. /s'ɨli/	--->	[s'ɨri] or [s'iri]	'to be sick'
c. /əmi/	--->	[əmi] or [emi]	'mother'

Thus in comparing the data in (21) and (22), it can be seen that a coda consonant does not normally block umlaut unless it is the first part of a geminate. Given the umlaut rule in (20) which was motivated based on the data in (13), (16) and (19) we can account for the observation that geminates block umlaut by positing that geminates are moraic but coda consonants in general are not. If Korean geminate consonants are moraic then they would be predicted to block umlaut given the rule in (20), since the target and trigger vowels for umlaut would no longer be adjacent on the moraic tier. This is illustrated in (24) with the word [ənni] 'sister'.

```
(24) [ənni] *[enni] 'sister'
          μ  μ  μ
          |  |  |
          ə  n  i   (umlaut does not apply)
```

On the other hand, in the words in (21) where the target vowel is in a syllable closed by a non-geminate consonant, umlaut still occurs since the target vowel and the trigger vowel are adjacent on the moraic tier. This is shown in (25) with the word [næmbi] 'kettle'.

```
(25) /nampi/ ---> [næmbi] 'kettle'
            μ     μ
            |     |
          n a m b i   (umlaut does apply)
```

The generalization that thus emerges is that umlaut applies only if the target vowel is in a monomoraic syllable. It applies in data like in (13) and (21) where the syllable with the target vowel would be monomoraic, but it does not apply if the target vowel is in a bimoraic syllable as in (19) and (22). Specifically, if the target vowel is long or in a syllable closed by a geminate umlaut fails to occur. Thus, only CVV and CVG syllables are being treated as bimoraic while CV and CVC syllables pattern as monomoraic.

4. Conclusion

In conclusion, there are languages in which CVG syllables function as bimoraic while CVC syllables function as monomoraic. Such languages are problematic for Tranel's proposed principle of Equal Weight for Codas since a coda consonant that is part of a geminate contributes to the weight of the syllable whereas other coda consonants do not. Moreover, the patterning of CVC and CVG as heavy is also problematic for Zec's (1988) sonority-based approach to moraification. Zec's theory predicts that in a language where an obstruent in a coda contributes to the weight of a syllable, a sonorant in a coda must also contribute to the weight of a syllable. However, the Hindi stress pattern, exemplified by the data in (11), is counter to Zec's prediction. For example in (11q), *áttaalikaaye* 'attics', stress falls on the initial syllable which is closed by an obstruent. However in (11m), *silváane* 'to stitch', stress does not fall on the initial syllable even though it is closed by a sonorant. This would constitute an example in which a syllable closed by an obstruent makes a syllable heavy where a syllable closed by a sonorant does not contribute weight. Thus the patterning of CVG syllables as heavy and CVC syllables as light is potentially problematic for Zec's sonority-based approach.[2]

With respect to Selkirk's (1990) two root node theory of geminates shown in (6), a language that treats CVG syllables as heavy and CVC syllables as light is unexpected since Weight-by-Position would not seem to apply consistently to all coda consonants. Selkirk, though, discusses the possibility of languages treating only CVV and CVG syllables as heavy to the exclusion of all other syllable types. Selkirk does not discuss specific languages showing such a division (such as Hindi and Korean); however, she suggests that were such a division to occur, it could be handled within the two root node theory of geminates by having Weight-by-Position being constrained by the Coda Condition (Ito 1989). That is, Weight-by-Position would apply to a coda consonant only if it were not singly linked to a Root Node. In this way, a geminate would be assigned a mora from Weight-by-Position since it is doubly-linked, whereas a single coda consonant would not be assigned a mora. While Selkirk's idea of Weight-by-Position being constrained by the Coda Condition is very intriguing, one problem for it is that is that it seems to predict that a place assimilated coda nasal should also behave as moraic. However, this prediction is not correct as can be seen by the Korean data in (21a-d). In these words there is a coda nasal that is assimilated to a following onset, yet they do not behave as moraic. Thus the patterning of CVV and CVG as heavy remains problematic for Selkirk's two root node theory of geminates.

Finally, the question that needs to be addressed is if geminate consonants are underlyingly moraic and contribute weight to the syllable, how is it that there are languages like Selkup and Chuvash in (4) and (5) which have quantity-sensitive stress but ignore the moraic status of geminates? Here I would refer to Steriade (1991) and Hyman (1992), who show that different moraic projections may be required within the same language to account for different weight sensitive phenomena. For example, only a subset of moras may be relevant for stress. Thus, in Selkup and Chuvash, only moras dominating vowels are projected for stress; moras dominating consonants would not be relevant. Nonetheless, the Korean and

Hindi data presented in this paper show that a syllable closed by a geminate does act as bimoraic even when a syllable closed by a nongeminate does not act as such.

Acknowledgments

I would like to thank Mi-Hui Cho, Daniel Dinnsen, Sharon Inkelas, Gregory Iverson, Jonni Kanerva, Jong-Kyoo Kim, Yongsung Lee, Minsu Shim, and Jin-Young Tak for discussion on aspects of this paper. Any errors are my responsibility.

Notes

[1]All data presented come from Gupta (1987, 1988). The data reflect stress on monomorphemic words and on polymorphemic words where the affixes are not stress affecting. Like other researchers on Hindi stress, such as Pandey (1989), Gupta assumes that rules of stress placement apply after other rules affecting syllable structure. In the data in (11) a period represents a syllable boundary. I do not follow Gupta in syllabifying intervocalic geminates as being entirely in the coda. I give their standard syllabification.

[2]Zec (1988) does not explicitly discuss the moraic status of geminates, but in her discussion on Italian she seems to assume that geminates are underlyingly nonmoraic.

References

Davis, Stuart. 1990. Stress, syllable weight hierarchies, and moraic phonology. *ESCOL* 6.84-92.

Gupta, Abha. 1987. Hindi word stress and the obligatory branching parameter. *CLS* 23.134-148.

Gupta, Abha. 1988. Peculiarities of geminates in Hindi. Unpublished ms. University of Arizona.

Halle, Morris & Clements, George. 1983. *Problem book in phonology.* Cambridge: MIT Press.

Hayes, Bruce. 1981. *A metrical theory of stress rules.* Doctoral dissertation, MIT. Revised version distributed by Indiana University Linguistics Club, Indiana University, Bloomington, Indiana.

Hayes, Bruce. 1986. Inalterability in CV phonology. *Language* 62.321-351.

Hayes, Bruce. 1989. Compensatory lengthening in moraic phonology. *Linguistic inquiry* 20.253-306.

Hume, Elizabeth. 1990. Front vowels, palatal consonants, and the rule of umlaut in Korean. *NELS* 20.230-243.

Hyman, Larry. 1992. Moraic mismatches in Bantu. *Phonology* 9.255-265.

Ito, Junko. 1989. A prosodic theory of epenthesis. *NLLT* 7.217-259.

Krueger, John. 1961. *Chuvash manual.* Bloomington: Indiana University Publications.

Lee, Yongsung. 1993. *Topics in the vowel phonology of Korean.* Doctoral dissertation, Indiana University.

Ohala, Manjari. 1977. Stress in Hindi. *Studies in stress and accent* (Southern California Occassional Papers in Lingusitics, 4), ed. by Larry Hyman, 327-338. USC, Department of Linguistics: Los Angeles.

Ohala, Manjari. 1983 *Aspects of Hindi phonology*. Delhi: Motilal Banarsidass.

Pandey, Pramod. 1989. Word accentuation in Hindi. *Lingua* 7.37-73.

Selkirk, Elisabeth. 1990. A two root theory of length. *University of Massachusetts Occasional Papers* 14.123-171.

Sharma, Aryendra. 1969. Hindi word-accent. *Indian linguistics* 30.115-118.

Shukla, Shaligram. 1990. Syllable structure and word stress in Hindi. *The Georgetown journal of languages and linguistics* 1.237-247.

Steriade, Donca. 1991. Moras and other slots. *FLSM* 1.254-280.

Tranel, Bernard. 1991. CVC light syllables, geminates and moraic theory. *Phonology* 8.291-302.

Zec, Draga. 1988. *Sonority constraints on prosodic structure.* Doctoral dissertation, Stanford University.

Complex Palatal Geminates in Brazilian Portuguese

JAMES P. GIANGOLA
University of California, San Diego

0. Introduction

In the phonology of Brazilian Portuguese [BP], the palatal sonorants [ñ] and [λ][1] are exceptional in numerous ways with respect to other palatal and sonorant consonants. The palatal sonorants are subject to certain distributional restrictions, and they interact with stress placement in a way that other consonants do not. In addition, vowels are always nasalized before [ñ], but are nasalized before [n] and [m] only under certain conditions. Finally, [ñ] is generally pronounced as [ỹ] in colloquial speech, and [λ] realized as [y] or [l] in Non-Standard BP.

Traditionally, it has been assumed that [ñ] and [λ], like the other sonorants in BP, are represented as structurally simple phonemes (Hall 1943, Reid & Leite 1947). Within a feature system such as that in the Sound Pattern of English (Chomsky & Halle 1968), these segments are analyzed as [-anterior] coronals. Further, it has been assumed that the palatal sonorants are simply onsets, without the recognition of their

[1] For typographic convenience I use [ñ] and [λ] instead of IPA [ɲ] and [ʎ], respectively.

exceptionally coda-like properties (e.g. Quicoli 1990:321)[2]. If one adopts both these assumptions, then [ñ] and [λ] are idiosyncratic, and a natural class cannot be recognized.

In this paper, I argue, however, that [ñ] and [λ] are only apparently idiosyncratic. Under the hypothesis that [ñ] and [λ] are not simple segments, but are underlyingly geminates in BP, we can account for their idiosyncratic properties.

I propose, further, that the palatal sonorants in BP are complex coronal segments, underlyingly /n^y/ and /l^y/, represented with a secondary *vocalic* articulation (after Clements 1991). The Complex Segment Analysis facilitates an explanation of the informal and Non-Standard variants [ỹ], [l], and [y]. Further support for the complexity of [ñ] and [λ] is historical: in Latin, sequences consisting of a coronal sonorant plus a front vowel coalesced into a single segment, [ñ] or [λ].

This paper proceeds along the following course. Section 1 exposes the seemingly exceptional behavior of [ñ] and [λ]. Section 2 provides pertinent background on the basic facts of BP syllable structure, as well as the relevant theoretical background, i.e. Moraic Theory (Hayes 1989) and hierarchical feature organization (Clements 1991). In Section 3, I account for the apparent idiosyncracies of [ñ] and [λ] under the assumption that they are moraic and syllablified simultanesouly as coda and onset. In Section 4, I present both synchronic and diachronic evidence for the structural complexity of [ñ] and [λ].

1.0 The exceptional properties of BP palatal sonorants

1.1 Distributional restrictions

The palatal sonorants are always intervocalic, e.g. *sonho* [sõñu] 'dream' and *olho* [oλu] 'eye.' As the data in (1) show, labial and [+ant] coronal sonorants can occur as onsets following closed syllables, while the palatal sonorants cannot.

(1)	mesmo	[mež.mu]	'same, really'	*[mež.ñu]
	forno	[foχ.nu]	'oven'	*[foχ.ñu]
	caule	[kaw.li]	'stem'	*[kaw.λi]

The palatal sonorants never follow closed syllables. Further, palatal

---

[2] Quicoli's formulation of an [ñ]-only nasalization rule (his 'Nasalization subcase 3') presupposes that [ñ] is an onset. If it were analyzed as a geminate, the rule would be unnecessary, given his rule of nasalization from nasal codas (his 'Nasalization subcase 2').

sonorants are seldom found in word-initial position. Other palatal consonants may occur word-initially, e.g. *giz* [žis] 'chalk'. The palatal sonorants thus form a class by themselves distributionally.

Nonetheless, [ñ] may appear word-initially in a few rare words of foreign origin, exemplified in (2)-(3):

(2) Denasalization

a. Afro-Braz. creole	[ñ]á, [ñ]a[ñ]á → [yayá] iaiá	'Miss'
b. from Tupi	[ñ]andaia ~ [ž]andaia ~ [n]andaia	'kind of bird'

(3) Epenthesis

a. from Italian	[ñ]occhi → i[ñ]oque	'pasta dumpling'
b. from Tupi	[ñ]ambu ~ i[ñ]ambu	'kind of partridge'
c. from Tupi	[ñ]aca ~ i[ñ]aca	'body stench, B.O.'

In these borrowings, word-initial [ñ] either undergoes denasalization, as in (2), or triggers epenthesis, as in (3).

The same restrictions apply to [λ]. It does not appear word-initially, except for a few Spanish loans, e.g. *lhama* 'the Andean ruminant' and erudite *lhano* 'sincere, frank'. Furthermore, the infrequent third person indirect object clitic, *lhe*, is generally pronounced [li] (Thomas 1969).

If the palatal sonorants are freely allowed in onset poition, these distributional restrictions and loan-word modifications are puzzling.

1.2 Stress placement

Another idiosycracy of palatal sonorants is their role in determining stress placement. Just as Harris (1983) notes for Spanish, antepenult stress is impossible if the penult is heavy in BP. Consequently, antepenult stress is prohibited in words like *a.fói.to* 'bold' and *a.pós.to* 'bet', owing to the heavy penult. In contrast, antepenult stress is possible in *á.ci.do* 'acid' and *ár.vo.re* 'tree' since the penult is light.

When [ñ] and [λ] are the onsets of word-final syllables, stress can only fall on the penult, as in *aranha* [a.rã´.ñʌ][3] 'spider' and *canalha* [ka.ná.λʌ] 'scum, riff-raff'. Antepenultimate stress is impossible, e.g. *[á.rã.ñʌ] and *[ká.na.λʌ]. If the palatal sonorants are assumed to be simple onsets of the word-final syllable, one would expect stress placement to ignore the penult, and to allow antepenultimate stress in these cases. However, antepenult stress is impossible here.

In contrast, non-palatal sonorant onsets do not influence stress placement, e.g. *mús.cu.l̲o* 'muscle', *lâ.mi.n̲a* 'blade'. If [ñ] and [λ] are

---

[3] For typographic convenience, I use [ã] in place of nasal [ʌ].

analyzed simply as onsets, they are exceptional.

1.3 Vowel nasalization

A third idiosyncracy of the palatal sonorants is the behavior of [ñ] with respect to nasalization. Consider the data in (4) from Quicoli (1990), which illustrate the nasalization effects of [n] and [m] in onset position.

(4) Nasalization effects of onsets [n] and [m]

Stressed, nasal		Unstressed, oral		
grama	[grã´.mʌ]	gramado	[gra.má.du]	'grass - lawn'
pena	[pẽ´.nʌ]	penacho	[pe.ná.šu]	'feather - headdress'
fino	[fĩ´.nu]	afinado	[a.fi.ná.du]	'fine - tuned up'
fumo	[fũ´.mu]	fumaça	[fu.má.sʌ]	'tobacco - smoke'

Vowels preceding [n] or [m] are nasalized in a stressed syllable.

The 'exceptional' nasalization effect of [ñ] (Quicoli 1990) is illustrated in (5). Vowels preceding [ñ] are invariantly nasalized.

(5) Nasalization effects of [ñ]

Stressed, nasal		Unstressed, nasal		
banho	[bã´.ñu]	banhado	[bã.ñá.du]	'bath - bathed'
penha	[pẽ´.ñʌ]	penhasco	[pẽ.ñáš.ku]	'rock - cliff'
linho	[lĩ´.ñu]	linhaça	[lĩ.ñá.sʌ]	'linen - linseed'
punho	[pũ´.ñu]	punhado	[pũ.ñá.du]	'fist - fistful'

These data reveal that vowels immediately preceding [ñ] are always nasal, regardless of stress. In contrast, onsets [n] and [m] are preceded by nasal vowels only if these vowels are stressed.

2.0 Background

In this section, I present the theoretical underpinnings of the proposed analysis, drawing on feature geometry to characterize complex segments and moraic theory to characterize geminates. In addition, I outline the relevant aspects of basic BP syllabification.

2.1 Feature Geometry

The analysis of the BP palatal sonorants as structurally complex segments follows a basic model of feature organization such as in Clements (1991), in turn based on Clements (1985) and Sagey (1986).

Within a model such as Clements (1991), complex consonants are analyzed as having branching Place nodes. Partial representations of simple [t], [i] and complex [t^y] illustrate this model in (6).

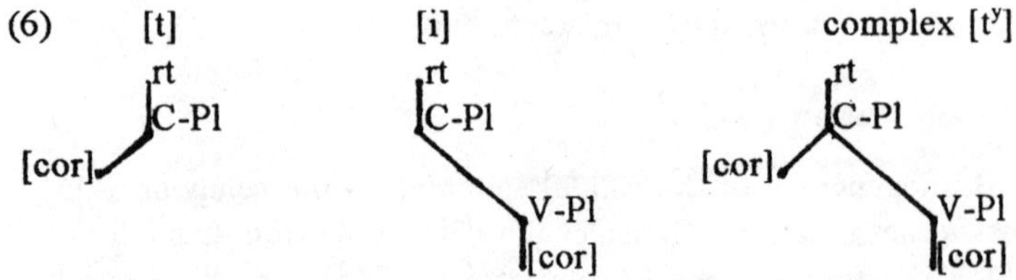

The representation of complex [tʸ] unites those of [t] and [i]. The place specifications of the complex palatal [tʸ] figure under both C-Pl and V-Pl nodes. In contrast, a simple palatal, e.g. [š], is represented with a single Place branch, where palatality devolves from the [-ant] feature, dependent on the coronal specification. While this simple representation may be appropriate for [ñ] and [λ] in other languages, I reject it for BP.

2.2 Moraic Theory

The proposed analysis assumes a theory of geminates, moraification and syllabification along the lines of Hayes (1989) (as well as Hyman 1985, McCarthy & Prince 1986, Zec 1988, and Itô 1989). An example such as *pardal* [paχ.dáw] 'sparrow' is syllabified from /pardal/ as in (7).

(7)

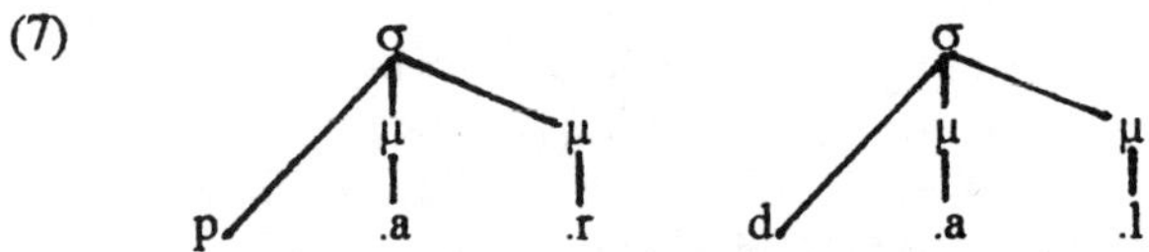

All vowels are moraic. Prevocalic consonants are attached to syllable nodes. Coda consonants are assigned weight positionally.

Geminates are moraic. The geminate's mora is associated simultaneously as the coda of one syllable and as the onset of the following syllable. Hayes' (1989) example of the syllabification of geminates is given in (8).

(8)

The root node of a geminate is unique in that it is doubly linked, serving as both an onset and a coda.

2.3 BP syllable structure

As in many of the world's languages, onsets are preferred in BP, while codas are avoided, exemplified in words like *pa.ra.le.le.pi.pe.do* 'cobblestone'. Onsetless syllables are acceptable when no consonant precedes, as in *ba.i.a* 'bay'. The preference for CV syllables in BP follows from a weak version of the Onset Condition (Steriade 1982, Itô 1986). That is, avoid $*_{\sigma}$[V....

The glides [y] and [w] are among the most common coda segments in BP, derivable from the corresponding unstressed high vowels after any another vowel. Allophones of /z/ also surface in the coda as [s], [z], [š], and [ž] (Lopez 1979).

The morphological alternations in (9)-(10) demonstrate another significant property of the BP coda.

(9)	Brasil	[bra.ziw]	'Brazil'
	brasileiro	[bra.zi.ley.ru]	'Brazilian'
(10)	cor	[koχ]~[koh]~[ko]	'color'
	cores	[ko.rIS]	'colors'

Onset [l] alternates with coda [w], in (9); onset [r] alternates with coda [χ] in the Carioca dialect of Rio de Janeiro, and with coda [h] or zero in the Northeastern dialects (e.g. Baiano), as shown in (10).

Two principles account for these alternations. First, a Coda Condition, formulated in (11), allows only sonorants in the coda (Waksler 1990, Zec 1988, Inkelas & Cho 1993, Goodman forthcoming).

(11) Coda Condition: * μ
|
[-son]

(Obstruent violations of the Coda Condition are resolved by epenthesis, as in *Bar.t[I] Sim.p[I].son.*) Second, these data suggest that when sonorants are syllabified as codas, the coronal specification is lost. This is formulated in (12) as a Coronal Delinking rule:

(12) Coronal Delinking: $C_{([+son])}\ ]_{\sigma}$
ǂ
[cor]

The rule requires that the coronal specification of coda consonants (which are always sonorants) be delinked.

The typically 'dark' pronunciation of Brazilian [l] suggests that it is at once coronal and dorsal, following Sproat and Fujimura (1993). By delinking the coronal articulator, we are left with a dorsal sonorant, namely [w]. In addition, the realization of /r/ in the coda as a voiceless continuant may bear some relation to the tendency for some Spanish dialects to spirantize and devoice [r] in certain environments, including the coda (Canfield 1981). Delinking the coronal articulator of voiceless [r] yields a voiceless back continuant in BP, i.e. [χ] or [h].

To sum up, codas in BP may consist of a glide or an allophone of /r/, realized as [χ]~[h]~Ø. An allophone of /z/ may also surface in the coda.

2.4 The Nasal Coda

In this section, we turn to the behavior of nasal consonants in the coda. There has been considerable debate in the literature on the status of nasal vowels and their relationship to nasal consonants (Hall 1943, Lüdtke 1953, Câmara 1953). In this section, I will present several arguments which support the claim that a non-surfacing nasal coda consonant is indeed the source of vowel nasalization.

The first argument is based on the distribution of the sonorant consonants in BP. We have seen that when /l/ and /r/ are syllabified as codas, they surface as [w] and [χ] (or [h]), respectively. Since the other coronal sonorants are permitted in the coda, it would be surprising if [n] were prohibited in coda position.

Second, nasal vowels generally occur in open syllables in BP, e.g. *conta* [kõ.tʌ] 'bill, bead', *[kõy.tʌ], *[kõw.tʌ].[4] Under the assumption that nasal consonants can be syllabified as codas, nasalize preceding vowels, but do not surface as a result of the Coronal Delinking rule (12), we avoid having to restrict the syllabification of nasal consonants in the coda, and we simultaneously account for the distribution of nasal vowels in superficially open syllables.

The Coronal Delinking rule extends straightforwardly to Vn$ sequences. Since the coronal specification of the nasal consonant no longer has a place of articulation, it cannot surface, and thus has no phonetic realization.

Third, nasal vowels have the same effect as coda consonants on the realizations of /r/ and /s/ (Câmara 1953). For example, both [r] and [χ] are possible intervocalically, as in *caro* [ka.ru] 'expensive' and *carro* [ka.χu] 'car'. Only [χ], however, is possible after a syllable closed by a consonant, as shown in *guelra* /gɛlra/ [gɛw.χʌ] 'fish gill' and *Israel* [iš.χa.ɛw] 'Israel'. Likewise, following nasal vowels, we find only [χ], as in *honra* [õ.χʌ] 'honor' and *genro* [žẽ.χu] 'son-in-law'. That is, oral vowels may be followed by either [χ] or [r], while nasal vowels and coda consonants are followed only by [χ].

Analogously, [z] and [s] both surface intervocalically, e.g. *teso* [te.zu] 'taut' and *teço* [te.su] 'I weave', but only [s] is possible after syllables

---

[4] Nasal diphthongs are generally word-final, e.g. *anão* [anãw̃′] 'dwarf' and *homem* [õ′mẽỹ] 'man'. There are two exceptions: *câimbra* [kãỹ′.brʌ] 'muscle cramp' and *muito* [mũỹ′.tu] 'much, many'.

closed by a consonant and after nasal vowels, e.g. *terço* [teχ.su] 'third' and *tenso* [tẽ.su] 'tense.[5]

While nasal vowels generally appear in open syllables, it is clear that they have the same effects on /s/ and /r/ as do syllables closed by a consonant. Câmara (1953) thus proposes that these superficially open syllables are closed by a nasal consonant earlier in the phonology.

Fourth, alternations between word-final nasality and intervocalic [n], e.g. *limão* [limãw̃'] 'lime' and *limonada* [limonádʌ] 'lime drink', suggest that a non-surfacing nasal coda is responsible for vowel nasalization.

Note that the proposed nasalization process, whereby [Vn.] becomes [Ṽ.] actually comprises two steps. One is the spreading of [nasal] from the coda to the nucleus, formalized in (13).

(13) Nasalization from the coda

The other step is the independently motivated process of Coronal Delinking (12).

3.0 The Geminate Analysis

In this section, I show that the idiosyncracies of the palatal sonorants can all be explained if [ñ] and [λ] are analyzed as geminates. On one hand, the distributional, metrical, and nasalization properties suggest that [ñ] and [λ] behave phonologically as coda segments. Native-speaker intuition and conventional core-syllabification, on the other hand, demand that they be onsets. The geminate analysis allows the palatal sonorants to participate as onsets *and* codas in the phonology of BP.

3.1 Distributional restrictions explained

Under the analysis that the palatal sonorants are geminates rather than simply onsets, the fact that they (1) are are always intervocalic, (2) are rarely word-initial, and (3) never follow a VG diphthong, is no longer exceptional given the nature of the coda in BP, which may consist of only one sonorant.

The epenthetic modification of [ñ]-initial loan words can now be seen as a move to repair the unsyllabifiable, moraic segment. The coda

---

[5] Exceptionally, [z] follows [ã] when *trans-* is prefixed to a vowel-initial root, e.g. *transação* [trãzasãw̃'] 'transaction'.

analysis accounts for why Italian [ñ]*occhi*, for instance, is unpronounceable as such in BP, since moraic [ñ] cannot be syllabified as an onset. The epenthesis of a word-intial vowel projects the syllable structure necessary for the syllabification of the mora-bearing sonorant, as shown in (14).

(14) Well-formed [ĩ̃ñɔkI]

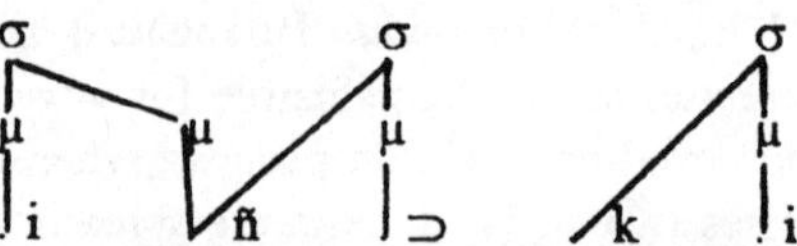

Furthermore, I claim that *[fiw.ñI] is an impossible form in BP since it constitutes a quantity violation of the Coda Condition, which allows only one sonorant per coda. The representation in (13) reveals the ill-formedness of *[fiwñI].

(15) Ill-formed *[fiw.ñI]

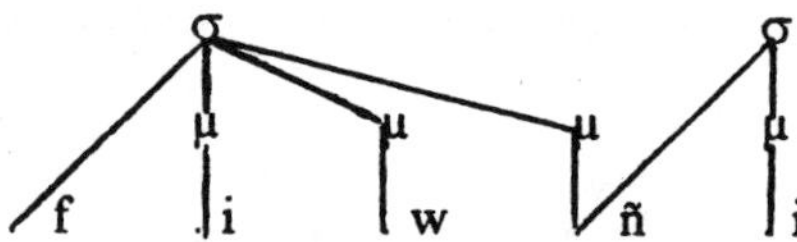

The first syllable of *[fiwñI] is tri-moraic, and thus ill-formed.

3.2 Stress placement explained

When palatal sonorants are the onsets of word-final syllables, they exceptionally prevent stress from falling on the antepenult. If we assume, however, that [ñ] and [λ] are geminates, we can easily account for their metrical effects. Since geminates contribute a mora to the preceding syllable, any syllable preceding a palatal sonorant is necessarily heavy, or bimoraic. The prosodic representation in (15) reveals that the penult of *canalha* [ka.ná.λʌ] is in fact heavy on the geminate analysis of [λ].

(16)

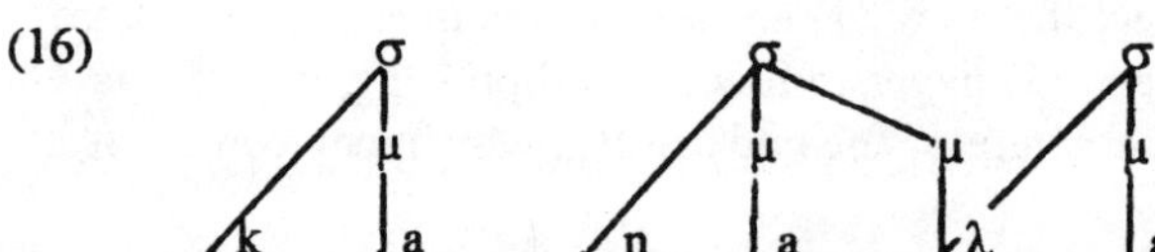

Recall that heavy penults prevent stress from falling on the antepenult (as noted in section 1.2). On the geminate analysis of palatal sonorants, it is therefore unsurprising that antepenult stress is impossible whenever palatal sonorants are 'onsets' in word-final syllables.

3.3 Nasalization explained

Recall that a stressed vowel immediately preceding onset [n] or [m] is nasal, as in *grama* [grã´.mʌ] 'grass', but not in *gramado* [gra.mádu] 'lawn'. This nasalization effect is analyzed as the result of the rule in (17) (cf. Nasalization from the Coda, given in 13).

(17) Nasalization from the Onset

$$V']_\sigma \; C$$
$$\quad [nas]$$

According to this rule, the nasal autosegment of onset [n] or [m] spreads to the preceding vowel of a stressed, open syllable.

If, as proposed, [ñ] is analyzed as a geminate rather than as simply an onset, there is no need for an additional rule to account for the fact that [ñ] nasalizes preceding vowels regardless of stress. Recall the rule of 'Nasalization from the Coda' (13). As a geminate, [ñ] is simultaneously syllabified as a coda, and thus nasalizes the preceding vowel. The geminate analysis of [ñ], along with rule of nasalization from the coda, accounts for the fact that [ñ] is always preceded by a nasal vowel.

We can contrast this analysis with one that posits an additional rule, such as in Quicoli (1990). His rule, given in (18), accounts for the nasalization effects of [ñ].

(18) Quicoli's [ñ]-Only Nasalization Rule

$$V \text{ -----> } [+nas] \; / \; \underline{\qquad} \begin{bmatrix} +nasal \\ +high \end{bmatrix}$$

Quicoli's rule regressively spreads nasalization to open syllables, even if they are unstressed. The rule reflects the assumption that [ñ], like [n] and [m], is a single segment syllabified simply as an onset.

The proposed analysis of [ñ] as a geminate obviates the need for this extra rule, since [ñ]-nasalization can be seen as a result of nasalization from the coda. At the same time, the proposed analysis accounts for the apparent idiosyncracies in the distribution and metrical effects of the palatal sonorants.

4.0 The Complex Segment Analysis

4.1 The proposal

I have argued that the palatal sonorants in BP are geminates, and that their 'exceptional' effects can be explained in terms of their moraic, geminate status. Why should palatal sonorants be underlyingly moraic, while other sonorants are not? I propose that [ñ] and [λ] form a natural class based on the complexity of their Place node, illustrated in (19) (based on Clements 1991).

(19) Proposed feature structure of BP palatal sonorants

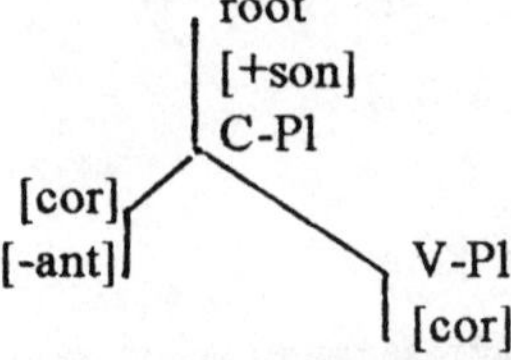

The C-Pl node dominates a coronal articulator as well as an additional vocalic branch, also specified for place.

I propose that the association of palatal sonorants with the mora is not at all arbitrary. Rather, the moraic character of [ñ] and [λ] can be motivated by their structural complexity. In particular, their distinct phonological weight can be related to the V-Place branch they bear.

Alternatively, if one suggests that [ñ] and [λ] are structurally simple, it becomes difficult to comprehend why these segments in particular should be moraic. It is unlikely that their moraic character somehow devolves from the fact that they are simply [-ant] coronal sonorants.

The Complex Segment Analysis that I have proposed is preferable to a simple segment analysis in that the former does not stipulate features. It refers to a natural class, namely, a class of consonants characterized by a V-Place branch; it refers to structure; it is essentially representational. In the following section, I adduce empirical evidence for the structural complexity of [ñ] and [λ].

4.2 Empirical Support for the Complex Segment Analysis

The Complex Segment Analysis allows an analysis of the colloquial and Non-Standard realizations of [ñ] and [λ] as instances of Place node simplification.

4.2.1 Colloquial BP

In colloquial BP, [ñ] is realized as nasal glide [ỹ], e.g. *venha* /ven^{y}a/ [vẽỹʌ] 'come!'. Since the root node of [ñ] occupies the coda of the first syllable, it meets the structural description for the Coronal Delinking rule. The C-Place coronal specification of [ñ] is therefore lost. Nevertheless, since [ñ] is complex, it still bears a V-Place [cor] branch. It thus surfaces as the nasal glide [ỹ].

The representation in (20) illustrates the relevant phonological processes resulting in colloquial [vẽỹʌ] from /venʸa/.

(20)

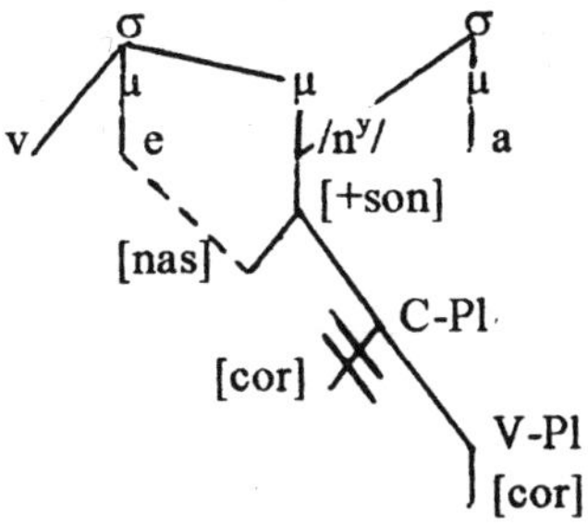

σ σ
μ μ μ
v e /nʸ/ a
[+son]
[nas]
C-Pl
[cor]
V-Pl
[cor]

Nasality spreads from coda to nucleus. Coronal Delinking severs the coronal C-Place branch, yet leaves a coronal V-Place specification in tact, thus accounting for the glide realization of [ñ].

Alternatively, if [ñ] were analyzed as a simple [-ant] coronal geminate /ñ/, then the [ñ] ~ [ỹ] alternation is truly puzzling. The mere fact of alternation now becomes difficult to motivate, without manipulations of major class nodes such as [+/- cons], e.g., a rule such as: [+cons] sonorants become [-cons] in the coda. One unfortunate consequence of such a rule is that we are then obliged to analyze coda [χ]~[h] as [-cons], rather than as the coronally delinked (and devoiced) [+cons] [r].

4.2.2 Non-Standard BP

The realizations of [λ] as [y] and [l] in Non-Standard BP, exemplified in (21), constitute evidence of the complexity of [λ].

(21)	Standard	Non-Standard	
a. filho	[fíλu]	[fíyu]	'son'
b. trabalhar	[trabaλáχ]	[t(r)abayá]	'to work'
c. mulher	[muλέχ]	[mulέ]	'woman'
d. colher	[koλέχ]	[kulέ]	'spoon'

Simplifications of [λ] to [y] are frequent, as in (21a, b). In the coda, Coronal Delinking deprives the C-Place node of its articulator, leaving only the V-Pl articulator. The segment [λ] surfaces as [y] in Non-Standard speech, in the same way that [ñ] surfaces as [ỹ] in colloquial speech.

Simplifications of [λ] to [l], as in (21c, d), are less common. Here, the C-Place articulator is preserved, and the consonant's V-Pl (coronal) articulator undergoes delinkage instead.

If, however, one analyzes [λ] as a simple [-ant] coronal, then the Non-Standard variants receive no explanation. The alternation between [λ] and [y] would again require a major class change from [+cons] to [-cons]. The alternation between [λ] and [l] would have to be handled by means of a change from [-ant] to [+ant]. Furthermore, under a simple segment analysis of [λ], there is no single phonological process which would result in either [l] or [y] on the surface. That is, the two surface forms cannot be related to a common principle, such as simplification.

4.2.3 The creolization of [ñ]

The lenition of [ñ] to a glide is not particular to BP but may be part of a more universal tendency to simplify underlyingly complex segments. The same phenomenon appears in Portuguese-based African creoles as well as in French-based Caribbean creoles. Valkhoff (1966) credits Barrena (1957) for the observation that in Annobón, an Afro-Portuguese Atlantic creole, oral vowel plus [ñ] can be realized as nasal vowel plus [y], as demonstrated in (22).

(22) Annobón Creole

[iña]	>	[ĩya]	'fingernail'
[uña]	>	[ũya]	'one' (fem.)
[govoña]	>	[govõya]	'shame'

These words correspond to Portuguese ***unha*** [ũñʌ], ***uma*** [ũmʌ], and ***vergonha*** [veχgõñʌ], respectively. Accompanying the simplification of [ñ] to [y], note that nasality spreads to the preceding vowel, just as in BP, where [ñ] and [ỹ] are always preceded by a nasal vowel.

In Martinican, a French-based Caribbean creole, French [ñ] and [ny] preceded by an oral vowel have become [y] preceded by a nasal vowel (Valkhoff 1966:132), as shown in (23):

(23)

French		Martinican Creole	
gagner	[gañe]	[gãye]	'earn'
panier	[panye]	[pãye]	'basket'
poignet	[pwañɛ]	[pɔ̃yɛt]	'wrist'

Note that the palatal sonorant nasalizes the preceding vowel, as in BP.

On the view that the palatal sonorants are structurally complex, the lenition of [ñ] to a nasal glide is unsurprising in the creoles of such diverse geographical locations. Understood as a structural simplification, this change epitomizes creolization phenomena.

4.3 Historical evidence

Latin [n] when followed by [i̯V] became [ñ] in Portuguese, exemplified in (24). Analogously, [l] or [ll] followed by [i̯V] became [λ], as in (25) (Williams 1986:91).

	Latin	Portuguese	Port. gloss
(24)	seniorem	se[ñ]or	'sir'
	teneo	te[ñ]o	'I have'
	vineam	vi[ñ]a	'come.1/3SG.IMPF'
(25)	filium	fi[λ]o	'son'
	mulierem	mu[λ]er	'wife'
	allium	a[λ]o	'garlic'
	malleare	ma[λ]ar	'to hammer'

Latin [n] became [ñ] between long, stressed [i] and [a] or [o], shown in (26) (Williams 1986:82).

(26)	gallī´nam	gali[ñ]a	'chicken'
	vicī´nam	vizi[ñ]o	'neighbor'
	vī´no	vi[ñ]o	'wine'

Latin [gn] became [yn], then [yñ], finally giving rise to [ñ] in Portuguese, exemplified in (27) (Williams 1986:94).

(27)	cognatum	cu[ñ]ado	'brother-in-law'
	pugnum	pu[ñ]o	'fist'

Vulgar Latin [gl] and [kl] became [λ] in Portuguese (Williams 1986:96). Perhaps the intermediate clusters were [yl] and [yλ], analogous to the evolution of [gn] to [ñ]. These cases are exemplified in (28).

(28)	apiculum	abe[λ]a	'bee'
	oculum	o[λ]o	'eye'
	tegulum	te[λ]a	'roof tile'

Sometimes the Latin geminates [ll] and [nn] correspond to Portuguese [λ] and [ñ], as in *beryllum* > *bri[λ]o*, but these were borrowed from Spanish (Williams 1986:85-6).

The BP palatal sonorants thus derive from Latin sequences of either a long, stressed [i] plus a coronal sonorant, as in (26), or a coronal sonorant plus [y] or unstressed, short [i], as in (24-25, 27-28). Historically, the development of the palatal sonorants can be portrayed as coalescence: here, a sonorant coronal consonant and [i] (or [y]) fuse into a single segment. I propose that they retained their original place nodes, a [cor] C-Place and a [cor] V-Place branch. This structural attribute renders them distinctively heavy, i.e. moraic, among consonants. The historical facts corroborate the Complex Segment Analysis.

5 Conclusion

The idiosyncratic properties of [ñ] and [λ] in BP can be explained once they are analyzed as geminates. Their restricted distribution and their metrical and nasalization effects can be accounted for by means of independently needed principles that relate to mora-bearing or coda segments, despite the conventional syllabification of [ñ] and [λ] as onsets.

These consonants form a natural class in that they bear a secondary vocalic articulation. I have claimed that this particular sort of structural complexity *motivates* the geminate analysis. That is, the geminate status and the Place node complexity of [ñ] and [λ] (for which there is ample evidence) should not be taken as arbitrary. Of course, there are languages, such as Italian, in which geminates cannot be characterized as consonants with a V-Pl branch. Nonetheless, the prosodic and feature-geometric characteristics of [ñ] and [λ] ought to be related in BP, especially in light of their development from Latin CV or VC sequences.

References

Barrena, N. 1957. Gramática annobonesa. Madrid: Consejo Superior de Investigaciones Científicas, Instituto de Estudios Africanos.

Canfield, D. Lincoln. 1981. Spanish pronunciation in the Americas. Chicago: Univ. of Chicago Press.

Câmara, João Mattoso, Jr. 1953. Para o estudo da fonêmica da língua portuguesa. Petrópolis, Rio de Janeiro: Editora Vozes.

Clements, George N. 1989. A unified set of features for cosonants and vowels, ms., Cornell Univ., Ithaca, NY.

Clements, George N. 1991. Place of articulation in consonants andvowels: a unified theory. Working Paper of the Cornell Phonetics Laboratory 5:77-123.

Goodman, Beverley. forthcoming. An integrated approach to the phonological feature hierarchy. Ithaca, NY: PhD dissertation, Cornell Univ.

Hall, Robert A., Jr. 1943. The unit phonemes of Brazilian Portuguese. Studies in Linguistics 1(15):1-6

Harris, James W. 1983. Syllable structure and stress in Spanish: a non-linear analysis. Linguistic Inquiry Monographs 8. Cambridge, MA: MIT Press.

Hyman, Larry M. 1985. A theory of phonological weight. Dordrecht: Foris Publications.

Inkelas, Sharon and Young-mee Yu Cho. 1993. Inalterability as pre-specification. Language 69(3):529-574.

Itô, Junko. 1986. Syllable theory and prosodic phonology. PhD dissertation, Univ. of Mass.

Itô, Junko. 1989. A prosodic theory of epenthesis. Natural Language & Linguistic Theory 7:217-260.

Lopez, Barbara Strodt. 1979. The sound pattern of Brazilian Portuguese (Cariocan dialect). PhD dissertation, UCLA.

Lüdtke, H. 1953. Fonemática portuguesa, 2: Vocalismo. Boletim de Filologia (Lisbon) 14:197-217.

McCarthy John & Alan S. Prince. 1986. Prosodic morphology, ms. from Univ. of Mass. Amherst & Brandeis Univ.

Pike, Kenneth. L. 1947. Phonemics: a technique for reducing languages to writing. Ann Arbor: University of Michigan Press.

Reed, David W. and Yolanda Leite. 1947. The segmental phonemes of Brazilian Portuguese: Standard Paulista dialect, in K. L. Pike, Phonemics, University of Michigan Press: Ann Arbor.

Quicoli, A. Carlos. 1990. Harmony, lowering and nasalization in Brazilian Portuguese. Lingua 80:295-331.

Sagey, Elizabeth. 1986. The representations of features and relations in non-linear phonology. PhD dissertation, MIT.

Sproat, Richard and Osamu Fujimura. 1993. Allophonic variation in English /l/ and its implications for phonetic implementation. Journal of phonetics 21(3):291-311.

Stavrou, Christopher. 1947. Brazilian Portuguese pronunciation. Philadelphia: David McKay Company.

Steriade, Donca. 1982. Greek prosodies and the nature of syllabification. PhD dissertation, MIT.

Valkhoff, Marius F. 1966. Studies in Portuguese and Creole. Johannesburg: Witwatersrand University Press.

Waksler, Rachelle. 1990. A formal account of glide-vowel alternation in prosodic theory. PhD dissertation, Harvard Univ.

Williams, Edwin B. 1986. Do latim ao português. Rio de Janeiro: Edições Tempo Brasileiro. (Trans. by A. Houaiss, From Latin to Portuguese, 1938, Oxford: Oxford Univ. Press.)

Zec, Draga. 1988. Sonority constraints on prosodic structure. PhD dissertation, Stanford Univ.

Prosodic Constituents in Poetic Meter

KRISTIN HANSON
University of British Columbia

1. Introduction

Linguists sometimes draw on poetics for evidence in support of hypothesized linguistic structures.[1] Such arguments rely on implicit assumptions about what the relation between poetic structure and linguistic structure is. A theory of poetic meter that makes the nature of the relation explicit has recently been proposed in Hanson and Kiparsky (1994), which includes the claim that for any meter one of the constituents of the prosodic[2] hierarchy -- mora (μ), syllable (σ), foot (ϕ) or prosodic word (λ) -- defines the maximum size of each abstract metrical position. The theory thus challenges a common assumption in both traditional and generative metrics that universally it is the syllable that defines a metrical position (Hayes 1983, Prince 1989), and also the more subtle assumption that each metrical position will necessarily be

---

1 This paper presents part of a broader analysis of English metrical systems developed in joint work with Paul Kiparsky. I would like to express my deep thanks to him for his insights which inform this paper, and absolve him of responsibility for any shortcomings in my development of them here. I would also like to thank Randy Schmidt for his assistance of all kinds, especially in scanning Milton. The work has been supported by UBC-HSS grant 5-70927.

2 The terms *prosodic* and *metrical* are both ambiguous in current linguistic usage. Here *prosodic* will be used consistently to refer to rhythmic structure in language, and *metrical* to rhythmic structure in poetry.

constituted by a well-formed constituent of a consistent type.[3] Here I will provide support for this claim about the role of prosodic constituents in poetic meter by showing that it provides an explanatory account of previously described differences in the iambic pentameter of two major English poets, Shakespeare and Milton.

Since its adaptation into English from syllable-based Romance forms during the Renaissance, the English iambic pentameter has been assumed to normally require a single syllable in each of its ten alternately weak and strong metrical positions (see section 2):

s s s s s
(1) The lion dying thrusteth forth his paw (R2 5.1.29)

But since that time it has also always been recognized that extra syllables may be allowed without compromising the metricality of a line. As the great metrist Saintsbury (1908) observes, 'It was all very well to lay down that English verse *must* consist of a certain number of syllables, but it could escape no one who had ever read a volume or even a very few pages of English poetry that it *did* consist of a very uncertain number of them.' Thus in Shakespeare, alongside (1) we also find such lines as (2) and (3) (Kiparsky 1977):

s s s s s
(2) a. Who? Silvia? Aye, Silvia, for your sake (TGV 4.2.23)
s s s s s
b. And take my milk for gall, you murdering ministers (Mac 1.5.48)
s s s s s
c. Weeds among weeds, or flowers with flowers gathered (Son 124.4)
s s s s s
(3) Come to one mark, as many ways meet in one town (H5 1.2.208)

Traditional metrics has dealt with such variation through the idea of 'trisyllabic substitution', the assumption that occasional extra syllables can be allowed provided they do not compromise any overall sense of the basic pattern (e.g. Saintsbury 1908, Fussell 1979). Following the foundational criticism of Halle and Keyser (1972), however, that this approach fails to distinguish explicitly what would compromise the basic pattern from what wouldn't, metrists in the generative tradition have instead sought to articulate rules which govern such aspects of metrical practice as variation in syllable count. Reflecting the assumption that the basic measure of English iambic meter is the syllable, such proposals have typically comprised a basic

---

3 See also Golston and Riad (1993) for another recent suggestion that the range and role of prosodic constituents in meter should be construed more broadly.

rule that a metrical position corresponds to a single syllable, and additional rules specifying allowable exceptions.

Thus Kiparsky's (1977) analysis of Shakespeare's iambic pentameter includes five rules by which two syllables instead of the normal one may correspond to a single metrical position.[4] Three PROSODIC RULES allow pairs of syllables that could plausibly be phonologically reduced to count as single syllables in the meter, though they need not necessarily be pronounced that way. By these rules, sequences of a high unstressed vowel followed by another unstressed vowel as in (2a), sequences of an unstressed vowel, a sonorant and another unstressed vowel as in (2b), and sequences of any two vowels as in (2c) may optionally be analyzed as single syllables. Two METRICAL RULES also allow two syllables to correspond to a single metrical position, but are distinguished precisely in that no phonological reduction is either plausible or assumed. Instead, metrical rules simply define exceptional cases where two phonologically distinct syllables may nonetheless count as a single metrical position. One such rule allows an unstressed nonlexical word to be disregarded, as in *in one* in (3). A second rule of RESOLUTION allows a sequence of a short vowel, a single consonant and a second short vowel ($\breve{V}C\breve{V}$) to count as a single position, as in *many* in (3).

But why should Shakespeare's metrical practice be governed by exactly these rules? What constrains the form of possible rules in a metrical description? The prosodic rules seem adequately explained by their basis in phonological reduction. But what is the basis of the metrical rules? Could extra syllables be permitted under entirely different rules in other poets' iambic practice? Could they be permitted under one of these rules but not the other?

On the theory of meter sketched in Hanson and Kiparsky (1994) these metrical rules are not required. Instead, the generalizations they express follow from the metrical position in Shakespeare's meter being defined not by the syllable but by the foot which figures in English phonology, the MORAIC TROCHEE. This analysis predicts that extra syllables in iambic meter should occur under both conditions expressed by these rules, or not at all. The case where they occur not at all is provided by Milton's iambic meter, in which the metrical position is genuinely defined by the syllable. Together, these two systems thus

---

4 A sixth rule of *extrametricality* (see section 5) also allows extra syllables at the ends of major metrical and/or prosodic constituents, as in (2c). It differs from the rules discussed here, however, in that the syllables here are not dependent on any higher level structure.

support the hypothesis that any prosodic constituent is available to define the position of a meter.

Section 2 will briefly sketch the relevant portion of the theory. Then sections 3 and 4 will show in detail how it explains the contrasting distribution of extra syllables in *King Lear*, celebrated by Saintsbury (1908) as the pinnacle of Shakespeare's achievement with trisyllabic substitution, and in *Paradise Lost*, representing a period of comparable stylistic maturity for Milton.

2. Metrical theory

The theory proposed in Hanson and Kiparsky (1994) constrains the possible form of the two fundamental components of any meter -- an UNDERLYING STRUCTURE of abstract METRICAL POSITIONS and a set of CORRESPONDENCE RULES which constrain possible mappings of the actual linguistic properties of a line into that underlying structure (Halle and Keyser 1972) -- by the assumption that meter is fundamentally a linguistic poetic form (Jakobson 1960, Kiparsky 1987) and specifically the one which derives from prosodic phonology (Hayes 1989). The two fundamental operations of prosodic phonology, parsing constituents into pairs, and assigning prominence to one element of the pair, provide the vocabulary of both components.

First, the underlying structure is always composed of a specified number of METRICAL FEET, each composed of two metrical positions, one STRONG, which is the head, and the other WEAK, in a specified order. Thus every meter has one of the forms in (4) as its underlying structure:

(4) a. w s w s w s w s ...
    b. s w s w s w s w ...

Second, the correspondence rules derive from setting three parameters. POSITION establishes the maximum size of a metrical position as one of the constituents given by the prosodic hierarchy, giving a rule like (5):

(5) Position: A metrical position contains at most ($\lambda/\phi/\sigma/\mu$).

In each case, the relevant form of the constituent is assumed to be the parsing form which figures in the language of the verse. For English, although analysis of its complex stress system is far from settled, we assume that among feet the moraic trochee as in (6a) (Hayes 1987) plays a role in the phonology (Kager 1989), and also that that foot type may include the form in (6b), with its highly restricted distribution defined by (prosodic) RESOLUTION (Hanson 1991, 1993a):

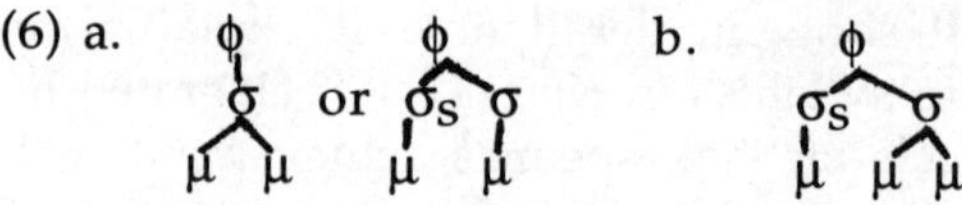

Two PROMINENCE parameters establish the contrast between weak and strong metrical positions: SITE chooses one of these positions to be subject to constraints on the linguistic prominence of the constituents in it, and TYPE specifies which kind of prominence in the prosodic phonology of the language is relevant, giving a rule roughly of the form in (7):

(7) Prominence: (Strong/weak) positions (must /must not) contain (heavy/stressed/strong) constituents.

The contrast between STRESS and STRENGTH bears elaboration because it is crucial to the typology of English metrical systems. Stress is by definition the property of being the head of a prosodic foot, and its presence is conveniently diagnosed in English by the fact that stressed syllables do not permit reduction of the syllable nucleus to [ə]. Thus in (8) for example, *fan-* , *-ta-* , and *fan* are all stressed (*[fəntæstik], *[fæntəstik], *[fən]), and therefore head feet:

(8)

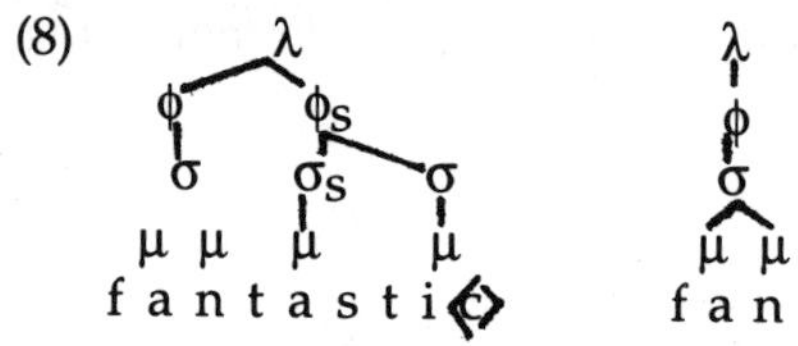

STRENGTH, on the other hand is the property of heading a branching consitutent (Liberman and Prince 1977). Therefore among the stressed syllables in (8) only *-ta-* is also strong. For English iambic pentameter only strength within the prosodic word is relevant.

A final assumption of the theory is that while lexical phonological structure is obligatorily respected by all poets, nonlexical structure is treated more variably (Hanson and Kiparsky 1994, Hanson 1993b, Hanson 1991). This is relevant here primarily with respect to the stress properties of nonlexical monosyllabic words. In English, some nonlexical words, typically those with long vowels such as *thou*, always have stress, as evidenced by their invulnerability to reduction (*[ə]). Others such as *but* may or may not have stress, depending on their position and on the intended meaning ([bʌt] or [bət]) (Zec and Inkelas 1988). But in either case, the feet responsible for such stress may be ignored in a scansion, occasionally or often depending on the poet, in a way that those of lexical words cannot.

3. Shakespeare

This theory has already been shown to provide an explanatory account of the most famous and extravagant example of variation in syllable count in English metrics, Hopkins' sprung rhythm, described in Kiparsky (1989) and reanalyzed in terms of stress in Hanson (1991). In this meter, a metrical position may contain nothing at all, a single stressed syllable (H́), a light stressed syllable followed by an unstressed syllable in the same word (ĹX), or any number of unstressed syllables (X*). All these possibilities follow from a single rule that a position contains at most a moraic trochee. This rule will be satisfied by a metrical position containing H́ as in (9a) or ĹX as in (9b) because it would contain exactly a foot, or X* as in (9c,d) because it would not need to be analyzed as containing any foot at all, but not structures like (9e,f,g) because it would contain a foot plus additional linguistic material:

(9)	a.	b.	c.	d.	e.	f.	g.
	φ	φ			φ	φ	φ
	σ	σ σ	σ	σ σ	σ σ	σ σ	σ σ
	μμ	μ μ	μ	μ μ	μμ μ	μμ μ	μ μμ
	keen	many	the	is your	comes your	sundry	akin

Thus, the phrase 'at most' crucially allows considerable variation, by defining only an upper bound for the linguistic content of each metrical position, and not a required constituent type.

Now sprung rhythm is fundamentally different from the English iambic pentameter in that it requires stress in all strong metrical positions. Iambic pentameter has no such requirement: for Shakespeare, Milton and indeed all English poets unstressed syllables are freely allowed in strong positions, just as stressed syllables are freely allowed in weak positions:

s s s s s
(10) a. Pluck the keen teeth from the fierce tigers' jaws (Son.19)

s s s s s
b. Works of day past, or morrow's next design (PL 5.33)

Only strong syllables are not allowed in weak position (Kiparsky 1977):[5]

(11) a. * Pluck immense teeth from enraged tigers' jaws
b. * Work's delights past, or morrow's next design

Thus, Shakespeare and Milton share rule (12):

(12) Prominence: Weak positions must not contain strong syllables.

But Kiparsky's two metrical rules for extra syllables described in section 1 suggest that with respect to what can constitute a metrical position, Shakespeare's iambic meter has more in common with sprung rhythm than with Milton's iambic meter. First, the metrical rule of resolution that allows a V̆CV̆ sequence to count as a single metrical position (*many* in (3)) most often applies to sequences where the initial syllable is stressed, in which case in English the following syllable must be unstressed. Thus it expresses the possibility of ĹX counting as a single metrical position, always strong because of (12). Such structures abound in *King Lear* :

s s s s s
(13) a. Yet, poor old heart, he holp the heavens to rain (5.3.140)
s s s s s
b. Here sir, but trouble him not -- his wits are gone (3.6.87)
s s s s s
c. A still soliciting eye, and such a tongue (1.1.231)
s s s s s
d. Her delicate cheek. It seem'd she was a queen, (4.3.13)
s s s s s
e. When majesty falls to folly. Reserve thy state, (1.1.149)
s s s s s
f. Sorrow would be a rarity most beloved (4.3.23)
s s s s s
g. Your horrible pleasure. Here I stand your slave. (3.2.19).
s s s s s
h. Sometimes with lunatic bands, sometimes with prayers. (2.3.10)

---

5 An exception is made at the beginning of major metrical and prosodic constituents; see for example *sorrow* in (13f), or *Uriel* in (24b). Milton also allows rare exceptions at the beginnings of prosodic feet where they coincide with beginnings of metrical feet (Kiparsky 1977), possibly in order to achieve trisyllabic cadences that the syllabic basis of his meter otherwise excludes.

s s s s s
To the Garden of bliss, thy seat prepar'd (8.299)

V̌CV̌ sequences where it is the second syllable which is stressed, in contrast, never count as single positions:

(14) * Yet, poor old heart, his life grows <u>akin</u> to death

Similarly, the metrical rule that allows an unstressed nonlexical word to be disregarded (*in one* in (3)) expresses the possibility that sequences of unstressed syllables, X*, may be single positions, and becomes more accurate stated that way. In almost[6] all cases in *King Lear* where one unstressed nonlexical word is disregarded, the other syllable in the position is also unstressed:

s s s s s
(15) a. <u>I am</u> made of that self metal as my sister (1.1.69)
s s s s s
b. As flies to wanton boys are we <u>to the</u> gods (4.1.36)
s s s s s
c. To seal <u>th'ac</u>cuser's lips. Get thee glass eyes, (4.6.170)
s s s s s
d. Draw, seem <u>to de</u>fend yourself; now quit you well (2.1.30)
s s s s s
e. That she would soon be here. <u>Is your</u> lady come? (2.4.184)
s s s s s
f. Gentle and low, an excellent thing <u>in a</u> woman (5.3.274)
s s s s s
g. And speak <u>'t ag</u>ain, my lord, no more with me (2.4.255)
s s s s s
h. <u>I had</u> thought, by ma<u>king this</u> well known unto you (1.4.205)
s s s s s
i. Pray you <u>now forg</u>et, <u>and forg</u>ive; <u>I am</u> old and foolish (4.7.83)

Lines where the other syllable is stressed as in (16) do not occur:

(16) *That she would soon be here. <u>Comes your</u> lady now?

If these generalizations are reformulated in this way, V̌CV̌ sequences with no stress which count as single positions by Kiparsky's

---

6 The exceptions are *<u>to'</u>obey* and *t<u>h'un</u>tented* where the second syllable has some secondary stress. This may reflect some not yet understood status of secondary stress, or it may reflect the residual effect of a conventional Elizabethan practice of reducing *to* and *the* before vowels, discussed more extensively below.

rule of resolution are still accounted for, but through their similarity to the X* structures of (15) rather than the ĹX sequences of (13):

```
                s        s        s        s     s
(17) a. The argument of your praise, balm of your age. (1.1.215)
                   s        s     s      s      s
     b. Strike flat the thick rotundity o' th' world (3.2.7)
               s      s     s     s     s
     c. Unmerciful lady, as you are I'm more (3.7.33)
```

This repartitioning of the metrical phenomena supports the reformulation in a subtle way, because it restores the traditional claim that lines like (13) have a distinct aesthetic effect in which stress is crucially implicated: 'If the stress in a verse may be illustrated by the tap of hammer on anvil, then resolution gives us the slight second blow or repercussion which follows whenever the hammer has been but slightly grasped' (Young 1928:76).

Putting these revised generalizations together with the uncontroversial fact that a metrical position can contain a single syllable, whether stressed or unstressed, what a single metrical position can contain in Shakespeare's iambic pentameter is H́, ĹX, or X*, just as Hopkins' sprung rhythm. The variation therefore follows from the same rule of position (though the prominence rules differ):

(18) Position: A metrical position contains at most ϕ (moraic trochee).

Before turning to the contrasting practice of Milton, it may be worth briefly considering two possible objections to this analysis. First, in light of the lines in (17) the lines in (13) appear to call into question the special status of ĹX on which the analysis depends, because in (13) ĹX is always followed by X, and could always therefore be analyzed as involving X* as in (17). In fact in other plays there are a few cases where ĹX is followed by H́, such as (3). But more important, for three syllable words, the cases like (13) where the initial syllable is light vastly outnumber those as in (17) where it is not. Given the assumption that a line is metrical if it can be mapped into the underlying structure in a way compatible with the rules which define the meter, it seems intuitively plausible that lines with multiple scansions should be metrically simpler, in that an acceptable mapping is more easily found. On the additional assumption that simpler lines might be expected to be more frequent than complex ones, then, the assumption that ĹX and X* are both allowable single positions explains the comparative frequency of lines like those in (13) in a way that admitting only X* cannot.

The second possible objection concerns the restrictiveness of the analysis.[7] Formally, the assumption that multiple syllables are allowed in a single position just in case all are unstressed together with the assumption that nonlexical stress may be ignored allows a number of structures which in fact occur only rarely. First, it allows metrical positions which contain even more than two syllables. This is a strength of the analysis for Hopkins, but a liability for Shakespeare; though it may possibly occur as in (19), it is clearly rare:

s s s s s
(19) a. I am mightily abus'd; I shuld ev'n die with pity (4.7.52)

s s s s s
b. And your disordered rabble make servants of their betters (1.4.256)

Second, it allows stressed nonlexical words in polysyllabic metrical positions. Again, though this may occur as in (15i), it is undeniably rare; even there it bespeaks Lear's degeneration. Finally, it allows two syllables in a single position as freely as one, yet one is much more common.

As with most issues in metrics, the answers probably lie partly with linguistic constraints and partly with artistic tradition. As described above, heavy nonlexical words would certainly receive postlexical stress, and other nonlexical words would tend to do so in alternating patterns. But although we know from his placement of the strong syllables of disyllabic nonlexical words in weak positions as in (20) that Shakespeare does sometimes ignore nonlexical stress (Hanson 1993), we also know that he doesn't do so often (Kiparsky 1977):

s s s s s
(20) And I will comment upon that offense (Son 89.2)

Thus the tendency to avoid precisely these structures that would include postlexical feet is expected.

Perhaps more important, however, is the fact that the iambic meter of modern English originated as a borrowed form that was consciously understood by poets of Shakespeare's time to be syllabic. This is evident from poets' own commentaries, from the practice of many of Shakespeare's predecessors who lack his rules for extra syllables discussed here, and from transcription and editing of Shakespeare even in his own time, as spellings are altered even in ways that obscure meanings to preserve an appearance of syllabicity. Thus it is hardly surpris-

---

7 I am grateful to Chris Golston for discussion of this issue during the presentation of this paper.

ing to find most metrical positions containing single syllables, at the same time that the formal possibility of more is developing.

5. Milton

Milton's meter and Shakespeare's are of course generally considered to be formally the same, both iambic pentameter. As we have seen, they share a prohibition in (12) on strong syllables in weak positions. But Milton's meter is strikingly different with respect to syllable count. Although it permits extra syllables under several rules (Weismiller 1989, Bridges 1921) and many critics therefore consider it equally characterized by 'trisyllabic substitution', its different aesthetic effect has always been recognized, and Weismiller (1989) in particular insists that it maintains a regular syllable count in a way that other English poets' meters do not. In fact, what Milton's practice in *Paradise Lost* excludes is precisely the possibilities of counting as single metrical positions LX and X*, the possibilities which for Shakespeare's meter support interpretation of the basic measure as a moraic trochee.

Although Milton uses various contractions and elisions, Weismiller (1989) argues that even the most phonologically implausible are intended to represent genuine reductions in syllable count. First, Milton permits extra syllables under all the prosodic rules illustrated in (2) above:

s s s s s
(21) a. Of Man's First Disobedience, and the Fruit (1.1)

s s s s s
b. Invoke thy aid to my advent'rous Song (1.13)

s s s s s
c. For those the race of Israel oft forsook (1.432)

Second, reflecting a convention common in 16th and 17th century metrical practice, he permits sequences of two vowels even across word boundaries to count as a single syllables:

s s s s s
(22) a. So were created, nor can justly accuse (3.112)

s s s s s
b. May I express thee unblam'd? since God is Light (3.3)

s s s s s
c. Anguish and doubt and fear and sorrow and pain (1.558)

s s s s s
d. To adore the Conqueror? who now beholds (1.323)

s s s s s
e. Who durst defy th'Omnipotent to Arms (1.49)
s s s s s
f. Whereto with speedy words th'Arch Fiend replied (1.156)
s s s s s
g. Created hugest that swim th'Ocean stream (1.202)

While many such examples involve two unstressed syllables, the presence of a few like (22f,g) which do not, together with the almost[8] complete absence of lines like Shakespeare's (15d-i) or (17) which have two unstressed syllables but no adjacent vowels, supports Weismiller's claim that Milton is assuming an artificial reduction, and not simply allowing positions to contain X*.

Third, again reflecting linguistic beliefs of the period (Weismiller 1989), Milton sometimes counts /l,m,n,r/ as nonsyllabic word finally:

s s s s s
(23)a. And where the river of Bliss through midst of Heav'n (3.358)
s s s s s
b. A Pillar of State; deep on his Front engraven (2.302)
s s s s s
c. Some Capital City; or less than if this frame (2.924)
s s s s s
d. Than to dwell here, driv'n out from bliss, condemned (2.86)
s s s s s
e. And now St. Peter at Heaven's Wicket seems (3.484)
s s s s s
f. The Portal shone, inimitable on Earth (3.508)

Here too, while many such sonorants are preceded by stressed light syllables, which are moreover scanned as strong, the presence of a few which are not as in (23e), together with the total absence of single positions containing ĹX where X is not a syllabic sonorant as in (13c-f,h), confirms that it is the conscious assumption about the nonsyllabicity of sonorants which is governing Milton's practice, and not the possibility of ĹX as a single position.

Finally, as for all poets in the English tradition, a handful of words like *Heaven* , *spirit* , *seven* , *evil and even* are treated as optionally monosyllabic:

---

8 There seems to be one counterexample, perhaps symbolic as is much of Milton's metrical usage:

Because thou hast heark'n'd to the voice of thy Wife (10.198)

s s s s s
(24) a. Within Heav'n's bound, unless Heav'n's Lord supreme (2.236)
s s s s s
b. Uriel, for thou of those sev'n Spirits that stand (3.654)

But whether these words are treated this way because of initial light stressed syllables or because of final syllabic sonorants, they are in a way the exceptions that prove the rule. The contrast between this tight list and the productivity of Shakespeare's rules couldn't be more striking.

Clearly Milton's practices raise questions about exactly how some of the less plausible metrical conventions for reduction of syllables he exhibits are best accommodated within a phonological theory of meter. But the absence of extra syllables under the two conditions found in Shakespeare that cannot be construed as what Weismiller (1989) calls 'irreducible triple rhythms', ĹX and X*, follows directly if Milton's meter is taken to be an instance of a genuine syllabic meter, with the following rule:

(25) Position: A metrical position contains at most a syllable.

5. Consequences

This analysis predicts several differences in the two poets' practices which are fully borne out. First, both poets allow an extrametrical weak position after a strong postion before a major metrical and/or prosodic boundary (Kiparsky 1977). For Milton, where the metrical position is always a syllable, it is at most a syllable that can be extrametrical:

s s s s s
(26)a. And high disdain, from sense of injured merit (PL 1.948)
s s s s s
b. Strange horror seize thee, and pangs unfelt before. (PL 2.703)

For Shakespeare, however, since two are possible as a position if both are unstressed, two may also be extrametrical Kiparsky (1977):

s s s s s
(27) a. Unless I spoke or look't or touch't or carv'd to thee (Err 2.2.118)
s s s s s
b. Indeed I heard it not, if then draws near the season (Ham 1.4.5)

Second, words with two adjacent unstressed syllables are treated in revealingly different ways. For Shakespeare, the two syllables may occupy either one position or two, and both possibilities are utilized equally:

s s s s s
(28) a. She hath pursued conclusions infinite (AC 4.8.17)
s s s s s
b. O infinite virtue, com'st thou smiling from (AC 4.8.17)

For Milton, however, each syllable must occupy its own position. Where a triple rhythm exists, it is created through the exceptional allowance of a strong syllable in an initial weak position (fn. 6):

s s s s s
(29) Infinite wrath, and infinite despair (PL 4.74)

Similarly, where two unstressed syllables fall between strong syllables, Shakespeare can scan them as a single position line-internally (Kiparsky 1977):

s s s s s
(30) This fortification, gentlemen, shall we see it? (Oth 3.2.5)

But for Milton such words can only be used line-initially, because only there can their initial strong syllable be in a weak position, permitting the second strong syllable to fall in a strong position without compromising the allocation of a single syllable to every metrical position:

s s s s s
(31) Justification towards God, and peace (PL 12.296)

These formal differences in turn may help explain the distinct aesthetic effects of the two poets' styles. English words and phrases abound with sequences of two unstressed syllables. The fact that Milton's syllable-based meter requires that one such syllable be in a strong position means that syllables are regularly endowed with metrical prominence greater than the prosodic prominence they have in ordinary speech, perhaps one source of the sense of great dignity and even exaltation associated with Milton's meter. The paramount property for which Shakespeare's meter, in contrast, has been celebrated, is its naturalness, and its ability to express the full gamut of human characters, emotions, and situations. This flexibility is likewise a direct consequence of his foot-based system, and the variety of metrical alignments that it permits.

6. Conclusion

This paper has argued that a theory that explains the described conditions under which extra syllables are permitted in English iambic pentameter reveals two separate traditions of that meter, Milton's which is genuinely based on the syllable, and Shakespeare's, which is actually based on the moraic trochee. The fact that both the syllable and the foot are required by metrical theory as ways to define the size of a metrical position supports a broad view that meter draws on the full range of structures available in prosodic phonology. This view in turn may help explain precisely why it is that when we experience meter, we sense that we are experiencing our own language in a heightened way. As Thompson (1966:10) put it, '[Meter] does for language what the forms of any art to for their materials. It abstracts certain elements from the experience of the senses and forms them into patterns ... The elements are ordered in patterns similar to those the senses experience all the time, but ... simpler and clearer, and ... having a kind of independent existence they do not have in everyday experience. The forms are used then to order a presentation of the everyday experience of the senses.' It is for this reason, then, that these metrical forms may also help reveal what the patterns of language actually are.

References

Bridges, Robert. 1921. *Milton's Prosody* . Oxford: Clarendon Press.

Fussell, Paul. 1979. *Poetic meter and poetic form* , rev. ed. New York: Random House.

Golston, Chris and Tomas Riad. 1993. 'Prosodic metrics'. Ms., University of California at Berkeley and Stockholm University.

Halle, Morris and S. J. Keyser . 1972. 'The iambic pentameter'. InW.K. Wimsatt (ed.),*Versification: major language types.* New York: New York University Press.

Hanson, Kristin. 1993a. 'Resolution: evidence from modern English metrics.' In Schafer, A. (ed.), *NELS 23* , University of Massachusetts at Amherst: GLSA.

Hanson, Kristin. 1993b. 'The distinction between lexical and non-lexical words in English metrics.' Paper presented at the 67th annual meeting of the LSA, Los Angeles, January 7-10.

Hanson, Kristin. 1991. *Resolution in modern meters.* Ph.D. dissertation, Stanford University, Stanford, California.

Hanson, Kristin and Paul Kiparsky. 1994. 'The best of all possible verse'. Ms., University of British Columbia and Stanford University.

Hayes, Bruce. 1989. 'The prosodic hierarchy in meter'. In Paul Kiparsky and Gilbert Youmans (eds.), *Phonetics and phonology, vol. 1: Rhythm and Meter* , San Diego: Academic Press.

Hayes, Bruce. 1987. 'A revised parametric metrical theory'. In *NELS 17,* vol. 1, University of Massachusetts at Amherst: GLSA.

Hayes, Bruce. 1983. 'A grid-based theory of English meter.' *LI* 14:357-394.

Jakobson, Roman. 1960. 'Linguistics and poetics'. In Thomas Sebeok (ed.), *Style in language* , Cambridge: MIT Press and J. Wiley & Sons.

Kager, Rene. 1989. *A metrical theory of stress and destressing in English and Dutch.* Doctoral dissertation, Rijksuniversiteit Utrecht, The Netherlands.

Kiparsky, Paul. 1989. 'Sprung rhythm'. In Paul Kiparsky and Gilbert Youmans (eds.), *Phonetics and phonology, vol. 1: Rhythm and meter* , San Diego: Academic Press.

Kiparsky, Paul. 1987. 'On theory and interpretation'. In Nigel Fabb et al. (eds.), *The Linguistics of writing,* New York: Methuen.

Kiparsky, Paul. 1977. 'The rhythmic structure of English verse'. *LI* 8: 189-247.

Prince, Alan. 1989. 'Metrical forms'. In Paul Kiparsky and Gilbert Youmans (eds.), *Phonetics and phonology, vol. 1: Rhythm and meter.* San Diego: Academic Press.

Saintsbury, George. 1908. *A history of English prosody from the twelfth century to the present day, vol. 2* .London: MacMillan.

Thompson, John. 1966. *The founding of English metre.* London: Routledge and Kegan Paul.

Weismiller, Edward. 1989. 'Triple threats to duple rhythm'. In Paul Kiparsky and Gilbert Youmans (eds.), *Phonetics and phonology, vol. 1: Rhythm and meter.* San Diego: Academic Press.

Young, Sir George. 1928. *An English prosody on inductive lines* . Cambridge: Cambridge University Press.

Zec, Draga and Sharon Inkelas. 1988. 'Phonological phrasing and the reduction of function words'. Ms., Stanford University.

Editions cited:

Shakespeare, William. *The Riverside Shakespeare.* G.Blakemore Evans (textual editor), Boston: Houghton-Mifflin Co., 1974.

Milton, John. *Complete poems and major prose* . Hughes, Merritt Y. (ed.). Indianapolis: The Bobbs-Merrill Co., 1957.

An Optimality-Theoretic Account of Rounding Harmony Typology

ABIGAIL R. KAUN
University of California, Los Angeles

1. Introduction

In this paper I present an analysis of the typology of Rounding Harmony systems within the framework of Optimality Theory (Prince & Smolensky 1993, McCarthy & Prince 1993a,b). Central to the analysis presented here is the claim that phonological systems are organized around principles of both articulation and perception. The goals of the paper are as follows: (i) to exemplify the range of attested Rounding Harmony patterns, (ii) to identify the perceptual and articulatory principles which give rise to these patterns, and (iii) to propose an explicit formal model which characterizes the role of these principles in grammar.

I propose that harmony is the grammatical reflex of a perceptual principle, which I am labeling 'Bad Vowels Spread.'[1] The ingredients of this principle are as follows. Assume there exists a set of perceptually difficult contrasts, and that vowels whose recoverability relies on the detection of such contrasts are relatively likely to be misidentified. Presumably, the probability that the value for some contrast will be accurately identified by the listener increases with increased exposure to the relevant value. In the representation in (a), feature [F] is non-harmonic, whereas in the representation in (b), feature [F] is harmonic and its temporal duration is extended:

---

[1]This conceptualization of harmony is inspired by Kari Suomi's (1983) theory of palatal (backness) harmony as a perceptually-motivated phenomenon.

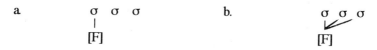

Under the view proposed here, the advantage of having harmony is that the temporal span of some perceptually vulnerable quality is extended.

The typology of Rounding Harmony systems is interesting in that Rounding Harmony rules nearly always impose conditions on the participating vowels which make reference to the height or backness tiers. For example, in Turkish we find the rule 'Spread the autosegment [round] rightward from vowel to vowel, but only if the target is [+high].' Despite the numerous possible forms which such conditions might take, it turns out that very clear patterns emerge, and only a small range of Rounding Harmony systems is attested.

Let us consider, by way of example, two systems found in Turkic, a language family in which Rounding Harmony is pervasive. The first of these is Turkish, which has the vowel inventory given in (1):

(1) Turkish Vowel Inventory

	Front		Back	
	Unround	Round	Unround	Round
High	i	ü	ı	u
Non-high	e	ö	a	o

Rounding Harmony in Turkish targets only high vowels: A high vowel following a syllable containing a rounded vowel surfaces as rounded. A non-high vowel, by contrast, is not subject to contextual rounding. Consider the nouns in (2), all of which contain the 'first (sg.) possessive' suffix /-(I)m/. As shown, the vowel of this suffix agrees with the vowels of the root in both backness and rounding:

(2) High Vowel Suffixes

a. kilim-im	'carpet-1.S'
b. ev-im	'house-1.S'
c. gül-üm	'rose-1.S'
d. köy-üm	'village-1.S'
e. kız-ım	'girl-1.S'
f. kaz-ım	'goose-1.S'
g. kuş-um	'bird-1.S'
h. koz-um	'walnut-1.S'

The nouns in (3) contain the 'plural' suffix /-lAr/, the low vowel of which agrees in backness, but not in rounding with the vowels of the root:

(3) Low Vowel Suffixes

a. kilim-ler	'carpet-PL'
b. ev-ler	'house-PL'

c. gül-ler 'rose-PL'
d. köy-ler 'village-PL'
e. kız-lar 'girl-PL'
f. kaz-lar 'goose-PL'
g. kuş-lar 'bird-PL'
h. koz-lar 'walnut-PL'

Harmony effects are observed across a span of multiple affixes, as shown in (4). The words in (a)-(h) contain the 'plural' suffix followed by the 'first (sg.) possessive' suffix. In these words, neither the low vowel of the 'plural' suffix nor the high vowel of the 'possessive' suffix undergoes Rounding Harmony. Thus, non-high vowels not only fail to undergo Rounding Harmony, they also block it. In the nouns in (i)-(p), the high vowel of the 'possessive' suffix is not prevented from undergoing Rounding Harmony. As expected, however, the low vowel of the 'plural' suffix which follows remains unrounded, even when preceded by rounded vowels:

(4) <u>Harmony Effects with Multiple Suffixes</u>

a. kilim-ler-im	'carpet-PL-1.S'	i. kilim-im-de	'carpet-1.S-LOC'
b. ev-ler-im	'house-PL-1.S'	j. ev-im-de	'house-1.S-LOC'
c. gül-ler-im	'rose-PL-1.S'	k. gül-üm-de	'rose-1.S-LOC'
d. köy-ler-im	'village-PL-1.S'	l. köy-üm-de	'village-1.S-LOC'
e. kız-lar-ım	'girl-PL-1.S'	m. kız-ım-da	'girl-1.S-LOC'
f. kaz-lar-ım	'goose-PL-1.S'	n. kaz-ım-da	'goose-1.S-LOC'
g. kuş-lar-ım	'bird-PL-1.S'	o. kuş-um-da	'bird-1.S-LOC'
h. koz-lar-ım	'walnut-PL-1.S'	p. koz-um-da	'walnut1.S-LOC'

Consider next the Rounding Harmony pattern found in the dialect of Kirghiz documented in Herbert & Poppe's grammar (1963). I will refer to this dialect as Kirghiz-B.[2] The vowel qualities of Kirghiz-B are like those of Turkish. There are two degrees of height, and rounding is contrastive among both the front vowels and the back vowels.

In Kirghiz-B, as in Turkish, underlying rounding contrasts are confined to the initial syllable of a word. Thus any instance of rounding in a non-initial syllable is the result of harmony. However, Rounding Harmony operates in a greater number of contexts, targeting high vowels, front vowels, and vowels which agree in height with the potential trigger. Thus, Rounding Harmony fails to apply in only one configuration: <u>uCa</u> surfaces in preference to <u>*uCo</u>.

To illustrate the operation of Rounding harmony in Kirghiz-B, consider the nouns in (5), which contain the 'ordinal' suffix, and those in (6), which contain the 'ablative.' In only one instance (6g) does a rounded vowel fail to trigger contextual rounding of a following vowel:

[2]Kirghiz-A, discussed below, refers to the dialect of Kirghiz reported in Comrie (1981).

(5) <u>High Vowel Suffixes</u>

a.	biri-inči	'one-ORD, *first*'
b.	beš-inči	'five-ORD, *fifth*'
c.	üč-ünčü	'three-ORD, *third*'
d.	tört-ünčü	'four-ORD, *fourth*'
e.	altı-ncı	'six-ORD, *sixth*'
f.	ǰıyırma-nčı	'twenty-ORD, *twentieth*'
g.	toguz-unču	'nine-ORD, *ninth*'
h.	on-unču	'ten-ORD, *tenth*'

(6) <u>Low Vowel Suffixes</u>

a.	iš-ten	'job-ABL'
b.	et-ten	'meat-ABL'
c.	üy-dön	'house-ABL'
d.	köl-dön	'lake-ABL'
e.	ǰıl-dan	'year-ABL'
f.	asan-dan	'Hasan-ABL'
g.	turmuš-tan (*turmuš-ton)	'life-ABL'
h.	tokoy-don	'forest-ABL'

Other Rounding Harmony patterns are found within Turkic and in other language families as well.

2. The Typology of Rounding Harmony

A thorough survey of Rounding Harmony phenomena yielded nine language types, including the two discussed in the preceding section. As far as I know, no other Rounding Harmony patterns are attested. For six of these nine types, Rounding Harmony is either unconditioned, or the conditions which are imposed on its application make reference only to the height of the participating vowels. That is, in those languages in which rounding contrasts are found among both the front vowels and the back vowels, the front and back vowels pattern alike with respect to Rounding Harmony. To represent the domain of harmony in these backness-neutral systems, I will employ the schematic notation given in (7):

(7) <u>Schematic Representation: Backness-neutral Rounding Harmony</u>

I = high vowel
A = non-high vowel

II:	trigger is [+high], target is [+high]
AA:	trigger is [-high], target is [-high]
IA:	trigger is [+high], target is [-high]
AI:	trigger is [-high], target is [+high]

The symbol 'I' represents a high vowel. 'A' represents a non-high vowel. The trigger is represented on the left, and the target is represented on the right. So the sequence 'II' represents a system in which Rounding Harmony is observed when the trigger and target are both high vowels, 'IA' represents a system in which [round] spreads from a high vowel onto a neighboring non-high vowel, and so on.

The first six Rounding Harmony types are given here, with representative languages listed for each type:

(8) Rounding Harmony Types 1-6

TYPE	DOMAIN	DESCRIPTION	LANGUAGES
Type 1	II, AA, AI, IA	*Harmony unrestricted*	Kirghiz-A (Comrie 1981)
Type 2	II, AI	*Target must be [+high]*	Nawuri (Casali 1993), Southern Paiute (Sapir 1930), Sierra Miwok dialects (Callaghan 1987, Broadbent 1964, Sloan 1991), Turkish (Lewis 1967), Tuvan (Krueger 1977)
Type 3	II, AA	*Trigger and target must agree in height*	Yawelmani Yokuts (Newman 1944, Kuroda 1967, Archangeli 1984), Galab (Steriade 1981)
Type 4	AA	*Trigger and target must both be [-high]*	Eastern Mongolian dialects (Svantesson 1985, Rialland & Djamouri 1984), Murut (Prentice 1974), Tungusic languages (Ard 1981, Sunik 1985, Avrorin & Lebedeva 1978)
Type 5	II	*Trigger and target must both be [+high]*	Hixkaryana (Derbyshire 1979), Kachin (Korn 1969), Tsou (Hsu 1993)
Type 6	II, AA, AI	*Trigger and Target must agree in height or target must be [+high]*	Yakut (Kreuger 1962)

In the remaining Rounding Harmony types, all of which are represented by Turkic languages, an asymmetry is observed between front vowels and back vowels. In these languages we find that Harmony is unrestricted when the trigger and target are front. When the trigger and target are back, conditions similar to those found in Types 2-6 are imposed on the application of Harmony. I will use Ü to represent a high front vowel, and Ö to represent a non-high front vowel. The remaining three Types are summarized in (9):

(9) Rounding Harmony Types 7-9

TYPE	DOMAIN	DESCRIPTION	LANGUAGES
Type 7	ÜÜ ÖÖ ÜÖ ÖÜ II AI	*Harmony unrestricted among [-back] vowels, among [+back] vowels, target must be [+high]*	Chulym Tatar (Korn 1969), Karakalpak (Menges 1947)
Type 8	ÜÜ ÖÖ ÜÖ ÖÜ II	*Harmony unrestricted among [-back] vowels, among [+back] vowels, trigger and target must both be [+high]*	Kyzyl Khakass (Korn 1969)
Type 9	ÜÜ ÖÖ ÜÖ ÖÜ II AA AI	*Harmony unrestricted among [-back] vowels, among [+back] vowels , trigger and target must agree in height, or target must be [+high]*	Kirghiz-B (Herbert & Poppe 1963), Altai (Korn 1969)

A summary of the typology is given in (10). Only those domains in which Rounding Harmony is attested are listed for each type:

(10) The Typology

Type 1:	II	AA	IA	AI
Type 2:	II			AI
Type 3:	II	AA		
Type 4:		AA		
Type 5:	II			
Type 6:	II	AA		AI
Type 7:	II			AI
	ÜÜ	ÖÖ	ÜÖ	ÖÜ
Type 8:	II			
	ÜÜ	ÖÖ	ÜÖ	ÖÜ
Type 9:	II	AA		AI
	ÜÜ	ÖÖ	ÜÖ	ÖÜ

Let us consider now what patterns emerge from the Typology in (10). How does the application of Rounding Harmony correlate with the height and backness dimensions? Stated differently, what conditions favor the application of Rounding Harmony? Based on the Typology in (10), we can conclude that high vowels are preferred as targets of Rounding Harmony over non-high vowels. By the same token, non-high vowels are preferred as triggers of Rounding Harmony. Furthermore, the application of Rounding Harmony is quite often blocked when the trigger and target disagree in height. Finally, in some instances (Types 7-9), Rounding Harmony is observed among front vowels while, in certain of the analogous back-vocalic contexts, Rounding Harmony fails to apply. We can thus conclude that the application of Rounding Harmony is favored when the trigger and target are front.

Feature Geometry theory is not designed to make predictions about the configurations in which spreading is likely to occur, or not to occur, when the occurence of spreading is conditioned by specifications on independent tiers. For example, it is difficult to imagine a Feature Geometric analysis which would explain why it is that high vowels are the preferred targets of Rounding Harmony, whereas non-high vowels are the preferred triggers of Rounding Harmony.

By contrast, Optimality Theory is well equipped to model the observed variation among harmony systems. Once one has identified the constraints which rule in favor of the spreading of harmonic features, the theory predicts that independent constraints which dictate a dispreference for spreading will also be operative. Such additional constraints might refer to how features associate and how they combine.

3. Optimality Theoretic Analysis

The basic tenets of Optimality Theory (Prince & Smolensky 1993, McCarthy & Prince 1993a,b) are as follows: The phonological rule is replaced by constraints on representations. These constraints are universal and may conflict with one another. Constraints are violable, and relative constraint ranking is language-specific. Given that Optimality Theoretic constraints are claimed to be universal, whereas their relative ranking is decided language-specifically, it is clear that Optimality Theory is inherently a model of linguistic typology, a possible linguistic system being one that is generated by some ranking of a fixed set of universal constraints.

The first category of constraints relevant here is what I am calling Contrast Constraints. Contrast Constraints characterize harmony as the grammaticization of a perceptually-driven phenomenon. Suppose that the [±F] contrast is a perceptually difficult contrast. Now, suppose that two competing representations for a given string are available, those given in (a) and (b) below:

a. σ σ σ
| | |
[±F][±F][±F]

b. σ σ σ
(all three linked to one)
[±F]

The decision to prefer (b) over (a) has the following positive consequences: First, over some span, the number of instances in which a [+F] vs. [-F] decision must be made is reduced to one. Second, the listener is provided with increased exposure to the feature value in question.

Of course the question which immediately arises is what constitutes a perceptually difficult phonological contrast? To answer this question, I want to pursue two hypotheses which are suggested by the observed typological facts. First is the role of Enhancement, as discussed in Stevens, Keyser & Kawasaki (1986). Typically, the [±labial] opposition and the [±back] opposition are mutually enhancing; front vowels are unrounded, back non-high vowels are rounded. When we say that [round] enhances [back], and vice-versa, what we mean is the following. Lip-rounding induces a lowering of F2. At the same time, the acoustic cue associated with back vowels is a relatively low F2 value. Therefore, the presence of lip-rounding reinforces the cue that a back vowel is indeed back. By the same token, the acoustic cue associated with front vowels is a relatively high F2 value, so the absence of lip rounding enhances the cue that a front vowel is indeed front. The hypothesis is that in languages in which the [±round] opposition and the [±back] opposition do not stand in a relationship of mutual enhancement, the perceptual cues available for recovering the backness and rounding values of a given vowel will be relatively weak. And indeed, we find that Backness Harmony and Rounding Harmony are very frequently found in languages in which the features [round] and [back] are not mutually enhancing. For instance, Backness Harmony is observed in Hungarian and Finnish. In these languages lip-rounding enhances [+back], but among the front vowels, the rounding and backness dimensions are not mutually enhancing. Both Backness Harmony and Rounding Harmony are observed in many Turkic languages. In these languages the roundness and backness dimensions are never mutually enhancing: Rounding contrasts obtain among both the front vowels and the back vowels.

The second factor which I will claim contributes to the perceptual difficulty of a given contrast involves relative articulatory magnitude. It has been observed that non-high rounded vowels tend to be less rounded than high rounded vowels. And similarly, front rounded vowels tend to involve less lip-rounding and/or protrusion than the analogous back rounded vowels. This pattern is demonstrated strikingly in Linker's dissertation (1982) on labial activity in vowels, in which the articulation of vowels in English, French, Cantonese, Swedish and Finnish was studied. Based on these observations, and the results of the present survey of Rounding Harmony phenomena, we may entertain the following hypothesis. In contexts in which the articulatory manifestations of the [±round] opposition are relatively small, they will give rise to relatively small acoustic differences. As a consequence, weaker perceptual cues will be available for determing whether a given vowel is rounded or unrounded. This hypothesis is supported by the results obtained in Terbeek's (1977) investigation of the factors which contribute to perceptual distances in the vowel space. Terbeek's study investigated the perceptual distance among 12 monophthongs. Speakers of five languages served as subjects: English, German, Thai, Turkish, and Swedish. For each of these subjects some, but not all of the monophthongs were similar to vowels occuring in the listener's native language. Six perceptual dimensions were identified, which Terbeek labeled as shown in (11):

(11) Perceptual Dimensions of Vowel Quality (Terbeek, 1977)

Back vs. Nonback (1)
Back vs. Nonback (2)
Low vs. Nonlow
High vs. Nonhigh
Round vs. Nonround
Peripheral vs. Central

Along the Round vs. Nonround continuum, the rounded vowels positioned themselves as shown schematically here (relative distance not shown):

(12) <u>The Round vs. Nonround Continuum</u> (Terbeek, 1977)

u o ü ö

<-----------------------------

Note that this arrangment indicates that non-high vowels and front vowels are perceived as relatively unrounded: The high vowels lie on the higher end of the scale relative to the non-high vowels, and the back vowels lie on the higher end of the scale relative to the front vowels.

I suggest that where a particular contrast is perceptually difficult, that difficulty has as its direct grammatical correlate a constraint of the "Bad Vowels Spread" family:

(13) <u>The "Bad Vowels Spread" Constraint Family</u>

Contrast	Corresponding Constraint
a. Rounding among non-high vowels	**EXTEND[RD]if[-HI]**
b. Rounding among front vowels	**EXTEND[RD]if[-BK]**
c. Contrastive Rounding (without [back] enhancement)	**EXTEND[RD]**

In addition to Contrast Constraints, I propose two constraints on feature combinations. Why is it that Rounding Harmony systems avoid the creation of non-high rounded vowels? The answer to this question is that lip-rounding in combination with low jaw position is dispreferred. This dispreference is manifested in cross-linguistic vowel inventory patterns. In Maddieson's *Patterns of Sounds* (1984), low rounded vowels are virtually non-existent. A further asymmetry exists among the mid vowels. We find that mid back rounded vowels are often higher than their front unrounded couterparts. The reverse scenario is unattested in Maddieson's survey. Within the framework of Optimality Theory, the dispreference for lip-rounding in combination with low jaw position can be assumed to have a direct correlate in grammar, and I will label the relevant constraint '***ROLO.**'[3]

A second pattern observed in the typology of Rounding Harmony systems involves the avoidance of sequences of rounded vowels which disagree in height. This pattern falls into the general class of phenomena whereby like segments tend to assimilate to like segments. I propose that the failure of Rounding Harmony to apply when it would create a sequence

---

[3]Chomsky & Halle (1968, Ch. 9) claim in Marking Convention XI that the unmarked value of [±round] is [-round] in the context of [+low]. ***ROLO**, while clearly related, makes a different claim. ***ROLO** states that lip-rounding and relatively low jaw position are incompatible. I do not, at this point, offer an explicit interpretation of the property 'relatively low jaw position.'

of different-height vowels multiply linked to a single [round] autosegment is related to the fact that the rounding gesture associated with non-high vowels is different from that associated with high vowels (Linker 1982). The relevant constraint, which I am labeling **UNI[RD]**, states that a single autosegment should have a uniform execution mechanism throughout its span of association. The representation in (b) incurs a **UNI[RD]** violation, whereas the representation in (a) does not:

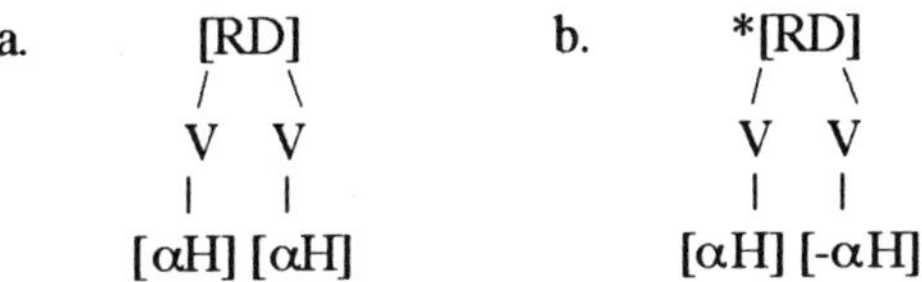

4. Excursus: Another Uniformity Effect

Padgett (1991) has observed that while nasal assimilation to stops is prevalent, nasal assimilation to fricatives is typically avoided. Padgett cites such asymmetries in English, Zoque, Lithuanian, Aguaruna, Attic Greek, and other languages. Under Padgett's analysis, [±continuent] is a dependent of the Place node, and the failure of nasals to assimilate to fricatives is the result of universal marking conditions which disallow nasal fricatives. This solution is problematic, however, in that contrastively nasalized fricatives do exist, being found in languages such as Zande (Tucker 1959) and Mumuye Zing (Shimizu 1983). Furthermore, Padgett cites a small number of cases in which nasals do in fact assimilate to continuants, including Icelandic, Kikongo and Swahili.

I suggest that the failure of nasals to assimilate to continuants is a Uniformity effect, the relevant constraint being **UNI[PL]**. Consider the sequence n̲+s̲. Both consonants involve a coronal articulation. The articulations are not uniform, however. For the nasal stop, the tongue is sealed around the sides and front of the palate, whereas for the fricative, the center of the tongue is grooved and there is no seal across the front of the palate. By contrast, the oral gestures involved in the articulation of the nasal and the stop in a n̲+t̲ sequence are equivalent. **UNI[PL]** is responsible for the fact that nasals tend not to assimilate to continuants in place of articulation. As an Optimality-Theoretic constraint, however, **UNI[PL]** is violable, as evidenced in such languages as Icelandic, Kikongo and Swahili.

5. Constraint Interaction

To show how the proposed constraints may interact with one another, let us consider Rounding Harmony Type 9, represented by Kirghiz-B. Recall that in Kirghiz-B, Rounding Harmony is unrestricted when the vowels in question are front. When the vowels are back, Rounding Harmony applies if the trigger and target agree in height, or if the target is a high vowel. A purely Feature Geometric rule for Kirghiz-B is given in (14):

(14) Rounding Harmony in Kirghiz B: Feature Geometry

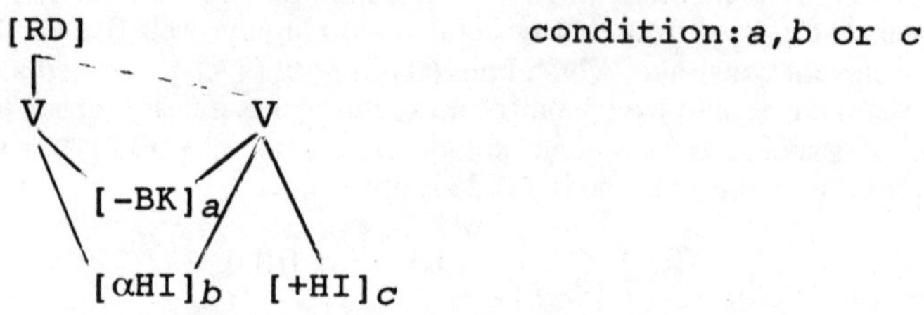

This rule states that the autosegment [round] spreads rightward from vowel to vowel, provided that at least one of three conditions is met: The vowels are [-back], the vowels agree in height, or the target is [+high]. In the vocabulary of rules which is clearly required for Kirghiz-B, any conceivable Rounding Harmony system can be represented. Thus, this type of analysis makes no predictions regarding the range of Rounding Harmony systems which will be attested. It is often supposed that the simplest rule will be the most widely attested. This prediction is clearly wrong, since Rounding Harmony systems can very rarely be characterized adequately with the simplest available rule: Spread [round] from vowel to vowel.

Tableaux showing how the proposed constraints can be ranked to generate the Kirghiz-B system within Optimality Theory are given in (15) and (16):

(15) Tableau for Kirghiz B: Back Vocalic Words

	EXT[RD] if [-BK]	EXT[RD] if [-HI]	*[ROLO]	EXT[RD]	UNI[RD]
→ u-u	√	√	√	√	√
u-ɨ	√	√	√	*	√
→ o-o	√	√	**	√	√
o-a	√	*	*	*	√
u-o	√	√	*	√	*
→ u-a	√	√	√	*	√
→ o-u	√	√	*	√	*
o-ɨ	√	*	*	*	√

(16) Tableau for Kirghiz B: Front Vocalic Words

	EXT[RD] if [-BK]	EXT[RD] if [-HI]	*[ROLO]	EXT[RD]	UNI[RD]
→ ü-ü	√	√	√	√	√
ü-i	*	√	√	*	√
→ ö-ö	√	√	**	√	√
ö-e	*	*	*	*	√
→ ü-ö	√	√	*	√	*
ü-e	*	√	√	*	√
→ ö-ü	√	√	*	√	*
ö-i	*	*	*	*	√

Crucially, the constraints which conspire to block Rounding Harmony, namely ***ROLO** and **UNI[RD]** must be ranked lower than those which dictate that contrastive rounding must spread when the trigger is either front or non-high. So **EXTEND[RD]if[-BK]** and **EXTEND[RD]if[-HI]** are ranked above ***ROLO** and **UNI[RD]**. The effects of ***ROLO** are observable, in that the sequence uCa surfaces in preference to the sequence uCo. Thus, ***ROLO** must outrank **EXTEND[RD]**. The constraints **EXTEND[RD]** and **UNI[RD]** are never decisive in Kirghiz-B, but in other Rounding Harmony types they are ranked higher, and their effects are indeed observable.

I have proposed five constraints to characterize the typology of Rounding Harmony. These are listed in (17):

(17) Summary of Proposed Constraints

EXTEND[RD]if[-HI]
EXTEND[RD]if[-BK]
EXTEND[RD]
***[ROLO]**
UNI[RD]

Now, it is the case that 5 constraints can be ranked in 120 unique orders (5!). Thus, 120 distinct grammars are available on the basis of the five constraints which I have proposed. Many of these various rankings produce the same surface pattern, however, and in fact the 120 grammars yield only 12 Rounding Harmony types. I have listed these in (18):

(18) Predicted Rounding Harmony Typology

(√= attested)

√Type 1:	II	AA	IA	AI
√Type 2:	II			AI
√Type 3:	II	AA		
√Type 4:	II	AA		
√Type 5:	II	AA		
√Type 6:	II	AA		AI
√Type 7:	II			AI
	ÜÜ	ÖÖ	ÜÖ	ÖÜ
√Type 8:	II			
	ÜÜ	ÖÖ	ÜÖ	ÖÜ
√Type 9:	II	AA		AI
	ÜÜ	ÖÖ	ÜÖ	ÖÜ
Type 10:	II			AI
	ÜÜ			ÖÜ
Type 11:	II			
	ÜÜ	ÖÖ		
Type 12:	II	AA		
	ÜÜ	ÖÖ	ÜÖ	ÖÜ

Of the 12 types predicted by this model, the first 9 are the attested patterns, indicated with check marks. Only three unattested types are predicted by this model, namely types 10-12.

To conclude, I have demonstrated that clear patterns emerge from a systematic examination of the typology of Rounding Harmony systems. These patterns yield to functional explanations, that is the systems 'make sense.' I claim that the observed systems are natural because the ingredients of grammar are natural. The ingredients of grammar are principles of perception and articulation. With the advent of Optimality Theory, we are in a position to model formally the interactions of such principles and, as I have shown, to formulate an explicit model of linguistic typologies.

References

Archangeli, Diana. 1984. *Underspecification in Yawelmani phonology and morphology.* Doctoral dissertation, MIT.

Ard, Josh. 1981. A sketch of vowel harmony in the Tungus languages, in *Studies in the languages of the USSR*, ed. by Bernard Comrie.

Avrorin, V. & Y. Lebedeva. 1978. *Orochkiye teksty i sovar.* Leningrad.

Broadbent, Sylvia. 1964. *The Northern Sierra Miwok language.* University of California publications in Linguistics 38.

Callaghan, Catherine. 1987. *Northern Sierra Miwok Dictionary.* University of California publications in Linguistics 110.

Casali, Roderic. 1993. Labial Opacity and Roundness Harmony in Nawuri, in *UCLA Occasional Papers in Linguistics* No. 13, ed. by Danial Silverman & Robert Kirchner.

Chomsky, Noam & Morris Halle. 1968. *The sound pattern of English.* MIT Press.

Comrie, Bernard. 1981. *Languages of the Soviet Union*. Cambridge University Press.

Derbyshire, Desmond. 1985. *Hixkaryana and linguistic typology*. SIL publications. UT Austin.

Hahn, Reinhard. 1991. *Spoken Uyghur*. University of Washington Press.

Herbert, Raymond & Nicholas Poppe. 1963. *Kirghiz manual*. Indiana University publications. Uralic and Altaic Series, vol. 33.

Hsu, Chai-Shune. 1993. Tsou Phonology. ms., UCLA.

Kaun, Abigail. forthcoming. *The typology of rounding harmony: An optimality-theoretic approach*. Doctoral dissertation, UCLA.

Kirchner, Robert. 1993. Turkish round and back harmony and disharmony: An Optimality Theoretic account. ms., UCLA.

Korn, David. 1969. Types of labial vowel harmony in the Turkic languages. *Anthropological Linguistics* 11.

Krueger, John. 1962. *Yakut manual*. Indiana University publications, Ural-Altaic Series 21.

Krueger, John. 1977. *Tuvan manual*. Indiana University publications, Ural-Altaic Series 126.

Kuroda, S-Y. 1967. *Yawelmani Phonology*. Research monograph no. 43. MIT Press.

Ladefoged, Peter & Ian Maddieson. forthcoming. *Sounds of the world's languages*.

Lewis, G.L. 1967. *Turkish grammar*. Oxford University Press.

Lindblad, Vernon. 1990. Neutralization in Uyghur. unpublished MA thesis, University of Washington.

Linker, Wendy. 1982. *Articulatory and acoustic correlates of labial activity in vowels: A cross-linguistic study*. Doctoral dissertation, UCLA. Published by *UCLA WPP* 56.

Maddieson, Ian. 1984. *Patterns of sounds*. Cambridge University Press.

McCarthy John & Alan Prince 1993a. *Prosodic morphology I: constraint interaction and satisfaction*. ms., UMass and Rutgers University.

McCarthy John & Alan Prince. 1993b. *Generalized alignment*. Technical Report #3 of the Rutgers Center for Cognitive Science, Rutgers, New Jersey.

Menges, Karl. 1947. *Qaraqalpaq Grammar*. King's Crown Press. New York.

Newman, Stanley. 1944. *The Yokuts language of California*. The Viking Fund Publications in Anthropology #2, New York.

Odden, David. 1991. Vowel Geometry, *Phonology* 8.

Prentice, D.J. 1971. *The Murut languages of Sabah*. Pacific Linguistics, Series C, No. 18.

Prince, Alan & Paul Smolensky. 1993. *Optimality Theory Constraint interaction in generative grammar*. ms., Rutgers University and University of Colorado at Boulder.

Rialland, Annie & Redouane Djamouri. 1984. Harmonie vocalique, consonantique et structures de dépendance dans le mot en mongol khalkha. Bulletin de la Société de Linguistique de Paris, vol. 79.

Sapir, Edward. 1930. *Southern Paiute, a Shoshonean language*. Proceedings of the American Academy of Arts and Sciences 65: 1-3.

Shimizu, K. 1983. *The Zing dialect of Mumuye: A descriptive grammar*. Helmut Buske. Verlag, Hamburg.

Sloan, Kelly. 1991. *Syllables and templates: Evidence from Southern Sierra Miwok*. Doctoral dissertation, MIT.

Steriade, Donca. 1993. Positional neutralization. *NELS* 24.

Steriade, Donca. 1981. Parameters of metrical vowel harmony rules: The underlying representation of harmonic vowels. ms., MIT.

Stevens, Kenneth, Samual K. Keyser & Haruko Kawasaki. 1986. Toward a phonetic and phonological theory of redundant features, in *Invariance and variability in speech processes,* ed. by Joseph Perkell & Dennis Klatt. Lawrence Erlbaum Associates, London.

Sunik, O. 1985. *Ulchskiy yazyk: Issledovaniya i materialy*. Leningrad.

Suomi, Kari. 1983. Palatal Harmony: A Perceptually Motivated Phenomenon? *Nordic Journal of Linguistics* 6:1-35.

Svantesson, Jan-Olaf. 1985. Vowel harmony shift in Mongolian. *Lingua* 67:283-327.

Terbeek, Dale. 1977. *A cross-language multidimensional scaling study of vowel perception*. Doctoral dissertation, UCLA. Published by UCLA WPP 37.

Tucker, A. with P. Hackett. 1959. *Le groupe linguistique zande*. Annales du Musé Royal du Congo Belge. Science de l'homme, Linguistique, vol. 22. Tervuren.

Extrasyllabic Consonants and Compensatory Lengthening

YEN-HWEI LIN
Michigan State University

1. Compensatory Lengthening and Moraic Licensing

In his typological study of Compensatory Lengthening (CL), Hayes (1989) makes two important claims. First, since CL processes conserve mora count (Moraic Conservation), CL never results from the loss of a moraless onset consonant. Second, CL is confined to languages that have a preexisting syllable weight contrast. It is assumed that segments are exhaustively syllabified. All nuclear vowels are linked to moras; a coda segment is assigned a mora if the language in question treats the VC rime as heavy. Therefore, only deletion of a syllable nucleus or a moraic coda segment could trigger CL.

Based on evidence from Bella Coola phonology and morphology, Bagemihl (1991) argues for the Simple Syllable Hypothesis as in (1a) and claims that some consonants must be left unaffiliated to a syllable phonologically. He then proposes the notion of Moraic Licensing as in (1b) and suggests that in some languages unsyllabified consonants may persist throughout the derivation and be exempt from stray erasure if they are moraic.

(1) a. Simple Syllable Hypothesis: no incorporation or adjunction of extensive series of consonants or consonants that violate sonority constraints.

b. Moraic Licensing: In the marked case, an unsyllabified segment is licensed if it is linked to a mora; segments unlinked to a mora are stray erased. (In the unmarked case, a segment is unlicensed if it is not linked to a syllable.)

In the normal situation, Prosodic Licensing in (2) requires that every segment be linked to a syllable; unlicensed segments would either be saved by stray epenthesis or deleted by Stray Erasure at the end of each cycle (Itô 1989). On the other hand, Moraic Licensing accounts for a marked case of Prosodic Licensing in which a stray consonant is properly licensed if it is linked to a mora; that is, only a moraless unsyllabified consonant is subject to Stray Erasure.

(2) Prosodic Licensing (Itô 1986, 1989)
Every phonological unit (segment, syllable, and foot) must be dominated by higher prosodic structure.

With the suggestion that some languages allow moraic consonants to be unsyllabified, one would expect to find a case of CL which occurs as a result of deletion of an extrasyllabic moraic consonant. This paper argues that CL in Piro (an Arawakan language spoken in Peru) is one such case. According to the analysis of Piro phonology in Lin (1987), Piro seems to present a counterexample to Hayes' claims (Lin 1988). First, CL in Piro appears to result from the loss of an onset consonant. Second, Piro has no preexisting syllable weight contrast but allows CL to occur. In this paper, I will demonstrate that a new account that recognizes the existence of extrasyllabic consonants in Piro is not only consistent with various phenomena in Piro phonology and phonetics, but also supports Moraic Licensing and Hayes' theory of CL.

The organization of the paper is as follows. I will first discuss previous analyses of syllable structure, syncope, and CL in Piro. The problems posed by Piro for Hayes' theory of CL are identified in §3. A proposal incorporating Moraic Licensing will then be presented in §4.

2. Syllable Structure, Syncope, and CL in Piro

The Piro underlying vowels and consonants are given in (3). In terms of distribution, Piro has no vowel-initial words, nor words ending in consonants. With the exception of a few single-consonant affixes (e.g. /n-/ 'my'), all underlying morphemes begin with one or two consonants and end in a vowel.

(3)							
a.	vowels	i	u	e	o	a	(/u/=high back unrounded)
b.	stops:		p	t		k	
c.	affricates:			ts	tš	tx	
d.	fricatives:			s	š	x	(/x/ = palatal spirant)
e.	nasal spirant:					h̃	
f.	flaps:			l	r		
g.	nasals & glides:		m	n	w	y	

Piro has been analyzed to have only open syllables, which allow up to three consonants in the syllabic onset (Matteson 1965, Lin 1987). Examples are given in (4). Three-consonant clusters are rare and result from morphological concatenations that involve single-consonant affixes, as shown in (5).

(4) Syllable Structure: (C)(C)CV

a. CV	h̃a	'water'	te.no	'tall'	ki.ni.ma	'bead bracelet'
b. CCV	šyo	'bat'	slo.ta	'clam'	tla.h̃wa	'toad'
c. CCCV	ph̃ya	'vapor'	nkno.ya.te	'my turtle'		

(5) a. n-knoyate → nknoyate 'my turtle'
b. rasuka - m - ta - na → rasukamtna 'they ran right away'

One important aspect of Piro syllabic phonology, as observed by Lin (1987, 1993), is that no sonority constraints are placed on the combinations of consonants. The examples in (6) show that any two consonants can occur in either order. Notice that Piro also allows geminate clusters as in (6g).

(6)				
a.	**tp**a	'curve'	**pt**o	'...'s group'
b.	**mw**enutu	'cheap'	**wm**ah̃atya	'we lack'
c.	**wy**optota	'we receive'	**yw**alitxa	'hip'
d.	**ks**u	'tube'	**sk**ota	'low abdomen'
e.	**tm**ennu	'flaw'	**mt**enotu	'short'
f.	**sm**ota	'blunt point'	**ms**a	'empty corn cob'
g.	**nn**ika	'I eat'	**ww**uh̃ene	'our child'

The only exceptions to such considerable freedom of consonant clustering are the combinations of fricatives and affricates that are similar in place and/or manner of articulation. The non-permissible clusters include fricative clusters (e.g. *sx, *xx), affricate clusters (e.g. *tstx), t + affricate (e.g.*tts), and affricate + fricative (e.g. *tss) (Matteson 1965, Lin 1987). These cooccurrence restrictions may be accounted for by OCP motivated filters, rather than by sonority constraints. Except for these limited non-permissible clusters, all other consonant combinations, including geminates, can be syllabified. The distinction between permissible and nonpermissible clusters is crucial to the analysis of syncope as we will see below.

In (7), I quote from Matteson (1965) the phonetic description of Piro syllables and her arguments for treating all consonants as onset elements. The important points are (i) that complete phonetic closure does not occur in normal speech, (ii) that the closure of syllables is highly variable, and (iii) that word initial clusters still need to be described as onset clusters.

(7) Matteson (1965:23-24)

A syllable consisting of CCV or CCCV is initiated by a weaker controlled syllable pulse or pulses with at least partial release(s) following each vocoid or syllabified consonants, with continued build-up even during the release, and with reinforcement by a strong pulse initiating the final syllabic unit...

In a sequence one syllable may be phonetically closed by the onset of the initial consonant of the following syllable. This closure is particularly common with nasal consonants. The degree of closure fluctuates from zero to complete closure with rearticulation of the consonant as a part of the following syllable. The latter extreme does not occur in normal speech, but in slow, exaggerated, hypostatic utterance...

all consonants are treated as belonging to the same syllable as the following vowel because (1) the closure of the syllables is freely fluctuating; (2) the patterns CV, CCV, CCCV occur word initially and so must be described whether or not closed syllables are also described; (3) the consonant invariably shares part of the muscular movement of the syllable pulse that produces the following vowel.

We have seen the arguments in favor of syllabifying all consonants as syllable onset based on segmental distributions and phonetic considerations. We now examine a phonological argument based on the behavior of a syncope rule. According to Lin (1987), syncope is the major lexical phonological rule in Piro. Morpheme final vowels are deleted whenever suffixation of a certain group of morphemes occurs, unless the deletion would result in tri-consonantal clusters. There are two groups of suffixes: one triggers syncope and the other does not; this division is arbitrary and has to be lexically marked. The cyclic syncope rule and representative examples are given (8). (The suffixes that do not trigger syncope are written in capitals in this paper.) In (8a), the suffix /NA/ belongs to the group that does not trigger syncope, so the vowel of the stem is retained. (8b) shows that deletion of the final vowel of the stem /koko/ is blocked because such deletion would create a tri-consonatal cluster. In (8c) the final vowel of the stem is deleted; the derived consonant cluster [ky] has the effect of blocking syncope on the next cycle.

(8) Syncope: V → ø / VC __ + CV (cyclic)

a. wuylaka + NA + ru
'we hit' 'verb theme suffix' 'him'
→ wuylakana - ru
→ wuylakan_ru 'we hit him'

b. koko + yma + ru + NE
'uncle' 'with' 'entity' 'plural'
→ kokoyma + ru + NE
→ kokoymaru + NE
→ kokoymarune 'with uncles'

c. nika + ya + waka + lu
'to eat' 'locative' 'place' 'it'
→ nik_ya + waka + lu
→ nikyawaka + lu
→ nikyawak_lu
→ nikyawaklu 'to eat it there'

There are, however, exceptions in which syncope applies unexpectedly. In examples (9ab), the fricative consonant clusters do not block syncope as one would expect. Compare these two examples with (8c) above and (9c) where the newly created clusters block syncope on the next cycle.

(9) a. kna + mtasa + xe + kaka
'pole' 'hollow' 'lasting' 'stem suffix'
→ knamtas x kaka (→ knamta:xkaka) 'lanky'

b. ptso + tsotaxi + xi + ĥima
'a little' 'postpositive' 'small member' 'postpositive'
→ ptsotsotax x ĥima (→ ptsotsota:xĥima) 'a little bit'

cf. c. kawa + kaka + ka + na
'bathe' 'causative' 'passive' 'them'
→ kawkak kana (→ kawka:kana) 'bathe themselves'

Lin (1987) reformulates the syncope rule to be sensitive to syllabic configuration as in (10). The rule states that only the vowel of a simple CV syllable is subject to deletion. On the assumption that the first member of a fricative cluster cannot be syllabified due to language specific cooccurrence restriction as mentioned above, syncope applies in the case of (10a) because there is only one syllabified consonant and the structure description of the rule is met. What is crucial for this syncope rule to work is to syllabify all permissible clusters, including some geminates, as onset clusters (as in (10b)) so that the syncope rule is blocked.

(10) Syllable sensitive syncope:

```
                                   V → ø / X C __ + CV
                                              \/
                                              σ
a.     σ                                 σ
      /|                                /|
    CCV + CVCV       (9a)            CCV + CVCV   (9b)
    ||ǂ   ||||                       ||ǂ   ||||
    sxe   kaka                       xxi   hima

b.     σ                                σ
     //|                              //|
    CCV + CVCV       (8c)            CCV + CV      (9c)
    |||   ||||                       |||   ||
    kya   waka                       kka   na
```

Now that we have reviewed the major evidence for the no coda hypothesis for Piro syllable structure, we now turn to the CL data. Examples in (11) show how long segments are derived in Piro. In (11ab), degemination applies to stops, but in (11cde) word-initial sonorant geminates are not subject to degemination. Word-internal consonant deletion leads to CL of the preceding vowel: in (11fg) degemination applies, and in (11hij) deletion occurs when a non-permissible cluster is created. Examples without CL involve identical nasal clusters, as the examples in (11k) show. Examples in (11lm) are cases where these processes are optional. Identical obstruent clusters are subject to obligatory degemination; the first consonant of a non-permissible cluster is deleted. Degemination applies to glides optionally but never to identical nasal stop clusters. The generalizations are summarized in (12).

(11) Degemination/consonant deletion and CL

<u>Prefixation with/without Deletion</u>

a. p + pawata → pawata
'you' 'make a fire' 'you make a fire'

b. t + tšiyah̃ata → tšiyah̃ata
'she' 'to weep' 'she weeps'

c. n + nika → nnika
'I' 'eat' 'I eat'

d. w + wuh̃ene → wwuh̃ene
'our' 'child' 'our child'

e. m + mah̃ata + KA + ti → mmah̃atakati
'privative' 'lack' 'nominal' 'individual' 'lacking'

Suffixation, Syncope, Deletion, and CL

f. ø + nika + ka → ni**kk**a → **ni:ka**
'he' 'to eat' 'passive' 'he is eaten'

g. h̃ira + re + TA → h̃i**rr**eta → **h̃i:reta**
'drink' 'relational' 'theme closure' 'to drink'

h. h̃itsrukate + tši → h̃itsruka**ttš**i → **h̃itsruka:tši**
'...'s chief' 'absolute' 'chief'

i. kose + xe + TA → ko**sx**eta → **ko:xeta**
'to pull' 'always' 'to always pull'

j. xitxi + tši → xi**txtš**i → **xi:tši**
'...'s foot' 'absolute' 'foot'

Suffixation, Syncope, No CL or Optional CL

k. xema + maka → xe**mm**aka
'he hears' 'subjunctive' 'he would hear'
h̃ina + ne → h̃i**nn**e
'rain' 'genitive' 'rain'

l. ruhi...TA + h̃ima → ru**h̃h̃**imata → **ru:h̃imata** / **ruɣ̃h̃imata**
'he answers' 'it is said'

m. kih̃le + YA + yi → **kih̃leyyi** / **kih̃le:yi**
'good' 'for' 'you' 'good for you '
rawa + wu → **rawwu** / **ra:wu**
'he takes' 'us' 'he takes us'

(12) a. Obligatory degemination & deletion, (and obligatory CL word-medially): Geminate stops; non-permissible clusters
b. No degemination word-initially, optional degemination and CL word-medially: yy, ww, h̃h̃
c. No degemination nor CL both word initially and medially: mm, nn

It is important to note that Piro has no underlying length contrast: all surface geminate consonants are derived by morphological concatenation and/or syncope, and all surface long vowels occur as a result of consonant deletion and CL.

3. The Problems

If we accept the previous analyses of Piro phonology, the problems for Hayes' theory of CL become obvious. The first problem is that CL in Piro results from the loss of an onset segment because all syllables are considered open, and all word internal consonant clusters are treated as complex onsets. Given that Lin's (1987) analysis has an unusual treatment of word-medial geminates as being tautosyllabic, such as the [kk] cluster in (13b), one is tempted to solve the problem by allowing word-internal codas in Piro, i.e. allowing complex onsets only word-initially. As shown in (14), if we accept word-medial codas, then Piro has a typical CL process that results from the deletion of a coda segment (e.g. Steriade 1982, Wetzel and Engin 1985).

(13) a. kose + xe + TA → ko. sxeta → ko:xeta 'to pull'
b. ø + nika + ka → ni. kka → ni:ka 'he is eaten'
c. rawa + wu → ra.wwu / ra:wu 'he takes us'

(14) a. kose + xe + TA → kos.xeta → ko:xeta
b. ø + nika + ka → nik.ka → ni:ka

Without further stipulation, the coda hypothesis, however, does not really solve the problem. The crucial question to ask is: does Piro have the weight-by-position rule? That is, is there evidence for heavy CVC syllables in Piro? If not, then according to Hayes' moraic theory all CVC syllables in Piro should be considered light, and deletion of a coda segment would not lead to CL. Therefore, we need to investigate if there is independent evidence to posit a heavy/light syllable weight contrast in Piro. Recall that Piro does not have an underlying length contrast, so there is no syllable weight contrast based on underlying long/short distinctions. One important source of evidence for possible syllable weight contrast comes from the stress system. The Piro stress rules in (15) are postlexical and apply to phonological words. In (16), we can see that this is a syllabic trochaic system in which stress assignment is weight-insensitive. The derivation in (16c) illustrates stress assignment in relation to other phonological rules. Notice that in (16bc), both of the derived long vowels are also ignored by stress assignment. Since there is no evidence for a syllable weight contrast, there is no weight-by-position rule and the coda would not bear a mora. Our problem remains because deletion of a suggested coda consonant in theory would not trigger CL, unless one further stipulates that the coda in Piro is assigned a mora by default despite the lack of independent evidence.

(15) Piro Stress (Matteson 1965)
a Primary stress on the penultimate syllable
b. Secondary stress on the initial syllable
c. Tertiary stress on alternating syllables counting from the initial syllable.

(16) a. pè.tšitš.ih̃ì.mat.ló.na   'they say they stalk it'

b. rù.ta:.ká.na   'he arrived'

c. ruptxaka + kaka + lewa + TA + na
'they help' 'reciprocal' 'characteristic' 'theme closure' 'they'

Syncope → ruptxak_kak_lewat_na
Degemination/CL → ruptxa:kaklewatna
Stress → rùptxa:kàklewátna
'they characteristically help each other'

In sum, the problems posed by Piro for Hayes' theory are: first, CL in Piro results from the loss of an onset segment, and second, CL occurs in a language that has no underlying length contrast or preexisting syllable weight contrast.

4. The Proposal

I would like to propose an analysis, summarized in (17), that I consider better motivated than the coda hypothesis with default mora assignment. I suggest that the parsing template for syllabification is simply CV. All other consonants are moraic but unaffiliated to syllables, and CL results from deletion of such extrasyllabic consonants.

(17) a. Syllable template: CV

b. All other consonants are unsyllabified but licensed by moras.

c. Deletion of an extrasyllabic consonant leads to CL.

The motivation for the proposal lies in several phonological and phonetic facts which indicate that the consonants left out by normal CV syllabification are both extrasyllabic and moraic. First, as we have seen, in a sequence of C_1C_2V, C_1 can be the first half of a geminate, which occurs both word-medially and word-initially (cf. (11ck)). This, together with the fact that deletion of C_1 leads to CL, suggests that C_1 is moraic. Second, the general lack of sonority constraints on consonant clusters becomes a natural consequence if C_1 is considered extrasyllabic. Third, phonetically speaking, since phonetic closure of syllables is highly variable, as Matteson describes, one could assume that C_1 can be adjoined either to the preceding or following syllable by phonetic implementation. I have not, however, found any phonological evidence for postlexical adjunction, so C_1 may not belong to any syllable after all. Finally, at the phonetic level, there is evidence supporting C_1 as both extrasyllabic and moraic: in examples like /šwamkalo/ [š^{ə}wam̩kálo] 'spider', C_1 is either syllabic or followed by a transitional vowel.

Let me briefly comment on the phonetic syllabicity phenomena. Piro has an elaborate system of phonetic syllabicity alternations. Matteson states that the phonetic syllabic component serves to facilitate the transition from consonant to consonant in a cluster. Lin (1993) suggests that phonetic syllabicity involves coarticulation effects of the extrasyllabic consonant and the following onset consonant. Some more examples are given in (18). Note that the rules apply both word initially and word internally, suggesting that initial and internal clusters are treated as being the same. This is strictly a phonetic phenomenon and insensitive to any phonological rules. For example, (19) and (20) show that if the transitional vowel were considered a phonological syllabic nucleus, incorrect forms would be derived by syncope and stress assignment.

(18) Syllabic consonants and transitional vowels (for more examples see Lin (1993), Matteson and Pike (1958), Matteson (1965)).

a. Stop + Fricative / Fricative + Stop

k^{ə}su	'...'s house'	**s̩k**ota	'low abdomen'
ɦi**p^{ə}s**olu	'its size'	ɦi**s̩p**utaka	'cause to fall from an edge'

b. Fricative + Sonorant / Sonorant + Fricative

s^{ə}mota	'blunt point'	**m̩s**a	'empty corn cob'
ɦo**š^{ə}**i	'it's a forest'	ɦi**n̩š**i	'its tail'

c. Nasal + Sonorant / Sonorant + Nasal

m̩wenutu	'cheap'	**w̩m**aɦat^{i}ya	'we lack'
pi**m̩r**i	'another'	nu**r̩m**ak^{ə}lu	'I would drink it'

(19) a. nika + ya → ni**ky**a → niki**y**a + waka
→ niki**yw**aka + lu → nikiywa**kl**u
→ *nikiywa**kə**lu 'to eat it there'

b. yoɦima + xitxa → yoɦi**m̩x**itxa → yoɦi_xitxa + ka
→ yoɦixi**tx**ka → yoɦixi**tx**ə**k**a + na → yoɦixitxə**kn**a
→ *yoɦixitxə**kə**na 'they were commanded to hide'

(20) a. t^{ə}nìk^{ə}lokat^{ə}nák^{ə}lu 'she swallows him again'
rùp^{ə}xa:kàk^{ə}ewát^{ə}na 'they characteristically help each other'

b. * t**ə̀**nik**ə̀**lok**à**tənak**ə́**lu * r**ù**pətx**à**:kak**ə̀**lewat**ə́**na

I now present sample derivations in (21) to illustrate my proposal. Following Hyman (1985) and Bagemihl (1991), I assume that every segment starts with a mora underlyingly, and a consonant loses its mora when it is incorporated into onset position. In (21ab), after vowel deletion, Parasitic Delinking (Hayes 1989) removes the syllable node. The stray consonant retains the mora but stays unaffiliated to any syllable. Consonant delinking then leaves behind an empty mora and triggers CL. In a monomorphemic form as in (21c), stray consonants are unlinked to a syllable and phonetically interpreted as moraic. (21d) shows an example of word-initial geminates.

```
(21) a. UR              →    Syllabification, suffixation, syncope
                               σ    σ
                               |    |
        μ μ μ μ                μ    μ  +  μ μ
        | | | |               /|   /ǂ     | |
        n i k a               n i  k a    k a

   →  Syllabification   →    Cons delinking, CL, syllabification
        σ       σ              σ    σ
        |       |              |\   |
        μ   μ   μ              μ μ  μ
       / |  | / |             /|/ǂ/|
        n i  k  a              n i  k a         [ni:ka]

     b. UR              →    Syllabification, suffixation, syncope
                               σ    σ
                               |    |
        μ μ μ μ                μ    μ  +  μ μ
        | | | |               /|   /ǂ     | |
        k o s e               k o  s e    x e

   →  Syllabification   →    Cons delinking, CL, syllabification
        σ      σ               σ      σ
        |      |               |\     |
        μ  μ   μ               μ μ    μ
       / | |  /|              / |/ǂ  /|
        k o s  x e             k o s  x e       [ko:xe]

     c. UR              →    Syllabification
                                  σ      σ  σ
                                  |      |  |
        μ μ μ μ μ μ μ μ          μ  μ μ   μ  μ
        | | | | | | | |          | /| |  /| /|
        š w a m k a l o          š w a m k a l o    [šᵊwam̩kalo]

     d. UR              →    Syllabification
                                  σ  σ
                                  |  |
        μ   μ μ μ μ              μ  μ  μ
        |   | | | |              |/ |  /|
        n + n i k a              n  i k a        [nnika]
```

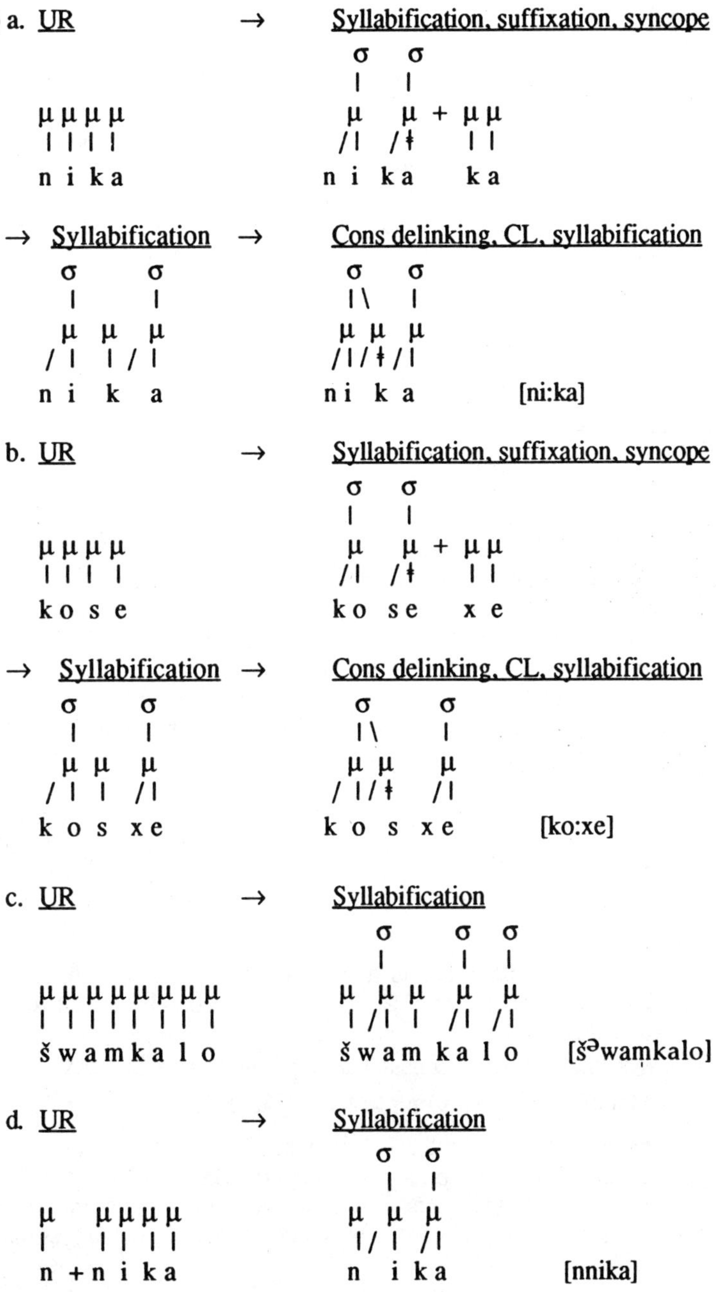

Consider now how this proposal may account for the exceptional cases of syncope in (9). Recall that non-permissible clusters and other permissible clusters behave differently with respect to syncope. Since this contrast has been considered an important piece of evidence for the existence of complex onsets, it is crucial to show that this set of data can be accounted for by the proposed analysis. The detailed arguments have been worked out in Lin (in prep). Here I briefly outline the new analysis of syncope. First, syncope is blocked if the application would result in more than one unaffiliated moraic consonant. Deletion of the first consonant of a non-permissible cluster is proposed to be a persistent rule (Myers 1991) that applies whenever the structure description of the rule is met. The deletion rule is immediately followed by CL to preserve the stranded mora. The relevant part of the derivation of (9a) is given in (22a), where we can see that by the time that syncope is to apply at the next cycle, we no longer have a condition that would block the syncope rule. In contrast, degemination of stops is proposed to be a postlexical rule. Since syncope is a lexical cyclic rule, stop geminates (which have to wait until the postlexical level to degeminate) would block vowel deletion at the lexical level, as shown in (22b).

(22) a. ...asa + xe → as_xe → a:xe → a:xe + kaka → a:x_kaka
b. ...kaka + ka → kak_ka + na → kakkana → ka:kana ((9c))

I have argued that by adopting simple CV syllable structure and Moraic Licensing, we are able to account for various phonetic and phonological facts in Piro without having to posit the problematic complex onset. The competing alternative, i.e. the moraic coda hypothesis, may work technically but suffers from several shortcomings. First, phonetic syllabicity for coarticulation effects and the general lack of complete closure of syllables appear to undermine the appeal of the coda hypothesis. Second, there is no independent phonological motivation for the existence of a heavy CVC syllable. The only motivation is to salvage the moraic account of CL. Third, we still have to posit extrasyllabic consonants in the language anyway because word-initial consonant clusters and word medial tri-consonantal clutters can not be exhaustively syllabified, as illustrated by the examples in (23ab).

(23) a. After CVC syllabification, additional word-initial consonants (including first halves of geminates) still need to be described as extrasyllabic: [n.ni.ka] 'I eat'; [š.wam.ka.lo] 'spider'
b. Word-medial tri-consonantal clusters cannot be exhaustively syllabified: ĥa.su.kam.t.ka.ka 'cause to run'

We have now reached the conclusion that the Simple Syllable Hypothesis together with Moraic Licensing provides the most satisfactory analysis. CL in Piro is still a process of Moraic Conservation but remains a counterexample to Hayes' prediction about the types of languages that may exhibit CL: Piro has no preexisting weight contrast but allows CL to occur. I would like to suggest some modification of the notion of preexisting weight distinctions. Hayes' prediction remains valid if we redefine the notion of weight distinctions to include both the bimoraic/monomoraic syllable ($\mu\mu$ vs. μ) contrast in the unmarked case and the moraic/moraless (μ vs. ø) contrast between the syllabified and the unsyllabified consonants in the marked case. If such redefinition is accepted, the prediction is that any language conditioned by Moraic Licensing potentially would exhibit the CL phenomenon.

5. Conclusion

In conclusion, I have dismissed a putative counterexample to Hayes' theory of CL and provided a new case of CL that is predicted to exist by Hayes' and Bagemihl's proposals. This analysis lends support to Bagemihl's proposal that extrasyllabic consonants not subject to stray erasure must be moraic. The suggestion that CL may occur in languages that have either a syllable weight contrast or a consonant weight contrast leads us to believe that it is the general weight contrast of a language, not just its syllable weight contrast, that determines whether CL may occur.

References

Bagemihl, Bruce. 1991. Syllable structure in Bella Coola. LI. 22.589-646.
Hayes, Bruce. 1989. Compensatory lengthening in moraic phonology. LI. 20.253-306.
Hyman, Larry. 1985. A theory of phonological weight. Dordrecht: Foris.
Itô, Junko. 1989. A prosodic theory of epenthesis. Natural Language and Linguistic Theory. 7.217-260.
Lin, Yen-Hwei. 1987. Theoretical implications of Piro syncope. NELS. 17.409-423.
Lin, Yen-Hwei. 1988. Compensatory lengthening in Piro. Paper presented at Annual Meeting of the Linguistic Society of America, New Orleans.
Lin, Yen-Hwei. 1993. Sonority and postlexical syllabicity in Piro. CLS. 28. 333-344.
Lin, Yen-Hwei. in preparation. Moraic structure in Piro. ms. Michigan State University.
Matteson, Esther and Kenneth L. Pike. 1958. Non-phonemic transition vocoid in Piro (Arawak). Miscellanea Phonetica. 3.22-30.
Matteson, Esther. 1965. The Piro (Arawakan) language. University Publications in Linguistics. 42. Berkeley: University of California Press.
Myers, Scott. 1991. Persistent rules. LI. 22.315-344.
Steriade, Donca. 1982. Greek prosodies and the nature of syllabification. Cambridge, Massachusetts: MIT Ph.D. dissertation.
Wetzels, Leo and Engin Sezer. (ed.) 1985. Studies in compensatory lengthening. Dordrecht: Foris.

Alignment with Place Nodes: An Analysis of Lexical Domain Distinctions in Japanese

HIROMU SAKAI
University of California, Irvine

0. Introduction

The goal of this paper is to provide an analysis of contrasting patterns of syllabification in the native and the non-native vocabularies of Japanese. We assume the framework of OPTIMALITY THEORY (Prince and Smolensky (1993), McCarthy (1993), McCarthy and Prince (1993a,b), Yip (1993a,b)). In particular, the theory of GENERALIZED ALIGNMENT proposed by McCarthy and Prince (1993b) plays a central role in our analysis. Generalized alignment is a set of constraints with a general format shown in (1).

(1) Generalized Alignment:
Align (Cat1, Edge1, Cat2, Edge2) = $_{def}$
$\forall$ Cat1 $\exists$ Cat2 such that Edge1 of Cat1 and Edge2 of Cat2 coincide, where Cat1, Cat2 $\in$ PCat $\cup$ GCat / Edge1, Edge2 $\in$ {Right, Left}

These constraints require all the relevant edges of category Cat1 to coincide with some edge of category Cat2, where Cat1 and Cat2 are restricted to either morphological or prosodic categories. In this paper, we argue that a principled analysis of lexical domain distinctions in Japanese can be provided if we include place nodes in the set of categories edge-aligned with morphological categories.

Once we include place nodes in the set of categories to be edge-aligned, a constraint (2) can be derived from the format (1), which we will call ALIGN-PLACE (ALIGN-P henceforth).

(2) ALIGN-P: Align (MCat, Edge1, Place, Edge2)

(2) requires the left or right edge of the category MCat to coincide with the left or right-most element instantiated by the place node. Consider the structures in (3).

(3) a.

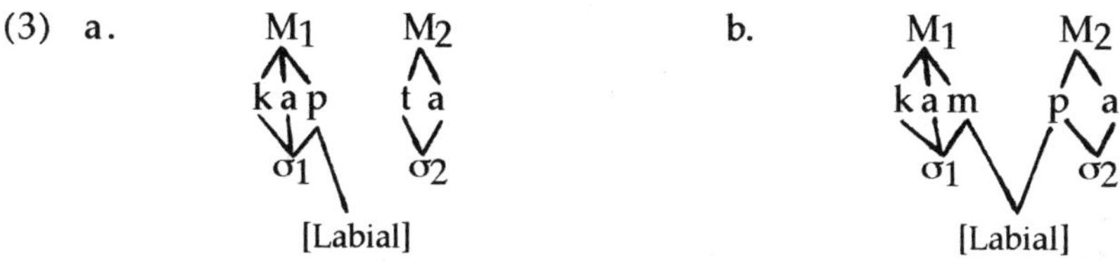

In the structure (3a), ALIGN-P is satisfied on the right edge of the morpheme M1, because the right edge of M1 coincides with the rightmost element instantiated by the place node [Labial]. In contrast, ALIGN-P is violated in the structure (3b), where the place node [Labial] is linked across the morpheme boundary, because the right edge of M1 is not the rightmost element instantiated by the place node [Labial]. Note also that another member of the set of alignment constraints, ALIGN-R, which requires coincidence of the right edge of M1 and the right edge of syllables , is satisfied in both of the structures.[1]

The relative ranking of ALIGN-P and ALIGN-R characterizes two different types of languages or vocabularies. If ALIGN-P is ranked above ALIGN-R in a language or vocabulary, structures like (3b) are less likely to be observed. Contrastingly, if ALIGN-R is ranked above ALIGN-P in another language or vocabulary, structures like (3b) are more likely to be observed. It is therefore possible that two languages or vocabularies are exactly like each other but contrast only in the ranking of these two constraints. We will argue that lexical domain distinctions in Japanese can best be characterized in this way.

---

1 A different view is proposed in McCarthy and Prince (1993a) . In their analysis of Axininca Campa, they attribute the ungrammaticality of (3b) type structures to a violation of ALIGN-R. This is not consistent with Prince and Smolensky (1993), who point out that (3b) type structures are grammatical in Lardil, and argue that ALIGN-R is satisfied in this type of structure. In our view, the contrast between Axininca Campa and Lardil can be attributed to the different rankings of ALIGN-R and ALIGN-P.

1. Theoretical Assumptions

Before going into a discussion of the Japanese data, we want to introduce a set of theoretical assumptions. We follow essentially the theory proposed in Prince and Smolensky (1993), and incorporate some of the proposals of McCarthy (1993).

In Optimality Theory, the role of grammar, which consists of a set of constraints ranked in a language-particular way, is to select an output among the candidates generated by the function GEN. GEN can in principle supply candidates with any structure, so long as it observes the principles called CONTAINMENT and CONSISTENCY OF EXPONENCE. We define these principles in (4).

(4) CONTAINMENT:
Lexical specifications of each morpheme must be fully instantiated.
CONSISTENCY OF EXPONENCE:
Lexical specifications of each morpheme cannot be altered.

To be more specific, CONTAINMENT requires that lexically specified elements cannot be literally removed from the representations. CONSISTENCY OF EXPONENCE requires that epenthetic elements can never be a part of morphemes. The term 'lexical specification of a morpheme M' (which is called 'underlying representation' in McCarthy (1993)) refers to a string of feature-bundles represented in the Lexicon. They are associated with a mora if necessary (in vowels or long consonants).

We also assume a set of basic constraints such as CODA, ONSET, PARSE, and FILL(M_{SEG} / M_{MORA}). They are defined in (5).

(5) CODA: A coda consonant must share place features.
ONSET: A syllable must have an onset.
PARSE: A node must be dominated by a mother node.
FILL(M_{SEG} / M_{MORA}): Representations must be minimal.

CODA requires that coda consonants must share place features with the following consonants. ONSET requires that syllables must have onsets, and PARSE requires that every element must be incorporated into a higher prosodic structure.

As for the constraint FILL, it is argued in Prince and Smolensky (1993) that epenthetic elements violate FILL because the contents of epenthetic elements are not fully-specified. McCarthy (1993), however, argues that GEN can fully specify the contents of epenthetic elements. As McCarthy points out, this makes it impossible to identify epenthetic elements by structural incompleteness. He therefore proposes the constraints M_{SEG} and M_{MORA}, which respectively require segments and morae to be parts of some morpheme. We further develop McCarthy's idea, and assume M_{SEG} and M_{MORA} to be restrictions on excessive elements in representations. In our interpretation, these constraints require representations to be minimal without violating CONTAINMENT or CONSISTENCY OF EXPONENCE. Epenthetic elements thus violate M_{SEG} or M_{MORA} because representations can satisfy these principles without having those elements. Since the term FILL is widely used in the literature, we continue using the term FILL unless it is necessary to distinguish M_{SEG} from M_{MORA}.

2. Ranking of Basic Constraints in Japanese

The lexicon of the Japanese language consists of several distinct lexical domains as discussed in McCawley (1968), Shibatani (1990), and Itô and Mester (1993). Among them are the native (or Yamato) vocabulary and the non-native vocabulary. The non-native vocabulary is further divided into the Sino-Japanese vocabulary and the Foreign vocabulary. In this section, we will set up the ranking of the basic constraints CODA, PARSE, ONSET, and FILL.

First of all, coda consonants are prohibited except as parts of geminates or homo-organic nasal+obstruent clusters. If unsyllabifiable clusters are created by morphological operations, they are resolved by vowel epenthesis. Examples are given in (6).[2]

(6) a. kak 'write' + tai 'DESIDERATIVE' ---> ka.k𝕀.tai. 'want to write'
kat 'win' + masu 'POLITE' ---> ka.ch𝕀.ma.su. 'win (polite)'
b. tet + dou ---> te.ts𝕌.dou. 'railway'
gak + sei ---> ga.k𝕌.sei. 'student'

In (6a), a consonant-final stem is concatenated with a consonant-initial suffix in the Yamato vocabulary.[3] (6b) is the case of compounding between a consonant-final stem and a consonant-initial stem in Sino-

---

2 We use outlined capitals for epenthesized elements. For instance, 𝕌 represents an epenthesized high back vowel and ℝ represents an epenthesized coronal liquid.

3 We assume the vowel 𝕀 in these examples to be epenthetic following the analysis of McCawley (1968). The vowel epenthesis further triggers palatalization of *t* in the second example.

It should also be noted that the past/perfective morpheme *-ta* behaves differently. It triggers gemination rather than epenthesis as shown in *kat + ta* ---> *katta*. This pattern, however, is widely assumed to be the result of historical change called 'on.bin' in traditional Japanese grammar (cf. Vance (1987), Shibatani (1990)). We therefore assume that the other auxiliaries show the unmarked pattern of suffixation.

Japanese.[4] In either case, unsyllabifiable consonants trigger vowel epenthesis. This is because violation of CODA or PARSE is more serious than a violation of FILL.[5]

Second, onsetless syllables are restricted in morpheme-internal positions.[6] If onsetless syllables are created in morpheme-internal positions as a result of suffixation, consonant epenthesis takes place to provide an onset. Examples are given in (7), where a vowel-final stem is combined with a vowel-initial suffix, and the epenthetic consonant ℝ is inserted as proposed by Itô and Mester (1989).

(7) mi 'see' + areru 'PASSIVE' ---> mi.ℝa.re.ru. 'be seen'
ki 'wear' + eba 'PROVISIONAL' ---> ki.ℝe.ba. '(if you) wear'

The consonant epenthesis pattern shows that FILL can be violated in order to avoid an ONSET violation. These patterns indicate that the ranking of the basic constraints must be CODA, PARSE, ONSET >> FILL.

3. Ranking of Alignment Constraints

Our next task is to incorporate alignment constraints into the ranking scheme. We start with the two alignment constraints proposed by McCarthy and Prince (1993b). They are defined in (8).

(8) ALIGN-L: Align (Stem, L, PrWd, L)
ALIGN-R: Align (Stem, R, σ, R)

ALIGN-L requires the left edges of all the stems to coincide with the left edges of some prosodic words, and ALIGN-R requires the right edges of all the stems to coincide with the right edges of some syllables. The effects of these constraints can be widely observed in Japanese. First,

---

4 We assume that these Sino-Japanese stems are underlyingly CVC, following the analysis of Itô (1986) and Tateishi (1986). In the first example, the underlying stop *t* is affricated as a result of an independent process.

5 The choice of epenthetic vowels varies among the vocabularies. In the native vocabulary, a high front vowel 𝕀 is selected. In Sino-Japanese, a high back vowel 𝕌 appears in most of the stems. However, 𝕀 is found with a limited number of stems as in *it* 'one' > *ich𝕀*, *nit* 'day' > *nich𝕀*. Although there is a tendency for harmony between the inserted vowel and the stem vowel, it is not decisive, as shown in *sit* 'quality' > *sit𝕌*, *hit* 'necessity' > *hit𝕌*. Itô (1986) suggests that the palatalization of stem final consonants is related to the choice of epenthetic vowels. We leave the topic open for future research.

6 Although onsetless syllables are strictly restricted to word-initial positions in Old Japanese, Modern Japanese allows a limited number of onsetless syllables in morpheme-internal positions. We do not have a principled account for the lack of consonant epenthesis in those cases.

onsetless syllables are not restricted in morpheme-initial position as shown in (9).

(9) Yamato: inu 'dog', erabu 'select', arau 'wash', uru 'sell', oru 'fold'
Sino-Japanese: i 'stomach', eN 'circle', ai 'love', uN 'fortune'

This indicates that ALIGN-L must be satisfied even if ONSET is violated. ALIGN-L is thus ranked above ONSET .

Second, if a vowel-final stem is concatenated with a vowel-initial suffix, hiatus is resolved by consonant epenthesis. This consonant epenthesis is obligatory even if the vowel sequence can form a single nucleus morpheme-internally. Consider the following examples.

(10) a. kie.ru. 'disappear', o.shie.ru. 'teach'
b. ki 'wear' + eru 'POTENTIAL (substandard)'
---> ki.ℝe.ru. *kie.ru. 'be able to wear'
mi 'see' + eba 'PROVISIONAL'
---> mi.ℝe.ba. *mie.ba. '(if you) see'

(10a) shows that the sequence *kie* is a possible syllable morpheme-internally. However, (10b) shows that the same sequence triggers consonant epenthesis if it is created by morpheme concatenation. This shows that ALIGN-R is ranked above FILL, because vowel coalescence would crucially violate ALIGN-R.

At the same time, ALIGN-R must be ranked below PARSE and CODA, because vowel epenthesis is obligatory even if it causes a violation of ALIGN-R in morpheme-final position as shown in (6).

Summarizing so far, we have established the constraint ranking shown in (11).

(11) CODA, PARSE >> FILL: Epenthesis rather than deletion
ONSET >> FILL: Consonant epenthesis for onsetless syllables
CODA, PARSE >> ALIGN-R: Vowel epenthesis is obligatory even in morpheme-final position
ALIGN-R >> FILL: Consonant epenthesis rather than vowel coalescence
ALIGN-L >> ONSET: Onsets are optional morpheme-initially

The overall ranking scheme is shown in (12).

(12) CODA, PARSE >> ALIGN-R >> FILL
ALIGN-L >> ONSET >> FILL

4. Contrast between Vocabularies

Up to this point, the native and the non-native vocabularies do not show any substantial difference. However, a clear contrast emerges if consonant clusters are created by morpheme concatenation.

Let us first look at the cases of Sino-Japanese vocabulary. In Sino-Japanese, stem-final consonants are restricted to either coronal or velar voiceless stops.[7] If unsyllabifiable clusters are created by morphological operations, different options are chosen according to the kind of consonants involved in the clusters. With coronal-final stems, consonant clusters are changed into geminates.[8] Examples are shown in (13).

(13) net + tou ---> net.tou. 'hot water'
net + ki ---> nek.ki. 'enthusiasm'
net + fuu ---> nep.puu. 'hot wind'

In contrast, velar-final stems are geminated only if they are followed by velar-initial stems as in (14a). Otherwise, clusters are resolved by vowel epenthesis as in (14b).

(14) a. gak + ki ---> gak.ki. 'musical instrument'
b. gak + tai ---> ga.kU.tai. *gak.kai. * gat.tai. 'musical band'
gak + fu ---> ga.kU.fu. *gak.ku. *gap.pu. 'musical score'

We argue that the ranking in (12) can explain these patterns along the line of analysis proposed by Itô (1986), if we accept the following two assumptions.

(15) Assumption 1: Features or segments can simultaneously belong to more than one morpheme.
Assumption 2: Final consonants do not have place features in so-called 'coronal-final' stems.

Assumption 1 means that features or segments can be ambiguous with respect to their morphological affiliations. As a consequence of this assumption, the function GEN can directly create an output such as

---

7 Except for nasals, which are often assumed to be vocalic in moraic positions.

8 It should be noted that clusters are never changed into geminates if the second member of the cluster is [+voice]. An independent restriction on geminate consonants is responsible for this pattern. That is, voiced geminates (except nasals) are strictly prohibited in the non-foreign vocabulary of Japanese .

gak.kai.in (16) without violating CONTAINMENT or CONSISTENCY OF EXPONENCE.[9]

(16)

$\sigma 1$ $\sigma 2$

g a k + k a i ---> g a k a i

M_1 M_2

Since geminate consonants can ambiguously belong to both of the morphemes M_1 and M_2, the lexical specification of each morpheme is fully realized in this output.[10]

Contrastingly, GEN cannot create an output with a geminate from an input with two distinct consonants, because it would violate either CONTAINMENT or CONSISTENCY OF EXPONENCE. For example, the lexical specification of the second stem 'tai' is not fully realized in (17a).

(17) a.

$\sigma 1$ $\sigma 2$

g a k + t a i ---> g a k a i

M_1 M_2

b.

$\sigma 1$ $\sigma 2$

g a k + t a i ---> g a k <t> a i

M_1 M_2

Consequently, given an input with a cluster of two distinct consonants, the only way to obtain a geminate output is to underparse one of the consonants as in (17b).

Assumption 2 is essentially the proposal of Itô (1986).[11] Since there is no lexical specification for the stem-final consonant, GEN can provide an output structure something like (18).

---

9 In other words, GEN provides the structure of 'fusion' discussed in McCarthy (1986), Itô (1986).

10 Assumption 1 has a close connection to a theoretical issue concerning the OCP (McCarthy (1986)). Since GEN is allowed to create doubly-linked structures across-morpheme boundaries, it might be argued that a necessary distinction between morpheme-internal geminates and a sequence of identical segments across morpheme boundaries would be obscured. This is not the case, however. ALIGN-P always requires non doubly-linked structures across morpheme-boundaries, although the strength of requirement varies across languages depending on the relative ranking of ALIGN-P.

11 It is likely that coronal underspecification is restricted to stem-final position in Sino-Japanese, because the place contrast is degenerate only at this position. See Itô and Mester (1989) for arguments that coronal underspecification is limited to liquids in the Yamato vocabulary.

(18)

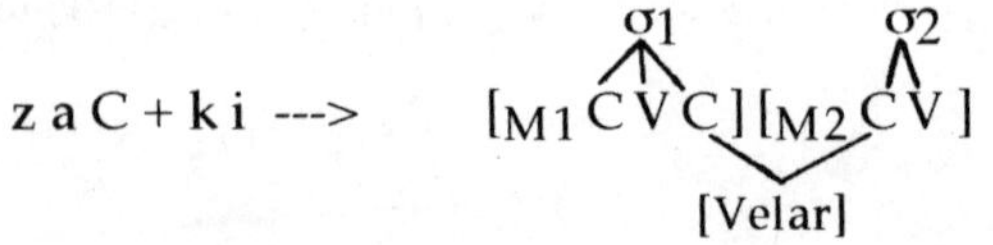

$\sigma 1$ $\sigma 2$

z a C + k i ---> [M1 C V C] [M2 C V]

[Velar]

In (18), the place node of the following consonant is linked to the stem-final consonant. Since the place feature [velar] can still be a part of M2 by Assumption 1, this structure satisfies CONTAINMENT and CONSISTENCY OF EXPONENCE.[12]

Bearing these assumptions in mind, let us examine the relevant cases one by one using constraint tableaux. Tableau (19) represents the combination of a velar-final stem 'gak' with a coronal-initial stem 'tai'. [13]

(19) gak + tai ---> ga.k𝕌.tai. *gak.kai.

	CODA	PARSE	ALIGN-L/R	FILL
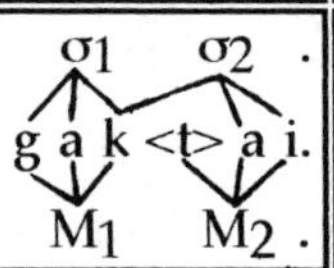 $\sigma 1$ $\sigma 2$. g a k <t> a i. M_1 M_2 .		* !	* ALIGN-L	
» ga.k]𝕌.[tai			* ALIGN-R	*
gak.][tai.	* !			
ga<k>.][tai.		* !		

Since the candidate with the geminate necessarily involves underparsing, it is ruled out as a PARSE violation. Since the other candidates violate highly ranked constraints such as PARSE or CODA, the one with vowel epenthesis must be selected.

If a velar-final stem is concatenated with a velar-initial stem, the candidate with the geminate consonant can be provided by GEN without involving underparsing. As shown in tableau (20), the candidate with geminate consonants satisfies all the relevant constraints in this case.

---

12 Note that doubly-linked features are not required to belong to both of the morphemes by Assumption 1. Consequently, M1 does not violate CONSISTENCY OF EXPONENCE in (18).

13 The symbol '»' in tableaux indicates the optimal candidate.

(20) gak + kai ---> gak.kai. *ga.kU.kai

	CODA	PARSE	ALIGN-L/R	FILL
σ1 σ2 . » g a k a i . M1 M2 .				
ga.k]U.[kai.			* !ALIGN-R	*

The output with the geminate must therefore be selected.

Finally, if the so-called 'coronal-final stems' are combined with consonant-initial stems, the candidate with geminate consonants should be selected based on the same considerations. Summarizing , the cases involving consonant clusters are fully explained by the constraint ranking we have established.

Let us turn to the Yamato vocabulary. Unfortunately, the ranking in (12) cannot explain the paradigm of compounding in the Yamato vocabulary. In the native vocabulary, consonant clusters are always resolved by epenthesis no matter what kinds of consonants are combined.

(21) a. kat + toru ---> ka.ch I.to.ru. 'note'
kat + kakeru ---> ka.chI.ka.ke.ru. 'about to win'
b. kak + tomeru ---> ka.kI.to.me.ru. 'write down'
kak + kaeru ---> ka.kI.kae.ru. 're-write'

(21a) shows the pattern with coronal-final stems, and (21b) shows the pattern with velar-final stems. Clusters trigger vowel epenthesis in all of the examples in (21).

The clearest contrast can be observed in the paradigm of velar-final stems as shown in (22).

(22) Yamato: kak + kakeru ---> ka.kI.kae.ru. * kak.kae.ru.
Sino-Japanese: gak + kai ---> * ga.kU.kai. gak.kai.

The two lexical domains thus sharply contrast with each other.

5. Deriving Lexical Domain Distinctions

We argue that the contrast observed in (22) can be properly characterized by ALIGN-P , which we now define as (23).

(23) ALIGN-P (Stem, R, Place, R)

(23) requires the right edge of every stem to coincide with the rightmost element instantiated by some place node.

In the Sino-Japanese vocabulary, we assume that ALIGN-P is ranked below other alignment constraints. This ranking makes the effect of ALIGN-P virtually invisible in Sino-Japanese. Our explanation for the Sino-Japanese vocabulary can thus be maintained without any modification. For example, in the case of concatenation of two identical consonants, the candidate with the geminate violates ALIGN-P, but the candidate with epenthesis violates ALIGN-R. Since the ranking is ALIGN-R >> ALIGN-P, the candidate with the geminate must be selected as in (24).

(24) Sino-Japanese (N+N compounding): gak + kai ---> gak.kai.

	ALIGN-L	ALIGN-R	ALIGN-P	FILL
» gak.][kai. [Velar] .			*	
ga.k]𝕌.[kai.		*!		*

Let us turn to the Yamato vocabulary. We crucially assume that ALIGN-P is ranked above ALIGN-R in the Yamato vocabulary. Since the candidates with hetero-morphemic geminates always violate ALIGN-P, this ranking excludes the possibility of gemination resulting from morpheme concatenation. Tableau (25) illustrates this point.

(25) Yamato (V+V compound): kak +kae(ru) ---> ka.k𝕀.kae.(ru.)

	ALIGN-L	ALIGN-P	ALIGN-R	FILL
»ka.k]𝕀.[kae			*	*
kak.][kae. [Velar] .		*!		

(26) represents the case of a consonant cluster created by suffixation. Even if the consonants have the same place feature, they cannot be geminated because they would violate ALIGN-P.

(26) Yamato (Suffixation): kat + tai ---> ka.chI.tai.

	ALIGN-L	ALIGN-P	ALIGN-R	FILL
» ka.ch]I.tai			*	*
kat.]tai. [Coronal].		*!		

We are thus given two sets of constraint rankings as shown in (27).

(27) Yamato:
CODA, PARSE, ALIGN-L, ALIGN-P >> ALIGN-R >> ONSET >> FILL
Sino-Japanese:
CODA, PARSE, ALIGN-L, ALIGN-R >> ALIGN-P >> ONSET >> FILL

Notice that the constraint rankings for these two vocabularies are exactly alike, except for the relative ranking of ALIGN-P and ALIGN-R. The similarity and contrast between the two vocabularies are thus clearly characterized in our account.

6. Double Epenthesis in Loanwords

Our analysis can be further supported by the pattern of double-epenthesis in loanword phonology, which we assume to be a part of the non-native vocabulary of Japanese. In loanword phonology, unsyllabifiable sequences of sounds are modified into syllabifiable ones by vowel epenthesis as shown in (28).[14]

(28) 'class' ---> kU.ra.sU.
'strike' ---> sU.tO.rai.kU.

In word-final position, another pattern is observed. Word-final consonants trigger not only vowel epenthesis but also gemination as shown in (29).[15]

---

14 The quality of epenthesized vowels is predictable from the quality of the preceding consonants as pointed out by Lovins (1973); Mid front O follows alveolars, high front I follows palatals, and high back U appears elsewhere.

15 There are some restrictions on this pattern. First, voiced stops are sometimes not geminated as in (1).

(1) 'pub' ---> pabu
'log' ---> rogu

In addition, liquids are never geminated as shown in (2). These patterns are related to the restrictions on voiced geminates in Japanese.

(2) 'pill' ---> piru
'hill' ---> hiru

(29) mat ---> mat.TO.
cup ---> kap.PU.
kick ---> kik.KU.

Although geminate consonants are also found in word-internal positions, their characteristics are quite different. The paradigm in (30) clearly shows that the distribution of word-internal geminates is closely related to the stress pattern of the original words. That is, geminates are observed only after stressed syllables.

(30) a. 'cótton' ---> kot.toN.
'pépper' ---> pep.paa.
'lúcky' ---> rak.kii.
'éssay' ---> es.sei.
b. 'éditor' ---> e.di.taa.
'guitár' ---> gi.taa.

This shows that what appears to be geminated are the ambisyllabic consonants of Kahn (1976). We therefore assume that these consonants are doubly-linked in the source language, and the doubly-linked structure is directly brought into Japanese.

Word-final gemination has totally different properties; it is not sensitive to the stress pattern as shown in (31a). More interestingly, as shown in (31b), coda consonants in closed syllables are never geminated word-internally.

(31) a. 'básket' ---> ba.su.ket.TO.
'góssip' ---> go.ship.PU.
'pícnic' ---> pi.ku.nik.KU.
b. 'nápkin' ---> nap.U.kiN.
'chápter' ---> cha.PU.taa.
'dóctor' ---> do.kU.taa.
'pícture' ---> pi.kU.chaa.

Second, nasals or fricatives are not geminated in word-final position as shown in (3), even though these consonants allow gemination word-internally (eg. *'hammer' > hammaa, 'essay' > essei*).
(3) 'ham' ---> hamu
'bus' ---> basu

Finally, consonants after long vowels or diphthongs are never geminated.
(4) 'meat' ---> mii.to.
'tape' ---> tee.pu.

This can be attributed to the restriction on super-heavy syllables in Japanese. In this paper, we abstract away from these properties, and concentrate on the final/non-final contrast.

These facts clearly indicate that 'word-finality' plays a central role in double-epenthesis, i.e. double-epenthesis is 'edge-oriented'. This suggests that alignment constraints are responsible for this phenomenon.

In fact, the pattern of double-epenthesis is expected in our analysis, because only the candidates with double epenthesis satisfy ALIGN-R as shown in (32).

(32) 'kick' ---> kik.𝕂𝕌.

	ALIGN-R	ALIGN-P	FILL
ki. k] 𝕌.	* !		*
» kik.] 𝕂𝕌.		*	* *

Rather, what is unexpected is the lack of double-epenthesis in Sino-Japanese. For example, the citation form of a consonant final stem 'gak' is not *gak.𝕂𝕌.* but *ga.k𝕌.*, even though the latter violates ALIGN-R.

The candidates with double-epenthesis clearly involve insertion of more elements than the candidates with simple-epenthesis. This suggests that the constraint FILL, i.e. M_{SEG} or M_{MORA}, might be responsible for the contrast. However, M_{SEG} cannot determine the output, because M_{SEG} must be ranked lower than ALIGN-R as we have discussed in section 4. The crucial example is shown in (33), which involves consonant epenthesis between a hetero-morphemic vowel sequence.

(33) ki + eba ---> ki.ℝe.ba.

	ALIGN-R	M_{SEG}
» ki.]ℝe.ba.		*
ki]e.ba.	* !	

Consider now the prosodic nature of double-epenthesis. It is clear that double-epenthesis involves more insertion of morae than simple-epenthesis. The impossibility of double-epenthesis can be attributed to M_{MORA}, because double-epenthesis violates M_{MORA} more seriously than simple-epenthesis. If M_{MORA} is ranked above ALIGN-R, the lack of double-epenthesis in Sino-Japanese is expected. This is shown in (34).

(34) Sino-Japanese: gak ---> ga.kU.

	M_{MORA}	ALIGN-R	ALIGN-P	M_{SEG}
μ μ. » g a. k] U.	*	*		*
μ μ μ. g a k.] KU.	**!		*	**

Contrastingly, if M_{MORA} is ranked below ALIGN-R in the Foreign vocabulary, the double-epenthesis pattern must be preferred. Notice that the ranking M_{MORA} >> ALIGN-R does not affect our analysis of consonant epenthesis, because what is inserted is not a mora but a segment in this case.

7. Summary

Summarizing, the analysis of syllabification patterns leads us to the following structure of Lexicon of the Japanese, where different lexical domains are characterized by the different ranking of constraints.

(35) Structure of the Lexicon of Japanese:

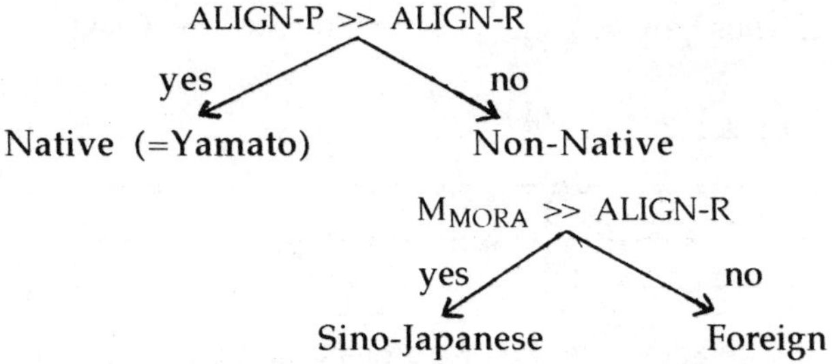

In (35), the native/non-native distinction is characterized by the ranking difference between ALIGN-R and ALIGN-P. Within the non-native vocabulary, the ranking difference between M_{MORA} and ALIGN-R characterizes the distinction between the Sino-Japanese vocabulary and the Foreign vocabulary. The lexical domain distinctions are thus clearly characterized by constraint ranking in Japanese.

Acknowledgement

I am grateful to Moira Yip and Bernard Tranel for helpful comments and suggestions. I also benefitted from discussions with my colleagues in the Linguistics Department at UC Irvine. Thanks to Yoko Sakai for drawing my attention to loanwords. Needless to say, all shortcomings are mine.

References

Itô, Junko. 1986. *Syllable Theory in Prosodic Phonology.* Doctoral Dissertation, University of Massachusetts. (Published by Garland Press, New York.)

____ 1989. A Prosodic Theory of Epenthesis. *Natural Language and Linguistic Theory* 7, pp. 217-259.

Itô, Junko and Ralf-Armin Mester. 1989. Feature Predictability and Underspecification: Palatal Prosody in Japanese Mimetics. *Language* 65, pp. 258-293.

____ 1993. *Japanese Phonology: Constraint Domains and Structure Preservation.* ms., University of California, Santa Cruz.

Kahn, Dan 1976. *Syllable-based Generalizations in English Phonology.* Doctoral Dissertation, MIT.

Kuroda, Shige-Yuki 1965. *Generative Grammatical Studies in the Japanese Language.* Doctoral Dissertation, MIT. (Published by Garland Press, New York.)

Lovins, Julie. B. 1973. *Loanwords and the Phonological Structure of Japanese.* Doctoral Dissertation, University of Chicago.

McCarthy, John J. 1986. OCP Effects: Gemination and Antigemination. *Linguistic Inquiry* 17, pp. 207-63..

____ 1993. *The Parallel Advantage: Containment, Consistency, and Alignment.* Rutgers Optimality Workshop.

McCarthy, John J. and Alan S. Prince. 1993a. *Prosodic Morphology.* ms., University of Massachusetts and Rutgers University.

____ 1993b. *Generalized Alignment.* ms., University of Massachusetts and Rutgers University.

McCawley, James. D. 1968. *The Phonological Component of a Grammar of Japanese.* The Hague: Mouton.

Prince, Alan S. and Paul Smolensky 1993. *Optimality Theory: Constraints Interaction in Generative Grammar.* ms., Rutgers University and University of Colorado.

Shibatani, Masayoshi 1990. *The Languages of Japan.* Cambridge University Press.

Tateishi, Koichi 1986. *What is syllabification in Sino Japanese Morphemes ?* ms,. University of Massachusetts.

Vance, Timothy J. 1987. *An Introduction to Japanese Phonology.* State University of New York Press, Albany.

Yip, Moira 1993a. Cantonese Loanword Phonology and Optimality Theory. *Journal of East Asian Linguistics* 2, pp. 261-291.

_____ 1993b. *The Interaction of ALIGN, PARSE-Place and ECHO in Reduplication.* Rutgers Optimality Workshop.

The Learnability of Optimality Theory

BRUCE TESAR & PAUL SMOLENSKY
University of Colorado at Boulder

In Optimality Theory (Prince & Smolensky 1993), Universal Grammar provides a set of highly general universal constraints which apply in parallel to assess the well-formedness of possible structural descriptions of linguistic inputs. Grammar is characterized through optimization: the possible structural description of an input that optimally satisfies the constraints is the grammatical one.

Evidence for this Optimality-Theoretic characterization of Universal Grammar is provided elsewhere; most work to date addresses phonology: see Prince & Smolensky 1993 (henceforth, 'P&S') and the several dozen works cited therein, notably McCarthy & Prince 1993; initial work addressing syntax includes Grimshaw 1993 and Legendre, Raymond & Smolensky 1993. For computational results concerning parsing in Optimality Theory, see Tesar 1994. Here, we address learnability.

As the number of constraints hypothesized for Universal Grammar grows, the number of possible grammars grows extremely quickly: faster than exponentially. Does there exist a learning procedure which is efficient, in the sense that the number of informative pieces of data required to determine the target language grows much slower than exponentially? If not, the kind of UG provided by Optimality Theory is very unlikely to render language acquisition feasible given a realistic number of constraints. In this paper we present a simple, provably correct learning procedure which efficiently converges from an initial state to any target language.

*Computer Science Department, Boulder CO 80309-0430; {tesar,smolensky}@cs.colorado.edu

0. Optimality Theory

The novel features of the learnability problem, and the character of the learning algorithm, depend on a number of the detailed properties of Optimality Theory. We begin with a self-contained presentation of the relevant principles of the theory, to the level of detail required for presentation of the learning algorithm. We consistently exemplify the principles, and in §2, the learning algorithm, using the Basic CV Syllable Structure Theory of P&S (§6), which we develop concurrently.

0.1 Constraints and Their Violation

(1) **Grammars are functions.**
A grammar is a specification of a function which assigns to each input a unique structural description or OUTPUT. (A grammar does not provide an algorithm for computing this function, e.g., by sequential derivation.)

In CV theory, an input is a string of Cs and Vs, e.g., /VCVC/. An output is a parse of the string into syllables, which we notate as follows:

(1′)	a.	.V.CVC.	= $[_\sigma$ V] $[_\sigma$ CVC]
	b.	⟨V⟩.CV.⟨C⟩	= V $[_\sigma$ CV] C
	c.	⟨V⟩.CV.C□́.	= V $[_\sigma$ CV] $[_\sigma$ C□́]
	d.	.□V.CV.⟨C⟩	= $[_\sigma$ □V] $[_\sigma$ CV] C

[A □ or □́ denotes a syllable position which is empty: not filled by an input segment. It is phonetically realized by some epenthetic consonant (□) or vowel (□́). Unparsed segments ⟨X⟩ are not phonetically realized.] What (1) asserts is that the grammar assigns to the input /VCVC/ one structural description, e.g., one of the possibilities listed under (1′.a–d). Which one gets assigned is determined by subsequent principles.

(2) GEN.
Universal Grammar provides the set of possible inputs, the set of possible outputs, and a function GEN which, given any input *i*, generates the set of candidate outputs GEN(*i*), for *i*. The input *i* is a substructure contained within each of its candidate outputs in GEN(*i*).

In the CV case, for any input *i*, the candidate outputs in GEN(*i*) consist in all possible parsings of the string into syllables, including the possible over-

and underparsing structures exemplified above in (1′.b-d). All syllables are assumed to contain a Nucleus position, with optional preceding Onset and following Coda positions. Here we adopt what P&S (§6) dub the Basic CV Syllable Structure Theory, in which the simplifying assumption is made that the syllable positions Onset and Coda may each contain at most one C, and the position Nucleus may contain at most one V.

(3) **Universal constraints.**
Universal Grammar provides a set of universal constraints which assess the well-formedness of candidate outputs for a given input in parallel (i.e., simultaneously). Given a candidate output, each constraint assesses a set of MARKS each of which corresponds to one violation of the constraint; the collection of all marks assessed a candidate c is denoted MARKS(c).

The CV constraints we will deal with here are as follows:

(3′) **Universal CV Syllable Structure Constraints.**

ONS	Syllables have onsets.
−COD	Syllables do not have codas.
PARSE	Underlying material is parsed into syllable structure.
FILL^{Nuc}	Nucleus positions are filled with underlying material.
FILL^{Ons}	Onset positions (when present) are filled with underlying material.

0.2 Optimality and Harmonic Ordering

The central notion of optimality now makes its appearance. The idea is that by examining the marks assigned by the universal constraints to all the candidate outputs for a given input, we can find the least marked, or optimal, one: this is the one and only well-formed parse that may be assigned to the input. The relevant notion of 'least marked' is not the simplistic one of just counting numbers of violations. Rather, in a given language, different constraints have different strengths or priorities: they are not all equal in force. When a choice must be made between satisfying one constraint or another, the stronger must take priority. The result is that the weaker will be violated in a well-formed surface structure.

(4) **Constraint Ranking, Harmonic Ordering, and Optimality.**
The grammar of each language RANKS the universal constraints in a DOMINANCE HIERARCHY; when constraint $\mathbf{C}_1$ dominates another $\mathbf{C}_2$ in the hierarchy, we write $\mathbf{C}_1 \gg \mathbf{C}_2$. The ranking is total: the

hierarchy determines the relative dominance of every pair of constraints:

$$C_1 \gg C_2 \gg \cdots \gg C_n$$

A grammar's constraint hierarchy induces on all the candidate outputs a HARMONIC ORDERING as follows. Let *a* and *b* be two candidate parses with sets of marks MARKS(*a*) and MARKS(*b*). To compare *a* and *b*, first cancel all the marks they have in common, getting lists of 'uncancelled' marks: MARKS′(*a*) and MARKS′(*b*); now, no mark occuring in one list occurs in the other. Then determine which list of uncancelled marks contains the worst mark: a mark assessed by the highest-ranking constraint violated in the two lists. This candidate is LESS HARMONIC or HAS LOWER HARMONY than the other; if it is *a*, then we write: $a \prec b$. (We also sometimes write MARKS(*a*) ≺ MARKS(*b*).) For a given input, the most harmonic of the candidate outputs provided by GEN is the OPTIMAL candidate: it is the one assigned to the input by the grammar. Only this optimal candidate is well-formed; all less harmonic candidates are ill-formed.

We can illustrate harmonic ordering in the CV case by examining a table of marks under the assumption that the universal constraints have been ranked by a particular grammar as follows:

(4′.a) **Constraint Hierachy for L_1:**

ONS ≫ −COD ≫ FILL^{Nuc} ≫ PARSE ≫ FILL^{Ons}

In the following CONSTRAINT TABLEAU, the most dominant constraints in L_1 appear to the left:

(4′.b) **Constraint Tableau for L_1**

Candidates	ONS	−COD	FILL^{Nuc}	PARSE	FILL^{Ons}
/VCVC/ →					
☞ *d.* .□V.CV.⟨C⟩				*	*
b. ⟨V⟩.CV.⟨C⟩				* *	
c. ⟨V⟩.CV.C□́.			*	*	
a. .V.CVC.	*	*			

The candidates in this tableau have been listed in harmonic order, from highest to lowest Harmony; the optimal candidate is marked manually (determining that this candidate is optimal requires demonstrating that it is more harmonic than any of the infinitely many competing candidates). Starting at the bottom of the tableau, let us verify that $a \prec c$. The first step is to cancel common marks: here, there are none. The next step is to determine which candidate has the worst mark, i.e., violates the most highly ranked constraint: it is *a*, which violates ONS. Therefore *a* is the less harmonic. In determining that $c \prec b$, we first cancel the common mark *PARSE; *c* then earns the worst mark of the two, *FILL^{Nuc}. We see the importance of retaining multiple marks in the comparison of *b* to *d*: one *PARSE mark cancels, leaving MARKS′(*b*) = {*PARSE} and MARKS′(*d*) = {*FILL^{Ons}}. The worst mark is the uncancelled *PARSE incurred by *b*: so $b \prec d$.

The final central principle of Optimality Theory is:

(5) **Typology by Re-Ranking.**
Cross-linguistic variation is principally due to variation in language-specific rankings of the universal constraints. Analysis of the optimal forms arising from all possible rankings of the constraints provided by Universal Grammar gives the typology of possible human languages. Universal Grammar may impose restrictions on the possible rankings of its constraints.

In the CV theory, Universal Grammar imposes no restrictions on the ranking of the constraints we have discussed here (3′). Analysis of all possible rankings of these constraints reveals that the resulting typology of basic CV syllable structures is an instantiation of Jakobson's typological generalizations (Jakobson 1962, Clements & Keyser 1983): see P&S:§6. In this typology, syllable structures may have required or optional onsets, and, independently, forbidden or optional codas.

1. The Learning Problem in Optimality Theory

Substantive knowledge of language in Optimality Theory thus consists in knowledge of the universal set of possible inputs, outputs and GEN (2); of the universal constraints (3); of the ranking of those constraints particular to the language (4); and of the lexicon providing the particular underlying forms in the language-particular inputs. Under the assumption that what is universal in this knowledge is not learned but innate, what remains then to be learned is the lexicon and the constraint ranking. Concerning acquisition of the lexicon, the reader is referred to discussion in P&S: §9. Here we assume that the learner has a hypothesized lexicon in hand, and faces the problem of learning the ranking of known (or, for that matter, merely hypothesized) constraints.

The initial data for the learning problem are pairs consisting of an input and its well-formed (optimal) parse. For example, the learner of the CV language L_1 might have as an initial datum the input /VCVC/ together with its well-formed parse .□V.CV.⟨C⟩ (4′.b). Together with this single piece of explicit positive evidence comes a large mass of implicit negative evidence. Every alternative parse of this input is known to be ill-formed; for example, the faithful parse *.V.CVC. is ill-formed. Thus the learner knows that, with respect to the unknown constraint hierarchy,

.V.CVC. ≺ .□V.CV.⟨C⟩

Furthermore, corresponding harmonic comparisons must hold for every sub-optimal parse.

Thus each single piece of positive initial data conveys a large amount of inferred comparative data of the form:

[sub-optimal parse *sub-opt* of input *i*] ≺ [optimal parse *opt* of input *i*]

Such pairs are what feed our learning algorithm. Each pair carries the information that the constraints violated by the sub-optimal parse *sub-opt* must out-rank those violated by the optimal parse *opt*, that, in some sense, we must have MARKS(*sub-opt*) ≫ MARKS(*opt*), or more informally, LOSER-MARKS ≫ WINNER-MARKS. The algorithm we now present is nothing but a means of making this observation precise, and deducing its consequences.

2. The Recursive Constraint Demotion (RCD) Algorithm

Before giving a general description of the algorithm, we first illustrate its use. In §2.1 we show how the algorithm learns the language L_1 from the single positive example which we have discussed, /VCVC/ → .□V.CV.⟨C⟩; we then show how the algorithm learns a different language L_2 from its (different) parse of the same input. Then in §2.2 we give a general but somewhat informal statement of the algorithm.

2.1 An Example: Learning CV Syllable Structure

In L_1, the correct parse of /VCVC/ is .□V.CV.⟨C⟩. This fact forms our starting point, one initial datum. Table (4′.b) gives the marks incurred by the well-formed parse (labelled *d*) and by three ill-formed parses. From this table we form the following table of MARK-DATA PAIRS:

(6) **Mark-data Pairs (L_1)**

sub-opt $\prec$ *opt*	LOSER-MARKS = MARKS(*sub-opt*)	WINNER-MARKS = MARKS(*opt*)
$a \prec d$	{*ONS, *−COD}	{*PARSE, *FILL^{Ons}}
$b \prec d$	{*PARSE, *PARSE}	{*PARSE, *FILL^{Ons}}
$c \prec d$	{*PARSE, *FILL^{Nuc}}	{*PARSE, *FILL^{Ons}}

In order that each sub-optimal output *sub-opt* be less harmonic than the optimal output *opt*, the marks incurred by the former, MARKS(*sub-opt*) must collectively be worse than MARKS(*opt*). According to (4), what this means more precisely is that *sub-opt* must incur the worst uncancelled mark, compared to *opt*. So the first step in the learning algorithm is to cancel the common marks in (6):

(7) **Mark-data Pairs after Cancellation (L_1)**

sub-opt $\prec$ *opt*	LOSER-MARKS = MARKS′(*sub-opt*)	WINNER-MARKS = MARKS′(*opt*)
$a \prec d$	{*ONS, *−COD}	{*PARSE, *FILL^{Ons}}
$b \prec d$	{~~*PARSE~~ *PARSE}	{~~*PARSE~~ *FILL^{Ons}}
$c \prec d$	{~~*PARSE~~ *FILL^{Nuc}}	{~~*PARSE~~ *FILL^{Ons}}

The cancelled marks have been struck out. Note that the cancellation operation which transforms MARKS to MARKS′ is only well-defined on PAIRS of sets of marks; e.g., *PARSE is cancelled in the pairs $b \prec d$ and $c \prec d$, but not in the pair $a \prec d$. Note also that cancellation of marks is done token-by-token: in the row $b \prec d$, one but not the other mark *PARSE in MARKS(b) is cancelled. As we will see, the algorithm is sensitive not to absolute numbers of marks, but only to whether *sub-opt* or *opt* incurs more marks of a given type. (Optimality Theory recognizes a relative distinction between greater- or fewer-violations of a constraint, but not an absolute quantitative measure of degree of constraint violation.)

The table (7) of mark-data after cancellation is the data on which the rest of the algorithm operates.

The second part of the algorithm proceeds recursively, finding first the constraints that may be ranked highest while being consistent with the mark-data pairs, then eliminating those constraints from the problem and starting over again to rank the remaining, lower, constraints. Conceived as a sequence of passes, the first pass through the data determines the highest-ranking constraints, the next pass the next-highest ranking constraints, and so forth down the hierarchy. If the data provide enough information to completely determine the total ranking, then only one constraint will be returned by each pass. In general, however, the result of the algorithm will be a STRATIFIED HIERARCHY of the form:

(8) **Stratified Domination Hierarchy**

$$\{C_1, C_2, ..., C_3\} \gg \{C_4, C_5, ..., C_6\} \gg ... \gg \{C_7, C_8, ..., C_9\}$$

The constraints C_1, C_2, ..., C_3 comprise the first stratum in the hierarchy: they are not ranked with respect to one another, but they each dominate all the remaining constraints. A stratified hierarchy may not totally harmonically order all candidate outputs for a given input, since it fails to specify the relative ranking of constraints which may conflict. This has the consequence, discussed below in §4.1, that the output of the algorithm may fail to decide between candidates for which relevant training data is unavailable.

N.B.: Henceforth, 'hierarchy' will mean 'stratified hierarchy'; when appropriate, hierarchies will be explicitly qualified as 'totally ranked.'

The initial state of the learner can be taken to be the completely degenerate stratified hierarchy in which all the constraints are lumped together in a single stratum. Learning proceeds to refine this hierarchy into a sequence of smaller strata. Each pass of the algorithm begins with a set of not-yet-ranked constraints, and ends by selecting some of them to constitute the next-lower stratum in the hierarchy. At each step, mark-data pairs which are accounted for by the already-ranked constrants are eliminated from the mark-data table (7), so that only not-yet-ranked constraints are left in the table.

The key observation is this:

(9) **Key observation.**

For any given pair, if an uncancelled mark is incurred by the winner, then it must be dominated by a mark incurred by the loser: otherwise, the winner wouldn't win (this is the Cancellation/Domination Lemma of P&S:130,148,221). Therefore, any constraint assessing an uncancelled mark to the winner cannot be among the highest ranked constraints in the set, and cannot be output as part of the next stratum. Conversely, any constraint that does not assess a mark to any winner can enter the next stratum, since no evidence exists that it is dominated by any of the remaining constraints.

We now show how to deduce the hierarchy for L_1 from the data in (7).

When the algorithm begins, the not-yet-ranked constraints comprise the entire universal set (3′.a–e):

not-yet-ranked-constraints = {ONS, −COD, PARSE, FILL^{Nuc}, FILL^{Ons}}

Examining the rightmost column of the mark-data table (7) we see that two marks, *PARSE and *FILL^{Ons}, appear in the list of uncancelled winner marks. So the two constraints PARSE and FILL^{Ons} must be dominated by other constraints (those violated by the corresponding losers); they cannot be the highest-ranked of the *not-yet-ranked-constraints*. This leaves:

(9.a) *highest-ranked-constraints* = {ONS, −COD, FILL^{Nuc}}

which constitutes the output of the first pass: these three constraints form the highest stratum in the hierarchy. The data do not support any distinctions in ranking among the three, so none are made. Now we have

(9.b) *not-yet-ranked-constraints* = {PARSE, FILL^{Ons}}

Now that the highest ranked constraints have been determined, the list of mark-data pairs can be trimmed down by removing any mark-data pairs that are completely accounted for by the constraints selected as highest. This is the case if at least one of the marks incurred by the loser of a pair is among the highest ranked constraints. Such a mark is guaranteed to dominate all of the corresponding winner's marks, because all of the winner's marks were disqualified from being ranked highest.

So we eliminate from the mark-data table every row in which any of the highest-ranked constraints appear. In the current example, we eliminate the pair $a \prec d$ because *ONS appears (or, alternatively, because *−COD appears), and also the pair $c \prec d$, because *FILL^{Nuc} appears. The new mark-data table is thus:

(9.c) **Mark-data Pairs (L_1, After First Pass)**

sub-opt $\prec$ *opt*	LOSER-MARKS	WINNER-MARKS
$b \prec d$	{~~*PARSE~~ *PARSE}	{~~*PARSE~~ *FILL^{Ons}}

At the end of the first pass, we now have the first (highest) stratum (9.a), a reduced list of not-yet-ranked constraints (9.b), and a reduced mark-data table (9.c). Crucially, the reduced mark-data table involves only the *not-yet-ranked-constraints*, so we can now recursively invoke the same algorithm, using the remaining data to rank the remaining constraints. This initiates the next pass.

Repeating this process with the reduced mark-data table (9.c), we examine the rightmost column of the table, and observe that of the two *not-yet-ranked-constraints* (9.b), only one, FILL^{Ons}, appears. The remaining constraint, then, is output as the next stratum of highest-ranked constraints:

(9.a′) *highest-ranked-constraints* = {PARSE}

This leaves

(9.b′) *not-yet-ranked-constraints* = {FILL^{Ons}}

The final step of the second pass is to trim the mark-data table, eliminating rows in which the *highest-ranked-constraints* appear. This eliminates the only row in the table, so that the new mark-data table is empty.

(9.c′) **Mark-data Pairs (L_1, After Second Pass)**: none

The result of the first two passes is the highest segment of the stratified hierarchy:

{ONS, −COD, FILL^{Nuc}} ≫ {PARSE}

The third pass operates on an empty mark-data table. Since there are no marks in the rightmost column of such a table, no remaining constraints must be dominated: all the not-yet-ranked constraints are output as the highest-ranked. In this case, that is the one remaining constraint FILL^{Ons}.

(9.a″) *highest-ranked-constraints* = {FILL^{Ons}}

This leaves

(9.b″) *not-yet-ranked-constraints* = {}

so the algorithm terminates, with the final result:

(10) **Learned Stratified Hierarchy for L_1:**
{ONS, −COD, FILL^{Nuc}} ≫ {PARSE} ≫ {FILL^{Ons}}

This result represents a class of totally-ranked constraint hierarchies all of which give rise to the target language L_1: the same optimal outputs arise regardless of the ranking of the three highest constraints. One of these refinements of the learned stratified hierarchy (10) is the particular total ranking given in (4′.a): this is but one of the correct hierachies for the target language.

The language L_2 is assumed to be generated by a different underlying ranking:

(4′.c) **Constraint Hierachy for L_2:**

ONS ≫ −COD ≫ FILL^{Ons} ≫ PARSE ≫ FILL^{Nuc}

It is easy to see how the course of learning L_2 differs from that of L_1, assuming the learner's initial datum is the parse of the same input, /VCVC/, which is now ⟨V⟩.CV.C□́. (candidate *c* in (1′)). The mark-data table used by the algorithm, containing the marks of *sub-opt* ≺ *opt* pairs after cancellation, is now:

(11) **Mark-data Pairs after Cancellation (L_2)**

sub-opt ≺ *opt*	LOSER-MARKS	WINNER-MARKS
a ≺ *c*	{*ONS, *−COD}	{*PARSE, *FILL^{Nuc}}
b ≺ *c*	{~~*PARSE~~ *PARSE}	{~~*PARSE~~ *FILL^{Nuc}}
d ≺ *c*	{~~*PARSE~~ *FILL^{Ons}}	{~~*PARSE~~ *FILL^{Nuc}}

This table is identical to its L_1 counterpart (7) except that the marks *FILL^{Nuc} and *FILL^{Ons} are interchanged. The result of the algorithm is therefore the same as before, (10), with this exchange made.

(12) **Learned Stratified Hierarchy for L_2:**

{ONS, −COD, FILL^{Ons}} ≫ {PARSE} ≫ {FILL^{Nuc}}

Again, this stratified hierarchy is correct: its further refinements into totally-ranked hierarchies, including the one we singled out in (4′.c), all give rise to L_2.

That these CV languages can each be learned completely from a single positive example attests to the power of the implicit negative data which comes with each positive example in Optimality Theory.

2.2 General Statement of the RCD Algorithm

Given:

universal-constraints = a set of universal constraints

initial-data = a set of well-formed outputs of the target language *L*

We assume that *L* arises from some (not necessarily unique) total ranking *R* of the universal constraints.

To Find:

A stratified hierarchy in which these are the optimal parses of their corresponding inputs.

We proceed via an intermediate step in which *initial-data* is prepared for the algorithm.

2.2.1 Data Preparation

Given:

universal-constraints = a set of universal constraints
initial-data = a set of well-formed outputs of the target language *L*

Generate:

a. For each output in *initial-data* (*opt*), choose a set of sub-optimal competitors (*sub-opt*)
b. Make a table of these pairs, *sub-opt* ≺ *opt*, listing the marks incurred by the *sub-opts* in one column, LOSER-MARKS, and the marks incurred by *opts* in another, WINNER-MARKS.
c. The result is *mark-data* =

sub-opt ≺ *opt*	LOSER-MARKS = MARKS(*sub-opt*)	WINNER-MARKS = MARKS(*opt*)
...	...	...

2.2.2 Recursive Constraint Demotion (RCD)

Given:

universal-constraints = a set of universal constraints
mark-data = a table of pairs of mark lists (LOSER-MARKS, WINNER-MARKS)

To Find:

A stratified hierarchy with respect to which each of the LOSER-MARKS is less harmonic than its corresponding WINNER-MARKS.

RCD Algorithm:

Set *not-yet-ranked-constraints* = *universal-constraints*

I. Mark Cancellation

For each pair (LOSER-MARKS, WINNER-MARKS) in *mark-data*:

a. For each occurrence of a mark *C in both LOSER-MARKS and WINNER-MARKS in the same pair, remove that occurrence of *C from both.

b. If, as a result, no WINNER-MARKS remain, remove the pair from *mark-data*.

II. Recursive Ranking

a. Output *highest-ranked-constraints* = all the constraints in *not-yet-ranked-constraints* which do not appear in the column WINNER-MARKS of *mark-data*; these form the highest-ranked stratum of the *not-yet-ranked constraints*.

b. Remove the *highest-ranked-constraints* from the *not-yet-ranked-constraints*.

c. Remove all rows from *mark-data* which contain any marks assessed by the *highest-ranked-constraints*.

d. Call Recursive Ranking again, with the reduced *mark-data* and the reduced *not-yet-ranked-constraints*.

Note that in step c of Recursive Ranking, the relevant marks (those assessed by the *highest-ranked-constraints*) can only appear in the column LOSER-MARKS; for any constraint contributing a mark to the column WINNER-MARKS is not, by step a, among the relevant constraints (those in *highest-ranked-constraints*).

2.3 Informal Analysis of the Algorithm

Observe first that multiple uncancelled tokens of the same type of mark in the *mark-data* table, either for winner or loser, have the same effect as a single token. For in Recursive Ranking step a, we simply determine which constraints assess no marks at all in the WINNER-MARKS column: whether a single token or multiple tokens of a mark appear makes no difference. Then in Recursive Ranking step b, a row is removed from *mark-data* if it contains any marks at all assessed by the *highest-ranked-constraints*; multiple tokens of a mark type have the same effect as a single token. Thus, for efficiency considerations below, we can assume that in Mark Cancellation Initialization step a, if a row of the *mark-data* table contains multiple tokens of the same type of mark after cancellation, duplicates are eliminated, leaving at most one token of each type. In other words, in the initial mark-data table prior to cancellation, what really matters is, for each constraint, which of *sub-opt* or *opt* incurs more violations of the constraint C; if it is *sub-opt*, then a token of the mark *C appears in the column LOSER-MARKS; if it is *opt*, then the token of *C appears instead in the column WINNER-MARKS. What matters in the assessment of optimality is only which of two candidates more seriously violates each constraint: not any absolute magnitude of violation.

The correctness of the algorithm should be clear. The *highest-ranked-constraints* output at each pass of the algorithm are exactly the constraints which need not be dominated in order to explain the available *mark-data*; the remaining *not-yet-ranked-constraints*, by contrast, must be dominated and so cannot be highest-ranked.

We now show that the algorithm must terminate. On each pass of the algorithm, at least one constraint must be output. For suppose not. That would mean that every one of the *not-yet-ranked-constraints* appears in the column WINNER-MARKS, i.e., as an uncancelled mark of an optimal form. But that would mean that every one of the *not-yet-ranked-constraints* must be dominated by one of the other *not-yet-ranked-constraints*: which means there is no ranking of these constraints which is consistent with the *mark-data*, in contradiction to the basic assumption that the *mark-data* derive from some ranking of the given constraints.

So on each pass, at least one constraint is eliminated from the *not-yet-ranked-constraints*. Thus the number of passes required cannot be more than the number of universal constraints: call this N_{constr}. The number of steps required for each pass cannot exceed the number of uncancelled marks in the *mark-data* table: each mark in the column WINNER-MARKS is examined in Recursive Ranking step (a) to ensure that its corresponding constraint will not be output as a *highest-ranked-constraint*, and, in the worst case, each mark in the column LOSER-MARKS must be examined in Recursive Ranking step (c) to determine which rows must be eliminated from *data*. The number of uncancelled marks per row of the table can't exceed the number of constraints N_{constr}, so the total number of steps per pass can't exceed $N_{constr}N_{pairs}$, where N_{pairs} is the number of rows in the initial *mark-data* table, i.e., the number of pairs *sub-opt* ≺ *opt* used.

So the number of steps required for all the passes can't exceed

$$(N_{constr})^2 N_{pairs}$$

In the worst case, the RCD algorithm is quadratic in the number of constraints, and linear in the number of mark-data pairs. This makes the algorithm quite efficient, although further work is required to investigate efficiency issues in the choice of *sub-opt* ≺ *opt* pairs.

3. Discussion

3.1 General Constraint Demotion

RCD is actually one member of the Constraint Demotion (CD) family of learning algorithms for Optimality Theory. These alorgithms are all based on the same core idea: demote constraints in the hierarchy just as far as necessary to ensure that each winner mark is dominated by a loser mark.

CD algorithms vary in how they accept input data. The RCD algorithm processes all data in one batch. The On-Line CD algorithm processes one mark data pair at a time. Others fall between these two extremes.

3.2 Ties

If two candidates are assessed exactly the same set of marks by the universal constraints, then they are equally harmonic (regardless of constraint ranking). If it should happen that such a tie should occur for the most harmonic candidate output for an input, then the two outputs are both optimal, both well-formed, with the interpretation of free alternation.

If two outputs for a single input tie for optimality in virtue of incurring identical marks, no harm is done the algorithm by incorrectly assuming that one of them is sub-optimal: see Tesar & Smolensky 1993.

3.3 Implicit Negative Evidence and the Subset Principle

The Subset Principle (e.g., Berwick 1986; Wexler and Manzini 1987) has been proposed as a way of explaining how children avoid overgeneralization. Motivation for the Subset Principle has come from the argument that, because children respond only to explicit, positive evidence, they have no way of recovering from overgeneralization.

Because Optimality Theory defines grammaticality in terms of optimality, candidates which compete with the observed form are available as implicit negative evidence. This permits learning in Optimality Theory to recover from overgeneralization without recourse to the Subset Principle, and without explicit negative evidence.

3.4 Nature of the Learning Data

It is possible to obtain the results here, which are entirely independent of the content of the universal constraints, because the learner is assumed to have access to full structural descriptions. These generally include information which is not directly perceptible (e.g., in the CV theory, unparsed input segments). In current research, we are studying whether comparable learnability results can be obtained given less rich learning data.

Acknowledgements

We are most grateful for important comments and encouragement from Alan Prince, Géraldine Legendre, Jane Grimshaw, and Bruce Hayes. Special thanks go to Esther Hunt and Bill Raymond for typing assistance. Tesar acknowledges the support of an NSF Graduate Fellowship, and both authors acknowledge the support of NSF grant IRI-9213894.

References

Berwick, Robert. 1986. *The acquisition of syntactic knowledge.* MIT Press, Cambridge, MA.

Clements, G. N and S.J. Keyser. *CV Phonology*. Cambridge, MA: MIT Press.

Grimshaw, Jane. 1993. Minimal projection, heads, and inversion. Ms. Rutgers University, New Brunswick, NJ.

Jakobson, Roman. 1962. *Selected writings 1: phonological studies*. The Hague: Mouton.

Legendre, Géraldine, William Raymond, and Paul Smolensky. 1993. Analytic typology of case marking and grammatical voice. Proceedings of the *Berkeley Linguistics Society*, 19.

McCarthy, John and Alan Prince. 1993. *Prosodic Morphology I: constraint interaction and satisfaction*. Ms. University of Massachusetts, Amherst, and Rutgers University, New Brunswick, NJ. To appear as a Linguistic Inquiry Monograph, MIT Press, Cambridge, MA.

Prince, Alan and Paul Smolensky. 1993. *Optimality Theory: Constraint Interaction in Generative Grammar.* Technical Report CU-CS-696-93, Department of Computer Science, University of Colorado at Boulder, and Technical Report TR-2, Rutgers Center for Cognitive Science, Rutgers University, New Brunswick, NJ. March. To appear as a Linguistic Inquiry Monograph; Cambridge, MA: MIT Press.

Tesar, Bruce. 1994. Parsing in Optimality Theory: A Dynamic Programming Approach. Technical Report CU-CS-714-94, April 1994. Department of Computer Science, University of Colorado, Boulder.

Tesar, Bruce, & Paul Smolensky. 1993. Learnability of Optimality Theory: An Algorithm and Some Basic Complexity Results. Technical Report CU-CS-678-93, October 1993. Department of Computer Science, University of Colorado, Boulder.

Wexler, Kenneth & M. Rita Manzini. 1987. Parameters and learnability in binding theory. In *Parameter setting*, eds. T. Roeper and E. Williams. Reidel, Dordrecht.

Alignment in Cairene Arabic

CAROLINE WILTSHIRE
Brown University

I. Introduction

Generalized Alignment, as originated by McCarthy and Prince (1993), claims to account for special edge effects that were previously described in terms of extrametricality and extraprosodicity. This paper develops an Alignment-based account of Cairene Arabic word-edge phonology and shows the need for extending the ALIGN family of constraints to phrases. At the same time, however, the account raises questions about the theory's ability to capture generalizations at word and phrase edges and suggests advantages to the more traditional accounts.

I.A. Optimality Theory (OT)

Alignment theory is developed within the framework of Optimality theory (Prince and Smolensky 1993). In this framework, a

---

*Thanks to Diane Brentari and Stuart Davis for comments on an earlier draft of this paper. Due to limitations of space, I have not addressed the question, raised by Davis, of how to analyze syncope, but interested readers are referred to McCarthy (1993) for an analysis of a similar issue.

phonological grammar consists solely of constraints, as opposed to rules; whether and how the grammar should include levels with reranked constraints remains under discussion. In OT, a function called GEN produces a set of candidate output forms from an input form by making any number of changes to the input form. The set of candidates are evaluated by violable constraints, which are universal but ranked on a language-specific basis. The ranking is absolute in that no number of violations of a lower ranked constraint can force a violation of a higher ranked constraint.

I.B. Alignment Theory

Alignment theory deals with the treatment of edges within OT, formulating constraints on how various constituents are aligned with each other. At its most general, an alignment constraint takes the form in (1):

(1) Alignment Constraint -- General Form

ALIGN (Cat1, Edge1, Cat2, Edge2) $=_{def}$ For any Cat1, there exists some Cat2 such that Edge1 of Cat1 and Edge2 of Cat2 coincide, where Cat1, Cat2 $\in$ {PCat U GCat}, and Edge1, Edge2 $\in$ {Right, Left}.

An edge of one category, whether phonological or morphological, is constrained to align with an edge of another category, also either phonological or morphological. In (2), some specific examples are given:

(2) Specific Alignment Constraints

A-L$_{\text{stem-PW}}$ Align (Stem, L, PrWd, L)
Every stem begins at the left edge of some prosodic word.

A-R$_{\text{PW-}\sigma}$ Align (PrWd, R, σ, R)
Every Prosodic Word ends at the right edge of some σ.

Extrametricality and extraprosodicity effects then result from the interaction of alignment constraints like A-R$_{\text{PW-}\sigma}$ with constraints such as PARSE and NOCODA. The intuition behind this interaction is that a constraint that matches, for example, word and syllable boundaries, is ranked high enough to force extra consonants to be parsed into a coda at a word boundary despite causing a violation of the medial syllable structure restrictions.

McCarthy and Prince illustrate this interaction with an example from Kamaiurá, a language with no medial codas which nonetheless allows a single word-final consonant. To capture this distribution, an $\text{A-R}_{\text{stem-}\sigma}$ constraint is ranked above a constraint against codas, and both of these are ranked above the faithfulness constraints PARSE and FILL, which require the input and output to resemble each other maximally.

(3) Constraints in Kamaiurá (McCarthy and Prince 1993: pp. 20, 37)

$\text{A-R}_{\text{stem-}\sigma}$ >> NOCODA >> FILL >> PARSE

$\text{A-R}_{\text{stem-}\sigma}$	Every stem ends at the right edge of a σ.
NOCODA	Syllables do not have codas.
FILL	Prohibit []; i.e., fill σ positions with underlying segments.
PARSE	Prohibit <α>; i.e., parse underlying segments into σ.

Alignment constraints play no role medially in a word; there the NOCODA constraint is unviolated, as in (4a), and it is enforced in this case by allowing violations of the lowest ranked constraint, PARSE. However, when a violation would arise word-finally, as in (4b), a final consonant is forced into the coda of the final syllable by the higher ranked ALIGN constraint.

(4a) No violations medially: /hutka/ --> [.hu.ka.] 'laugh'

Candidates	$\text{A-R}_{\text{stem-}\sigma}$	NOCODA	FILL	PARSE
☞ .hu.<t>ka.|				*
.hut.ka.|		*!		
.hu.t[].ka|			*!	

(4b) violation word-finally: /apot/ --> [.a.pot.] 'I jump'

Candidates	$\text{A-R}_{\text{stem-}\sigma}$	NOCODA	FILL	PARSE
☞ .a.pot.|		*		
.a.po.<t>|	*!			*
.a.po.t|[]	*!		*	

The symbol ☞ indicates the candidate that is both chosen by the constraints as ranked and attested in the language. The symbol ☹ will indicate a form chosen by the ranking under consideration, when that form is not the form found in the language.

Here the final consonant has been analyzed as belonging to the word-final syllable. However, in some languages, we have evidence for analyzing the final consonant or its moraic content as being outside the final syllable -- that is, attached directly to the prosodic word or dominated by an appendix node apart from the final syllable, as shown in (5):

(5) **Cairene Prosodic Word**

```
      PrWord               PrWord
     /    |\              /   |  \
    σ     σ \            σ    σ   Ω
   / |\  / |  \         / |\  / |  |
  C V C C V   C         C V C C V C
  m á k t a   b         m á k t a b
```

For instance, in Cairene Arabic, a single final consonant does not make a final syllable attract stress as it does in a medial syllable. Although a final consonant is phonotactically acceptable in a coda, we still analyze the word-final consonant as falling outside the final syllable; hence we require a constraint on the alignment of prosodic words, A-$R_{stem\text{-}PW}$ (6a). This constraint may conflict with the A-$R_{PW\text{-}\sigma}$ constraint of (2) when the stem contains material beyond that permitted in a syllable.

(6a) A-$R_{stem\text{-}PW}$ ALIGN (Stem, R, PrWd, R)
Align right edge of stem and right edge of Prosodic Word. (McCarthy and Prince 1993:48, fn 40)

In order to prevent consonants from attaching directly to prosodic words in languages which do not allow this option, McCarthy and Prince cite a constraint against extra consonants in this position, namely NOAPPENDIX from Sherer (1993). As I will show, this constraint may also be used to keep extra consonants to a minimum in languages which do allow them:

(6b) **NOAPPENDIX (NoΩ)** Consonants are not attached directly to the Prosodic Word. Alternatively stated, the appendix (Ω) does not dominate consonants.

Ranking A-R$_{\text{stem-PW}}$ (6a) above NOAPPENDIX (6b) will allow consonants to be directly attached to the prosodic word as necessary for Cairene Arabic. Note that any limitations on the form of a coda consonant no longer play a role in determining what is permitted at word-edge, since the final consonant need not be analyzed as a coda to satisfy the ALIGN constraint.

(7) Appendix C to Prosodic Word: /apot/ --> [.a.po.t] 'I jump'
] = right edge of word, | = right edge of stem

<table>
<tr><th>Candidates</th><th>A-R_{stem-PW}</th><th>NOCODA</th><th>NOΩ</th><th>FILL</th><th>PARSE</th></tr>
<tr><td>☞.a.po.t|]</td><td></td><td></td><td>*</td><td></td><td></td></tr>
<tr><td>.a.po.]<t>|</td><td>*!</td><td></td><td></td><td></td><td>*</td></tr>
<tr><td>.a.po.t|[]]</td><td>*!</td><td></td><td></td><td>*</td><td></td></tr>
</table>

A-R$_{\text{PW-}\sigma}$ must also be ranked lower than A-R$_{\text{stem-PW}}$ for the top candidate to be optimal, since the form no longer ends the word at a σ boundary.

Because exceptional consonants are permitted at word-edges by overriding syllable constraints with constraints on alignment, the problem remains of capturing precisely what exceptions are allowed in edge positions. The constraint NOΩ can help here; consider a fictional underlying form with two consonants word-finally, and its candidate outputs in (8) below.

(8) additional C to Prosodic Word: /apont/ --> [.a.po.nt]?

<table>
<tr><th>Candidates</th><th>A-R_{stem-PW}</th><th>NOCODA</th><th>NOΩ</th><th>FILL</th><th>PRSE</th></tr>
<tr><td>.a.po.nt|]</td><td></td><td></td><td>**!</td><td></td><td></td></tr>
<tr><td>.a.po.]<nt>|</td><td>*!*</td><td></td><td></td><td></td><td>**</td></tr>
<tr><td>☞ .a.po.<n>t|]</td><td></td><td></td><td>*</td><td></td><td>*</td></tr>
<tr><td>.a.pon.t|]</td><td></td><td>*!</td><td>*</td><td></td><td></td></tr>
</table>

If the NoΩ constraint ranks above one of the faithfulness constraints, then when more than a single consonant is stem-final, a violation of lower constraints, FILL or PARSE, reduces the number of violations of the NoΩ constraint to produce a more optimal candidate. By violating FILL or PARSE, the violations of NoΩ can be reduced to a minimum, namely a single consonant, without violating the dominant ALIGN constraint. When a single consonant is stem-final, however, violations of FILL and PARSE also cause violations of ALIGN, and hence create only worse candidates as in (7).

Since no language allows an unconstrained number of consonants in the appendix position, the constraints limiting appendix content must always be ranked above some constraint whose violations will result in limited appendices. Again note that NOCODA and other syllable related constraints (such as *COMPLEX, discussed below for Cairene) cannot play much of a role in choosing the successful candidate's word-edge limitations.

II. Cairene Arabic

II.A. Syllabification Data

Cairene Arabic syllabification has been widely discussed in the generative phonology literature, for instance by Broselow (1979, 1980), Itô (1988, 1989), McCarthy and Prince (1990), and Rice (1990). Cairene has long and short vowels, with only a single consonant allowed in onset or coda (9a). However, as in (9b), two consonants may appear word-finally:

(9) **Syllable types medially:** CV CVV CVC
and finally: CV CVV CVC CVVC CVCC

a) nabíiha	'intelligent'	anaStaréet	'I bought'
katábt	'I/you(m) wrote'	?akálti	'you ate'
kátab	'he wrote'	káanit	'she was'
b) gabr	'algebra'	wagh	'face'
?ibn	'son'	Tamy	'silt'
waD9	'situation'	tebn	'hay'

Main stress falls on one of the last two syllables of a word: the final syllable if it has a long vowel or ends with two consonants, otherwise the penult:

(10) Stress in Cairene Arabic

Penult		Ultima (superheavy)	
kátab	'he wrote'	kitáab	'book'
káanit	'she was'	safírt	'I traveled'
máktab	'office'		

The final consonant in Cairene words has been analyzed as extraprosodic in Rice (1990), as a degenerate syllable in McCarthy and Prince (1990), and as licensed by an appendix in Wiltshire (1992). By contrast to a coda consonant or vowel in a final syllable, the word-final consonant does not contribute to the weight of the final syllable. In all these analyses, we analyze a single final consonant and the second of two final consonants in the same way, as not being a member of the final syllable coda, even though phonotactically a single consonant normally belongs to a coda.

Syllabification in Cairene can freely cross word-boundaries, and both edges of the word are sites of phonological alternations. One source of evidence for phrasal syllabification is glottal stop insertion. Before a vowel-initial word, a glottal stop onset appears if no onset is supplied by the phrasal context. The added stop is unnecessary if the final consonant of the previous word occupies onset position in phrasal syllabification:

(11) Glottal stop insertion rule: **∅ --> ? / $_{\sigma}$[__ V**

a) #il# #mudarris# — [.**?**il.mu.dar.ris.]
'the teacher'

b) #kallim# #il# #mudarris# — [.kal.li.mil.mu.dar.ris]
'he spoke to the teacher'

c) #il# #?ahwa# — [.**?**il.?ah.wa.]
'the coffee'

d) #sirib# #il# #?ahwa# — [.si.ri.bil.?ah.wa.]
'he drank the coffee'

In (a) and (c), a glottal stop is inserted before phrase-initial /i/, while examples (b) and (d) show that the phrasal context of the word /il/ determines whether the rule need apply.

Epenthesis is also based on phrasal context, and prevents consonant clusters in onsets and codas by supplying an additional nucleus:

(12) Epenthesis rule: ∅ --> i / CC__C

Within words

a)	?ul + t + l + u	[?ultilu]
	said + 1sg-to-him	'I said to him'
b)	?ul + t + l + ha	[?ultilha]
	said + 1sg-to-her	'I said to her'
c)	katab + t + l + ha	[katabtilha]
	write + 1s-to-her	'I wrote to her'

Within phrases

d)	katabt gawaab	[katabtigawaab]
	you wrote letter	'you (m.) wrote a letter'
e)	bint nabiiha	[bintinabiiha]
	girl intelligent	'an intelligent girl'

In Cairene, this vowel appears after the first two consonants of a cluster, in the same way within and across words. As a result, no more than two consonants may cluster, within both words and phrases, and while two consonants may appear phrase-finally, phrase-initially we find only a single consonant. The environment of epenthesis in phrases shows that word boundaries are not sufficient to supply an extra consonant, as it appeared in (9b); it is only at a final phrase boundary that an additional consonant is allowed. Apparently consonant clusters in phrase-final position either need not be repaired, or cannot be repaired without violating a higher constraint.

II.B. Analysis within Alignment Theory

A full account of Cairene Arabic epenthesis will require extending the ALIGN constraints to phrases. However, ALIGN constraints on words alone play a role in the distribution of epenthetic glottal stops. We can analyze the facts using the constraints in (13):

(13) Constraints for Glottal Stop Epenthesis

ONS	Syllables have onsets.
FILL^{ONS}	ONS does not dominate [].
A-L$_{stem\text{-}\sigma}$	ALIGN (Stem, L, σ, L) Align L edge of every stem with L edge of some σ.
A-R$_{stem\text{-}\sigma}$	ALIGN (stem, R, σ, R) Align R edge of every stem with R edge of some σ.

The dominant, unviolated constraint is ONS, that syllables have onsets. The FILL^{ONS} constraint bars added onset positions with no underlying material, e.g., epenthetic glottal stops. Nonetheless, if ONS ranks above FILL^{ONS}, violations of FILL^{ONS} are expected in order to satisfy ONS.

In addition, ONS and FILL^{ONS} interact with the alignment constraints in (13). When an epenthetic glottal stop appears, the left-edge alignment between stem and syllable is violated. Similarly, if a consonant from a previous word syllabifies to fill an onset position, left-alignment is violated since the stem-initial vowel is not syllable-initial. Hence left-alignment is outranked by ONS. In the case of across-word syllabification, we see that both ONS and FILL^{ONS} violations are worse than a violation of the right-edge alignment of stem and syllable. The overall constraint ranking shown below (14) is illustrated in (15a) and (15b):

(14) Pairwise ranking Evidence

ONS >> FILL^{ONS}	Onsets filled with epenthetic glottal stops.
ONS >> A-L$_{stem\text{-}\sigma}$	To have an onset, stems do not left-align with σ (epenthetic stop or across-word syllabification).
ONS >> A-R$_{stem\text{-}\sigma}$	Misalign stem-final position to fill ONS position.
FILL^{ONS}>>A-R$_{stem\text{-}\sigma}$	Prefer cross-word syllabification to filled onset.

Overall: **ONS >> { FILL^{ONS} , A-L$_{stem\text{-}\sigma}$ } >> A-R$_{stem\text{-}\sigma}$**

(15a) Glottal stop epenthesis input: #il# #mudarris#

Candidates	ONS	FILL^{ONS} : A-L$_{stem\text{-}\sigma}$	A-R$_{stem\text{-}\sigma}$
☞ .?[il.mud...		* : *	
[.il.mud....	*!		

(15b) Across-Word syllabification   input: #kallim# #il# #mudarris#

Candidates	ONS	FILL^{ONS} : A-L$_{stem\text{-}\sigma}$	A-R$_{stem\text{-}\sigma}$
☞ .kal.li.m][il....		: *	*
.kal.lim].?[il..		*! : *	
.kal.lim].[il....	*!	:	

Thus the glottal stop epenthesis facts can be neatly handled by overriding the alignment constraints with the ONS and FILL^{ONS} constraints.

Vowel epenthesis, however, cannot be handled solely in terms of word alignments; in fact, such a treatment would lead to an apparent ranking paradox. First, an analysis of word-medial epenthesis. We expect such epenthesis to result from ranking constraints against complex onsets and codas above a constraint against added empty structure:

(16) **PARSE** — Prohibit <α>.
***COMPLEX** — σ positions are limited to single segments.
FILL^{NUC} — NUC does not dominate [].
ALIGN-σ — Align (σ, R, PrWd, R) (Mester & Padgett 1993)
Align R edge of every σ with R edge of some prosodic word.

Both *COMPLEX and FILL^{NUC} must rank below the PARSE constraint so that all underlying material will appear in the output. The ALIGN-σ constraint in (16) handles the placement of the epenthetic vowel after the second of three consonants, thus bringing the syllable edge closer to alignment with the right edge of the prosodic word (since NOCODA would not determine the location of epenthesis). ALIGN-σ is not crucially ranked with respect to the FILL^{NUC} and *COMPLEX constraints, but will be placed at the right edge of the following tables for ease of illustration. The rankings in (17) alone are sufficient for the medial epenthesis facts, as is shown in the table in (17a). There we see that the best candidate has an epenthetic nucleus word-medially, rather than parsing two consonants into a complex onset or coda, or failing to parse a consonant.

(17) Pairwise rankings:

PARSE >> FILL^{NUC}	Underlying consonants and vowels are all parsed even if that requires empty nuclei.
PARSE >> *CMPLX	Clusters are not repaired by failing to parse consonants.
***CMPLX >> FILL^{NUC}**	Clusters are repaired by epenthetic vowels.
PARSE >> ALIGN-σ	Segments are parsed into σs even though not every σ can end at the right edge of the Pr Wd.

Overall: **PARSE {>> *COMPLEX >> FILL^{NUC}**
{>> ALIGN-σ

(17a) input: ?ul + t + l + u

Candidates	PARSE	*COMPLEX	FILL^{NUC}	ALIGN-σ s1 σ2 σ3
?ult.lu		*!		- μ -
☞ ?ul.ti.lu			*	- μ μμ
?u.lit.lu			*	- μ μμμ!

Given that words in Cairene may end with two consonants, we must rank A-$R_{stem-PW}$ and NoΩ amongst the constraints. The right-edge alignment of stems with prosodic words must outrank the constraint against appendices in order to allow an additional consonant word-finally, and the constraint NoΩ must be ranked below FILL^{NUC} so that forms with appendices surface rather than forms with epenthesis. This ranking continues to give the right results for word-medial epenthesis, but word-finally will allow two consonants without epenthesis in order to align the right edge of the word with the right edge of the underlying material. Note that the optimal form in (18a) does not violate *COMPLEX:

(18) Pairwise comparison

PARSE >> NoΩ	Final clusters are parsed despite causing an Ω.
FILL^{NUC} >> NoΩ	Epenthetic vowels are not added to Ω.
A-$R_{stem-PW}$ >> NoΩ	Ωs to satisfy stem-word alignment.
***CMPLX >> NoΩ**	Ω rather than complex coda cluster.
***CMPLX >> FILL^{NUC}**	epenthetic vowels fix clusters medially.

Overall: { PARSE , A-$R_{stem\text{-}PW}$ } >> *COMPLEX >> $FILL^{NUC}$ >> NoΩ

(18a) input: bint#

Candidates	PARSE : A-$R_{stem\text{-}PW}$	*CMPLX	$FILL^{NUC}$	No-Ω
☞ .bin.t]	:			*
.bin.t]**i**	: *!		*	
.bin<t>.]	*! : *!			
.bi.n**i**t.]	:		*!	

In words that are medial in phrases, however, we do get epenthesis after two word-final consonants if they appear before a word-initial consonant. Using only word-based constraints, the same ranking that allows us [bint] in isolation without epenthesis (18a) would allow us [bint] in phrases (18b). That is, the same set of marks is incurred in the phrasal context for /#bint# #nabiiha#/ as were for /bint/, hence predicting the same result.

(18b) input: bint# #nabiiha

Candidates	PARSE:A-$R_{stem\text{-}PW}$	*CMPLX	$FILL^{NUC}$	*Ω
☹ .bin.t][na.	:			*
.bin.t]**i**[na.	: *!		*	
.bin<t>.][na.	*! : *!			
.bi.n**i**t.][na.	:		*!	

The form chosen by the ranking, *[bintnabiiha], is indicated with a ☹ because although it is predicted by the ranking, this is not the form produced by speakers of the language.

The problem is a ranking paradox between the ALIGN, NoΩ, and FILL constraints. Ranking NoΩ lowest, we can prevent epenthesis at word edges and satisfy alignment. However, phrase-medial violations of NoΩ are not tolerated, with ALIGN and FILL violations incurred instead:

(19) Ranking Paradox

Words:

*COMPLEX >> FILL^{NUC} — epenthesis medially

FILL^{NUC} >> NoΩ }
A-R$_{stem\text{-}PW}$ >> NoΩ } — prevents epenthesis finally

Phrases:

NoΩ >> FILL^{NUC} }
NoΩ >> A-R$_{stem\text{-}PW}$ } — epenthesis phrase-medially and word-finally

As (20) shows, ranking NoΩ higher than it was in (18a) will account for the appearance of /bint/ with epenthesis in phrases.

(20) input: bint# #nabiiha

Candidates	PRSE	*Ω	*CMPLX	FILL^{N}	A-σ	A-R
.bin.t][na.		*!				
☞ .bin.t]i[na.				*		
.bin<t>.][na.	*!					*
.bi.nit.][na.				*	μ!	

The ALIGN-σ constraint again enforces where the epenthesis is located. From the table in (20) we see that one way to resolve the ranking paradox is to allow two levels of constraint rankings, a word and a phrase level, with the NoΩ constraints crucially ranked differently in the different levels.

An alternative is to extend the ALIGN family of constraints to include constraints on the alignment of phrases as in (21a), and rank the phrasal and word alignment constraints independently (21b). This alternative allows us to evaluate all constraints simultaneously, giving the correct result of epenthetic vowels after word-final clusters in phrases, with extra consonants parsed at the end of a phrase, as in (22):

(21a) Phrasal Alignment:

A-R$_{PHRASE}$ — ALIGN (PrWd, R, Phrase, R)
Align R edge of PrWd with R edge of Pr Phr.

(21b) PARSE >> A-R$_{PHR}$ >> NOΩ >> FILL^{NUC} >> A-R$_{stem\text{-}PW}$

(22) Epenthesis medially but not finally input: #katabt# #gawaab#

Candidates	PRSE	A-R$_{PHR}$	*Ω	FILL^{Nuc}	A-R$_{st\text{-}PW}$
☞.ka.tab.t]i.ga.waa.b]			*	*	*
.ka.tab.<t>.]ga.waa.b]	*!		*		*
.ka.tabt.]ga.waab.]			**!		

Here, the ALIGN constraint on phrases is ranked above both FILL^{NUC} and NOΩ, so that two consonants are parsed in phrase-final position without epenthesis, while the ALIGN constraint on words is ranked below both in order to choose forms with epenthesis medially in phrases and words.

III. Discussion

However, both aesthetic and practical criticisms may be directed at this account. The aesthetic problem, first, is that nowhere in the analysis do we have thc simple generalization that only a single additional consonant appears at word and at phrase boundaries. Words and phrases look the same in Cairene; each consists of any number of well-formed syllables followed by a final single-consonant appendix. Instead of having this stated as a single constraint in the grammar of Cairene, it is broken up into a number of interactions of alignment in different domains ranked with respect to constraints on epenthetic nuclei and appendix structures. Accounts using an appendix licenser or extraprosodicity stated the generalization on the form of the appendix more positively and more simply.

Additionally, OT makes the interesting claim that manipulating the possible rankings of its universal constraints gives a typology of possible languages; however, we never want to rank NOΩ too low in the heirarchy, since its violations are always limited. Therefore, the set of all possible rerankings will overgenerate to produce unattested language types.

As for a practical problem in the analysis, remember that a single word-final consonant is analyzed as an appendix, outside of the final syllable, in the same way as the second member of a two-consonant final cluster. This was because such consonants do not count as weight-bearing codas as do syllable-final consonants in medial position.

To force a final consonant into the appendix rather than the coda, we might rank the NOCODA constraint above the NOΩ constraint, as attempted in (23a):

(23a) Single C: final Ω **kátab:** **.ká.ta.b**

Candidates	A-R$_{PHR}$	NOCODA	NO-Ω	Fill^{NUC}
☞ [.ka.ta.b]				
[.ka.tab.]		*!		
[.ka.ta.b]i	*!		*	

However, we have also ranked the NOΩ constraint above FILL^{NUC}, as in (21b), in order to get epenthesis to reduce NOΩ violations phrase-medially. If NOΩ dominates FILL^{NUC}, and NOCODA dominates NOΩ, we have NOCODA dominating FILL^{NUC}. This makes the wrong prediction that potential word-medial codas will also be removed by epenthesis.

Furthermore, if we force a single final consonant into an appendix by ranking NOCODA higher than NOΩ, a word ending in a two consonant cluster, such as /katábt/ in (23b) would have both of its final consonants wrongly analyzed as appendices, since that incurs lower marks than parsing either of them into coda position. However, the first of these consonants should be analyzed in the coda in order to bear weight and attract stress.

(23b) Two C cluster: one coda, one Ω **katábt** **ka.tab.t**

Candidates	A-R$_{PHR}$	NOCODA	NO-Ω	Fill^{NUC}
☹ [.ka.ta.bt]			**	
[.ka.tab.t]		*!	*	
[.ka.ta.bit]		*!		*

Therefore, it appears that we cannot get a single final consonant into the appendix without creating problems for our analysis of word-final clusters and word-medial coda consonants.

Thus an Alignment-based account which works well for glottal stop insertion appears to offer a less insightful account of the distribution of the appendix and epenthetic vowels in words and phrases than did traditional accounts. Because alignment is based on competing negative constraints, in the case of Cairene Arabic, it seems unable to capture simple generalizations that accounts using Extraprosodicity or an Appendix licenser had no difficulty stating.

REFERENCES

Broselow, E. 1979. Cairene Arabic syllable structure. *Linguistic Analysis* 5.4: 345-382.

________. 1980. Syllable structure in two Arabic dialects. *Studies in the linguistic sciences.* 10.2:1 3-24.

Itô, J. 1988. *Syllable theory in prosodic phonology.* New York: Garland press. 1986, PhD diss., University of Massachusetts, Amherst.

________. 1989. A prosodic theory of epenthesis. *Natural Language and Linguistic Theory* 7:217-259.

McCarthy, J. 1993. "The Parallel Advantage: Containment, Consistency and Alignment." Rutgers Optimality Workshop I.

McCarthy, J. and A. Prince. 1990. Prosodic Morphology and Templatic Morphology. in M. Eid and J. McCarthy, eds., *Perspectives on Arabic Linguistics II*, John Benjamins Publishing Company, Amsterdam, pp. 1-54.

________. 1993. *Generalized Alignment.* Technical Report #7 of the Rutgers Center for Cognitive Science, Rutgers, NJ.

Mester, A. and J. Padgett. 1993. Directional Syllabification in Generalized Alignment. Ms, posted on the Rutgers Archive.

Prince, A. and P. Smolensky. 1993. *Optimality Theory: Constraint Interaction in Generative Grammar.* Technical Report #2 of the Rutgers Center for Cognitive Science, Rutgers, NJ.

Rice, K. 1990. Predicting rule domains in the phrasal phonology. in S. Inkelas and D. Zec, eds., *The Phonology-Syntax connection.* Chicago: University of Chicago Press.

Sherer, T. 1993. *Prosodic Phonotactics.* PhD. diss, Univ. of Massachusetts, Amherst.

Wiltshire, C. 1992. *Syllabification and Rule Application in Harmonic Phonology,* Ph.D. diss., University of Chicago, Occasional Papers in Linguistics.

Syntax

The Complementation of Tense Auxiliaries in French

ANNE ABEILLÉ & DANIÈLE GODARD
UFRL & CNRS, Université Denis Diderot Paris-7

1. Introduction[1]

There seems to be no universal syntactic characterization of the category "auxiliary verb". Thc question must be raised for each language, and, even, for each set of auxiliaries in a given language, of which syntactic properties if any, distinguish them. Traditionally, French has two sets of auxiliaries (aux): those which are part of "compound tenses", or "tense auxiliaries", and the passive auxiliary. This article examines the first, *avoir* as in (1a) and *être* as in (1b):

(1)a. Jean a mangé à midi. *J. has eaten at 12 = ate at 12*
b. Jean est parti à midi. *J. is left at 12 = left at 12*

We propose here that they have a specific complementation: they are the head of a "flat VP", taking as complement sisters the past participle as well as the complements of the latter.[2] This analysis, which is empirically supported by observations independent of any specific framework, is easily and precisely implemented in the formalism of Head Driven Phrase Structure Grammar (HPSG, cf. Pollard & Sag 1987, 1994), which is based on feature structures and, crucially, makes available a feature sharing mechanism.

---

[1] This paper is part of a larger investigation of French syntax undertaken together with Philip Miller and Ivan Sag. We also thank A. Delaveau, J. Fodor, G. Green, J. Jayez, J. P. Koenig and J.-C. Milner.

[2] The core cases of *faire* illustrate the same structure, cf. Miller (1992), Abeillé et al. (1994).

There are three possible structures for tense auxiliaries: the flat structure (I) which we argue for here (Legaré & Rollin 1976, Fradin 1993);[3] the hierarchical structure (II) with the aux taking a VP complement (Pollock 1986, Manning 1992, and Gazdar et al. 1982 for English); and the verbal complex (III) where the aux and the participle together form a constituent (Emonds 1978). We show that only the first adequately represents the properties of tense auxiliaries in French.

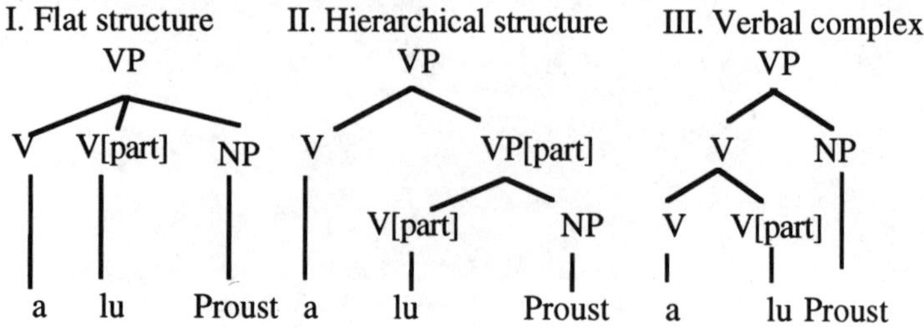

2. Four Arguments Against the Hierarchical Hypothesis

We present four arguments against structure II. First, there is absolutely no evidence for a VP complement, based on the classical constituency tests, as shown in Emonds (1978), Fradin (1993). While pronominalization, VP deletion or null complement anaphora, VP preposing, and cleft extraction show that the infinitival V complement of a control V forms a constituent with its complements, this is not so with the participle and its complements. We illustrate our point with pronominalization in (2-5)[4] and VP deletion (or null complement anaphora) in (6-7):[5]

(2) Jean peut venir, mais il ne le veut pas.
J. can come, but he it-does not want.

(3)a.* Jean n'est pas arrivé hier à l'heure au rendez-vous, mais Marie l'est.
J. is not arrived yesterday on time at the meeting, but M. it-is.

b.* Jean croyait avoir compris, mais il ne l'avait pas.
J. thought he had understood, but he it-had not.

(4) Que veut-elle ? – Partir. *What does she want? – To go away.*

(5)a.* Qu'est-elle ? – Partie. *What is she? – Gone.*

b.* Qu'a-t-elle ? – Vendu ses livres. *What has she? -- Sold her books.*

---

[3] Davies & Rosen (1988) formalize the same intuition in relational grammar.

[4] Pronominalization can be allowed with certain V's (? *Jean est déjà arrivé mais Marie ne l'est pas encore*), but these are copular constructions, not compound tenses, as shown by the present tense interpretation.

[5] Not all control V's allow this structure, cf. Zribi-Hertz (1986).

(6)a. Jean voudrait venir, mais il n'ose pas.
J. wants to come, but he doesn't dare.
b. Si Jean veut venir, il peut. *If J. wants to come, he can.*
(7)a.* Jean n'est pas arrivé, mais Marie est.
J. is not arrived, but M. is.
b.* Jean a fini son travail, mais Marie n'a pas.
J. has finished his work, but Mary hasn't.

There may well exist independent reasons for which each of these constructions is impossible. Yet, it must be acknowledged that the structure proposed in II is not supported by syntactic tests. An exception, at first sight, is coordination of sequences of V[part] and complements, which has usually been analyzed as in (8c), and to which we come back in § 3:

(8)a. Paul a parlé avec Marie et compris son erreur.
P. has spoken with Mary and understood his mistake.
b. Paul est arrivé à 10 heures et reparti à midi.
P. is arrived at 10, and gone away at noon.
c. NP Aux [[VP [part]] et [VP[part]]]

We analyze such structures as instances of Non Constituent Coordination (cf. "Paul donnera un livre à Gilles et un disque à Henriette", *P. will-give a book to G. and a record to H.*). Although we will not be able to give a formal treatment here, we assume a flat structure for the VP's of (8), with the aux taking as complement the concatenation of the two complement lists, cf. Abeillé & Godard (in prep.).

Second, the properties of manner adverbs, by which we mean *-ment* adverbs which cannot escape from the VP, cannot be accounted for within hypothesis II. Like other adverbs and non-argumental PPs, they occur between the aux and the participle (as well as after the participle); they do not occur in S-initial position:

(9)a. Jean a attentivement écouté son professeur.
J. has attentively listened to his teacher.
b.?? Attentivement, Jean a écouté son professeur.
Attentively, J. listened to his teacher.

There are two possibilities for generating the adverb in (9a) within hypothesis II: either it is dominated by the lower VP, as in structures A below, or by the higher VP, as in structures B. The difference between A1 and A2, between B1 and B2, is orthogonal to our reasoning, and we need not go into it here.

(10) Four possible Structures for V Adv VP[part] in II

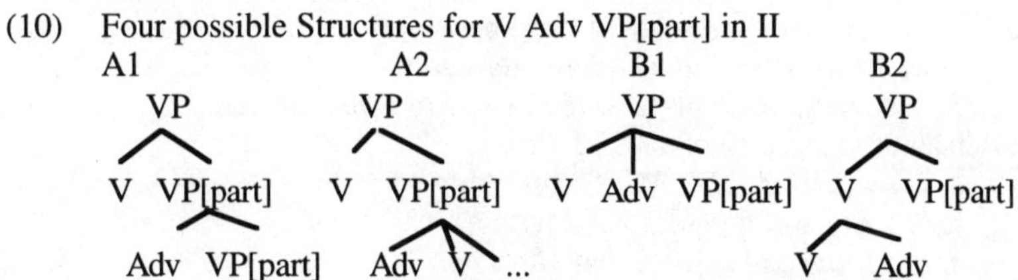

Structure A leads one to expect that the adverb may occur in VP-initial position, independently of the presence of an aux, before an absolute participial or an infinitival V. Although this is a legitimate position for some adverbs, like the time adverb in (11), this is not so for manner adverbs:

(11)a. Il s'était résolu à immédiatement partir pour le Japon.
He had decided to immediately go to Japan.
b. Immédiatement descendu, il a pu apprécier les dégâts.
Immediately gone down, he could evaluate the damage.

(12)a??Bruyamment sortis, les députés ont fait connaître leur désapprobation.
Loudly gone out, the M.P.'s made their disapproval known.
b. Sortis bruyamment, les députés ont fait connaître leur désapprobation.
Gone out loudly, the M.P.'s made their disapproval known.

(13)a.* Attentivement prendre des notes ne suffit pas à faire un bon étudiant.
To attentively take notes is insufficient to make a good student.
b. Prendre attentivement des notes ne suffit pas à faire un bon étudiant.
To take attentively notes is not sufficient to make a good student.

Thus, structure A is not adequate for manner adverbs.

Structure B leads one to expect that the adverb will have wide scope over a conjunction of participial VP's. This is not what we find. A manner adverb may not have wide scope over a sequence of participles and their complements: (14a) can only mean that Jean listened to his teacher with attention, and took notes; it cannot mean that Jean attentively took notes.

(14)a. Jean a attentivement écouté son professeur et pris des notes.
J. has attentively listened to his teacher and taken notes.

b. (14a) under hypothesis B1

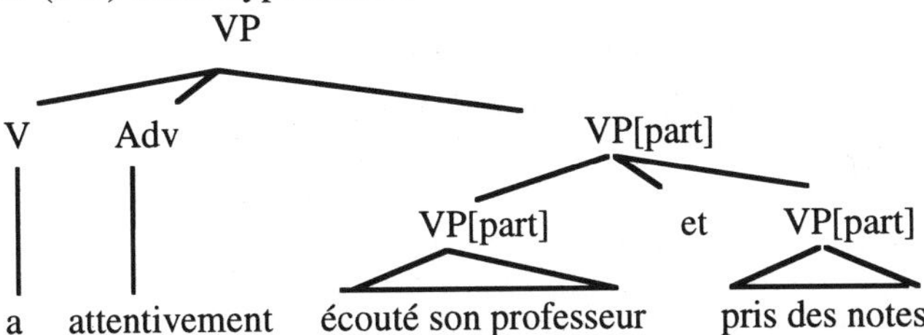

Structure B also makes the wrong predictions about the order of adverbs (see Jackendoff, 1972). Consider (15a), which contains a manner adv before the first participle and a time adv before the second one:

(15)a Paul a bruyamment réagi et immédiatement contre-attaqué.
P. has loudly reacted and immediately counter-attacked.
b. (15a) under hypothesis B1

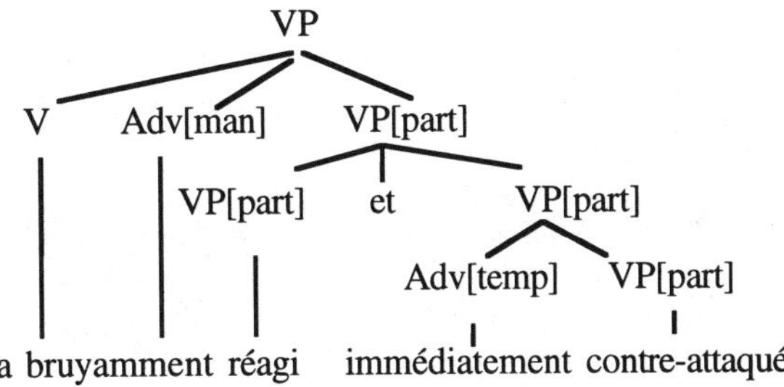

Recall that a time adv like *immédiatement* can occur before the non-finite V, as illustrated in (11); the structure under hypothesis IIB is given in (15b). Thus, if there is only one participle after the aux, we expect the manner adv to be able to precede the time adv since the structure would be as in (16):

(16)

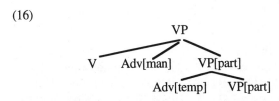

VP
V Adv[man] VP[part]
Adv[temp] VP[part]

But this is not the right order: a time adv (at least, most time adVs) must precede manner adv:

(17)a.??Jean a bruyamment immédiatement contre-attaqué.
J. has loudly immediately counter-attacked.
b. Jean a immédiatement bruyamment contre-attaqué.

We conclude that structure II cannot account for the positional, scopal, and word order properties of manner adVs.

Bounded dependencies in French offer a third argument against the hierarchical hypothesis. In contrast with English, *tough* constructions and *à* infinitival relative clauses involve a bounded dependency, as was recognized by Huot (1981), and Rizzi (1982) for the former, and Kayne (1974/75) for the latter. This property is illustrated in (18)-(19):

(18)a. Cette chanson est facile à apprendre.
This song is easy to learn.
b. On m'a donné un travail à finir pour demain.
I have been given some work to finish for to-morrow.

(19)a.* Cette chanson est facile à promettre d'apprendre.
This song is easy to promise to learn.
b.* On m'a donné un travail à prévoir de finir pour demain.
I have been given some work to plan to finish for to-morrow.

But the missing NP may be the complement of a participle which is itself the complement of an aux. Although not all examples of this sort are equally acceptable (there seem to be aspectual constraints), the following sentences show the structure to be unproblematic:

(20)a. C'est le genre de gens utiles à avoir fréquenté pendant sa jeunesse.
They are the type of people useful to have known during one's youth.
b. C'est le genre d'auteur utile à s'être attaché dès son premier livre.
They are the type of author useful to have attached to oneself from his first book.

(21)a. Le chef lui cherchait un test à avoir passé avec succès avant la fin du camp.
The counselor was trying to find for him a test to have successfully taken before the end of the camp.
b. On lui avait donné une somme à s'être avalé avant la fin du week-end.
He had been given a heavy book to have read before the end of the week- end.

This contrast follows from structures I and III: the missing NP is a complement of the infinitival aux (or of the verbal complex) in (20)-(21), whereas it is embedded inside a VP complement in (19). But it raises difficulties for structure II, where both the control V and the aux select a VP complement.

Finally, let us turn to causatives. As is well-known, the causee is realized in French either as an unmarked NP or an NP marked with *à* depending on properties of the infinitival V complement. We assume this to be the transitivity/ intransitivity distinction, for which the *faire* construction gives the strongest test, and which is a property of lexical Vs as such. This is illustrated in (22). The crucial point here is that the alternation is not specific to argument lists which are made of nominals, but is relevant for Vs with infinitival or tensed sentential complements, as observed in Burzio (1986) for Italian; very generally, Vs with an unmarked infinitival complement are treated as transitive by *faire*, as shown in (23):

(22)a. Paul fera sortir (* à) Jean.
*P. will-make leave Jean/ *to Jean.*
b. Paul fera passer son examen * (à) Jean.
*P. will-make take his exam *Jean. / to Jean.*

(23) Le juge fera avouer * (à) Jean être responsable de la tentative de corruption.
*P. will-make confess * Jean/ to Jean to be responsible for the corruption attempt.*

Thus, transitivity is more general than having an argument list of the form <NP, NP, ...>; it also characterizes Vs with a <NP, VP[unmarked]/S, ...> list. If the auxiliaries take a phrasal unmarked complement (by hypothesis, a VP), we expect them to be treated as transitive by *faire,* or, at least, to be treated in a consistent way. This is not what we find. In fact, when the sentence is acceptable (again, there are aspectual constraints), the realization of the causee depends entirely on the transitivity of the participle:

(24) Leur flair et leur ambition ont fait avoir fréquenté les gens qu'il fallait * (à) notre nouveau ministre et à sa femme.
Their flair and their ambition have made have known the right people to our new minister and his wife.

(25) La frugalité fait avoir vécu jusqu'à 110 ans (* à) notre fameuse concitoyenne, et la fera vivre encore longtemps.
Frugality makes have lived until 110 years our famous fellow-citizen, and will her-make live a long time.

Fréquenter is transitive, and *avoir* in (24) is treated as a transitive V; conversely, *vivre* is intransitive, and *avoir* is treated as intransitive in (25). It is difficult to see how these data can be accomodated within structure II. The aux, like all raising Vs, inherits its subject from the participle. Why should the realization of this argument depend not on the presence or the form of another complement, but on the transitivity of the head of its VP complement? In the hierarchical hypothesis, one has to admit that a V (the aux) with an argument list of the form <NP, VP> is transitive or intransitive depending on the transitivity of the head of the VP (the participial VP). Even if one accepted that transitivity is transmitted from the head V (the participle) to the VP – a move which requires further justification, given that the notion of a transitive VP is very unclear – it does not follow that a V (the aux) would itself inherit the classification of its complement VP. On the other hand, the data in (24)-(25) follow from structure I, where the aux takes as complements the complements of the participle; given that there is an implication between argument structure and transitivity (a V with an argument list of the form <NP, NP, ...> is transitive), it is clear that the aux also inherits the transitivity of the participle. In HPSG, we will use transitivity as a boolean feature.

The argument based on bounded dependencies is relatively dependent on a specific framework: if one takes the complement of a control V to be an S (rather than a VP), the difference between the constructions with an aux and those with a control V can be captured by a difference between VP and S complementation. However, the other arguments are framework-independent. The one based on the properties of manner adverbs illustrates basic syntactic methodology; the one based on causative constructions requires that one recognizes two things, which are framework independent: (a) the NP/ *à* NP alternation in a causative construction depends on the transitivity of the infinitival V, which is a lexical property; (b) in any standard view of argument and complement structures, a lexical property of the head of a VP complement is not transmitted to the V which is subcategorized for this VP.

3. A treatment in HPSG

The properties uncovered in the preceding paragraph could be captured in structure III as well as structure I. The reason why we prefer the latter is the following. The point of structure III is to represent the intuition that a sequence made of an aux + a participle + the complements has in a certain sense two heads: a morpho-syntactic one (the aux) and a semantic one (the participle). While we agree with this analysis, there are other means of representing this besides tree structure, which are better adapted to the purpose in a framework which uses feature structures. Thus, structure III appears to be an unnecessary complication compared to structure I.[6]

To summarize, the tense aux is the morpho-syntactic head of a VP; its SUBJ is identified with that of the participle (as is the case for all raising Vs); it inherits the complements and the transitivity of the participle; finally, the content of the participle (the relation) is transfered onto the aux. Appropriate schematic lexical entries are given in (26) and (27):

---

[6] In addition, structure III predicts dubious coordination data.

(26)

$$\begin{bmatrix} \text{PHON /avoir/} \\ \text{CAT} \begin{bmatrix} \text{HEAD [TENSE } \alpha \text{]} \\ \text{SUBJ } \langle [1] \rangle \\ \text{COMPS } \langle \text{ V}^0 \begin{bmatrix} \text{HEAD [MOOD part, TENSE past]} \\ \text{SUBJ } \langle [1] \rangle \quad \text{COMPS L} \\ \text{CONT [2]} \quad \text{TRANS } \beta \\ \textit{aux-avoir} \end{bmatrix} \rangle \oplus \text{ L} \end{bmatrix} \\ \text{CONT [2]} \cup \text{[LOC F(}\alpha\text{)]} \\ \text{TRANS } \beta \end{bmatrix}$$

aux-avoir

(27)

$$\begin{bmatrix} \text{PHON /être/} \\ \text{CAT} \begin{bmatrix} \text{HEAD [TENSE } \alpha \text{]} \\ \text{SUBJ } \langle [1] \rangle \\ \text{COMPS } \langle \text{ V}^0 \begin{bmatrix} \text{HEAD [MOOD part, TENSE past]} \\ \text{SUBJ } \langle [1] \rangle \quad \text{COMPS L} \\ \text{CONT [2]} \quad \text{TRANS } \beta \\ \textit{aux-être} \end{bmatrix} \rangle \oplus \text{ L} \end{bmatrix} \\ \text{CONT [2]} \cup \text{[LOC F(}\alpha\text{)]} \\ \text{TRANS } \beta \end{bmatrix}$$

aux-avoir

Identical value for two features is represented by identity of the tag, and $\cup$ means unification. Thus, the values of the feature SUBJ for the aux and that of the feature SUBJ for the participle are identical (tag [1]). To represent the inheritance of the complements, here the list L, we use the mechanism of argument composition proposed in Hinrichs & Nakazawa (1990, 1994): the aux takes as complements the lexical participle (V^0), which remains unsaturated for its complements L, and the list L. The transitivity (TRANS) is also shared (tag β). We leave aside the precise formulation of the semantic import of the aux, just noting that it is a localization of the relation inherited from the participle ([2]), which is a function of the morphological tense (α).

The aux and the participle are specified with the sort *aux-être/avoir*, which indicates whether the V combines with the aux *être* or *avoir*. Note that aux *être* combines itself with *avoir* (in "surcomposés": *Quand Jean a été arrivé...* When J. has had arrived). Although we cannot enter into this question here, we see this as a morphological matter, which cannot be reduced to any other property. The bulk of aux-être Vs is made of the reflexives (Vs of the form se-V) plus some thirty intransitive Vs (in standard French), which have to be listed. Examples of VP's headed by an aux are (28) and (29):

(28) a attentivement lu ce livre (*has attentively read this book*)

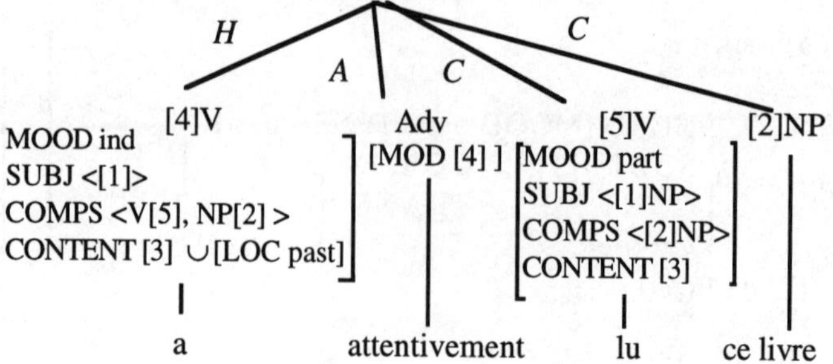

(29) a montré le livre à Marie. (*has shown the book to M.*)

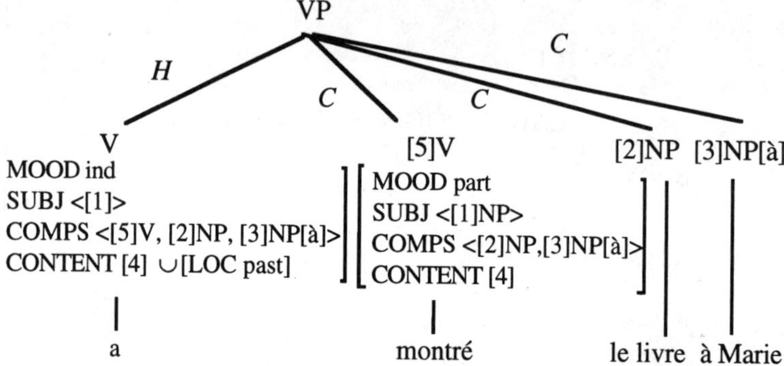

In addition to the lexical entry for the aux, a complete analysis for these VP's requires the specification of Immediate Dominance Schemata and Linear Precedence Statements. Each given phrase must unify with one of the Immediate Dominance Schemata. We have the following set:

(30) Immediate Dominance Schemata

a. Subject-Head schema

X	--->	HEAD-DTR, SUBJ-DTR
[COMPS <>]		[LEX -]

b. Head-Comp-Adjunct schema (French):

X	--->	HEAD-DTR, COMPS-DTRS*, ADJ-DTRS*
		[LEX +]

(where * denotes the Kleene star)

c. Head-Adjunct schema

X	--->	HEAD-DTR,	ADJ-DTR
		[SYNSEM [1]]	[MOD [1]]

Schemata (30a, c) are as in Pollard & Sag (1994). Schema (30a) corresponds to an S, and (30c) is needed when an adverb is adjoined to a VP, for instance, as in (11). Instead of the schema proposed in P & S for the Head-Complement structure, we have (30b), which may be more parochial (although it has been proposed for German in Kasper, 1994).[7] In French, adverbs and PPs are freely interspersed with complements, and the simplest way to get this is to have both complements and adjuncts at the same level of structure. Thus, adjuncts may be allowed either by the schema (30b) or the schema (30c). The VP's in (28) and (29) both unify with the schema in (30b); only the VP in (28) takes advantage of the possibility of having an adjunct daughter.

The Linear Precedence Statements are given in (31):

(31) Linear Precedence statements
  a. X < H [LEX -]
  b. H [LEX +] < X
  c. V[LEX +] << X
  d. Adv [time1] < Adv [man]

(31a) accounts for the leftward position of the adverb adjoined to VP as well as for the position of the subject to the left of the VP, since anything (X) which is at the same level as a non lexical head (H [LEX -]) precedes (<) it. (31b) says that the lexical head, hence the V^0, is the first element in its phrase. (31c) orders complements along an obliqueness hierachy (<<), such that lexical Vs come before all elements (X) that follow them on the COMPS list. This explains why the participle, as a complement, must precede the others, but may be preceded by adjuncts, which may occur between the aux (the head) and the participle (the first complement):

(32)a.* Paul a son travail terminé.
  P. has his work finished.
 b.* Paul s'est à Jeanne adressé.
  P. is (=has) to Jeanne adressed himself.

(33)a. Paul a vraisemblablement attentivement lu Proust.
  P. has probably attentively read Proust.
 b. Paul s'est vraisemblablement résolu à lire Proust.
  P. is (=has) probably decided to read Proust.

---

[7] Another difference to English is that, in this schema, X is not necessarily saturated (COMPS <>). Bounded dependencies such as those mentioned in § 2, are represented with a (complement or relative) infinitival VP missing its direct complement (COMPS <NP>).

Finally, (31d) states that, as we have seen, time adverbs in a general way precede manner adverbs. As for the class of time adverbs (*hier, demain*) which do not follow this rule, they do not belong to the Adv [time1] class.

Clitic climbing immediately follows from our analysis: since the complements of the participle are complements of the aux, they are cliticized under the same conditions as ordinary complements. Following the analysis of cliticization in Miller (1992), Miller & Sag (1993), clitics are affixes, the morphological realization of a feature (CLTS) on the V. To get a non empty CLTS value corresponding to an argument, a V undergoes two lexical rules (Complement Extraction and Complement Cliticization), cf. Sag & Godard (1993). Schematic lexical entries for two Vs with non empty CLTS value, a ditransitive one (*lui donnera,* as in *lui donnera un livre*) and aux *avoir* (as in *lui a donné un livre*) are given in (34):

(34)a. lui-donnera

[CLTS {[1] NP[*à*$_1$]3fsg}
SUBJ <[3]>
COMPS <[2]NP[acc]>
ARG-S <[3], [2], [4][LOC [1]]>]

b. lui-a

[CLTS {[1] NP[*à*$_1$]3fsg}
SUBJ <[3]>
COMPS <[5]V^0 [SUBJ <[3]> COMPS <[2]NP[acc], [4]>], [2]>
ARG-S <[3], [5], [2], [4][LOC [1]]>]

Another advantage of our representation is that it easily captures the "surcomposés" forms (compound tenses involving two auxiliaries), thanks to the transitivity of the complement sharing mechanism. A VP such as *a eu chanté* (has had sung) is analyzed as flat with the main aux taking as complements both the participal aux and the lexical participial. The arguments presented in § 2 carry over to these constructions.

4. In Defense of Lexicalism

Our account espouses the strict lexicalism of HPSG, which eschews functional categories such as syntactic Tense. Instead, we have rich feature structures for Vs where morphological attributes such as Mood and Tense appear as Head features:

(35) SYNSEM|CAT| HEAD verb [MOOD α, TENSE β ...]

Such an approach runs counter to the idea that French offers empirical arguments in favor of functional categories (Pollock, 1989). We briefly show that, even within Pollock's own system, French data give no evidence in favor of functional categories.

Pollock's argumentation makes crucial use of the order of the constituents found in the following sentences:

(36) Il avouait ne pas lire Proust/ Il ne lit pas Proust.
He admitted ne-not to read P./ He ne-reads not Proust.

(37)a. Il avouait fréquemment lire Proust. *He admitted to frequently read P.*
b. Il avouait lire fréquemment Proust. *He admitted to read frequently P.*

The negation *pas* precedes the infinitival V, but follows the tensed V; the adverb (*fréquemment*) may follow or precede the infinitival V. To account for this ordering, Pollock proposes the following: there are two functional categories, Tense and Agr, separated by the Negation (*pas*); VP is governed by Agr, and adVs are adjoined to the left of VP. Thus, sequentially, the categories are, from left to right: Tense- Negation- Agr- Adv- V. The surface orders are obtained via movement of the V over the adVs and the negation. In tensed Ss, the V moves out of the VP to Agr, and then to Tense; consequently, the tensed V always precedes *pas*. In infinitivals, the V optionally moves to Agr over the adv; consequently, the adv may precede or follow the V, but *pas* always precedes it. For this argumentation to hold, two points must be made independently: (a) the infinitival V moves, while the adv occurs in one position only; (b) the tensed V moves, while the negation occurs in one position only, which is the same for infinitival and tensed Ss. We briefly show that these points cannot be made.

The idea that the infinitival V has moved in (37b) rests on the following hypothesis: when an adverb occurs immediately after the infinitival V (before the complements), then, it is left-adjoined to the VP in D.S. (as well as surface structure). This is problematic. Iatridou (1990) has already argued that one may imagine other derivations for these adVs. We can strengthen the argument: within Pollock's system of analysis, there is no way to avoid a different D.S., and a different derivation.

Sentential adVs of the *vraisemblablement/ fréquemment* ("probably, frequently") class may occur before the Vinf, and are thus likely candidates for left adjunction to the VP.[8] Other adVs may not occur preverbally, e.g. some time adVs like *demain* ("tomorrow") and manner adVs with active Vs (cf. examples (12)):

---

[8] Adv's of the *bien* class ("well") (cf. Kayne, 1975) also occur before the Vinf. However, we should leave them aside, because they are in fact adjoined to the lexical V rather than the VP (for instance, they may not have wide scope over a coordination), a structural possibility which was proposed by di Sciullo & Williams (1987) for adv's in general.

(38)a.* Il se promet de demain aller à la plage.
He is looking forward to to-morrow going to the beach.
b. Il se promet d'aller à la plage demain.
c. Il se promet d'aller demain à la plage.

Pollock proposes that adVs of the second class be adjoined to the right of the VP in D.S. and that the complements may be moved to the right of the right-adjoined adv. Thus, (38b) illustrates the D.S. position, and (38c) the sequence resulting from the movement of the complement *à la plage*.

Going back to adVs of the first class, we see that not only can they occur before the infinitival V, and immediately after it, as expected, but also at the end of the VP, following the complements:

(39)a. Il était tout excité de fréquemment aller au Japon.
He was really excited about frequently going to Japan.
b. Il était tout excité d'aller fréquemment au Japon.
c. Il était tout excité d'aller au Japon fréquemment.

The difficulty for Pollock's proposal concerns the order in (39c): to get the adv in final position, one must accept that it may be right-adjoined to the VP (whether it is generated to the right of the VP, or generated to the left and moved to the right does not matter). In any case, the adv *fréquemment* in (39c) is in the same position as the adv *demain* in (38b). Consequently, it is not possible to avoid getting two derivations for sentences such as (39b): one where the V has moved to the left of the (left-adjoined) adv, as is proposed, and one where the complement has moved to the right of the (right-adjoined) adv (as is proposed for *demain* in (38b)). But if there exists an alternate derivation for (37b), in which the V has not moved to the left of the adv, then, the order which this sentence illustrates (V[inf] + adv + complement) does not constitute an empirical argument in favor of the movement of the V out of the VP. If the V has not moved, the argument in favor of the existence of a functional category Agr to which it would have moved disappears.

Secondly, taking the data in (36)-(37) as evidence in favor of the existence of functional categories supposes that the negation *pas* occurs in the same position independent of whether the V is infinitival or tensed. Again, this is very problematic. There is good evidence that the negation which precedes the infinitival V is left-adjoined to the VP: it can have wide scope over a conjunction of VP's, as shown for instance by the fact that *pas* licenses in the second member of a coordination an NP of the form *de* N, whose occurrence is restricted to certain contexts, negative ones in particular (cf. (40a)). But the negation which follows the V does not license such an NP in a second conjunct and thus cannot be left-adjoined to VP. Since the infinitivals *avoir* and *être* may be either followed or preceded by the negation *pas*, (40b) stands in crucial contrast with (40a):[9]

(40)a. Il reconnaît ne pas avoir écrit d'article là-dessus, ou même fait d'exposé sur le sujet en général.
He recognizes ne-not to have written of-article on it or even given of- lecture on the subject in general.
b.?? Il reconnaît n'avoir pas écrit d'article là-dessus ou même fait d'exposé sur le sujet en général.
He recognizes ne-have not written of-article on it or even given of-lecture on the subject in general.

This contrast cannot be understood if the negation occupies the same position in both cases. There is no reason why moving the aux to a position to the left of the negation (as would be the case in (40b)) should change the licensing scope of the negation over the complements. To conclude, Pollock's account of the ordering facts illustrated in (36)-(37), which uses functional categories syntactically distinct from V, rests on two hypotheses which have both been shown to be inadequate.

5. Conclusion

We have shown, on the basis of four empirical arguments (classical constituency tests, properties of manner adverbs, bounded dependencies and *faire* constructions) that French tense auxiliaries cannot have a VP complementation, and we propose to analyze them as (morpho-syntactic) heads of a flat VP. HPSG provides a natural framework for this analysis since it allows the aux to inherit the arguments and the semantics of the following participle. We conclude with a more general argument in favor of such a lexicalist approach, which is based on rich feature structures and avoids the need for functional categories such as Tense or Agr. We show in particular that Pollock's (1989) split Infl hypothesis is not empirically supported for French.

References

Abeillé Anne, Danièle Godard & Philip Miller. 1994. The Syntactic Structure of French Causative Constructions. *69th LSA Meeting*, Boston.
Abeillé Anne & Danièle Godard. in prep. A Lexicalist Approach to Non Constituent Coordination. ms, U. Paris-7.
Burzio Luigi. 1986. *Italian syntax : a Government and Binding approach,* Dordrecht: Reidel.
Davies, William & Carol Rosen. 1988. Union as Multipredicate Clauses.

[9] The contrast illustrated in (40) characterizes the use of so-called "standard speakers".

Lg 64. 52-88.
Di Sciullo, Anne-Marie & Edwin Williams. 1987. *On the Definition of Word*. Cambridge: MIT Press.
Emonds, Joe. 1978. The verbal complex V' V in French. *LI*. 9-2.151-175.
Fradin, Bernard. 1993. *Organisation de l'information lexicale: l'interface morphologie-syntaxe dans le domaine verbal*. Doctorat d'Etat, U. Paris 8.
Gazdar, Gerald, Georges Pullum & Ivan A. Sag. 1982. Auxiliaries and Related Phenomena in a Restrictive Theory of Grammar, *Lg* 58. 591-638.
Hinrichs, Erhard & Tsuneko Nakazawa. 1990. Subcategorization and VP Structure in German, in Hughes, Shaun & Salmon (eds), *Proceedings of the 3rd Symposium on German Linguistics*. Amsterdam: J. Benjamins.
Hinrichs, Erhard & Tsuneko Nakazawa. 1994. Linearizing Auxs in German Verbal Complexes, in J. Nerbonne, K. Netter, C. Pollard (eds), *German Grammar in HPSG*, forthcoming.
Huot, Hélène. 1981. *Constructions infinitives du français : le subordonnant de*. Genève: Droz.
Jackendoff, Ray. 1972. *Semantic Interpretation in Generative Grammar*. Cambridge: MIT Press.
Iatridou, Sabine. 1990. About Agr(P). *LI* 21.551-577.
Kasper, Robert. 1994. Adjuncts in the Mittelfeld, in J. Nerbonne et al (eds).
Kayne, Richard. 1974-75. French Relative *que*. *Recherches Linguistiques de Vincennes* II.40-61, III.27-92.
Kayne, Richard. 1975. *French Syntax: the Transformational Cycle*. Cambridge: MIT Press.
Legaré, Luc & Jacques Rollin. 1976. Syntaxe de l'auxiliaire en français. *NELS VI*, *Recherches Linguistiques à Montréal*, 187-195.
Manning, Christopher. 1992. *Romance is so Complex*. CSLI Report, Stanford University.
Miller, Philip. 1991. *Clitics and Constituent Sructure*. PhD Thesis, Utrecht University (published New York: Garland, 1992)
Miller, Philip & Ivan. A. Sag. 1993. French Clitic Movement without Clitics or Movement, *68th LSA Meeting*, Los Angeles.
Pollard, Carl & Ivan. A. Sag. 1987. *Information-based Syntax and Semantics*. CSLI series (distrib. University of Chicago Press).
Pollard, Carl & Ivan A. Sag. 1994. *Head-driven Phrase Structure Grammar*. Chicago: UCP and Stanford: CSLI Publications.
Pollock, Jean-Yves. 1989. Verb Movement, Universal Grammar and the Structure of IP, *LI* 20.365-424.
Sag, Ivan A. & Danièle Godard. 1993. Extraction of de-phrases from the French NP, M. Gonzales (ed), NELS 24, UMass. Amherst.
Rizzi, Luigi. 1982. *Issues in Italian Syntax*. Dordrecht: Reidel.
Zribi-Hertz, Anne. 1986. *Relations anaphoriques en français*. Doctorat d'Etat, U Paris-8.

The Conditions on pro and the ECP

ELABBAS BENMAMOUN
University of Illinois at Urbana-Champaign

1. Introduction

In Moroccan Arabic (MA), the subject can be phonologically null:

(1) qrat   lə-ktab
    read.3SF the-book
    `She read the book'

Within the Principles and Parameters (P&P) framework it is proposed that the subject position in (1) is filled by the null pronominal element *pro* (Chomksy 1982).[1] As to the conditions that constrain the distribution of *pro*, it is argued by Rizzi (1986), among others, that this linguistic object is subject to two independent conditions, identification/recoverability and licensing. In MA, for instance, identification requires the presence of a local head that carries the appropriate agreement features (person, number and gender) to identify the null pronominal. Licensing, on the other hand, requires that the null pronominal be assigned Case.

---

[1] As is well known, MA like the other Arabic dialects, allows for both the SVO and the VSO orders (Mohammad 1989, Benmamoun 1992, Fassi Fehri 1993, and Aoun, Benmamoun & Sportiche 1994).

The separation of identification and licensing has both empirical and conceptual advantages. Empirically, it derives the contrast between thematic *pro* and expletive *pro*. Thus, while both types of null pronominals require licensing they diverge as far as identification is concerned. For example, in MA while a thematic *pro* must be identified there is no such requirement on expletive *pro*. The evidence for this contrast comes from the fact that a thematic *pro* in MA can only occur in the context of a head that carries all the agreement features necessary for identification like the verb in (1). If a head, such as the adjective or the participle in (2), does not carry all the agreement features, particularly person, thematic *pro* is not allowed:[2]

(2) a. *(huwa) mriD
he sick.MS
`He is sick'

b. *(huwa) naʕəs
he sleeping.MS
`He is sleeping'

Notice that while the adjective and the participle carry gender and number, they do not carry the person feature that is necessary to license the thematic null pronominal.[3]

By contrast the null expletive seems to be able to occur in the contexts where the thematic null pronominal cannot as shown in (3):[4]

(3) a. Sʕib ʕli-hum yʒiw
difficult on-them come
`It is difficult for them to come'

---

[2] Unlike SA, in MA, gender distinctions are restricted to the singular form of the verb and the participle.

[3]See Borer (1984), Kentowicz (1989) and Fassi Fehri (1993).

[4] For a thorough analysis of the expletive subject in SA see Mahammad (1989). See also Fassi Fehri (1993).

b. Dahər bəlli Salma kanət hna
appearing.MS that Salma was here
`It appears that Salma was here'

c. waʒəb ʕli-hum yʒiw
necessity on-them come
`It is necessary for them to come'

In (3a,b,c) the expletive null pronominal occurs in the context of an adjective, participle and noun respectively which do not carry the person agreement features.

That there is an expletive pronominal in the subject position of the predicates in (3) is evident in Standard Arabic (SA) as convincingly demonstrated in (Mohammad 1989). As is well known, in SA, the complementizer *ʔanna* assigns accusative Case to the embedded subject:

(4) samiʕtu ʔanna l-walad-a mariiDun
(I) heard that the-boy-Acc sick
`I heard that the boy is sick'

If the embedded subject is a pronominal it surfaces as an accusative clitic on *ʔanna*:

(5) samiʕtu ʔanna-hu mariiDun
(I) heard that-him sick
`I heard that he is sick'

Interestingly, when the embedded subject is an expletive it also surfaces as an accusative clitic on *ʔanna*

(6) samiʕtu ʔanna-hu min l-waaʒibi ʕalay-ka ʔan taħdura
(I) heard that-it from the-duty on-you to come
`I heard that you must come'

This suggests that there is an expletive subject in (7).

(7) min l-waaʒibi ʕalay-ka ʔan taħDura
from the-duty on-you to come
`You must come'

But if there is an expletive *pro*, it is clearly different from thematic *pro* in that it does not require identification by agreement features on a head.

Therefore, by separating identification from licensing one can derive the differences and similarities between thematic pro and expletive *pro*. They are both subject to licensing by a Case assigner. But only thematic *pro* is subject to identification.

As mentioned above this division of identification and licensing has also conceptual advantages. It parallels the ECP (Aoun et al. 1987 and Rizzi 1986, 1990). According to Aoun et al., empty NP positions in particular are subject to two independent conditions.[5] They must be antecedent governed (or bound in the sense of the theory of Generalized Binding of Aoun 1986) and they must also be head governed.[6] These two conditions belong to different components of the grammar PF and LF respectively. Rizzi (1986, 518) in turn points out that there is a parallelism between the conditions on null pronominals and the ECP; the ECP's head government seems to parallel licensing while antecedent government/binding seems to parallel identification.

However, while the two conditions subsumed under the ECP can be fulfilled by different objects, chain formation and head government, in Rizzi's (1986) analysis of *pro* both identification and licensing are fulfilled by the same head governing the null pronominal "...pro is allowed to occur through government by a head belonging to a language-specific set of licensers, and its content is recovered through nonstandard binding by the licensing head" (Rizzi 1986, 540). In the following sections, we shall provide empirical arguments that show that, like the ECP, the two conditions on *pro* can be fulfilled by different objects. Then, we discuss the conceptual content of the parallelism between the ECP and the conditions on *pro*.

---

[5]Null elements that are not relevant to LF are only subject to licensing. One such element is the expletive discussed above. Another element is the null complementizer in English (Aoun et al. 1987).

[6]We adopt the definition of government in Aoun and Sportiche (1981) in terms of maximal projection (A governs B if all maximal projections dominating A dominate B and vice versa).

2. The Separation of Identification and Licensing

The generalization that identification and licensing require the same lexical head to carry the features that license and identify *pro* is empirically incorrect. There are null subject languages where it is clear that tense and agreement occur on different lexical heads. As shown in detail in Benmamoun (1992) in negative sentences in SA, tense and agreement occur on different lexical heads, tense on the negative and agreement on the verb:[7]

(8) a. Salmaa daxalat
Salma entered.3FS
`Salma entered'

b. Salmaa lam tadxul
Salma Neg.Past entered.3FS
`Salma did not enter'

(9) a. Salmaa sa-tadxul
Salma Fut-enter.3FS
`Salma will enter'

b. Salmaa lan tadxula
Salma Neg.Fut enter.3FS
`Salma will not enter'

In (8a) and (9a) the verb carries both tense and agreement while in (8b) and (9b) the verb carries agreement and the negative carries tense.[8]

---

[7]In Benmamoun (1992) this type of evidence was taken as a strong argument for the split Infl hypothesis proposed by Ouhalla (1988) and Pollock (1989). Note that the facts in Arabic indicate that if there is a subject agreement projection it should be located lower than tense and negation.

[8]The negative must be adjacent to the verb (Mohammad 1989 and Moutaouakil 1991):

Under an analysis where categories such as Tense, Agreement and Negation occupy independent projections, a sentence such as (8b) would have a representation as in (10)[9]

(10) $[_{TP}$ Salma$_i$ $[_{T'}$ lam$_j$ $[_{NegP}$ t_j $[_{Agrs\text{-}P}$ t_i $[_{Agrs'}$ tadxul$_k$ $[_{VP}$ t_i $[_{V'}$ $t_k]]]]]]]$

If identification and licensing are required to be performed by inflections on the same head, the prediction is that a null pronominal should not be allowed because the licensing head (tense) and the identifying head (agreement) occur on different lexical hosts, negation and the verb respectively.[10] This prediction is clearly not borne out as (11) shows:

(i) a. Salmaa lam tadxul
Salma Neg.Past enter
`Salma did not enter'

b.*lam Salmaa tadxul
Neg.Past Salma tadxul

However, this cannot be taken to show that the tensed negative is a clitic or a prefix on the verb. As shown in (ii) two tensed negatives can be conjoined which is usually not the case with bound elements:

(ii) a. Salmaa lam wa lan tadxula
Salma Neg.Past and Neg.Fut enter
`Salma did not and will not enter'

[9]We assume with Mohammad (1989) and Fassi Fehri (1993) that the subject in Arabic originates within the VP
projection. See also Aoun, Benmamoun and Sportiche (1994). In this paper, it is assumed that the negative raises to Neg in the syntax. This is not entirely obvious (Benmamoun 1992).

[10]In Arabic, at least, nominative Case seems to be assigned by tense and not agreement. There is strong evidence for this assumption. For instance, if the subject is embedded under an ECM verb, it surfaces as an accusative clitic although the embedded verb carries agreement features.

(11) a. lam yadxuluu
Neg.Past enter.3MP
`They did not enter'

b. lan yadxuluu
Neg.Fut enter.3MP
`They will not enter'

Further evidence that the licenser and the identifier may occur on different lexical heads comes from MA. As shown in Benmamoun (1992), MA uses the modal ɣadi for future tense reference. This modal may inflect for gender and number. The lexical verb, in contrast, inflects for person, number and gender:[11]

(12) a. Salma ɣada təmʃi
Salma will.SF go.3FS
`Salma will go'

b. lə-wlad ɣadyən yəmʃiw
the-children will.P go.3P
`The children will go'

(i) Salma bɣat-u yəmsi
Salma wanted-him go.3MS
`She wanted him to go'

[11]In addition to the inflected form of the modal, there is a non-inflected free form ɣadi and a clitic (bound) form ɣa:

(i) lə-wlad ɣadi yəmʃiw
the-children will go.3P
`The children will go'

(ii) lə-wlad ɣa-yəmʃiw
the-children will-go.3P
`The children will go'

See Benmamoun (1992) for more details.

Assuming that the modal is located in T and that it assigns nominative Case, it follows that, like in the context of tensed negatives, if there is a *pro* it will be licensed by the modal and identified by the verb that carries the crucial person feature necessary for identification. The modal cannot identify *pro* since it does not carry the person feature.

(13) a. ɣada təmʃi
will.SF go
`She will go'

b. ɣadyən yəmʃiw
will.P go.3P
`They will go'

Given the above facts we are led to conclude that, like the ECP, licensing and identification may be performed by different elements.

Attributing identification and licensing to features on the same lexical head is not necessary. In his paper, Rizzi was mainly concerned with null objects in Italian which are found in constructions like (14):

(14) Gianni fotografa nude
`Gianni photographs nude'

Rizzi provides several arguments that (a) the object position is syntactically projected and (b) that it is occupied by a pronominal element *pro* with arbitrary interpretation:[12]

(15) Gianni fotografa pro_{arb} nude

pro is identified via coindexation with a slot in the thematic grid of the verb and licensed by the verb that governs it.[13]

---

[12]But see Authier (1989). Regardless of the precise nature of the element in the object position in Italian (if there is any) it does not directly bear on the main point of this paper.

[13]Since *pro* has arbitrary interpretation [+human, +generic, +plural], Rizzi proposes a rule that assigns the arb feature to the slot in the thematic grid of the verb. *pro*, then, acquires this feature via coindexation with the

However, sentences such as (16) are problematic.

(16) *----vengono fotografati ....nude
`(they) are photographed nude

This sentence is ungrammatical when the surface subject has the same arbitrary interpretation as the object has in (15). In order to block a representation of (17) where the subject originates as an arbitrary object *pro*, which undergoes NP movement that is standard with passives, Rizzi proposes that the *pro* module must apply "at (or not earlier than) S-Structure". This insures that *pro* must be licensed in the same position where it is identified. If *pro* remains in the object position it cannot be licensed because the passive verb cannot assign Case. If *pro* moves to the subject position it can only be licensed and identified by Infl. But the features in Infl can only identify *pro* as a definite, rather than arbitrary, pronoun.

Rather than attributing the ill-formedness of the above sentence to identification, let us assume that *pro* is identified and interpreted as arbitrary in the object position but cannot move to the subject position because the agreement features in Infl are not compatible with the feature matrix of this pronominal and therefore the two elements cannot enter into Spec-head agreement relation.

However, there is an alternative representation, independently available in the syntax of Italian when the NP is lexical, that this analysis does not rule out. Suppose that the object *pro* remains in the object position and is linked to an expletive *pro* in the subject position:

(17) pro Infl vengono fotografati pro_{arb} nude

One way to rule this out is to require that licensing and identification be carried out by features on the same lexical head. However, this solution is no longer tenable given the above facts from Arabic. Now, the main generalization that emerges from (17) is that, unlike lexical NPs, *pro* cannot get licensed by entering in a chain relation with the expletive pro

---

governing verb.

which is in a Case position.[14] That is, *pro* must be in a Case position overtly. There is strong empirical evidence for this generalization. There are several arguments to support it but due to lack of space I will focus on one piece of evidence. As is well known, in Standard Arabic, when the subject is in the postverbal position it agrees with the verb in person and gender only. On the other hand, when the subject is in the preverbal position agreement is in person, number and gender (Mohammad 1989, Benmamoun 1992, Fassi Fehri 1993 and Aoun, Benmamoun and Sportiche 1994):

(18) a. daxala T-Tullab-u
entered.3SM the-students-Nom
`The students entered'

b. T-Tullab-u daxaluu
the-students-Nom entered.3PM
`The students entered'

In the context of auxiliary verbs, if the subject is after the auxiliary and before the verb, it agrees with the former in person and gender and with the latter in person, number and gender:

(19) a. kaana T-Tullab-u yadrusuun
was.3SM the-students-Nom study.3PM
`The students were studying'

b. T-Tullab-u kaanuu yadrusuun
the-students-Nom were.3PM study.3PM
`The students were studying'

Interestingly, when the subject is a null pronominal, both the auxiliary verb and the lexical verb must carry full agreement (Benmamoun 1992, 141):

(20)*a. kaana yadrusuun
was.3SM study.3PM

---

[14]A stronger claim would be that there is no Case transfer (via chain formation) even with lexical NPs. The facts traditionally derived by this mechanism may need to be reanalyzed in terms of LF movement (Chomsky 1993) or alternative Case relations (Belletti 1988).

b. kaanuu yadrusuun
were.3PM study.3PM
`They were studying'

Assuming that full agreement and particularly number agreement obtains when the subject is in the preverbal position (in Spec-head relation) the facts in (20b) suggest that the null pronominal is in the preverbal position. Notice in particular that movement of *pro* to the preverbal position cannot be due to identification because the lexical verb carries all the agreement features that are necessary to identify it.[15]

Thus, the reason why (17) is ill-formed in Italian is that the null pronominal is not in Spec-head agreement relation with its licenser. In this respect, it parallels (20) in Arabic which is ill-formed for the same reason. Both (17) and (20) violate the generalization that the null pronominal must be in a Case position and correlatively that chain formation is not a device that licensing of *pro* can resort to. This is what we should expect if licensing is to be conceptually parallel to the head government part of the ECP. Licensing is a local relation between a head and its governee (and/or specifier).

Before closing this section it is worth mentioning that linking licensing and identification by requiring that they be performed by features on the same lexical head is consistent with the recent proposal of Chomsky (1993) that agreement, as a syntactic projection, plays a crucial role in Case assignment. Assuming the structure in (21), where tense and agreement occupy independent projections, Chomsky suggests that the nominative Case feature originates with T.[16]

---

[15]According to Aoun, Benmamoun and Sportiche (1994) there is always agreement between the subject and the verb. The reason why number agreement does not show up under the VSO order in SA, when the subject is a lexical NP, is that this non-inherent feature may not be retained after verb movement. The number feature is retained with pronouns because it is inherent.

[16]Incidentally, this cannot be the correct structure for the Arabic sentences. If inflectional morphemes such as Tense and subject Agreement head their own syntactic projections, in order to get the right inflection on

(21) [$_{CP}$ Spec [$_{C'}$ C [$_{AgrS''}$ Spec [$_{AgrS'}$ AgrS [$_{TP}$ T [$_{AgrO''}$ Spec [$_{AgrO'}$ AgrO [$_{VP}$]]]]]]]]

While the nominative Case feature originates in T, it must be checked in Agr-S''. This obtains by moving Tense (together with its lexical host) to the head of AgrS''. The subject NP is in turn forced to move (overtly or covertly depending on the strength of the features involved) to Spec AgrS''. Thus, both tense and agreement play a role in Case assignment (Checking/licensing). In the present context, this implies that agreement plays a role in both identification and licensing of pro.[17] However, this analysis cannot be maintained in the context of the facts from Arabic, especially tensed negatives in Standard Arabic as illustrated in (22). In these sentences the negative carries tense and the verb carries agreement. This clearly shows that agreement does not play a role in Case assignment/checking because the Case feature (originating with tense) is located on the negative while the agreement features are located on the verb.[18]

(22) a. pro lam yadxuluu
Neg.Past enter.3MP
`They did not enter'

b. pro lan yadxuluu
Neg.Fut enter.3MP
`They will not enter'

To sum up, the parallelism between the ECP and the conditions on *pro* can be maintained. The trace of a moved NP is subject to recoverability and head government with the former obtaining via antecedent government/binding and the latter under head government (probably at different interface levels). The null pronominal is subject to

---

the right host, Tense must be projected higher than subject agreement with negation in between.

[17]For null objects, AgrO-P would also play a role in Case assignment (Checking) and identification.

[18]See Benmamoun (1993) for further arguments against the postulation of an independent agreement projection.

identification/recoverability and licensing with the former obtaining via agreement (in Arabic) and the latter via Case assignment.

3. Parallelism between the conditions on pro and the ECP

The question that arises is whether this parallelism has any conceptual content. Can there be unified conditions on *pro*, traces and other null elements? Consider the parallelism between the head government part of the ECP and the licensing condition on *pro*. Both elements seem to require licensing at the same component or level of representation. According to Aoun et al. (1987) the head government part of the ECP should apply in PF. In Chomsky's minimalist theory this implies that it should obtain by Spell-Out (overtly).[19] This seems to be the case as far as *pro* is concerned. Recall that a null pronominal must be in Spec-head agreement relation with its Case assigner.
Under minimalism this implies that the Case of *pro* must be checked by Spell-Out (overtly).

If this is correct it suggests that the head government part of the ECP and the licensing condition on *pro* can be reduced to a general licensing condition on empty NP positions in particular, namely that they be licensed locally by head government (or Spec-head agreement).

On the other hand, the antecedent government/binding part of the ECP parallels the identification/recoverability condition on *pro*. Interestingly, chain formation seems to be relevant to both of them. Consider the derivation and representation of (22a). Let us assume that the negative is generated as head of NegP and then moved to T. Subject *pro* is generated in Spec VP and the moved to Spec TP. Notice that the identification task falls on the verb because it carries all the agreement features (and particularly person). The licensing task, on the other hand, falls on Tense. Recall also that *pro* must move to the Spec of TP to get Case:

---

[19]This is an oversimplification. The exact nature of the level of representation where the head government part of the ECP applies remains to be determined. What is clear is that it is a level that seems to use the X'schema.

(23) TP
pro$_i$ T'
T NegP
Neg+T Neg VP
lam$_k$ t_k t_i V'
V
yadxuluu

In (23) *pro* is identified by virtue of being in a chain relation with its trace which is in Spec-head agreement with the verb carrying the agreement features. However, there is another alternative that does not appeal to the notion of chain. Suppose that D-Structure is a legitimate level of representation. Then, one can assume that *pro* is identified at D-Structure in Spec VP and then moved to Spec TP to be licensed. However, this analysis only holds when it is the lexical verb that identifies the null pronominal. But this is not always the case. In other contexts, a functional head may be the only element carrying the agreement features that identify *pro*. This situation, for instance, obtains in the context of the copular negative *laysa* (be not) in SA. This negative inflects for person, number and gender and therefore can identify a null pronominal:

(24) lastu naaʔiman
neg.1S sleeping
`I am not sleeping'

Assuming that the null pronominal is generated within the lexical projection containing the participle (for the thematic role to be assigned locally), for *pro* to be identified it has to move to the Spec of the projection containing the negative copula.[20] This in turn entails that identification does not take place at D-Structure. Therefore, I will assume, in the spirit of Aoun et al. and minimalism that identification is an LF process and that chain formation is a key mechanism for carrying it out. This is what we should expect if the recoverability of thematic *pro* and the antecedent government/binding condition on traces are to be reduced to one unified condition governing the distribution of such elements.

---

[20]The negative copula is restricted to the present tense. I will assume with Eisle (1988) and Fassi Fehri (1993) that there is an abstract present tense projection. *pro* moves to the specifier of this projection to be licensed.

* Thanks to Joseph Aoun, James Yoon and Sandro Zucchi for comments and discussions.

References

Aoun, Joseph. 1986. *Generalized Binding*. Holland: Foris, Dordrecht.

Aoun, Joseph, Norbert Hornstein, David Lightfoot, and Amy Weinberg. 1987. Two Types of Locality. *Linguistic Inquiry* 18, 537-577.

Aoun, Joseph, Elabbas Benmamoun, and Dominique Sportiche.1994 Agreement and Conjunction in Some Varieties of Arabic. *Linguistic Inquiry* 25, 195-220

Authier, Mark. 1989. Arbitrary Null Objects and Unselective Binding. *The Null Subject Parameter*, ed. by Jaeggli, Osvaldo, and Kenneth Safir, 45-67. Holland, Kluwer Academic

Benmamoun, Elabbas. 1992. *Functional and Inflectional Morphology: Problems of Projection, Representation and Derivation*. Doctoral dissertation, USC, Los Angeles.

Benmamoun, Elabbas. 1993. Agreement and the Agreement Projection in Arabic. *Studies in Linguistic Sciences*. 23, 1-11, University of Illinois.

Belletti, Adriana. 1988. The Case of Unaccusatives. *Linguistic Inquiry* 19, 1-34.

Borer, Hagit. 1984. *Parametric Syntax*. Holland: Foris, Dordrecht.

Chomsky, Noam. 1992. *Some Concepts and Consequences of the Theory of Government and Binding*. Cambridge, Massacusetts: MIT Press.

Chomsky, Noam. 1993. A Minimalist Program for Linguistic Theory. *The View from building 20*: Essays in Honor of Sylvain Bromberger, ed. by Kenneth Hale and Samuel Keyser, 1-52. Cambridge, Massachusetts: MIT Press.

Eisele, John. 1988. *The Syntax of Tense, Aspect, and Time Reference in Cairene Arabic*. Doctoral dissertation, University of Chicago.

Fassi Fehri, Abdelkader. 1993. *Issues in the Structure of Arabic Clauses and Words*, Holland: Kluwer Academic.

Kenstowicz, Michael. 1989. The Null Subject Parameter in Modern Arabic Dialects. *The Null Subject Parameter*, ed by Jaeggli, Osvaldo, and Kenneth Safir, 363-275, Holland: Kluwer Academic.

Mohammad, Mohammad. 1989. *The Sentence Structure of Arabic*. Doctoral dissertation, USC, Los Angeles.

Moutaouakil, Ahmed. 1991. NEGATIVE CONSTRUCTIONS IN ARABIC: TOWARDS A FUNCTIONAL APPROACH. *Budapest Studies in*

Arabic 3-4, ed by Devengi, Kinga, and Tamas Ivanyi, 263-296. Budapest.

Ouhalla, Jamal. 1988. *The Syntax of Head Movement, A Study of Berber*. Ph.D dissertation, University College London, England.

Pollock, Jean-Yves. 1989. Verb Movement, UG and the Structure of IP. *Linguistic Inquiry* 20, 365-424.

Shlonsky, Ur. 1994. Semitic Clitics. MS. Universite de Geneve.

Rizzi, Luigi. 1986. Null Objects in Italian and the Theory of pro. *Linguistic Inquiry* 17, 501- 558.

Rizzi, Luigi. 1990. *Relativized Minimality*. Cambridge: MIT Press.

Is Wh-in-Situ Really in-situ? Evidence from Malay and Chinese*

PETER COLE & GABRIELLA HERMON
University of Delaware

1. Introduction

Since the seminal work of Huang (1982) it has been widely accepted that in languages with no overt wh movement, wh-in-situ universally undergoes covert wh movement, and, hence, is always subject to restrictions on movement. Although in Huang it was argued that the movement in question is LF wh movement, to which it was widely assumed that only the ECP but not subjacency applied, more recently Nishigauchi (1990), Watanabe (1992 and 1993) and others, arguing against Huang, have contended that in Japanese (and presumably also Chinese) wh questions obey the wh island condition, which is assumed to derive from subjacency. While Nishigauchi, Watanabe and others have argued that the movement in question is operator movement in the syntax rather than LF wh movement, these analyses share the claim that wh-in-situ involves covert movement.

In contrast to the covert movement approach, a number of authors have argued in favor of interpreting wh-in-situ without movement, either by means of coindexation of the wh-in-situ with a Q marker, as in Baker (1968) and (1970), or by means of interpretive devices in the semantics, as in Reinhart (1993). Reinhart has argued that in the context of the Minimalist Framework of Chomsky (1992), the choice of LF movement in some languages but not in others is not a possible analysis: In the

Minimalist Framework there can be no parametric differences among languages with regard to whether movement takes place in the syntax or LF since these components do not constitute separate linguistic levels.[1] What authors in both the movement and the non-movement camps share is the assumption that a unified approach to wh-in-situ is appropriate: For both groups of authors, the question is whether universally wh-in-situ involves movement or not.[2]

In this paper we shall argue that there are in fact two different types of wh-in-situ, with clearly contrasting syntatic properties. While one type requires covert movement (which we will take to be null OP movement rather than LF wh movement, following Watanabe and others), the second type involves interpretation in-situ. Our arguments are based on the contrast between wh-in-situ in Malay on the one hand and in Chinese on the other: We shall show that in Malay wh-in-situ does not involve covert movement, but is in-situ at all stages in the derivation, while in Chinese a covert movement analysis is justified by the data.[3] Furthermore, while wh-in-situ in Malay does not involve covert movement, following the analysis of Indonesian of Saddy (1991), we shall argue that Malay exhibits an additional type of wh construction that involves both overt movement and subsequent covert movement. We conclude, therefore, 1) that wh-in-situ is typologically not a unified phenomenon requiring a unified treatment in universal grammar; and 2) that languages are not parameterized into those with covert movement and those with direct in-situ interpretation. In this paper our emphasis is on laying out the arguments for these claims rather than on providing a detailed analysis of the principles of UG which would account for the observed typological differences. We hope to return to the latter topic in the future.

2. Wh Questions in Malay

It is useful at this point to provide a short sketch of the properties of wh questions in Malay on which our analysis is based. There are three types of wh questions found in Malay, wh which is moved to its position of understood scope, wh-in-situ and partially moved wh. These possibilities are illustrated in (1)-(3):

(1) Wh Moved to its Scopal Position[4]

a. Siapa$_i$ (yang)[5] [Bill harap [yang[6] t$_i$ akan membeli baju untuknya]]?
Who (that) Bill hope that will buy clothes for him?
'Who does Bill hope will buy clothes for him?'

b. Kenapa$_i$ [awak fikir [dia pergi t$_i$]]?
Why you think he leave?
'Why do you think he left?'

(2) Wh-in-situ

a. Ali memberitahu kamu tadi [Fatimah baca apa]?
Ali informed you just now Fatimah read what?
'What did Ali tell you just now Fatimah was reading?'

b. Bill harap [guru itu akan mendenda siapa]?
Bill hope teacher that will punish who?
'Who does Bill hope that teacher will punish?'

(3) Partially Moved Wh

a. Ali memberitahu kamu tadi [$_{CP}$ apa$_i$ yang [$_{IP}$ Fatimah baca t_i]]?
Ali told you just now what that Fatimah read ?
'Ali told you just now, what was Fatimah reading ?'

b. Kamu percaya [$_{CP}$ ke mana$_i$ yang [$_{IP}$ Mary pergi t_i]]?
You believe to where that Mary go?
'Where do you believe that Mary went?'

c. John fikir [kenapa$_i$ yang Mary rasa [Ali dipecat t_i]]?
John think why that Mary feel Ali was fired
'John thinks why Mary felt Ali was fired ?'

In (1) the wh words siapa 'who' and kenapa 'why' have moved from a position within the complement clause to the beginning of the matrix clause, a position which, as in English, we take to be the specifier of the matrix CP. In contrast, in (2), as in Chinese and Japanese, the wh words apa 'what' and siapa 'who' remain in-situ in the complement clause. As in similar examples in Chinese and Japanese, the wh words are understood to have scope over the sentence as a whole, just as in (1), and need not be D-linked (Pesetsky 1987). Finally, in (3), as in one type of wh question in Ancash Quechua (discussed in Cole and Hermon 1994), the wh words apa 'what' and ke mana 'to where' have moved to the beginning of the clause in which they originate or to the beginning of the intermediate clause, to the pre-comp position. We take this position to be the specifier of the subordinate CP. Note particularly that in (3c) kenapa 'why' has moved entirely out of its own clause to the beginning of the intermediate clause. This movement is incompatible with a clause internal scrambling analysis of partial wh movement. Again, as in (1) and (2), the wh word is understood to have scope over the entire sentence.

When the wh form is an argument, all three options (fully moved wh, wh-in-situ and partially moved wh) are possible, as was illustrated in (1)-(3). However, when the wh form is an adjunct, wh-in-situ is less than completely well-formed. In the case of kenapa 'why' and bagaimana 'how' (and other words meaning 'why' and 'how'), wh-in-situ is completely ill-formed, but in the case of di mana 'where', there is only a slight reduction in grammaticality:[7]

(4) a. Kenapa Fatimah menangis?
Why Fatimah cry?
'Why did Fatimah cry?'

b. *Fatimah menangis kenapa?
Fatimah cry why?
'Why did Fatimah cry?'

(5) a. Bila kau nak ke pasar?
when you want to market?
'When are you going to the market?'

b. *Kau nak ke pasar bila?
you want to market when?
'When are you going to the market?'

(6) a. Di mana Ali membeli pangasapuri?
at where Ali buy condominium
'Where did Ali buy a condominium?'

b. ?Ali membeli pangsapuri di mana?
Ali buy condominium at where?
'Where did Ali buy the condominium?'

Compare (6), in which di mana is an adjunct, with (7), in which di mana is a complement. While (6) is of somewhat reduced grammaticality, (7) is completely well-formed:

(7) a. Di mana Fatimah tinggal?
At where Fatimah live?
'Where does Fatimah live?'

b. Fatimah tinggal di mana?
Fatimah live at where?
'Where does Fatimah live?'

3. Wh-in-situ in Relative Clauses in Malay

We shall now examine each type of wh question in Malay with regard to the extent to which it appears to obey (or create) island restrictions. We shall show that while overtly moved wh in Malay (both fully and partially moved) obeys subjacency, wh-in-situ does not. We shall first consider relative clauses.

Overt wh movement in Malay is not possible from relative clauses:

(8) Relative Clauses

a. *Di mana$_i$ [kamu fikir [Ali suka [perempuan yang tinggal t_i]?
At where you think Ali like woman that live?
'You think Ali likes woman who lives where?'

b. *Dengan siapa$_i$ [kamu sayang [perempuan [yang telah berjumpa t_i]?
With who you love woman that already meet
'You love the woman who met who?'

Turning now to wh-in-situ, the sentences of (9) show that in-situ wh forms can appear in relative clauses:

(9) Relative Clauses

a. Kamu fikir [Ali suka [perempuan [yang tinggal di mana]]]?
you think Ali like woman that live at where
'You think Ali likes women who live where ?'

b. Kamu sayang [perempuan [yang telah berjumpa siapa]]?
You love woman that already meet who ?
'You love the woman who met who?'

4. Wh-in-situ in Islands in Japanese and Chinese

The examples of (9) would appear to show that unlike overtly moved wh, wh-in-situ is not subject to syntactic islands created by subjacency, and hence, does not involve movement. But work on Japanese and Chinese suggests that relative clauses alone do not provide sufficient evidence that wh-in-situ in Malay does not obey subjacency. It is shown by Nishigauchi (1990) that in Japanese wh-in-situ can occur inside relative clauses but not in wh islands:

(10) Wh-in-situ in Relative Clause in Japanese
Kimi-wa [[dare-ga kai-ta] hon]-o yomi-masi-ta ka
you-T who-N write-P book-acc read-P Q
'You read books that who wrote?'

(11) Wh-in-situ in Wh Island
*Tanaka-kun-wa [dare-ga nani-o tabeta-ta-ka] oboe-te-i-masu-ka
T. who-N what-acc eat-P-Q remember-is-Q
'Who does T. remember bought what?'

The same facts would appear to hold for Chinese:

(12) Wh-in-situ in Relative Clause in Chinese
ni xihuan [$_{NP}$ nage [$_{CP}$ t_i yao mai shenme] OP_i de ren_i]
you like that want buy what comp man
'You like the man who wants to buy what??'

(13) Wh-in-situ in Wh Island[8]
*Wo wenguo Zhangsan [shei maile shenme].
I ask Zhangsan who buy what
'Who did you ask Zhangsan bought what?'

The discrepancy between judgements regarding wh-in-situ in relative clauses and wh-in-situ in wh islands is explained by Nishigauchi on the basis of two assumptions: 1) Subjacency applies to both syntactic and LF movement. 2) Wh-in-situ in relative clauses involves "massive pied-piping".[9] Thus, in (10), according to Nishigauchi, the entire relative clause has been pied-piped to the matrix specifier of CP, and no movement out of the island has taken place.

In contrast, in the case of the wh island, LF pied-piping is claimed not to be possible. Thus, on the assumption that wh-in-situ involves covert movement, wh-in-situ inside a wh island will result in ungrammaticality which cannot be avoided by pied-piping. The just cited facts from Japanese and Chinese raise doubts regarding the conclusion drawn from the Malay examples in (9) that subjacency does not apply to wh-in-situ in Malay.

5. Wh-in-situ and Islandhood in Malay

It is necessary, therefore, to determine whether the well-formedness of wh-in-situ in Malay is limited to relative clauses, or whether it extends to other island environments as well. As the examples which follow show, the pattern found in Malay contrasts sharply with that in Japanese and Chinese. While in Japanese and Chinese matrix interpretation for wh-in-situ inside a wh island is difficult or impossible, in Malay such an interpretation is well-formed. On the one hand, the (a) sentences of (14)-(15) show that overt extraction from a wh island is ungrammatical. The (b) sentences, on the other hand, show that a matrix interpretation for wh-in-situ inside wh islands is possible:

(14)
a. *Apa$_i$ kamu tanya Ali siapa beli t$_i$?[10]
what you ask Ali who buy
'What did you ask Ali who bought?'
b. Kamu tanya Ali siapa beli apa?[11]
you ask Ali who buy what
'What did you ask Ali who bought?'
(15)
a. *Apa kamu ingin tahu Ali baiki di mana?[12]
what you wonder Ali fix where
'What do you wonder where Ali fixed?'
b. Kamu ingin tahu Ali baiki apa di mana?
you wonder Ali fix what where
'What do you wonder where Ali fixed?'

Thus, the examples of (14) and (15) show that wh-in-situ in Malay differs from wh-in-situ in Japanese and Chinese in allowing a matrix interpretation for wh words within wh islands. These facts could not be accounted for by abstract pied-piping.

There are two additional arguments that the occurrence of wh-in-situ in Malay is not due to pied-piping. First, since it is generally believed that "massive pied-piping" is restricted to relative clauses (and constructions with the same structure as a relative clause), it would be expected that pied-piping would not be possible from sentential subjects. But in Malay, while wh-in-situ is possible in sentential subjects, overt movement from sentential subjects is not:

(16) Overt Wh Movement From Sentential Subject
*[$_{CP}$ Siapa$_i$ [t'$_i$ yang [Ali mengahwini t$_i$]] mengecewakan ibunya].
who that Ali married upset his mother
'Who did that Ali married upset his mother?'
(17) Wh-in-situ in Sentential Subject
[Yang Ali mengahwini siapa] mengecewakan ibunya.
that Ali married who upset his mother
'Who did that Ali married upset his mother?'

On the assumption that the pied-piping of sentential subjects is not possible, examples like (17) constitute an argument that wh-in-situ in Malay does not involve movement.

Second, covert wh movement in Japanese and Chinese can have the effect of creating wh islands, which can block other, overt movement. On the assumption that the gap in relative clauses in Chinese is due to the movement of a null operator in the syntax, relativization into indirect questions provides a test for the claim that wh-in-situ in Chinese involves covert movement. Consider the sentences of (18) and (19):

(18) Relativization of Locative
a. Relativization into Indirect Question Using Resumptive Pronoun
[$_{NP}$ nage [$_{CP}$ wo wenguo ni [$_{CP}$ ta$_i$ zai nali gongzuo] OP$_i$ de] ren$_i$] shi
that I asked you he at where work comp man is
wode pengyou.
my friend
'The man who I asked you if he works where is my friend.'
b. Relativization into Indirect Question Leaving Gap
??[$_{NP}$ nage [$_{CP}$ wo wenguo ni [$_{CP}$ t zai nali gongzuo] OP$_i$ de] ren$_i$] shi
that I asked you at where worked comp man is
wode pengyou.
my friend
'The man who I asked you if works where is my friend.'
(19) Relativization of Argument
a. Relativization into Indirect Question Using Resumptive Pronoun
[$_{NP}$ nage [$_{CP}$ wo wenguo ni [ta$_i$ maile shenme] OP$_i$ de] ren$_i$] shi wode
that I asked you he bought what comp man is my
friend
pengyou
'The man who I asked you if he bought what is my friend.'

b. Relativization into Indirect Question Leaving Gap
??[$_{NP}$ nage [$_{CP}$ wo wenguo ni [$_{CP}$ t maile shenme] OP_i de] ren_i] shi
that I asked you bought what comp man is
wode pengyou
my friend
'The man who I asked you if he bought what is my friend.'

The examples of (18) and (19) show that in Chinese wh-in-situ creates wh islands: The wh word in indirect questions moves to specifier of CP of its clause, thereby blocking the movement of OP to that position. Thus, these examples constitute strong evidence that wh-in-situ in Chinese is subject to subjacency.[13]

Returning to Malay, there is a sharp contrast between examples (18) and (19) in Chinese on the one hand, and similar sentences in Malay on the other:

(20) Relativization Into Indirect Question in Malay
a. Relativization into Wh island Created by Overt wh movement
*Orang itu_i [$_{CP}$ OP_i yang saya tanya [$_{CP}$ di $mana_j$ [t_i bekerja t_j]]]
person that that I ask at where work
ialah abang saya.
is brother my
'The person who I asked where he worked is my brother.'
b. Relativization into Wh Island Created by Overt Movement Using Resumptive Pronoun
Orang itu_i [OP_i yang saya tanya [di $mana_j$ dia_i bekerja t_j]] ialah
person that that I ask at where he work is
abang saya.
brother my
'The person who I asked where he worked is my brother.'
c. Relativization into Putative Wh Island Allegedly Created by Wh-in-situ (**no** islandhood)
Orang itu_i [OP_i yang saya tanya [t_i bekerja di mana]] ialah abang
person that that I ask work at where is brother
saya.
my
'The person who I asked where he worked is my brother.'
(21) Relativization Into Indirect Question in Malay
a. Relativization Into Wh Island Created by Overt Wh Movement
*$Lelaki_i$ [OP_i yang [kamu tanya [apa_j [t_i beli t_j]]] ialah abang saya.
man that you ask what buy is brother my.
'The man who you asked bought what is my brother.'

b. Relativization into Putative Wh Island Allegedly Created by Wh-in-situ (**no** islandhood)
Lelaki$_i$ [OP$_i$ yang [kamu tanya [t$_i$ beli apa]]] ialah abang saya.
man that you ask buy what is brother my.
'The man who you asked bought what is my brother.'

The sentences of (20) and (21) show that in Malay, while overt wh movement creates a wh island that can block relativization, wh-in-situ does not have that effect. This is in contrast to the situation in Chinese, in which wh-in-situ does create wh islands. Thus, we conclude that despite superficial similarities between wh-in-situ in Malay and wh-in-situ in Chinese and Japanese, wh-in-situ in Malay does not create wh islands.

6. Wh-in-situ and the ECP

The hypothesis that wh-in-situ in Malay does not involve movement, covert or overt, also predicts that wh-in-situ in Malay will be well-formed in environments in which movement would violate the ECP. Unfortunately, we have not been able to test these predictions. Two subcases of the ECP should, in principle, be testable: the "that trace filter" and the constraint against the occurrence of adjuncts inside adjunct clauses. These predictions, however, turn out to be untestable in Malay.

First, the predictions regarding the "that trace" filter are not testable because sentences similar to English "that trace" violations are well-formed in Malay even when overt movement takes place:

(22) Siapa$_i$ Bill harap [$_{CP}$ t'$_i$ yang [$_{IP}$ t$_i$ akan membeli baju
who Bill hope that will buy clothes
untuknya]]]?
for him
'Who does Bill hope will buy clothes for him ?'

Thus, the well-formedness of wh-in-situ in "that trace" environments is inconclusive.

Secondly, as shown earlier, with the exception of <u>di mana</u> 'where', adjuncts cannot occur in-situ, regardless of whether the environment in which the adjunct occurs is itself an adjunct or an argument. Thus, again, we cannot test the prediction made by the movement hypothesis that wh-in-situ obeys the ECP. It should be noted that 'where' adjuncts do not provide a useful test since even in Chinese, according to Huang (1982), 'where' behaves as though it were an argument, and can appear inside adjunct clauses. Thus, we are unable to test whether, as would be predicted by the non-movement hypothesis, wh-in-situ can appear in environments from which the ECP would prohibit movement.

It should be noted, however, that in the case of Ancash Quechua, another language in which wh-in-situ does not respect subjacency, wh-in-situ can appear in environments which are, for overt movement, blocked by the ECP.[14] This is illustrated in (23) for "<u>that</u> trace" effects:

(23) a. Ill-formed Extraction of Complement Subject in Ancash Quechua

*Pi-taq Fuan musyan [e tanta-ta ruranqan-ta]?
who-acc Juan knows bread-acc made-acc
'Who does Juan know that made bread?'

b. Well-Formed Wh-in-situ in Complement Subject Position

Fuan musyan [pi tanta-ta ruranqan-ta]?
Juan knows who bread-acc made-acc
'Juan knows that who made bread?'

Thus, in the absence of evidence to the contrary, we shall assume that wh-in-situ is exempt from the ECP in languages like Malay (and Ancash Quechua) in which it is exempt from subjacency.

To summarize, we have argued so far 1) that Huang, Nishigauchi and others are correct in claiming that in Chinese and Japanese wh-in-situ involves covert movement, 2) that in Malay, like Ancash Quechua, wh-in-situ is not subject to islandhood constraints and, hence, does not involve covert movement.

7. Partial Movement and Islandhood

We shall now turn from wh-in-situ to the partially moved wh construction, and shall show that the properties of this construction require both overt syntactic movement and covert movement. Consider (3) (repeated):

(3) Partially Moved Wh
Ali memberitahu kamu tadi [$_{CP}$ apa$_i$ yang [$_{IP}$ Fatimah baca t$_i$]]?
Ali told you just now what that Fatimah read ?
'Ali told you just now, what was Fatimah reading ?'[15]

As was noted by Saddy for Indonesian, not only is partial movement subject to subjacency with respect to the overt movement, but subjacency also applies when an island boundary intervenes between the surface position of the wh word and the specifier of CP representing the scope of the wh word:

(24) a. Wh-in-situ
Kamu sayang [perempuan [yang telah berjumpa siapa]]?
You love woman that already meet who?
'You love the woman who met who?'

b. Partially Moved Wh
*Kamu sayang [perempuan [dengan siapa yang telah jumpa]]?
You love woman with who that already meet ?
'You love the woman who met who?'
(25) a. Wh-in-situ
Kamu sayang [perempuan [yang telah makan apa]]?
You love woman that already eat what?
'You love the woman who ate what?'
b. Partially Moved Wh
*Kamu sayang [perempuan [apa yang telah makan]]?
You love woman what that already eat?
'You love the woman who ate what?'

In the examples of partially moved wh just cited, the wh word is within the relative clause. No overt movement over a barrier has occurred. Yet the sentence is ungrammatical. These sentences are in contrast with wh-in-situ, which can appear with impunity inside a relative clause. The ungrammaticality of partial movement within an island leads to the conclusion (reached by Saddy) that while wh-in-situ does not undergo covert movement, partially moved wh does. Thus, we conclude that partial overt movement requires further covert movement to the scopal specifier of CP, ruling out the possibility that partially moved wh is interpreted by a non-movement mechanism such as coindexing in the position to which it moves in the syntax.

8. Conclusions

We have argued that languages exhibit two distinct types of wh-in-situ, type one, typified by the distribution of wh-in-situ in Chinese and Japanese, in which wh-in-situ respects subjacency and the ECP and type two, typified by that found in Malay and Ancash Quechua, in which wh-in-situ does not respect movement constraints. This state of affairs can be captured by assuming that wh-in-situ of type one involves covert operator movement while wh-in-situ of type two requires interpretation in-situ. Malay is of special interest because, in addition to exhibiting direct interpretation of wh-in-situ, there is a partially moved construction which has the characteristics of covert operator movement in addition to overt movement to an intermediate spec of CP.

The typological differences between Malay and Chinese raise a number of questions which we cannot answer here. First, is it merely an arbitrary fact about the grammar of a language whether wh forms undergo overt movement, covert operator movement or are radically in-situ? Put differently, can the typological differences just described be derived from the interaction among independently motivated properties of the language in question and principles of universal grammar, or must they be stipulated? As observed by Cheng (1991), Aoun and Li (1993) and Watanabe (1992), inter alia, languages which do not exhibit overt movement seem to have wh-phrases which are not inherently question operators, but rather bound variables, and are also used as non-interrogative indefinite expressions. Hence, movement of a null operator rather than the wh-phrase may be the only way of satisfying the wh-criterion in these languages. It has also been noted (most recently by Aoun and Li 1993) that languages like Chinese have overt question markers in some higher functional projection (such as C). Malay and Ancash, in contrast, allow optional Q markers on the wh-word itself. The base position of the Q marker may then predict whether a language will have null operator movement or true in-situ interpretation. While space does not allow us to develop this idea here, we hope to do so in a later work.

Finally, is it universally the case that partially moved wh requires further covert operator movement to the scopal spec of CP rather than direct interpretation at the point where the wh-form occurs on the surface? We believe that this is the case and that this fact follows from limiting direct interpretation to argument positions, hence forcing further covert movement from Spec CP (an A'-position). Oversimplifying somewhat, this follows from the semantic interpretation mechanism suggested by Reinhart (1993), which seems to be limited to nominal arguments and excludes adjuncts. Again, we hope to address these issues in a later work.

Notes

---

* We would like to express our appreciation to a number of our friends and colleagues, who made comments on the ideas expressed in this paper: Lisa Cheng, Sandy Chung, David Gil, Jim Huang, Mashudi Kader, Jeff Lidz, K.P. Mohanan, Tara Mohanan, Tanya Reinhart, Christina Tortora, Chengchi Wang. Many of the ideas in this paper were inspired by the work of Doug Saddy on a closely related language, Bahasa Indonesia. Special thanks are also due to our Malay consultants in Singapore. The research reported on here was conducted while we were on visiting appointments at the National University of Singapore. We would like to express our gratitude to the Department of English at NUS for providing us with an excellent environment for our work.

1 This is one of several sort of arguments provided by Reinhart against LF movement of wh-in-situ. It should be noted that Reinhart does not discuss the operator movement hypothesis. It would not appear that, at least without significant modification, her arguments against LF movement would go through against operator movement.

2 An exception is Pesetsky (1987), who argues that certain instances of wh-in-situ are "D-linked" and hence are interpreted in-situ while others are not D-linked, and, hence, undergo movement. In addition, Aoun and Li (1993) treat certain instances of wh-in-situ as involving coindexation and others as involving covert movement, but they do not explicitly discuss the question of the universality of covert movement.

3 Our analysis of Malay is similar to and partially derived from that of Saddy (1991 and 1992)) on Indonesian. While Malay and Indonesian are closely related, the facts regarding wh extraction in these two languages are somewhat different. See discussion below.

4 In order to make our presentation less complicated, we omit traces in spec of CP except where their presence is relevant to the point being made.

5 It has been argued by Kader (1976) and later authors that wh questions employing yang are instances of clefts or focus movement, the structure of which may be similar to (i):

(i) [It is who_i [OP_i that Bill hopes [t_i will buy clothes for him]]]

As reported by Saddy and others, wh fronting in Bahasa Indonesia requires the presence of yang, and sentences like (1a) would be ill-formed if yang were not present. This, however, is not the case in the Malay of our informants, for whom wh fronting without yang is an option. Whatever may be the status of questions with yang, we assume that those without yang are not clefts but rather simply instances of syntactic wh movement. See footnote 17 for additional arguments against the assumption that all wh questions involve focus movement.

6 According to Saddy (1991), yang cannot be used as a complementizer in Bahasa Indonesia. Rather, bahawa is used. In the Malay of our informants, yang is normally used as a "that" complementizer. Bahawa has a decidedly literary flavor.

7 The fact that 'where' adjuncts are only of slightly reduced grammaticality in situ parallels the fact that in Chinese 'where' adjuncts behave like arguments in that they can occur inside adjunct clauses. See Huang (1982) for examples.

8 Sentences like these were claimed by Huang (1982) to be multiply ambiguous, including the reading in which 'who' and 'what' have matrix scope. This was taken to be an argument that wh in situ in Chinese is not subject to subjacency. But speakers find it very difficult to judge these sentences. Apparently, only the indirect question reading (in which the wh words only have scope over the embedded clause) is fully acceptable without special intonation etc. It would seem that it is the consensus among native speakers of Chinese that the wh words in (13) cannot have matrix scope. If the judgements reflected in (13) are correct, such examples show that subjacency does apply to wh-in-situ in Chinese.

9 Watanabe (1992) adapts Nishigauchi's "massive pied-piping" to the covert operator movement hypothesis. In Watanabe's treatment, a null operator is found in specifier of DP of the relative clause as a whole, outside the island. This null operator is coindexed with the wh form inside the island. The coindexing relationship does not involve movement, and, therefore, is not

subject to subjacency. Movement of the operator to matrix specifier of CP occurs entirely outside the island.

While this analysis provides a solution to Watanabe's problem of how to account for cases which he has dealt with as pied-piping, it must be noted that Watanabe's analysis makes use of coindexing rather than pied-piping, and thereby raises the question of whether there is a principled basis for determining when coindexing will be possible in a language that makes use of operator movement. If coindexing were completely unconstrained, it would be expected that Japanese would exhibit no islandhood restrictions rather than a subset of the restrictions found, for example, in English.

10 Overt movement of siapa 'who' rather than apa 'what' is also ill-formed.

11 This sentence also has an (irrelevant) interpretation in which the scope of both wh words is the lower clause. The same is true for the examples which follow.

12 Overt movement of di mana 'where'instead of apa 'what' is also ungrammatical.

13 These examples are consistent both with the application of subjacency at LF to elements undergoing LF wh movement and with the hypothesis that subjacency applies in the syntax and wh-in-situ in Chinese involves syntactic movement of a null operator.

14 Wh-in-situ in Ancash Quechua is discussed in Cole and Hermon (1994) inter alia.

15 It might be wondered whether partially moved wh is restricted to focus questions like (i):

(i) Apa yang kamu beli.
what that you buy
'What did you buy?'

which have been analyzed as clefts (Kader (1976), Saddy (1991), Alsagoff (1992) and Cheng (1991) inter alia. We believe that this is not the case. First, partially moved wh can occur without yang:

(ii) Ali sangka apa Fatimah baca?
Ali suspect what Fatimah read?
`What did Ali suspect Fatimah was reading?'

Secondly, while yang is used in focus questions with arguments like apa 'what' and siapa 'who', it cannot occur with adjuncts like kenapa 'why' and bagaimana 'how':

(iii)

a. Kenapa with yang

*Kenapa yang awak buat?
Why that you do?
`Why did you do it?'

b. Kenapa without yang

Kenapa awak buat?

Why you do?

`Why did you do it?'

But when a wh adjunct is partially moved, it can occur before yang:

(iv) Partially moved kenapa with yang

Kamu agak [kenapa yang Ali dipecat]?

You guess [why that Ali was fired]?

`Why do you guess Ali was fired?'

Thus, we conclude that the yang occurring in with partially moved wh is the complementizer yang. It should be noted that these examples provide the basis for an argument against extending to Malay the claim made in Cheng (1991) for Indonesian that all instances of wh movement are clefts.

References

Alsagoff, Lubna Shariffa. 1992. Topic in Malay: the other subject, PhD dissertation, Stanford University.

Aoun, Joseph and Audrey Li. 1993. "Wh-Elements in-situ: syntax or LF?", Linguistic Inquiry 24: 199-238.

Baker, C. Lee. 1968. Indirect questions in English, PhD dissertation, University of Illinois, Urbana.

Baker, C. Lee. 1970. "Note on the description of English questions: the role of an abstract question morpheme", Foundations Of Language 6: 197-219.

Cheng, Lisa. 1991. On the typology of wh-questions, PhD dissertation, MIT.

Cole, Peter and Gabriella Hermon. 1994. "Is there LF wh movement?", Linguistic Inquiry 25: 239-262.

Chomsky, Noam. 1992. "A minimalist program for linguistic theory", MIT Occasional Papers in Linguistics 1.

Hermon, Gabriella. 1985. Syntactic Modularity. Foris Press, Dordrecht.

Huang, C.T. James. 1982. Logical relations in Chinese and the theory of grammar, PhD dissertation, MIT.

Kader, Mashudi. 1976. The syntax of Malay interrogatives, PhD dissertation, Simon Fraser University.

Nishigauchi, Taisuke. 1990. Quantification in the theory of grammar. Kluwer Academic, Dordrecht.

Pesetsky, David. 1987. "Wh-in-situ: movement and unselective binding", in E. Reuland and A. ter Meulen (eds.) The representation of (in)definiteness, MIT Press.

Reinhart, Tanya. 1993. "Wh-in-situ in the framework of the minimalist program", presented at the Utrecht Linguistics Colloquium, October 1993.

Saddy, Douglas. 1991. "Wh scope mechanisms in Bahasa Indonesia", in L. Cheng and H. Demirdash (eds.) More Papers on Wh-Movement, MITWPL 15.

Saddy, Douglas. 1992. "A versus A-bar movement and WH fronting in Bahasa Indonesia", manuscript, University of Queensland, Australia.

Watanabe, Akira. 1992a. "Wh-in-situ, subjacency and chain formation", MIT Occasional Papers in Linguistics 2.

Watanabe, Akira. 1992b. "Subjacency and s-structure movement of wh-in-situ", Journal of East Asian Linguistics 1:3.

Pair List Answers With Floated Quantifiers

VIVIANE DÉPREZ
Rutgers University

1.Introduction

Much of the works on question/quantifier interactions focuses on the interpretation of questions with universally quantified NPs in argument positions and characteristically ignore universal quantifiers which occur in non-argumental positions such as the floating quantifiers in (1b) and the binominal quantifier in (1c).

(1)	a. **Chacun** de ces étudiants a lu deux livres. Each of the students read two books.	Argument Q
	b. Les étudiants ont **chacun** lu deux livres. The students have each read two books.	Floating Q
	c. Les étudiants ont lu deux livres **chacun**. The students have read two books each.	Binominal Q

The goal of this paper is to present an analysis of the interaction of questions with universal terms in non-argument positions and to compare these interactions with that of their argument counterpart. Due to space constraints, this paper concerns floated quantifiers (FQs) only[1]. French is used for the comparison,

[1] Binominal quantifiers are discussed in Deprez (1993).

primarily because it presents a construction which helps strengthen our point, but the conclusions reached should generalize (with relevant variants) to other languages with comparable quantification phenomena.

After showing that questions with non-argumental quantifiers vary significantly in their ability to license pair-list answers standardly taken to signify the wide scope of a universal quantifier over a question term, I argue that the observed variation is determined by two distinct factors. These are, on the one hand, the plural/singular status of the question term and on the other hand the syntactic position of the non-argumental quantifier. The proposed analysis makes use of both factors in demonstrating that the observed variation with list answers cannot be taken to stem from scope interactions between the question term and the FQ. I propose instead that they result from the fact that the semantic contribution of an FQ to the sentence denotation varies with its syntactic position and interacts with questions accordingly. The central claim is that FQs in sentential adverb positions are interpreted as non-scopal weak distributors enforcing a pragmatic weak distributivity over groups or plural variables, while FQs in VP adverbial positions are interpreted as low scope quantifiers binding singular variables. This proposal accounts for 1) the observed variation with list answers in argument questions and 2) inner island effects created by the presence of FQs in adjunct questions.

2. The problem

It is well known that questions with universal quantifiers in subject position such as (2a) are ambiguous in that they admit at least two kinds of answers, an individual answer as in (3a) and a pair-list answer as in (3b). In constrast, questions with universal quantifiers in object positions as in (2b) are unambiguous, admiting only the individual answer.

(2) a. Who does everyone like? QP>WH & WH>QP
b. Who likes everyone? *QP>WH & WH>QP

(3) a. Individual answer: John
b. Pair-list answer: Mary likes John and Julie likes Bill.

(4) a. $\forall$x (person x) which (person y) x likes y QP>WH
b. which (person x) $\forall$y (person y) x like y WH>QP

This distinction is often assumed to reflect a distinction in scope, with the pair-list answer signifying the wide scope of the universal term over the WH, as in (4a), and the individual answer the low scope of the universal term as in (4b). Taking first pair-list answers as a diagnostic, consider questions with FQs. A first observation is that FQs appear to contrast systematically with argument quantifiers (AQ) in failing to license pair-list answers. Consider for instance (5). As the felicity of the continuation sentence "please make a list" indicates, (5a) with an AQ can have the reading in (5'a) where the quantifier has wide scope allowing the pairing of individual children with distinct books. But the same continuation sentence is unfelicitous with the FQ in (5b). (5b) can only be understood as asking about a single book which each of the children have read and no pairing of individual children with distinct books is possible.

(5) a. Dites-moi quel livre **chacun** de ces enfants a lu. Faites-en une liste.
Tell me which book each of the children read. Please make a list of them.
b. Dites-moi quel livre ces enfants ont **chacun** lu. #Faites-en une liste

(5') a. Tell me for ∀x (child x) which y (book y) x read y
Tell me for each child which book he has read.
b. Tell me which y (book y) ∀x (child x) x read y
Tell me which book is such that each child has read it.

The same constrast can be observed in (6) where the list answer is felicitous only as an answer to (6a) with the AQ and not to (6b) with the FQ. Here again (6b) is understood to be a question about a single patient which has been examined by each of the nurse as spelled out in (6'b):

(6) a. Dites moi quel malade **chacune** de ces infirmières a examiné.
Marie a examiné Jean et Julie, Pierre.
Tell me which patient each of these nurses has examined.
b. Dites moi quel malade ces infirmières ont **chacune** examiné.
#Marie a examiné Jean et Julie, Pierre.
Tell me which patient these nurses have each examined.

(6') a. Tell me ∀x (nurse x) which y (patient y) x has examined y
b. Tell me which y (patient y) ∀x (nurse x) x has examined y

(5) and (6) thus suggest that, in contrast to their argumental counterpart, FQs generally have low scope with respect to question terms. This concurs with Williams'(1982) observation that FQs have a more restricted scope than their argument counterpart even in non-question contexts such as the one in (7). In (7a), the AQ *each of the professors*, can have wide scope over the matrix subject as represented in (7'a). But this possibility is excluded with the FQ, in (7b), which must have the reading represented in (7'b). Similarly for the French examples in (8), the AQ can have wide scope but the FQ cannot:

(7) a. Some student believes each of the professors to be incompetent.
b. Some student believes the professors to each be incompetent in a way.

(7') a. ∀x (professor x) ∃y (student y) y believes x to be incompetent
b. ∃y (student y) ∀x (professor x) y believes x to be incompetent in some way

(8) a. Quelqun aurait vu **chacun** des garcons en train d'embrasser une fille.
b. Quelqun aurait vu ces garcons en train de **chacun** embrasser une fille.
Someone would have seen (each of) these boys each kissing a girl.

(8') a. ∀x (garcon x) ∃y (personne y) y a vu x embrasser une fille
b. ∃y (personne y) ∀x (garcon x) y a vu x embrasser une fille

Since the low scope of FQs appears to be independent of question contexts, it is quite doubtful that the absence of pair-list answers in (5 and 6b) above could be attributed to the ECP or the Path Containment Condition in line with May's (1985) account for (2b). Questions with FQs appear, in any event, to be more parrallel to those not subject to the ECP as (2a) since they involve a subject related quantifier and wh-movement from a properly governed object position and can thus satisfy the PCC. This suggests that the PCC/ECP cannot be responsible for blocking the wide scope construal of the FQ and some other principle must be involved. It is apparent that, at S-structure, the FQs c-commands neither the question terms in (5) and (6) nor the matrix subject in (7) and (8). Thus, an obvious way to capture their obligatory low scope is to ensure that, at LF, they remain in the same positions[2]. If so, the distinction observed between AQs and FQs can now derive from the fact that the former can undergo QR (or its equivalent) but the latter cannot as descriptively stated in (9).

(9) Floated quantifiers cannot undergo QR.

If FQs cannot move at LF, they will have to be interpreted in their S-structure position. If so, May's Scope Principle will predict that an FQ adjoined to or located in the specifier of VP can take scope over the subject, but not further up. This is sufficient to derive the correct reading of (5b) and (6b) with the LF structure (10). In (10), the VP adjoined *chacun* is unable to form a Σ-sequence with the question term and consequently, it cannot interact with it in scope.

---

[2] The assumption in (9) contrasts with Heim, Lasnik and May's (1992) proposal that the quantificational part of *each other* can undergo LF movement. If correct, the conclusion reached in this paper instead supports Williams' (1992) proposal that the distributivity present in plurals and in reciprocals do not involve scope.

(10) LF: $[_{CP}$ WH$_i$ $[_{IP}$ NP...$[_{VP}$ chacun $[_{VP}$ ..t$_i$.]]]]

Similarly, in the non-question context of (7) and (8), the VP adjoined FQs correctly fail to have scope over the matrix subject. Thus (9) appears to account elegantly for the facts reviewed so far. Incidentally, it should be clear that (9) does not need to be independently stipulated. There are indeed a number of ways to derive it from more general principles depending in part on the syntactic structure chosen for FQs. If FQs are adverbials in adjoined/A'Spec positions, (9) can derive from general Economy considerations ('Greed' in Chomsky 1993) which will prevent LF movement of elements already in A' or operator position by Spell-Out. Such a constraint is independently needed to ensure, for instance, that VP adverbs cannot acquire sentential scope through LF movement or that overtly moved WH elements cannot not undergo further LF movement out of their Spell Out Spec CP positions. If, on the other hand, FQs are "stranded quantifiers" containing the trace of a moved NP as in (11a) (Sportiche 1988), (9) could derive from the Proper Binding Condition, since further LF raising as in (11b) will lead to a structure where the NP trace is not bound by its antecedent:

(11) a. Spell-Out $[_{CP}$ WH $[_{IP}$ NP$_i$... [chacun t$_i$]...]]
b. LF: *$[_{CP}$ WH $[_{IP}$ [chacun t$_i$] $[_{IP}$ NP$_i$... t$_i$..]]]

Further evidence, however, shows that this simple analysis is too strong. A careful look at the data reveals, indeed, that there are questions with floated quantifiers which do admit pair list answers. In questions such as (12), for instance, pair-list answers have been judged to be possible and even fairly natural both in French and English:

(12) a. Qui ont-elles **chacune** aimé? Marie a aimé Jean, et Sue Paul.
Whom do they each like? Mary likes John and Sue, Paul.
b. Je me demande ce que ces enfants ont **chacun** recu pour Noel?
Julie a recu un train électrique et Jean un ours en peluche.
I wonder what these children have each received for Christmas?
Julie received an electric train and John a teddy bear.
c. Dites-moi quels hommes ces journalistes auraient **chacune** du interviewer. Marie aurait du interviewer Clinton et Sue le pape.
Tell me which man these journalists should each have interviewed.
Mary should have interviewed Clinton and Sue the Pope.

The availability of pair-lists answers in (12) is disturbing as it suggests that, in contrast to our earlier conclusion, FQs can sometimes take wide scope over question terms. Moreover, since here, as above, FQs do not overtly c-command the question term, this means that within a May-style approach to pair list answers, QR of FQs must be possible, in full contradiction with (9). We are now faced with a dilemna and must assume either that QR freely applies to all universal terms, including FQs --- in which case the absence of wide scope in (5) to (8) will have to result from some constraint on QR ---, or maintain (9),in which case the pair-list answers of (12) will have to derive from something other than scope. In what follows, evidence will be presented that this second approach is preferable. First, it seems clear that since FQs have generally narrow scope in non-question context, it is (12), not (5) and (6), which is exceptional. Second, since, as discussed above, the low scope of FQs in (5) and (6) cannot be subsumed under known constraints such as the ECP or the PCC, an independent constraint on QR would be needed. Third, and perhaps most importantly, Krifka (1992) and Srivastav (1992) have argued that pair-list answers must independently be recognized to have two distinct sources, one resulting from quantificational interactions with questions and another resulting from pragmatic interpretations of plurals. As I will show, pair-list answers found with FQs are clearly distinct from the former and show many properties of the latter. If so, there is no need to invoke QR for (12), and (9) can be fully maintained.

3. Two types of list answers

It has often been noted, that pair-list answers are not limited to questions with quantificational subjects but are also possible in questions with plural subjects. Thus (13a) can have an individual plural answer (13b) and a list answer (13c):

(13) a.What have these boys rented?
Plural individual answer
b.The Paper and The Piano.
List answer
c.(In fact) John rented The Paper and Bill The Piano.

Krifka (1992) and Srivastav (1992) have argued that pair-list answers with plurals subjects differ fundamentally from the ones resulting from WH interactions with universal quantifiers. They do not involve relative scope, but are the spell out of a relation understood but left unspecified in the plural answer. As such, list answers with plurals subjects are not distinct from plural answers themselves. They are only a disambiguating strategy which serves to clarify an understood relation among the parts of two plural groups. Thus (13c) is simply a more informative variant of the plural answer (13b) which specifies the relation that the group of boys bears to the group of rented movies, not a distinct answer. With (13b), indeed, we don't know whether the two movies were rented together or separately by the boys or whether one boy rented two movies and the other only one and so on. In principle, these are all possible readings of the plural answer and the list simply makes clear which one was in fact the presupposed one. Confirming that plural answers and their list counterparts are in some sense "the same" is the fact that they have the same entailments. In contrast, the list answer and plural answer of questions with quantificational subjects such as (14) have clearly distinct entailments:

(14) a. What has each boy rented?
Plural individual answer
b.The Paper and The Piano.
= (John has rented both movies and Bill has rented both movies)
List answer
c.(*In fact) John rented The Paper and Bill The Piano.

(14b) entails that each boy has rented both movies. That is, there is a pairing of each boy to all rented movies, i.e. the low scope reading. (14c), on the other hand, entails that each boy has rented a single distinct movie. That is, there is a pairing of individual boys to individual movies. Evidently, the list answer here is not an explanation of the plural answer. It involves a distinct computation of the pairing of boys and movies. Further differences between the two types of list-answers are shown in (15) and (16). Since list-answers with plural subjects spell out relations between two plural groups, they manifest no subject object assymetry as shown in (15).

(15) Who rented these movies?
John rented The Paper and Bill The Piano.

Moreover, they are only possible in questions where both the question term and the subject are plural. If the question is semantically singular as in (16a), the list answer is impossible:

(16) a.Which movie have the boys rented?
Plural individual answer:
The Paper
List answer:
*John has rented The Paper and Bill The Piano.
b.Which movie has each boy rented?
John has rented The Paper and Bill The Piano.

In contrast, as shown in (16b), in questions with quantificational subjects the list answer remains possible even when the question is singular.

The distinctions between the two types of list answers can be seen as a consequence of the difference in the force of the distributivity inherent to plural predication vs quantificational interaction. As illustrated in (17), plural distributivity differs significantly from quantificational distributivity (Williams 1991):

(17) a. The boys fought each other. Weak distributivity
b. Each of the boys fought the other. Strong distributivity

Both (17a-b) are distributive. But while (17a) can be true in a situation in which two of the boys are fighting a third one, (17b) cannot be. That is, in (17a) the fighting can be understood as global, but in (17b) it must involve each of the boys against each of the other boys. Plural distributivity which does not enforce a fully uniform mapping was dubbed weak-distributivity by Williams. Quantificational distributivity, which must verify the truth of a relation on one individual at a time is called strong distributivity. To distinguish the two, Williams (1991) argued that in (17a) *each* is a non-scopal weak distributor which ranges over plural variables, that is groups with parts, while in (17b), *each* is a scope taking strong distributive quantifier which binds singular atomic variables and enforces the calculation of the distributive relation one boy at a time.

The difference between to two kinds of list answers noted above can be thought of as parallel: list answers with plural subjects are non-quantificational, spelling out an understood weak distributive relation between groups. List-answers with quantificational subjects, on the other hand, give in extension the output of a function which pairs individuals one at a time.

Returning to questions with FQs, we now have the tools to determine whether they involve a weakly distributive plural interaction or a quantificational interaction. In this regard, questions with FQs are particularly interesting since they feature both a plural subject and a distributive quantifier. What follows will show that FQs in fact interact with questions in two different ways. On one hand, they can function as weak distributors over plural variables. In this case, they lead pair-list readings which are identical to the one generated by the interaction of plurals with question terms. On the other hand, they can function as true quantifiers. In this case, they have necessary low scope and are incompatible with a list reading of any sort.

Turning to the first point, consider again the contrast between (5) and (6) where list answers are impossible and (12) where list answers are possible. Note that the central difference between the former and the latter resides in the type of question terms used. In (12), on one hand, we find plural question terms and question terms such as *who* and *what* which although morphologically singular are semantically unmarked for plurality. In (5) and (6), on the other hand, we find only singular *which* phrases which are known to be both morphologically and semantically singular and to presupose uniqueness. The generalization is now clear. List readings are possible with semantically plural question terms and impossible with singular ones. That the plurality of the question term is an essential factor in the availability of the list answer is confirmed by the fact that the mere replacement of the question term in (5b) and (6b) by their plural counterparts is sufficient to make a list answer possible. This is shown in (18):

(18) a. Je veux savoir quels livres ces enfants ont **chacun** lu. Faites en une liste par enfant.
I want to know which books these children have each read. Make a list per child.

b. Dites moi quels malades ces infirmières ont **chacune** examiné. Marie a examiné Jean et Paul et Sue, Pierre.
Tell which patients these nurses have each examined. Marie has examined John, and Paul and Sue, Peter.

Recall that, as discussed above, the plural vs. singular nature of the question term matters only for list answers with plurals, not for the quantificational one. Thus (18) and the contrast between (12) and (5) and (6) offer solid evidence that the list answers found in questions with floated quantifiers do not result from the wide scope quantification but rather from the interaction of the plural subject with the question term. This is further supported by the fact, shown in (19), that list answers to questions with floated quantifiers can have the same entailment as their plural answer. The former functions as an explication of the latter as shown by the use of the expression *plus précisement* 'more precisely':

(19) Dites moi quels élèves elles ont **chacune** voulu aider financièrement Jean, Paul et Pierre. Plus précisément, Marie a voulu aider Jean et Paul et Sue, Pierre.
Tell me which students they each wanted to help financially. John, Paul and Peter. More precisely, Mary wanted to help John, and Paul and Sue, Peter.

As a result, we can now conclude that it is not necessary to posit any means of scoping out the FQ to obtain the list-reading in (12). In such cases, I propose that FQs are construed as a non-scopal weak distributors which ensure, perhaps only pragmatically, the distributive reading of a plural subject. As such, the FQs are largely equivalent in meaning to distributive adverbs such as *individually, separately or respectively* which, as shown in (20), are also compatible with plural cooperative list answers:

(20) Dites-moi quels élèves Marie et Sue ont individuellement/ séparément/ respectivement/ voulu aider financièrement. Marie a voulu aider Jean et Paul et Sue, Pierre.
Tell me which student Mary and Sue individually/ separatly/ respectively wanted to help financially. Mary wanted to help John, and Paul and Sue, Peter.

Like FQs, these adverbs do not interact in scope with question terms but only ensure the distributive reading of the plural subject. Summing up, I have provided evidence that list answers which arise in questions with FQs do not stem from the wide scope of the FQ over the question term but rather from the fact that the FQ is interpreted as a non-scopal weak distributor which serves to disambiguate the reading of a plural predication. Consequently, the idea that FQs do not undergo QR can be maintained.

4. The syntactic position of floated quantifiers

The non-scopal weak distributor reading is not the only interpretation that FQs can have in questions. The availability of list-answers, indeed, is not solely constrained by the plurality of the question term but also by the syntactic position in which FQs occur. As (21) shows, FQs in French can occupy a variety of syntactic positions along a string of auxiliaries, modals and VPs.

(21) a. Les infirmières examineront $[_{VP}$ **chacune** deux malades].
The nurses will each examine two patients.
b. Elles ont $[_{VP/AGRP}$(**chacune**) $[_{VP}$ examiné (**chacune**) deux malades]].
They have (each) examined (each) two patients.
c. Elles auraient (**chacune**) du $[_{VP}$ (**chacune**) examiner (**chacune**) deux malades].
They should (each) have (each) examined (each) two patients.
d. Elles voudraient (**chacune**) pouvoir $[_{VP}$ (**chacune**) examiner (**chacune**) deux malades].
They wanted (each) to be able to (each) examine (each) two patients.

Comparing (21) with (22) and (23) which illustrate the respective positions in which VP adverbs and sentential adverbs can occur, reveals that FQs can appear in both positions.

(22) <u>VP adverb positions:</u>
a. Les infirmières examineront $[_{VP}$ **soigneusement** deux malades].
The nurses will examine carefully two patients.

(22) b. Elles ont [$_{VP/AGRP}$ **OK** examiné [$_{VP}$ **OK** deux malades]].
They have OK examined OK two patients.
c. Elles auraient * du [$_{VP}$ **OK** examiner **OK** deux malades].
They should have examined two patients.
d. Elles voudraient * pouvoir [$_{VP}$ **OK** examiner **OK** deux malades.
They would like to be able to examine two patients.

(23) <u>IP adverb positions:</u>
a. Elles examineront **probablement** [$_{VP}$ deux malades] demain.
They will probably examine two patients tomorrow.
b. Elles ont **OK** [$_{VP}$ examiné * deux malades] hier.
They have examined two patients yesterday.
c. Elles auraient **OK** [$_{VP}$ du * examiner * deux malades] hier.
They should have examined two patients yesterday.
d. Elles voudraient **OK** [$_{VP}$ pouvoir * examiner * deux malades] demain.
They wanted to be able to examine two patients tomorrow.

In other words, like VP adverbs, FQs can adjoin to projections of VP (or AGROP) and like sentential adverbs, they can adjoin to projections of IP (or TP/AGRSP). What is interesting is that these two attachment sites have different effects in questions with FQs. As (24) shows, when FQs occur in clear sentential adverb positions, as before a modal, the list answer is possible.

(24) a. Dis-moi quels malades ces infirmières ont **chacune** [$_{VP}$ du examiner] hier. Marie a du examiner Jean et Paul et Sue, Pierre.
Tell me for each nurse, which patients she had to examine yesterday. Mary had to examiner Jean & Paul and Sue, Pierre.

b. Dites-moi lequels elles voudraient **chacune** [$_{VP}$ pouvoir examiner] demain. Marie voudrait pouvoir examiner Jean et Paul, et Sue Pierre.
Tell me for each nurse which patients she would like to be able to examine tomorrow. Mary wanted to be able to examine Jean, and Paul and Sue, Pierre.

But when they occur in clear VP adverb positions, as after an untensed verbal form in (25) or after a modal in (26), the list reading is not possible even with a plural question term. (25a), in contrast to (24), is a question about patients who have been examined by each nurse. There is no pairing of individual nurses with individual patients but rather of the group of all patients to each nurse. This reading, which is paraphrased after the = sign in (25), clearly corresponds to the low scope of the quantifier with respect to the question term. In (25), the plural answer and the list answer have clearly different entailments. The plural answer is here understood as giving the extension of the set of patients examined by each nurse, while the list answer, on the other hand, implies a pairing of individual nurses with individual patients, which is impossible here.

(25) a. Dis-moi quels malades elles ont [$_{VP}$ du examiner **chacune**] hier.
Tell me which patients are such that each nurse had to examine them yesterday.
<u>Plural answer:</u>
Jean, Paul et Pierre = Mary had to examine J P & P and Sue did too.
<u>List answer:</u>
*Marie a du examiner Jean et Paul et Sue, Pierre.
Mary had to examine Jean, and Paul and Sue, Pierre.

b. Dis-moi lesquels elles voudraient [$_{VP}$ pouvoir examiner **chacune**] demain.
Tell me which ones are such that each nurse would like to be able to examine them tomorrow.
<u>Plural answer:</u>
Jean, Paul et Pierre = Mary would like to be able to examine J, P&P and Sue would too.
<u>List answer:</u>
*Marie voudrait pouvoir examiner Jean et Paul et Sue, Pierre.
Mary wanted to be able to examine Jean and Paul and Sue, Pierre.

(26) a. Dis-moi quels malades elles ont [$_{VP}$ du **chacune** examiner] hier.
Tell me which patients are such that each nurse had to examine them.
<u>List answer:</u>
*Marie a du examiner Jean et Paul et Sue, Pierre.
Mary had to examine Jean and Paul and Sue, Pierre.
b. Dis-moi lesquels elles voudraient [^{VP} pouvoir chacune examiner] demain.
Tell me which patients are such that they each would like to be able to each examine him tomorrow.

The contrast between (24) and (25)/(26), suggests that FQs can interact with questions in two distinct ways. They are interpreted either as weak distributors which range over plural variables or as distributive quantifiers with low scope. These two distinct possibilities correlate with the syntactic position of the quantifier. Only FQs which occur in sentential adverbial positions can have the weak distributor reading. FQs which occur in VP adjoined positions are low scope quantifiers. As sentential adverbs, FQs have an interpretation largely equivalent to that of distributive adverbs. In this regard, note that as shown in (27), these distributive adverbs are typically sentence adverbs which cannot occur in VP adverb positions.

(27) Sentential adverb positions:
a. Elles examineront **respectivement/individuellement** deux malades.
They will respectively/ individually examine two patients tomorrow.
b. Elles ont OK examiné * deux malades hier.
They have examined two patients yesterday.
c. Elles ont OK du * examiner * deux malades hier.
They should have examined two patients yesterday.
d. Elles voudraient OK pouvoir * examiner * deux malades demain.
They wanted to be able to examine two patients tomorrow.

This suggests that the distinction we have seen between the two interpretations of FQs is more generally symptomatic of the different contribution that sentential adverbs and VP adverbs make to the computation of a sentence denotation. The contribution of the former to the sentence meaning seems in general more pragmatically relevant, as if sentential adverbs did not fully enter the compositional calculus of the denotation of a proposition. This is what in our view is here reflected in the behavior of FQs. As weak distributors in sentential adverb positions, FQs only pragmatically ensure the distributive reading of a plural predication. As full VP quantifiers, they have low scope since they do not undergo QR and enter in the compositional computation of a distributive relation.

5. Floated quantifiers and inner island effects

Interesting support for the conclusions reached above on the basis of an analysis of list answers with FQs comes from considering the effects of FQs in non-argument questions. As is known, only non-argument questions show a sensitivity to inner islands. Typical cases of such effects are illustrated by the French split *combien* extraction in (28a) which is blocked when moving over an intervening quantificational adverb such as *beaucoup* 'many' in (28b):

(28) a. Combien as-tu lu de livres?
How many books did you read?
b. *Combien as-tu **beaucoup** lu de livres?
How many books did you read a lot of?

Szabolcsi and Zwartz (1993) [3] have recently argued that weak island effects in general and inner island effects in particular are scope effects. In brief, weak island

[3] See also De Swart (1992), E.Kiss (1993) and Dobrovnie-Sorin (1992).

effects arise whenever question terms are forced to take wide scope over intervening scope bearing elements. Wide scope question terms must receive a `specific' or `referential' interpretation, a possibility open only to question terms ranging over individuals, typically argument NPs, and not to question terms ranging over more complex entities such as manners, reasons and amounts. Hence, the argument/adjunct assymetry. Recall that we have proposed above that FQs can be interpreted either as low scope quantifiers or as non-scopal weak distributors depending on their syntactic positions. If weak island effects are scope effects, this proposal makes the interesting prediction that low scope FQs should create inner island effects, since they are scope bearing elements over which wh-adjunct must take scope, while FQs interpreted as weak distributors should not, since they are not scope bearing elements. The contrast between (29) and (30) shows this prediction to be fully verified. Typically, VP attached FQs block the split extraction of *combien* while IP attached FQs do not.

(29) VP floated quantifiers --> inner island effects

a.Combien de malades ont-elles du [$_{VP}$ (**chacune**) examiner (**chacune**)] hier?

a'*Combien ont-elles du [$_{VP}$ (**chacune**) examiner (**chacune**) de malades hier?

(lit.) How many had they each to examine of patients yesterday?

b.Dis-moi combien de malades elles voudraient pouvoir [$_{VP}$ (**chacune**) examiner (**chacune**)] demain.

b'*Dis-moi combien elles voudraient pouvoir [$_{VP}$ (**chacune**) examiner (**chacune**) de malades] demain.

(lit.) Tell me how many they wanted to be able to each examine of patients tomorrow.

c.(?)Dis-moi combien de malades elles ont [$_{VP}$ examiné (**chacune**)] hier.

c'*Dis-moi combien elles ont [VP examiné (**chacune**) de malades] hier.

(lit.) Tell me how many they have examined each of patients yesterday.

(30) IP floated quantifiers --> no inner island effects

a.(?)Dis-moi combien elles ont (**chacune**) du [$_{VP}$ examiner de malades] hier. (vs 33a')

(lit.) Tell me how many they have each had to examine of patients.

b.(?)Dis-moi combien elles ont (**chacune**) [$_{VP}$ examiné de malades] hier

(lit.) Tell me how many they have each examined of patients.

As shown in (31), furthermore, distributive sentential adverbs like *respectively* behave here again exactly like IP attached FQs in not blocking *combien* extractions.

(31) Distributive sentential adverbs --> no inner island effects

a. Dis-moi combien Marie et Sue ont **respectivement** du [$_{VP}$ examiner de malades] hier.

Tell me how many patients Marie and Sue have respectively had to examine yesterday.

b. Dis-moi combien Marie et Sue ont **respectivement** [$_{VP}$ examiné de malades] hier.

Tell me how many patients Marie and Sue have respectively examined.

The effects of FQs and distributive sentential adverbs in non-argument questions thus provide strong confirmation both for the analysis of FQs proposed here and for the scope approach to weak islands.

To conclude, this paper has argued that FQs in questions behave in two differents ways. First, in sentential adverb positions, FQs act as non-scopal weak distributors which pragmatically ensure the distributive reading of a plural predication. As such, they permit plural cooperative list answers and do not induce island effects. Second, in VP adverb positions, FQs act as low scope distibutive quantifiers and as such are incompatible with list answers and induce island effects. We have taken this dual behavior to reveal a split in the way different types of adverbs contribute to the denotation of a sentence. For sentiential adverbs the contribution is more pragmatic, for VP adverbs it is compositionally semantic. The behavior of distributive sentential adverbs such as *respectively* in questions provides support for this view.

References

Chomsky, Noam. 1993. A minimalist program for linguistic theory. Kenneth Hale and Samuel Jay Keyser (eds) *The view from building 20: Essays in linguistics in honor of Sylvian Bromberger*. Cambridge: MIT Press.

Déprez, Viviane. 1993. On the Opacity of floated *chacun*, ms, Rutgers.

Déprez, Viviane. 1993. The weak island effect of floating quantifiers, E. Benedicto & J.A Runner (eds) *Functional Projections*, UMOP 17, UMass Amherst.

Dobrovnie-Sorin, Carmen. 1992. What does QR raise? ms, Paris:CNRS

Enc, Murvet. 1991. The Semantics of Specificity, *Linguistic Inquiry* **22**, 1-25.

Kiss, Katalin E. 1993. Wh-movement and specificity, NLLT.

Heim, Irene, Howard Lasnik and **Robert May**. 1991. On "Reciprocal Scope", *Linguistic Inquiry*, **22**:1, 173-192.

Krifka, Manfred. 1992. Definite NPs aren't Quantifiers, *Linguistic Inquiry* **23**:1, 156-163.

May, Robert. 1985. *Logical Form:Its Structure and Derivation*, Cambrige, MIT Press.

Sportiche, Dominique. 1988. A theory of floating quantifiers and its corollaries for constituent structure, *Linguistic Inquiry* 19: 425-449.

de Swart, Henriette. 1992. Intervention effects, Monotonicity and Scope, in C.Barker & D. Dowty (eds), *SALT II: Proceedings of the Second Conference on Semantics and Linguistic Theory*, Ohio State University Working papers in Linguistics 40.

Srivastav, Veneeta. 1992. Two Types of Universal Terms in Questions, Proceedings of NELS 22, GLSA, UMass, Amherst.

Szabolcsi, Anna and Frans Zwarts, 1993. Weak Island and Algebraic Semantics for scope taking, *Natural Language Semantics* **1**, 235-284.

Szabolcsi, Anna. 1992. Weak Islands, Individuals, and Scope, in C. Barker D. Dowty (eds), *SALT II: Proceedings of the 2nd Conference on Semantics and Linguistic Theory*, O.S.U Working papers in Linguistics 40.

Williams, Edwin. 1982. The NP cycle, *Linguistic Inquiry*, **13**:2, 277-295.

Williams, Edwin. 1991. Reciprocal scope, *Linguistic Inquiry*, **22**:1, 159-173.

Are You Right? On Pronoun-Postposing and Other Problems of Irish Word-Order[1]

NIGEL DUFFIELD
McGill University

Consider the Irish sentence in (1):

1. Chonaic Máire an fear sa tsráid i nDoire inné
saw Mary the man in-the street in Derry yesterday
Mary saw the man in the street in Derry yesterday

Recent theoretical proposals, including those of Chomsky (1992) and Kayne (1993), have interesting implications for standard treatments of the VSOX word-order in finite clauses illustrated by this example, whether as Verb-movement to C^o (Deprez & Hale 1986), or as V^o-movement to a projection of Infl, with VP-internal subjects in situ (McCloskey 1992 i.a.). This recent work has re-opened the debate not just regarding the position of the finite verb in these structures, but also with respect to the position of both subjects and objects. Assuming the now standard 'split-Infl' approach to functional projections, the candidates in (2) present themselves as plausible analyses of finite VSO word order (with $I^{1,2,3,}$ etc indicating possible sub-projections of Infl — Agr^s, T^o, Agr^o, Neg^o, etc.):

2. a. subject in [Spec, V^{max}], object in [NP, VP], verb in I^o
   b. subject in [Spec, IP^1], object in [NP, VP], verb in C^o
   c. subject in [Spec, IP^1], object in [Spec, IP^2], verb in C^o
   d. subject in [Spec, IP^1], object in [Spec, IP^2], verb in I^o

This does not, of course, exhaust the theoretical options available: in particular, given the possibility of functional categories internal to the VPmax (Travis 1991, forthcoming, Noonan 1994), one could postulate object-movement without requiring subject-movement (a version of (2a)); nevertheless, these seem to cover the most commonly-accepted analyses.

Proponents of some version of (2a), including Sproat (1985), Duffield (1990), Dooley Collberg (1990), Guilfoyle (1990), McCloskey (1992), have advanced distributional arguments to show that the verb cannot have raised to the highest functional projection in finite clauses, i.e. as high as C°. Such evidence includes the absence of any complementary distribution between complementizer elements and the finite verb; in Modern Irish, there are no root/non-root asymmetries of the type which both characterize and motivate verb-raising to C° analyses (e.g. in the Germanic languages):

3. a. Nach *gc*uireann sé ar a suaimhneas iad?
NEG-Q put he on their ease them
Doesn't he put them at their ease?

b. Deir sí [nach *gc*uireann sé ar a suaimhneas iad]
says she NEG-COMP put he on their ease them
She says that he doesn't put them at their ease.

Further evidence for (2a) includes: the possibility of preverbal adverbial placement, exemplified in (4), which should be ruled out by universal constraints if this involved adjunction to CP (cf. (4b)) but which follows straightforwardly if these examples are instances of adjunction to IP; and the option of having pre-verbal negative polarity phrases in narrative-fronting contexts (McCloskey 1992), shown in (5), which McCloskey (1992) accounts for in terms of a C°-I° (Comp-lowering) analysis:

4. a. Deiridís [an chéad Nollaig eile [go dtiocfadh sé aníos]] (30)
they-used-to-say the first Xmas other comp-would-come-he up
They used to say that next christmas he would come up

b. *The man last Xmas that Peter saw

5. a. [Aon cheo difir [ní dhein sé t]] (*cf.* 100)
any tiny-thing difference NEG make it t
It doesn't make the tiniest bit of difference

Finally, there are the facts of preverbal initial consonant mutation (ICM), discussed extensively in Duffield (1991, forthcoming), and exemplified in (7); facts which I have argued previously can be given a principled syntactic account in terms of the MUTATION HYPOTHESIS in (6). This hypothesis requires that the verb does not generally raise as high as C°:

6. Mutation Hypothesis
   a. Lexicalized C° triggers eclipsis (*urú*/voicing/nasalization)
   b. Lexicalized T° triggers lenition (*séimhiú*/spirantization)

7. a. Deir sé [$_{CP}$ go*bp*ógann sí é]
   says he COMP kiss she him
   he says that she kisses him

   b. [$_{TP}$ Ní-or *ph*óg sí é]
   NEG-PAST kiss she him
   She didn't kiss him

By contrast, proponents of a movement-to-Comp analysis of VSOX word-order, as in (2b) and (2c), have focused on other data. Here, two types of distributional evidence have been considered particularly relevant. First, there is the well-attested impossibility of placing any constituent, including sentential and temporal adverbials, between the complementizer (or complementizer-like elements) and the finite verb, exemplified in (8):

8. a. *go ar ndóighe/inné bfhaca sí/Máire an fear
   COMP of course/yesterday see-PAST she/Mary the man
   ..that Mary ofcourse/yesterday saw the man.

   b. *..gu-r ar ndóighe/inné chuir sí/Máire an cheist air
   C-PAST of course/yesterday put she/Mary the question to-him
   that she/M. of course/yesterday asked him the question

Related to this is the observation that, phonologically at least, the complementizer, verb-stem and inflectional elements jointly form a tightly-bound complex; with inflectional elements, such as Tense, Aspect and Agreement patterning more closely with either the verb-stem or the complementizer head, depending on the particular verb-form selected; compare the distribution of Tense morphology in (8a) and (8b) above.

Finally, the facts of object-placement in non-finite clauses with SOV word order (previously treated in Duffield (1990), Noonan (1992)) have been adduced by some researchers as evidence for an analysis in which all of the relevant constituents (verb, subject and object) are raised out of the maximal thematic VP in finite clauses (as in analysis (2c,d)). This is the line pursued, for example, in the Minimalist proposal of Bobaljik & Carnie (1992), Carnie & Bobaljik (1993), where it is proposed that even in finite clauses in Irish, the subject must move at least to [Spec,TP] before Spell-Out for Case-checking purposes, with the object NP occupying [Spec,Agr°P]:

9. a. [Ba mhaith leat [é Máire a phósadh]
   You-would-like him-ACC Mary-ACC ptc marry-VN
   You would like him to marry Mary.

   b. [$_{TP}$ é ... [$_{AgroP}$ Máire$_i$ [$_{Agro}$ a phósadh t_i]]]

There is, I believe, quite compelling evidence for Object-Raising in non-finite clauses, with the preverbal particle *a* heading its own functional projection (Duffield 1990, forthcoming, Noonan 1992).[2] However, even if (9b) is the correct analysis of non-finite constructions — whilst noting that these data are also compatible with a VP-internal Object-Raising analysis — it obviously does not follow without additional arguments that finite constructions must work the same way. Cross-linguistically, it is unclear that the scope of subject-movement is always identical in finite and non-finite clauses; if anything, the available empirical evidence suggests the contrary (cf. Pollock 1989, Rizzi 1993, Henry (forthcoming)).

In short, the evidence so far adduced seems consistent with all of the VSOX analyses in (2). This paper proposes a way of partially reconciling some of these positions. The present proposal is empirically motivated by a new analysis of pronoun-placement in finite clauses. On the basis of this, it will be suggested that the Bobaljik & Carnie (1992) proposal — namely that the verb, subject and object are all raised to some higher position — is on the right track, but that, quite literally, it does not go far enough.

The derivation to be argued for is schematized in (10) (over) as a first approximation: in finite clauses, the TP containing the entire VSO complex is raised to a Specifier position [Spec,WP], immediately below but independent of C^o. (Rather than being an arbitrary label, W is here intended to indicate 'Wackernagel'; this node has been posited independently by a number of researchers for both Romance and Germanic languages, and has been assigned various labels: Agr^1 (Cardinaletti & Roberts 1991), Agr^s (Zwart 1992), Top^o (Müller & Sternefeld 1993), F^o (Uriagareka 1993).

The movement involved here can be viewed as a type of generalized topicalization operation, akin to the type of VP-topicalization observed in Germanic Verb-second. Although such an analysis may seem quite implausible at first glance, it turns out to have some useful empirical consequences for the analysis of other questions in Irish syntax apart from the derivation of VSOX order, as we shall see directly.

As may be clear, the main conceptual motivation for this analysis is due to recent work by Emonds (1992) and Kayne (1993), in which rightward functional projections are universally excluded. For Kayne (1993), this prohibition follows from the theory of Linearity. A major consequence of Kayne's (1993) Linear Correspondence Axiom (LCA) is to exclude from UG both right-headed structures and any rightward-movement, either of heads or of other constituents. In most cases, the LCA correctly derives commonly-observed left-right asymmetries without further stipulation or resort to extra-grammatical principles.[3] For Emonds (1992), the restriction is on rightward specifiers of functional categories only. This constitutes a stipulated principle of UG, and is motivated largely by cross-linguistic observations.

10.

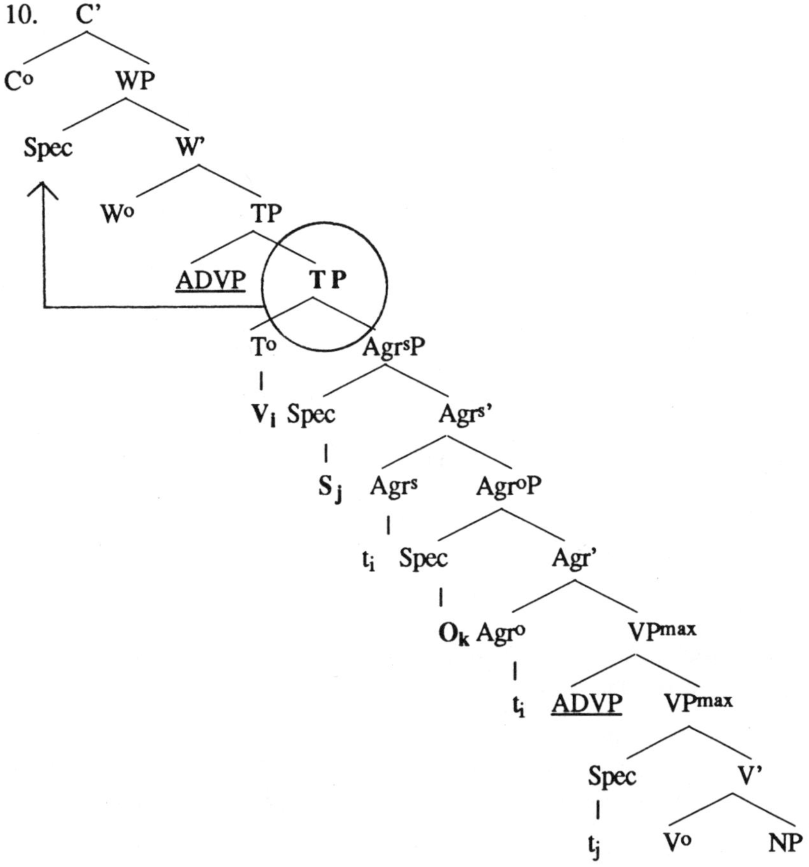

Keeping these theoretical concerns in mind, let us now consider one of three recalcitrant cases of apparent rightward or downward movement in Irish, a language which is otherwise, to quote Chung & McCloskey (1987) 'massively regular[ly] head-initial'. The three phenomena of interest are listed in (11): the phenomena in (11b) and (11c) will be addressed in future work. We focus here on the surface configuration schematized in (11a), the phenomenon traditionally termed PRONOUN-POSTPOSING.

11. a. config I: C°-V°-S-X-pro-(X) Pronoun-Postposing
    b. config II: N° (ADJP) POSS-NP Rightward Specifiers of NPs
    c. config III: ADVP/NPI C°-V°-S Complementizer Lowering

Consider the distribution of object-pronouns in the examples in (12-14) below, which illustrate the phenomenon known standardly as pronoun-postposing, whereby object pronouns in finite clauses occur on the right-periphery of the clause. (In finite clauses (13,14), rightward pronouns are virtually oligatory; in the small-clause cases in (14), the movement has more of an optional character). The main point to observe in these examples is that divergence from regular VSOX word-order is restricted to pronouns, specifically to weak pronouns: neither full noun-phrases nor contrastive or emphatic (tonic) pronouns may ever occur in this position.[4]

I. Pronoun-Postposing: (underlining = X constituent; **bold** = weak pronoun distribution)

12. a. Bhrís sé **í** (an chathaoir/í féin) leis an ord aréir (O'Siadhail 1989)
broke he it (the chair/that one) with the hammer last night
He broke the chair with the hammer last night.

b. Bhris sé leis an ord aréir **í** (*an chathaoir/*í féin)
broke he with the hammer last night it/the chair/that one
He broke it last night with the hammer

13. a. D'inis sé **é** (an scéal/eisean) do Bhríd
told he it (the story/that) to Bríd
He told the story to Bríd

b. D'inis sé do Bhríd **é**/(*an scéal/*eisean)
told he to Brídthe story/it/that
He told it to Bríd

14. a. Ba annamh [sa bhaile **é**]
COP rare him at home him
He was rarely at home

b. Chuala mé [ag ceol **iad**]
heard I PROG sing-VN them
I heard them singing.

As the examples in (14) — adapted from Chung & McCloskey (1987) — illustrate, it is not just weak object pronouns that can appear right-peripherally: assuming the SMALL CLAUSE analysis of Chung & McCloskey (1987), it appears that subject pronouns in small clauses appear in this position also. Importantly, however, the option of subject pronoun-postposing is restricted to selected small clauses, a point returned to below.

Although pronoun-postposing is generally analyzed as a rightward adjunction to some VP projection (cf. Chung & McCloskey 1987), it should be clear that an adjunction analysis can provide no principled explanation for the weak-pronoun restriction. Indeed, from either formal or functional perspectives, adjunction of exclusively light constituents is very puzzling; standardly, it is heavy elements that are extraposed in this way (cf. also Hawkins (1990)).

Instead of resembling a rightward adjuction, this contrast between weak pronouns and other argument NPs is much more reminiscent of the leftward object-movement found in other more familiar Indo-European languages.

The most natural treatment of this pronoun-distribution, therefore, would seem to be to relate it directly either to the type of OBJECT-SHIFT operative in Germanic languages (discussed in Koopman 1990, Johnson 1991, Jonas & Bobaljik 1993 i.a), or — by treating the Irish weak-pronoun as a clitic head — to assimilate its distribution with other types of object-cliticization; that is, to treat is as a type of WACKERNAGEL EFFECT (along the lines of Cardinaletti & Roberts 1991, Sportiche 1992, Zwart 1992, Uriagareka 1993).

The first type of movement, Object Shift, is generally analyzed as a type of specifier-movement applying obligatorily to pronouns and optionally to full noun-phrases. As the Icelandic examples in (15) — from Johnson (1991) — illustrate, object NPs are raised out of the VP whenever the lexical verb itself moves.

15. a. ad Jón keypti **bókina** ekki
COMP J. bought book not
John didn't buy the book

b. ad Jón keypti ekki **bókina**
c. ad Jón keypti ekki **HANN**
d. *ad Jón keypti ekki **hann**
e. ad Jón keypti **hann** ekki

The relevant point to note from these examples is that lexical NPs can also move to this (putatively VP-external) position in Icelandic. Hence, even if Object-shift did turn out to determine the basic s-structure position of object noun-phrases in Irish, as Bobaljik & Carnie (1992) have proposed, it could not account for the weak pronoun vs. NP distinction that we are concerned with here, for the simple reason that lexical NPs may never occur in this position.

By contrast, if we adopt the second possibility, to treat Irish weak pronouns as X° categories, following Kayne (1990), then we straightforwardly expect the distributional constrast observed in (12-14): Irish weak pronouns would then pattern with the clitic pronouns found in more familiar Western Indo-European languages, exemplified in (16-18). In all of these latter cases, the weak (clitic) pronoun occupies some position other than the object-shifted position, a position that is not available to maximal projections. (The examples in (18) — from Zwart (1992) — show that this position can be very high indeed: Dutch object clitics, unlike full NPs, can appear in the matrix clause of ECM constructions, apparently raising out of their own clause, and crossing the embedded subject position).

16. a. je **te** vois/*je **toi** vois/*je **l'homme** vois
I see you/the man

17. a. Jan heeft gisteren **haar** gekust
J. has yesterday her kissed
J. kissed her yesterday

b. Jan heeft **haar** gisteren gekust
c. Jan heeft **'r** gisteren gekust
d. *Jan heeft gisteren **'r** gekust

18. a. dat ik [Jan **het boek**] heb zien lezen
COMP I [J. the book] have seen read
that I have seen John read the book

b. dat ik [Jan **'t**] heb zien lezen
c. ***dat ik het boek$_i$** [Jan t_i] heb zien lezen
d. dat ik **'t** [Jan] heb zien lezen

Up to now, the obvious problem for an analysis that treats Irish weak pronouns as X° categories is that it seems to require a rightward functional head within IP. This assumption is not only problematic given the general theoretical considerations just discussed; it also contradicts everything that has been determined about the directionality of functional heads in Irish (cf. Chung & McCloskey 1987, Duffield 1990, Ernst 1992). Of the hitherto analyzed functional projections, C°, Agr^s, T°, and Agr^o can all be demonstrated to be head-initial.

If we exclude the logical possibility that Irish is not a natural language — respecting neither the Head Movement Constraint and its variants, nor general functional constraints on extraposition of heavy constituents — only one possibility remains: there is no postposing in these examples. Instead, these are instances of Light Predicate Raising — to borrow Larson's (1988) term — rather than any sort of rightward-movement at all.[5] In other words, Irish sentences involving weak pronouns exhibit the quite standard underlying distribution schematized in (19). Irish is distinguished from, say Dutch, by the generalized specifier-movement proposed in (10) above: the only formal difference between Irish and Dutch, is that in Irish almost all other lexical material underlyingly to the right of W° has raised to [Spec, WP]:

19. C° ----- W° ----- IP^{1,2,3,n} -------- VP^{max}
|
('t , 'r (Dutch), te (French), thú, é (Irish))

It might be supposed, in line with Minimalist assumptions, that this movement is motivated by a GREED requirement that finite TPs check some 'strong' featural property by moving to [Spec,WP]: in V2 languages, this is achieved by head-movement of the finite-verb; whereas in Irish, the other option, namely specifier-movement, is chosen. Alternatively, one might view this movement in terms of (c-)selection: complementizers obligatorily select for TPs; WP can satisfy this selectional requirement only by hosting a finite Tense-feature either in its head — giving rise to V2 effects in Germanic — or by hosting TP in its Specifier position, (satisfying selection through [Spec, Head] Agreement).

Since neither of these explanations does much more than to recapitulate the fact of the observed distribution — in the absence of an independent mechanism for determining strength of features or selectional requirements — it had better be the case that this proposal at least has some further empirical consequences, in addition to accounting for pronoun-placement.

First, there are some related diachronic facts. As the examples in (20) from Acquaviva (1990) illustrate, Old Irish did in fact display quite familiar Wackernagel effects: pronominal elements appeared pre-verbally in finite clauses, infixed between complementizers and the finite verb. Subsequently, these elements either disappeared or were reanalyzed in one of two ways. Some were reanalyzed as past-tense morphemes, giving rise to the *d'*-/-*r* alternations shown in (21). (This reanalysis distinguishes Irish from the closely-related Scottish Gaelic, which does not show this alternation). Alternatively, these pronominals came to be reanalyzed as relative particles of the type illustrated in (22b), particles devoid of any phi-features.

20. a. ní-**m**-charatsa infir
    not-me-love the men
    people do not love me

    b. con-**did** moladar
    that-it praises-3sg
    so that he praises it

21. do *th*uig// A-r *th*uig mé an tseanbhean.
    PAST understand I// Q-PAST understand I the old woman
    I understood// Did I understand the old woman

For both cases, however, I have argued elsewhere that these reanalyzed pronominals occupy T° synchronically (Duffield 1991): given that object relativization is perfectly compatible with right-ward pronouns, the current proposal then entails a representation for (22b) like that in (23) (next page). Given this structure, it becomes unsurprising that these particles are no longer interpreted as pronominal elements; by hypothesis, Tense cannot host pronominal clitics.

22. a. an chabhair [$_{CP}$ a *dt*ugann siad daoibh í]
    the help PTC give-PRES they to-you it
    the help that they give you (it)..

    b. an chabhair$_i$ [$_{TP}$ a *th*ugann siad daoibh x$_i$]
    the help PTC give-pres they to you ec
    the help that they give you..

In addition to permitting a relatively straightforward diachronic re-analysis of preverbal clitics, the representation in (23) offers a way of accounting for certain anomalies of adverbial placement and adverbial order in Irish finite clauses that are not adequately explained by previous analyses.

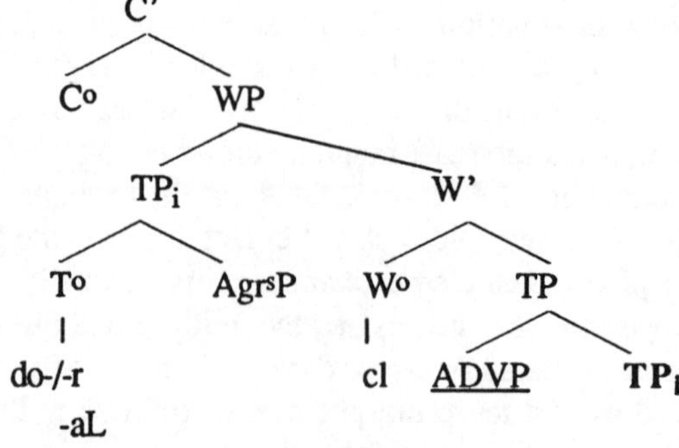

The distributional constraint that we are chiefly concerned with here is the restriction on placing adverbials between lexical subject and object NPs in finite contexts, whenever the object NPs are not weak pronouns. The example in (24) adapted from Ernst (1992) illustrates this restriction with various types of adverbial element:

24. *Chuir sé fosta/go díchéilli/cheana féin an tuairim in iúl dom
put he also/foolishly/already the proposal known to-me
He also/foolishly/already put the proposal to me

This constraint on placing adverbials, particularly sentential adverbials, between subject and object is not observed to my knowledge in any other Western Indo-European language, whether or not it has overt Object-Shift. On an account in which the subject and object NPs are moved separately to higher specifier positions, this restriction must simply be stipulated in the grammar (cf. Ernst 1992).

On the present account, however, these restrictions follow reasonably directly. Suppose that sentential and temporal adverbials are adjoined either to WP, or to TP, but no lower, that is, not within the thematic projections. In a language such as German, adverbial-medial order (X S AdvP O Y) can be obtained by raising the subject NP to a specifier position higher than Tense. In Irish, however, subjects do not move alone to [Spec,WP], rather it is the entire TP that is raised, according to the present proposal. This analysis correctly predicts the two main distributions for sentential and temporal adverbials in Irish as being either clause-initial or clause-final; no further language-particular stipulations are required to derive this result.

An additional consequence of this proposed derivation is that it offers a possible account of the *order* of adverbial phrases in Irish. Ó Siadhail (1989) cites Ward's (1974) study of adverbial placement, where it is claimed that the hierarchy in (25) represents the unmarked linear order of adverbial elements. Although O'Siadhail notes that there are many exceptions to this rule, it is nonetheless interesting to note that this order — in which time adverbials invariably follow place and manner adverbs — is just the opposite of the unmarked order in Germanic:

25. Ward's (1974) hierarchy (from Ó Siadhail 1989):
directionals > positional locatives > manner adverbials > prepositional phrases > time expressions

This would be quite unexpected if Irish VSOX word-order were just a special case of V-movement-to-Infl or to Comp (that is, if Irish were Verb-second without the first constituent). However, adopting the derivation in (10), we can preserve a common underlying hierarchy of adverbial-placement cross-linguistically: in Irish, manner adverbials and prepositional phrases — which are presumably adjoined within the maximal VP — will be raised with the VSO complex to [Spec,WP], to yield the marked precedence-relations that Ward (1974) describes.

Returning now to the distribution of weak pronominals, it is instructive to consider those constructions, in which pronoun-postposing — Light Predicate Raising in our terms, applies either partially, optionally or, most significantly, not at all. Let us consider the cases of partial LPR first, since these are the least problematic.

Several researchers, including Chung & McCloskey (1987) and Ó Siadháil (1989), have noted that pronoun-postposing does not always result in the pronoun appearing on the right periphery of the clause; in many cases, the pronoun may appear to the left of long adjuncts, or even between adjuncts, as example (26) illustrates. All of these orders can be derived under the present analysis, by adjoining the right-peripheral adverbial phrase to TP. However, our analysis correctly predicts that 'stranding' temporal adverbs such as *aréir* in (26) should be preferred over stranding manner adverbials or subcategorized locational PPs; i.e. that positions (3) and (4) should be preferred over (1) and (2) in (26). This is because the word-order with manner adverbials to the right of 'postposed' pronouns — i.e. pronouns under W° — could only be derived by adjoining manner adverbials to the higher TP prior to TP raising to [Spec,WP]. Given the standard assumption that manner adverbials are adjoined within the maximal VP, sentences such as that in (27) are correctly predicted to be marginal, if not ungrammatical.

26. Fágadh é ina luí $\uparrow_1$ ar an talamh $\uparrow_2$ taobh thiar den scioból $\uparrow_3$ aréir $\uparrow_4$
Was left it in-its lying _ on the ground _ behind the barn _ last night _
It was left lying on the ground behind the barn last night.

27. ??Gortaíodh aréir é go holc
was-injured last night him badly
He was injured there last night

It should again be clear that the traditional adjunction analysis of rightward pronouns can provide no principled account either of the general constraints on adverbial placement or of the more specific facts of adverbial order and its interaction with optional LPR; whereas all of these follow fairly directly from the present proposal.

Next, we may reconsider the small-clause cases, exemplified in (28) and (29). Chung & McCloskey's original observation was that pronoun-postposing in small clauses — LPR in our terms — is possible only if the small clause is selected by some higher predicate; the adjective *annamh* 'rare' in (28a) and the verb *chuala* 'heard' in (28b). By contrast, whenever the small clause is unselected, as in (29), postposing is excluded.

Perhaps the most promising way to treat this contrast under the current proposal would be to assume that the right-peripheral pronoun in (28) is actually in the W° position of the *higher* matrix clause, not of the small clause at all. The derivation of (28a) would then be as in (30). On this analysis, movement to [Spec,WP] would be driven by the same finite Tense feature as in regular finite clauses. This would immediately account for the impossibility of postposing in (29), where no WP is projected.[6]

28. a. Ba annamh [sa bhaile é]
cop rare him at home him
He was rarely at home

b. Chuala mé [ag ceol **iad**]
heard I prog sing-VN them
I heard them singing.

29. a. *agus [sa bhaile é]
and [at home him]
and him at home

b. *agus [ag ceol é]
and [sing-VN him]
and him singing

30.

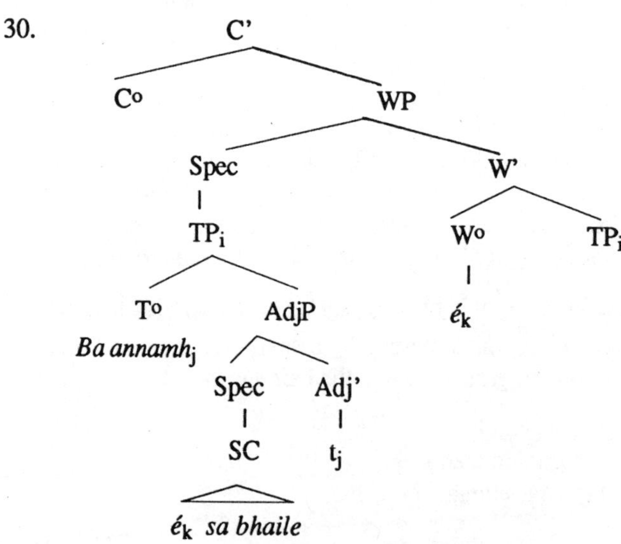

On this analysis, the clitic distribution in this derivation would be directly comparable to the Dutch ECM facts that were presented in (18) above, discussed in Zwart (1992).

Lastly, we should reconsider the status of *non*-finite clauses, mentioned briefly at the beginning of this paper. As was illustrated in (9) above, Northern dialects of Modern Irish show SOVX order in non-finite clauses.[7] The relevant point to note now about non-finite clauses is that they never permit 'pronoun-postposing': weak and strong object pronouns and lexical NPs show exactly the same pre-verbal distribution in non-finite contexts.

Whereas this contrast between finite and non-finite clauses with respect to pronoun-placement is quite unexpected on any account such as that of Bobaljik & Carnie (1992), in which subjects and objects occupy the same position irrespective of the finiteness of the clause, it once again follows fairly directly from the present proposal, on the assumption that it is the +finite/Tense feature of TP which motivates LP-raising to [Spec,WP] and which in turn gives rise to the 'pronoun-postposing' effect.

To summarize, we have tried to show that there is a reasonable amount of conceptual and empirical support of the prima facie rather unlikely proposal in (10). In addition to providing a principled treatment of adverbial placement and order, diachronic reanalyses, and differences in clause-type with respect to pronoun-placement, the present proposal offers a way of reconciling the various analyses of VSOX word-order in Irish that have previously been advanced. Proponents of the V^o-I^o analysis in (2a) are partly correct in so far as the verb does not move all the way to Comp, at least not in the syntax.[8] Proponents of the V^o-to-C^o analysis (2b,c) are correct in so far as the verb does move beyond the highest Infl projection. Proponents of (2d) are correct in assuming that the verb, subject and object all move in the overt syntax, even though the type of movement proposed here is quite different from that proposed in, for example, Bobaljik & Carnie (1992).

Finally, the current analysis offers a new perspective on the relationship between Celtic and Germanic word-order. In both cases, basic word-order in finite clauses is determined by the featural properties of a functional head below Comp and above Infl. The observed contrasts between Irish and, say, Dutch are reduced to one theoretically-sanctioned difference: whether these featural properties are satisfied by head-movement (Dutch) or Specifier-movement (Irish). Although much more work needs to be done to justify this proposal, this would seem to be a quite desirable preliminary result.

Notes

1. I am very grateful to Joseph Aoun, David Adger, Richard Kayne, and Máire Ní Chiosáin for their comments on and reaction to this paper. The usual disclaimers apply: reponsibility for errors and inaccuracies remains mine alone.

2. Different researchers have assigned this node various labels: cf. also Ramchand (1992), Adger (1994) for Scots Gaelic.

3. Recently, Chomsky (1993: class lectures) has apparently called into question whether Kayne's definition of linearity in terms of sets of ordered terminal pairs may not in fact be compatible with head-finality, unless some further stipulation is added. I will not pursue this matter further here, noting only that whatever the theoretical underpinnings for the exclusion of rightward heads may be, it constitutes a more restrictive proposal about UG options for the projection of phrase-structure than was previously available; as such, it is presumably to be welcomed, provided that apparent counter-examples can be treated in a principled manner.

4. This is not strictly accurate: formal registers of Munster do optionally permit the apparent postposing of a restricted set of intransitive (unaccusative) subject NPs. This is observed in O Siadhail (1989:217). However, it can be shown that this 'postposing' — which is argued in Duffield (in prep) to be another case of Light Predicate Raising— involves a different structural position from that occupied by the object-pronouns in the (b) examples here. These facts do not materially affect the descriptive generalization presented here, namely, that full object noun-phrases cannot appear on the right periphery of the clause.

5. In fact, as has been pointed out to me (R. Kayne, p.c.) this is not a strictly accurate appropriation of Larson's term given that in the current proposal, the predicate-phrase is moving directly to a specifier-position, rather than to a head-position via reanalysis. Nevertheless, the proposal is intended in the same spirit, and allows us to dispense with rightward-movement in these cases.

6. Alternatively, one might analyze the contrast between (28) and (29) in terms of selection and designation — adopting Müller & Sternefeld's (1993) terminology: it might be that WP is always selected, that small clauses are really WPs, but that it is only designated — triggering movement to its Specifier position, whenever either (i) a lower finite TP moves into its Spec or (ii) a higher predicate directly selects it, as in (28).

7. Southern dialects also show SOV order whenever the subject is PRO; if the subject is overt, however, SVOX order is required. This dialect constrast is discussed in Duffield (1990, forthcoming); see also Noonan (1994). The fact of this contrast, although interesting for other reasons, has no direct bearing on the present discussion, since neither dialect permits rightward pronouns in non-finite clauses: i.e. [S V_{infin} X Obj-pron] is ungrammatical in all dialects.

8. At this point, I leave open the possibility of complementizer-lowering, as proposed in McCloskey (1992), to handle the cases illustrated in (4) and (5) above. In Duffield (in prep.), however, it will be argued that most of these cases can also be treated without requiring any lowering in the syntax.

References

Acquaviva, P. 1990. The Syntactic Function of Lenition and Nasalization in Old Irish, ms. Scuola Normale Superiore, Pisa.

Adger, D. 1994. Aspect, Agreement and Measure Phrases in Scottish Gaelic, ms., Centre for Cognitive Science, University of Edinburgh.

Bobaljik, J. & A. Carnie 1992. A Minimalist Approach to some Problems of Irish Word Order. *Proceedings of the 12th Annual Harvard Celtic Colloquium*, Harvard University.

Carnie, A. & J. Bobaljik 1993. A note on the position of Subjects and Object Raising, ms. MIT.

Cardinaletti A. & I. Roberts 1991. Clause Structure and X-second, ms., University of Geneva.

Chomsky, N. 1993. A Minimalist Program for Linguistic Theory. In K. Hale & S.J. Keyser (eds). *The View from Building 20: Essays in honor of Sylvain Bromberger*. Cambridge, MIT Press.

Chung, S. & J. McCloskey 1987. Government, Barriers and Small Clauses in Modern Irish. *LI* 18, 173-237.

Deprez, V. & K. Hale Resumptive Pronouns in Irish, in *Proceedings of the 1985 Harvard Celtic Colloquium*, Harvard University, Cambridge, Massachusetts.

Dooley Collberg S. 1990. An Expanded-Infl Syntax for Modern Irish, *Working Papers 36*, Dept. of Linguistics, Lund University.

Duffield, N. 1990. Movement and Mutation in Modern Irish. In T. Green & S. Uziel (eds), *MIT Working Papers in Linguistics 12: Student Conference in Linguistics 1990*. Cambridge, MA: MITWPL.

Duffield, N. 1991. Negation, Minimality and Irish Relative Clauses. *CLS* 27:II Chicago, IL.

Duffield, N. forthcoming. *Particles and Projections of Irish Syntax*. Dordrecht: Kluwer.

Emonds, J. 1992. Talk delivered at the Conference on Comparative Celtic Syntax, June 1992, Bangor, Gwynedd.

Ernst, T. 1992. Phrase-Structure and Directionality in Irish. *JL* 28.2

Guilfoyle, E. 1990. Functional Categories and Phrase-Structure Parameters. Doctoral dissertation, McGill University.

Hawkins, J. 1990. A Parsing Theory of Word Order Universals.*LI* 21, 223-26.

Henry, A. forthcoming. *Dialect Variation and Parameter-setting: a study of Belfast English and Standard English. Oxford University Press.*

Kayne, R. 1990. Romance Clitics, Verb-Movement and PRO, LI 22, 647-686.

Kayne, R. 1993. The Antisymmetry of Syntax, ms. CUNY.

Johnson, K. 1991. Object Positions. *NLLT*

Jonas, D. & J. Bobaljik 1993. Specs for Subjects. *MIT Working Papers in Linguistics: Papers on Case & Agreement I.* Cambridge, MIT.

Koopman, H. 1990. The Syntactic Structure of the Verb-particle Construction. Ms. UCLA.

McCloskey, J. 1992. On the Scope of Verb-movement in Irish. Working Paper 92-10, Linguistics Research Center, UC, Santa Cruz.

Müller, G. & W. Sternefeld. 1993. Improper Movement & Unambiguous Binding. *LI* 24, 461-508.

Noonan, M. 1992. Case & Syntactic Geometry. Doctoral dissertation, McGill University.

Noonan, M. 1994. VP internal and VP external Agr_oP: evidence from Irish. *WCCFL XIII* , UC, San Diego (this volume).

Ó Siadhail, M. 1989. *Modern Irish: Grammatical structure and dialectal variation.* Cambridge: Cambridge University Press.

Pollock, J.Y. 1989. Verb-Movement, Universal Grammar, and the Structure of IP. *LI* 20, 365-424.

Ramchand, G.C. 1992. Aspect Phrase in Modern Scottish Gaelic.*NELS 23.* Amherst: GLSA.

Rizzi L. 1993. Some Notes on Linguistic Theory and Language Development, ms. University of Geneva.

Sproat, R. 1985. Welsh Syntax and VSO structure. *NLLT 3,173-216.*

Travis, L. 1991. Derived Objects, Inner Aspect and the Structure of VP, NELS 20.

Travis, L. forthcoming. *Inner Aspect and the Structure of VP.* (working title) Dordrecht::Kluwer.

Uriagereka, J. 1993. Why do Clitics move where? Paper presented at *Going Romance*, University of Utrecht, The Netherlands, December 1993.

Ward, A. 1974. The grammatical structure of Modern Irish, Doctoral thesis, Dublin University.

Zwart, C. J. 1992. Verb Movement and Complementizer Agreement. Ms. MIT/Groningen.

Causative Binding and the Minimal Distance Principle

PATRICK FARRELL
University of California, Davis

1. Introduction

The MINIMAL DISTANCE PRINCIPLE (MDP) (Rosenbaum 1970, Chomsky 1980, Larson 1991, Huang 1992), stated in a simple form in (1), is meant to account for the fact that the implicit subject of the embedded infinitival phrase (i.e., PRO) in examples such as (2) must be bound by the direct object of the main verb — rather than by the subject, as would be allowed under purely binding-theoretic accounts of control (Manzini 1983, Koster 1984, Borer 1989).

(1) *Minimal Distance Principle*
The controller of a complement clause must be the closest c-commanding NP.

(2) Bert$_j$ forced/persuaded/convinced Ernie$_i$ [PRO$_{i/*j}$ to remain seated].

This paper is devoted primarily to showing that there is a more general principle of binding in LEXICAL CONCEPTUAL STRUCTURE (LCS) that yields this effect of the MDP, if control is characterized as a lexical

Thanks to Farrell Ackerman, Jean-Pierre Koenig, S.-Y. Kuroda, and Steve Lapointe for useful discussion of issues treated in this paper. All errors or shortcomings are mine alone.

binding phenomenon as proposed in Jackendoff (1990), and secondarily to exploring some of the theoretical consequences and implications of adopting this approach to control. Although the proposed explanation for the MDP effect is essentially semantic, it goes beyond alternative semantic explanations (see, for example, Jackendoff 1972, Foley and Van Valin 1984, Farkas 1988, Sag and Pollard 1991, Cutrer 1993, Farrell 1993) in that it reduces the MDP to an independently needed principle of lexical binding, rather than substituting a semantic principle for it, thus substantially simplifying control theory.

2. Conceptual structure and causative verbs

2.1. Simple lexical causatives

It has long been recognized that lexical causative verbs, some typical examples of which are *kill* ('cause to become dead'), *break* ('cause to become broken'), and *open* ('cause to become open'), are best analyzed as syntactically atomic verbs (see Fodor 1970, Jackendoff 1990). Given that the causative interpretation of such verbs is due to their conceptual semantics, the lexical entry of *open* as used in *The burglar opened the window* would be as in Figure 1.

$$\begin{bmatrix} \text{V}, \underline{\quad} \text{NP}_j \\ \text{LCS:} \begin{bmatrix} \text{CAUSE ([}\alpha\text{], [GO ([}\beta\text{], [TO (OPEN)])])} \\ \text{AFF ([ ]}^{\alpha}_{i}\text{, [ ]}^{\beta}_{j}\text{)} \end{bmatrix} \end{bmatrix}$$

Figure 1. Lexical entry for *open*

A standard subcategorization frame is shown above the LCS. The latter is a semantic decomposition, in which primitive predicates, such as CAUSE and GO, combine with arguments in ways determined by general principles. Based on the framework presented in Jackendoff (1990), this LCS utilizes both a THEMATIC TIER, concerned with causation, motion, and location, and an ACTION TIER with the predicate AFF, which is intended to represent the roles of actor and patient.[1] The external argument (or thematically most prominent

---

[1] These roles are more precisely something like proto-agent and proto-patient in the sense of Dowty (1991), as the arguments of AFF may be the acting/controlling/volitional participant and the acted on/affected participant to varying degrees or in different ways. For Jackendoff, these differences are generally accounted for by subcategorization of AFF (AFF [±volitional], AFF^+, AFF^- etc.), a feature of his analysis that is suppressed here for the sake of simplicity only.

argument) — bearer of the subscript index *i* — is the actor, or the first argument of AFF. Not indicated in the subcategorization frame, the external argument is by convention realized as the subject in syntactic structure (in an active clause). Greek letters are used to indicate ARGUMENT BINDING in LCSs. As the acting participant is also the causing participant, the actor argument binds the first argument of CAUSE. This binding relation is indicated by showing the content of the bound argument to be the Greek letter superscripted on the binding argument. Whereas the first argument of AFF is open, the first argument of CAUSE is filled as a consequence of being bound. Given the convention that there may be at most one syntactic expression of the LCS chain created by an open argument and its filled bound arguments (see Jackendoff's 1990 Linking Condition), the fact that there is exactly one NP that corresponds to the actor (i.e., *the burglar* in *The burglar opened the window*) follows from the fact that the other role that the actor plays (i.e., causer of the subevent) is that of a bound and filled argument. The first argument of GO, the so-called theme, is bound by the second argument of AFF, the patient, which is expressed as a direct internal argument, as indicated by the matching subscript indices in the LCS and in the subcategorization frame. In short, the important lexical properties of causative *open* are that it means something like (3a) and the correspondence between its meaning and its syntax is as given in (3b).[2]

(3) a. *X* acts on *Y* in such a way as to cause *Y* to go into the state of being open.
b. There is a direct object NP in syntactic structure corresponding to *Y* and a subject corresponding to X.

2.2. Morphological causatives

This analysis of English lexical causatives suggests an analysis of the cross-linguistically common phenomenon of morphological causativization according to which a lexical entry such as in Figure 1 is derived from another lexical entry in conjunction with a morphological process. Consider the following examples, which illustrate a relatively productive affixally-mediated causativization process in Berber (discussed in Guerssel 1986, 1987, Lumsden and Trigo 1987, and Alalou and Farrell 1993).

---

[2] Of course *open* can also be used with a non-causative meaning, as in *The door opened*. I assume that causative *open* is related to non-causative *open* by a process of lexical derivation.

(4) a. Y-gn wrba
3MsgS-sleep boy
'The boy is sleeping.'[3]

b. Y-ss-gn wryaz arba
3MsgS-CAUS-sleep man boy
'The man put the boy to sleep.'

Alalou and Farrell argue that the causative prefix *ss-* in Berber has the lexical entry shown in Figure 2.[4]

$$\begin{bmatrix} \text{Affix, \_\_ V} \\ \text{LCS:} \begin{bmatrix} \text{CAUSE ([}\alpha\text{], [Event ...[}\beta\text{]...])} \\ \text{AFF ([ ]}^{\alpha}\text{, [ ]}^{\beta}\text{)} \end{bmatrix} \end{bmatrix}$$

Figure 2. Lexical entry of *ss-*

The affixation process involves insertion of the LCS of the base verb as the second argument of the CAUSE predicate in the LCS of *ss-*. As indicated in Figure 2, one of the arguments of the base verb (the external argument by default) is necessarily bound by the second argument of AFF in the LCS of *ss-*.[5] Thus, affixing *ss-* to *gn* 'sleep', for example, results in the creation of the lexical entry shown in Figure 3.

$$\begin{bmatrix} \text{V, \_\_ NP}_j \\ \text{LCS:} \begin{bmatrix} \text{CAUSE ([}\alpha\text{], [SLEEP ([}\beta\text{])])} \\ \text{AFF ([ ]}^{\alpha}_{i}\text{, [ ]}^{\beta}_{j}\text{)} \end{bmatrix} \end{bmatrix}$$

Figure 3. Lexical entry of *ss-gn*

---

[3] The following abbreviations are used in glosses:

CAUS = causative prefix	DAT = dative pronominal clitic
F = feminine	FV = focal vowel
M = masculine	PR = present tense
PS = past tense	S = subject
sg = singular	3 = third person

[4] The second argument of CAUSE in Figure 2 could be a state as well as an event. For the sake of simplicity alone, I do not make the event/state distinction here and elsewhere in this paper.

[5] More specifically, following the parametrized principle proposed in Alsina (1992), Alalou and Farrell claim that in Berber the bound argument is either the argument most in control or an affected argument of the subordinate event.

One important claim of this analysis is that morphological causativization, at least in some languages, is a lexical derivational process, as opposed to a syntactic incorporation of the sort proposed in Baker (1988) and Li (1990). Alalou and Farrell (1993) argue for the correctness of this claim for Berber based, for example, on the interaction of causativization and noun formation. A non-eventive noun can be created from an eventive verb in Berber by adding nominal morphology. Some examples are given in (5).

(5)	**verb**	**derived noun**
	rɣ 'be warm'	*anrɣi* 'heat'
	uru 'write'	*tirra* 'writings'

It is clear that deverbal nouns of this kind do not have the same syntactic arguments as the corresponding verbs, since the verb's complement cannot be expressed as the noun's complement:

(6) a. T-aru tmṭut tabrat
3FsgS-write woman letter
'The woman wrote the letter.'
b. * tirra n tbratin
writings of letters
'writings of letters'

For present purposes, the interesting fact about this sort of noun formation is that it can apply to causativized verbs, as shown in (7).

(7)	**verb**	**causativized verb**	**derived noun**
	nɣ 'hurt'	*ss-nɣ* 'make hurt'	*a-ss-nɣi* 'a hurt'
	nd 'churn'	*ss-nd* 'make churn'	*ta-ss-ndut* 'churned stuff'
	irid 'wash'	*ss-ird* 'make wash'	*am-ss-ird* 'washing place'
	ɣli 'cross'	*ss-ɣli* 'make cross'	*a-ss-ɣli* 'crossing place'

Since this is a category-changing process in which syntactic arguments are deleted, it must be a lexical one, that is, one which has lexical entries as input and output. Since causativization feeds noun formation, it too must be a lexical process.

Further evidence for this claim comes from ways in which causativization interacts with anticausativization and a certain class of psych verbs in Berber. Similar analyses and arguments for this general approach to the phenomenon are presented for Berber in

Guerssel (1987), for Chichewa and other Bantu languages in Alsina (1992), and for various languages in Falk (1991).[6]

A second important claim of this analysis is that the causative affix has a patient argument. This claim is supported by the following examples, which illustrate a standard test for the patient relation.

(8) a. Mayd-as yskr wryaz i wrba?
what-DAT do man to boy
'What did the man do to the boy?'
b. * Y-annay-t
3MsgS-see-him
'He saw him.'
c. Y-wt-t
3MsgS-hit-him
'He hit him.'
d. Y-ss-gn-t
3MsgS-CAUS-sleep-him
'He put him to sleep.'

(8a) is a question about the kind of event in which the boy was affected in some way by the man. (8c) is an appropriate response, unlike (8b), because the verb 'hit' denotes an event in which the action of one participant affects another, whereas 'see', whose object is thematically a percept, does not. The well-formedness of (8d) indicates that *ss-gn* denotes essentially the same kind of event as 'hit'; the sleeper is construed as being affected by the activity in which the causing participant engages. If the superficial object is a patient, it must be so as a result of the causative affixation, since *gn* itself is a monadic activity verb whose argument is an actor only.

Alsina (1992) presents similar examples from Chichewa in support of the claim that the causative affix has a patient argument in this language. He shows that this analysis also explains several other phenomena. For example, as shown in (9), it is not possible to

---

[6] In these other works, causativization is technically treated as an operation on argument structure (as in Grimshaw 1990). Following Jackendoff, I assume that recognition of LCSs, which are a kind of semantically elaborated argument structure, precludes the need for a distinct level of representation known as argument structure. Dubinsky, Lloret, and Newman (1988) find evidence for both lexical and syntactic morphological causatives in Oromo. For present purposes, it is not important that some languages might have syntactically derived morphological causatives. Rather, it is important that morphological causatives are lexically derived at least in some languages.

causativize a verb such as *onēka* 'appear' whose sole argument is a clause.

(9) a. Zi-ku-ónék-a kutí nyā́ni a-na-póny-á
8 S-PR-appear-FV that 1a baboon 1 S-PS-throw-FV
mpira pa tsîndwi
3 ball 16 roof
'It appears that the baboon threw a ball on the roof.'

b. * Njōvu i-ku-ónék-ets-a kutí ...
9 elephant 9 S-PR-appear-CAUS-FV that
'The elephant makes it appear that ...'

The ungrammaticality of (9b) can be attributed to the fact that the causative suffix in Chichewa has a patient argument that must bind one of the arguments of the base verb and a verb such as *onēka* has no argument that can be construed as a patient. Alsina shows further that the interaction of idiom formation and unspecified object deletion with causativization supports the conclusion that the causative suffix has a patient argument.

Summarizing to this point, lexical causative verbs such as English *break, kill,* and *open* as well as morphological causatives in some languages (Berber and Chichewa for example) have a kind of LCS in which the patient argument of the AFF predicate binds into the event argument of CAUSE. This binding relationship, being represented solely in the LCS, cannot be characterized in terms of a relationship between nodes in a phrase-marker, and thus cannot be regulated by a syntactic principle such as the MDP.[7]

3. Object control as causative binding

An explanation for the MDP effect with object control verbs emerges from two observations. First, the fact that it is the patient of causative verbs that binds into the event argument of the CAUSE predicate is not an idiosyncrasy; rather, it is completely predictable and therefore attributable to a general principle. Second, control verbs with object controllers are semantically causative and have both a patient argument and an event argument. The principle that ensures that it is the

[7] Although one might posit a lexical level of syntactic argument structure (as in Hale and Keyser 1993) that would allow the MDP to regulate this kind of binding. I do not pursue this possibility here, as I assume that LCSs are needed in any case and otherwise obviate the need for such a further level of representation.

patient of a causative event that binds into an embedded event argument accounts for object control, if control is treated as a kind of lexical binding.

Whereas causative verbs with LCSs of the kind illustrated in Figures 1 and 3 are ubiquitous across languages, the logically possible type of causative verb with the LCS shown in Figure 4 appears not to occur at all.

$$\begin{bmatrix} \text{V}, \_\_\ \text{NP}_j \\ \text{LCS:} \begin{bmatrix} \text{CAUSE}\ ([\alpha], [\ldots[\alpha]\ldots]) \\ \text{AFF}\ ([\ ]_i^{\alpha}, [\ ]_j^{\beta}) \end{bmatrix} \end{bmatrix}$$

Figure 4. Lexical entry of non-occurring causative verb type

That is to say, there are no simple lexical causative verbs in English, or apparently any language, such as the hypothetical *blip* in (10), which would have the lexical entry shown in Figure 5.

(10) *The girl blipped the boy.
'The girl acted on the boy causing herself to blip.'

$$\begin{bmatrix} \text{V}, \_\_\ \text{NP}_j \\ \text{LCS:} \begin{bmatrix} \text{CAUSE}\ ([\alpha], [\text{BLIP}\ ([\alpha])]) \\ \text{AFF}\ ([\ ]_i^{\alpha}, [\ ]_j^{\beta}) \end{bmatrix} \end{bmatrix}$$

Figure 5. Lexical entry of **blip*

Similarly, it appears that no language has the kind of morphological causativization illustrated by the hypothetical Berber examples in (11), where *dd-* is a causative morpheme with the lexical entry shown in Figure 6.

(11) a. Y-gn wrba
3MsgS-sleep boy
'The boy is sleeping.'

b. * Y-dd-gn wryaz arba
3MsgS-CAUS-sleep man boy
'The man acted on the boy in such a way as to fall sleep.'

$$\begin{bmatrix} \text{Affix, } \_\_ \text{ V} \\ \text{LCS:} \begin{bmatrix} \text{CAUSE ([}\alpha\text{], [}_{\text{Event}} \ldots [\alpha] \ldots \text{])} \\ \text{AFF ([ ]}^{\alpha}\text{, [ ]}^{\beta}\text{)} \end{bmatrix} \end{bmatrix}$$

Figure 6. Lexical entry of hypothetical **dd-*

The impossibility of this general type of causative lexical entry suggests that there is a principle governing lexical binding such as (12).[8]

(12) *Causative binding principle (CBP)*
Given an LCS with a CAUSE predicate *C*, its associated AFF predicate *A*, and an event argument *E* of *C*, the second argument of *A* binds into *E*.

Now, given that object control verbs such as *force, persuade,* and *convince* are causative verbs that differ from verbs such as *open, break,* and *kill* (see Figure 1) essentially only in that the content of their event argument is open and they are subcategorized for a clausal complement that expresses this open argument, their schematic lexical entry would be as shown in Figure 7.[9]

$$\begin{bmatrix} \text{V, } \_\_ \text{ NP}_j \text{ CP}_k \\ \text{LCS:} \begin{bmatrix} \text{CAUSE ([}\alpha\text{], [}_{\text{Event}} \ldots [\beta] \ldots \text{]}_k\text{)} \\ \text{AFF ([ ]}_i^{\alpha}\text{, [ ]}_j^{\beta}\text{)} \end{bmatrix} \end{bmatrix}$$

Figure 7. Lexical entry of object control verbs

Crucially, the CBP guarantees that no other LCS would be possible. The patient argument (the second argument of AFF) must be the binder of the embedded argument, which is realized as PRO in the

[8] Jackendoff (1990: 145) hints at the possibility of such a principle. Given that conceptual structure is a model of human cognition, the claim is essentially that humans conceptualize causation in such a way as to entail (12), something which presumably follows ultimately from laws of the physical universe that motivate this conceptualization of causation.

[9] Of course, there are various semantic distinctions between object control verbs that I ignore here. For example, *persuade* and *convince* differ from *force* in that they are verbs of communication. However this distinction is encoded in LCSs, I assume that both types of verb would have the core LCS shown in Figure 7.

syntax.[10] Thus the object control effect of the MDP simply follows from the independently needed CBP.[11]

---

[10] Presumably the realization of this argument as PRO can be seen as resolving a conflict between the Extended Projection Principle (Chomsky 1981), which requires that a clause have a syntactically realized subject, and the Linking Condition of Jackendoff (1990), which essentially requires that an LCS chain correspond to a single position in the syntax. Alternatively, the conflict might be resolved by analyzing the embedded infinitival phrase as syntactically subjectless (see, for example, Brame 1976, Gunji 1987, Bresnan 1982, Gazdar et al. 1985, and Culicover and Wilkins 1986).

[11] It has long been recognized that resultative predicate adjectives, as in *The man painted the house red*, must be construed with a co-argument that is a direct internal argument (Simpson 1983, Rappaport and Levin 1988, Carrier and Randall 1992) or, more precisely, a patient (Jackendoff 1990, Goldberg 1991). Although a complete analysis of resultatives would take us too far afield here, it is worth noting that this fact, for which Huang (1992) invokes a syntactic control analysis and the MDP, is minimally consistent with the CBP, given an analysis of the LCS of resultatives of the sort proposed in Jackendoff (1990). However, Chinese resultative V-V compounds (as discussed in Huang 1992) pose a potential problem for the CBP. In many cases the CBP is clearly respected. For example, (ia) can only mean that Lisi was awakened, which would follow from the CBP, if the LCS of *ku-xing* is roughly as indicated.

(i) a. ta ku-xing-le Lisi.
he cry-awake-ASP Lisi
'He cried and awoke Lisi.'
LCS: *X* acts on *Y*, by crying, causing *Y* to become awake.

b. ta chi-bao fan le
he eat-full rice ASP
'He ate rice and got full'
LCS[1]: *X* acts on *Y*, by eating, causing *X* to become full.
LCS[2]: *X* acts on *Y* causing *Y* to fill the digestive tract of *X*.

The problem is that in the case of such compounds as *chi-bao* 'eat-full' the subject/actor is necessarily interpreted as the undergoer of the change of state, as illustrated by (ib). This is surprising if (ib) has an LCS such as indicated by LCS[1]. However, it is not clear why it could not be said to have the equally reasonable LCS[2], in which case it would conform to the CBP.

4. Consequences and further issues

4.1. Difficulties with syntactic MDP

One nice consequence of the proposed analysis is that like other semantic approaches to the controller choice question, it overcomes various more or less well-known difficulties with the MDP and other c-command based approaches (see, among others, Jackendoff 1972, 1987, Williams 1985, Sag and Pollard 1991, Farrell 1993). For example, within nominalizations the controlling NP need not be the syntactically closest NP (see 13a), nor a c-commanding NP (see 13b), nor even a syntactically expressed NP (see 13c).

(13) a. the soldier's$_i$ orders from the army [PRO$_i$ to return home]
b. my advice [PP to the students$_i$] [PRO$_i$ to study harder]
c. the boss's order ø$_i$ [PRO$_i$ to mop the kitchen]

If controller choice is a matter of lexical binding governed by the CBP and the essential content of the LCSs of verbs and their nominal counterparts is the same, it is as expected that the patient is always chosen as controller regardless of how or if it is syntactically expressed.

4.2. The problem of *promise*

A well-known problem for the MDP (Jackendoff 1972, 1987, Larson 1991) is that there is a small class of control verbs including *promise, vow, commit*, and a few other semantically similar verbs whose subject is generally the controller even though there may be a closer potential controller, as illustrated by (14).

(14) I$_i$ promised the children$_j$ [PRO$_{i/*j}$ to return home early].

The proposed lexical binding approach to the controller choice issue suggests a plausible explanation for subject control in such cases. The direct object of *promise* is the participant to whom the commitment is made (the commissee) and is not substantially affected by the action, as evidenced by the fact that, unlike the object of an object control verb such as *force*, it fails the pseudocleft test of affectedness, as shown by the following examples.

(15) a. What I did to *those guys* was force *them* to finish the job.
b. * What I did to *those guys* was promise *them* to finish the job.
c. What I did to myself was promise those guys to finish the job.

On the other hand, (15c) shows that the participant most affected by the action is actually the actor, who essentially self-commits to causing something to occur. It is therefore reasonable to assume that *promise* has a lexical entry along the lines shown in Figure 8.

$$\begin{bmatrix} \text{V, \_\_NP}_j\ \text{CP}_k & \\ \text{LCS:} & \begin{bmatrix} \text{COMMIT ([}\alpha\text{], [TO ([ ]}^{\gamma}{}_j\text{)], [CAUSE ([}\alpha\text{], [}_{\text{Event}} \ldots[\beta]\ldots]_k\text{)])} \\ \text{AFF ([ ]}_i^{\alpha}\text{, [}\alpha\text{]}^{\beta}\text{)} \end{bmatrix} \end{bmatrix}$$

Figure 8. Lexical entry of *promise*

By the CBP, the second argument of AFF is necessarily the binder into the caused event. The argument expressed as the direct object, being simply a commissee and not an acted upon participant, is not an argument of AFF and hence not the binder. The argument expressed as subject binds the second argument of AFF,[12] which in turn binds into the event argument. Subject control with verbs of commitment such as *promise* is therefore in accordance with the CBP.[13]

---

[12] It is not particularly unusual for the second argument of AFF to be lexically bound by the first argument of AFF. This is presumably the way to treat intransitive verbs of grooming for example (*bathe, dress, shave,* etc.), as in Jackendoff (1990), as well as verbs such as *move* (as in *The man moved across the room*), which has an LCS like 'X acts on X causing X to go somewhere'. An alternative analysis of *promise* and verbs of commitment, considered in Farrell (1993), is that they simply have no second argument on the action tier. Under this analysis, the CBP would have to be reformulated so as to allow/require actor binding in the absence of a patient.

[13] As is well known, the commissee may under certain conditions be the controller, as in the case of (i).

(i) I promised the kids$_i$ [PRO$_i$ to be able/permitted/allowed to watch TV].

Farrell (1993) argues for an analysis of this kind of controller shift that is consistent with the claims of the CBP. The idea, in a nutshell, is that this use of *promise* is the commitment-to-transfer-of-possession use found for example in *I promised the kids a new TV*. As with other dative-shift transfer-of-

4.3. The broader picture of complement control

Representative examples of the kinds of predicates that allow or require complement control are shown in (16), three main semantic classes being distinguished (based on Sag and Pollard 1991).

(16) *Influence*
order, persuade, permit, command, direct, advise, convince, impel, induce, pressure, prompt, encourage, urge, ask, cause, force, etc.
Commitment
promise, swear, contract, pledge, commit, vow, try, intend, refuse, choose, decline, decide, attempt, etc.
Orientation
want, desire, wish, long, prefer, hope, need, expect, aspire, hate, be eager, be able, etc.

What these predicates have in common is that they have an event argument that may (and typically must) be expressed as a clausal complement with an implicit subject (PRO) that is bound by another of their arguments. What is needed specifically for control verbs is a principle along the lines of (17).

(17) *Control principle*
The event argument of verbs of influence, commitment, and orientation may/must be expressed as a clause whose subject corresponds to a lexically bound argument in conceptual structure.

Under the proposed analysis, nothing more needs to be said specifically about control verbs, since the problem of controller choice is handled by a more general principle of lexical binding. Verbs of influence and commitment are causative verbs.[14] The object of the

---

possession verbs, the direct object is construed as an affected recipient. It is therefore the second argument of an AFF predicate, and thus a legitimate controller by the CBP. The transfer-of-possession reading is possible with an embedded infinitive only when it expresses subject potentiation, as in (i), presumably by analogy with such (abstract) transfer-of-possession cases as *I promised the kids permission to watch TV*.

[14] Of course, not all of these involve the standard causation that characterizes verbs such as *force*. I assume that their LCSs nevertheless all contain the generalized force-dynamic predicate CS of Jackendoff (1990), which is subcategorized according to outcome (for example, *pressure* and *try*

former and the subject of the latter is the second argument of AFF and therefore the binder of the embedded argument, in accordance with the CBP. Verbs of orientation are not causative and hence not governed by the CBP. In any case, they have only one argument other than the complement clause and thus only one potential controller.

References

Alalou, Ali, and Patrick Farrell. 1993. Argument Structure and Causativization in Berber. *Journal of African Languages and Linguistics* 14.155–186.

Alsina, Alex. 1992. On the Argument Structure of Causatives. *Linguistic Inquiry* 23.517–556.

Baker, Mark C. 1988. *Incorporation: A Theory of Grammatical Function Changing*. Chicago: University of Chicago Press.

Borer, Hagit. 1989. Anaphoric AGR. *The Null Subject Parameter*, ed. by Osvaldo Jaeggli and Kenneth J. Safir, 69–109. Dordrecht: Kluwer.

Brame, Michael K. 1976. *Conjectures and Refutations in Syntax and Semantics*. Amsterdam and New York: Elsevier.

Bresnan, Joan. 1982. Control and Complementation. *The Mental Representation of Grammatical Relations*, ed. by Joan Bresnan, 282–390. Cambridge, Mass.: MIT Press.

Carrier, Jill, and Janet H. Randall. 1992. The Argument Structure and Syntactic Structure of Resultatives. *Linguistic Inquiry* 23.173–234.

Chomsky, Noam. 1980. On Binding. *Linguistic Inquiry* 11.1–46.

———. 1981. *Lectures on Government and Binding*. Dordrecht: Foris.

Culicover, Peter, and Wendy Wilkins. 1986. Control, PRO, and the Projection Principle. *Language* 62.120–153.

Cutrer, L. Michelle. 1993. Semantic and Syntactic Factors in Control. *Advances in Role and Reference Grammar*, ed. by Robert D. Van Valin Jr., 167–195. Amsterdam and Philadelphia: John Benjamins.

Dowty, David. 1991. Thematic Proto-Roles and Argument Selection. *Language* 67.547-619.

Dubinsky, Stanley, Maria-Rosa Lloret, and Paul Newman. 1988. Lexical and Syntactic Causatives in Oromo. *Language* 64.485–498.

Falk, Yehuda N. 1991. Causativization. *Journal of Linguistics* 27.55–79.

---

with undetermined outcome vs. *force* with successful outcome). Technically, the CBP should be formulated in terms of CS rather than CAUSE.

Farkas, Donka. 1988. On Obligatory Control. *Linguistics and Philosophy* 11.27–58.

Farrell, Patrick. 1993. The Interplay of Syntax and Semantics in Complement Control. Proceedings of Semantics and Linguistic Theory III, Cornell University.

Fodor, Jerry A. 1970. Three Reasons for Not Deriving 'Kill' from 'Cause to Die'. *Linguistic Inquiry* 1.429–438.

Foley, William A., and Robert D. Van Valin Jr. 1984. *Functional Syntax and Universal Grammar*. Cambridge and New York: Cambridge University Press.

Gazdar, Gerald, Ewan Klein, Geoffrey K. Pullum, and Ivan A. Sag. 1985. *Generalized Phrase Structure Grammar*. Cambridge, Mass.: Harvard University Press.

Goldberg, Adele. 1991. A Semantic Account of Resultatives. *Linguistic Analysis* 21.66–96.

Grimshaw, Jane. 1990. *Argument Structure*. Cambridge, Mass.: MIT Press.

Guerssel, Mohamed. 1986. *On Berber Verbs of Change: A Study of Transitivity Alternations*. Lexicon Project Working Papers 9. Cambridge, Mass.: Center for Cognitive Science, MIT.

———. 1987. Berber Causativization. *Current Approaches to African Linguistics (Vol. 4)*, ed. by David Odden, 197–208. Dordrecht: Foris.

Gunji, Takao. 1987. Japanese Phrase Structure Grammar: A Unification-Based Approach. Dordrecht: D. Reidel.

Hale, Kenneth, and Samuel Jay Keyser. 1993. On Argument Structure and the Lexical Expression of Syntactic Relations. *The View from Building 20: Essays in Honor of Sylvain Bromberger*, ed. by Kenneth Hale and Samuel Jay Keyser, 53–109. Cambridge, Mass.: MIT Press.

Huang, C.-T. James. 1992. Complex Predicates in Control. *Control and Grammar*, ed. by Richard K. Larson, Sabine Iatridou, Utpal Lahiri, and James Higginbotham, 109–147. Dordrecht: Kluwer.

Jackendoff, Ray S. 1972. *Semantics in Generative Grammar*. Cambridge, Mass.: MIT Press.

———. 1987. The Status of Thematic Relations in Linguistic Theory. *Linguistic Inquiry* 18.369–411.

———. 1990. *Semantic Structures*. Cambridge, Mass.: MIT Press.

Koster, Jan. 1984. On Binding and Control. *Linguistic Inquiry* 15.417-443.

Larson, Richard K. 1991. *Promise* and the Theory of Control. *Linguistic Inquiry* 22.103–140.

Li, Yafei. 1990. X°-Binding and Verb Incorporation. *Linguistic Inquiry* 21.399–426.

Lumsden, John, and Loren Trigo. 1987. The Causative, Passive, and Reciprocal in Berber. *Lexicon Project Working Papers 14*, ed. by Kenneth Hale and Mohamed Guerssel, 79–101. Cambridge, Mass.: Center for Cognitive Science, MIT.

Manzini, Maria Rita. 1983. On Control and Control Theory. *Linguistic Inquiry* 14.421–446.

Rappaport, Malka, and Beth Levin. 1988. What to Do with θ-Roles. *Syntax and Semantics 21: Thematic Relations*, ed. by Wendy Wilkins, 7–36. San Diego: Academic Press.

Rosenbaum, Peter S. 1970. A Principle Governing Deletion in English Sentential Complementation. *Readings in English Transformational Grammar*, ed. by Roderick A. Jacobs and Peter S. Rosenbaum, Waltham, Mass.: Blaisdell.

Sag, Ivan A., and Carl Pollard. 1991. An Integrated Theory of Complement Control. *Language* 67.63–113.

Simpson, Jane. 1983. Resultatives. *Papers in Lexical-Functional Grammar*, ed. by Lori Levin, Malka Rappaport, and Annie Zaenen, 143–157. Bloomington, Indiana: Indiana University Linguistics Club.

Williams, Edwin. 1985. PRO and Subject of NP. *Natural Language and Linguistic Theory* 3.297–315.

XP-PREPOSING IN SPANISH

MARÍA-LUISA JIMÉNEZ
Georgetown University

1. Introduction*

This paper argues that there are two distinct classes of XPs that may prepose in Spanish, those that block movement of the subject to [Spec,IP] and those that do not. We take the subject to be base-generated VP-internally. As the subject does not obligatorily move to [Spec,IP] in Spanish, when it does, we take it to be a case of preposing, similar to that of other constituents. We believe that XPs that block movement of the subject to [Spec,IP] do so because they have also moved to [Spec,IP]. On the other hand, we argue that those XPs that do not block preposing of the subject to [Spec,IP] do not move to this position but to [Spec,CP] instead.

This paper also argues that XP-preposing, with the exception of that of WH-phrases, is motivated from within the interpretative component of the grammar. XPs that move to [Spec,IP] are to be interpreted as foci, while XPs that move to [Spec,CP] are to be interpreted as links, in Vallduví's (1990) terms.

* This paper is an expanded version of the paper 'Spec,IP in Spanish: a focus position', presented at the WCCFL XIII, held at University of San Diego in March 1994. I am indebted to Raffaella Zanuttini and Paul Portner, who reviewed earlier versions of this paper and helped me with their insightful comments. I want to thank all the participants at WCCFL XIII for comments and support. Needless to say, they do not necessarily agree with the conclusions presented here. Finally, I want to dedicate this work to my dear friends Kathleen, Gustavo, Julia and Mila, my parents, Luis and Herminia, and my brother Luis.

2. XP-Preposing in Spanish

2.1. The underlying word order in Spanish

Spanish has been argued to be an SVO language. Recent proposals (Contreras (1991), Bonet (1991), inter alia) have challenged this assumption and have alternatively proposed that VOS is the underlying order in Spanish.[1] They both assume that the subject is base-generated in the specifier of VP that they argue to be to the right of the V-bar instead of to the left.[2] In this light, a pre-verbal subject is always a derived one, contrary to proposals (cf. Rizzi (1982a)) according to which post-verbal subjects are derived.

The fact that, contrary to the case in English, the subject in Spanish does not need to move to [Spec,IP] in order to receive case, supports the claim that post-verbal subjects are the basic ones. We illustrate this in (1), where the underlined constituent is the subject of the sentence:

(1) a. *Ha llamado mi madre esta mañana.*
Has called my mother this morning
'My mother has called this morning'

b. *Mi madre ha llamado esta mañana.*
'My mother has called this morning'

Contrary to Bonet (1990) and Contreras (1991), we take the subject in Spanish to be base-generated VP-internally in a specifier position to the left of the maximal projection (Koopman & Sportiche (1988)). Following Suñer (1991), we believe that V moves to I in Spanish. As a result, we believe that a post-verbal subject is one that remains in its base-generated position, while a pre-verbal subject is one that has undergone preposing.

2.2. Constituents that may be preposed

The fact that the subject may remain VP-internally in Spanish has interesting consequences. One of them is that it allows other constituents, e.g. NPs, PPs, AdvPs, to appear in sentence initial position. For example, in (2a), the AdvP *ayer* 'yesterday' remains in situ, while in (2b) it is

---

1 Bonet (1991) actually writes about Catalan, but she points out that her proposal can also be extended to Spanish.

2 We believe that this claim, although attractive, is problematic for theory internal reasons. It is difficult to maintain that the VP is the only maximal projection with a specifier to the right, especially if one takes seriously Kayne's (1993) proposal that specifiers, which he claims to be cases of adjunction, are always to the left of the head.

preposed. As illustrated in (2c), when *ayer* preposes, the subject has to remain in its base-generated position:

(2) a. *Susana llegó ayer.*
Susana arrived yesterday

b. *Ayer llegó Susana.*
Yesterday arrived Susana

c. **Ayer Susana llegó.*
Yesterday Susana arrived

'Susana arrived yesterday'

PPs and AdvPs are the constituents that most often prepose in Spanish, with the exception of NP subjects.[3] The preposing of an NP that is not the subject of the sentence, although grammatical, is a much more marked operation.[4] In (3b,c) and (4b,c), we provide examples of a preposed PP and a non-subject NP, respectively (these constituents are underlined). As in (2c), when a PP or an NP preposes, the subject must remain VP-internally, as illustrated in the (c) examples:

(3) a. *María vive en Barcelona.*
María lives in Barcelona

b. *En Barcelona vive María.*
In Barcelona lives María

c. * *En Barcelona María vive.*
In Barcelona María lives

'María lives in Barcelona'

(4) a. *Juan odia los aviones.*
Juan hates the planes

b. *Los aviones odia Juan.*
The planes hates Juan

---

[3] NPs, PPs and AdvPs are not the only constituents that may prepose in Spanish; VPs and IPs, to mention just a few, may also appear in a sentence initial position. In this paper we will not address these other cases.

[4] Fontana (1993) argues that NP-preposing was a quite common phenomenon in Old Spanish which, due to the development of left-dislocated structures, became, with time, much more restricted .

c. * *Los aviones Juan odia.*
The planes Juan hates

'Juan hates planes'

In other cases, the preposing of a constituent does not block the movement of the subject. As we illustrate in (5c)-(7c), a preverbal subject and a preposed XP may co-occur (we underline the constituents that undergo preposing):

(5) a. *Juan conoció a su novia en Barcelona.*
Juan met to his girlfriend in Barcelona

b. *En Barcelona conoció Juan a su novia.*
In Barcelona met Juan his girlfriend

c. *En Barcelona Juan conoció a su novia.*
In Barcelona Juan met his girlfriend

'Juan met his girlfriend in Barcelona'

(6) a. *Juan se compró un coche ayer.*
Juan himself bought a car yesterday.

b. *Ayer se compró Juan un coche.*
Yesterday himself bought Juan a car

c. *Ayer Juan se compró un coche.*
Yesterday Juan himself bought a car

'Juan bought himself a car yesterday'

(7) a. *Elisa se bebió la botella de coñac de su padre.*
Elisa 'clitic' drank the bottle of brandy of her father.

b. *La botella de coñac de su padre se la bebió Elisa.*
The bottle of brandy of her father 'clitic' it drank Elisa

c. *La botella de coñac de su padre Elisa se la bebió.*
The bottle of brandy of her father Elisa 'clitic' it drank

'Elisa drank her father's bottle of brandy'

The preposing of an NP, PP or AdvP in Spanish is optional; as we have shown in the examples above, the XP may prepose or may remain in situ. We take this optionality as support that this movement is not syntactically-driven. Although optional XP-preposing is a syntactic operation that, as such, obeys the usual constraints on movement (i.e. SUBJACENCY, ECP), we believe that the motivations behind XP preposing are not syntactic. In the sections to follow, we will argue that these motivations belong to the interpretative component of the grammar.

2.3. Constituents that must be preposed

Contrary to NPs, PPs and AdvPs, which, as we have seen, may optionally prepose in Spanish, WH-phrases must prepose by the level of LF. Interestingly, certain WH-phrases do not allow the subject to raise when they prepose, in a similar fashion to those preposed XPs that also block movement of the subject, as shown in (2)-(4).We illustrate this point in (8) (the underlined XP is the subject of the sentence):

(8) a. *¿Dónde vive tu primo Julio?*
Where lives your cousin Julio?

b. *¿*Dónde tu primo Julio vive?*
Where your cousin Julio lives?

'Where does your cousin Julio live?'

Not all WH-phrases require the subject to remain VP-internally, though. As Jiménez (1994) points out, WH-phrases that are linked to the discourse, in Pesetsky's (1987) terms, do not block movement of the subject to [Spec,IP]:

(9) a. *¿A cuál de los amigos de Ignacio lo invitó Susana a su cumpleaños?*
To which one of the friends of Ignacio him invited Susana to her birthday?

b. *¿A cuál de los amigos de Ignacio Susana lo invitó a su cumpleaños?*
To which one of the friends of Ignacio Susana him invited to her birthday?

'Which one of Ignacio's friends did Susana invite to her birthday party?'

2.4. Where do preposed XPs move to?

Summarizing the facts on XP-preposing in Spanish, only WH-phrases must undergo preposing in Spanish. Other XPs, e.g. NPs, PPs and AdvPs, to give just a sample, may prepose as well, but in these cases the movement of the XP is optional. We have also pointed out that a first group of constituents, illustrated in examples (2)-(4), block the movement of the subject to [Spec,IP] when they prepose, a phenomenon which we also observed in the case of WH-phrases that are not linked to the discourse. On the other hand, a second group of preposed XPs, that we exemplified in (5)-(7), do not block the movement of the subject; in this group we included WH-phrases that are linked to the discourse, following Jiménez (1994).

The distribution facts on XP-preposing in Spanish suggest that not all constituents have the same landing site. The fact that WH-phrases (except those that are linked to the discourse) and NPs, PPs and AdvPs which belong to the first group are in complementary distribution with a subject in [Spec,IP], suggests that these constituents move to the same position, namely, [Spec,IP]. In (10) we illustrate that WH-phrases and preposed constituents of the first group are in complementary distribution with each other as well:

(10) *¿*Dónde ayer fue tu hermano?*
Where yesterday went your brother?
'Where did your brother go yesterday?'

Interestingly, although the AdvP *ayer* 'yesterday' cannot follow the WH-phrase *dónde* 'where', it is free to precede it. We take this fact as evidence that, in each case, *ayer* moves to a different position:

(11) *Ayer ¿dónde fue tu hermano?*
Yesterday where went your brother?
'where did your brother go yesterday?'

Claiming A-bar movement to [Spec,IP] is not new in the literature. Goodall (1991a,b), Bonet (1990), Fontana (1993) and Vallduví (1990), inter alia, have defended the A-bar status of [Spec,IP] in Spanish and have proposed that WH-phrases land in this position, given the fact that they are in complementary distribution with a subject in [Spec,IP]. We suggest that, in addition to WH-phrases, XPs of the first group also move there.[5]

On the other hand, the fact that WH-phrases that are linked to the discourse and NPs, PPs and AdvPs which belong to the second group are compatible with a subject in [Spec,IP], suggest that they do not land in this position. For this reason, we propose that they move to another position, which we believe to be [Spec,CP].

---

[5] Fontana (1993) takes the fact that WH-phrases and subject negative phrases are also in complementary distribution to propose that both move to [Spec,IP]. Goodall (1991a,b) proposes that WH-phrases in Spanish move to [Spec,IP] before moving to their final landing site, [Spec,CP]. We refer the reader to these papers for extensive discussion.

2.5. Other proposals on XP-preposing

There have been other approaches to XP-preposing in the literature. Rivero (1980) and Hernanz and Brucart (1987), inter alia, have proposed that examples such as (2b,c)-(4b,c), which they call instances of TOPICALIZATION, involve movement of the XP appearing in sentence initial position. On the other hand, they believe that there is no movement involved in examples such as (5b,c)-(7b,c), which they claim to be cases of LEFT-DISLOCATION. In these latter cases, the XP is base-generated sentence-initially as an adjoined element.

Campos and Zampini (1990) give conclusive arguments to propose that, only in cases like (7), is the sentence initial XP actually base-generated sentence-initially and resumed by a clitic (*la* 'it-fem.' in this particular example). The NP *la botella de coñac* 'the bottle of brandy' in (7) is not sensitive to the usual island constraints, such as the WH-ISLAND CONSTRAINT that we illustrate in (12). Campos and Zampini (1990) take this fact as a strong indication that there is no movement involved in this case:

(12) *La botella de coñac de su padre no sé [CP cuándo[IP se la bebió Elisa]].*
The bottle of brandy of her father not I know when herself it Elisa drank
'I don't know when Elisa drank her father's bottle of brandy'

If the NP had moved from inside the lower IP, it would not have been able to stop at [Spec,CP] because this position would be taken by the WH-phrase *cuándo* 'when'. Consequently, we would expect (12) to be marginal as one barrier is crossed in this derivation. Contrary to these predictions, the sentence is perfectly grammatical. Nevertheless, if one believes the proposal that WH-phrases move to [Spec,IP] in Spanish, the landing of *cuando* would be [Spec,IP], instead of [Spec,CP], which could be, then, an available escape hatch for the NP. As a consequence, (12) could, in fact, involve movement.[6] We would still have to justify, though, the presence of the clitic, which is necessary to maintain the grammaticality of the sentence.

Campos and Zampini (1990) propose that, in cases such as (5)-(6), the sentence initial XP has actually moved from inside the VP and has adjoined

---

[6] Our claim that *cuando* 'when' is in [Spec,IP] of the embedded clause is supported by the fact that WH-phrases in Spanish block movement of the subject to [Spec,IP], both in main and embedded clauses, as Torrego (1984), among others, has pointed out. The subject in (18), *Elisa*, cannot move to [Spec,IP], as we illustrate in (i):

(i) * La botella de coñac de su padre no sé cuándo Elisa se la bebió.

to CP.[7] The fact that these preposed XPs can co-occur with a WH-phrase that has undergone movement is evidence for their claim that preposed XPs adjoin to CP:

(13) *En Barcelona ¿cómo conoció Juan a su novia?*
In Barcelona how met Juan his girlfriend?
'How did Juan meet his girlfriend in Barcelona?'

(14) *Ayer ¿dónde durmió Gustavo?*
Yesterday where slept Gustavo?
'Where did Gustavo sleep yesterday? '

In our system, WH-phrases that are not linked to the discourse move to [Spec,IP], therefore, [Spec,CP] is an available landing site for the preposed XPs. Consequently, it seems more elegant to us to propose that *en Barcelona* 'en Barcelona' and *ayer* 'yesterday' do not adjoin to CP but move into its Spec position.[8] In order to give a unified account for these preposing facts, it would also be desirable for us to propose that, even in cases where the preposed XP is an NP and it is resumed VP-internally by a clitic, there is movement involved and that the presence of the clitic is required for other reasons. Obviously, this proposal needs more argumentation; as it is not essential for the main proposal of this paper, we leave it open for future research.

3. XP-preposing & the level of interpretation

3.1. Motivations for XP-preposing

In this section we will address the issue of what triggers the preposing of an XP other than a WH-phrase in Spanish. Let us take into consideration the following sentence:

(15) a. *Mi hermano volvió ayer de vacaciones.*
My brother returned yesterday from vacation

b. *Ayer volvió mi hermano de vacaciones.*
Yesterday returned my brother from vacation

c. *Ayer mi hermano volvió de vacaciones.*
Yesterday my brother returned from vacation

---

[7] We refer the reader to their paper for arguments to support theit claim that these constructions involve movement.

[8] If one follows Kayne's (1993) system, where specifiers and adjuncts are the same thing, it would make no difference to claim movement to [Spec,CP] or adjunction to CP.

'My brother returned from his vacation yesterday'

In (15) the AdvP *ayer* 'yesterday' may appear in three different positions within the sentence. In (15a), it remains in situ, while in (15b,c) *ayer* preposes; in (15b), the subject remains in situ, while in (15c) it also preposes. As we have pointed out in the previous section, this movement does not have a syntactic motivation, contrary to what happens with WH-phrases. Our next step is to argue that the motivations for XP-preposing belong to the interpretative component of language.

The truth conditions of (15a,b and c) do not seem to be affected by the position of the AdvP *ayer*. Following Stump (1985), we propose that (16) is a possible translation for the three sentences in (16):

(16) λt [ayer (t) & past (t) & venir (mi hermano)]

After all the temporal elements are incorporated into the translation, the time variable is bound by an existential quantifier; as a consequence, *ayer* does not take scope, and its position does not affect the truth conditions of the sentence:

(17) ∃ t [ayer (t) & past (t) & venir (mi hermano)]

The position of the AdvP *ayer* does affect the felicity conditions of (15a,b and c), though. For example, only (18b) is a felicitous answer to the WH question in (18a), while (18c and d) are an unfelicitous response:

(18) a. *¿Quién volvió ayer de vacaciones?*
Who returned yesterday from vacation?
'Who returned from his vacation yesterday?'

b. *Mi hermano (volvió ayer de vacaciones).*
My brother returned yesterday from vacation

c. # *Ayer volvió mi hermano de vacaciones.*
Yesterday returned my brother from vacation

d. # *Ayer mi hermano volvió de vacaciones.*
Yesterday my brother returned from vacation

'My brother returned from his vacation yesterday'

On the contrary, only (19b) is a felicitous response to (19a):

(19) a. *¿Cuándo volvió tu hermano de vacaciones?*
When returned your brother from vacation?
'When did your brother returned from his vacation?'

b. *Ayer (volvió mi hermano de vacaciones).*
Yesterday returned my brother from vacation

c. # *Mi hermano volvió ayer de vacaciones.*
My brother returned yesterday from vacation

d. # *Ayer mi hermano volvió de vacaciones.*
Yesterday my brother returned from vacation

'My brother returned from his vacation yesterday'

Summarizing, our data indicates that the preposing of NPs, AdvPs and PPs in Spanish does not affect the truth conditions of a sentence, although it does affect its felicity conditions. In the next section, we will review some work on the syntax, semantics and pragmatics of FOCUS and TOPIC, in an attempt to account for the preposing facts that we have described so far. At the end of this paper, we will come back to the sentences in (19) in order to account for the infelicity of the c and d examples.

3.2. The level of interpretation: focus and topic

The notions of focus and topic have been extensively addressed in the literature, but very often mean different things for different people. In this section we will briefly present some theories of focus and topic; we will take from them those concepts that are crucial to explain our data.

Syntacticians, within the GB framework, have argued that there is a syntactic feature, [+F], which all constituents that are foci share. In an operation that is known in the literature as FOCUS RAISING (Chomsky (1976), Brody (1981), Chomsky (1981), Culicover and Rochemont (1983), among others), a focused constituent, which has quantificational force, needs to raise in order to have scope over its quantificational domain. Focus Raising is analyzed as an instance of A-bar movement to a position adjoined to IP.

As for the concept of topic, GB syntacticians over the last two decades have tried to define it in purely syntactic terms, by calling a left-dislocated XP adjoined to the IP/CP node the topic of a sentence. We believe that using the term topic to refer to an XP in sentence initial position may be confusing, because it does not always correspond to what has been called a topic in the semantic tradition.

The notion of focus has also been of major concern for semanticists. Of particular interest is the observation that the focus of a sentence tends to associate with scalar particles such as *only* and *ever,* and also with adverbs like *always,* a phenomenon known in the literature as ASSOCIATION WITH FOCUS. One of the most influential pieces of work on this issue is Rooth

(1985). This work views focus as introducing a set of alternatives, creating then a domain of quantification. The role of scalar particles is to choose one of the alternatives within this set.

Halliday (1967) defines focus as the only informative part of the utterance; the counterpart of focus is the OPEN-PROPOSITION, which is defined as a piece of shared knowledge between the hearer and the speaker. Halliday's open-proposition is quite similar to the Prague School's notion of topic.

Heim (1982) argues that sentences with a quantifier in them have a tripartite structure, which consists of an OPERATOR, a RESTRICTOR and a NUCLEAR SCOPE. Using Heim's tripartite framework, Partee (1991) proposes that the focus of a sentence would fall under the nuclear scope, while the topic, which she defines much in the line of Halliday's open-proposition, would be within the restrictor.

Diesing (1992) proposes the so-called MAPPING HYPOTHESIS, according to which material from IP is mapped into the restrictor, while material from VP is mapped into the nuclear scope (p.10). Although Diesing does not particularly address the issue of focus in her theory, she does briefly in her discussion of bare plurals. She proposes that focused bare plurals have to be inside the VP, that is, the nuclear scope, before reaching LF in order to be interpreted as such. She points out that, although this kind of movement is not syntactically overt in English, it is in other languages such as German.

Vallduví (1990) has a somehow different approach to the subject of focus and topic. He argues that INFORMATICS is another part of the linguistic aparatus, in which informational relations are interpreted. He also proposes that there is another level of representation in the grammar, different from D-S, S-S, LF and PF, which he calls IS (INFORMATION STRUCTURE). Sentence material is organized at S-structure depending on its informational function. Once this material is informatically organized, it is mapped into a pure IS representation, which is later interpreted in the Informatics component. Vallduví's (1990) proposal differs from Heim (1982), Partee (1991) and Diesing (1992) in proposing that sentence structure does not only interface with Logical Semantics but also with Informatics. Vallduví (1990) divides the sentence into focus and GROUND. His notion of focus is quite in the line of Halliday's; he defines it as the only informative contribution to the hearer's knowledge. What he considers to be the ground is basically the same than Halliday's (1967) open-proposition and the Prague School's topic. The ground is further divided into the LINK and the TAIL. Since the notion of tail is not crucial for our discussion, we will not introduce it here. As for the link, it serves as a pointer to where the information, the focus, has to be entered within the knowledge-store system of the speaker (p. 59);[9] because of its function, the link must appear sentence initially.

3.3. XP-preposing and the interpretation of the sentence in Spanish.

In this section we want to argue that, in order for the hearer and the speaker to accomplish a successful communication, sentential constituents have to be arranged in a particular way. We believe that the VP is generally the part of the sentence where informative material is contained; in this respect, we follow Diesing (1992), who believes that focal material has to be inside the VP by LF. Following Halliday (1967), inter alia, we consider that all informative material is focal. In (20b) we illustrate a sentence in which the whole VP is the focus of the sentence:

(20) a. *¿Qué hace Pedro para ganarse la vida?*
What does Pedro to earn the living?
'What does Pedro do to earn his living?'

b. *Vende coches de segunda mano.*
Sells cars of second hand
'He sells second-hand cars'

When the informative part of a sentence is not the whole verb phrase but only one constituent, we believe that the VP becomes Vallduví's (1990) ground or Halliday's (1967) open-proposition, i.e. shared knowledge between the speaker and the hearer. We want to propose that Spanish has two strategies to express that the whole VP is no longer focal, but that the informational part of the sentence falls only on one constituent. The first option is to move the XP to [Spec,IP], a position that is always available in Spanish, as we have argued in this paper. Although this movement to [Spec,IP] affects the felicity conditions of the sentence, it leaves unaltered its truth conditions.

The second option for a constituent to be singled out and be interpreted as the focus of the sentence is to remain in situ and get intonational prominence. Gundel (1988) argues that in languages like English, where sentence stress is quite free and can virtually fall anywhere, intonational prominence is used in order to mark focus. On the other hand, in languages like French or Spanish, in which the sentence stress is always fixed clause-finally, word order is the device the most likely to be used.

We illustrate our proposal of how a constituent is interpreted as a focus in Spanish in (21). In (21a) the WH-phrase *dónde* 'where' requests new

---

9 Vallduví (1990) develops a whole theory of how the speaker's knowledge is stored; due to lack of space, we refer the reader to that work for discussion.

information; the PP *en Madrid* 'in Madrid' is the focus of (21b), because it answers the WH-word and is, then, the informational part of the sentence. In this case, the speaker chooses to mark where the focus of the sentence falls by preposing the XP to [Spec,IP]. In (21c), he chooses to do it by putting intonational prominence on the PP:

(21) a. *¿Dónde vive Susana?*
Where lives Susana
'Where does Susana live?'

b. *En Madrid (vive Susana).*
In Madrid lives Susana

c. *Susana vive EN MADRID.*
Susana lives in Madrid
'Susana lives IN MADRID'

We also want to argue that CP is the domain reserved for links in Spanish, in Vallduví's (1990) terms. Vallduví's link is very similar in distribution to what syntacticians call topic. We prefer to use the term link over topic for two reasons; first, in this way, we are able to avoid confusion with the topic and, second, because the term 'link' captures the idea that this XP in sentence-initial position 'links' the sentence to the previous discourse. Although we borrow Vallduví's terminology, we do not wish to commit ourselves to his theory of Informatics.

Vallduví argues that, because of their informational task, links are inherently sentence-initial (p.84). Usually, the subject of a sentence fulfils the role of a link; in those cases in which the link is an XP other than the subject, this constituent has to move sentence initially.

If XPs that are to be interpreted as links must move, and if we accept that non-D-linked WH-phrases move to [Spec,IP] in Spanish, [Spec,CP] seems a likely landing site for links. In (22b) we provide an example in which the pre-verbal subject fulfils the role of a link; assuming that the subject is generated VP-internally and may remain there in Spanish, we propose that *Roberto*, the subject, has moved from inside the VP to [Spec,CP]. In (23b) the link is the AdvP ayer, which must then raise to [Spec,CP] while the subject remains inside the VP as part of the focus:

(22) a. *¿Qué sabes de Roberto?*
What you know of Roberto?
'What is going with Roberto? '

b. *Roberto se acaba de marchar de viaje.*
Roberto himself finished of to leave of trip
'Roberto has just left on a trip'

(23) a. *¿Qué hicistes ayer?*
What you did yesterday?
'What did you do yesterday?'

b. *Ayer vino Roberto a visitarme.*
Yesterday came Roberto to visit me
'Roberto came to visit me yesterday'

Not all pre-verbal subjects are interpreted as links, though. In (18b), which we repeate here as (24b), the pre-verbal subject *mi hermano* 'my brother' provides the information requested by the WH-phrase *quién* 'who'. Consequently, *mi hermano* is not to be interpreted as a link but as a focus. We then propose that in (24b) the subject does not move to [Spec,CP] but to [Spec,IP]:

(24) a. *¿Quién volvió ayer de vacaciones?*
Who returned yesterday from vacation?
'Who returned from his vacation yesterday?'

b. *Mi hermano (volvió ayer de vacaciones).*
'My brother returned from vacation yesterday'

Before ending this paper, we would like to go back to the examples in (19) and explain why (19c,d) are unfelicitous. We repeat the example as (25) for convenience:[10]

(25) a. *¿Cuándo volvió tu hermano de vacaciones?*
When returned your brother from vacation?
'When did your brother returned from his vacation?'

b. *Ayer (volvió mi hermano de vacaciones).*
c. # *Mi hermano volvió ayer de vacaciones.*
d. # *Ayer mi hermano volvió de vacaciones.*

'My brother returned from his vacation yesterday'

The AdvP *ayer* 'yesterday' provides the information requested by *cuándo* 'when', the WH-phrase in (25a). Consequently, *ayer* is a focus and, in order to be interpreted as such, it may prepose to [Spec,IP] or it may get intonational prominence. In (25b), the AdvP moves to [Spec,IP], is then interpreted as a focus and, as a result, the sentence is felicitous. In (25d), the subject *mi hermano* 'my brother' appears pre-verbally and following *ayer*, which means that the AdvP cannot possibly be in [Spec,IP], but in [Spec,CP] instead. We believe that in (25d) *ayer* is a link, while it should

---

[10] As the glosses for this examples are in (19), we do not provide them. We only include the translation.

be a focus, and *mi hermano* is a focus, while it should be a link, being this the reason why the sentence is infelicitous. Finally, (25c) is infelicitous because *ayer* is neither in [Spec,IP] nor does it have intonational prominence.

4. CONCLUSION

In this paper we have argued that, contrary to WH-phrases, there is another group of constituents that optionally prepose in Spanish. Among them we have included NPs, PPs and AdvPs. The group of XPs that may prepose further divides into two groups; XPs that block movement of the subject to [Spec,IP] belong to the first group, while XPs that do not block this movement belong to the second one. We have accounted for these facts by proposing that constituents which belong to the first group move to [Spec,IP], this being the reason why they are in complementary distribution with preverbal subjects. On the other hand, XPs of the second group move to [Spec,CP] when they prepose; as a consequence, they are able to co-exist with a subject in [Spec,IP].

We have also argued that optional XP-preposing in Spanish is motivated from within the interpretative component of the grammar. Although XP-preposing does not affect the truth conditions of a sentence, it does affect its felicity conditions.

We have followed Diesing (1992) in taking the VP to be the domain where the informational material of the sentence is represented; following Halliday (1967), among others, we have called this informational material the focus of the sentence. We have proposed that XP-preposing to [Spec,IP] allows one constituent to be singled out as the only focal element in the sentence; due to this focus operation, material inside the VP is no longer focal, but part of the ground (Vallduví (1990)) or open-proposition (Halliday (1967)). Finally, we have proposed that XPs that are to be interpreted as links (Vallduví (1990)), move to [Spec,CP].

References

Bonet, Eulalia. 1990. Subjects in Catalan. *MIT Working Papers in Linguistics* 13.1-26.

Brody, J. 1981. Binding Theory and the Generalized ECP. Presented at NELS XII, at MIT, and at 1982 GLOW in Paris.

Campos, Hector & Mary Zampini. 1990. Focalization strategies in Spanish. *Probus, vol. 2.1.*, 47-64. Holland: Foris Publications,

Contreras, Helles. 1991. On the position of Subjects. *Perspectives on phrase structure: head and licensing*, vol.25, ed. by Rothstein. New York: Academic Press.

Culicover, P. & M. Rochemont. 1983. Stress and Focus in English. *Language* 59.123-165.

Chomsky, Noam. 1976. Conditions on rules of Grammar. *Linguistic Analysis* 1.75-109.

Chomsky, Noam. 1981. *Lectures on Government and Binding*. Dordrecht: Foris.

Diesing, Molly. 1992. *Indefinites*. Cambridge: the MIT Press.

Fontana, Josep María. 1993. A residual A-bar position in Spanish. To appear in the proceedings of WCCFL XII.

Goodall, Grant. 1991a. Spec of IP and Spec of CP in Spanish WH-questions. Presented at LSRL XXI.

Goodall, Grant. 1991b. On the status of Spec of IP. To appear in the proceedings of WCCFL X.

Gundel, J. 1988. Universals of topic-comment structure. *Studies in syntactic typology*, ed. by M. Hammond, E. Moravcsik & J. Wirth, 209-39. Amsterdam/Philadelphia: John Benjamins.

Halliday, M.A.K. 1967. Notes on transitivity and theme in English, part II. *Journal of Linguistics* 3.199-224.

Heim, Irene. 1982. *The semantics of definite and indefinirte noun phrases*. Doctoral dissertation, University of Massachussetts.

Hernanz, María Luisa. & Josep María Brucart. 1987. *La sintaxis*. Barcelona: Crítica.

Jiménez, María Luisa. 1994. Subject-verb inversion in Spanish. Paper presented at the LSA annual meeting.

Kayne, Richard. 1993. The antisymmetry of syntax. CUNY unpublished ms.

Koopman, Hilda. & Dominique Sportiche. 1988. Subjects. UCLA unpublished ms.

Partee, Barbara. 1991. Topic, Focus and Quantification. *Proceedings of SALT I*, ed. by S. Moore & A. Wyner, 159-87.

Pesetsky, David. 1987. WH-in-situ: movement and unselective binding. *The representation of (in)definiteness*, ed. by Reuland & ter Meulen, 98-129. Cambridge: MIT Press.

Rivero, María Luisa. 1980. On left-dislocation and topicalization in Spanish. *Linguistic Inquiry* 11.363-93.

Rizzi, Luigi. 1982. *Issues in Italian syntax*. Dordrecht: Foris.

Rooth, M. 1985. *Association with Focus*. Ph.D. dissertation, University of Massachusetts.

Stump, Gregory. 1985. *The semantic variability of absolute constructions*. Dordrecht: D. Reidel Publishing Company.

Suñer, Margarita. 1991. Indirect questions and the structure of CP: some consequences. *Current Studies in Spanish Linguistics*, ed. by Hector Campos & Fernando Martínez-Gil. Washington, D.C.: Georgetown University Press.

Torrego, Esther. 1984. On inversion in Spanish and some of its effects. *Linguistic Inquiry* 15.103-29

Vallduví, Enric. 1990. *The informational component*. Ph.D. dissertation, University of Pennsylvania.

Type Underspecification and On-line Type Construction in the Lexicon

JEAN-PIERRE KOENIG* & DANIEL JURAFSKY* †
University of California, Berkeley & International Computer Science Institute*†*

1 Introduction

Many recent lexical and syntactic theories have used TYPE HIERARCHIES to model linguistic generalizations, including valence alternations, morphological generalizations, subregularities, and positive exceptions (Bobrow & Webber 1980; Flickinger *et al.* 1985; Hudson 1984; Lakoff 1987; Pollard & Sag 1987; Jurafsky 1992; Briscoe *et al.* 1994; Pollard & Sag 1994).

Despite these successes, current type hierarchies are unable to model LEXICAL PRODUCTIVITY: the kind of productive patterns which occur in morphologically recursive languages, lexical borrowing and learning, and productive valence alternations (Hankamer 1989; Pinker 1989). This failure is due to the traditional conception of lexical types as generalizations over actual fully specified entries, functioning like redundancy rules. A lexical type hierarchy gives us an inventory of the word classes in a language, but does not tell us how to use productive processes like inflection to create new forms.

To model lexical productivity, we propose to underspecify the type hierarchy. For example, rather than store a type for each surface form of each word of the language, we store a single type for each root and each productive morphological template. Then these types are combined on-line to build types for surface forms in processing or producing an utterance, by an algorithm we call ON-LINE TYPE CONSTRUCTION. Thus some of the burden typically borne by the lexical type hierarchy is shifted to the processing component, which combines these types on-line.

Although our system is embedded in the specific framework of CONSTRUCTION GRAMMAR (Fillmore *et al.* 1988; Kay 1990; Lakoff 1987; Goldberg 1991; Goldberg 1992; Koenig 1993), it is directly applicable to any typed theory such as HPSG. In fact, we show that on-line type construction can advantageously replace mechanisms like lexical rules which are used in HPSG to model lexical productivity.

2 Typed Lexicons

Theories of typed lexicons (Flickinger *et al.* 1985; Pollard & Sag 1987) rely on the intuition that lexical entries can be grouped into classes with common properties. These common properties can then be stated of the class as a whole, each member of the class inheriting the properties. This process of abstraction can proceed recursively; classes are grouped into more abstract classes, and so on. This set of words and classes and their relations is called a TYPE HIERARCHY. Consider the sample HPSG-style partial type hierarchy with English lexemes in Figure 1. (Our diagrams omit branches of the hierarchy for expository purposes).

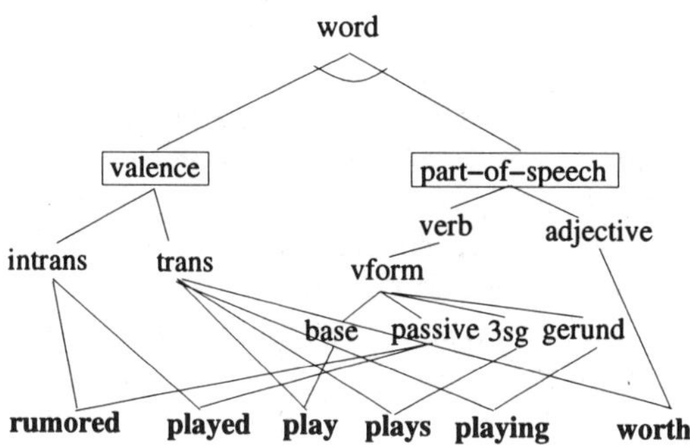

Figure 1: Part of a type hierarchy for HPSG

The generalization that **rumored** and **played** are both intransitive is captured by positing a class **intrans** with inheritance links to both **rumored** and **played** and which includes all properties common to intransitive verbs. This type **intrans** together with a similar general class **trans** PARTITION the type **valence** in our simple hierarchy. This means that any verb must belong to exactly one of the types **intrans** or **trans**. We call this a DISJUNCTIVE interpretation of type inheritance, since set-theoretically, objects which are of type **word** will belong either to the class **intrans** or the class **trans**.

The fact that **rumored** has both an intransitive valence and is a verb while **worth** is both transitive and an adjective is modeled by classifying words along multiple DIMENSIONS. These dimensions, (such as **valence** or **part-of-speech**) are represented in the diagram inside boxes. We mark a curved line on the link between **word** and the two dimensions **valence** and **part-of-speech**, indicating that every word must be specified for both valence and part-of-speech. The link from **valence** to **trans** indicates that the type **trans** is relevant for the **valence** dimension.

We call the relation between a type like **word** and its dimensions like **part-of-speech** a CONJUNCTIVE interpretation of type relations, since words must be specified for both part-of-speech and valence.

As mentioned above, although current type hierarchies have a number of advantages as a device for capturing generalizations, they are incapable of modeling productive processes. Notice in Figure 1 that the lexicon lists even the result of productive inflectional processes, such as *playing* and *played*.

3 On-Line Type Construction

We argue that to model all forms of lexical productivity, we need both a context-free approach to morphology (Selkirk 1982 and others) and a radical underspecification of the type hierarchy. This paper focuses on this second proposal, called ON-LINE TYPE CONSTRUCTION.[1] The gist of the proposal is that lexical entries are stored radically underspecified in the grammar. For example, Figure 2 shows part of the type hierarchy for Construction Grammar. The details of the hierarchy will be discussed later; the important intuition for now is that there is only one type for the lexeme *play*. In contrast to the compiled-out lexicon in Figure 1, we don't need to list a type for the inflected forms *playing*, *played*, etc. These forms of the word *play* are derived while interpreting or producing an utterance by combining *play* with inflectional templates. Since each of these forms is a new type, we call this TYPE CONSTRUCTION. We refer to our algorithm as ON-LINE to emphasize that types are not combined in advance.

Our on-line type construction algorithm is a modification and extension of one of Carpenter's (1992) algorithms for off-line type construction. In this paper we cannot give the formal details of the algorithm.[2] Instead, we will work through an extended example, showing how a type inference system presented with the sentences in (1) builds a fully specified entry for the various

[1] Neither type underspecification nor context-free morphology is sufficient by itself. Context-free morphology is ill-suited to model valence alternations which are not mediated by morphophonological change, such as extraposition. Type underspecification alone is not capable of handling the recursive aspects of morphology.

[2] Happily, constructing types on-line requires only a minor change in the mathematics of Carpenter's algorithm for off-line type construction from a choice-network, allowing us to rely on his axiomatization. This is true because we can view the compiled-out type lattice as virtually present, although the entire lattice is not actually constructed. Thus any time his axioms refer to a join on the lattice, where a compiled-out type lattice merely looks up the join (via the greatest lower bound operation), the underspecified network must actually perform a complete unification at parse-time. If we interpret join in this manner, the only parts of Carpenter's axiomatization that need to be changed are those referring to the fail-type. Informally, the join of two types will produce the fail type if the feature structures associated with the two types fail to unify.

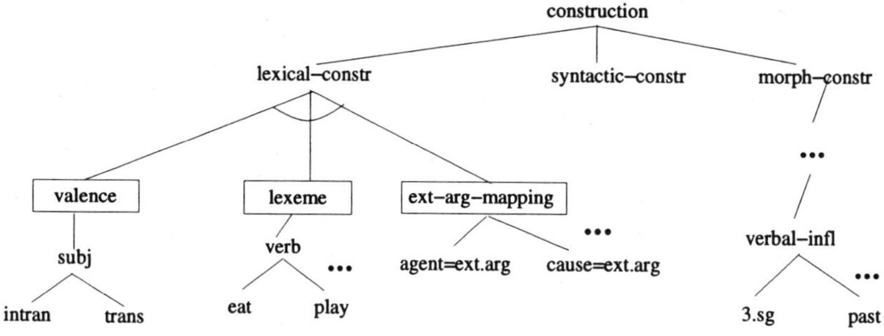

Figure 2: Part of the Construction Grammar Type Hierarchy

forms and valences of the word *play*. Figure 3 shows a simplification of the Construction Grammar type hierarchy with the newly-constructed types indicated in bold italic and connected by dotted lines.[3] As we mentioned

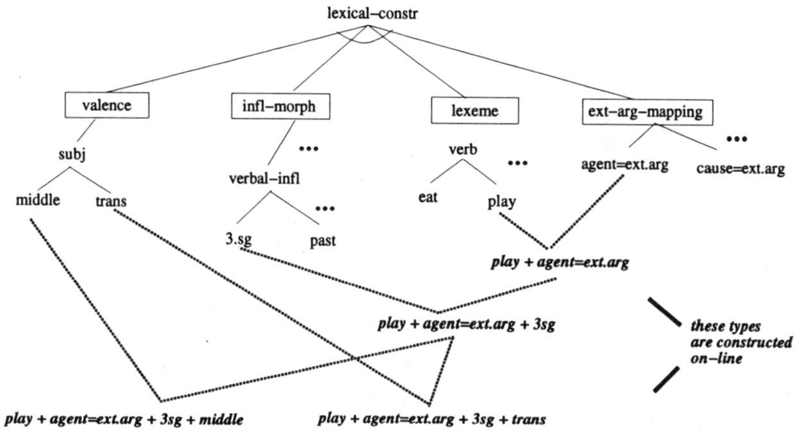

Figure 3: Example of On-Line Type Construction

before, the lexical dimension is underspecified because lexemes like *play* only specify stem phonology; predictable forms like *plays* or *played* are not present in the hierarchy. Consider (1a), which has the form *plays*.

(1) a. Claudio plays the sonata.
b. This sonata plays well on a piano-forte.
c. Carla played the sonata you love so much.

[3] For expository purposes, we (wrongly) assume in this figure that inflectional morphology is not modeled via context-free templates, but is a dimension of **lexical-constr.**

In order to determine the features of the fully-specified entry *plays*, we must construct a new type from the hierarchy. Since *plays* is a sub-type of **lexical-construction**, and **lexical-construction** has four dimensions we know that *plays* will need to be a subtype of exactly one type in each of the four dimensions **lexeme, external-argument mapping, inflection**, and **valence**.

Suppose that the system has determined that the form *play* is of lexeme type **play**. Only some of the types in the other dimensions are compatible with lexeme **play**. For example, since play has an agent argument (and not an experiencer) only the **agent=ext.arg** type in the **external-argument mapping** dimension is compatible with it. The two types can be combined into a more specified entry in which the external-argument is specified as the player of the playing event, as shown in Figure 4[4]. We can read the new feature structure as specifying a STEM "play", a semantic form with two arguments, of which the PLAYER is the external-argument, and a valence (subcategorization) set with two elements.

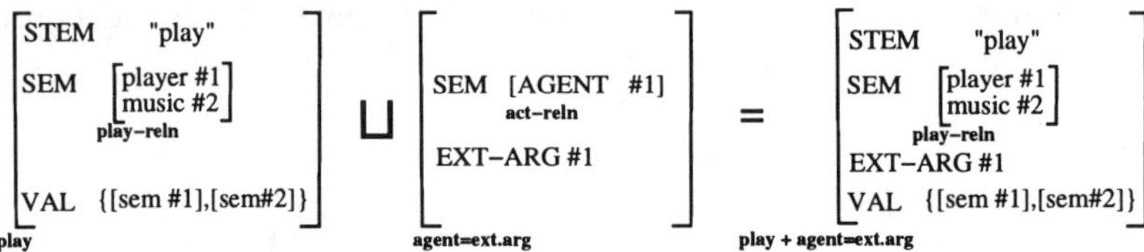

Figure 4: The Constructed Type *play + agent=ext.arg*

Similarly, the only morphological type compatible with the form *plays* is the **3sg** type. We can therefore combine the type **3sg** with the type **play+agent=ext.arg** to derive the new type **play+agent=ext.arg+3sg**. Finally, we must choose between the middle and transitive valence templates (in this simplified graph). Combining each of them with the entry we've got so far creates two new types: **play+agent=ext.arg+3sg+middle** and **play+agent=ext.arg+3sg+trans**. These types are now fully-specified, but only the transitive type is compatible with the input (intuitively middles do not have objects). Sentences (1b) and (1c) would be analyzed similarly, although other choices would be made along the inflectional or valence dimensions.

4 Advantages of On-Line Type Construction

The last section illustrated how on-line type construction models lexical productivity, by combining underspecified abstract entries with valence and morphological templates. In this section, we show how type construction provides a motivated and direct solution to well-known morphological and valence problems. These include positive and negative exceptions, subregularities,

[4]Types are indicated in boldface to the lower left of the feature structure. Pound signs indicate identity of structure.

the need for conjunctive versus disjunctive rule blocks, and suppletive stem selection. In each case we also compare our on-line typing approach to the only previous model of lexical productivity within a typing system, the LEXICAL RULE approach assumed by HPSG. [5]

Our approach to lexical productivity — in addition to a context-free morphology — is to underspecify lexical entries and derive fully-specified entries on-line. The HPSG approach is to use a compiled-out type hierarchy to capture common properties of words, and lexical rules to handle productivity. Lexical rules in HPSG apply on-line to map fully-specified lexical entries into new fully-specified entries. On-line application means that the rules are used to build new lexical entries at the time of interpreting or producing an utterance. [6]

In HPSG, for example, the fact that the verb *eat* has both transitive and passive realizations as in (2)–(4) might be captured with a valence affecting lexical rule, while the morphological relation between *eats* and *ate* might be captured with an inflectional lexical rule.

(2) John ate a sandwich
(3) John eats a sandwich every day
(4) The sandwich was eaten

Figure 5 represents a simplified passive lexical rule, whose effect is basically to suppress the subject requirement and make an intransitive verb out of a transitive verb.

CAT	V	⟹	CAT	V
FORM	active		FORM	passive
VAL	<#1 NP, #2 NP> subj obj		VAL	<#2 NP> subj

Figure 5: A simplified passive lexical rule

4.1 Exceptions and Subregularities It is well-known that lexically-governed processes are subject to exceptions (Lakoff 1970). Consider the verb *rumored* in (5):

[5] We discuss here the theory of lexical rules sketched in Pollard & Sag (1987) and Pollard & Sag (1994). As we have recently become aware, some HPSG scholars have a view of the lexicon much closer to the one advocated in this paper (see for example Krieger & Nerbonne (1993) and Riehemann (1993)). We see this unexpected convergence of results as significant, although we cannot compare their approach to ours in this paper.

[6] Earlier theories of lexical rules assumed the REDUNDANCY interpretation of lexical rules, in which the lexicon contains all forms and the rule acts as a redundancy marker. Goldberg (1991) presents a number of linguistic arguments against this redundancy interpretation. Jurafsky (1992) argues that the redundancy interpretation is inconsistent with the Strong Competence Hypothesis of Bresnan & Kaplan (1982).

(5) a. It was rumored that the meeting would not be held.
b. *John rumored that the meeting would not be held.

As (5) shows, there is no active form of the verb *rumored*. Verbs of this sort are traditionally referred to as POSITIVE EXCEPTIONS, since verbs like *rumored* can be thought of as obligatorily undergoing the passive rule or transformation.

We handle verbs like *rumored* in our system by declaring them as subtypes of type **passive**. Thus *rumored* will correctly inherit all the morphological and syntactic properties common to all passives. In addition, this pretyping will prevent the active template from applying, since the active and passive types are incompatible, thus explaining the lack of an active form. By contrast, ordinary transitive lexemes like *love* can combine with either active or passive templates, because they are not pre-typed to either. Figure 6 shows these examples in our typed system. The absence of any inheritance link between **love** and either the **passive** or **transitive** constructions means it can combine with either provided they contain information compatible with its own. [7]

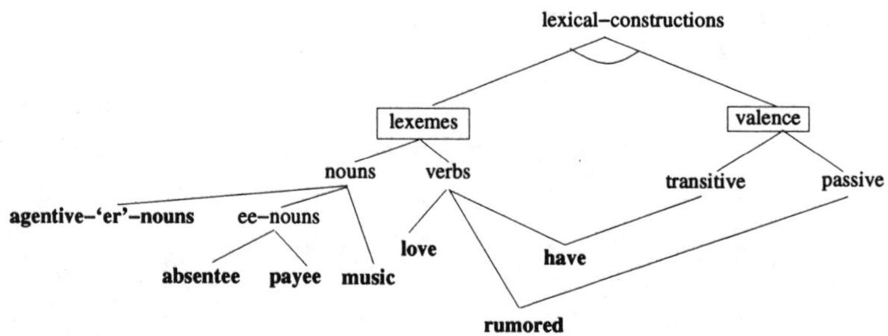

Figure 6: Positive and Negative Exceptions in a On-line Typing System

By contrast, a lexical rule system models positive exceptions by marking the offending lexical item with rule-specific *exception features*. A lexical rule will not apply to any lexical item which is marked with its exception feature. Since **rumored** is obligatorily passive we will need to specify in the entry for **rumored** the feature [PASSIVE-LEX-RULE –] to insure that the passive-lexical rule cannot apply. But in addition to marking the entry with this feature, a lexical rule system must still mark **rumored** as an instance of the passive type, because it acts syntactically like other passive forms. Thus

[7] Note also that so-called negative exceptions to the passive lexical-rule like *have* (although cf. Pinker (1989)) are also handled via *pre-typing* of the relevant entries.

(6) a. *The house was had by many people
b. This house was owned by many people

Abeillé (1990) gives other examples of negative exceptions from French.

the entry will be marked twice, once for being a passive template, and once for being an exception to the passive lexical rule. The on-line typing system accomplishes the same results with only type information.

More generally, on-line type construction allows us to model the difference between fully productive and semi-productive or subregular patterns via the structure of the type hierarchy. For example, Jurafsky (1992) proposes to capture the subregularity relating deverbal nouns in **-ee** (*addressee, employee*) by positing a super-type **-ee-nouns** representing semantically and morphophonologically common information. Since this type is not completely productive, it must be defined extensionally: each word it applies to must be listed in the stored hierarchy, as shown in Figure 6.[8] By contrast, the productive morphological construction **agentive-'er'-nouns** (*builder,mower*) is a leaf in the hierarchy; the lexemes it applies to are not stored in the grammar as a special class of stem. Thus 'builder' and 'mower' are constructed on-line, while 'absentee' is stored in the lexicon.

The positive and negative exceptions to regular processes discussed above are thus a special case of subregularities.

4.2 Stem selection algorithms for suppletive stems The combination of the AND/OR hierarchy and on-line type construction also allows for a direct account of suppletive stems. Consider the French lexeme *aller* in (7a)–(7d), whose various forms are based on four different suppletive stems, *all-*, *ir-*, *v-*, and *aill-*, respectively. Each stem occurs in an idiosyncratic morphological environment. The stem *ir-*, for example, is used in the future and conditional, the stem *v-* for the singular present indicative and imperative and third person plural present indicative, etc. (7) also exemplifies the many different valence and semantic entries for *aller*; it can mean 'go', 'leave', 'fit', etc. Significantly, these semantically different entries for *aller* all share the four stems; each entry can appear with any of the stems, and the endings which attach to these stems are regular. In Aronoff's (1976) terms, there are many French words which correspond to a single morpheme *aller*.

(7) a. Marc *allait* à Paris.
Marc go.impf to Paris
Marc went to Paris'

b. Marc s'en *ira*.
Marc refl of.it go.fut
Marc will leave.

c. Ce costume te *va* bien.
This suit you go.pr well
This suit fits you well (lit. goes well to you)

[8] The figure is somewhat simplified and does not show the internal structure of the **agentive-er-nouns** and **ee-nouns** constructions.

d. Il faut que tu y *ailles*
It must.pr that you there go.subj.pr
You must go there.

The system we propose can elegantly represent stem selection by associating with *aller* a bi-dimensional lexeme of entries and stems, with each stem leaving underspecified the endings to be filled in by the morphological-templates, as shown in Figure 7. Any actual form of *aller* combines one entry subtype and one stem subtype of *aller* together with the ordinary valence, inflectional and other templates. Note that the **/v/-** or **/ir/-** stems in the figure prespecify some morphosyntactic features. These features will constrain the contexts of occurrences of words derived from these stems.[9]

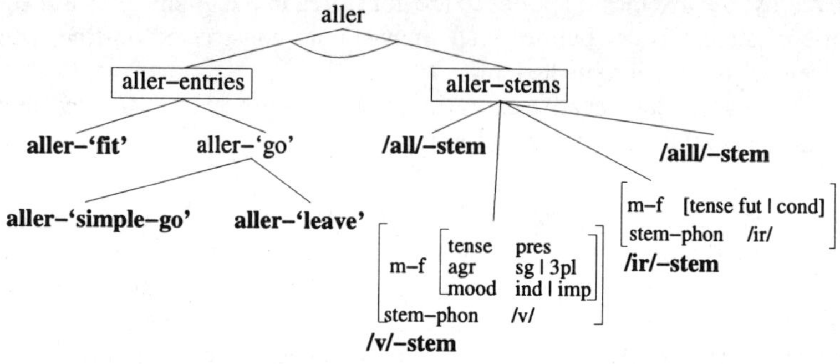

Figure 7: The type hierarchy for the French lexeme *aller*

By contrast, to insure the proper selection of stem in context, the lexical rules responsible for tense and person-endings in French must be sensitive to which of the four stems is appropriate in the sentence's morphosyntactic environment. A lexical rule (or hybrid) approach might propose an abstract *aller* entry shared by the more specific entries ('go', 'leave', 'fit'), as in our approach. However, in order to capture these generalizations about stems without type underspecification, this abstract entry would need to include ad-hoc features representing the phonology of all four possible 'stems' of *aller* and the morphological environments which condition them, duplicating independently-needed features. Moreover, when applying to *aller* inflectional lexical rules would need to implement a choice system, to insure that the correct stem is supplied for each morphological feature bundle. The AND/OR hierarchy assumed by such a hybrid system already implements such a choice system; thus implementing it via lexical rules is particularly inelegant.

[9] As suggested to us by Bill Ladusaw (p.c.) the same strategy can be profitably used for more mundane cases, like English *says* and *does*, which (although orthographically regular) have an irregular allomorph of the verbs with a lowered vowel when followed by the third-singular affix. Each verb would have associated with it a set of forms with specific stem-phonology.

4.3 AND/OR Trees and Conjunctive vs. Disjunctive Rule Application

Another advantage of combining on-line type construction and AND/OR trees is that it can account for what has been called CONJUNCTIVE AND DISJUNCTIVE RULE APPLICATION (Anderson 1992). For example, Inkelas & Orgun (1993) have shown cases in Turkish in which more than one affix applies on a given cycle. We can model this obligatory concatenation of morphemes on the same cycle by using the dimension (AND) part of the type hierarchy to encode the fact that any form must express each of a certain set of affixes.

This section gives a simple example using the Latin verbal inflectional system. For the purposes of this example, we'll assume that the three affixes we consider belong to the same cycle. The structure of Latin verbs is represented informally in (8):

(8) *stem-(aspect)-(tense/mood)-(agreement+pass/act)*
ama-v-isse-m 'I wish I had loved'
ama-ba-r 'you were loved'

Figure 8 shows our proposal for a partial type hierarchy for Latin. It specifies that to construct a Latin verb one must choose a lexeme (here **amare**), and combine it with one template from each of three classes of choices: aspect-affix templates, tense/mood-affix templates, and person/voice ending templates.

In the case of **amavissem** in (8), the only choices compatible with the input form are the nodes at the end of branches a, b, c, and d, i.e. the **amare** lexeme, and the **perfect**, **past-subjunctive**, and **1st-singular-active** affix types. Thus the ordinary logic of AND/OR graphs, required independently for dimensional type systems, accounts for the Latin data with no additional morphology-specific mechanism.

By comparison, the lexical rule approach would need an ad-hoc device to account for the same data. Since these affixes are productive, each would be introduced by a productive lexical rule. Whereas ordinary lexical rules map words onto words, applying only one of these rules does not derive a well-formed word in this case. The three rules must apply together, and in sequence. We refer to this circumstance as a LEXICAL RULE CHAIN. Indeed, the situation is even somewhat more complex, since for affixes 2 and 3 (mood/tense and person endings), there are several possible values for the affixes. This means that capturing Latin verbal morphology with lexical rules requires chains of disjunctive sets of lexical rules. The on-line type construction algorithm avoids this unnecessary machinery.

5 An Ordering Paradox and Other Problems with Lexical Rules

Combining types via our on-line type construction algorithm is order-independent. It is therefore immune to ordering paradoxes, by contrast to rule-based approaches, like the lexical rule approach to valence alternations taken in classical HPSG.

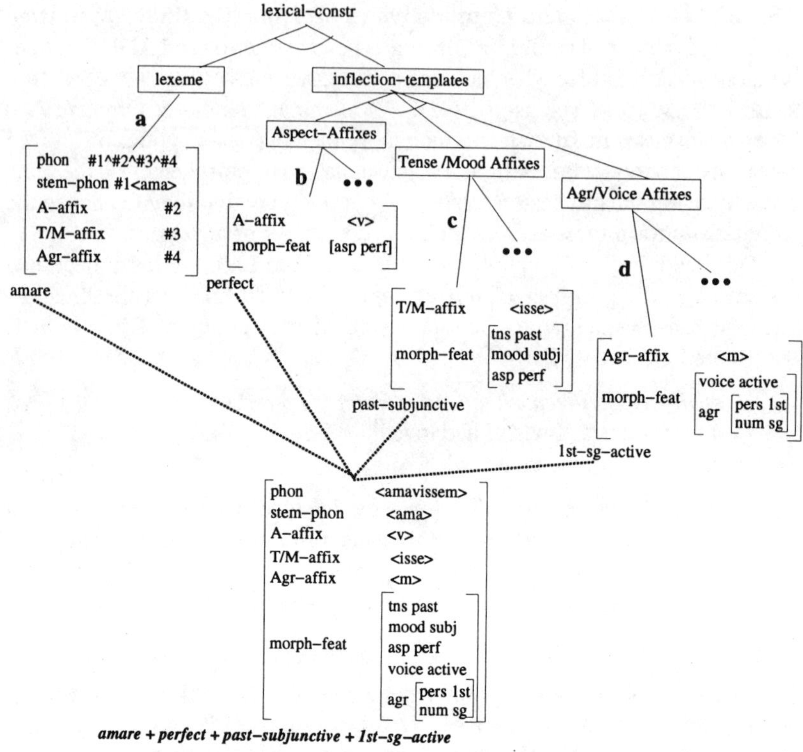

Figure 8: Latin Morphology: A Simplified Example

Data from the French passive-reflexive and impersonal-inversion valence constructions provide such a paradox. Consider (9), which illustrates the basic transitive use of the verb *vendre* 'to sell'.

(9) Jacques vend des livres
Jacques sell.pr indef books
Jacques sells books

(10) illustrates the middle or passive-reflexive use of the same verb (*se vendre*).[10] The lexical rule approach would derive *se vendre* (as in (10)) from *vendre* (as in (9)) via a passive-reflexive lexical rule which moves the object into subject position and adds a reflexive marker which agrees with the subject. (Notice that the reflexive clitic (*t'* or *nous*) agrees with the subject.)

[10]In all examples involving first or second person pronouns, the pronoun refers metonymically to the author of the book being sold.

(10) a. A la dernière foire du livre tu t'es bien vendu.
At the last book fair you sold well

b. A la dernière foire du livre nous nous sommes bien vendus.
At the last book fair we sold well

Figure 9 sketches the lexical rule in an HPSG-style notation.

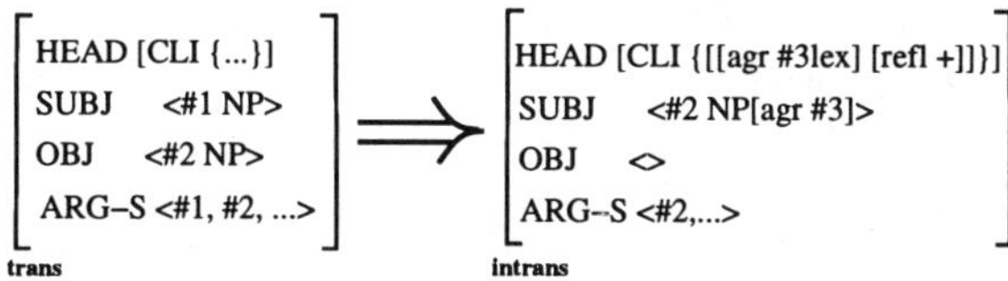

Figure 9: The Passive Reflexive Lexical Rule

(11) illustrates the impersonal-inversion valence of *se vendre*. The lexical rule approach would derive this valence of *se vendre* via an impersonal-inversion lexical rule which moves the subject into object position and adds an expletive subject *il*.

(11) Il se vend deux cent livres par an à Paris
It 3rd.refl sell two hundred books by year to Paris
'Two hundred books are sold each year in Paris'

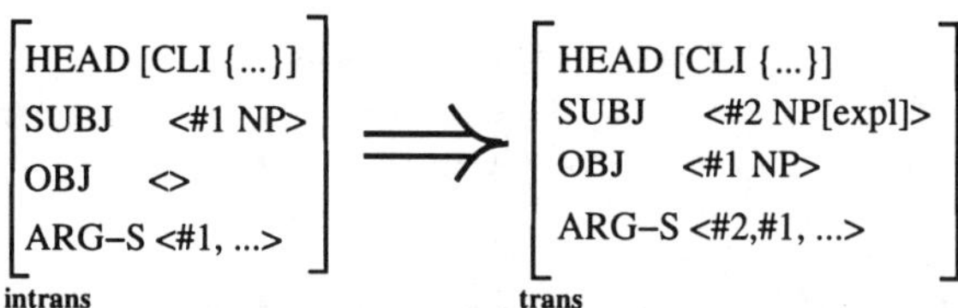

Figure 10: The Impersonal Inversion Lexical Rule

Figure 10 sketches the impersonal inversion rule. Note that this rule must apply after the passive-reflexive rule. The contrast between (12) and (13) shows that the impersonal-inversion construction only applies to intransitive verbs. It cannot therefore apply directly to the transitive form of *vendre*, as shown in (14).

(12) Il est arrivé deux personnes
it be.pr arrive.ppt two people
Two people arrived.

(13) *Il mange des champignons Jacques
It eats.pr indef mushrooms Jacques
Jacques eats mushrooms.

(14) *Il vend des livres Jacques
It sell.pr indef books Jacques
Jacques sells books.

(14) is bad because we must first derive an intransitive valence by applying the passive-reflexive lexical rule. In other words, the passive-reflexive feeds the impersonal-inversion rule. We sketch this as follows:

(15) Jean a vendu un livre $\overset{pass-refl}{\Rightarrow}$ Un livre s'est vendu $\overset{imp-inv}{\Rightarrow}$ Il s'est vendu un livre.
(16) Jean a vendu un livre $\overset{imp-inv}{\Rightarrow}$ *Il a vendu un livre Jean

Unfortunately, there are other agreement facts which show that the impersonal inversion construction must apply before the passive-reflexive rule, causing an ordering paradox. We mentioned above that the reflexive clitic introduced by the passive-reflexive lexical rule must agree with the subject. Note that in sentences where both lexical rules have applied ((17a) below), the reflexive clitic agrees with the expletive subject introduced by the impersonal inversion construction. Thus (17aa) is ungrammatical because the reflexive clitic *t'* agrees with the extraposed pronoun *toi*.

(17) a. *A la dernière foire du livre, il ne t'est bien vendu que toi.
At the last fair of.the book it not refl.2sg be.pr well sell.ppt that you
At the last book fair only you sold well.

b. (?)A la dernière foire du livre, il ne s'est bien vendu que toi.
At the last fair of.the book it not refl.3sg be.pr well sell.ppt that you
At the last book fair only you sold well.

Intuitively, the clitic must be introduced after the surface subject is in place. Since in (17a) the surface subject is introduced by the impersonal inversion rule, the passive reflexive rule which introduces the clitic must follow the inversion rule.

But we showed above that the passive-reflexive rule must apply before the impersonal-inversion construction, to create the appropriate intransitive environment for the application of the impersonal construction. Hence the ordering paradox.[11]

[11] This paradox does not depend on the details of our description of the passive reflexive rule. For example, one might abstract the reflexive clitic agreement facts away from the rule itself, making them constraints on all reflexive verbs which would be inherited by the output of the rule. Since the reflexive rule and the clitic agreement information are now separated, we might attempt to order the inheritance of the reflexive type differently from the passive-reflexive rule. However, this proposal solves the ordering paradox by introducing an inelegant and otherwise unmotivated non-monotonicity: requiring inherited information to apply after other lexical rules.

Our underspecified approach to lexical productivity does not run into any ordering paradox, since patterns do not apply in any order. The passive-reflexive construction (using an HPSG-like notation for comparison with the lexical rule approach) is sketched in Figure 11. The construction says that the valence requirement corresponding to the external-argument is lexically satisfied, and that the subject agrees with a clitic-affix. The impersonal-inversion construction, also in Figure 11 says that one valence requirement is assigned the object function and the subject is an expletive NP. Both patterns, together with other linking patterns, account for the data in (9)–(17a).

[SEM[CONT[EXT–ARG #4]]
HEAD [CLI {[[agr #1] [refl +]]}]
SUBJ <#2 NP[agr #1]>
OBJ <...>
LEX–SAT {#3[SEM|CONT #4]}
ARG–S {#2, #3, ...}]

passive–reflexive

[SUBJ <#1 NP[expl]>
OBJ <#2 NP>
ARG–S {#1, #2, ...}]

impersonal–inversion

Figure 11: The Passive Reflexive and Impersonal Inversion Valence Constructions

The crucial difference between the two treatments lies in the fact that the lexical rule approach operates on fully specified entries. It must therefore decide before the final valence-affecting rule applies which argument is the subject of the output of the passive-reflexive rule and will have to agree with the reflexive clitic.

Finally, we turn to computational considerations. Consider trying to parse the Latin form *amavissem* in (8). Since this word contains productive tense, aspect, and mood suffixes, it will not be listed in the lexicon. So in order to find the lexical entry for this word, we must recover its base form, say the infinitive *amare* 'to love'. How can we do this? If inflection is represented by lexical rules, we must run the lexical rules *backwards*, one at a time, stripping off phonological material at the right-edge of the word at each step, til we come to the base verb, and can check the lexicon.

But now we need to build the proper feature structure for the input form *amavissem*, and so we will have to run each lexical rule forwards again starting from the base infinitive verb to build the surface form!

The lexical rule approach requires this inefficient computation because lexeme-specific information is stored in a specific fully specified base form.[12] Our underspecified type system eschews this extra computational cost entirely,

[12]We wish to stress again that this argument rests on the assumption that lexical rules map fully specified and inflected words into fully specified and inflected words, without employing the kind of underspecified entries or context-free morphology we propose.

since lexical entries are stored radically underspecified and there is only one abstract entry for all inflectional and valence alternates of a word.

This argument shows that the lexical rule approach has a greater computational cost than on-line type construction.

6 Conclusion

We have introduced a new theory of on-line type construction for inheritance-based grammars like Construction Grammar or HPSG which, together with a context-free theory of morphology, accounts for productivity in the lexicon. Because it is based on type theory, our model retains the ability of types to model positive exceptions and subregularities. Because the lattice of types is constructed on-line, we can directly model true productivity in the lexicon.

We have also shown that this direct way of modeling lexical productivity has distinct advantages over other approaches to lexical productivity in lexically oriented theories like HPSG. This includes the ability to model exceptions to productive processes, complex stem suppletion like French *aller* and complex inflectional morphology all without proposing additional mechanisms like exception features or lexical rule chains. Our system also avoids ordering paradoxes which plague lexical rules, like their transformational ancestors.

To conclude, we would like to emphasize an implicit theme of our on-line model, when compared with compiled-out type hierarchies (Carpenter 1992). Where a compiled-out theory lists all possible linguistic types in the grammar, our model shifts some of the burden of representing linguistic knowledge out of the grammar and into the computational processes of generation and interpretation. To a certain extent, recent theories of on-line lexical rules (Pollard & Sag 1994) have made this same shift from earlier redundancy models by allowing new forms to be added to the lexicon. But our model shifts even more out of the grammar, as the underspecified lexicon includes no fully-specified lexemes, only blueprints for their eventual construction. In current work we are examining an extension of this use of the processing component, to model other lexical phenomena like blocking.

Acknowledgments

We thank Bob Carpenter, Tony Davis, Chuck Fillmore, Sharon Inkelas, Paul Kay, Bill Ladusaw, Orhan Orgun, Carl Pollard, Ivan Sag, participants in the Berkeley Typed Feature Structure seminar, and the WCCFL talk audience for valuable comments on the content of this paper. All remaining errors are ours.

References

ABEILLÉ, ANNE. 1990. Lexical and syntactic rules in a tree adjoining grammar. In *Proceedings of the 28th ACL*, 292–298, Pittsburgh, PA.

ANDERSON, STEPHEN. 1992. *Amorphous Morphology*. Cambridge: Cambridge University Press.

ARONOFF, MARK. 1976. *Word Formation in Generative Grammar*. Cambridge: MIT Press.

BOBROW, ROBERT J., & BONNIE WEBBER. 1980. Knowledge representation for syntactic/semantic processing. In *Proceedings of the First National Conference on Artificial Intelligence*, 316–323. Morgan Kaufmann.

BRESNAN, JOAN, & RONALD M. KAPLAN. 1982. Introduction: Grammars as mental representations of language. In *The Mental Representation of Grammatical Relations*, ed. by Joan Bresnan. Cambridge, MA: MIT Press.

BRISCOE, TED, ANN COPESTAKE, & ALEX LASCARIDES, 1994. Blocking. manuscript.

CARPENTER, BOB. 1992. *The logic of typed feature structures*. Cambridge: Cambridge University Press.

FILLMORE, CHARLES J., PAUL KAY, & M. C. O'CONNOR. 1988. Regularity and idiomaticity in grammatical constructions: The case of let alone. *Language* 64.501–538.

FLICKINGER, DANIEL, CARL POLLARD, & THOMAS WASOW. 1985. Structure-sharing in lexical representation. In *Proceedings of the 23rd ACL*, 262–267, Chicago.

GOLDBERG, ADELE E. 1991. On the problems with lexical rule accounts of argument structure. In *Proceedings of the 13th Annual Cognitive Science Conference*, 729–733, Chicago.

—— 1992. The inherent semantics of argument stucture: the case of the English ditransitive construction. *Cognitive Linguistics* 3.37–74.

HANKAMER, JORGE. 1989. Morphological parsing and the lexicon. In *Lexical Representation and Process*, ed. by William Marslen-Wilson, 392–408. Cambridge, MA: MIT Press.

HUDSON, RICHARD. 1984. *Word Grammar*. Oxford: Basil Blackwell.

INKELAS, SHARON, & ORHAN ORGUN. 1993. Level economy, derived environment effects, and the treatment of exceptions. In *Proceedings of the Workshop on Recent Developments in Lexical Phonology*, ed. by Richard Wiese. Düsseldorf: H. Heine Universität.

JURAFSKY, DANIEL, 1992. *An On-line Computational Model of Human Sentence Interpretation: A Theory of the Representation and Use of Linguistic Knowledge*. Berkeley, CA: University of California dissertation. Available as UC Berkeley Computer Science Division TR #92/676.

KAY, PAUL. 1990. Even. *Linguistics and Philosophy* 13.59–216.

KOENIG, JEAN-PIERRE. 1993. Linking constructions vs. linking rules: Evidence from French. In *Proceedings of the 19th BLS*, 217–231, Berkeley, CA.

KRIEGER, HANS-ULRICH, & JOHN NERBONNE. 1993. Feature-based inheritance networks for computational lexicons. In *Inheritance, Defaults, and the Lexicon*, ed. by Ted Briscoe, Valeria de Paiva, & Ann Copestake, 90–136. Cambridge: Cambridge University Press.

LAKOFF, GEORGE. 1970. *Irregularity in Syntax*. New York: Holt, Rinehart, and Winston.

——. 1987. *Women, Fire, and Dangerous Things*. Chicago: University of Chicago Press.

PINKER, STEVEN. 1989. *Learnability and Cognition: The acquisition of argument structure*. Cambridge: MIT Press.

POLLARD, CARL, & IVAN A. SAG. 1987. *Information-Based Syntax and Semantics: Volume 1: Fundamentals*. Chicago: University of Chicago Press.

——, & ——. 1994. *Head-Driven Phrase Structure Grammar*. Chicago: University of Chicago Press.

RIEHEMANN, SUSANNE, 1993. *Word Formation in Lexical Type Hierarchies*. University of Tuebingen thesis.

SELKIRK, ELISABETH. 1982. *The Syntax of Words*. Cambridge: MIT Press.

ACTIVE PASSIVES

ANOOP MAHAJAN
University of California, Los Angeles

1. Introduction

Descriptive fact: There is a passive (like) construction in Hindi in which the underlying object is not made the surface subject and, more importantly, the underlying subject is *not* a surface adjunct phrase (it remains an active subject). This construction then is an ACTIVE construction (and this construction will therefore be called an ACTIVE Passive in this paper) despite having an instrumental subject and characteristic passive morphology as shown in (1) below (compare with active (2)):

(1) šikaariyõõ dwaaraa haathii maaraa gayaa
hunters by elephant-ms-sg. kill-perf go-perf-ms-sg.
The elephant was killed by the hunters.

(2) šikaariyõõ ne haathii maaraa
hunters erg elephant kill-perf -ms-sg
The hunter killed the elephant.

Theoretical relevance of ACTIVE Passives: If (1) is indeed an active construction (as I will argue below), it raises a number of theoretical issues.

Some of these issues are:

(3) (i) Why does the passive agent retain all of its subject properties (except for not having nominative/ergative case)?

(ii) Why does the underlying object fail to become the surface subject despite the characteristic passive (Case absorbing) morphology in the verbal complex (cf. Sobin,1985; also Goodall,1993)?

(iii) What is the status of ACTIVE Passives with respect to theories that correlate properties of passives with Burzio's generalization or with the Case/theta absorption properties of *-en* morpheme (cf.Jaeggli,1986; Baker,Johnson and Roberts,1989)?

(iv) Why are constructions like (2) not widespread? In particular, why do languages like English lack a parallel construction with the same properties?

Summary of the main results of this paper: I will suggest that the agent in ACTIVE Passives is a surface structural subject and that is the reason why it behaves like a subject and that is also the reason why the object does not become a subject in such constructions. The role of passive morphology is to provide a context for the assignment of instrumental morphology to the agent. The underlying object is assigned Case the same way as objects get in normal active ergative constructions, i.e., from AGR (cf. Mahajan,1989). I will also suggest that Burzio's generalization does not hold in these construction types (and possibly in all oblique subject constructions). The fact that English-like languages exhibit effects of Burzio's generalization in passive constructions is because such languages do not allow oblique subjects in general, as opposed to languages like Hindi that have a variety of oblique subjects and consequently the passive *by* phrase is demoted and the underlying object is moved to the subject position. The analysis pursued in this paper will motivate a view of passives which is very much like the classical derivational view of passives in earlier transformational grammars.

Outline of the paper: I will argue that the construction exemplified in (1) is indeed an active construction. This will be done by providing evidence that the underlying subject in such constructions retains all its subject properties despite having oblique morphology (section 3) and that the underlying object remains a surface object and is not made a subject at any stage of the derivation (section 4). I will then sketch out an analysis for the properties that this construction exhibits (section 5). A discussion of the theoretical issues raised above in (i)-(iv) will conclude the paper (sections 6-8).

2. Background

Constructions with properties similar to Hindi ACTIVE Passives are reported to exist in related languages like Marathi (cf. Rosen and Wali, 1989; Joshi, 1991; similar type of facts from certain North Russian dialects have been reported by Timberlake, 1976). However, the construction that I discuss here appears to have somewhat different properties from the constructions that Rosen and Wali (1989) discuss. In particular, it will become evident from the properties of ACTIVE Passives discussed in this paper that they do not fall in either of the two classes of Marathi Passives discussed by Wali and Rosen. I will, however, not discuss the relevant differences between Marathi and Hindi in this paper. Mohanan (1990) discusses a range of facts from a dialect of Hindi which are also partially similar to the ones discussed below. However, there are significant differences between the dialect that I discuss in this paper and the dialect that Mohanan reports. An example of the construction (relevant to our discussion) that Mohanan discusses is in (5).

(4) ravii se raam ko piiṭaa nahĩĩ gayaa (Mohanan,1990,p203)
Ravi-Inst Ram acc beat-perf not go-perf
Ravi could not (bring himself to) beat Ram.

Major differences between construction type (2) (the ACTIVE Passive) and Mohanan's (4) (called THE INSTRUMENTAL SUBJECT CONSTRUCTION by Mohanan) are: (i) the dialect (which has construction type (2)) that I discuss here does not require negation *nahii* that is required in regular passives and in the instrumental subject construction discussed by Mohanan (also see Kachru,1980; Pandharipande,1981; Davison,1982). (ii) this dialect allows the subject to take a regular oblique ending *dwaaraa* (as in (2) above) rather than the instrumental marker *se* that instrumental subjects require (cf. Mohanan,1990, p.203-205) (iii) construction type illustrated in (2) does not have a capabilitative meaning associated with it as does the instrumental subject construction (4) reported by Mohanan.[1]

---

[1] The capabilitative meaning aspect of Hindi passives has been discussed in many treatments of the Hindi Passive constructions (for a comprehensive discussion, see Pandharipande, 1981). It appears that the presence of the *se* instrumental ending (on the agent) is more strongly associated with the capability meaning that the *dwaaraa* ending used in (2). It is not entirely clear whether the differences that I am describing between the facts reported by Mohanan and the facts reported here are dialectal or whether (1) represents a distinct oblique subject construction in addition

3. Subject of ACTIVE Passives

To argue that the underlying subject of ACTIVE Passive constructions like (1) is a surface subject, I will use a number of tests that indicate that the agent phrase in such constructions has the same properties as other 'normal' subjects have, i.e., I will compare ACTIVE Passive subjects with nominative and ergative subjects and show that they have the same structural properties. This is essentially the same strategy that is used in a number of papers in Verma (1976) and also by Wali and Rosen (1989) and Mohanan (1990); most of the tests are based on Keenan (1976). The tests that I use here are based on anaphor binding, pronominal coreference, control and extraction.

3.1. Anaphor binding: Agentive phrases in ACTIVE Passives can bind anaphors the same way that nominative subjects and ergative subjects can. This is shown in (5)-(7) below:

(5) salmaa$_i$ apne$_i$ ghar kaa nirikšaṇ karegii
Salma self's house gen examination do-fut-fem
Salma will examine self's house.

(6) salmaa$_i$ ne apne$_i$ ghar kaa nirikšaṇ kiyaa
Salma-erg self's house gen examination do-perf-masc
Salma examined self's house

(7) salmaa$_i$ dwaaraa apne$_i$ ghar kaa nirikšaṇ kiyaa gayaa
Salma by selfs home gen examination do-perf-masc go-perf masc
=Self's house was examined by Salma.

3.2. Antisubject Orientation of pronouns: As noted by Gurtu (1985), Mohanan (1990) and Srivastav-Dayal (1993), pronouns in Hindi have an anti-subject orientation. This fact is similar to the one found in Scandinavian languages like Icelandic (Thrainsson, 1979), Danish

---

to the instrumental subject construction described by Mohanan. The theoretical issues that are discussed here are not identical to the ones addressed by either Rosen and Wali (1989) or by Mohanan (1990). However, the empirical part of the discussion and the consequences of the solutions suggested here may have implications for the analyses provided in those studies. The converse may also be true. I will, however, not pursue a systematic comparison between Hindi and Marathi or between Mohanan's facts and analysis and the facts and analysis reported here.

(Vikner,1985) and in Norwegian (Hestvik,1992). Hestvik derives the antisubject orientation in Norwegian by postulating an LF pronominal movement to INFL (similar to LF movement of reflexives), the level at which binding principle B applies to yield the effect of disjoint reference between the subject and the pronoun. The crucial observation is that since subject is the only element that c-commands the pronoun at LF (after movement), we get anti-subject orientation and not anti-object orientation (see Hestvik,1992 for the details of this proposal). This analysis provides a test that can be used to check the subjecthood of an argument. (10) below indicates that the agentive phrase of ACTIVE Passives is in fact in SPEC IP (SPEC AGRPs) position ((8)-(9) illustrate the same fact for nominative and ergative subjects)

(8) salmaa$_i$ uske$_{*i}$ ghar kaa nirikšaṇ karegii
Salma her house gen examination do-fut-fem
Salma$_i$ will examine her$_{*i}$ house.

(9) salmaa$_i$ ne uske$_{*i}$ ghar kaa nirikšaṇ kiyaa
Salma-erg her house gen examination do-perf-masc
Salma$_i$ examined her$_{*i}$ house

(10) salmaa$_i$ dwaaraa uske$_{*i}$ ghar kaa nirikšaṇ kiyaa gayaa
Salma by her home gen examination do-perf-masc go-perf-masc
=Her$_{*i}$ house was examined by Salma$_i$.

3.3. Control into argument clauses: The behavior of agent phrases in ACTIVE Passives in subject control constructions indicates that they are subjects as indicated by (13) below:

(11) salmaa$_i$ [PRO$_i$ ghar jaanaa] caahtii thii
Salma home go-inf want-imp-fem be-pst-fem
Salma wanted to go home.

(12) salmaa$_i$ ne [PRO$_i$ ghar jaanaa] caahaa
Salma erg home go-inf want-perf-masc
Salma wanted to go home.

(13) salmaa$_i$ dwaaraa [PRO$_i$ ghar jaanaa] caahaa gayaa
Salma by home go-inf want-perf-masc go-perf-masc
=It was wanted by Salma to go home.

3.4. Control into adverbial clauses: As noted by Kachru, Kachru and

Bhatia (1976) and Mohanan (1990), control into conjunctive participle (*kar*) adverbial clauses can be used as a test for subjecthood. Agentive phrases of ACTIVE Passives also behave like subjects with respect to this test as indicated by (16) below.

(14) salmaa$_i$ [PRO$_i$ ghar jaa kar] mohan ko dããṭegii
Salma home go do Mohan ko scold-fut-fem
=Salma will scold Mohan after going home.

(15) salmaa$_i$ ne [PRO$_i$ ghar jaa kar] mohan ko dããṭaa
Salma erg home go do Mohan ko scold-perf-masc
Salma scolded Mohan after going home.

(16) salmaa$_i$ dwaaraa [PRO$_i$ ghar jaa kar] mohan ko dããṭaa gayaa
Salma by home go do Mohan ko scold-perf go-perf-masc
=Mohan was scolded by Salma after she went home.

3.5. Extraction out of an extraposed clause: This test can be used to show that the agent phrase of an ACTIVE Passive construction is an argument and has not been demoted to an adjunct status (this test does not distinguish between subjects and objects since they behave alike with respect to extraction in Hindi). In Hindi, extraposed clauses that are duplicated by an expletive *yah* in the object position act as islands for extraction. They yield the familiar argument/adjunct asymmetries with respect to extraction. Argument extraction from extraposed *yah* clauses yields a weaker (subjacency) violation while adjunct extraction yields a stronger (ECP) violation (cf. Mahajan,1990; 1993 and Srivastav,1991). (17) below illustrates the *yah* extraposition construction.(18)-(19) show that long distance NP scrambling and wh-scrambling yield subjacency type violations for subject extractions.

(17) salmaa yah soctii thii ki mohan ne raam ko maaraa
Salmaa it think-imp be-pst that Mohan erg Ram ko hit-perf
=Salma thinks *it* that Mohan hit Ram.

(18)??? mohan ne, salmaa yah soctii thii ki __ raam ko maaraa
Mohan erg Salma it think-imp be-pst that Ram ko hit-perf
=Mohan, Salma thinks that (he) hit Ram.

(19)??? kis ne, salmaa yah soctii thii ki __ raam ko maaraa
who erg Salma it think-imp be-pst that Ram ko hit-perf
=Who does Salmaa think that (he) hit Ram?

Extraction of adjuncts yields a stronger violation as shown by (21) below derived from (20). (22) indicates that in the absence of *yah*, adjunct extraction is possible, i.e., long distance adjunct extraction is not prohibited in general.

(20) salmaa yah soctii thii ki mohan ne raam ko ghar me maaraa
Salmaa it think-imp be-pst that Mohan erg Ram ko home at hit-perf
Salma thinks that Mohan hit Ram at home.

(21)*ghar me, salmaa yah soctii thii ki mohan ne raam ko__maaraa
home in, Salma it think-imp be-pst that Mohan erg Ram ko hit
=At home, Salma thinks that Mohan hit Ram.

(22) ghar me, salmaa soctii thii ki mohan ne raam ko __maaraa
home in, Salma think-imp be-pst that Mohan erg Ram ko hit
=At home, Salma thinks that Mohan hit Ram.

The extraction of *dwaaraa* agent phrases of ACTIVE Passives from inside an extraposed *yah* clause indicates that they behave like arguments rather than like adjuncts. (23) and (24) below have a status similar to that of argument extraction as in (18)-(19) above rather than that of an adjunct extraction case like (21) above.[2]

---

[2] This fact, while providing a clue about the status of the *dwaaraa* phrases in ACTIVE Passives (that it is an argument), raises an issue about the status of *by* phrases in English. Thus, while it is often argued that the agent phrase in English has the status of a structural adjunct (i.e., it is not in an A-position), its status with respect to extraction from within wh-islands yields weaker violations than that of adjunct extractions. (I) and (ii) below are weaker (subjacency like violations) compared to (iii) which is a stronger (ECP) violation.
(I) ??Who do you wonder whether John shot?
(ii) ???By whom do you wonder whether Bill was shot?
(iii)* How do you wonder whether Bill shot John?
If *by* phrases in English passives are base generated in an adjunct position then (ii) would be a problem since the trace of the passive agent will be ungoverned in (ii). (I should note that it has been suggested that the extraction of *by* phrases out of wh-islands does indeed show ECP effects (cf. Zubizarreta,1985, Roberts,1987) though this claim is not entirely consistent with the judgements that I obtained. A weaker status of *by* phrase extraction violations would support the idea that the extraction is from a theta governed position (a claim consistent with the idea developed in the later part of this paper).

(22) salmaa yah soctii thii ki mohan dwaaraa raam ko maaraa gayaa
Salmaa it think-imp be-pst that Mohan by Ram ko hit-perf go-perf
Salma thinks that Ram was hit by Mohan at home.

(23)???mohan dwaaraa salmaa yah soctii thii ki __ raam ko maaraa gayaa
Mohan by Salmaa it think-imp be-pst that Ram ko hit-perf go-perf
=By Mohan, Salma thinks that Ram was hit.

(24)???kis ke dwaaraa salmaa yah soctii thii ki __ raam ko maaraa gayaa
who gen by Salmaa it think-imp be-pst that Ram ko hit-perf go-perf
=By whom does Salma think that Ram was hit?

3.6. Summary of section 3: The syntactic behavior of *dwaaraa* phrases of ACTIVE Passives indicates that it is in the subject position. The last test indicates that the *dwaaraa* phrase is an argument with respect to movement and cannot be viewed as an adjunct for the purposes of extraction out of *yah* islands..

4. Object of ACTIVE Passives

In this section, I will show that the object in ACTIVE Passive construction behaves like a normal object in nominative/ergative constructions.

4.1. Agreement: The object in an ACTIVE Passive construction may or may not show agreement depending on its case marking. In that respect, it behaves in a manner similar to objects in ergative/ nominative constructions. (25)-(26) below indicate that the objects in ergative and in ACTIVE Passive constructions show agreement.

(25) raajaa ne jaŋgal ke saaree šer maar diye
king erg jungle gen all tiger(masc-pl) kill give-perf-masc-pl
The king killed all the tigers in the jungle.

(26) raajaa dwaaraa jaŋgal ke saaree šer maar diye gaye
king by jungle gen all tiger(masc-pl) kill give-perf-masc go-perf-m-pl
All the tigers in the jungle were killed by the king.

4.2. Morphological case: Objects in Hindi can be marked with a *-ko* ending that denotes specificity. (27), (28), (29) below indicate that in that respect objects in ergative constructions, nominative constructions and in ACTIVE Passive constructions do not differ (cf. Davison, 1988).

(27) raajaa ne saare šerõ ko maar diyaa
king erg all tigers ko kill give-perf-m-sg (def agr)
The king killed all the tigers in the jungle.

(28) raajaa saare šerõ ko maar degaa
king nom all tigers ko kill give-fut-m-sg
The king will kill all the tigers in the jungle.

(29) raajaa dwaaraa saare šerõ ko maar diyaa gayaa
king by all tigers ko kill give-perf-m-sg go-perf-m-sg (def agr)
All the tigers in the jungle were killed by the king.

4.3. Pronominal coreference. Pronouns in Hindi can corefer with objects. This is shown in an ergative construction (30) and a nominative subject construction in (31). As the ACTIVE Passive construction in (32) shows, the pronoun in this construction can corefer with the object indicating that the object has not moved to the subject position.

(30) siitaa$_j$ ne salmaa$_i$ ko uske$_{i/*j}$ ghar bhej diyaa
Sita erg Salma ko her home send give-perf
Sita sent Salma to her home.

(31) siitaa$_j$ salmaa$_i$ ko uske$_{i/*j}$ ghar bhej degii
Sita Salma ko her home send give-fut
Sita will send Salma to her home.

(32) siitaa$_j$ dwaaraa salmaa$_i$ ko uske$_{i/*j}$ ghar bhej diyaa gaya
Sita by Salma ko her home send give-perf go-perf
Salma was sent to her home by Sita.

4.4 Object Control: (33)-(34) below illustrate object control constructions with an ergative subject and a nominative subject respectively. (35) shows that the object is still capable of controlling in an ACTIVE Passive construction, i.e., it has not been promoted or demoted.

(33) raam$_i$ ne mohan ko [PRO$_i$ ghar jaane ke liye] kahaa
Ram erg Mohan ko home go-inf gen for told
Ram told Mohan to go home.

(34) raam$_i$ mohan ko [PRO$_i$ ghar jaane ke liye] kahegaa
Ram Mohan ko home go-inf gen for tell-fut
Ram will tell Mohan to go home.

(35) raam$_i$ dwaaraa mohan ko [PRO$_i$ ghar jaane ke liye] kahaa gayaa
Ram by Mohan ko home go-inf gen for tell-perf go-perf
Ram told Mohan to go home.

4.5. Object Extraction out of a *yah* extraposed clause: This test shows once again that the underlying object in an ACTIVE Passive remains an argument and is not demoted to an adjunct status (though this test does not show whether or not the object has been promoted). (36) and (37) below are both subjacency violations indicating the argumenthood of the object in the ACTIVE Passive construction.

(36) ??? mohan ko salmaa yah soctii thii ki
Mohan ko Salma it think-imp be-pst that
raam dwaaraa__maaraa gayaa
Ram by hit-perf go-perf
=Mohan, Salma thinks that (he) was hit by Ram.

(37)??? kis ko salmaa yah soctii thii ki
who ko Salma it think-imp be-pst that
raam dwaaraa __ maaraa gayaa
Ram by hit-perf go-perf
=Who does Salma think that (he) was hit by Ram?

4.6. Summary of the results so far: All the tests that we have conducted so far indicate that the *dwaaraa* phrase of the ACTIVE Passives is a surface subject. Furthermore, the underlying object has not been promoted to the subject position. Therefore, ACTIVE Passives have, in fact, not undergone any change of grammatical functions : they are **active** constructions.

5. Analysis of ACTIVE Passives:

Suggestion: ACTIVE PASSIVE (1) is parallel to the active ergative construction given in (2) (both repeated below). It differs from (2) in that it has no passive auxiliary and the subject is ergative rather than a *by* phrase. In both (1) and (2), the verb is a perfect participle.

(1) šikaariyõõ dwaaraa haathii maaraa gayaa
hunters by elephant-ms.sg. kill-perf go-perf-ms.-sg.
The elephant was killed by the hunters.

(2) šikaariyõõ ne haathii maaraa
hunters erg elephant kill-perf
The hunter killed the elephant.

If we assume that perfect participles are not structural Case assigners in Hindi (cf. Mahajan, 1989) then the object will have to get a structural Case elsewhere in the sentence. Since the participle agrees with the object in (1) as well as in (2), let us assume, following Kayne (1989), that the object moves to SPEC AGRo, the site of participle agreement. This explains why the objects in active constructions and the objects of the ACTIVE Passive in (1) behave in an identical manner: both are in a canonical object position, which is SPEC AGRo. I assume that the passive auxiliary, while forming a complex predicate with the participle (cf. Saksena, 1978), projects its own AGR projection and can, therefore, agree with the object independently.[3] The overt subject case marking, ergative in (3) and *dwaaraa* (*by*) in (2), must then be tied to the nature of the verbal complexes. In (2), the verbal complex is a complex predicate containing (passive) auxiliary *gayaa*; in (3) there is no such auxiliary (in fact ergative constructions are not compatible with this auxiliary *gayaa*). Let us assume that the predicate in (2) assigns a lexical instrumental case if it contains the auxiliary `go' with a perfective main verb. In the absence of such an auxiliary, a lexical ergative case is assigned if the verb is transitive and perfective. However, in both instances, the subject is in its VP internal 'subject' position when the lexical case is assigned. This lexical assignment of case to the subject can be viewed as an instance of 'dependent case marking' in the sense of Marantz (1991) (though it applies internal to VP rather than to SPEC IP position as suggested by Marantz).

The lexically case marked subjects can now move to a VP external subject position (SPEC AGRs). This explains why the subjects in (2) and (3) behave identically with respect to all the subjecthood tests. They are underlying as well as surface subjects. Similarly, the underlying object

---

[3] This view of syntactic position of AGR projections is consistent with Travis (1991) where it is suggested that VP has AGR projections internal to it. Such positions may be structurally below the subject position, the subject being generated in the highest SPEC position of the VP shell (cf. Koopman and Sportiche, 1991). Alternatively, the object agrees with the participle and the auxiliary by moving through their SPEC positions directly.

moves to SPEC AGRPo position in active as well as ACTIVE PASSIVE constructions. It never moves to the SPEC AGRPs position in either construction and therefore it retains its object properties.

It should be noted that this sort of analysis is made possible only in theories that adopt the VP internal subject hypothesis. Previous theories of Passive with the Principles and Parameters approach did not have access to the ideas made available by the VP internal subject theories and therefore had NO position to fit the external argument in an A-position in passive constructions. That is, these theories had only two A-positions available within the IP and since both of these positions were required (in English) for the object and its trace, there simply was no A-position available for the underlying subject. VP internal subject hypothesis along with the articulated IP structure overcame this shortcoming by providing additional A-positions. If we base generate both the subject and the object internal to the VP, several possibilities become available. The analysis of Hindi ACTIVE Passives that I have outlined essentially exploits one of these possibilities. English, I will argue next, utilizes a somewhat different strategy for an independently motivated reason yielding a different output structure.

6. Differences between Hindi and English

Why does English not have a construction similar to Hindi ACTIVE Passives? That is, why is the external argument suppressed in English Passives (for detailed arguments for external argument suppression in English, see Grimshaw,1990)? Part of the answer to this question is that the English Passive *is* similar to the Hindi ACTIVE Passives at an underlying level but for some reason the *by* phrase of English is not allowed to move into the SPEC AGRPs position. That is, the subject in Passive constructions in English also starts out in the SPEC VP position and is assigned a lexical case marker *(by)* by the complex predicate comprising of the participle and *be* (which originates in a lower position than the normal AUX position (cf. Baker, Johnson and Roberts,1989)). Under this view, Hindi and English are underlyingly identical in the categorial assignment of instrumental P to the subject in participle+*be* constructions.

The crucial difference between Hindi and English then must be that Hindi allows oblique subjects in general while English does not (for evidence that Hindi allows a variety of oblique subject constructions, see papers in Verma (1976) and Mohanan (1990)). Is this a parametric difference between Hindi and English? I will not go into this question in this paper (see Mahajan ,1994, where it is suggested that this difference is tied (to some degree) to the fact that English has surface SVO order while Hindi is SOV).

If English does not allow *by* phrases to move into SPEC AGRPs (and this would be a subcase of English not allowing oblique subjects in general; for some relevant discussion from a somewhat different perspective see Bresnan and Kanerva,1989 and Bresnan,1994), then the SPEC AGRs position in English would have to be filled by the object. This would be forced by the Extended Projection Principle. Under this view, then, NP movement in English Passives is forced not for Case theory reasons but because of the Extended Projection Principle.

The *by* phrase in English appears in an adjunct position because it is not allowed in the subject position. In Hindi, the *by* phrase is allowed in the subject position therefore it is not *demoted* to an adjunct position. It appears in the subject position with all the properties of subjects.[4]

7.0. Consequences: Burzio's Generalization and Passives

If the agentive marking *dwaaraa* of Hindi (and *by* of English) are assigned as a lexical case to the thematic subject in the SPEC VP position then there is no straightforward reason for saying that the external theta role is not assigned in Passives. The analysis suggested here is not directly compatible with Burzio's generalization since Case absorption is not correlated with external theta role absorption. Burzio's generalization holds superficially for English Passives to the extent that the *by* phrase in English does not end up in an A-position. However, as I have indicated, that may have nothing to do with subject dethematization. Rather, that fact follows from the fact that since oblique (PP) subjects are not permitted in the subject position in English, they are moved out of the way to an adjunct position necessitating the object to fill the surface subject position. This movement is to satisfy the Extended Projection Principle and may or may not have anything to do with Case theory (I will not go into the fact that English Passives do not allow expletive subjects in Passives though that may be a relevant issue). This analysis then supports Marantz's (1991) observation that Burzio's generalization may not be about structural Case (see Marantz's discussion of Japanese (cf. Kubo,1989), Kichaga (cf. Bresnan and Moshi,1990) and Icelandic (cf. Zaenen, Maling and Thrainsson,1985; Sigurdsson,1991). In fact, Burzio's generalization does

---

[4] This leaves open the question of the *other* Passive construction(s) in Hindi which need to be investigated from the perspective of this paper (see Mohanan,1991 for some relevant discussion).

not hold for Hindi Passives (the same is true for Hindi ergative and dative subject constructions).

There is, however, a correlation between the inability of a verb to assign structural Case and its subject receiving a lexical case in Hindi. Thus the subjects of perfect participles receive an instrumental/agentive or ergative case while the subjects of experiencer predicates receive a dative case. Similarly, the subjects of nouns and verbal nouns get a genitive case. This suggests the idea that lexical cases are assigned by a variant of genitive assignment rule. that is, in [XP [$_{Y'}$ Y ZP]], where Y is a non Case assigning category, XP gets a lexical case, the form of which depends on Y. (Here 'non Case assigning' may be equated to non-verbal in some sense).[5]

8. Conclusion

I have outlined a view of ACTIVE Passives in Hindi and Passives in general that is very similar to the classical transformational view of passives. That is, the underlying structure of passive constructions contains VPs with thematic subjects as well as objects. While Hindi licenses the VP internal subject (in ACTIVE Passives) with its instrumental ending in SPEC AGRPs position, English cannot. Therefore, English *by* phrases are *moved* to an adjunct position.[6] This essentially entails that the effects of Burzio's Generalization will not be observed in certain construction types (like

[5] This analysis may account for the observation that quirky case marked subject constructions cannot be passivized (cf. Yip, Maling and Jackendoff,1987; Grimshaw,1990). Hindi Passives are quirky case marked constructions. Since they are already Passives in some sense (Case assignment, passive AUX etc), they cannot be further passivized (where one of the aspects of passivization is dealing with the subject case marking). Similarly, Hindi dative subject construction (another instance of a quirky case marked construction) cannot be passivized. But then again, the dative subject construction also has a non case assigning verb. One could argue that the fact that the Hindi ergative construction can be passivized is a counterexample to the generalization that quirky subject constructions cannot be passivized. However, this would be misleading since the derived structure in such passives would have an instrumental subject which under the analysis that I am suggesting gets its instrumental case inside the VP. That is, the passive of ergative is never ergative to start with.

[6] This view is not incompatible with Baker, Johnson and Roberts (1989) analysis. *-en* morpheme of English could be viewed as a clitic doubled off an adjunct position PP while the parallel morphology in Hindi could be viewed as a clitic doubled off an A-position PP. Many of the properties of Passives attributed to the *-en* morpheme can simply be attributed to the trace of the *by* phrase within the VP.

ACTIVE Passives in Hindi) while they will show up in parallel constructions in English type languages.

References:

Baker, M., K. Johnson and I. Roberts. 1989. Passive arguments raised. *LI* 20.219-251.

Bresnan, J. 1994. Locative inversion and the architecture of Universal Grammar. *Language* 70,72-131.

Bresnan J. and J. M. Kanerva. 1989. Locative inversion in Chichewa: A case study of factorization in grammar. *LI* 20.1-50.

Bresnan, J. and L. Moshi. 1990. Object asymmetries in comparative Bantu syntax. *LI* 21.147-85.

Davison, A. 1982. On the form and meaning of Hindi passive sentences. *Lingua* 58.149-179.

Davison, A. 1988. The case filter as motivation for move alpha. *Cornell Working Papers in Linguistics*, No. 8.

Goodall, G. 1993. On case and the passive morpheme. *NLLT* 11.31-44.

Grimshaw, J. 1990. *Argument structure*. Cambridge: MIT Press.

Gurtu, M. 1985. *Anaphoric relations in Hindi and English*. Doctoral dissertation, CIEFL, Hyderabad.

Hestvik, A. 1992. LF movement of pronouns and antisubject orientation. *LI* 23.557-594.

Jaeggli, O. 1986. Passive. *LI* 17.587-622.

Joshi, S. 1991. The passive and reversal construction in Marathi and the notion of `subject'. ms., Stanford University.

Kachu, Y. 1980. *Aspects of Hindi grammar*. Manohar publications, New Delhi.

Kachru, Y., B. Kachru and T. Bhatia. 1976. The notion 'subject': A note on Hindi-Urdu, Kashmiri and Panjabi. *The notion of subject in South Asian languages*, ed. by M.K. Verma, 79-108. South Asian Studies, University of Wisconsin, Madison.

Kayne, R. 1989. Facets of Romance past participle agreement. *Dialect variation and the theory of grammar*, ed. by P. Beninca. Dordrecht: Foris.

Kayne, R. 1993. Toward a modular theory of auxiliary selection. *Studia Linguistica* 47.3-31.

Keenan, E. 1976. Towards a universal definition of subject. *Subject and Topic*, ed. by C. Li, 247-302. New York: Academic Press.

Koopman, H. and D. Sportiche, 1991. The position of subjects. *Lingua* 85.211-258.

Kubo, M. 1989. Japanese passives. ms., MIT.

Mahajan, A. 1989. Agreement and agreement phrases. *MIT Working papers in Linguistics*, Volume 10.

Mahajan, A. 1990. *The A-A-bar distinction and movement theory*. Doctoral dissertation, MIT.

Mahajan, A. 1993. On Gamma marking adjunct traces in Hindi. *UCLA Occasional Papers in Syntax,* No. 11, 55-64.

Mahajan, A. 1994. Split ergativity, Auxiliary selection and word order directionality, *GLOW Newsletter* 32, Spring 1994.

Marantz, A. 1991. Case and licensing. *ESCOL* 1991.

Mohanan, T. 1990. *Arguments in Hindi*. Doctoral dissertation, Stanford University.

Pandharipande, R. 1981. *Passives in selected South Asian Languages*. Doctoral dissertation, University of Illinois, Urbana-Champaign.

Roberts, I. 1987. *The representation of implicit and dethematized subjects*. Dordrecht:Foris.

Rosen, S. and K. Wali, 1989. Twin passives, inversion and multistratalism in Marathi. *NLLT* 7.1-50.

Saksena, A. 1978. A reanalysis of the passive in Hindi. *Lingua* 46.339-353.

Sobin, N. 1985. Case assignment in Ukranian morphological passive constructions. *LI* 16.649-662.

Srivastav, V. 1991. *Wh dependencies in Hindi and the theory of grammar*. Doctoral dissertation, Cornell University.

Srivastav-Dayal, V. 1993. Binding facts in Hindi and the scrambling phenomena. ms., Rutgers University.

Sigurdsson, H. 1991. Icelandic case marked PRO and the licensing of lexical arguments. *NLLT* 9.327-363.

Thrainsson, H. 1976. Reflexives and subjunctives in Icelandic. *NELS* 6.225-239.

Thrainsson, H. 1979. *On Complementation in Icelandic*. New York: Garland.

Timberlake, A. 1976. Subject properties in the North Russian passive. *Subject and Topic*, ed. by C. Li, New York: Academic Press.

Travis, L. 1991. Derived objects, inner aspect, and the structure of VP. *NELS* 1991.

Verma, M. 1976. *The notion of subject in South Asian languages*, ed. by M.K. Verma, 79-108. South Asian Studies, University of Wisconsin, Madison.

Vikner, S. 1985. Parameters of binding and binding category in Danish. *Working Papers in Scandinavian Syntax*, University of Trondheim.

Yip, M., J. Maling and R. Jackendoff. 1987. Case in tiers. Language 63.216-250.

Zaenen, A., J. Maling and H. Thrainsson. 1985. Case and grammatical functions: The Icelandic passive. *NLLT* 3.441-483.

Zubizarreta, M.L. 1987. *Levels of representation in the lexicon and in the syntax*. Dordrecht:Foris.

Adjunction and Cyclicity

KEIKO MURASUGI & MAMORU SAITO
Kinjo Gakuin University & University of Connecticut

1. Introduction

Chomsky (1992) proposes to eliminate D-structure and S-structure altogether. Within this minimalist model, a phrase structure is built in a bottom-up fashion, and movement applies as the phrase structure is constructed. For example, in (1), the wh-phrase *what* moves to the embedded CP SPEC, before the embedded CP is combined with the matrix verb *wonder* to form the matrix V'.

(1) John wonders $[_{CP}$what$_i$ $[_{IP}$ Mary bought $\underline{t_i}]]$

In this paper, we discuss two 'adjunction paradoxes' that arose in the investigation of Japanese scrambling, and argue that they constitute supporting evidence for this conception of phrase structure building.

The two 'adjunction paradoxes' that we are concerned with involve operations of the following forms:

---

* The material in this paper was presented at the University of Connecticut and Cornell University. We would like to thank Zeljko Boskovic, Chris Collins, Susan Fischer, Howard Lasnik, Roger Martin, and Daiko Takahashi for helpful comments.

(2)a. ... $[_{XP}$ YP $[_{XP}$ ... *t* ...
|________|

b. YP ... $[_{XP}$ *t'* $[_{XP}$ ... *t* ...
|________| |________|

In (2a), YP simply adjoins to XP. In (2b), on the other hand, YP moves out of XP through the XP-adjoined position. In the following section, we discuss a case where XP=IP, and (2a) but not (2b) is allowed. In Section 3, we turn to a case where the 'paradox' occurs in the opposite direction, i.e., (2b) is allowed but (2a) is not. The relevant data involve long adjunction to VP. Finally, in Section 4, we argue on the basis of our analysis that adjunction, like substitution, is subject to strict cycle, or more precisely, to Chomsky's (1992) extension requirement.

2. Movement within and out of Relative Clauses

2.1. The IP Hypothesis

The first adjunction paradox arises when we consider scrambling within and out of relative clauses.[1] It has been argued extensively that Japanese relative clauses, and prenominal sentential modifiers in general, are not of the category CP, but of the category IP. (See, for example, Saito 1985, Sakai 1990, Murasugi 1990, 1991, and Tateishi 1991.) One direct piece of evidence for this hypothesis is that an overt complementizer can never appear in prenominal sentential modifiers. This is shown in (3a-b).

(3)a. [[Mary-ga John-ni $\underline{e}_i$ watasita] (*to/no)] hon_i
-nom -to handed book
(the book Mary handed to John)

b. [[John-ga sono hon -o nusunda] (*to/no)] syooko
-nom that book-acc stole evidence
(the evidence that John stole that book)

These examples show that an overt complementizer *to* or *no* cannot appear in a relative clause or a pure sentential modifier. This is expected if the prenominal sentential modifiers are of the category IP.

The fact in (3b) is particularly significant, since the complementizer *that* is obligatory in English pure complex NPs, as shown below in (3c-d).

---

[1] The material in this section is discussed in more detail but in a different form in Murasugi (1993).

(3)c. the claim [*(that) [Mary handed the book to John]]

d. the evidence [*(that) [John stole the book]]

Kayne (1981) and Stowell (1981) propose to derive this fact from the ECP. Their hypothesis is that when an overt complementizer is absent, there is an empty C and this empty category is subject to the ECP. Since the position of C is not properly governed in (3c-d), these examples, without *that*, are ruled out by the ECP. Given this analysis, the sentential modifier in (3b) cannot be a CP, since it is grammatical without an overt complementizer. If it were a CP, the empty C should be in violation of the ECP. (3b), thus, provide strong evidence that prenominal sentential modifiers in Japanese are IPs.

The IP hypothesis introduced above is consistent with the extraction facts discussed in the literature. As noted by Haig (1976) and Harada (1977), among others, Japanese scrambling obeys the complex NP constraint. The examples in (4) confirm their observation.

(4)a.??John-ni$_j$ [$_{IP}$Bill-ga [$_{NP}$[$_{IP}$Mary-ga t_j e_i watasita] hon$_i$]-o nusunda]
-to -nom -nom handed book-acc stole
(*Lit*. To John, Bill stole the book Mary handed)

b. ?sono hon -o$_j$ [$_{IP}$Bill-ga [$_{NP}$[$_{IP}$John-ga t_j nusunda] syooko] -o
that book-acc -nom -nom stole evidence-acc
mituketa]
found
(*Lit*. That book, Bill found the evidence that John stole)

These examples are only marginal, but are clearly worse than those in (5), which are perfect.[2]

(5)a. John-ni$_j$ [$_{IP}$Bill-ga [$_{CP}$Mary-ga t_j sono hon-o watasita to]
-to -nom -nom that book-acc handed that
omotteiru]
think
(To John, Bill thinks that Mary handed that book)

---

2 The island effects are, for some reason, generally weak with scrambling. See Kikuchi (1987) for discussion of comparative deletion in Japanese where the effects show up more clearly.

b. sono hon-o$_j$ [$_{IP}$Bill-ga [$_{CP}$John-ga $\underline{t}_j$ nusunda to] omotteiru]
that book-acc -nom -nom stole that think
(That book, Bill thinks that John stole)

The island effect observed above follows from the theory of Subjacency proposed in Chomsky (1986) and developed in subsequent works. The relative clause IP and the pure sentential modifier IP are not L-marked, and hence, are barriers for movement. If the movement crosses the barrier IP directly, it violates Subjacency. If, on the other hand, the movement can proceed via adjunction to the barrier IP, then the effect of the barrier can be nullified. The case of the relative clause is illustrated in (6).

(6)

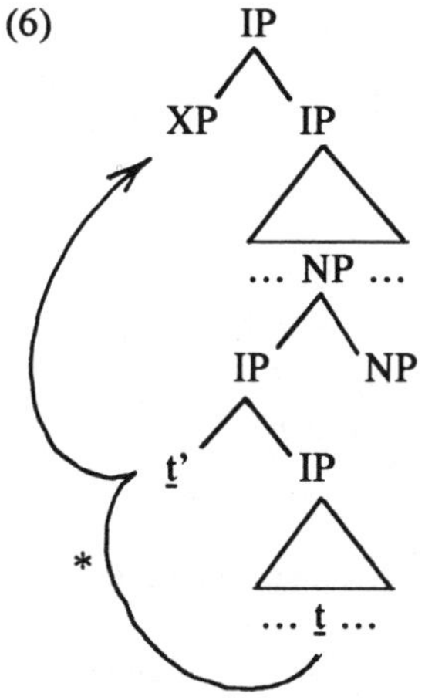

However, the prenominal sentential modifiers in (4) are adjuncts, and by assumption, adjunction to adjuncts is prohibited. Hence, the effect of those barriers cannot be circumvented by adjunction. Thus, we correctly predict that the examples in (4) are Subjacency violations.

2.2. The First Adjunction Paradox

So far, we have shown that prenominal sentential modifiers are IPs in Japanese, and further, that the extraction facts are consistent with this hypothesis. However, an interesting problem arises when we consider scrambling within the sentential modifiers. As shown in (7)-(8), a phrase can be scrambled and be adjoined to those prenominal IP modifiers.

(7)a. [$_{IP}$John-ni$_j$ [$_{IP}$Mary-ga $\underline{t}_j$ $\underline{e}_i$ watasita]] hon$_i$
-to -nom handed book
(the book Mary handed to John)

b. [$_{IP}$sono hon -o$_j$ [$_{IP}$John-ga $\underline{t}_j$ nusunda]] syooko
that book-acc -nom stole evidence
(the evidence that John stole that book)

(8)a. [$_{IP}$John-ni$_j$ [$_{IP}$Bill-ga [$_{CP}$Mary-ga $\underline{t}_j$ $\underline{e}_i$ watasita] to] omotteiru] hon$_i$
-to -nom -nom handed that think book
(the book Bill thinks Mary handed to John)

b. [$_{IP}$sono hon -o$_j$ [$_{IP}$Bill-ga [$_{CP}$John-ga $\underline{t}_j$ nusunda to] omotteiru] zizitu
that book-acc -nom -nom stole that think fact
(the fact that Bill thinks that John stole that book)

Here we have an apparent paradox. In the account for (4), we assumed crucially that adjunction to prenominal IP modifiers is not possible. But (7)-(8) show that scrambling can overtly adjoin phrases to those IPs.

What the discussion so far indicates, more precisely, is that adjunction to those IPs is possible if the movement terminates there, but not if the adjoined phrase moves on to a higher position. That is, relative clauses and pure sentential modifiers are possible targets for adjunction if they are the final landing sites, but not if they are intermediate landing sites. But why should this be so?

The minimalist model provides a direct solution to this problem. Recall that according to this model, movement can apply as the phrase structure is constructed. Thus, the movement in (7a), for example, can apply before the relative clause is combined with the relative head. This derivation is illustrated in (9).

(9)

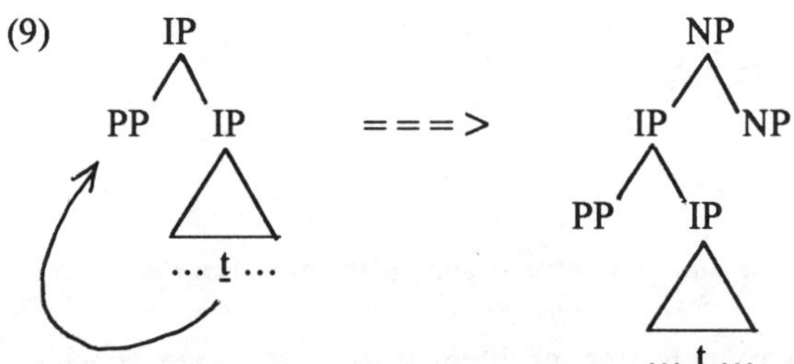

The PP *John-ni* is first adjoined to the relative clause IP, and then, the relative clause IP is combined with the relative head *hon*.[3]

Note here that the IP in (9) is an adjunct in relation to the relative head. Hence, it is reasonable to suppose that it gets adjunct status only when it is combined with the relative head. Then, if the relevant constraint prohibits adjunction to adjuncts, nothing prevents the adjunction of PP to IP in (9). Once the IP is combined with the head NP, it becomes an adjunct. But at this point, no movement takes place and hence no principle is violated. Thus, the grammaticality of (7)-(8) is correctly accounted for.

This analysis of (7)-(8) does not affect the previous account for (4a-b). In (4a), for example, a PP is scrambled out of the complex NP. Hence, the movement can take place only after the relative clause IP is combined with the relative head. But then, the relative clause IP already has adjunct status, and adjunction to this IP is prohibited. The effect of this IP as a barrier, consequently, cannot be circumvented by adjunction. Thus, it follows from the minimalist approach that the adjunction in (2a), but not that in (2b), is allowed when XP is an adjunct.

3. VP as Final and Intermediate Adjunction Sites

3.1. VP-adjunction as 'A-movement'

The second paradox arises with adjunction to VP. As shown in (10), both IP and VP are possible adjunction sites for scrambling.

(10)a. [$_{IP}$John-ga [$_{VP}$Mary-ni sono hon -o watasita]]
-nom -to that book-acc handed
(John handed that book to Mary)

b. [$_{IP}$sono hon-o$_i$ [$_{IP}$John-ga [$_{VP}$Mary-ni $\underline{t}_i$ watasita]]]

c. [$_{IP}$John-ga [$_{VP}$sono hon-o$_i$ [$_{VP}$Mary-ni $\underline{t}_i$ watasita]]]

---

3 This derivation is virtually identical to what Lebeaux (1988) proposes to account for examples like (i) and (ii).

(i) [$_{NP}$which book [$_{CP}$that John$_i$ read]] did he$_i$ like

(ii) *[$_{NP}$which picture of John$_i$] did he$_i$ like

He hypothesizes that relative clauses, and adjuncts in general, are inserted into the phrase structure after D-structure. Thus, in (i), the relative clause CP can be adjoined to the wh-phrase which book, after the wh-phrase moves to CP SPEC. Then, the pronoun he binds John at D-structure in (ii), but this binding need not obtain at any level in the case of (i).

However, as noted in Saito (1985), a difference between IP-adjunction and VP-adjunction emerges when we consider long-distance scrambling. (11b) and (12b) show that long-distance IP adjunction is fine. But (11c) and (12c) indicate that long-distance VP-adjunction results in marginality.

(11)a. [$_{IP}$John-ga [$_{VP}$Bill-ni [$_{CP}$Mary-ga sono hon -o motteiru to] itta]]
-nom -to -nom that book-acc have that said
(John said to Bill that Mary has that book)

b. [$_{IP}$sono hon-o$_i$ [$_{IP}$John-ga [$_{VP}$Bill-ni [$_{CP}$Mary-ga t_i motteiru to] itta]]]

c.??[$_{IP}$John-ga [$_{VP}$sono hon-o$_i$ [$_{VP}$Bill-ni [$_{CP}$Mary-ga t_i motteiru to] itta]]]

(12)a. [$_{IP}$John-ga [$_{VP}$Bill-ni [$_{CP}$Mary-ga sono mati-ni sundeiru to] itta]]
-nom -to -nom that town-in reside that said
(John said to Bill that Mary lives in that town)

b. [$_{IP}$sono mati-ni$_i$ [$_{IP}$John-ga [$_{VP}$Bill-ni [$_{CP}$Mary-ga t_i sundeiru to] itta]]]

c.??[$_{IP}$John-ga [$_{VP}$sono mati-ni$_i$ [$_{VP}$Bill-ni [$_{CP}$Mary-ga t_i sundeiru to] itta]]]

A similar contrast obtains with wh-movement and heavy NP shift in English: as is well known, wh-movement allows long-distance movement out of an embedded clause, but heavy NP shift does not.

(13)a. what$_i$ do you think that John bought t_i

b. *I have expected [that I would find t_i] since 1939 [$_{NP}$the treasure said to have been buried on that island]$_i$ (Ross 1967, Postal 1974)

What (11c) and (12c) show, then, is that VP-adjunction scrambling is subject to the 'right roof constraint', despite the fact that it is leftward movement. Put differently, if heavy NP shift also involves VP-adjunction, then the 'clause-boundedness' is not necessarily a characteristic of rightward movement, but it is a property of VP-adjunction.

The parallelism between VP-adjunction scrambling and heavy NP shift in fact goes further. It is noted in Saito (1985) that what results in marginality is more precisely long-distance VP-adjunction scrambling out of a finite clause. Long-distance VP-adjunction is allowed in a control structure, as shown in (14).

(14) [$_{IP}$John-ga [$_{VP}$sono hon -o$_i$ [$_{VP}$Bill-ni [PRO t_i mottekuru yooni] itta]]]
-nom that book-acc -to bring to said
(John told Bill to bring that book)

The same is true of heavy NP shift as noted in Postal (1974). His example in (15) shows that long-distance heavy NP shift is allowed out of a non-finite clause.

(15) I have expected [PRO to find t_i] since 1939 [$_{NP}$the treasure said to have been buried on that island]$_i$

Then, how should the locality effect on VP-adjunction scrambling be accounted for? The most plausible hypothesis, at this point, seems to be that VP-adjunction is A-movement.[4] It was noted in Mahajan (1989) that scrambling in Hindi is in general ambiguous between A and A' movement, but long-distance A-scrambling out of a finite clause is impossible. Japanese scrambling exhibits the same pattern, as noted in Tada (1990) and Saito (1992), among others. Let us consider the following examples:

(16)a.?*[[otagai$_i$ -no sensei]-ga karera$_i$-o hihansita]
each other-gen teacher-nom they -acc criticized
(*Lit.* Each other's teachers criticized them)

b. ?karera-o$_i$ [[otagai$_i$ -no sensei]-ga t_i hihansita]
they -acc each other-gen teacher-nom criticized

(17)a. *[[otagai$_i$ -no sensei]-ga [Hanako-ga karera$_i$-o hihansita to]
each other-gen teacher-nom -nom they -acc criticized that
itta]
said
(*Lit.* Each other's teachers said that Hanako criticized them)

b. *karera-o$_i$ [[otagai$_i$ -no sensei]-ga [Hanako-ga t_i hihansita
they -acc each other-gen teacher-nom -nom criticized
to] itta]
that said

---

4 This hypothesis was initially proposed in Tada (1990) for examples of short VP-adjunction scrambling like (10c), and was adopted for cases of long-distance VP-adjunction scrambling and heavy NP shift in Tada and Saito (1991). In what follows, we develop the account suggested in the latter work.

(16b) shows that a phrase preposed by clause-internal scrambling can serve as an A-binder for an anaphor. (17c), on the other hand, indicates that a phrase preposed out of a finite embedded clause cannot. A-scrambling, thus, seems clause-bound.

However, Mahajan (1989) notes also that long-distance A-scrambling is possible in a control structure in Hindi. Nemoto (1991) shows that here again, Japanese patterns like Hindi. Relevant examples are presented in (18).

(18)a. *[John-ga [[otagai$_i$ -no sensei]-ni [PRO karera$_i$-o homeru
-nom each other-gen teacher-to they -acc praise
yooni] tanonda]]
to asked
(*Lit.* John asked each other's teachers to praise them)

b. ?karera-o$_i$ [John-ga [[otagai$_i$ -no sensei]-ni [PRO t_i homeru
they -acc -nom each other-gen teacher-to praise
yooni] tanonda]]
to asked

c. ?[John-ga [karera-o$_i$ [[otagai$_i$ -no sensei]-ni [PRO t_i homeru
-nom they -acc each other-gen teacher-to praise
yooni] tanonda]]
to asked

The examples in (18) indicate that long scrambling out of a non-finite clause can be A-movement whether it is IP-adjunction (18b) or VP-adjunction (18c). Thus, clause-internal scrambling and long-distance scrambling out of a non-finite clause can be A-movement, but not long-distance scrambling out of a finite clause. VP-adjunction scrambling, then, seems to show exactly the same locality effect as A-scrambling. This, of course, suggests that the VP-adjoined position is an A-position.[5]

---

[5] Given the parallelism between VP-adjunction scrambling and heavy NP shift, we expect the latter to show the properties of A-movement with respect to binding. The relevant facts seem far from clear. But Daiko Takahashi (p.c.) points out that examples such as the following suggest that the prediction is in fact borne out:

(i)a. *Mary wanted [PRO to meet [$_{NP}$the men who had been accused of the crime]$_i$] until each other's$_i$ trials

b. ?Mary wanted [PRO to meet t_i] until each other's$_i$ trials [$_{NP}$the men who had been accused of the crime]$_i$

Given this hypothesis on the VP-adjoined position, the ill-formedness of (11c) and (12c) is not surprising. Since by assumption scrambling is an adjunction operation, the economy condition 'Minimize Chain Links' (in the sense of Chomsky and Lasnik 1991) forces the scrambled phrase to move through every possible adjunction site. In particular, the scrambled phrases in (11c) and (12c) must adjoin to the embedded CP (or C' in Fukui and Speas's 1986 theory) on the way to the VP-adjoined position. This movement is illustrated in (19).

(19) ... $[_{VP}$ XP_i $[_{VP}$ ... $[_{CP}$ $\underline{t}_i$' $[_{CP}$ ... $\underline{t}_i$ ...

If we assume, as seems reasonable, that any position within a C projection, including the CP/C'-adjoined position, is necessarily an A'-position, the chain in (19) is an improper chain of the form A-A'-A. Hence, (11c) and (12c) are ruled out as instances of improper movement. (See Takahashi 1992 and Fukui 1993 for relevant discussion on improper movement.)

The difference between (11c)/(12c) and (14) can be attributed to the presence/absence of a C projection in the embedded clause. Since Chomsky (1981), it has been widely assumed that the distribution of PRO is captured by the PRO theorem, which states that PRO occurs only in ungoverned positions. Hence, in a control structure such as (20), it has been assumed that a CP node is present in the embedded clause preventing the government of PRO by the matrix verb.

(20) John tried $[_{CP}$ $[_{IP}$ PRO to win the race]]

On the other hand, it is suggested in Chomsky and Lasnik (1991) that PRO is assigned 'null Case' by non-finite INFL. Extending this proposal, Martin (1992) argues that the distribution of PRO can be explained by that of null Case, and hence, that the PRO theorem is superfluous. Further, Boskovic (1993) argues that control complements in fact lack the C projection. Thus, *try* in (20) takes an IP complement. Given this hypothesis, it seems only reasonable to assume that there is no C projection in the embedded clause of (14). We suggest that this is why VP-adjunction can take place in this example without forming an improper chain.[6]

---

[6] We assume that PRO in the embedded subject position does not induce relativized minimality effect on the VP-adjunction scrambling in (14), because the movement is adjunction, not substitution to IP SPEC. (See R.K. Lee 1992, Abe 1993, and Takano 1994 for relevant discussion.) It should also be noted that we are assuming that the IP-adjoined position is ambiguous between A-position and A'-position, basically along the lines suggested

3.2. The Second Adjunction Paradox

As shown above, the hypothesis that the VP-adjoined position is an A-position allows us to account for the locality of VP-adjunction scrambling. But this hypothesis gives rise to the second adjunction paradox.

It was proposed in Chomsky (1986) that A'-movement, in general, can proceed via adjunction, in particular, VP-adjunction. Since then, evidence has been presented that this is in fact the case. (See Takahashi in prep. for detailed discussion on this point.) If we combine this hypothesis with Chomsky and Lasnik's principle 'Minimize Chain Links', it follows that A'-movement must proceed through every possible adjunction site, including the VP-adjoined position. A long-distance wh-movement, then, must take place as illustrated in (21).

(21) [$_{CP}$what$_i$ do [$_{IP}$you [$_{VP}$think [$_{CP}$ that [$_{IP}$John [$_{VP}$bought t_i]]]]]]
|_____||_____||______||_____||_____||______|

The long-distance A'-scrambling in (22) must proceed in a similar way.

(22) [$_{IP}$sono hon-o$_j$ [$_{IP}$Bill-ga [$_{VP}$ [$_{CP}$ [$_{IP}$John-ga [$_{VP}$ t_j nusunda]] to]
that book-acc -nom -nom stole that
omotteiru]]]
think
(That book, Bill thinks that John stole)

The preposed NP *sono hon-o* adjoins to the embedded VP, the embedded IP, the embedded CP (or C'), and the matrix VP, before it finally adjoins to the matrix IP.

The paradox arises when we compare the derivations of (11c) and (22). If we ignore the last step in the derivation of (22), it is exactly like that of (11c), that is, a long-distance VP-adjunction out of a finite clause. The two derivations are illustrated in (23).

(23) (11c) --------- [$_{IP}$ ... [$_{VP}$ NP$_i$ [$_{VP}$ ... [$_{CP}$ ... t_i
|_____??______|

---

in Webelhuth (1989), Tada (1990), and Saito (1992). We will discuss the A/A' properties of adjoined positions in more general terms later in this paper.

(22) --- $[_{IP}$ NP_i $[_{IP}$ ... $[_{VP}$ t_i' $[_{VP}$ ... $[_{CP}$ ... t_i

We concluded above that (11c) is not grammatical because the VP-adjoined position is an A-position, and A-movement out of a CP is prohibited. But then, why is long-distance VP-adjunction allowed in (22)? The same problem arises when we compare the derivation of (21) and that of the heavy NP shift example in (13b).[7]

The well-formedness of the derivation of (22) indicates that the long-distance VP-adjunction in this example can be A'-movement. The contrast between (11c) and (22), then, implies that the VP-adjoined position is an A-position as a final landing site, but is an A'-position as an intermediate landing site. If this is the correct generalization, the paradox noted above reduces to the problem of why the VP-adjoined position has this peculiar property.

Here, we would like to argue that the minimalist approach, when combined with a functional definition of 'maximal projection' suggested by Fukui (1986), among others, provides a straightforward answer to this problem. Fukui (1986) argues that the definition of X^{max} does not coincide with that of X", and further, that the former should be defined roughly as the highest projection of X. (See also Muysken 1982, Speas 1990, and the references cited there.) Let us assume, basically following this idea, that a phrase is construed as a maximal projection when (i) SPEC-head agreement takes place in the phrase, and (ii) the phrase is embedded as a complement, specifier, or adjunct. In the case of a V-projection, (i) is irrelevant, since SPEC-head agreement is limited to functional categories. Thus, a V-projection is maximal only when it is embedded, e.g. as a complement of I.

Let us now return to the contrast between (11c) and (22). Suppose, following the minimalist conception of phrase structure building, that scrambling applies as the phrase structure is constructed. Then, the VP-adjunction scrambling in (11c) takes place before the matrix VP is combined

---

7 Based on a similar problem, Fukui (1993) concludes that wh-movement does not go through the VP-adjoined position, and suggests to return to the COMP-to-COMP analysis of Chomsky (1973,1977). Although this may turn out to be correct, we will not adopt it here mainly because it does not seem compatible with the approach to various phenomena based on 'Minimize Chain Links'. (See Takahashi in prep. for relevant discussion.) In particular, if this economy condition forces the scrambling in (11c) to go through the CP/C'-adjoined position, it is not clear why it does not force VP-adjunction in examples like (22).

with I and embedded under the matrix I'. Hence, as illustrated in (24a), the adjunction is to a non-maximal projection of V. The situation is quite different in the case of the IP-adjunction scrambling in (22). Since the final landing site is the matrix IP, the matrix VP must already be embedded within the I-projection when the scrambling applies. The adjunction to the matrix VP in this case, then, is an adjunction to a maximal projection of V, as illustrated in (24b).

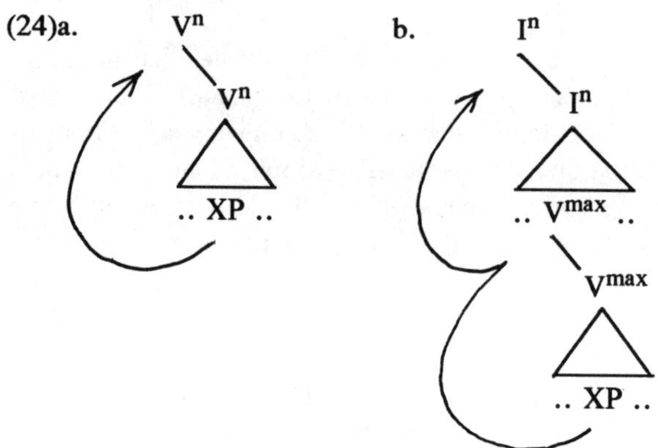

Thus, a clear distinction is drawn between VP-adjunction as the final step and VP-adjunction as an intermediate step in a form-chain operation.

Given this distinction, the contrast between (11c) and (22) is readily accounted for if a position adjoined to a non-maximal projection of V is necessarily an A-position, while a position adjoined to a maximal projection of V can be an A'-position. More generally, we can assume that an adjoined position is ambiguous (or undefined) with respect to A/A', basically along the lines suggested in Webelhuth (1989) and Tada (1990), with the following two exceptions:

(25)a. An adjunction to a projection of C is A'-movement.

b. An adjunction to a non-maximal projection of a lexical category is A-movement.

(25b) seems reasonable especially if only the higher V^n in (24a), for example, is construed as a maximal projection when the V-projection is embedded. Then, at that point, the adjoined position will be completely inside the maximal projection of V.

4. An Implication of the Proposed Analysis

We have shown above that the minimalist approach, or more specifically, the hypothesis that movement applies as the phrase structure is constructed, solves two adjunction paradoxes that arose in the investigation of Japanese scrambling. The two adjunction paradoxes, then, constitute supporting evidence for this conception of phrase structure building.

Before we conclude this paper, we would like to discuss one implication of our analysis for the general conception of adjunction. Note first that our analysis of (11c)/(12c) implies that the VP-adjunction scrambling in these examples not only can but must take place before the target VP is embedded under the I-projection. This is so, since if the scrambling can apply after the embedding occurs, then it can be adjunction to the maximal projection of V, exactly as the VP-adjunction in (24b), and hence, it can be A'-movement. But then, our analysis of (11c)/(12c) clearly fails.

This amounts to saying that scrambling, despite the fact that it is an adjunction operation, is subject to strict cycle, or more precisely, the extension requirement of Chomsky (1992). Chomsky (1992) suggests that substitution operations are subject to this requirement, but adjunction operations are not. The main reason for excluding adjunction here concerns head-movement. In the example (26a), the verb *are* is adjoined to INFL, as illustrated in (26b).

(26)a. They are intelligent

b.

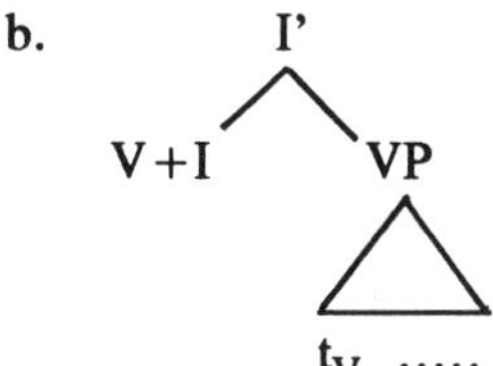

Since this adjunction can apply only after I and VP are combined to form I', this movement apparently cannot affect the top-most node of the target structure (I'). But as noted by Chomsky elsewhere (class lectures 1993), it is possible to reformulate the extension requirement so that it applies to head-movement as well: in (26b) V is adjoined to the head of I', and in this sense, the movement affects the I' node. Our analysis of VP-adjunction scrambling, then, supports this hypothesis. If it is correct, all syntactic operations, both substitution and adjunction, are subject to the extension requirement.

References

Abe, Jun (1993) *Binding Conditions and Scrambling without A/A' Distinction*, PhD dissertation, Connecticut.

Boskovic, Zeljko (1993) "Selection and Categorial Status of Infinitival Complements," ms. Connecticut.

Chomsky, Noam (1973) "Conditions on Transformations," in Stephen Anderson and Paul Kiparsky, eds., *A Festschrift for Morris Halle*, Holt, Rinehart & Winston, New York.

Chomsky, Noam (1977) "On Wh-Movement," in Peter Culicover, et al., eds., *Formal Syntax*, Academic Press, New York.

Chomsky, Noam (1981) *Lectures on Government and Binding*, Foris Publications, Dordrecht.

Chomsky, Noam (1986) *Barriers*, MIT Press, Cambridge.

Chomsky, Noam (1992) *A Minimalist Program for Linguistic Theory*, MIT Occasional Papers in Linguistics 1.

Chomsky, Noam and Howard Lasnik (1991) "Principles and Parameters Theory," ms. MIT and Connecticut.

Fukui, Naoki (1986) *A Theory of Category Projection and its Applications*, PhD dissertation, MIT.

Fukui, Naoki (1993) "A Note on Improper Movement," ms. UC Irvine.

Fukui, Naoki and Margaret Speas (1986) "Specifiers and Projection," *MIT Working Papers in Linguistics* 8.

Haig, John (1976) "Shadow Pronoun Deletion in Japanese," *Linguistic Inquiry* 7.2.

Harada, Shin-Ichi (1977) "Nihongo-ni 'Henkei'-wa Hituyoo-da," *Gengo* 6.10-11.

Kayne, Richard S. (1981) "ECP Extensions," *Linguistic Inquiry* 12.1.

Kikuchi, Akira (1989) "Comparative Deletion in Japanese," ms. Yamagata.

Lebeaux, David (1989) *Language Acquisition and the Form of the Grammar*, PhD dissertation, Massachusetts.

Lee, Rhanghyeyun Kim (1992) "Negative Polarity Items Licensing and the Nature of Neg Projection," ms. Connecticut.

Mahajan, Anoop K. (1989) "Weak Crossover and Scrambling in Hindi," ms. MIT.

Martin, Roger (1992) "On the Distribution and Case Features of PRO," ms. Connecticut.

Murasugi, Keiko (1990) "Overgeneration of *No*: Its Implications for Syntax and Acquisition Theory," the 15th BU Conference on Language Development.

Murasugi, Keiko (1991) *Noun Phrases in Japanese and English: A Study in Syntax, Learnability and Acquisition*, PhD dissertation, Connecticut.

Murasugi, Keiko (1993) "The Generalized Transformation Analysis of Relative Clauses and Island Effects in Japanese," ms. Kinjo Gakuin.

Muysken, Pieter (1982) "Parametrizing the Notion 'Head'," *Journal of Linguistic Research* 2.3.

Nemoto, Naoko (1991) "Scrambling and Conditions on A-Movement," *WCCFL* 10.

Nemoto, Naoko (1993) *Chains and Case Positions: A Study from Scrambling in Japanese*, PhD dissertation, Connecticut.

Postal, Paul (1974) *On Raising*, MIT Press, Cambridge.

Ross, John R. (1967) *Constraints on Variables in Syntax*, PhD dissertation, MIT.

Saito, Mamoru (1985) *Some Asymmetries in Japanese and their Theoretical Implications*, PhD dissertation, MIT.

Saito, Mamoru (1992) "Long Distance Scrambling in Japanese," *Journal of East Asian Linguistics* 1.1.

Sakai, Hiromu (1990) "Complex NP Constraint and Case-Conversions in Japanese," ms. UC Irvine.

Speas, Margaret (1990) *Phrase Structure in Natural Language*, Kluwer Academic Publishers, Dordrecht.

Stowell, Tim (1981) *Origins of Phrase Structure*, PhD dissertation, MIT.

Tada, Hiroaki (1990) "Scrambling(s)," the Ohio State Workshop on Japanese Syntax.

Tada, Hiroaki (1993) *A/A' Partition in Derivation*, PhD dissertation, MIT.

Tada, Hiroaki and Mamoru Saito (1991) "VP-Internal Scrambling," ms. MIT and Connecticut.

Takahashi, Daiko (1992) "Improper Movement and Chain Formation," ms. Connecticut.

Takahashi, Daiko (1993) "Minimize Chain Links," the 11th Annual Meeting of the English Linguistics Society of Japan.

Takahashi, Daiko (in prep.) *Minimality of Movement*, PhD dissertation, Connecticut.

Takano, Yuji (1994) "Scrambling, Relativized Minimality, and Economy of Derivation," *WCCFL* 13.

Tateishi, Koichi (1991) *The Syntax of 'Subjects'*, PhD dissertation, Massachusetts.

Webelhuth, Gert (1989) *Syntactic Saturation Phenomena and the Modern Germanic Languages*, PhD dissertation, Massachusetts.

VP internal and VP external AGRoP: evidence from Irish

MÁIRE B. NOONAN
University College Dublin

1.0 Introduction

This paper makes two points. The first is of general theoretical significance and bears on the question of the locus of AGRoP and questions of constraints on NP movement such as the economy principle of Shortest Movement and the equidistance requirement as proposed in Chomsky (1993). I will show that a certain type of object shift construction that is found in Irish infinitives poses a problem for the theory of Shortest Movement and equidistance. A solution is proposed which assumes an AGR-projection below the base position of the external argument. The second point bears more on a particular aspect of Irish syntax. It is argued that Irish shows signs of ergativity in infinitives.

* I would like to thank Máire Ní Chiosáin for help with the Irish data and for reading a draft of this paper. All faults of course remain mine.

1.1 VP projection and the site of AGRoP

Under the assumptions adopted in the minimalist approach of Chomsky (1993), NPs raise to the specifier of an appropriate AGR-projection for feature checking of Case features and of features associated with functional heads (V- and N-features). Raising occurs either in the overt syntax (before SPELL OUT), or covertly at LF. Features that are strong and thus visible at PF must be checked (i.e. eliminated) before SPELL OUT. In cases where features are not strong (i.e. not visible at PF), movement is delayed until LF in accordance with the economy principle Procrastinate. In this paper I am mainly concerned with raising of the object NP to Spec/AGRoP.

It has been observed in the literature that overt raising of the object to AGRoP is parasitic on overt verb raising (often referred to as Holmberg's generalisation, see Holmberg 1986). In the minimalist framework, the reason for this is derived from the economy principle of *Shortest Movement* (the minimalist version of the minimality condition, see Rizzi 1990): raising of the verb to AGRs makes Spec/AGRoP and Spec/AGRsP equidistant for the subject NP, therefore raising of the subject does not violate Shortest Movement (see Chomsky 1993:17). Note that this reasoning applies under the hypothesis that AGRoP is above the base-generated position of the subject NP. There is however another possibility, which is that the Case checking projection AGRoP is situated within a double layer VP. This idea is adopted in e.g. Sportiche (1990), Travis (1991), and Noonan (1992). Under this view VPs are assumed to project as Larsonian 'double layer' VP shells whenever a verb assigns an external argument (Noonan 1992). This layered VP consists of a inner VP headed by the lexical verb, a higher empty verb, and a functional projection (AGRoP, or AspectP (see Travis 1991)) within the layered VP shell. This is shown in the tree diagram under (1). [1]

---

[1] The works mentioned differ in certain respects. For Travis, the lower VP is headed by an VN. Hale & Keyser (1993) also adopt a Larsonian double VP shell for certain types of conflated verbs, but they assume these layers to be lexical relational representations. For them, the higher verb slot represents an empty 'abstract causative' verb. This view is crucially adopted in Noonan (1992a/b), but extended to syntactic representations.

(1)

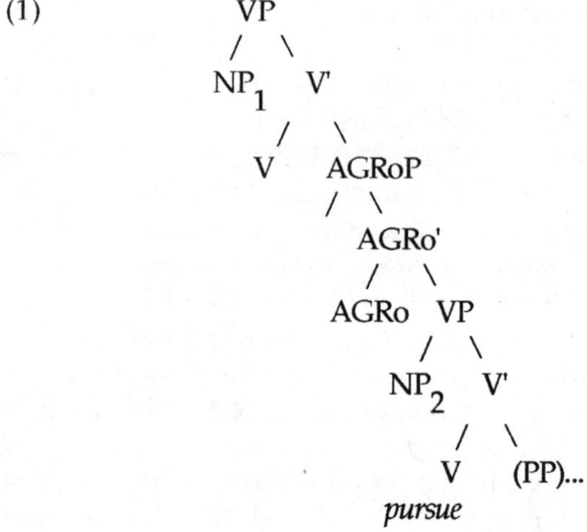

Note that under this view, the derivation of Holmberg's generalisation in terms of Shortest Movement is lost, since AGRoP is below the base-position of the subject. Object shift is thus expected to apply independent of overt verb raising to T or AGRs.

In this paper I present data from one dialect of Modern Irish which do indeed support such an approach, while posing a problem for the AGRoP external hypothesis. Another dialect, on the other hand, yields the opposite results, namely that AGRoP is outside the VP layer. Consequently, the conclusion of this paper is that there is an AGR projection both within and without the VP shell, and that the dialectal difference reduces to which one of them is activated in infinitives.[2]

2.0 Northern Irish

Irish is a head initial VSO language. Following a number of works I assume that in finite clauses the verb moves to INFL (T or AGRs, for present purposes the choice is not crucial), while the subject remains below Spec/AGRs.[3]

(2) a. Chonaic mé Seán.
saw I Seán 'I saw Seán.'

---

[2] Noonan (1992b) and Collins & Thráinsson (1993) assume an AGRP both within and without the VP shell, although in the latter work this is only assumed for double object constructions.

[3] The exact position of the subject is not of importance for this paper.

b. Thug mé cúig phunt do Chian.
gave I five pound to Cian
'I gave five pounds to Cian.'

In infinitives the verb does not raise to I. The expected word order therefore is SVO(XP). However, the attested word order is SOV(XP). This word order is furthermore accompanied by a preverbal leniting particle (henceforth *aL*).

(3) a. Ba mhaith liom [sibh an doras a phéinteáil]
I-would-like you(pl) the door aL paint
'I would like you to paint the door.'

b. Ba mhaith liom [Seán an caora a mheá ar an bhfeirm]
I-would-like Seán the sheep aL weigh on the farm
'I would like Seán to weigh the sheep on the farm.'

The preverbal leniting particle appears only with transitive verbs. It is therefore likely to be associated with accusative Case marking of the preverbal object NP.[4] I take aL to be an overt realisation of strong AGRo. Note that it is invariable, that is, it is abstract agreement which does not reflect overt person and number distinctions. Since AGR headed by aL contains strong features, it forces the object to raise to its specifier before SPELL OUT. The verb raises to AGRo, but no further, since it follows, and does not precede, the object. The subject, since it also precedes the object, must have raised from its base-position. The examples in (4) show that failure of the subject to raise to a position preceding the object results in ungrammaticality.

(4) a. *Ba mhaith liom [an doras a phéinteáil sibh]
I-would-like the door aL paint you(pl)
'I would like you to paint the door.'

b. *Ba mhaith liom [an caora a mheá Seán ar an bhfeirm]
I-would-like the sheep aL weigh Seán on the farm
'I would like Seán to weigh the sheep on the farm.'

---

4 Indeed, a Case theoretic account has been proposed in McCloskey & Sells (1988); they propose that it is an element adjoined to the VN, turning it into a Case assigning element and forcing the object to adjoin to the left of the VP (since aL assigns Case to the left). See also Duffield (1991), Noonan (1992b), and Guilfoyle (1993) for identifying aL with an agreement Case configuration.

2.1 The Problem

Note that the configuration of the examples such as (3) constitutes an exception to Holmberg's generalisation, as we observe overt object shift in the absence of verb raising. This construction thus poses a challenge to the analysis proposed in Chomsky (1993): since Spec/AGRo is not equidistant to the landing site of the raised subject, raising of the subject NP across the shifted object constitutes a violation of Shortest Movement (Chomsky 1993).[5] Note that the conflict would be circumvented if it could be shown that the subject moves to an A-bar position. However, there is evidence to the contrary, since the subject may bind an anaphor and license a bound pronoun with respect to the shifted object, i.e there are no WCO effects, (see Duffield 1991).

(5) a.*Ba mhaith liom a_1 máthair $gach_1$ cailín a fheiceáil
I-would-like her mother every girl aL see
'I would like her_1 mother to see every $girl_1$'

b. Ba mhaith liom [$gach_1$ cailín a_1 máthair a fheiceáil
I-would-like every girl her mother aL see
'I would like every $girl_1$ to see her $mother_1$'
[Duffield 1991:135]

These examples suggest strongly that the subject moves to an A-position. The syntactic tree diagram in (6) illustrates the problematic configuration of examples such as given in (3).

---

5 This conflict is noted in Bobaljik & Carnie (1992). They propose a solution that is linked to Irish default accusative Case marking of the subject from C. However, I fail to see how this solves the basic problem of NP-moving across the shifted object. Furthermore, the problem remains independent of default accusative Case, as will become clear in section 3.2 on southern Irish dialects.

(6)

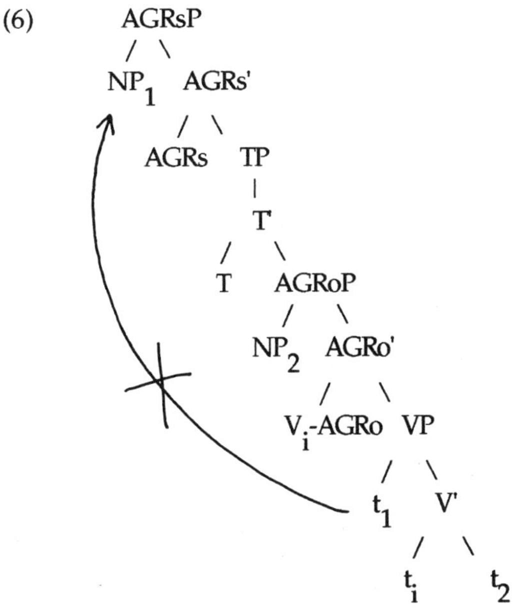

The question also arises as to how the subject of an infinitive is Case licensed, since the constructions dealt with here are not ECM constructions. Without addressing this question in detail here, I follow Chung & McCloskey (1987) in assuming that a default accusative Case is available for subjects of infinitives and small clauses in Irish. It is unclear where this default Case comes from, and whether is is assigned/checked under AGRs, since it is equally available in small clauses that do not contain INFL (see Chung & McCloskey 1987). It is equally unclear what forces the subject to raise before SPELL OUT. One possibility is that -TNS-AGRs licenses either null Case or default accusative Case, and that in the latter case its features are strong and force overt NP raising. I leave this matter open here.

2.2 VP-internal AGRoP

In order to maintain the definition of equidistance and the principle of Shortest Movement, I would like to propose that in Northern Irish (henceforth NI) infinitives the object shifts to an AGR projection within the double layer shell of the VP. Consequently there is no crossing of the subject and the object NPs, and raising of the subject would not violate Shortest Movement. In fact, under this view we do not have to assume that the subject raises, because its D-structure position precedes the derived object position.[6] The structure assumed in the present proposal is illustrated in (7), (strong AGRo highlighted):

(7)

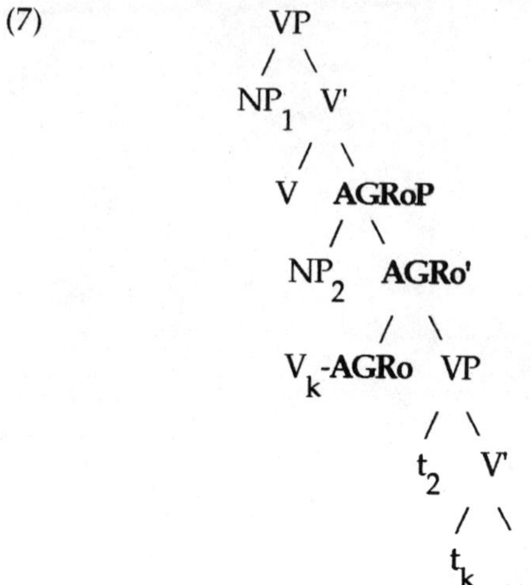

2.3 Ergativity in Irish Infinitives.

Since aL is associated with accusative Case, we do not expect it to occur with intransitive verbs, either unergatives or unaccusatives. In fact, aL does not occur with unergatives. However, somewhat surprisingly we do find it occuring with the unaccusative verbs *a bheith* 'be', *a dhul* 'go' and *a theacht* 'come'.

(8) a. Ba mhaith liom sibh a bheith anseo.
I-would like you(pl) aL be here
'I would like you to be here.'

---

[6] Data presented in Duffield (1991:142) involving NEG placement suggest that in fact both possibilities are attested: the subject remains *in situ* or raises:

(i) [gan Nóra an fear sin a phósadh] a ba mhaith leat
NEG Nóra that man aL marry you would like
'Not for Nóra to marry that man is what you want/
you want for Nóra not to marry that man.

(ii) [Nóra gan an fear sin a phósadh] a ba mhaith leat
Nóra NEG that man aL marry you would like
'Not for Nóra to marry that man is what you want/
you want for Nóra not to marry that man.

b. Ba mhaith liom sibh a dhul/a theacht.
I-would-like you(pl) aL go/ aL come
'I would like you to go/come.'

While this observation supports the hypothesis that the AGR-projection in question is VP-internal (hence only available for internal arguments), it is also surprising because it calls into question whether or not the particle aL is really associated with accusativity. In tensed clauses, the internal arguments of the verbs above do not appear in accusative Case, but raise to subject position and are marked nominative, just as is the case in any accusative language. If the aL case is an objective Case, then this implies that Burzio's generalisation does not hold in NI infinitives: objective Case is available in the absence of an external argument position.

In fact, the Case pattern exemplified in NI infinitives is not unlike that of many ergative languages: the internal argument of one-place verbs and the internal argument of two-place verbs are marked by the same case, namely absolutive (in this case accusative), while the external argument of an "unergative" verb appears in ergative Case. An example of this type of Case pattern is found in Basque. The relevant examples (from Laka 1993) are given below:

(9) a. emakumeak_{C1} emakumea_{C2} ikusi du
woman-the-E woman-the-A seen has
'The woman saw the woman'

b. emakumea_{C2} erori da
woman-the-A fallen is
'The woman has fallen'

c. emakumeak_{C1} barre egin du
woman-the-E laugh done has
'The woman has laughed.'

Under recent minimalist approaches, absolutive Case is seen as the equivalent of accusative Case, that is Case that is checked under AGRoP (the lower AGR-phrase).[7] Under this

---

7 See e.g. Bobaljiek (1992), Laka (1993). See also Shaer (1990), who argues against the traditional view that absolutive is equivalent to nominative Case, taking it rather to constitute a verbal case.

assumption, ergative languages do not obey Burzio's generalisation, since the availability of AGRo-Case marking does not depend on the existence of an external argument. A prevalent analysis within the minimalist approach to account for this fact is to propose that languages are parameterised as to whether AGRs or AGRo is active in mono-argumental clauses. In ergative languages AGRo is active, thus the single argument of an intransitive verb appears in AGRo-Case. In nominative/accusative languages, AGRs is active, thus the single argument of an intransitive verb surfaces in AGRs Case (= nominative).[8]

This analysis can be carried over to non-finite clauses: just as in tensed clauses, the active AGRP in English infinitives is also AGRsP (which licenses null case when dominating [-TNS]; see Chomsky & Lasnik 1991). Therefore, single arguments of intransitive verbs (in non-ECM contexts) are PRO, and only a second argument, if present, is licensed by accusative Case.

While Irish is nominative/accusative in tensed clauses[9], it exhibits an ergative Case pattern in infinitives. The active AGRP in Irish infinitives is AGRoP, so that if there is one single argument, it will be licensed in AGRoP (= aL-Case). AGRs in NI non-finites licenses either null Case (PRO) or accusative Case (henceforth [-TNS]-AGRs-Case, or default accusative).[10] [-TNS]-AGRs-Case only appears with a two argument verb. However, since the structural position of the active AGRoP is within the VP layer, it is only available for internal arguments, and not for a single external argument.[11]

---

[8] Note that this approach, though simple, in fact fails to account for Burzio's generalisation, because it does not have an explanation for why intransitive verbs whose single argument is an external argument may license an accusative NP (as long as this NP is either a cognate object, or thematically licensed independently, such as a subject of a resultative small clause), while intransitive verbs whose single argument is internal may never do so. For the purpose of this paper I leave this issue open. See Noonan (in progress) for a more thorough discussion of Burzio's generalisation in connection with ergativity.

[9] This is the case only in imperfective aspect and with non-stative verbs. See Noonan (1992 and in progress) for arguments that Irish stative and perfective predicates exhibit ergativity.

[10] What confuses the matter is the fact that both Cases are accusative. If instead of default accusative Case we had ergative Case, the situation would be much clearer. In order to distinguish between the accusative Case coming from [-TNS]/AGRs, and the one from AGRo I refer to the two as AGRs-Case and aL-Case, respectively.

[11] It is unclear whether ergative languages such as Basque, that is languages where the subject of "unergative" verbs appears in ergative Case, might be

2.4 The two AGRo-phrases

At this point I should address the question of what the nature of the two AGRo-phrases is, and why there should be two. Clearly the two functional Case checking projections are linked to one and the same structural Case and do not each correspond to a separate structural Case. In Noonan (1992a/b), I ascribe an important role to the inner AGRoP regarding the determination of accusativity; the presence of this functional category selected by a verb is crucial in the structural configuration that yields accusative Case. There are reasons to believe that the inner AGR-projection might be aspectual in nature. In fact, Travis 1991 assumes it to be an ASPECT phrase and supports this with data from Austronesian languages. Guilfoyle (1993), following Travis' VP-structure, suggests that the Case position in Irish infinitives is Spec/AspP.[12] There is also independent evidence coming from Irish suggesting that this is on the right track: in certain cases the aspectual progressive marker ag can be "turned" into aL. This occurs in cases where an NP is extracted from the aspectual phrase introduced by ag.[13] Last but not least there is Tenny's exhaustive study of the close interrelatedness of accusative Case and aspectual notions such as affectedness of the Case marked NP (see Tenny (1987).

I propose that the inner AGR phrase determines the availability of the structural Case, while the outer AGRoP is a further AGR projection to which the accusative marked NP ultimately raises (i.e. at the latest at LF),[14] and for which there appears to be independent evidence for the existence of the outer AGRoP, once coming from Germanic languages, which show that the object undergoes further A-movement across the subject, and from French, where word order facts also strongly support the assumption of a functional projection outside of V^{max}. (In fact, these data, first presented in Pollock (1989) and taken up by Chomky

---

accounted for in terms of the analysis which positions the active AGRoP VP-internally. See Laka (1993) for a different analysis, arguing that "unergatives" in Basque have an unincorporated internal argument in the sense of Hale & Keyser (1993).

12 Although for Guilfoyle, the Case coming from ASPECT appears to be independent of the verb (i.e. VN). This incidentally represents another possibility that might account for the fact that accusative appears to be available for internal arguments of unaccusative verbs in infinitives.

13 See Duffield (1991) for a discussion of the ag->aL rule.

14 See Sportiche (1992), who argues for yet another Case related projection, AccPhrase, which dominates TP and AGRsP.

(1991) represented the intial motivation for an AGRoP outside of the V^{max} constituent.)

3.0 Southern Irish Infinitives.

The word order and Case patterns in Munster Irish and other Southern Irish dialects (henceforth SI) differ from those in NI in important respects. The first thing to note is that the aL particle is not restricted to internal arguments as is the case in NI; it appears with any preverbal overt NP, whether this is an internal argument or an external argument of an intransitive verb (but not with PRO). Thus while there would be no aL in example (10) in NI, we do find it in SI:

(10) Ní thaitníonn leat [iad a chruinniú]
NEG pleases with-you them*aL* assemble
'It does not please you for them to assemble'

Since the AGR projection headed by aL is available for the external argument, we must conclude that its structural position is external to V^{max}. However, if AGRoP with strong features is outside the VP shell, then movement of the object NP to its specifier accompanied by raising of the subject NP would violate Shortest movement in the absence of verb movement (see the problematic configuration (6)). This conclusion seems to be compatible with the SI data: the only circumstance where the object raises to Spec/AGRoP is when there is no overt subject NP. If there is an overt subject NP, the object remains postverbal, while the subject raises to SPEC/AGRoP in place.[15] Consequently, with two overt NPs we observe the word order SVO, and when there is only one overt NP, we find SV or OV, respectively:

[15] The post-verbal object NP is marked with genitive Case, except in younger dialects, where we observe more and more occurences of post-verbal accusative objects in infinitives. The fact that the post-verbal object appears with genitive case has often been motivation for assuming Irish non-finite verbs to have the categorial status of VNs, unable to license accusative Case. Under this view, the aL particle is seen as an independent Case marking element (see for example McCloskey & Sells 1988, Duffield 1991, Guilfoyle 1993), analoguous to 'of'-insertion in English. My view differs, since I assume aL merely to be an overt realsiation of a strong feature which triggers a Spec/head agreement configuration being established before SPELL OUT.

(11) Ní thaitníonn leat [mé a dhíol an chaora]
NEG pleases with-you me *aL* sell the sheep(GEN)
'It does not please you for me to sell the sheep'

(12) Ní theastaíonn uaim [PRO an caora a dhíol]
NEG wants from-me the sheep *aL* sell
'I don't want to sell the sheep'

Let us assume that the PRO subject remains in situ until LF. Now raising of the object NP to SPEC/AGRoP across the PRO subject in Spec/VP causes no violation (V-raising to AGRo makes Spec/AGRoP and Spec/VP equidistant). This configuration is illustrated in tree diagram (13).

(13)

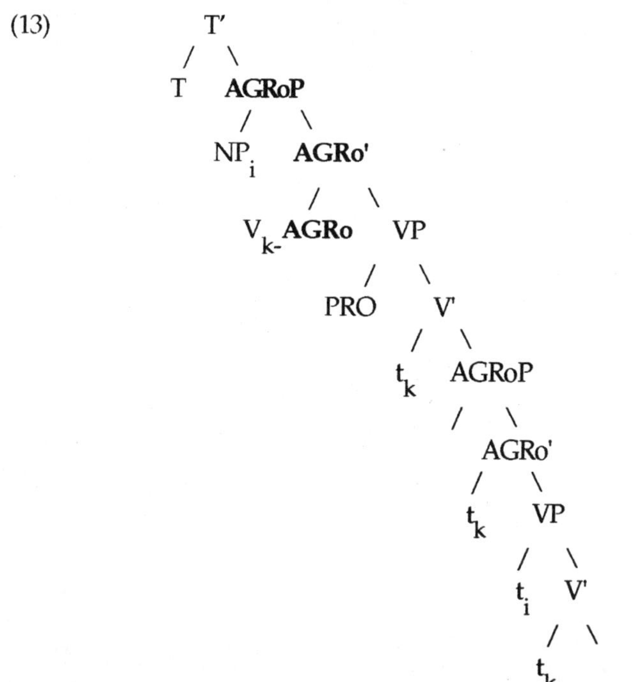

If the subject is overt, it cannot remain in its D-structure position. However, it is prevented from doing so by Shortest Movement, if the object is in Spec/AGRoP. Thus, in sentences with an overt subject NP, it is the subject NP that must raise to Spec/AGRoP and check the strong AGRo-features, while the object NP must remain in situ and appears marked with GEN Case (see (11)). This is expected, because if it was bearing accusative Case, it would have to raise to

Spec/AGRoP at LF to check features. Spec/AGRoP, however, is taken up by the subject NP which has raised there in the overt syntax. It cannot raise to Spec/AGRsP either because of Shortest Movement (see Chomsky, this is the classic argument why crossing of subject and object NPs is necessary). As a result, the object is Case marked in a different way, namely through genitive Case.[16,17]

3.1 Ergativity in SI

As in NI, we are once more faced with a Case pattern that is more akin to the Case pattern found in ergative languages than to one from nominative/accusative languages: the internal argument of a transitive verb (where the external argument is PRO), and the external argument of an intransitive (in this dialect it makes no difference whether the verb is 'unaccusative' or 'unergative') are licensed under the same Case checking projection (= aL-Case). However, the circumstances that the features of AgroP are strong and that the verb does not raise higher than AGRo conspire in such a way that a type of anti-passive construction is forced in those cases where both arguments are overt: the object bears genitive case.[18]

---

16 For the purpose of this paper, I shall leave the question open how and where genitive Case is checked. See Duffield (1991: 121-22) for an analysis that assumes the genitive object to incorporate into VN to be Case licensed. Apparently there is a tendency observed amongst younger speakers towards marking the post-verbal object accusative Case. Here, we might assume that the object raises to VP-internal Spec/AGRoP.

17 See also Guilfoyle (1993), who argues that SI dialects do not project a double layered VP (or more precisely, that the matrix verbs select for an Aspect phrase rather than a VP in SI), therefore there are never two NPs preceding the verb in AGRo (for her this is ASP). That analysis is problematic for a very general theory of argument projection which takes arguments to occupy identical stuctural positions universally (see Hale & Keyser 1993), and across categories (see e.g. Valois 1991 for the view that NPs project their arguments in parallel fashion to VPs). This means that if the external argument is sometimes generated in the specifier of a higher VP with an empty abstract V at D-structure, it should be generated there in general. The problem is that SI infinitives do appear with external arguments; I therefore maintain the projection of double layered VPs also in SI infinitives. A similar critique applies to Duffield's solution in terms of varying base-generated positions of the external argument.

18 In fact, speakers of many southern dialects avoid infinitives with two overt NPs altogether and prefer using a finite complement clause instead.

3.2 Raising constructions in SI

Although our analysis works well with the constructions considered sofar, there is a set of constructions in SI that remain problematic for the principle of Shortest Movement and the definition of equidistance. These are raising predicates, two examples of which are given below (see McCloskey 1984, Stowell 1989):

(14) a. Thiocfadh le Ciarán$_k$ [t$_k$ teach a cheannach]
come(COND) with Ciarán house aL buy
'Ciarán could buy a house'

b. Caithfidh Ciarán$_k$ [t$_k$ teach a cheannach]
must Ciarán a house aL buy
'Ciarán must buy a house.'

Note that in both examples the object moves to Spec/AGRoP, since it precedes the verb. If these are in fact instances of NP movement of the embedded subject to matrix subject position, then the question arises, why movement of the subject across the shifted object is not in conflict with Shortest Movement: in the absence of further verb movement, the Spec/AGRsP (or Spec/TP, whichever specifier the subject moves through on its way to the matrix clause) and Spec/AGRoP are not equidistant for the subject in Spec/VP. We are in fact confronted with precisely the problematic configuration of (6).

These cases indicate that we might need to abandon a narrow version of Shortest Movement or revise the definition of what counts as equidistant, as NP movment across a shifted object in the absence of V-raising appear to be possible.

However, I would like to suggest a different possibility. It is apparently the case that SI infinitives are only able to license one overt argument with accusative Case. Apparently, AGRsP dominating [-TNS] in SI does not license overt Case but only null Case, so that AGRoP is available to the object only if the subject does not need to be Case licensed.[19,20] Let us assume now that while in NI the "active" AGR-phrase is exclusively the VP internal one,

---

[19] This analysis was adopted in Noonan (1992b).

[20] However, default accusative Case definitely is available in small clauses in SI also.

in SI it may be either the inner or the outer AGR-projection. The VP-external AGRo is activated when there is either an overt external NP argument to raise to its specifier, or when the subject is PRO and remains in situ, so that the object may raise to the external AGRoP. In those cases where the subject raises to the matrix clause by NP-movement, the outer AGRoP cannot be activated, as there is no NP to raise and check its features, since the object NP may not move to it specifier without that a violation of shortest movement results.

In conclusion, I have argued that Irish shows evidence for the existence of an AGRoP both within and without of the double layer VP. In NI, the VP-internal AGRo-phrase has strong features and triggers object shift (aL only occurs with internal arguments), whereas in SI either of the AGR-phrases may have strong features. I have furthermore argued that Case patterns in Irish infinitives are ergative in nature.

References

Bobaljek, Jonathan & Andrew Carnie. 1992. A Minimalist Approach to Some Problems of Irish Word Order. Ms. MIT.

Chomsky, Noam. 1991. Some Notes on Economy of Derivation and Representation. In R. Freidin (ed). *Principles and Parameters in Comparative Grammar.* MIT Press. Cambridge, Mass.

Chomsky, Noam. 1993. A Minimalist Program for Linguistic Theory. In Kenneth Hale & Samuel Keyser (ed) *The View from Building 20.* The MIT Press. Cambridge, Mass.

Chomsky, Noam & Howard Lasnik. 1991. Principle and Parameters Theory. In: J. Jacobs, A. von Stechow, W. Sternefeld, & T. Venemann. Syntax: An International Handbook of Contemporary Reearch. Berlin: de Gruyter.

Chung, Sandra & James McCloskey. 1987. Government, Barriers, and Small Clauses in Modern Irish. *Linguistic Inquiry* 18:173-237.

Collins, Chris & H. Thráinsson. 1993. Object Shift in Double Object Constructions and the Theory of Case. Ms. Cornell University.

Duffield, Nigel. 1991.*Particles and Projections.* PhD diss. USC, Los Angeles. CA.

Guilfoyle, Eithne. 1993. VNPs, Finiteness and External Arguments. *NELS* 24.

Hale, Kenneth & Samuel Keyser. 1993. On Argument Structure and the Lexical Expression of Syntactic Relations. In Kenneth Hale & Samuel Keyser (ed) *The View from Building 20.* The MIT Press. Cambridge, Mass.

Holmberg, Anders. 1986. Word Order and Syntactic Features in the Scandinavian Languages and English. Doctoral dissertation. University of Stockholm, Stockholm.

Laka, Itziar. 1993. Unergatives that assign ergative, unaccusatives that assign accusative. In Bobaljik J. & Phil et al (eds) *MITWPL.* MIT. Cambridge, Mass.

McCloskey, James 1984. Raising, Subcategorisation and Selection in Modern Irish. *NLLT* 1:441-485.

Noonan, Máire 1992a. Statives, Perfectives, and Accusativity: the importance of being HAVE. In Jonathan Mead (ed).*WCCFL* 11. Stanford Linguistics Association.

Noonan, Máire. 1992b. *Case and Syntactic Geometry.* PhD diss. McGill University. Montreal.

Noonan, Máire. (in progress). On Burzio's Generalisation and Ergativity in Irish. Ms. University College Dublin.

Pollock, Jean-Yves. 1989. Verb movement, Universal Grammar, and the Structure of IP. *Linguistic Inquiry* 20:365-424.

Shaer, Benjamin. 1990. Functional Categories, Reference and the Nature of the Eskimo Verb. Paper presented at GLOW.

Sportiche, Dominique. 1990. Movement, Agreement and Case. Ms. UCLA.

Sportiche, Dominique. 1992. Clitic Constructions. Ms. UCLA.

Stowell, Timothy. 1989. Raising in Irish and the Projection Principle. *NLLT* 7:317-359.

Tenny, Carol. 1987. *Grammaticalising Aspect and Affectedness.* PhD diss., MIT, Cambridge, Mass.

Travis. Lisa. 1991. Derived Objects, Inner Aspect and the Structure of VP. *NELS* XXII.

Valois, Daniel. 1991. *The Internal Syntax of DP.* PhD diss. UCLA, Los Angeles, CA.

Weak Crossover, Scope, and Agreement in a Minimalist Framework*

PIERRE PICA & WILLIAM SNYDER
UQAM & CNRS & Massachusetts Institute of Technology

0. Introduction

The first section of our paper presents a novel theory of weak crossover effects, based entirely on quantifier scope preferences and their consequences for variable binding. The structural notion 'crossover' plays no role. The second section presents a theory of scope preferences, based on assumptions of Chomsky's (1993) minimalist framework. The proposed theory ascribes a central role to the AGR-P system of case-checking.

* The authors wish to thank F. Beghelli, N. Chomsky, I. Heim, H. Hoji, N. Hornstein, R. Kayne, H. Lasnik, K. Safir, E. Williams, and the audience at WCCFL XIII, especially V. Deprez and S. Iatridou, for their many helpful comments and suggestions. All errors remain our own. Portions of this work were presented at the New Jersey Linguistics Circle, May 1994. This work was partly supported by the Social Sciences and Humanities Research Council of Canada Grant n° 411-92-0012 (Pica); and by an NSF Fellowship in linguistics, an NSF Research Traineeship in linguistics and cognitive science, and the McDonnell-Pew Center for Cognitive Neuroscience at MIT (Snyder).

I.Weak Crossover

I.1. Standard Accounts of WCO: The 'Crossover' Configuration

Since (Postal 1972), weak crossover effects (as in 1) have generally been attributed to a constraint stated in terms of a structural 'crossing' configuration, or similarly in terms of structural notions such as 'leftness' or 'bijection'. A recent formulation is (2), drawn from (Lasnik & Stowell 1991), which is taken to apply at LF after QR.[1]

(1) a. ?? Who_i does his_i mother like t_i
  b. ?? His_i mother likes everyone_i

(2) In a configuration where a pronoun P and a trace T are both bound by a quantifier Q, T must c-command P. (Lasnik & Stowell 1989)

In this paper we argue *against* accounts of WCO in terms of directionality, bijection, or crossover, including the approach in (2).

I.2. Scope Preferences and Grammaticality

A major goal of this paper is to make the following methodological point: A 'dispreferred' scope reading should not be treated as 'fully grammatical'. The standard argument that variable binding should even be possible in (1b), for example, comes from the possibility of a wide-scope reading of *everyone* in the parallel example (3).

(3) Someone likes everyone

Yet, it is independently acknowledged that in (3) the wide-scope reading for *everyone* is strongly dispreferred, especially by informants who have not received extensive training in formal logic. The standard assumption, which we challenge, is that even 'dispreferred' scope readings are to be treated as 'fully

---

1 Lasnik & Stowell take (2) as a descriptive generalization compatible with most of the data in the WCO literature. In the course of their paper, however, they argue that the range of WCO effects in fact observed is more restricted than would be expected under (2), a point to which we shall return.

grammatical'.

I.3. Weak Crossover Effects as a Failure of Variable Binding

We shall now argue that the classical cases of 'WCO' effects should be attributed to a difficulty in variable binding, rather than a constraint of the type in (2). On this view, the classical cases of 'WCO' are 'weak' violations precisely because it is at least marginally possible to obtain wide scope on the QP or *wh*-word at the point of interpretation. To the extent that wide scope is dispreferred in an example such as (1b), however, we take variable binding of the pronoun by the QP to be correspondingly dispreferred.

This is the opposite logic of all the standard accounts. In our view, to the extent that a 'crossover' configuration holds at the point of interpretation, the sentence is in fact grammatical. To the extent that the sentence is ungrammatical, this is because of the difficulty in allowing the QP or *wh*-expression to serve as a binder for the pronoun; in other words, because of the difficulty in *obtaining* the crossover configuration at LF.

The first part of our argument is that the acceptability of a WCO configuration involving a quantified NP is *directly proportional* to the acceptability of a wide-scope reading of the (lower) quantifier in parallel examples involving two quantifiers, as illustrated in (4-8a,b).[2] (Several of these examples are drawn from Barss & Lasnik 1986.)

(4) Double object datives
   a. * John gave someone everything (Wide Scope on *everything*)
   b. * John gave its_i owner every $paycheck_i$
   c. * $What_i$ did John give its_i owner t_i
   d. * John gave his_i own master $Fido_i$

---

[2] In (4-8a), we are concerned with the scope preferences obtained with 'neutral' focus, such as focus on the verb or the proper name. While focus is probably present in some form in every sentence, the *parallellism* among the a-d examples under each of (4-8) is our crucial point, and this parallellism should obtain as long as the sentences are all focused in the same way. Although our proposals in the second part of the paper may provide a candidate explanation for the effects of focus on scope, we will not address this issue here. For a broader discussion of the 'complex predicate' constructions employed in (4-8), see also Snyder & Stromswold (in review).

(5) Perceptual reports[3]
  a. * Mary saw someone greet everyone
      (Wide Scope on *everyone*)
  b. * Mary saw his_i host greet $everyone_i$
  c. * Who_i did Mary see his_i host greet
      (contrast, 'Who did Mary see Fred greet')
  d. * Mary saw his_i own host greet Ted_i

(6) Monotransitives
  a. ?? Someone likes everyone (Wide Scope on *everyone*)
  b. ?? His_i mother likes $everyone_i$
  c. ?? Who_i does his_i mother like
  d. ?? His_i own mother likes Ted_i

(7) Prepositional datives
  a. Mary gave something to everyone (Wide Scope on *everyone*)
  b. ? Mary gave his_i paycheck to $everyone_i$
  c. ? To $whom_i$ did Mary give his_i paycheck
  d. ? Mary gave his_i own paycheck to Ted_i

(8) *Put*-locatives
  a. Mary put something on every box (Wide Scope on *every box*)
  b. ? Mary put its_i label on every box_i
  c. ? On what box_i did Mary put its_i label
  d. ? Mary put its_i own label on the box_i

Many of the judgements in (4-8) vary across English speakers, and for this reason Snyder (1994) has conducted a psycholinguistic investigation on native English-speakers (all of them non-linguists) to evaluate the predicted positive correlation between the relative grammaticality of the a and b sentences for each of double object datives (4), monotransitives (6), and prepositional datives (7). Despite some variability in the relative ranking of the three sentence types across speakers, and despite the difficulty in eliciting judgements of scope preferences, the study found the predicted correlation at a statistically significant level (as indicated in 9).

(9) $r = .490, t\,(28) = 8.83, p < .006$

---

3 The same pattern of judgements obtains for corresponding *make*-causatives.

We can extend our analysis in terms of scope preferences to *wh*-words, as demonstrated by the parallel judgements for the (b) and (c) examples in (4-8). Recent work (including Heim 1987, Chierchia 1993, among others) indicates that the traditional notion of 'scope' of a *wh*-word is too simplistic. We will adopt the proposal of Heim 1987 (cf. also Chomsky 1964, pp. 38-40), according to which *wh*-expressions are decomposed into a *wh*-feature and an existential expression, for purposes of interpretation. On this view, the *wh*-feature in a *wh*-question is typically interpreted in SPEC CP, where it indicates that the sentence is to be interpreted as a *wh*-question. The existential component of the *wh*-expression is interpreted in a lower position, where its scope relative to other quantifiers can vary.

We propose that (i) the portion of a *wh*-expression responsible for binding a lower variable is the existential component, and that (ii) the scope preferences affecting the existential component are the same as those affecting a simple quantified NP. (Again, we will discuss a theory of scope preferences in the second part of the paper.) On these assumptions, the judgements in (4-8c) are directly accounted for.[4]

The second part of our argument is that the cases in which a wide-scope reading of the lower quantifier is most fully acceptable are those in which the lower quantifier is contained in a prepositional phrase (e.g. 7a, 8a). Crucially, the parallel WCO

---

4 In the restrictive relatives of (i) we find the same pattern as for *wh*-questions in (4c), (6c), and (7c). We are led to an analysis of restrictive relatives that is parallel to our account of *wh*-questions. For example, the relative pronoun (or null operator) may be interpreted as bifurcated into a relative-clause marking feature interpreted in C^0/CP, and a pronominal element preferentially interpreted in the same position as a simple quantified NP. Note also that the head noun (*paycheck, person*) of the restrictive relative is not a suitable antecedent for a bound variable pronoun, nor is the NP containing the restrictive relative. This is as expected, if a variable must be bound by a c-commanding maximal projection.

i. 'WCO' effects in restrictive relatives
  a. * No [paycheck which$_i$ Mary gave its$_i$ owner t$_i$] has been found
  b. ?? No [person who$_i$ his$_i$ mother likes t$_i$] is allowed in the support group (cf. Postal 1971, among others)
  c. ? No [person to whom$_i$ Mary gave his$_i$ paycheck t$_i$] is allowed ...

configurations are only very mildly ungrammatical in (7-8b,c), much less so than the standard examples of 'WCO' in monotransitives (6b,c).[5] Moreover, the 'residue' of WCO (7-8b,c) is plausibly related to some difficulty in variable binding out of the PP structure .[6] In (7-8c) we take the preposition to undergo LF movement as part of the oblique argument.

Third, the *his own* construction in English, in order to be licensed, must be c-commanded by its antecedent at LF (cf. Fiengo & Higginbotham 1984). As predicted by our account, but not by standard treatments of WCO, the grammaticality of the *his own* construction is directly proportional both to the grammaticality of

---

5 Lasnik & Stowell (1991) discuss a number of cases where WCO effects are predicted by standard accounts of WCO, yet are absent. Our own approach provides an account for most or all of these cases. For example, lack of WCO effects in topicalization and non-restrictive relatives (i,ii) is predicted on our account (in §II), to the extent that the topic or the head of the relative cannot be interpreted in any trace position lower than the pronoun. Unfortunately, L&S's evidence is confounded by their use of non-quantificational NPs:

i. $John_i$, OP_i his_i mother likes t_i (Guéron 1986:62)
ii. $John_i$, who_i his_i mother likes t_i, ... (cf. L&S 1991, and references therein)

Postal (1993), in a reply to L&S, brings up examples of the type in (iii), which he takes to show that true quantified topics do yield WCO effects. As illustrated in (iv-v.b), however, Postal's claim does not hold up in other cases. Indeed, not only do (iv-v.b) seem relatively acceptable, but the contrast in judgements for (iii), with and without coindexing, is not at all clear for us.

iii. Everybody $else_i$, I told $his_{j/*i}$ wife that I had called t_i (Postal 1993)
iv. a. Anybody $else_i$ would have quit his_i job
b. Anybody $else_i$, his_i boss would have fired t_i
v. a. Everybody $else_i$ likes his_i mother
b. Everybody $else_i$, his_i mother likes t_i

6 Some support for this view comes from the fact that the equivalents of 7b,c are fully grammatical in French (ia,b) (see also Snyder 1992). Kayne (1975) has argued, on the basis of coordination facts, that *à*-phrases serving as dative arguments are NPs rather than PPs in French. The more general pattern of WCO effects in French, as discussed by Postal (1993), is more complex, however, and remains somewhat mysterious on all currently available accounts.

i. a. Marie a donné sa_i paye à tout le $monde_i$
`Mary gave his_i check to $everyone_i$'
b. À qui_i Marie a-t-elle donné sa_i paye?
'To $whom_i$ has Mary given his_i check?'

the wide-scope reading on the corresponding quantifier example, and to the grammaticality of the corresponding WCO configurations, as illustrated in (4-8d). On the scope theory that we will now present, this parallelism follows from the 'preferred' position of interpretation for an NP. On our account, such preferences extend to definite descriptions as well as to *wh*-expressions and QPs.

II. A minimalist theory of quantifier scope preferences

In this section we present a very simple theory of quantifier scope preferences. The proposals represent work in progress, indeed in its early stages. Given the vastness and complexity of the literature on quantifier scope, we cannot hope to do justice here to the full range of related issues. As will become apparent, our approach relates in potentially interesting ways to recent work by Diesing (1992), Beghelli (1992), and others. Our hope is that these various lines of work will ultimately prove to be mutually compatible. We are especially indebted to Norbert Hornstein for several key suggestions, although the details of our proposals diverge in significant ways from Hornstein's own (1994) scope theory.[7]

II.1. Outline of the theory

In developing a theory of quantifier scope preferences, our starting point has been Chomsky's (1993) proposal that LF reconstruction to an A-position is 'obligatory if syntactically possible'. This has the effect that if 'QR', in the conventional sense of A-bar movement and adjunction at LF, occurs at all, it is effectively 'undone' prior to the point of semantic interpretation. Sportiche (1994) has recently argued, for independent reasons, that adjunction operations should be eliminated from the grammar entirely. If correct, Sportiche's arguments independently lead us to question the conventional view of QR as an LF adjunction operation.

---

7 Hornstein (1994) has developed a theory that, like ours, is based on interpretation of QPs in the A-positions available under Minimalist assumptions. The major ways in which our work differs from Hornstein's are that we develop a theory of scope *preferences*, we relate WCO effects to scope preferences (as opposed to linking), and we provide a somewhat different treatment of 'complex predicate' constructions, especially double object and prepositional datives.

A major motivation for LF adjunction as the basis of QR in (May 1977) was the need for scopal positions in which to interpret quantificational expressions. If we adopt the AGR-P theory of case-checking and the VP-internal subject hypothesis, however, we introduce as a consequence a number of A-positions that can potentially serve as scopal positions, a possibility exploited, for example, in the system of (Diesing 1992). We will assume here that A-movement, as well as A-bar movement, can trigger predicate abstraction, so that there should be no obstacle to treating the SPEC of an AGR-P as a scopal position.

We will assume a theory of LF reconstruction in terms of the 'copy' theory of traces developed in (Chomsky & Lasnik 1992) and (Chomsky 1993). This assumption will have important consequences for our treatment of scope in VP-ellipsis constructions.

The essential points of our theory of scope preferences are given in (10).

(10) a. The *preferred* syntactic position in which to interpret a DP (quantified or otherwise) is the position in which its Case is checked. (i.e. SPEC AGRsP for subjects, SPEC AGRoP for objects bearing structural accusative Case).

We assume, perhaps controversially, that PP arguments, like DP arguments, must be checked in a VP-external SPEC AGR-P position by LF.

(10) b. Argument PPs are preferentially interpreted in a checking position intermediate between T^0 and VP.

Below we will motivate (10b) on empirical grounds. We assume that the checking position for PP arguments can be generated either immediately above, or immediately below, AGRoP. The final component of our theory is (10c).

(10) c. It is marginally possible to interpret a DP in its theta-position (subject to the requirement of Full Interpretation).

If we assume a restrictive account of quantifier interpretation in which internal object positions of a transitive verb are not scopal (that is, if we avoid a flexible-types approach), then (10c) will only affect the interpretive possibilities for subjects: A quantified subject may be interpreted either in SPEC AGRsP or (with marginal acceptability) in SPEC VP.[8]

II.2. Application of the Theory to Selected Examples.

Let us now examine how the proposals in (10) account for the evidence in (4-8). Recall that the relevant scope judgements all assume 'neutral' focus, without focus on either QP. The preferred interpretation of a monotransitive example such as (6a) follows from interpretation of the quantified subject in SPEC AGRsP, and interpretation of the quantified object in SPEC AGRoP:

(11) a. Preferred interpretation of (6a):
someone AGRs everyone AGRo [VP t likes t]

The marginally possible interpretation in which *everyone* receives wide scope, follows from interpretation of the object in SPEC AGRoP,

---

8 One place where we differ with Hornstein (1994) is on the standard question of whether ellipsis should be handled by LF copying or PF deletion. Hornstein adopts an LF-copying approach, but we find that this approach is inconsistent with an A-position approach to quantifier scope. For example, in (ii.a), the existential QPs can take narrow scope:

(ii) a. Some girl likes every teacher, and some boy does too.
b. A friend of mine went to every party, and a bassoonist did too.

For both Hornstein and us, the existential QPs in (ii.a) must be interpreted in SPEC VP, yet this means that LF-copying of the non-elliptical VP into the elliptical VP should over-write *some boy* with *some girl*, leading not to the observed narrow scope reading, but to an unavailable interpretation: 'Some girl likes every teacher, and some girl likes every teacher too'. We propose instead that VP ellipsis is accomplished through PF deletion of defocused material (cf. Tancredi 1992). The material is required to be parallel to corresponding overt material, but this requirement is checked at LF. When two SPEC VPs stand in a contrastive focus relation (ii.a), the [+F] material is subject to a weaker parallelism constraint that does not require identity. This weaker constraint is nonetheless violated in (ii.b), where only the narrow-scope reading of the universal QP is allowed. An important consequence of our minimalist approach is that the parallelism constraint can be stated entirely on the LF representation, without stipulating parallel derivations. This follows if we take VP ellipsis to be in reality AGR-P ellipsis (i.e. everything under T^{o}), because there is only one scope position (AGRsP) above T^{o}. Hence, we avoid the standard problem of two QPs raising and adjoining to IP in different orders in the two conjuncts (which has led others to stipulate parallel derivations as well as parallel LF representations).

but interpretation of the subject in VP-internal subject position:

(11) b. Marginally possible interpretation of (6a):
AGRs everyone AGRo [VP someone likes t]

The full ambiguity found in *to*-datives (7a) (as well as *put*-locatives, 8a) follows from interpretation of the PP (*to*-phrase) in a position either immediately above, or immediately below, SPEC AGRoP.[9]

(12) a. Wide-scope interpretation of lower QP in (7a):
Mary$_i$ AGRs [to everyone]$_j$ AGRpp something$_k$ AGRo [VP t_i gave t_k t_j]

(12) b. Narrow-scope interpretation of lower QP in (7a):
Mary$_i$ AGRs something$_k$ AGRo [to everyone]$_j$ AGRpp [VP t_i gave t_k t_j]

Notice that the system in (10) correctly captures the scope preferences applying to the subject and prepositional object in a *to*-dative. In (12c), *someone* preferentially takes wider scope than *everyone*, but can marginally take narrow scope.

(12) c. Someone gave a present to everyone

This follows if *to everyone* is interpreted between T^0 and VP (10b), and if *someone* is interpreted either in SPEC AGRsP (the preferred location) or in VP-internal subject position (the dispreferred location).

We attribute the apparent lack of ambiguity in scope relations

---

[9] The examples (7a) and (8a) of course show only that the prepositional argument can take wider scope than the direct object. The examples (i-ii) show that the direct object can also take wide scope over the PP with no loss of grammaticality.

(i) Mary gave every story to a (different) reporter
(ii) Mary put every letter in a (different) box

There is a tendency for an existential quantifier in the PP to be interpreted specifically in (i-ii), but this tendency can be easily overcome with addition of a modifier such as *different*.

found in double object datives (4a) to the presence of a phonologically null P^o which takes the lower object as its complement. On our account, this null P^o contrasts with the overt P^o in *to*-datives (7a) or *put*-locatives (8a), in that the null P^o blocks both variable binding and quantifier 'scoping' out of the PP. Thus, even though the PP is interpreted in a checking position intermediate between T^o and VP, there is no way for its complement to bind or take scope over a DP in SPEC AGRoP or in SPEC VP.

(13) a. $John_i$ AGRs $someone_j$ AGRo $[_{PP}$ P^o everything$]_k$ AGR_{PP}
$[_{VP}$ t_i gave t_j $t_k]$
b. $John_i$ AGRs $[_{PP}$ P^o everything$]_k$ AGR_{PP} $someone_j$ AGRo
$[_{VP}$ t_i gave t_j $t_k]$

(The LF in 13b, while possible, corresponds to a proper subset of the interpretations available in 13a.) Thus, the narrow scope interpretation of the lower (universal) QP in (4a) is the only available interpretation under the principles in (10).[10]

The analysis in (13) is comparable to a proposal of Hoffman (1991), in which the null P^o would correspond to the preposition *with* in (14a). (In the use of a null P^o 13 also resembles proposals of Kayne 1984 and Pesetsky 1994, among many others.) Interestingly, the *present-with* construction parallels the double object dative (4) with respect to scope, WCO, and licensing of *his own*, as illustrated in (14a-d).

(14) *Present-with* constructions
a. * Mary presented someone with everything
(Wide scope on *everything*)
b. * Mary presented its_i owner with every $check_i$
c. * With $what_i$ did Mary present its_i owner t_i
d. * Mary presented his_i own master with $Fido_i$

We are led to conclude that the *with*-phrase in (14), like the PP in

---

10 Strictly speaking, in (13a) there is also the possibility of 'independent' scope relations between the two QPs; this is the only possibility in (13b). In these examples, however, the 'independent' scope interpretation yields the same truth conditions as a wide scope reading of the existential.

(13), is a barrier to variable binding and quantifier scope. Thus, it appears that the choice of preposition determines whether the preposition's object can bind or take scope over a DP that the PP c-commands.[11]

If both internal arguments of a triadic predicate are interpreted outside the VP, we predict that when the subject takes narrow scope relative to either internal argument (by being interpreted in SPEC VP), it must take narrow scope relative to the other internal argument as well. This prediction is borne out, as shown in (15a-b).

(15) a. Someone$_i$ gave everyone his$_i$ business card
b. Someone$_i$ gave every good book to his$_i$ friend

In 15a-b, the requirement that the existential QP bind a variable in one of the internal arguments can be satisfied only if the existential takes wider scope than *both* internal arguments. Hence, wide scope on the universal quantifier is blocked in both examples.[12]

Although the proposals in (10) are somewhat stipulative in their present form, we would like to suggest that they may be derived from Pica's (1994) theory of the AGR-P system and its role in the visibility of syntactic arguments. The general idea is that the AgrP system serves as an alternative to the widely assumed mechanism of 'syntactic indexing'. On this approach, NPs are

---

[11] One place where *present-with* constructions diverge from double-object datives is in antecedent-contained deletion (ACD), as in (i). A preliminary investigation suggests to us that overt prepositions as in (ib) tend to interfere with ACD, for reasons that are unclear.

(i) a. John gave Frank everything that I did (Hornstein 1994, p.192)
b. ?* John presented Frank with everything that I did

[12] Hornstein (1984:194) notes an example similar to (15a), and arrives at a similar conclusion, except that he treats the two internal arguments of a double object dative as together forming a SC-like constituent, which is checked as a unit in SPEC AGRoP. This approach raises obvious problems for the analysis of indirect passives, where only the first of the two internal arguments moves to SPEC AGRsP. Also, Hornstein does not address the ambiguity of scope relations between the internal arguments of prepositional datives, or the obligatoriness of narrow scope on the existential in (15b). If Hornstein were to accept an explanation in which the two internal arguments of a prepositional dative are checked in separate AGR-Ps, then his idea that there is only one AGR-P for both internal objects of a double object dative would again be called into question.

normally related, via the AgrP system, to what Pica terms a 'cognitive value' (adapting the terminology of Heim 1993) in the discourse representation, and thus become visible to interpretive processes. We suggest that NPs are necessarily interpreted (i.e. take scope) in the position in which they become visible. Interpretation in a non-Case-checking position such as SPEC VP, while possible, is a more 'costly' option that perhaps depends on visibility through incorporation (cf. Marantz 1984, Baker 1988).[13]

II.3. Major Conceptual and Empirical Advantages.

A major conceptual advantage of our approach is that it marks a return to the direct account of relative quantifier scope in terms of *LF c-command relations between quantifiers*. This was the approach of (May 1977), but was abandoned for example in (May 1985) and in (Aoun & Li 1989, 1993). The latter accounts depend on additional mechanisms to derive possible scope relations from the LF structural relations holding between quantifiers. A further conceptual advantage is that we provide a predictive theory of quantifier scope *preferences*, in contrast to most if not all prior accounts.

---

13 This approach is consistent with several additional facts concerning scope preferences in raising and passive constructions. If we assume that an NP can receive a 'cognitive value' in any SPEC AGR-P position through which it passes in the course of having its features checked, then we account for the relative lack of scope preferences in (i) and (ii), as compared with (iii).

i. Something was given to everyone
(LF: something AGRs [to everyone] AGRpp (something) AGRo)
ii. Almost everyone seems (t) to like Mary
(LF: almost everyone AGRs seems (almost everyone) AGRs Mary AGRo)
iii. Someone spoke to everyone
(LF : someone AGRs [to everyone] AGRpp [$_{VP}$ (someone) ...])

In (i) the surface subject is an underlying direct object, and (arguably) passes through SPEC AGRoP on the way to SPEC AGRsP; the relative scope of the universal and existential quantifiers is fully ambiguous in (i). In (ii) the matrix subject is generated in VP-internal subject position of the embedded clause, but presumably passes through a SPEC AGRsP position in the embedded clause before raising to SPEC AGRsP in the matrix clause; the relative scope of the quantifier and the verb *seems* is again highly ambiguous. In (iii), however, the surface subject is not an underlying direct object; the only way for it to be interpreted lower than the indirect object is through the more 'costly' option of being interpreted in SPEC VP. (On the structure of 'dyadic' *to*-datives as in (iii), see also Snyder & Stromswold, in review.) In (iii) the preference is for wide scope on the existential quantifier.

A major empirical advantage of our approach is that it provides a very natural explanation for the role of S-structure c-command relations in determining quantifier scope relations, discussed by Huang (1982), Frey (1993), and Krifka (1994), among others. This is because S-structure positions in most cases correspond to the preferred position of interpretation for a quantified DP.

Similarly, our approach provides a very natural account of Aoun & Li's (1989) generalization that two quantified DPs have ambiguous scope relations if and only if their A-chains overlap. For the cases discussed by Aoun and Li, this generalization follows on our account from the fact that a quantified subject is preferentially interpreted in SPEC AGRsP, but with marginal acceptability can also be interpreted in VP-internal subject position. If a second quantifier is Case-checked in a position between SPEC AGRsP and the VP-internal subject position, then its A-chain overlaps with that of the subject, and precisely then our system allows the subject to be interpreted either inside or outside the scope of the second quantifier. A further empirical advantage of our system is that it explains the generalization that quantifier scope is overwhelmingly clause-bounded.[14] This generalization follows on our account from the obligatory nature of reconstruction, in most cases, to an A-position.[15]

III. References

Abusch, Dorit. 1994. The scope of indefinites. To appear in *Natural Language*

---

[14] Abusch (1994) has presented some apparent counterexamples to this generalization, in which indefinites seemingly take clause-external scope. Kratzer (1994) has argued, however, that the apparently extra-clausal scope of these indefinites is in fact a 'pseudoscope' phenomenon. According to Kratzer, these indefinites really take clause-internal scope, but appear to take wider scope because of an interpretive dependence on a variable bound from outside the clause.

[15] The cases where our account permits clause-external scope are those in which a quantified element undergoes clause-external movement to satisfy a morphological checking relation, and then is syntactically blocked from reconstruction. For example, reconstruction may be syntactically blocked if part of the QP undergoes incorporation into the head of a clause-external XP; Chomsky (1993) gives an example involving *wh*-movement of the phrase *which picture of himself*, with incorporation of *-self* into a clause-external antecedent. The apparent ability of *focus* to license clause-external scope would follow on our account if focus involves LF movement and incorporation into a phonologically null (or at least non-segmental) 'focus-marker'.

Semantics 2.

Aoun, Joseph and Audrey Yen-Hui Li. 1989. Scope and constituency. *Linguistic Inquiry* 20.141-172.

Aoun, Joseph and Audrey Yen-Hui Li. 1993. *Syntax of scope*. Cambridge, MA: MIT Press.

Baker, Mark. 1988. *Incorporation: A theory of grammatical function-changing*. Chicago: University of Chicago Press.

Barss, Andrew and Howard Lasnik. 1986. A note on anaphora and double objects. *Linguistic Inquiry* 17.347-354.

Beghelli, Filippo. 1992. A minimalist approach to quantifier scope. *Proceedings of NELS* 23, 65-80. Amherst, MA: GLSA.

Chierchia, Gennaro. 1993. Questions with quantifiers. *Natural Language Semantics* 1.181-234.

Chomsky, Noam. 1964. *Current Issues in linguistic theory*. The Hague: Mouton.

Chomsky, Noam. 1993. A minimalist program for linguistic theory. *The view from Building 20: Essays in honor of Sylvain Bromberger*, ed. by Ken Hale and Samuel Jay Keyser, 1-52. Cambridge, MA: MIT Press.

Chomsky, Noam and Howard Lasnik. 1992. Principles and parameters theory. *Syntax: An international handbook of contemporary research*, ed. by J. Jacobs, A. von Stechow, W. Sternefeld, and T. Vennemann Berlin: Walter de Gruyter.

Diesing, Molly. 1992. *Indefinites*. MIT Press: Cambridge, MA.

Fiengo, Robert and James Higginbotham. 1984. Opacity in NP. *Linguistic Analysis* 7.395-421.

Frey, Werner. 1993. *Syntaktische Bedingungen für die semantische Repräsentation. Über Bindung, implizite Argumente und Skopus*. (Studia Grammatica XXXV). Berlin: Adademie Verlag.

Guéron, Jacqueline. 1986. Coréférence et structures topicalisées. *La Grammaire Modulaire*, ed. by Mitsou Ronat and Daniel Couquaux. Paris: Minuit.

Heim, Irene. 1987. Where does the definiteness restriction apply? Evidence from the definiteness of variables. *The representation of (in)definiteness*, ed. by Eric Reuland and Alice ter Meulen, 21-42. Cambridge, MA: MIT Press.

Heim, Irene. 1993. Anaphora and semantic interpretation: A reinterpretation of Reinhart's approach. SfS-Report-07, Eberhard-Karls-Universität Tübingen.

Hoffman, Mika. 1991. *The syntax of argument-structure-changing morphology*. Doctoral dissertation, MIT.

Hornstein, Norbert. 1994. The grammar of LF: From GB to Minimalism. (To be published by Blackwell.) Ms., University of Maryland.

Huang, C.-T. James. 1982. *Logical relations in Chinese and the theory of grammar*. Doctoral disseration, MIT.

Kayne, Richard. 1975. *French syntax: The transformational cycle.* Cambridge, MA: MIT Press.

Kayne, Richard. 1984. Connectedness and binary branching. Dordrecht: Foris.

Kratzer, A. 1994. Scope or pseudoscope? Are there wide-scope indefinites? Paper presented at MIT, Cambridge, MA, 1 April 1994.

Krifka, Manfred. 1994. Focus and operator scope in German. Paper presented at the Linguistic Society of America Annual Meeting, Boston, MA, January 1994.

Lasnik, Howard and Tim Stowell. 1991. Weakest crossover. *Linguistic Inquiry* 22.687-720.

Marantz, Alec. 1984. *On the nature of grammatical relations*. Cambridge, MA: MIT Press.

May, Robert. 1977. *The grammar of quantification*. Doctoral disseration, MIT.

May, Robert. 1985. *Logical form: Its structure and derivation*. Cambridge, MA: MIT Press.

Pica, Pierre. 1994. On the disjoint agreement principle. To appear in *Essays on modularity: Projections, interfaces and modules*, ed. by Anna-Maria DiSciullo. Cambridge, UK: Oxford University Press.

Pesetsky, David. 1994. *Zero-syntax: Experiencers and cascades (Final Version).* MIT ms.

Postal, Paul. 1971. *Cross-over phenomena*. New York: Holt, Rinehart, and Winston.

Postal, Paul. 1993. Remarks on weak crossover effects. *Linguistic Inquiry* 24.539-556.

Snyder, William. 1992. Chain-formation and crossover. Generals Paper, MIT.

Snyder, William. 1994. A psycholinguistic investigation of weak crossover, islands, and syntactic satiation effects. Poster presented at CUNY Sentence Processing Conference, CUNY Graduate Center, New York , 17 March 1994.

Snyder, William and Karin Stromswold. In review. The structure and acquisition of English dative constructions. Cambridge, MA: MIT ms.

Sportiche, Dominique. 1994. Adjuncts and adjunction. *GLOW Newsletter* 32.54-55.

Tancredi, Chris. 1992. *Deletion, Deaccenting, and Presupposition.* Doctoral dissertation, MIT.

Explaining the Syntactic Consequences of 'Rich' Agreement Morphology: On the Licensing of V-to-AgrS Raising and pro

BERNHARD ROHRBACHER
University of Pennsylvania

Morphologically 'rich' subject-verb agreement is often held responsible for V-to-AgrS raising and pro-drop. But the precise definition of 'rich' agreement is the subject of much debate, and the question of why it triggers V-to-AgrS raising is usually not addressed at all or answered in a stipulative fashion. Moreover, a unified agreement-based account for V-to-AgrS raising and pro-drop has yet to be developed. This paper takes on these tasks and argues that affixes of paradigms which distinctively mark all person features are listed in the lexicon and inserted under AgrS where they attract the verb and give content to AgrSP so that AgrSPSpec can remain empty. Affixes of paradigms which fail to distinctively mark one or both of the person features are generated directly on the verb, leaving AgrS empty. There is no motivation for the verb to move to this position and AgSPSpec must be filled in order to give content to AgrSP.*

1 V-to-AgrS Raising

In embedded clauses that aren't complements of bridge verbs (i.e. in environments that do not allow head movement to C), the finite verb appears

---

* For reasons of space, I can only draw a rough sketch of this proposal. Moreover, many relevant issues cannot even be mentioned here. For a more thorough treatment along slightly different lines, see Rohrbacher (1993). Work on this paper was partially supported by the NSF grant SBR-8920230.

preadverbially in some Germanic SVO languages (cf. the Icelandic example in (1a)) but postadverbially in others (cf. the Faroese example in (1b)).

(1) a. Jón harmar adh María læsti ekki bókina.
J. regrets that M. read not book-the
'John regrets that Mary didn't read the book.' (Icelandic)

b. Har vóru nógv fólk, eg ekki kendi.
there were many people I not knew
'There were many people I didn't know.' (Faroese)

This contrast is standardly taken to reflect V-TO-AGRS RAISING (or verb movement to the highest inflectional head) in Icelandic (cf. (2a)) versus V-IN-SITU (or verb movement to at most an intermediate inflectional head) in Faroese (cf. (2b)).

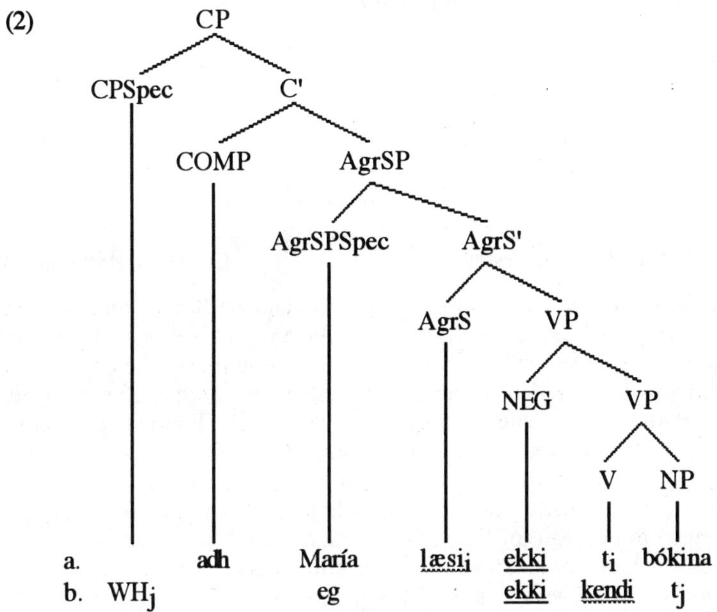

Vikner (1991) argues that (1a) involves free CP-RECURSION and verb movement to C above AgrS. Conversely, one could claim that (1a) involves verb movement to an intermediate inflectional head below AgrS. But the sentence in (3) cannot be analyzed along either of these lines: Here CP recursion (which blocks extraction) is excluded and the indefinite subject cannot be in VPSpec (since it precedes negation) or AgrOPSpec (since the features of the object have to be checked in this position) and must instead be in TPSpec. Therefore the verb in front of the indefinite subject must be in AgrS.

(3) [$_{CP}$ Thessa bók$_i$ [$_{C'}$ tel ég [$_{CP}$ t_i [$_{C'}$ adh [$_{AgrSP}$ thadh
this book believe I that there
[$_{AgrS'}$ hafi$_j$ [$_{TP}$ sumir menn$_k$ [$_{T'}$ t_j [$_{AgrOP}$ t_i [$_{AgrO'}$ t_j [$_{VP}$ ekki
have some men not
[$_{VP}$ t_j [$_{VP}$ t_k lesidh t_i]]]]]]]]]]]]
read
'I believe that some men haven't read this book' (Icelandic)

A contrast similar to that in (1) exists in the Romance languages. In nonfinite and simple finite clauses, European Portuguese exhibits ENCLISIS (cf. (4)) while Brazilian Portuguese exhibits PROCLISIS (cf. (5)).

(4) a. A Ana espera ver -te esta tarde.
the A. wants to-see you this afternoon.
b. A Maria deu- lhe esse livro ontem.
the M. gave- him this book yesterday.
(European Portuguese)

(5) a. Ela quer me ver.
she wants me to-see
'She wants to see me.'
b. O Pedro me chamou ontem.
the P. me called yesterday
'Peter called me yesterday.' (Brazilian Portuguese)

Kayne (1991) argues that enclisis and proclisis in Italian and French infinitives, respectively, is due to verb movement past the clitic in Italian and lack of such movement in French. By the same token, the contrast in (4,5) indicates that the European Portuguese verb raises higher than its Brazilian Portuguese counterpart (Galves 1989:fn26). Following Hegarty (1993), I assume that object clitics are adjoined to AgrO and that AgrO can be interpolated into the structure at the end of the derivation. In European Portuguese, where the verb raises to AgrS before AgrO is interpolated, the clitic appears to the right of the verb to which it encliticizes. In Brazilian Portuguese, where the verb remains in situ in overt syntax, the clitic appears to the left of the verb to which it procliticizes.

Additional evidence supporting this conclusion comes from the distribution of empty referential inanimate objects. In European Portuguese, these elements are barred from sentential subjects and other islands for movement. In Brazilian Portuguese, the same construction is wellformed (cf. (6)).

(6) Que a IBM venda *e* a particulares surpreende- me.
That the IBM sells (it) to individuals surprises me
'That IBM sells it to private individuals surprises me.'
(*European Portuguese, √Brazilian Portuguese)

Raposo (1986) proposes that in European Portuguese, *e* is the trace of an empty operator which has moved to the matrix topic position in violation of the SENTENTIAL SUBJECT CONSTRAINT (cf. (7)).

(7) $[_{CP}$ Op_i $[_{AgrSP}$ $[_{NP}$ $[_{CP}$ $[_{AgrSP}$ NP_j $[_{AgrS'}$ V_k $[_{VP}$ t_j t_k t_i]]]]] ...]]

The absence of a comparable island violation in Brazilian Portuguese has led Farrell (1990) to conclude that here *e* is an instance of pro. But Galves (1989,1990) points out that Raposo's analysis can be extended to Brazilian Portuguese if, in this language, the subject remains in TPSpec, thus leaving the AgrSPSpec of the sentential subject available as a topic position. As a consequence, the operator does not have to move out of its minimal clause and no violation of the Sentential Subject Constraint incurs (cf. (8)). This analysis implies that the verb following the subject in TPSpec does not move past Tns.

(8) $[_{CP}$ $[_{AgrSP}$ $[_{NP}$ $[_{CP}$ $[_{AgrSP}$ Op_i $[_{TP}$ NP_j $[_{T'}$ V_k $[_{VP}$ t_j t_k t_i]]]]]] ...]]

In summary, there is reason to believe that the verb moves to AgrS in Icelandic and European Portuguese but not in Faroese and Brazilian Portuguese.

2 Agreement Morphology

Platzack & Holmberg (1989) were the first to relate the contrast in (1) to the relative 'richness' of overt subject-verb agreement in the two languages. Recent proposals in this vein include Roberts (1993) and Falk (1993). In both, overt number agreement either requires or allows V-to-AgrS raising. According to Roberts, overt number agreement turns AgrS into a defective category that requires verb raising to become morphologically wellformed (cf. (9)). According to Falk, overt number agreement turns AgrS into a governor for the trace of verb raising, a precondition for the latter. V-to-AgrS raising remains optional unless overt person agreement prevents recovery of AgrS's content by the finiteness feature [+F] in C (cf. (10)).

(9) AGR^{-1} is postulated if there is overt distinct morphological plural marking (Roberts 1993:267)

(10) a. agreement in person: turns I^o into a governor, its content is not recoverable by [+F].

b. agreement in number: turns I^o into a governor, its content is recoverable by [+F].

c. tense: does not turn I^o into a governor, its content is recoverable by [+F]. (Falk 1993:198)

The V-to-AgrS languages Icelandic (cf. (11a)) and European Portuguese (cf. (11b)) clearly have overt number agreement. Roberts argues on the basis of the first weak conjugation in (12a) that the V-in-situ language Faroese lacks overt number agreement. This conjugation is compatible with the assumption that the plural form of the indicative present is a bare stem (with the stem-final vowel deleted before suffix-initial vowels). But all other conjugations (which together account for roughly 60% of all Faroese verbs) are incompatible with this assumption. The indicative preterite, preterite participle and imperative singular forms of e.g. the second weak conjugation in (12b) force the conclusion that the final vowel of the indicative present plural forms does not belong to the stem and instead constitutes an overt plural marker. This plural marker presumably also shows up in (12a) where it is identical to the stem-final vowel that deletes in its presence. It thus turns out that Faroese has overt number agreement as does Brazilian Portuguese (cf. (13)) and Roberts's and Falk's theories wrongly predict that both languages should require/allow V-to-AgrS raising.

(11) a. ICELANDIC segj-a 'say'

INDICATIVE PRESENT	SG	PL
1ST	seg-i	segj-um
2ND	seg-ir	seg-idh
3RD	seg-ir	segj-a

b. EUROPEAN PORTUGUESE compra-r 'to sell'

INDICATIVE PRESENT	SG	PL
1ST	compr-o	compr-amos
2ND	compra-s	compr-am
3RD	compra	compr-am

(12) a. FAROESE kasta 'throw'

	SG	PL
INDICATIVE PRESENT		
1ST	kast-i	kasta
2ND	kasta-r	kasta
3RD	kasta-r	kasta
INDICATIVE PRETERITE		
	kasta-dhi	kasta-dhu
PRETERITE PARTICIPLE		
	kasta-dhur	
IMPERATIVE		
	kasta	kast-idh

b. FAROESE nevn-a 'name'

	SG	PL
INDICATIVE PRESENT		
1ST	nevn-i	nevn-a
2ND	nevn-ir	nevn-a
3RD	nevn-ir	nevn-a
INDICATIVE PRETERITE		
	nevn-di	nevn-du
PRETERITE PARTICIPLE		
	nevn-dur	
IMPERATIVE		
	nevn	nevn-idh

(13) BRAZILIAN PORTUGUESE fala-r 'to speak'

INDICATIVE PRESENT	SG	PL
1ST	fal-o	fala
2ND	fala	fala-m
3RD	fala	fala-m

There is however a sense in which subject-verb agreement is 'richer' in the V-to-AgrS languages Icelandic and European Portuguese than in the V-in-situ languages Faroese and Brazilian Portuguese, although upon closer examination this difference turns out to involve person and not number agreement. In order to make the vague notion of morphological richness more precise, let us assume that person agreement is formally represented by the privative features [1st] and [2nd] and that a privative feature is DISTINCTIVELY MARKED when the forms bearing it differ overtly from the forms not bearing it. Thus both [1st] and [2nd] are distinctively marked in the Icelandic plural (cf. (11a)) and the European Portuguese singular (cf. (11b)) since the forms bearing these features differ overtly from each other and from the 'third' person and infinitival forms. Since [1st] is not distinctively marked in the Icelandic singular and [2nd] is not distinctively marked in the European Portuguese plural, I will say that these features are MINIMALLY DISTINCTIVELY MARKED in these languages. Turning to the V-in-situ languages Faroese and Brazilian Portuguese, we now see that in these languages [2nd] is not minimally distinctively marked since in both singular and plural the forms for second and 'third' person are indistinguishable.

This correlation between minimal distinctive marking of the person features [1st] and [2nd] on the one hand and V-to-AgrS raising on the other hand is not restricted to the languages discussed so far. Table 1 summarizes the feature marking and verb raising facts from synchronic and diachronic dialects of the Germanic VO languages. All V-in-situ languages fail to distinctively mark at least one of the two person features and all languages with minimal distinctive marking of both features have V-to-AgrS raising. There are only two V-to-AgrS dialects without minimal distinctive marking, Middle Scots and Kronoby Swedish. Both were or are in close contact with other V-to-AgrS languages (Old Norwegian and Finnish, respectively) and should probably be explained differently from the rest (cf. Rohrbacher (1993)). With this caveat in mind, it appears that V-to-AgrS raising occurs in exactly those languages whose subject-verb agreement minimally distinctively marks both of the person features [1st] and [2nd].

As indicated in table 1, all Germanic VO languages with minimal distinctive marking of [1st] and [2nd] also exhibit minimal distinctive marking of the number feature [pl], and the same is true for the Romance languages (cf. the European Portuguese paradigm in (11b)). These data are therefore compatible with the assumption in Rohrbacher (1993:118) that V-to-AgrS raising requires minimal distinctive marking of not only [1st] and [2nd], but also [pl]. The validity of this assumption is difficult to check because subject-verb agreement systems reflecting person but not number are very rare crosslinguistically: Only 12 (or 5%) of the 237 languages in the sample of the world's languages analyzed in Siewierska and Bakker (1994) have an agreement system of this kind. Given these numbers, it is hardly surprising that there does not seem to be an unambiguous V-to-AgrS or V-in-situ language with person but not number agreement. But there is at least one pro-drop language which fits the bill (Miskitu, cf. section 3). Since I argue in this paper that V-to-AgrS and pro-drop are licensed by the same type of agreement, I will assume that the less restrictive generalization at the end of the previous paragraph is correct and that minimal distinctive marking of the number feature [pl] is irrelevant with respect to the licensing of V-to-AgrS raising and pro-drop.

	[1st]	[2nd]	[pl]	V-to-AgrS
Faroese	√		√	
Hallingdalen Norwegian			√	
Early Modern English		√	(√)	
English			(√)	
Danish				
Norwegian				
Swedish				
Yiddish	√	√	√	√
Icelandic	√	√	√	√
Middle English	√	√	√	√
Old Danish	√	√	√	√
Old Norwegian	√	√	√	√
Old Swedish	√	√	√	√
Älvdalen Swedish	√	√	√	√
Middle Scots				√
Kronoby Swedish				√

Table 1: Distinctive Feature Marking and V-to-AgrS Raising in the Germanic VO Languages

Why should there be this correlation between minimal distinctive marking of the person features and V-to-AgrS raising? I would like to suggest that the reason has to do with the fact that [1st] and [2nd] (and only they) are REFERENTIAL FEATURES: If overtly distinguished, they usually identify the subject as either the speaker(s), the hearer(s), or other(s). Number and gender features do not play a comparable role since the context of discourse often contains more than one singular (or plural) entity and more than one feminine (or masculine or neuter) entity. In other words, if subject-verb agreement is marked for either first, second or 'third' person, this tells us much more about what the subject refers to than if subject-verb agreement is marked for either singular or plural or for either feminine, masculine or neuter. Let us then assume the following.

(14) AgrS is a referential category with lexically listed affixes in exactly those languages where regular subject-verb agreement minimally distinctively marks all referential AgrS-features such that in at least one number of one tense, the person features [1st] and [2nd] are distinctively marked.

According to (14), AgrS is referential and its affixes are (like all referential elements) lexically listed in languages where subject-verb agreement minimally distinctively marks both of the referential AgrS-features [1st] and [2nd]. Inserted under AgrS at D-structure, the agreement affix triggers V-to-AgrS raising at S-structure since it must be bound at this level. This is schematically represented in (15a). AgrS is nonreferential and its affixes are (like all nonreferential elements) lexically unlisted in languages where subject-verb agreement fails to distinctively mark one or both of the referential AgrS-features [1st] and [2nd]. AgrS is empty at D-structure and nothing forces verb movement to this position at S-structure. Postsyntactically, the abstract agreement features on the verb are spelled out as proposed in Anderson (1992). This is schematically represented in (15b). Alternatively, one could assume that V-in-situ languages inflect the verb already in the lexicon as proposed in Chomsky (1992).

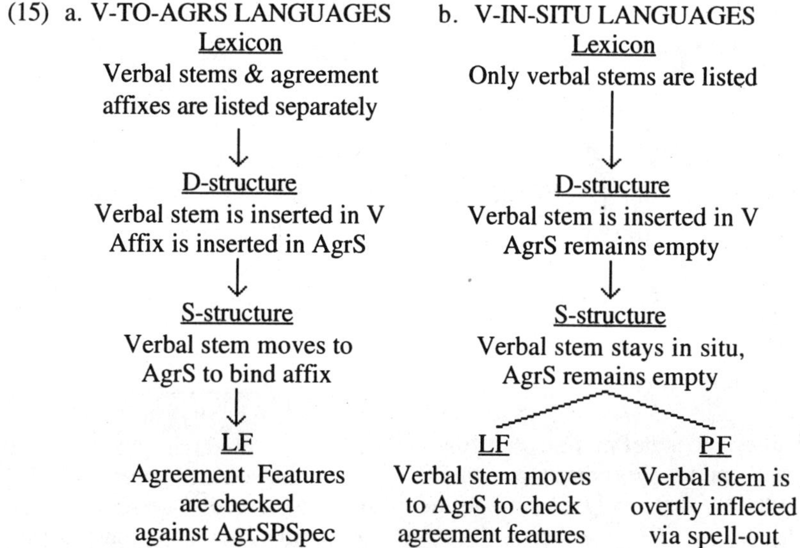
(15) a. V-TO-AGRS LANGUAGES
Lexicon
Verbal stems & agreement affixes are listed separately
D-structure
Verbal stem is inserted in V
Affix is inserted in AgrS
S-structure
Verbal stem moves to AgrS to bind affix
LF
Agreement Features are checked against AgrSPSpec
b. V-IN-SITU LANGUAGES
Lexicon
Only verbal stems are listed
D-structure
Verbal stem is inserted in V
AgrS remains empty
S-structure
Verbal stem stays in situ, AgrS remains empty
LF
Verbal stem moves to AgrS to check agreement features
PF
Verbal stem is overtly inflected via spell-out

Let us now go through two concrete examples, namely the radically different derivations of the virtually identical verb forms *thu/tú kastar* 'you dream' in Icelandic and Faroese. Icelandic minimally distinctively marks all referential AgrS-features and therefore its agreement affixes have the lexical entries listed in (16a). In the presence of the second person singular subject *thu*, the affix *-(v)r* is inserted under AgrS at D-structure as shown in (16b) (otherwise the derivation crashes at LF when feature checking takes place). Since *-(v)r* must be bound in order to be morphologically wellformed, the verb raises to AgrS at S-structure as shown in (16c).

(16) ICELANDIC

a. Lexicon

present	[1st]	[2nd]	
	-(v)	-(v)r	-(v)r
[pl]	-um	-idh	-a

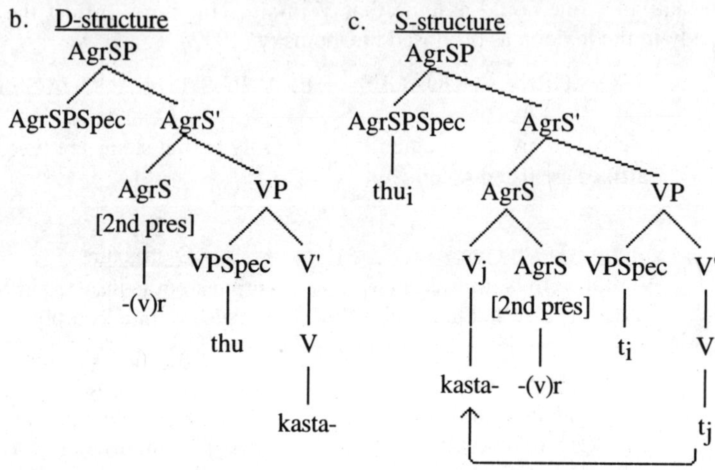

Faroese does not minimally distinctively mark the referential AgrS-feature [2nd] and therefore its agreement affixes do not have lexical entries. At D-structure, AgrS is empty and in the presence of a second person singular subject the verb is assigned the abstract agreement features [2nd pres] as shown in (17a) (otherwise the derivation again crashes at LF). At S-structure, the verb can remain in situ since the empty AgrS is wellformed as shown in (17b). Postsyntactically, the verb undergoes the most specific SPELL-OUT RULE that is compatible with its abstract agreement features, in our case the second of the three rules in (17c).

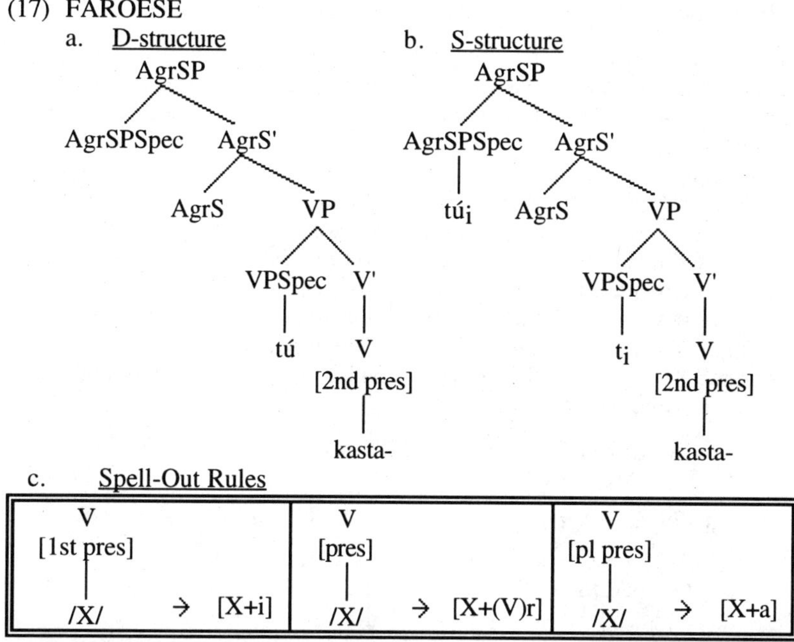

In summary, 'rich' agreement minimally distinctively marks the referential AgrS-features [1st] and [2nd] and triggers V-to-AgrS raising because its affixes are lexically listed and inserted under AgrS at D-structure.

3 Pro-drop

It is well-known that REFERENTIAL SMALL PRO SUBJECTS are licensed in languages like Japanese (cf. (18a)) without any overt agreement and in languages like Spanish (cf. (18b)) with a lot of overt agreement, but not in languages like English (cf. (18c)) with just a little overt agreement.

(18) a. Ø Sasimi -o taberu-Ø.
sashimi -ACC eat
'She eats sashimi.' (Japanese)

b. Ø Habl {-o / -as / -a} Espanol. (Spanish)

c. {I / you / she} speak {-Ø / -Ø / -s} Spanish

Speas (1993:14) proposes the principle of ECONOMY OF PROJECTION in (19) to account for this distribution.

(19) Project XP only if XP has [phonetic or semantic] content.

This principle requires the specifier or the head of each projection to be phonetically or semantically filled. In languages like Japanese without any overt agreement, AgrS is not posited and TP is the highest inflectional projection. Since Tns is always semantically filled, TPSpec can remain phonetically empty and referential pro subjects are possible. In languages like Spanish or English with overt agreement, AgrSP is posited as the highest inflectional projection. Since AgrS is always semantically empty, it or AgrSPSpec must be phonetically filled. In languages like Spanish with rich agreement, an agreement affix is generated in AgrS, AgrSPSpec can hence remain empty and referential pro subjects are possible (cf. (20a)). In languages like English with poor agreement, no agreement affix is generated in AgrS, AgrSPSpec must hence be filled and referential pro subjects are impossible (cf. (20b,c)).

(20)

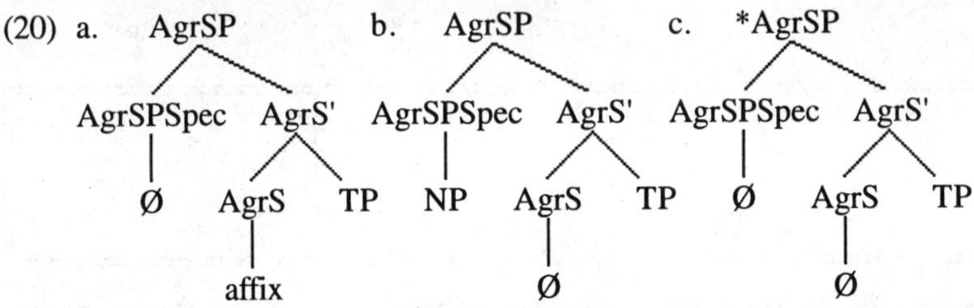

Speas argues that a language has rich agreement if its inflectional paradigm obeys MORPHOLOGICAL UNIFORMITY as defined in (21).

(21) An inflectional paradigm P in a language L is morphologically uniform for feature F iff P has only derived inflectional forms expressing F. (Speas 1993:34)

A look at European and Brazilian Portuguese reveals however that morphological uniformity is irrelevant in this connection and it is instead the minimal distinctive marking of the referential AgrS-features [1st] and [2nd] which licenses pro (just as it triggers V-to-AgrS raising) by base-generating the agreement affixes under AgrS. Both the European Portuguese paradigm in (11b) and the Brazilian Portuguese paradigm in (13) are morphologically nonuniform since each contains derived as well as nonderived inflectional forms expressing the feature [pl] (cf. the first and 'third' person singular). A theory based on (21) therefore predicts that neither language allows referential pro subjects. As discussed in section 2, European but not Brazilian Portuguese minimally distinctively marks all referential AgrS-features. A theory based on (14) therefore predicts that European but not Brazilian Portuguese allows referential pro subjects. The latter predictions are borne out by the facts. Moreover, figures 1 and 2 below (taken from Duarte 1993) show that Brazilian Portuguese lost pro precisely after the distinctively marked DIRECT SECOND PERSON singular (which is still visible in the European Portuguese paradigm in (11b)) had been lost, leaving only the INDIRECT SECOND PERSON forms which are identical with the 'third' person forms and hence not distinctively marked (cf. (13)). Note that this change affected only distinctive feature marking and not morphological uniformity. The former and not the latter must therefore be responsible for the licensing of referential pro subjects.

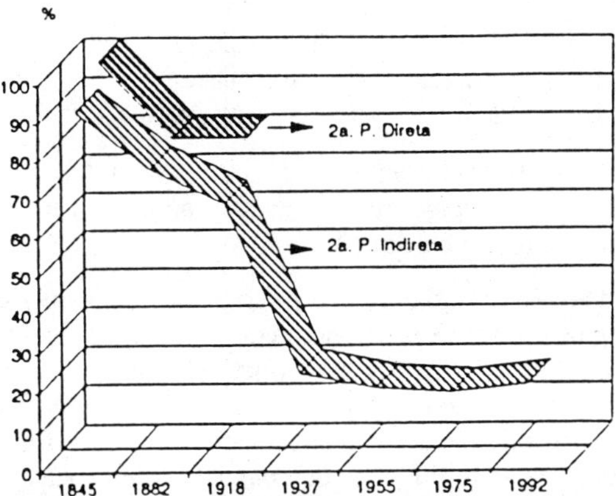

Figure 1: Subject pro w/ Direct & Indirect 2nd Person (Duarte 1993:113)

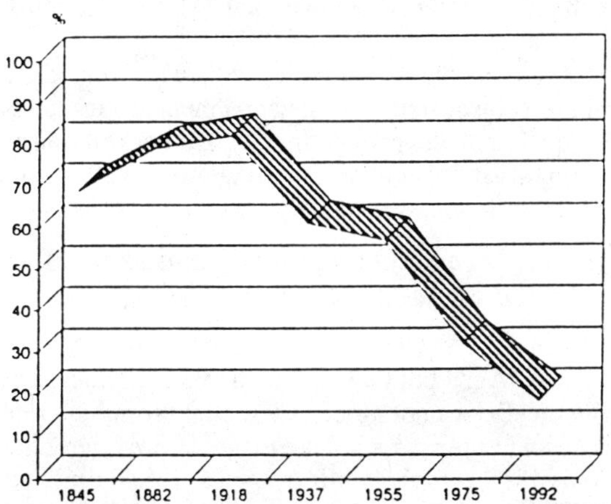

Figure 2: Subject pro w/ 1st Person (Duarte 1993:115)

As mentioned in section 2, the distribution of pro-drop provides direct evidence that lexically listed (and hence syntactically active) agreement affixes must minimally distinctively mark the person features [1st] and [2nd] but need not do so with respect to the number feature [pl]. Mike Dickey and Ken Hale (p.c.) pointed out to me that in the Amerind language Miskitu, subject verb agreement minimally distinctively marks [1st] and [2nd] but not [pl] (cf. (22)). Since Miskitu is right-headed, it is unclear whether it is an V-to-AgrS or V-in-situ language. Referential pro subjects are however clearly licensed (cf. (23)), and in the absence of a phonetically realized subject in AgrSPSpec the highest inflectional projection must satisfy Economy of Projection via a lexically listed agreement affix in AgrS.

(22) MISKITU atk-aia "to buy"

	PRESENT		PAST		FUTURE	
	SG	PL	SG	PL	SG	PL
1ST	atk-isna	atk-isna	atk-ri	atk-ri	atk-amna	atk-amna
2ND	atk-isma	atk-isma	atk-ram	atk-ram	at(k)-ma	at(k)-ma
3RD	atk-isa	atk-isa	atk-an	atk-an	at(k)-bin	at(k)-bin

(23) Yang [_e_ plun atk-ram] ba piak-amna.
I food buy-2nd.pst the cook-1st.fut
'I will cook the food you bought' (Miskitu)

We have arrived at a unified theory for the triggering of V-to-AgrS raising and the licensing of pro subjects. In languages where the referential AgrS-features [1st] and [2nd] are minimally distinctively marked, the agreement affixes are listed in the lexicon and inserted under AgrS at D-structure where they attract the verb and give content to AgrSP whose specifier (and the subject) can hence remain empty. In languages where at least one of the referential AgrS-features is not minimally distinctively marked, the agreement affixes are not lexically listed and AgrS remains empty, a situation in which the verb can stay in situ and AgrSPSpec must be filled by an overt subject to give content to AgrSP.

One question this theory must answer is why Icelandic does not allow referential pro subjects although its agreement affixes are base generated under AgrS as evidenced by the fact that the verb raises to this position. I propose that in Icelandic, referential pro is actually licensed but cannot be identified, following the idea by Jaeggli and Hyams (1988) that

(24) AGR can identify an empty category as (thematic) pro iff the category containing AGR Case-governs the empty category.

Let us assume that in V2 LANGUAGES such as Icelandic, the subject is Case-governed not by AgrS but by C, an idea that is of course by no means new. Since Icelandic C does not agree, referential pro subjects cannot be identified. This account predicts a V2 language allows referential pro subjects if and only if its complementizer agrees with the subject (cf. Platzack 1993). This prediction is borne out by the Bavarian data in (25). Additional examples from West Flemish and Frisian are given in (26).

(25) a. Ob *(du) nach Minga kummst.
b. Obst (du) nach Minga kummst.
whether you to Munich come
'whether you come to Munich.' (Bavarian)

(26) a. Kpeinzen dank (ik) goan kommen.
I-think that-1sg I go come
'I think that I will come.' (West Flemish)

b. Hy tinkt datst (do) jûn komst.
he thinks that-2sg you tonight come-2sg
'He thinks that you'll come tonight.' (Frisian)

4 Conclusions

Chomsky (1989:44) suggests that 'parameters of UG relate not to the computational system, but only to the [lexical entries of functional elements]'. The proposal in this paper is compatible with this suggestion: Languages are not parameterized for V-to-AgrS raising and pro-drop as such, but merely for the presence or absence of lexical entries for their agreement affixes. While a positive setting of this parameter will trigger V-to-AgrS raising and allow pro-drop, a negative setting will prohibit both. Much recent work inspired by the quote at the head of this paragraph bases the setting of parameters on abstract properties of functional elements. This procedure encounters the problem of circularity, since abstract properties of functional elements are supposed to explain syntactic phenomena that are in turn the only available evidence for the abstract properties in question. The proposal in this paper avoids this trap. The language-specific lexical status of the agreement affixes depends on the concrete shape (instead of abstract properties) of the agreement paradigm. The latter has to be learned in the true sense of the word and does not follow from e.g. the position of the finite verb or the phonetic appearance of the subject. I propose that in fact all syntactic learning is of this sort: It concerns the concrete morphological properties of the functional elements. Once these are acquired, the syntax of the language follows. This is the simplest (and therefore default) theory of 'syntactic' parameterization - whether it can be maintained remains to be seen.

References

Anderson, Stephen. 1992. *A-morphous morphology*. Cambridge: Cambridge University Press.

Chomsky, Noam. 1989. Some notes on economy of derivation and representation. *MIT Working Papers in Lnguistics* 10.43-74.

Chomsky, Noam. 1992. *A minimalist program for linguistic theory*. (MIT Occasional Papers in Linguistics, 1) Cambridge: MITWPL.

Duarte, Maria. 1993. Do pronome nulo ao pronome pleno: a trajetória do sujeito no potuguês do Brasil. *Português Brasileiro: Uma viagem diacronica*, ed. by Ian Roberts and Mary Kato, 107-128. Campinas: Editora da UNICAMP.

Falk, Cecilia. 1993. *Non-referential subjects in the history of Swedish.* Doctoral dissertation, Lund University.

Farrell, Patrick. 1990. Null objects in Brazilian Portuguese. *Natural Language and Linguistic Theory* 8.325-346.

Galves, Charlotte. 1989. L'objet nul et la structure de la próposition en portugais du Brésil. *Revue des Languages Romanes* 93.305-336.

Galves, Charlotte. 1990. V movement, levels of representation and the structure of S. Talk given at GLOW 13, London.

Hegarty, Michael. 1993. The derivational composition of phrase structure. Manuscript, University of Pennsylvania.

Jaeggli, Osvaldo and Nina Hyams. 1988. Morphological uniformity and the setting of the null subject parameter. *NELS* 18.238-253.

Kayne, Richard. 1991. Romance clitics, verb movement, and PRO. *Linguistic Inquiry* 22.647-686.

Platzack, Christer. 1993. Complementizer agreement and argument clitics. *Working Papers in Scandinavian Syntax* 50.25-54.

Platzack, Christer and Anders Holmberg. 1989. The role of AGR and finiteness in Germanic VO languages. *Working Papers in Scandinavian Syntax* 43.51-76.

Raposo, Eduardo. 1986. On the null object in European Portuguese. *Studies in Romance linguistics*, ed. by Osvaldo Jaeggli and Carmen Silva-Corvalán, 373-390. Dordrecht: Foris.

Roberts, Ian. 1993. *Verbs in diachronic syntax. A comparative history of English and French*. Dordrecht: Kluwer.

Rohrbacher, Bernhard. 1993. *The Germanic VO languages and the full paradigm: A theory of V to I raising*. Doctoral dissertation, University of Massachusetts at Amherst.

Siewierska, Anna and Dik Bakker. 1994. The distribution of subject and object agreement and word order type. *Eurotyp Working Papers* 6.83-126.

Speas, Margaret. 1993. "Null arguments in a theory of economy of projection". Manuscript, U Mass Amherst.

Vikner, Sten. 1991. *Verb movement and the licensing of NP-positions in the Germanic languages*. Doctoral dissertation, University of Geneva.

Extraction Without Traces

IVAN A. SAG & JANET DEAN FODOR*
Stanford University & Graduate Center, CUNY

1. Introduction

Phonetically unexpressed syntactic constituents have been a familiar ingredient of syntactic analyses of extraction for many years. But traceless analyses of long distance filler-gap dependencies have also been formulated, by Gazdar et al. (1984), Steedman (1987, 1988), and Kaplan and Zaenen (1989). In this paper we present a new traceless analysis cast within the framework of Head-driven Phrase Structure Grammar (Pollard and Sag 1987, 1994), which permits a simple and elegant, lexically-based account of unbounded dependency constructions. It provides a basis for dealing with a variety of constraints on extraction, with idiosyncratic lexical extraction 'signatures', and with strong crossover phenomena, and it is compatible with contraction phenomena at 'gap' sites, and with the current psycholinguistic results about how extraction constructions are processed. None of this requires the postulation of phonologically empty constituents of any kind.

Earlier HPSG analyses did assume the existence of WH-trace, which was imported into GPSG, and thence into HPSG, on the basis of a long tradition of 'independent evidence' for empty elements in extraction gaps. But somewhat suprisingly, when one takes stock and examines carefully what the empirical support for WH-trace amounts to, it turns out that there is none. WH-trace has been motivated primarily by

*We thank Peter Sells, Geoff Pullum, and Josef Taglicht for comments on an earlier version of this paper. Our collaboration was supported in part by NSF Grant SBR-9309588 to Stanford University.

theory-internal considerations which, however telling they may be, do not travel well from one theoretical framework to another. For instance, a theory which employs binding principles to constrain extraction gaps will want gaps to contain empty pronominals/anaphors, but this won't be a relevant consideration in a theory that imposes comparable constraints by other means. Also, a theory which posits one kind of empty constituent could find it more parsimonious, in terms of the generalizations expressed by UG principles, to posit **more** than one type of empty constituent. But again, such an argument may have no bite in the context of a different set of theoretical assumptions. This is why special interest has always attached to the theory-independent arguments in favor of WH-trace that have been developed over the years. These could settle the issue about empty constituents, and about many other matters besides, inasmuch as the treatment of extraction is interlinked with that of many other related linguistic phenomena. Evidence for WH-trace, if decisive, would direct theory development towards those frameworks into which empty constituents do fit naturally. The fact that traceless analyses of the extraction facts can be constructed would be a minor curiosity but not of central interest.

The major lines of evidence that have been cited for WH-trace, other than the extraction facts themselves, are: (i) failure of *wanna* contraction over a gap; (ii) failure of auxiliary contraction preceding a gap; (iii) impossibility of floated quantifiers preceding a gap; and (iv) psycholinguistic results. We will address and update the discussion of each of these phenomena. In each case, it turns out that the force of the arguments has declined the longer they have been considered. Our summary will show that the preponderance of evidence at present is either against, or at least neutral with respect to, the existence of WH-trace.[1]

2. Evidence for WH-Trace

2.1. Wanna Contraction

Want and *to* contract to *wanna* in (1)a and (1)b where PRO intervenes (in theories which assume PRO), but not in (1)c, where WH-trace (__) intervenes.

(1) a. Does Kim_i want PRO_i to (wanna) go to the movies?

b. Who_j does Kim_i want PRO_i to (wanna) go to the movies with $\_\__j$?

[1]Our discussion is limited to WH-trace; we do not discuss other empty constituents except as they happen to be relevant to WH-constructions. Note, though, that evidence of types (i)–(iv) has generally been seen as **strongest** for WH-trace, and weaker or non-existent for other empty elements such as PRO or NP-trace.

c. Who$_j$ does Kim$_i$ want __ $_j$ to (*wanna) go to the movies?

It has been widely accepted that the explanation for (1)c is that WH-trace is visible to the contraction rule which creates *wanna*. The invisibility of PRO (and NP-trace) for purposes of this rule has been attributed to lack of Case: only Case-marked NPs appear in PF – alternatively, NPs not requiring Case are free to appear in other PF-positions where they would not interfere with contraction. The generality of such an account is compromised, however, by the fact that nominative Case-marked WH-trace does not block contraction of an auxiliary onto a preceding verb (Bresnan, 1971; Schachter, 1984).

(2) a. Who$_i$ does Kim think __ $_i$ is (think's) beneath contempt?

b. Who$_i$ does Kim think __ $_i$ will (think'll) be late?

c. What$_i$ does Kim imagine __ $_i$ has (imagine's) been happening?

The contrast between (1)c and the examples in (2) is a serious problem. Chomsky (1986) proposed a rule ordering solution. Empty constituents are deleted at PF; *think's*-contraction applies after they are deleted, but *wanna*-contraction applies before. As Chomsky notes, this would fit well with current theorizing only if the ordering could be shown to follow from general principles, but so far it has not.

It is often supposed that Bresnan's (1971) account of auxiliary contraction can explain this difference between nominative and accusative WH-trace. Bresnan proposed that, unlike the reduced *to* in *wanna*-contraction, the reduced auxiliary in *think's*-contraction is a proclitic; in (2)a, for instance, the *'s* is associated not to *think* on its left but to *beneath* on its right. Then, of course, the WH-trace does **not** intervene between the auxiliary and its host in (2). However, as noted by Lakoff (1972), the reduced auxiliary exhibits phonetic sensitivity to the verb on its left, not to the word on its right. In (2)a the *'s* is unvoiced after */k/*, while in (2)c it is voiced after */n/*; in both examples it is followed by voiced */b/*. Zwicky (1970) noted also that there is sensitivity to the syntactic properties of the left context. For auxiliary contraction following an overt subject there are contrasts such as *You'd enjoy it* but **Kim and you'd enjoy it*. Attempts to save the procliticization analysis (e.g. Klavans 1985) run into other problems; see Fodor (1993) for details. The fact is that Bresnan's proposal was made prior to the introduction of empty constituents into syntactic theory; it works well in a theory without traces, but cannot be adapted successfully to fit into a theory with traces.

Think's-contraction is extremely general; it applies to all matrix verbs which permit a tensed complement clause without *that*, and to all auxiliaries (with some individual variation with respect to the extent of the reduction). But *wanna*-contraction is extremely limited; it applies to only a handful of matrix verbs that take *to*-complements. Consider *gonna, hafta,* **intenna* (*intend to*), **lufta* (*love to*), **meanna* (*meant to*). The arbitrariness of this set suggests that there is no rule, but just a collection of lexical facts. A small number of subject-control verbs alternate with a colloquial form (e.g., *wanna*) which has exactly the same syntactic and semantic properties except that the complement it selects is a base form without *to*. The alternating form no doubt had its historical source in contraction and merger of *to* with the verb, but no synchronic derivation is motivated.

Note that though a verb such as *wanna* is irregular in certain ways, every one of its oddities has some precedent. The lack of *to* is evidenced by modals, *let*, and *make* (*I let him go, I made him cry*). The lack of inflection (**He wannas leave*) and the limitation to contexts where inflection is not required (*We wanna leave,* **He wanna leave*) are shared by the exceptional verb *beware* (*Beware of the dog!,* **John bewares the dog.* **John beware the dog.*; see Fodor, 1972) and by the 'serial verb' *go* (*Every day I go fetch the paper,* **I have often gone fetch(ed) the paper*). Thus, though verbs such as *wanna* and *hafta* (with its third-singular present form *hasta*) are clearly exceptional, there is no reason to suppose that they are impossible. And the assumption that the English lexicon contains these verbs solves a number of problems that attend the postulation of a **rule** of *wanna*-contraction (e.g. the anomalous regressive assimilation required to derive *hafta* and *hasta* – cf. the progressive pattern of other verb combinations, e.g. *eats [s], craves [z]*). In addition, this lexical analysis predicts the configurational restrictions on the distribution of *wanna* discussed by Postal and Pullum (1982) and references therein.

Now if there is a rule of *think's*-contraction and no rule of *wanna*-contraction, then there remains no evidence for the blocking of any rule by any intervening empty constituent. The reason (1)c is ungrammatical is not that a trace is present, not that a rule is blocked, but just that *wanna* is a subject control verb (as in (1)a and (1)b), and in any case a lexical item cannot contain within it the gap associated with a WH-filler.[2] The apparently contradictory observations that accusative WH-trace does block contraction while nominative WH-trace does not, are now very simply resolved, on the assumption that inter-

[2]It is often claimed that there are 'dialects' where examples like (1)c are grammatical. In such a variety, *wanna* contraction presumably is a phonological rule, one that applies only in the configuration: [*want* [*to* VP]], a configuration shared by all of (1)a-c in an analysis (like the one we present below) which countenances neither PRO nor WH-trace.

vening empty constituents are irrelevant to phonological contraction processes. Whether they are irrelevant because they are not visible at PF, or because they do not exist at any linguistic level, cannot be determined on these grounds, but must be decided in some other fashion.

2.2. Auxiliary Contraction

WH-trace has also been held to play a crucial role in the explanation of the observation by King (1970) that the contraction of auxiliaries is prohibited immediately preceding an extraction gap or the site of ellipsis.

(3) a. The butcher is laughing and the baker is (*baker's) too. [VP-Ellipsis]

b. How tall do you think she is (*'s) __ ? [WH-Extraction]

Bresnan's (1971) analysis (see above) assumed that the auxiliary cliticizes onto the following word **prior** to ellipsis or extraction, and thereby prevents the ellipsis or extraction from occurring. More recent treatments within theories that employ empty constituents typically assume that ellipsis/extraction precedes cliticization, and that cliticization onto a phonologically unrealized constituent is impossible. However Selkirk (1984) (also Sells 1983; see also unpublished work by Sharon Inkelas and Draga Zec) shows that these facts follow from known principles of metrical phonology, which account for many other facts besides. As noted by Barss (1993), Selkirk's theory subsumes the think's-contraction phenomenon discussed above, as well as King's observations.[3] We follow Barss's exposition here.

The essence of Selkirk's proposal is that the English phonological rule of Monosyllabic Destressing is subject to a constraint that the grid column to which it applies may not be followed by a silent demibeat. The Monosyllabic Destressing rule applies to function words such as auxiliaries. Once stress is reduced, the auxiliary becomes eligible for vowel reduction, which in turn is the precondition for auxiliary contraction. However, silent demibeats are obligatorily added to the right edge of a metrical grid, as shown in (4)b.

[3]Barss (1993: nt. 24) suggests a syntactic treatment of *think's*-contraction which feeds the prosodic component, and which rests crucially on movement traces. However, one of its premises seems to be incorrect. Barss claims that *Who do you think's available?* is more acceptable than *Who do you think's altruistic?* because *available* is a stage-level predicate while *altruistic* is an individual-level predicate. Consideration of further data suggests, to the contrary, that *think's contraction* is more acceptable when it does not create a sequence of adjacent stresses.

(4) a.

				x	
	x			x	
x	x	x		x	x
x	x	x	x	x	x
the	ba	ker	is	laugh	ing

(the baker's laughing)

b.

	x			
x	x	x	x	
x	x	x	x	x
the	ba	ker	is	

(*the baker's)

Thus auxiliary contraction is impossible at the right edge of a metrical grid, e.g. at the end of a clause. Likewise, auxiliary contraction is blocked in the context of an appositive, as in (5), since appositives are preceded and followed by silent demibeats that inhibit the contraction.

(5) *The baker's, I think, laughing outside.

For present purposes the most important aspect of Selkirk's treatment of these contraction phenomena is that it makes no reference to phonetically empty syntactic entities. Contraction is blocked not by the **presence** of an empty constituent, but the **absence** of any overt constituent following the auxiliary. The descriptive scope of Selkirk's analysis is arguably superior to any treatment based on empty elements (and is certainly no less explanatory), but it is completely neutral with respect to the existence of such elements. Thus these contraction facts do not offer any support for the existence of WH-trace.[4]

2.3. Floated Quantifiers

Floated quantifiers may not appear directly before an extraction site:

(6) a. They (all) were (all) completely satisfied.

b. How satisfied do you think they all were __ ?

c.*How satisfied do you think they were all __ ?

These contrasts have also been explained (Baker 1971, Sag 1980) in terms of WH-trace. The precise nature of the trace-based account of

[4]Selkirk's is not the only prosodically based approach imaginable. For example, an alternative, stress-based account of these same auxiliary contraction contrasts has been suggested by Inkelas and Zec (1993). Certain unresolved issues remain, e.g. the exact nature of the prosodic boundary in examples like *I'll prepare lunch, and you can | dinner* (our thanks to Josef Taglicht for examples). Such cases may warrant appeal to independent principles requiring some degree of stress on remnants in gapping and pseudogapping constructions. However, as far as we are aware, none of the likely approaches to these problems need or would benefit from the postulation of traces.

these facts has been a matter of some debate (see Ernst 1983 and the references cited there). But in each analysis, the presence of a WH-trace interacted with some other rule or constraint to ensure that examples like (6)c are never derived. Baker discussed proposals for enriching the grammar to allow traces to be visible in some contexts and invisible in others; Sag's proposal included a surface filter in addition to the traces he assumed.

Interestingly, there is a straightforward account of the data in question that involves no such complexities. Brodie (1983) and Dowty and Brodie (1984) have proposed that floated quantifiers be treated as base-generated adjoined modifiers, as shown in (7).

(7)

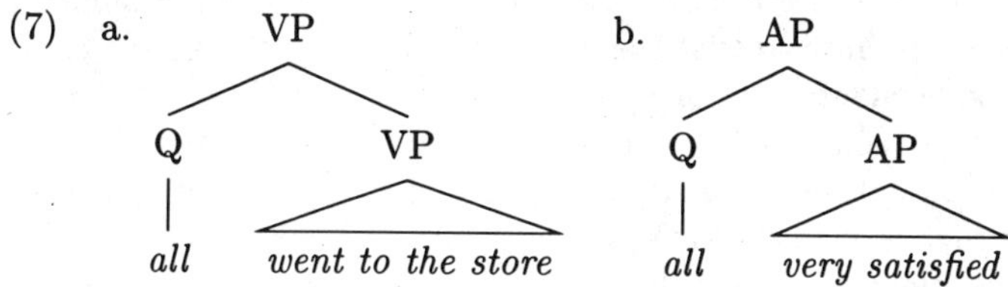

This analysis thus likens floated quantifiers syntactically to VP-adjoined adverbs.[5] As Dowty and Brodie argue at length, this syntactic analysis provides an appropriate basis for an account of the full range of semantic constraints on the floated quantifier construction. In addition, it provides a solution to certain longstanding problems facing movement-based alternatives, e.g. the fact that *None of the classes have all finished the exam* would have to be derived from a D-structure that should also give rise to **All (of) none of the classes have finished the exam.*

And crucially, though this point is not made by Dowty and Brodie, the treatment of floated quantifiers as adjoined modifiers interacts perfectly with a traceless theory of extraction. If extraction and ellipsis involve no trace (e.g. if (6) involves no AP trace), then there is no node for these elements to adjoin to. The ungrammaticality of examples like (6) above is then a simple and direct consequence of the Brodie/Dowty proposal, just in case the grammar of extraction posits no traces for floated quantifiers or other adjoined modifiers to modify. This is a much simpler and more elegant account than any of the trace-based alternatives in the literature.

[5]There are similar contrasts involving VP modifiers like *(n)ever* (*How satisfied do you think they ever are* __ *?*; **How satisfied do you think they are ever* __ *?*). These pose the same problem as floated quantifiers and are amenable to the same solution.

2.4. Psycholinguistic Results

The experimental data on sentence processing that have been offered as evidence for movement traces indicate that at a gap position, the meaning of the filler (antecedent) phrase is mentally activated. This has been argued for NP-trace by Bever and McElree (1988) and MacDonald (1989), and for WH-trace by Nicol and Swinney (1989), Hickok (1993), Nicol (1993) and others. This work had its origin in previous studies which had shown that overt pronouns and anaphors activate their antecedents during sentence processing. The idea was that if an extraction gap harbors a silent species of pronoun, it should show just the same sort of behavior as an overt pronoun. Antecedent activation does indeed occur in both cases. However, this fact does not suffice to establish that an empty constituent is present in the extraction examples. The experimental findings are **compatible** with the presence of an empty constituent, but no more than that. They are equally compatible with any other linguistic analysis which supports a processing model in which a fronted WH-phrase is semantically integrated into the sentence meaning when the processor associates it with the gap position. This could of course be so even if there is no empty category at that position. In either case, the processor would have to be using local information about the verb and any other arguments or adjuncts associated with it, in order to determine that this **is** the gap position, and to integrate the WH-phrase into the sentential semantics. Thus on almost any model, with or without traces, the relevant processing could be expected to occur at or around the gap position.

What would it take to show, on the basis of sentence processing, either that there is, or that there is not, a syntactic entity in an extraction gap? Fodor (1993) noted that no psycholinguistic finding could even in principle qualify as evidence for empty constituents unless it were established that the data pertained to the **syntactic** processing or representation of the sentence. But for all we know at present, the experimental techniques that have been used to study gap processing to date might be providing information about **semantic** processing only. If so, they would be completely uninformative about traces, because they wouldn't tell us whether the sentence meaning is computed from a trace or from a traceless gap in the syntax. This objection is particularly telling in the case of NP-trace, since its only sturdy experimental support derives from a post-sentential recall task, which almost certainly taps semantic representations in memory rather than syntactic structure or on-line syntactic processing. By contrast, WH-constructions show antecedent reactivation even when the experimental paradigm (cross-modal priming) is one that more plausibly does tap on-line syntactic processing. But the logical point still stands. Even if the syntactic sensitivity of the cross-modal experiments were definitively established, this would not – **could** not – demonstrate the existence of a syntactic **entity** in the gap. This is because any syntactic activity detected at a gap site would be equally explicable as due to the syntactic processes by which the parser detects the gap, i.e., deduces that a constituent is 'missing' at that point.

Pickering and Barry (1991) have argued recently for the contrary position, that sentence processing facts demonstrate that there is **no** empty element in an extraction gap. The empirical basis for their claim resides in certain indications that WH-phrase interpretation occurs not when the gap site is processed but when the governing verb (or other thematic role assigner) is processed. Often these coincide, as in example (8) from Nicol and Swinney 1989; the role-assigning verb is *accused*, and the gap immediately follows it (assuming canonical word order; see Pickering and Barry for discussion). But the verb and the gap are separated when a prepositional phrase argument of a transitive verb is fronted, or the second object of a double object dative construction. In (9), the role-assigning verb is *gave*, and the gap occurs 34 words later.

(8) The policeman saw the boy that the crowd at the party accused GAP of the crime.

(9) That's the prize which we gave [every student capable of answering every single tricky question on the details of the new and extremely complicated theory about the causes of political instability in small nations with a history of military rulers] GAP.

(10) We gave [every student capable of answering every single tricky question on the details of the new and extremely complicated theory about the causes of political instability in small nations with a history of military rulers] [a prize].

Pickering and Barry note that (9) does not, at least intuitively, exhibit the usual awkwardness that occurs when a long constituent is followed by another constituent, as in (10). No experimental data are available, but informal impressions suggest that the word *which* in (9) is assigned its semantic role when *gave* is received. There is no sign that the processor is attaching any constituent, even a phonologically null constituent, into the tree after the long noun phrase. Pickering and Barry also observe that a sentence like (11), in which two gap sites occur at the end, creating a doubly center-embedded structure, does not exhibit the extreme difficulty normally associated with doubly center-embedded constructions, as in (12). Again, this suggests that no constituents, empty or otherwise, are being attached after *tea* in (11).

(11) John found the saucer [on which Mary put the cup [into which I poured the tea GAP] GAP].

(12) John found the saucer [which Mary put the cup [which I poured the tea into GAP] on GAP].

Pickering and Barry wanted to conclude from these facts that WH-trace is not just unnecessary in extraction gaps but is provably absent.

There are all sorts of details here that might be questioned. But it is more useful to put minor objections aside and focus on the general line of argument, which is novel and interesting. It is not, however, convincing. Gorrell (1993) and Gibson and Hickok (1933) have pointed out, in defense of empty constituents, that the Pickering and Barry facts are equally compatible with a sentence processing device which posits WH-trace whenever it has sufficient information to do so (or at least, to make a reasonable guess), and builds the trace into the correct position in the tree though in advance, sometimes, of encountering words that precede it structurally. Thus a WH-trace could be postulated as *gave* is processed in (9), but the trace could be located structurally to the right of the complex indirect object NP whose details the processor must then continue to fill in. What we have here is a dissociation of the **time** at which the trace is postulated and the **position** in the string at which it is placed. But such dissociation is very common in sentence processing. It has been a familiar assumption for years that predictable tree nodes can be constructed in advance – for instance, that on encountering a nominative NP the processor could construct an associated VP node, though not yet knowing what the VP will consist of or whether other words will intervene first. Pickering (1993) acknowledges this point and retreats to a parsimony argument: the data give 'very good grounds to abandon empty categories, since there is then no **processing** reason to postulate their existence' (p. 175 [Pickering's emphasis]).

In short, it appears that a theory with empty elements has the flexibility to absorb data showing antecedent reactivation at the gap site **or** at the verb, and that only a theory without traces, such as Pickering and Barry's, or the HPSG analysis we present below, actually engages with the psycholinguistic facts. Pickering (p.193) says that his model 'makes some clear empirical predictions. In particular, it should not be possible to find experimental effects of any kind at the assumed gap location.' What little experimental data there are do not support this strong claim, and indeed it is not clear that Pickering's model is or should be committed to it. Nicol (1993) tested sentences such as (13), where four words separate the gap from the verb.

(13) [To which pilot] did [the soldier who was recovering from an ill-

ness in San Francisco] send [some new popular cassettes] GAP on Wednesday morning?

Nicol observed reactivation of the antecedent noun *pilot* both following the verb and at the gap. Though she notes that additional controls are needed to eliminate alternative possibilities, she suggests that a thematic role is tentatively assigned to the WH-phrase when the verb is processed, and that this assignment is checked at the gap site, giving rise to antecedent activation at both points. This seems very plausible. For the processor to check the gap position is essential. At the verb, it can only guess the role of the WH-phrase, and there are many examples in which an initial guess later proves to be incorrect. For instance in (14)a the processor typically assumes that *which book* is the object of *read*, and only later discovers that it must be the object of *from*. In (14)b there is a tendency to guess that *which boys* is the direct object of *introduce* and then be surprised on finding that *introduce* is followed by an overt direct object.

(14) a. Which book did you read to the children from?

b. Which boys did you introduce Sandy to?

Thus, the argument structure of the verb can suggest a **possible** role for the WH-phrase, but that role can be maintained only if there is no other phrase that needs it, and no obligatory role elsewhere in the sentence that lacks lexical realization. This is a fact about sentences, and any efficient processing system must respect it, regardless of whether the grammar that the processor operates with acknowledges WH-trace or not.

Thus the final judgement, at least until or unless other forms of argument can be devised, is that the processing data are neutral with respect to the linguistically important issue of whether a syntactic constituent is or is not present in an extraction gap. There is agreement now on both sides of the debate that antecedent reactivation is not decisive evidence in favor of empty constituents, and also that 'it is not possible to **disprove** the existence of empty categories' on the basis of Pickering and Barry's examples (Pickering, p. 175). The two accounts – no empty categories versus empty categories anticipated by the parser – 'are empirically indistinguishable with respect to the type of data under consideration' (Gibson and Hickok, p. 160). This doesn't mean that there are no facts of interest about filler–gap constructions that psycholinguistic experiments can reveal. For instance, the fact that NP-movement gaps and WH-movement gaps behave differently in the cross-modal priming experiments is potentially of some significance. It suggests that the two kinds of dependency have a different linguistic status, as is the case in HPSG (see below). Experimantally distinguishing different kinds of linguistic dependency (e.g. syntactic, lexical, or semantic) is valuable and is something that psycholinguistic methods may allow us to do. However, that is not the same as distinguishing syntactic phenomena with empty constituents from syntactic phenomena without empty constituents, which, at the present level of experimental sophistication, we have no idea how to do.

3. An HPSG Extraction Analysis

Following Pollard and Sag (1994: chap. 9), we assume a lexical rule that removes an element from a word's COMPS list, placing that complement instead onto the value (a list) of the feature SLASH.[6] Intuitively, SLASH encodes information about the element(s) that are missing from a phrase (i.e. about the 'gaps' that the 'slashed' phrase contains). This complement extraction lexical rule, shown in (15), thus creates lexical items whose valence is reduced by one complement, but whose SLASH value contains precisely the information associated with the missing complement.

(15) Complement Extraction Lexical Rule:

$$\begin{bmatrix} \text{COMPS} & \langle \ldots, \boxed{1}, \ldots \rangle \\ \text{SLASH} & \langle\, \rangle \end{bmatrix} \Rightarrow \begin{bmatrix} \text{COMPS} & \langle \ldots, \quad, \ldots \rangle \\ \text{SLASH} & \langle \boxed{1} \rangle \end{bmatrix}$$

Within a lexical rule, all properties of the input (e.g. semantic role assignment) that are not explicitly modifed remain unchanged in the corresponding output. Thus, the effect of this rule will be to map lexical entries like *hates*$_1$ into counterparts like *hates*$_2$:

(16) hates$_1$ hates$_2$

$$\begin{bmatrix} \text{HEAD} & \text{verb[fin]} \\ \text{SUBJ} & \langle \boxed{1}\text{NP[nom]}_{3s} \rangle \\ \text{COMPS} & \langle \boxed{2}\text{NP[acc]} \rangle \\ \text{ARG-S} & \langle \boxed{1}, \boxed{2} \rangle \\ \text{SLASH} & \langle\, \rangle \end{bmatrix} \Rightarrow \begin{bmatrix} \text{HEAD} & \text{verb[fin]} \\ \text{SUBJ} & \langle \boxed{1}\text{NP[nom]}_{3s} \rangle \\ \text{COMPS} & \langle\, \rangle \\ \text{ARG-S} & \langle \boxed{1}, \boxed{2} \rangle \\ \text{SLASH} & \langle \boxed{2}\text{NP[acc]} \rangle \end{bmatrix}$$

By default, a lexical entry has the empty list as its value for a nonlocal feature such as SLASH. Lexical entries that result from the lexical rule in (15), however, contain non-empty SLASH specifications

[6] For expository convenience, we will treat SLASH values as synsem objects, ignoring the important distinction between LOCAL and SYNSEM values.

that will percolate up the tree until an appropriate binding environment is found in accordance with principles we explicate in a moment. Thus only *hates*$_2$, not *hates*$_1$, may terminate a filler-gap dependency, as illustrated in (17). Through a cascade of identities, the filler at the top of the dependency is linked to the relevant position of the argument structure of *hates*$_2$. Extraction is thus treated entirely in terms of constraint satisfaction, rather than transformational derivation.

What guarantees that the SLASH value lexically specified on *hates*$_2$ percolates to higher elements in a tree like (17)? Universal grammar contains a principle – the NONLOCAL Feature Principle – which governs the 'percolation' of all NONLOCAL features. Here we restrict our attention to the NONLOCAL feature SLASH, which functions much as it did in the analysis first proposed by Gazdar (1981). The value of SLASH is a list, rather than a category (as it was in Gazdar's analysis), and NLFP defines a phrase's SLASH value in terms of an 'append' operation that collects the SLASH values of the phrase's daughters in left-to-right (first-to-last) order.

(17)

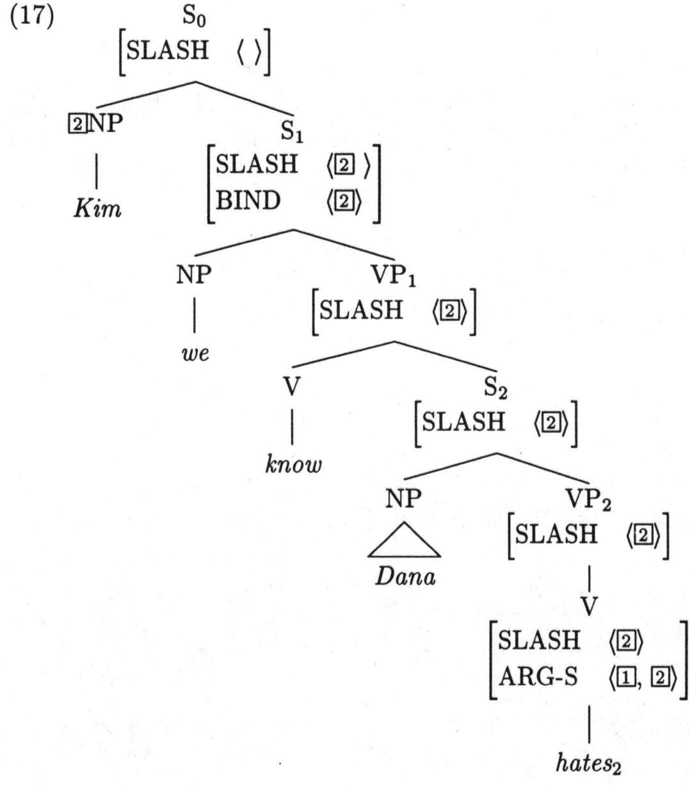

(18) NONLOCAL Feature Principle (NLFP)

For each NONLOCAL feature F in a local structure α^0 whose head-daughter is α^h:

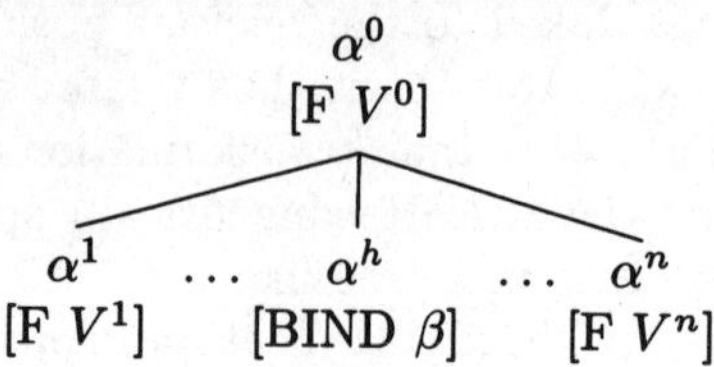

$V^0 = append(V^1, \ldots, V^n) - \beta$

(18) says that the SLASH value of a phrase is the list that results ¿From first appending the daughters' SLASH values – in left-to-right order – and then removing from that list whatever element (possibly none) the head-daughter binds off (specified as the value (possibly empty) of the feature BIND).[7]

To see how this works, let us reconsider the tree in (17), bottom up. (For convenience, empty list values of SLASH and BIND are suppressed; thus, for example, the V node over *hates*$_2$ has an implicit empty list value for BIND.) Consider VP$_2$. Since it has only one daughter, the append of all the daughters' SLASH values is identical to that daughter's SLASH value, i.e. is just the list ⟨[2]⟩. And since that daughter is also the head-daughter whose BIND value is the empty list, VP$_2$'s SLASH value is ⟨[2]⟩ minus nothing at all, i.e. just ⟨[2]⟩. The NP sister of VP$_2$ is specified as [SLASH ⟨ ⟩], hence if we consider S$_2$, we see that the append of its two daughter's SLASH values is again ⟨[2]⟩; and since its head daughter (VP$_2$) has an empty BIND value, it follows from the NLFP that S$_2$'s SLASH value is also the singleton list ⟨[2]⟩. By similar reasoning, NLFP guarantees that *hate*$_2$'s SLASH value is passed all the way up to S$_1$ in (17).

How does SLASH-binding happen in (17)? This is a consequence of the schema in (19) that licenses the highest local tree in (17):

[7]For the sake of uniformity, we treat BIND values as possibly empty lists and – as list difference. In practice, however, the BIND values (like the list values of the feature SUBJ) contain at most one member.

(19) Slash-Binding Schema:

$$X \rightarrow \boxed{2}\text{Filler-Dtr}, \quad \text{Head-Dtr}\begin{bmatrix}\text{SLASH} & \langle\boxed{2}\rangle \\ \text{BIND} & \langle\boxed{2}\rangle\end{bmatrix}$$

The $\boxed{2}$s in (19) represent feature structure identities between the filler-daughter and the head-daughter's SLASH and BIND values. These identities, taken together with the NLFP, cause the SLASH-binding to be just as indicated in (17). The SLASH value of S_0 is the empty list: $\langle\boxed{2}\rangle$ (the append of the filler-daughter's empty SLASH value and the head-daughter's nonempty SLASH value) minus $\langle\boxed{2}\rangle$ (the BIND value of the head-daughter).[8] SLASH percolation thus stops at S_0, a complete sentential constituent.

In the remaining paragraphs, we comment briefly on several features of the extraction analysis just sketched. First, since our analysis (like its GPSG and HPSG predecessors) encodes information about extraction dependencies via the percolation of SLASH specifications, such information is systematically registered on nodes that dominate the extraction site. This in turn predicts that information about the extraction should be available for selection by lexical items that appear at intermediate levels within an extraction dependency. The wealth of evidence that such selection does indeed exist throughout the world's languages (see, e.g. Hukari and Levine 1994) is striking confirmation of this approach.

Second, because our analysis, unlike earlier SLASH-based accounts, treats the value of the SLASH feature as a list (rather than simply a category or a set of categories), the nested dependency condition (Fodor 1978; Pesetsky 1982) can be simply stated within the grammar. That is, the contrast between (20)a,b can be made to follow from the fact that binding like that specified in the lexical entry of an *easy*-type adjective can only access the **first** member of the (infinitival complement's) SLASH value.

(20) a. [Gorbachev's innocence]$_j$, [my friend in Minsk]$_i$ was easy to talk to $\_\__i$ about $\_\__j$.

b.*[My friend in Minsk]$_i$, [Gorbachev's innocence]$_j$ was easy to talk to $\_\__i$ about $\_\__j$.

[8] Specialized instances of (19), which we cannot discuss here, allow an account of various SLASH-binding constraints particular to relative or interrogative constructions. Also, a second clause must be added to the formulation of NLFP in (18) in order to take account of parasitic gaps.

The NLFP ensures that this initial SLASH element (lexically coindexed with the subject of *easy*) will always be associated with the leftmost gap within the infinitival complement (e.g. the missing object of *to* in the phrase *talk to* __ *about* __), forcing the higher binder (the topicalized NP) to bind the rightmost gap.

Third, the lexically based theory of extraction just sketched provides a natural account of lexical exceptions – both positive and negative. For example, the contrast between (21)a,b (first noted by Kayne (1984)) is treated entirely within the lexicon.

(21) a. This student, I can assure you __ to be trustworthy.

b.*I can assure you [this student] to be trustworthy.

The lexical entry for *assure* selects a subject, one object, and a VP complement. *Assure* is also specified as [SLASH ⟨NP⟩], where the the NP on this SLASH list is coindexed with the VP complement's unexpressed subject. This lexical entry can thus only occur at the bottom of a filler–gap dependency. This analysis seems superior to the one considered by Fodor (1992), where *assure* takes an otherwise nonexistent subcategorization frame: two objects (the second marked as phonetically null, i.e. a WH-trace) and a VP complement. And there are apparently varieties of English where the object of certain verbs, e.g. *make* and *let* are unextractable:

(22) a. You let Sandy go home early.

b. %Who did you let go home early?

c. Who did you let Sandy go to visit?

In such varieties, *let* and/or *make* are simply exceptions to the complement extraction lexical rule. Note that this does not mean that extraction is blocked from the VP complement, as in (22)c.

And finally, our traceless extraction analysis is compatible with an account of strong crossover stated in terms of Principle C. The HPSG Binding Theory spelled out in Pollard and Sag (1994: sec. 6.8.3) is stated in terms of a nonconfigurational notion of obliqueness-command, (o-command), which is argued at length to be superior to approaches based on the familiar notion of c-command. O-command relations are defined recursively, and hence extend to the argument structures of verbs within embedded constituents. Thus the highest subject (*we*) in a topicalized structure like (17) is the least oblique element of the highest argument structure (ARG-S list of the highest verb *know*) and *we* o-commands all the elements in the argument structure lists of the subordinate verbs. Since the filler in (17) is identified with the object in the lowest verb's argument structure, the filler is also o-commanded by the higher subject *we*. Principle C, which bars a nonpronominal from being coindexed with an o-commanding expression, thus rules out the standard cases of strong crossover:

(23) a. *Clinton$_i$, he$_i$ thinks we should support.

b. *Who$_i$ does she$_i$ think we should support.

Because the complement extraction lexical rule removes elements from a verb's COMPS list, but leaves its ARG-S list intact, the argument structure relations necessary for the binding theory account of strong crossover remain intact – without appeal to WH-traces.

4. Summary and Conclusions

Trace theory has gone largely unquestioned within Government Binding theory, and was so well-entrenched that it became a feature also of other theoretical frameworks. However, it is appropriate for any theory to take stock from time to time to see whether its principles and theoretical postulates are continuing to do useful work as the system has evolved. Except for Government Binding theory, it appears that the theory-internal motivation for phonologically empty syntactic entities is minimal. In Combinatory Categorial Grammar, extraction is accomplished through judicious use of combinators, rendering traces quite unnecessary. Similarly, traces have little to contribute to an LFG extraction analysis based on the notion of functional uncertainty.

In HPSG it has turned out on closer scrutiny that the real work of constructing and constraining long distance dependencies is done by the feature SLASH which marks the path from filler to gap; the existence of a syntactic element at the bottom of the path in the gap position is not critical. Because of this, it is very important to note that syntactic theories are not under any **external** pressure to postulate empty constituents in WH-gaps. The arguments for empty constituents that have been based on *wanna* contraction, auxiliary contraction, and floated quantifiers were ingenious, and were the right kinds of arguments to bring to bear on the issue, but as further work has been directed toward them they have simply evaporated. And though psycholinguistic experimentation may one day, as we must hope, be able to reveal the mental representation of extraction constructions more clearly, the current verdict must be that psycholinguistics has not yet succeeded in finding a technique for addressing the theoretically crucial difference between **empty** and **absent** constituents. It is important to pursue all these lines of investigation, and we can't anticipate what interesting arguments for or against empty constituents might yet emerge. But at present our conclusion is that analyses of extraction must be evaluated on their descriptive and explanatory merits in accounting for the extraction facts; other domains provide no evidence that will decide the matter.

References

Altmann, G. T. M. and Richard Shillcock, eds. 1993. *Cognitive Models of Speech Processing: The Second Sperlonga Meeting.* Hillsdale, NJ: Lawrence Erlbaum Associates.

Baker, C. Leroy. 1971. Stress level and auxiliary behavior in English. *LI* 2: 167–181.

Barss, Andrew 1993. Transparency and visibility: sentence processing and the grammar of anaphora. In Altmann and Shillcock, eds. Pp. 401–451.

Bever, Thomas G. and Brian McElree. 1988. Empty categories access their antecedents during comprehension. *LI* 19: 35–43.

Bresnan, Joan. 1971. Contraction and the transformational cycle in English. Unpublished ms. distributed by Indiana University Linguistics Club.

Brodie, Belinda. 1983. *English Adverb Placement in Generalized Phrase Structure Grammar.* M.A. Thesis, Ohio State University.

Chomsky, Noam. 1986. *Knowledge of Language: Its Nature, Origin, and Use.* New York: Praeger.

Dowty, David R. and Belinda Brodie. 1984. The semantics of "floated" quantifiers in a transformationless grammar. WCCFL 3. Stanford: Stanford Linguistics Association.

Ernst, Thomas. 1983. More on adverbs and stressed auxiliaries. *LI* 14: 542–549.

Fodor, Janet D. 1972. Beware. *LI* 3: 528–535.

Fodor, Janet D. 1978. Parsing strategies and constraints on transformations. *LI* 9: 427–473.

Fodor, Janet D. 1992. Islands, learnability, and the lexicon. *Island Constraints: Theory, Acquisition, and Processing*, ed. Helen Goodluck and Michael Rochemont. Boston: Kluwer Academic Publishers. Pp. 109–180.

Fodor, Janet D. 1993. Processing empty categories: a question of visibility. In Altmann and Shillcock, eds. Pp. 351–400.

Gazdar, Gerald. 1981. Unbounded dependencies and coordinate structure. *LI* 12: 155–184.

Gazdar, Gerald, Ewan Klein, Geoffrey K. Pullum, and Ivan A. Sag. 1984. Foot features and parasitic gaps. *Sentential Complementation*, ed. W. Geest and Y. Putseys. Dordrecht: Foris. Pp. 83–94.

Gibson, Edward and Hickok, G. 1993. Sentence processing with empty categories. *Language and Cognitive Processes* 8, 147-161.

Gorrell, Paul. 1993. Evaluating the direct association hypothesis: A reply to Pickering and Barry. *Language and Cognitive Processes* 8: 129–146.

Hickok, G. 1993. Parallel parsing: evidence from reactivation in garden-path sentences. *Journal of Psycholinguistic Research* 22: 239–250.

Hukari, Thomas and Robert D. Levine. 1994. Adjunct extraction. *WCCFL 12*.

Inkelas, Sharon and Draga Zec. 1993. Auxiliary reduction without empty categories: a prosodic account. *Working Papers of the Cornell Phonetics Laboratory* 8: 205–253.

Kaplan, Ronald and Annie Zaenen. 1987. Long-distance dependencies, constituent structure, and functional uncertainty. *Alternative Conceptions of Phrase Structure*, ed. Mark Baltin and Anthony Kroch. Chicago: U. of Chicago Press.

Kayne, Richard. 1984. *Connectedness and Binary Branching*. Dordrecht: Foris.

King, Harold V. 1970. On blocking the rules for contraction in English. *LI* 1: 134–136.

Klavans, Judith L. 1985. The independence of syntax and phonology in cliticization. *Language* 61: 95–120.

Lakoff, George. 1972. The arbitrary basis of transformational grammar. *Language* 48: 76–87.

MacDonald, Maryellen C. 1989. Priming effects from gaps to antecedents. *Language and Cognitive Processes* 4: 1–72.

Nicol, Janet L. 1993. Reconsidering reactivation. In Altmann and Shillcock, eds. Pp. 321–347.

Nicol, Janet and David A. Swinney. 1989. The role of structure in coreference assignment during sentence comprehension. *Journal of Psycholinguistic Research* 18: 5–19.

Pesetsky, David. 1982. *Paths and Categories.* Doctoral dissertation, MIT.

Pickering, Martin. 1993. Direct association and sentence processing: a reply to Gorrell and to Gibson and Hickok. *Language and Cognitive Processes* 8: 163–196.

Pickering, Martin and Guy Barry. 1991. Sentence processing without empty categories. *Language and Cognitive Processes* 6: 229–259.

Pollard, Carl and Ivan A. Sag. 1987. *Information-Based Syntax and Semantics, Volume 1: Fundamentals.* CSLI Lecture Notes Series No. 13. Stanford: Center for the Study of Language and Information. [Distributed by University of Chicago Press]

Pollard, Carl and Ivan A. Sag. 1994. *Head-Driven Phrase Structure Grammar.* Chicago: University of Chicago Press and Stanford: CSLI Publications.

Postal, Paul M. and Geoffrey K. Pullum. 1982. The Contraction Debate. *LI* 13: 122–138.

Sag, Ivan A. 1980. A further note on floated quantifiers, adverbs, and extraction sites. *LI* 11: 255-257.

Schachter, Paul. 1984. Auxiliary reduction: An argument for GPSG. *LI* 15: 514–523.

Selkirk, Elizabeth. 1984. *Phonology and Syntax: The Relation between Sound and Structure.* Cambridge, MA: MIT Press.

Sells, Peter. 1983. Juncture and the phonology of auxiliary reduction in English. U. Mass. *Occasional Papers in Linguistics. Vol. 8*, ed. Toni Borowsky and Dan Finer. Amherst: GLSA.

Steedman, Mark. 1987. Combinatory grammars and parasitic gaps. *NLLT* 5: 403–439.

Steedman, Mark. 1988. Combinators and grammars. *Categorial Grammars and Natural Language Structures*, ed. Richard Oehrle, Emmon Bach, and Deirdre Wheeler. Dordrecht: Reidel.

Zwicky, Arnold M. 1970. Auxiliary reduction in English. *LI* 1: 323–336.

Scrambling, Relativized Minimality and Economy of Derivation*

YUJI TAKANO
University of California, Irvine

1 Introduction

In this paper, two major questions are addressed regarding Relativized Minimality. First, the possibility of deriving Relativized Minimality from considerations of Economy of Derivation is explored. Second, the difference between *wh*-movement in English and scrambling in Japanese with respect to Relativized Minimality effects is considered. I will propose that if we adopt the 'free movement hypothesis', which allows adjunction freely, we can in fact derive the effect of Relativized Minimality from Economy of Derivation, specifically, from the interaction of two Economy principles, 'Shortest Link' and 'Greed'. I will show that the proposed approach can account for the difference between *wh*-movement and scrambling by making crucial reference to the different feature-checking processes involved in the two operations.

* I am indebted to Lisa Cheng, Naoki Fukui, Terri Griffith, Toru Ishii, Mamoru Saito, Hiromu Sakai, Shin Watanabe, and Mihoko Zushi for helpful comments and suggestions on earlier versions of this paper. A first version of this paper was presented at the symposium 'On the Minimalist Program', held during the 65th General Meeting of the English Literary Society of Japan (1993, Tokyo University). I wish to thank the audience there and the audience in San Diego for their questions and comments.

2 Relativized Minimality: Toward an Economy Account

Rizzi (1990) has shown that the effect of 'minimality' for movement is relative to the relationship between the type of movement and the status of an intervening element, and has proposed to account for this effect in terms of the general principle in (1), called RELATIVIZED MINIMALITY:[1]

(1) α-movement is blocked by an intervening element in β, where α and β are of the same type:
A'-movement is blocked by an intervening element in an A'-specifier;
A-movement is blocked by an intervening element in an A-specifier; and
X^0-movement is blocked by an intervening element in an X^0-position.

The following examples show the effect of Relativized Minimality:

(2)a. *To $whom_i$ do you wonder $what_j$ John gave t_j t_i?
b. *$John_i$ seems that it is likely t_i to win.
c. *Be_i John will t_i coming?

In (2a), *wh*-movement moves *to whom* over *what* in [Spec, CP], an A'-specifier, and results in a *wh*-island violation. In (2b), NP-movement moves *John* over *it* in [Spec, IP], an A-specifier, and yields a case of 'superraising'. In (2c), X^0-movement moves *be* over *will* in an X^0-position, causing a violation of the Head Movement Constraint (see Travis 1984, Baker 1988). All these cases fall under Relativized Minimality.[2]

Rizzi's proposal is intuitively very plausible, and gives us new insight into the issues concerning bounding. At the same time, however, it raises a new question as to why Relativized Minimality should hold at all. We might reasonably ask whether Relativized Minimality can be shown to follow from deeper considerations.

Addressing this question, Chomsky (1993a) and Chomsky and Lasnik (1993) suggest a way of deducing Relativized Minimality from Economy of

---

[1]Rizzi formulates Relativized Minimality as a condition on (antecedent) government. In this paper, I reinterpret his proposal and formulate it as a condition on movement, essentially following Chomsky and Lasnik (1993).

[2]Rizzi's original proposal takes a *wh*-island violation induced by adjunct extraction to be a typical case showing that A'-movement is blocked by an intervening A'-specifier, resting on the well-known observation that argument extraction out of a *wh*-island yields a less deviant result than adjunct extraction out of a *wh*-island. In this paper, I focus on the fact that argument extraction does show a *wh*-island effect, ignoring the observed difference in acceptability.

Derivation. Specifically, they suggest that Economy of Derivation includes the following general principle:

(3) Minimize chain links.

They claim that this principle has the effect of minimizing each link of a chain, and, by doing so, will account for the effect of Relativized Minimality. Let us refer to the principle in (3) as SHORTEST LINK.

There are several ways of implementing this general idea. One possibility is to directly appeal to Shortest Link in accounting for the Relativized Minimality effect. Let us consider (2a), repeated here as (4):

(4) *To $whom_i$ do you wonder [$what_j$ John gave t_j t_i]?

The derivation commonly assumed for (4) is given in (5):

(5) [$_{CP1}$ to $whom_i$ C1 you wonder [$_{CP2}$ $what_j$ C2 John gave t_j t_i]]

We might say that in this derivation, *to whom* does not make the shortest possible link, since it skips the closest 'potential landing site' for *wh*-movement, namely [Spec, CP2], and that because of this, the derivation is excluded as a violation of Shortest Link. On this view, then, movement cannot skip any potential landing sites. Let us refer to this view as a 'potential landing site approach'.[3]

There are several problems with this move, however. First, in order to maintain the potential landing site approach, we must spell out the concept 'potential landing site' for movement, which seems to be a nontrivial task.

Second, note that the derivation given in (5) does not take into consideration the possibility of intermediate adjunction. More specifically, if we adopt the 'free movement hypothesis', which allows adjunction freely, the *wh*-phrase *to whom* should be able to adjoin to CP2 on the way to [Spec, CP1], unless some independent condition blocks the intermediate adjunction. Since nothing seems to block it, we must conclude that (4) also has the following derivation:[4]

---

[3]Frampton (1991) suggests an interpretation of Rizzi's proposal which is essentially parallel to the potential landing site approach, though his suggestion is not formulated in terms of Economy of Derivation.

[4]Chomsky (1986) suggests that adjunction to arguments is prohibited for theta theoretic reasons. However, this suggestion is hard to maintain, especially under the assumptions that theta theory only applies to LF representations (Chomsky 1993a), and that intermediate traces delete at LF (Lasnik and Saito 1984, Chomsky 1991, Chomsky and Lasnik 1993).

(6) $[_{CP1}$ to whom$_i$ C1 you wonder $[_{CP2}$ t_i' $[_{CP2}$ what$_j$ C2 John gave t_j t_i]]]

Here *to whom* 'successive cyclically' moves to [Spec, CP1], via adjunction to CP2.

However, allowing this derivation poses a problem for the potential landing site approach. Chomsky (1993a) argues that the Spec position of XP and the position adjoined to XP share a fundamental property with respect to their relation to the head X. More specifically, he proposes that both positions are within the CHECKING DOMAIN of X. This implies that the two positions are simply 'indistinguishable' in terms of their relation to the head. Based on this intuition, Chomsky further claims that two positions are EQUIDISTANT from other positions if they are within the same checking domain.[5] Given this, then, the position adjoined to CP2 and [Spec, CP2] in (6) are equidistant from t_i, since they are within the checking domain of C2. If this is the case, it follows that *to whom* does not 'skip' [Spec, CP2] in (6). Given that the potential landing site approach relies crucially on the assumption that Relativized Minimality effects arise when movement skips a potential landing site, the approach cannot be maintained if we allow the derivation in (6).

Finally, consider the following examples from Japanese:

(7)a. $[_{IP1}$ Mary-ni$_i$ $[_{IP1}$ Tom-ga $[_{IP2}$ sono hon-o$_j$ $[_{IP2}$ John-ga t_j t_i ageta
-dat -nom that book-acc -nom gave
to]] itta]]
that said
'(Lit.) To Mary, Tom said that that book, John gave'

b. $[_{IP1}$ NY-e$_i$ $[_{IP1}$ Tom-ga $[_{IP2}$ Boston-kara$_j$ $[_{IP2}$ John-ga t_j t_i itta
-to -nom -from -nom went
to]] omotteiru]]
that think
'(Lit.) To NY, Tom thinks that from Boston, John went.'

As Fukui (1986) observes, scrambling in Japanese, unlike *wh*-movement in English, does not show Relativized Minimality effects. Thus in (7a) *Mary-ni* is scrambled from within IP2 to the front of the sentence, moving past

---

[5]The exact formulation of Chomsky's proposal is the following:

(i) Two positions are equidistant from γ if they are in the same minimal domain.

The MINIMAL DOMAIN consists of the checking domain and the INTERNAL DOMAIN (corresponding to the complement position). For present purposes, we limit our attention to the checking domain in the text account.

sono hon-o, which is also scrambled from within IP2. Similarly, in (7b) *NY-e* is scrambled past *Boston-kara*, which is also scrambled. These examples show that scrambling is not affected by the presence of an element that is already scrambled. Given that English equivalents involving *wh*-movement do exhibit the Relativized Minimality effect, this fact poses a problem for the potential landing site approach. Apparently, scrambling can skip a potential landing site for scrambling.

These considerations indicate that the potential landing site approach, as it stands, has problematic aspects to it. On the other hand, the Chomsky-Lasnik suggestion -- that Relativized Minimality might be reduced to considerations of Shortest Link -- seems to have intuitive plausibility. In the next section, I will propose an alternative way of implementing this idea which resolves the problems that we have seen above.

3 Deriving Relativized Minimality: Free Movement, Shortest Link, and Greed

Continuing to assume the free movement hypothesis, we see that (4) has two derivational possibilities, (5) and (6), repeated here:

(5) $[_{CP1}$ to $whom_i$ C1 you wonder $[_{CP2}$ $what_j$ C2 John gave t_j $t_i]]$

(6) $[_{CP1}$ to $whom_i$ C1 you wonder $[_{CP2}$ t_i' $[_{CP2}$ $what_j$ C2 John gave t_j $t_i]]]$

Now the question is how we resolve this ambiguity of derivation. A natural move will be to claim that Shortest Link plays a role here; more specifically, that given Shortest Link, the derivation in (6) blocks the derivation in (5). To put it differently, Shortest Link chooses (6) over (5), since the former has shorter links. Thus, in general terms, Shortest Link, coupled with the free movement hypothesis, forces a derivation to proceed successive cyclically via adjunction, even when an intermediate [Spec, CP] is filled.[6]

The next question to ask is what blocks (6). Notice that in (6) *to whom* first adjoins to CP2. Recall now that the position adjoined to CP2 is within the checking domain of C2. This means that the *wh*-feature of *to whom* can be checked in this position, on the assumption that in principle,

[6]We assume that the derivations (5) and (6) both converge; otherwise, they cannot be compared against Shortest Link. Following Chomsky (1993a), we assume that two derivations are 'alternative derivations' only if (i) they converge, and (ii) they yield the same LF structure.

C can check a *wh*-feature more than once.[7] Nevertheless, it moves further into [Spec, CP1] to derive (6). If so, this step, namely the step from the position adjoined to CP2, violates GREED, another Economy principle proposed by Chomsky (1993a):

(8) Movement of α is legitimate only if it is necessary for satisfaction of morphological properties of α itself.

Greed is a stronger version of the Last Resort principle, requiring every instance of movement to be a 'self-serving' last resort. The step from the position adjoined to CP2 in (6) is not necessary for satisfaction of the *wh*-feature of *to whom*, and hence violates Greed. Thus on this view, the *wh*-island effect is ultimately attributed to a violation of Greed.

One question that immediately arises in this connection is why (9) is ungrammatical in English, if the embedded C can check a *wh*-feature more than once:

(9) *I wonder to whom what John gave.

Following the general idea proposed by Cheng (1991), I suggest that the ungrammaticality of (9) is due to the principle of PROCRASTINATE, which states that movement operations must be carried out in LF whenever possible (see Chomsky 1993a). In English, the only requirement on *wh*-checking is that some *wh*-phrase occupy [Spec, CP] if its head is [+wh], but nothing requires other *wh*-phrases to move overtly. Thus overt movement of *to whom* in (9) is not required, and hence is blocked by Procrastinate.[8]

Now let us consider the example in (10):

(10) What$_i$ do you think that John bought t_i?

Under our approach, Shortest Link always forces successive cyclic movement. This uniquely determines the optimal derivation for (10), as shown in (11):

---

[7]This assumption is incompatible with Chomsky's (1993a) claim that a head disappears after it has carried out feature checking. On the other hand, there is some independent reason to believe that a head must remain even after it has checked some feature. For example, assuming that in-situ *wh*-phrases in English undergo LF movement to get their *wh*-features checked by [+wh] C (see Huang 1982), [+wh] C must be present after it has checked the *wh*-feature of the *wh*-phrase that has undergone overt movement. The same argument carries over if so-called 'multiple *wh*-movement' as seen in languages like Bulgarian and Romanian (see Rudin 1988) involves multiple *wh*-checking.

[8]On the other hand, in 'multiple *wh*-movement' languages, *wh*-phrases themselves have some feature that requires them to move overtly. See Cheng 1991 for relevant discussion.

(11) $[_{CP1}$ what$_i$ C1 you think $[_{CP2}$ t$_i$' $[_{C2}$ that] John bought t$_i$]]

There is nothing wrong with this derivation; in particular, the step from [Spec, CP2] satisfies Greed, since C2, being a [-wh] complementizer, does not have the ability to check the *wh*-feature of *what*. Thus standard cases of successive cyclic *wh*-movement follow straightforwardly.

The proposed approach carries over to cases involving NP-movement. Consider (12), a case of superraising:

(12) *John$_i$ seems that it is likely t$_i$ to win

The derivation that has traditionally been assumed for (12) is (13):

(13) $[_{IP1}$ John$_i$ seems that $[_{IP2}$ it $[_{I2}$ is] likely $[_{IP3}$ t$_i$ to win]]]

Here *John* moves into [Spec, IP1] directly. However, under the free movement hypothesis, the following derivation should also be possible:

(14) $[_{IP1}$ John$_i$ seems that $[_{IP2}$ t$_i$' $[_{IP2}$ it $[_{I2}$ is] likely $[_{IP3}$ t$_i$ to win]]]]

In this derivation, *John* adjoins to IP2 on the way to [Spec, IP1]. Then (13) is blocked by (14) (Shortest Link), and (14) is in turn excluded by Greed, since the position adjoined to IP2 is internal to the checking domain of I2, and thus the Case feature of *John* can be checked there.[9]

Standard cases of successive cyclic NP-movement follow straightforwardly, just like successive cyclic *wh*-movement. Consider (15) and its optimal derivation (16):

(15) John$_i$ seems t$_i$' to be likely t$_i$ to win.
(16) $[_{IP1}$ John$_i$ seems $[_{IP2}$ t$_i$' $[_{I2}$ to] be likely $[_{IP3}$ t$_i$ to win]]]

In (16) the step from [Spec, IP2] satisfies Greed, given that I2 is infinitival, and thus cannot check the Case feature of *John*.

---

[9]Here I assume that the IP-adjoined position is an 'L-related' position (see Chomsky 1993a). Thus the derivation given in (14) does not involve 'improper movement'. See Fukui 1993b for discussion of improper movement. Note also that this analysis rests crucially on the assumption that a Case feature can be checked in the IP-adjoined position. On the other hand, the fact that there seem to be no known cases where more than one NP is checked for Case by the same I might cast doubt on this assumption. However, I suspect that this gap is accidental. Note that in general, there are two positions per clause in which Case features are checked, e.g. [Spec, Agr-s] and [Spec, Agr-o], and further that only argument NPs need to be checked for Case. This situation might make multiple Case checking unnecessary.

Now let us return to the scrambling cases, repeated below, which posed a problem for the potential landing site approach:

(7)a. [$_{IP1}$ Mary-ni$_i$ [$_{IP1}$ Tom-ga [$_{IP2}$ sono hon-o$_j$ [$_{IP2}$ John-ga t_j t_i ageta
-dat -nom that book-acc -nom gave
to]] itta]]
that said
'(Lit.) To Mary, Tom said that that book, John gave'

b. [$_{IP1}$ NY-e$_i$ [$_{IP1}$ Tom-ga [$_{IP2}$ Boston-kara$_j$ [$_{IP2}$ John-ga t_j t_i itta
-to -nom -from -nom went
to]] omotteiru]]
that think
'(Lit.) To NY, Tom thinks that from Boston, John went.'

In our approach, this fact follows with the minimal assumption that scrambling in Japanese is not motivated by feature checking (see Fukui 1986, 1993a and Saito 1989). In other words, the landing site of scrambling is not a position for feature checking. Then it follows that movement of *Mary-ni* and *NY-e* in (7) is not affected by the presence of the scrambled elements. To see why this is so, let us consider the following derivation for (7a), which satisfies Shortest Link:

(17) [$_{IP1}$ Mary-ni$_i$ [$_{IP1}$ Tom-ga [$_{IP2}$ t_i' [$_{IP2}$ sono hon-o$_j$
[$_{IP2}$ John-ga t_j t_i ageta to]]] itta]]

The crucial step is the one where *Mary-ni* moves from the position adjoined to IP2. Since scrambling is nonfeature-checking movement, the position adjoined to IP2 has nothing to do with feature checking, and hence the step in question does not violate Greed. This ensures that the effect of Relativized Minimality is never induced when scrambling 'moves over' a scrambled phrase.[10]

[10] In fact, the conclusion should be made more general. Given that scrambling is not feature-checking movement, it is further predicted that (i) a scrambled phrase will not affect feature-checking movement, and (ii) scrambling will not be affected by an element that has undergone feature-checking movement. Although space limitation precludes discussion of this topic here, the predictions in fact seem to be borne out. See Takano 1994 for relevant discussion.

4 Extensions of the Shortest Move-and-Greed Approach

4.1 Relevance of Feature Checking for the Theory of Bounding

We have seen that the proposed approach correctly accounts for standard cases involving *wh*-movement and NP-movement. Note that this approach maintains the traditional claim, originating from Chomsky (1973), that movement must be carried out in a successive cyclic way. However, it crucially departs from traditional approaches in that, coupled with the free movement hypothesis, it also requires successive cyclic movement via adjunction when intermediate Spec positions are filled. As a result of this, unacceptable cases are attributed to a violation of Greed, caused by the presence of a feature-checking head.

This approach has further consequences and implications. First, it implies that the correct generalization about Relativized Minimality effects should refer to the properties of the moved elements and the intervening heads concerning feature checking, rather than their X-bar theoretic status, as Rizzi originally proposed.[11] In the case of *wh*-movement, the relevant feature is a *wh*-feature, whereas in the case of NP-movement, it is a Case feature. Then it follows that *wh*-movement is blocked by an intervening *wh*-checking head, whereas NP-movement is blocked by an intervening Case-checking head. This seems consistent with the observations made in the traditional literature. The discussion in the previous section of the difference between *wh*-movement and scrambling also supports this move.

Note that the idea that feature-checking heads play a central role in determining certain bounding effects is far from new, and can be traced back to Fukui's (1986) work on the parametric difference between English and Japanese (see also Fukui and Speas 1986, Kuroda 1988). Fukui argues that in English, (functional) categories 'close off' because of the function of agreement, whereas in Japanese, categories never close off because of lack of agreement features in the language, and that this is responsible for certain differences between the two languages. Particularly relevant to our concern is his claim that multiple *wh*-movement is impossible because the projection gets 'closed' by agreement when one *wh*-phrase moves into [Spec, CP], thereby blocking further application of *wh*-movement, whereas multiple scrambling is possible because the projection is always 'open' due to lack of agreement (see also Fukui and Saito 1993 for extensions of this general idea). It is then clear that our approach shares the fundamental claim with Fukui's proposal that feature checking plays a crucial role in determining the effect of certain aspects of bounding.

Another consequence of our approach is that it accounts easily for the fact that there are no known cases where base-generated adjuncts block *wh*-

[11]This intuition is shared by Abe (1993) and Ferguson (1993), though they take different directions than ours to implement the idea.

movement or NP-movement, since the positions of adjuncts do not enter into a feature-checking relation to any head. Similarly, the fact that so-called 'weak islands' do not affect argument extraction (see Cinque 1990, Rizzi 1990) can be accounted for, given that such factors as negation and factivity have nothing to do with *wh*-checking (or Case checking).[12]

4.2 Movement out of a Moved Element

Our approach also has consequences for an empirical domain that has been considered to be totally unrelated to Relativized Minimality. Consider the following example:

(18) *Who$_i$ do you wonder [which picture of t$_i$]$_j$ Mary bought t$_j$?
(Lasnik and Saito 1992; "*" mine)

Such examples as this are always degraded. To put it differently, *wh*-movement out of a *wh*-moved phrase yields a deviant result. At first sight, the deviance of (18) seems to be unrelated to Relativized Minimality effects. However, in our analysis, Shortest Link, together with the free movement hypothesis, forces the following derivation, where *who* first adjoins to CP2 and then moves to [Spec, CP1]:

(19) [$_{CP1}$ who$_i$ C1 you wonder [$_{CP2}$ t$_i$' [$_{CP2}$ [which picture of t$_i$]$_j$ C2 Mary bought t$_j$]]]

This derivation is therefore excluded by Greed, since the position adjoined to CP2 is in the checking domain of C2, which checks a *wh*-feature, and thus further movement of *who* is blocked.

Given this account, it is obvious that our approach treats examples like (19) on a par with *wh*-island violations. In other words, *wh*-island cases and cases like (19) now receive a unified account which has been impossible in traditional approaches.

Scrambling in Japanese behaves differently in this regard. As Saito (1985) observes, scrambling out of a scrambled phrase is always allowed:

---

[12]If this approach to weak islands is on the right track, the fact that they affect adjunct extraction must be accounted for on grounds independent of Relativized Minimality. See Szabolcsi and Zwarts 1992 for a semantic, rather than syntactic, approach to this effect.

(20)a. $[_{IP1}$ Mary-ni$_i$ $[_{IP1}$ Tom-ga $[_{IP2}$ [John-ga t_i atta to$]_j$ $[_{IP2}$ Bill-ga t_j
-dat -nom -nom met that -nom
omotteiru to]] itta]]
think that said
'(Lit.) Mary$_i$, Tom said that [that John met t_i]$_j$, Bill thinks t_j.'

b. $[_{IP1}$ NY-e$_i$ $[_{IP1}$ Tom-ga $[_{IP2}$ [John-ga t_i itteiru to$]_j$
-to -nom -nom have-gone that
$[_{IP2}$ Bill-ga t_j omotteiru to]] itta]]
-nom think that said
'(Lit.) To New York$_i$, Tom said that [that John has gone t_i]$_j$, Bill thinks t_j.'

Again, the difference follows from the nonfeature-checking nature of scrambling. Suppose that (20a) is derived as follows:

(21) $[_{IP1}$ Mary-ni$_i$ $[_{IP1}$ Tom-ga $[_{IP2}$ t_i' $[_{IP2}$ $[_{IP3}$ John-ga t_i atta to$]_j$ $[_{IP2}$ Bill-ga t_j omotteiru to]]]] itta]]

Here IP3 first adjoins to IP2. Then *Mary-ni* adjoins to IP2, and moves further to IP1. The derivation satisfies Greed, since the position adjoined to IP2 is not a position for feature checking.

Thus our approach explains in a unified way why *wh*-movement out of a *wh*-moved element results in a degraded status, whereas scrambling out of a scrambled element does not exhibit the same property, another desirable consequence of the approach.

4.3 X^0-Movement

So far, we have restricted our attention to cases involving XP-movement. Let us now turn to cases involving X^0-movement. First, notice that examples like (2c), noted previously, no longer represent Relativized Minimality effects in our sense:

(2)c. *Be$_i$ John will t_i coming?

To see why this is so, let us consider the general effect of 'Subject Aux Inversion' in English. Following the insight that goes back to den Besten (1983), suppose that there is a close connection between C and I. If we interpret this intuition in current terms, we might say that I, probably Tense, needs to be checked by C (Chomsky 1993b; see also Pesetsky 1982, Stowell 1982, Watanabe 1993). In English, this checking usually takes place in LF. However, under certain restricted contexts, such as question and negation, the raising of I takes place in overt syntax, probably because the relevant feature of C is strong under such contexts. If this is correct, it follows that movement of *be* in (2c) violates the Last Resort principle (which is now part of Greed), since it is not motivated by anything. Thus cases like (2c) are now excluded as trivial cases of a Last Resort violation.

Let us turn to more complicated cases. Baker (1988) observes that noun incorporation (NI) to V is impossible from the NP which is a complement of P. The relevant situation is shown in (22):

```
(22)        VP
           /  \
       N+V    PP
        ↑    /  \
        X   P   NP
         \       |
          `------t
```

Notice that under our assumptions, Shortest Link always forces X^0-movement to proceed via successive cyclic adjunction. Thus in the case of (22), the correct derivation has to be as shown in (23):

```
(23)        VP
           /  \
       N+V    PP
        ↑    /  \
        `-t'+P   NP
           ↑      |
           `------t
```

Then the question is what is wrong with this derivation. In order to address this question, we must consider what motivates NI in terms of feature checking. Baker (1988) claims that NI has the effect of satisfying the Case filter. Given this, it seems reasonable to suppose that NI is motivated by Case checking, as suggested by Chomsky (1993b) and Ferguson (1993). Then it follows that movement of N from the position adjoined to P in (23) violates Greed, since P checks a Case feature.

Note that there are other cases which seem to show that X^0-movement can 'skip' an intervening X^0-position. For example, Baker and Hale (1990) discuss cases where NI seems to 'skip' D (assuming the 'DP analysis' of noun phrases).[13] It has also been observed by Kayne (1989), Roberts (1991), and others that clitic movement can 'skip' intervening heads such as V. It also seems that verb raising can 'skip' Neg (assuming that negation heads NegP; see Kayne 1989, Pollock 1989, Laka 1990, Chomsky 1991). What is the difference between these cases and the NI cases discussed above?

---

[13] See Zushi 1993 for a possible counterargument to this conclusion.

Although full discussion of this issue takes us too far afield, I will just sketch out a possible direction to take. Recall that our analysis does not allow a head to skip another head in the first place; a head must always move by successive cyclic adjunction. Crucial for us, then, is the properties concerning feature checking of the moved heads and the intervening heads. In fact, such grammatical cases as mentioned above seem to follow under our approach, if the relevant properties of the moved heads and those of the intervening heads are properly understood. Thus it seems that such grammatical cases all involve intervening heads which do not enter into any checking relation to the moved heads. If this is correct, those cases can be treated on a par with standard cases of successive cyclic *wh*-movement and NP-movement (see section 3).[14]

5 Conclusion

In this paper, we have developed a new theory of movement according to which Relativized Minimality is deduced from the interaction of two Economy principles, Shortest Link and Greed. Following the suggestion of Chomsky (1993a) and Chomsky and Lasnik (1993), we started out with a 'potential landing site approach', which attempts to derive Relativized Minimality directly from the effect of Shortest Link. We have shown that this approach, as it stands, has several problematic aspects to it, though as a first approximation, it has sufficient intuitive plausibility. Keeping intact the original insight of the Chomsky-Lasnik suggestion, we have proposed an alternative approach according to which movement makes free use of adjunction in the spirit of the free movement hypothesis, and as a result of this, Shortest Link forces successive cyclic movement via adjunction even when intermediate Spec positions are filled. This has made it possible to analyze standard cases of Relativized Minimality as violations of Greed. We have seen that the proposed approach accounts for the difference between *wh*-movement and scrambling by making crucial reference to their different properties concerning feature checking, and has further consequences and implications which fall outside the range of traditional approaches.

References

Abe, Jun. 1993. *Binding conditions and scrambling without A/A'*

---

[14]Note that if we pursue this approach to X^0-movement, we might be able to eliminate so-called 'substitution into X^0-position' proposed by Rizzi and Roberts (1989) and Roberts (1991). This, if indeed possible, will be a desirable move, given that the proposed operation poses a nontrivial problem from an X-bar theoretic point of view.

distinction. Doctoral dissertation, University of Connecticut.

Baker, Mark. 1988. *Incorporation: A theory of grammatical function changing*. Chicago: University of Chicago Press.

Baker, Mark and Ken Hale. 1990. Relativized minimality and pronoun incorporation. *Linguistic Inquiry* 21.289-97.

Besten, Hans den. 1983. On the interaction of root transformations and lexical deletive rules. *On the formal syntax of Westgermania*, ed. by W. Abraham, 47-131. Amsterdam: John Benjamins.

Cheng, Lisa L.-S. 1991. *On the typology of wh-questions*. Doctoral dissertation, MIT.

Chomsky, Noam. 1973. Conditions on transformations. *A Festschrift for Morris Halle*, ed. by Stephen R. Anderson and Paul Kiparsky, 232-86. New York: Holt, Rinehart and Winston.

Chomsky, Noam. 1986. *Barriers*. Cambridge, Mass: MIT Press.

Chomsky, Noam. 1991. Some notes on economy of derivation and representation. *Principles and parameters in comparative grammar*, ed. by Robert Freidin, 417-54. Cambridge, Mass: MIT Press.

Chomsky, Noam. 1993a. A minimalist program for linguistic theory. *The view from Building 20: Essays in linguistics in honor of Sylvain Bromberger*, ed. by Kenneth Hale and Samuel Jay Keyser, 1-52. Cambridge, Mass: MIT Press.

Chomsky, Noam. 1993b. Prospects for minimalism. Talk given at the University of California, Irvine.

Chomsky, Noam and Howard Lasnik. 1993. Principles and parameters theory. *Syntax: An international handbook of contemporary research*, ed. by J. Jacobs, A. von Stechow, W. Sternefeld, and T. Vennemann. Berlin: Walter de Gruyter.

Cinque, Guglielmo. 1990. *Types of A-bar dependencies*. Cambridge, Mass: MIT Press.

Ferguson, Scott. 1993. Notes on the shortest move metric and object checking. *Harvard working papers in linguistics* 3, ed. by Höskuldur Thráinsson, Samuel Epstein, and Susumu Kuno, 65-80. Cambridge, Mass: Department of Linguistics, Harvard University.

Frampton, John. 1991. Relativized minimality, a review. *The Linguistic Review* 8.1-46.

Fukui, Naoki. 1986. *A theory of category projection and its applications*. Doctoral dissertation, MIT.

Fukui, Naoki. 1993a. Parameters and optionality. *Linguistic Inquiry* 24.399-420.

Fukui, Naoki. 1993b. A note on improper movement. *The Linguistic Review* 10.111-26.

Fukui, Naoki and Mamoru Saito. 1993. Agreement, X'-compatibility, and the theory of movement. Unpublished manuscript, University of California, Irvine and University of Connecticut.

Fukui, Naoki and Margaret Speas. 1986. Specifiers and projection. *MIT working papers in linguistics* 8, ed. by Naoki Fukui, Tova Rapoport, and

Elizabeth Sagey, 128-72. Cambridge, Mass: Department of Linguistics and Philosophy, MIT.

Huang, C.-T. James. 1982. *Logical relations in Chinese and the theory of grammar*. Doctoral dissertation, MIT.

Kayne, Richard. 1989. Null subjects and clitic climbing. *The null subject parameter*, ed. by Osvaldo Jaeggli and Kenneth Safir, 239-62. Dordrecht: Kluwer.

Kuroda, S.-Y. 1988. Whether we agree or not: A comparative syntax of English and Japanese. *Papers from the second international workshop on Japanese syntax*, ed. by William Poser, 103-43. Stanford: Center for the Study of Language and Information, Stanford University.

Laka, Itziar. 1990. *Negation in syntax: On the nature of functional categories and projections*. Doctoral dissertation, MIT.

Lasnik, Howard and Mamoru Saito. 1984. On the nature of proper government. *Linguistic Inquiry* 15.235-89.

Lasnik, Howard and Mamoru Saito. 1992. *Move α: Conditions on its application and output*. Cambridge, Mass: MIT Press.

Pesetsky, David. 1982. *Paths and categories*. Doctoral dissertation, MIT.

Pollock, Jean-Yves. 1989. Verb movement, universal grammar, and the structure of IP. *Linguistic Inquiry* 20.365-424.

Rizzi, Luigi. 1990. *Relativized minimality*. Cambridge, Mass. MIT Press.

Rizzi, Luigi and Ian Roberts. 1989. Complex inversion in French. *Probus* 1.1-30.

Roberts, Ian. 1991. Excorporation and minimality. *Linguistic Inquiry* 22.209-18.

Rudin, Catherine. 1988. On multiple questions and multiple wh fronting. *Natural Language and Linguistic Theory* 6.445-501.

Saito, Mamoru. 1985. *Some asymmetries in Japanese and their theoretical implications*. Doctoral dissertation, MIT.

Saito, Mamoru. 1989. Scrambling as semantically vacuous A'-movement. *Alternative conceptions of phrase structure*, ed. by Mark Baltin and Anthony Kroch, 182-200. Chicago: University of Chicago Press.

Stowell, Tim. 1982. The tense of infinitives. *Linguistic Inquiry* 13.561-70.

Szabolcsi, Anna and Frans Zwarts. 1992. Weak islands and an algebraic semantics for scope-taking. Unpublished manuscript, University of California, Los Angeles and Rijksuniversiteit Groningen.

Takano, Yuji. 1994. Economy of derivation, relativized minimality, and proper binding. Unpublished manuscript, University of California, Irvine.

Travis, Lisa. 1984. *Parameters and effects of word order variation*. Doctoral dissertation, MIT.

Watanabe, Akira. 1993. *Agr-based case theory and its interaction with the A-bar system*. Doctoral dissertation, MIT.

Zushi, Mihoko. 1993. Subject-object asymmetry in noun incorporation. Paper presented at Western Conference on Linguistics '93.

Idioms, Patterns and Anthropocentricity

GERT WEBELHUTH
University of North Carolina

1. Overview of the Paper[1]

The central contribution of this paper is the presentation of the results of an empirical syntactic and semantic study of nearly 400 German idioms. Section 2 of the paper introduces a number of previous claims about the structure of idioms and tests these against the German corpus. It is shown that none of the proposals are without counterexamples. In section 3, further generalizations from the corpus are derived and exemplified.

2. Previous Claims

In this section four proposals about universal constraints on the structure of idioms are presented and tested against the corpus.[2]

---

1 I would like to thank Farrell Ackerman for the important contributions he has made to my thinking about idioms. The interested reader can find more material on this subject and another, larger, empirical study of German idioms, in Webelhuth and Ackerman (1994).

I would also like to express my gratitude to Ivan Sag, Geoffrey Nunberg, Tom Wasow, and Martin Everaert for making their manuscripts and articles on idioms available to me. While I disagree with some of their views, their insights were important starting points for what to look for in my empirical material and the conclusions I ultimately draw. I alone bear the responsibility for mistakes and oversights in this paper.

2 Strict space limitations do not allow me to provide much detail of the four theories to be discussed. The reader is encouraged to consult the original papers for more information.

The corpus consists of 386 verbal idioms from Lupson (1984) that contain at least one non-frozen grammatical function. Fully sentential

The first proposal comes from Coopmans and Everaert (1988, 79). They propose (1):

(1) The idiom formation that X^0 undergoes can only affect its direct θ-role.

Our corpus contains many idioms consisting of a verb and a frozen direct object consistent with the proposal. (2) is an example:

(2)
X hat einen Dickschädel
X has a thick-skull
'X is stubborn'

However, there are also many frozen expressions in idioms that are usually not analyzed as direct θ–role recipients. One class involves idioms with frozen indirect objects as in (3) [the indirect object is underlined]:

(3) Idioms with Frozen Indirect Objects

a.
X traut dem Frieden nicht
X trusts the peace not
'It's too good to last'

b.
X öffnet dieser Sache Tür und Tor
X opens this matter door and gate
'X opens the floodgates to this matter'

c.
X macht seinem Herzen Luft
X makes his heart air
'X gives vent to X's feelings'

A particularly productive type of idiom contains a frozen locative adverbial (for a similar observation on English see Kiparsky (1987)). Many of these locatives are not arguments of the verb at all; those that are would not usually be considered direct arguments. A few representative examples are given in (4):

(4) Idioms with Locative Adverbials

a.
X sucht eine Stecknadel in einem Heuhaufen
X seeks a needle in a haystack
'X looks for a needle in a haystack'

---

idioms were excluded because the present paper deals with the relative properties of frozen and non-frozen positions in sentences containing idioms.

b. X hat etwas auf dem Herzen
X has something on the heart
'X has something on X's mind'

c. X findet ein Haar in der Suppe
X finds a hair in the soup
'X finds something to moan about'

Finally, the idioms in (5) contain frozen adjuncts of other types: (a) contains an instrumental, (b) contains the negation adjunct and a frequency adverb:

(5) Idioms with Other Adjuncts

a. X schlägt zwei Fliegen mit einer Klappe
X hits two flies with one flap
'X kills two birds with one stone'

b. X läßt sich das nicht zweimal sagen
X lets refl that not twice say
'X doesn't need to be told that twice'

Baltin (1987, 6) posits a constraint on idioms which casts the net slightly larger than Coopmans' and Everaert's proposal:

(6) ... the participants in the idiom always involve the head of a phrase and the head of one of its complements (examples *make headway, keep track of, keep tabs on).* [Footnote omitted]

This proposal accounts for the idioms in (3) but the examples in (4) and (5) are counterexamples to it. Another large class of problematic cases comes from structures with frozen adjective phrases within NPs that are parts of idioms. (7) presents examples of this type. The underlined adjective (phrase) in each case is not selected by the verbal head of the idiom nor do the adjective (phrase) and the noun stand in a head-complement relation:

(7) Idioms with Attributive Adjectives

a. X spielt die beleidigte Leberwurst
X plays the insulted liverwurst
'X plays the prima donna'

b. X schluckt die bittere Pille
X swallows the bitter pill
'X bites the bullet'

c. X spielt die erste Geige
X plays the first violin
'X calls the tune'

The third approach to idioms we consider comes from Van Gestel (1989, 1992):[3]

(8) For any idiom X^m, X^m contains all and only fixed material.

Of the approaches we have seen up to this point this one is the most liberal since it refers only to constituency, irrespective of the thematic or grammatical-functional relationships between the idiom's daughters. (8) is probably consistent with all the examples presented so far.

However, even this proposal faces a multitude of counterexamples from the German corpus, including all of the examples in (9) which instantiate a very productive type of idiom. Here the idiom consists of a verb and a preposition (and perhaps additional material) but, crucially, the object of the preposition is non-frozen. These idioms thus all violate (8) because there is a non-fixed position within the otherwise completely idiomatic constituent.

(9) Idioms with Frozen Prepositions Whose Object is Non-Frozen

a. Bei X ist eine Schraube locker
with X is a screw loose
'X has a screw loose'

b. Bei X ist Hopfen und Malz verloren
with X is hops and malt lost
'X is a dead loss'

c. X macht nicht viel Federlesens mit Y
X makes not much feather gathering with Y
'X wastes no time on Y'

d. X macht kurzen Prozeß mit Y
X makes short process with Y
'X gives Y short shrift'

The examples in (10) present further challenges to the claim that idioms are constituents containing all and only fixed material. (10a) is an idiomatic

3 These papers have not been accessible to me at the time of writing. Van Gestel's claim (8) is reported in Everaert (1993, 47). It would appear that a similar claim is presupposed by Larson (1988, 340) in an argument for his double-VP analysis of ditransitive verbs in English.

main clause (note that the finite verb is in second position and that the existential particle *es,* which is restricted to the first position of main clauses in German, appears here. The minimal category that contains all the fixed material of the idiom is thus the S-node. But embedded within that constituent we find a non-fixed indirect object, represented by X.

(10) Other Counterexamples to (8)

a. Es läuft X kalt über den Rücken
it runs X cold over the back
'Something sends a shiver down X's spine'

b. Ich weiß nicht wo X der Kopf steht
I know not where X the head stands
'X does not know whether X is coming or going'

In (10b) the whole matrix clause is fixed as are the question word, the subject, and the verb of the embedded clause. Nevertheless, deeply embedded within the subordinate clause we find a free indirect object. (8) predicts that such idioms don't exist.

Finally we move to Marantz (1984, 27) where we find the following observation:

(11) ... there are countless object idioms in English like *kick the bucket* while subject idioms that are not also full phrasal idioms are rare, if they exist at all.

Marantz took (11) to be evidence for his view of theta theory that objects are theta-marked directly by the verb but that external arguments receive their theta role compositionally from the verb phrase containing the verb and its internal arguments.

Unlike the earlier claims we examined, Marantz's narrowly circumscribed observation carries over well to the German data. My corpus contains only 16 subject idioms that aren't fully phrasal. These are presented in (12):

(12) Idioms with Frozen Subjects

a. X reißt die Geduld
X tears the patience
'X's patience is wearing thin'

b. X raucht der Kopf
X smokes the head
'X's head is spinning'

c. X brummt der Schädel
X buzzes the head
'X's head is throbbing'

d. X rutscht das Herz in die Hose
X slides the heart into the trousers
'X's heart sinks into X's boots'

e. X stehen die Haare zu Berge
X stand the hairs on mountains
'X's hair stands on end'

f. X fällt ein Stein vom Herzen
X falls a stone from the heart
'It's a load of X's mind'

g. Es läuft X kalt über den Rücken
it runs X cold over the back
'Something sends a shiver down X's spine'

h. X steht das Wasser bis zum Hals
X stands the water up to the neck
'X is up to X's neck in it'

i. X ist eine Laus über die Leber gelaufen
X is a louse over the liver run
'Something is bugging X'

j. Ich weiß nicht wo X der Kopf steht
I know not where X the head stands
'X does not know whether X is coming or going'

k. Bei X ist eine Schraube locker
with X is a screw loose
'Someone has a screw loose'

l. Bei X ist Hopfen und Malz verloren
with X is hops and malt lost
'X is a dead loss'

m. Wie steht es um X?
how stands it about X
'How is X doing?'

n. Was fehlt X denn?
what lacks X then
'What's wrong with X?'

o. X bringen keine zehn Pferde dahin
X bring no ten horses there
'Wild horses wouldn't drag X there'

p. Wo drückt es X denn?
where presses it X then
'What's troubling X?'

Observe that none of the examples in (a)-(n) contains a direct object, and that all of their frozen subjects are non-agentive. This invites an analysis in terms of unaccusativity which would locate the surface subject within the VP at D-structure where it can be directly theta-marked by the verb. Only (o) and (p) resist such an analysis due to the facts that both already contain a direct object distinct from the subject (namely the free X position) and that the surface subject in (o) would appear to be a proto-agent in the sense of Dowty (1991) and hence not qualify as an underlying direct object. All in all, however, while Marantz's proposal cannot be universally correct, it provides the basis for a very strong markedness statement concerning idioms.

Because Marantz's proposal focuses exclusively on subjects, it would not appear to be sufficiently general to account for another strong tendency in German idioms. As the table (13) shows, not only subjects but also indirect objects show a powerful resistance to occur frozen in idioms:

(13) The Resistance of Grammatical Functions to Idiomatization

	Number	Percent
Idioms with a frozen IO:	3	1.8
Idioms with a frozen SU:	16	9.8
Idioms with a frozen DO:	144	88.3

We leave the second section of this paper with the following two firmly established empirical generalizations:

(14) Generalizations to Take Away from This Section

1. Idioms do not have to be phrase-structural constituents.
2. Subject and indirect object idioms are much rarer than direct object idioms.

3. Other Generalizations Derived from the German Corpus

We will now take a closer look at the properties of the argument structure and the subcategorization frame of idioms. The corpus yields particularly interesting generalizations in this regard.

We begin by inspecting the list of the nouns that appear as the heads of the frozen subjects in the 16 subject idioms and as the heads of the 3 indirect object idioms:

(15) The head nouns of the subject in subject idioms

Geduld	patience
Kopf	head
Schädel	head/skull
Herz	heart
Haare	hair
Stein	stone
Es	it
Pferde	horses
Wasser	water
Laus	louse
Schraube	screw
Hopfen	hops
Malz	malt
Was	what

(16) The head nouns of the indirect object in IO idioms

Friede	peace •
Sache	affair
Herz	heart

Note the striking absence of nouns referring to human beings in (15) and (16). Compare this with the first few nouns contained in an article from an arbitrarily chosen German newspaper:

(17) The head nouns of subjects in a recent newspaper article

Kirche	church
Anglikaner	Anglicans
Gegner und Gegnerinnen	male and female opponents
Diakoninnen	female deacon
Gemeinde	community
Gäste	guests

Millionenpublikum	an audience of millions
Ereignis	event
Kathedrale	cathedral
Dekan	dean
Applaus	applause
Diakoninnen	female deacon
Bischof	bishop
der	he

11 of the 14 nouns taken from this article (those which are italicized) refer to human beings or collections of human beings. With indirect objects one would doubtlessly find a similar result. On the basis of (15)-(17) we state two further generalizations:

(18) The head nouns of frozen subjects and indirect objects

3. The referents of the SUBJ and IO functions are in general more likely to be HUMAN than NON-HUMAN. These are precisely the functions that are least likely to be frozen in idioms (cf. Nunberg, Sag, and Wasow 1994).

4. However, when these functions (i.e. SUBJ and IO) ARE fixed in idioms, their conventional interpretation typically is NON-HUMAN.

The data just discussed of course suggest the conclusion that subjects and indirect objects occur in idioms relatively rarely precisely *because* they so frequently refer to human beings. The following two counts are designed to shed more light on this possibility. (19) is concerned with the argument structure of idioms. In total, the 386 idioms in the corpus take 523 arguments (= non-frozen positions). I have classified each of these arguments according to whether it should denote a human being, a non-human entity, or whether it is compatible with both interpretations according to the selectional restrictions imposed by the idiomatic predicate. The results are striking: more than 8 out of 10 open argument positions of idiomatic predicates are reserved for NPs referring to human beings, with another 4.8 % being compatible with a human or a non-human interpretation.

(19) The Aboutness of Idioms I: Open Positions

Database 386 idioms

Open positions 523

Selectional Restrictions on open positions	Absolute	Percent
HUMAN	440	84.1
NON-HUMAN	58	11.1
VAGUE	25	4.8
-----	-----	-------
ALL	523	100.0

Having established that idioms are stereotypically about human beings, let us now ask what kinds of nouns occur frozen in idioms. The results are stunning as well, as (20) shows:

(20) The Aboutness of Idioms II: The Conventional Meaning of the Head Nouns of Frozen Positions

Conventional Meaning	Absolute	Percentage
BODY PARTS/HUMAN FOODS	117	30.3
CULTURE/TOOLS	130	33.7
MENTAL PROPERTIES	24	6.2
	-----	------
	271	70.2

Body parts, foods: hand, mouth, ears, porridge, foot, tip of the nose, ...
Culture, tools: blanket, little house, track, one-way street, wheels, ...
Mental properties: happiness, fears, understanding, spirits, question, ...

Almost one third of all the idioms in the corpus contain a noun in a frozen position that conventionally refers to a human body part or a food for human consumption. Another 33% contain nouns that refer to human culture or tools used by humans. Fully 70% of all idioms contain a frozen noun that in its conventional interpretation is likely to occur in a sentence that is "about" a human being or a group of human beings.

What about the remaining 30% that do not contain such an NP? It turns out, as is shown in (21), that many of these idioms contain verbs that in their conventional interpretation refer specifically to human participants, e.g. *to kick, to open oneself up, to sit down, etc.:*

(21) Frozen Verbs from the Remaining 30 % of the Idioms

verschwinden	disappear
treten	kick
greifen	grip
schlagen	hit

fallen	fall
aus sich herausgehen	open oneself up
geraten	get
gehen	go
kommen	come
sich setzen	sit down
sich legen	lie down
schleichen	move silently and slowly
sich werfen	to throw oneself
tanzen	dance
leben	live
beissen	bite
hängen	hang
stehen	stand
hauen	hit
bleiben	stay
sitzen	sit
lachen	laugh
dienen	serve
...	

The data just presented can be summed up in the following two generalizations:

(22) The Arguments and Syntactic Dependents of Idiomatic Predicates

5. There is a very strong preference for idiomatic predicates to assign theta-roles to their free arguments containing the entailment +HUMAN.

6. There is a very strong preference for idiomatic predicates to contain nouns or verbs that stereotypically cooccur with a +HUMAN NP.

Having established preferences affecting the argument structure and the subcategorization of idioms, it is natural to turn to the question of *linking,* i.e. how the arguments of the idioms are realized by the grammatical functions governed by the idiom.

First, we restate and illustrate a linking generalization that is widely cited in the literature and well supported by our data:

(23) The Linking Properties of Idioms I

7. Idiomatic predicates usually have formally identical non-idiomatic counterparts (cf. Weinreich 1969, and others). The idiomatic predicate's semantic valency usually is identical to or smaller than that of its non-idiomatic counterpart.

(24) is typical in this regard. The expression has both an idiomatic interpretation and a literal one (which is very unlikely to be true) and while the literal interpretation involves a two-place predicate, the idiomatic interpretation involves only a one-place functor:

(24) X brummt der Schädel
X buzzes the head
'X's head is throbbing'

But there are further constraints on linking, including the one in (25) which to my knowledge has not been noticed before:

(25) The Linking Properties of Idioms II

8. Agentive arguments of idiomatic predicates must meet the same linking constraints as agentive arguments of non-idiomatic predicates, i.e. there are no idiomatic predicates whose agent is expressed as an IO, a DO, a GENITIVE, or the object of a preposition that cannot mark agents in non-idiomatic predicates.

This generalization is supported by all the sentences in (26), among others. (26a) is unremarkable since the idiom has only one non-frozen grammatical function which happens to be the subject interpreted as an agent. In (26b, c), however, the agent could theoretically be realized either as the non-frozen subject or the non-frozen indirect object. It is realized as the subject, however. Realizing the agent as a direct object, a genitive, or the object of a preposition is ruled out as well, as is shown by (26d-f).

(26) Agents of Idiomatic Predicates Are Subject to the Same Linking Conventions as Agents of Non-idiomatic Predicates

a. SUBJ/AG wirbelt viel Staub auf
X kicks a lot of dust up
'X causes a great stir'

b. SUBJ/AG verpaßt IO einen Denkzettel
X gives Y a think-note
'X teaches Y a lesson'

c. SUBJ/AG fällt IO ins Wort
X falls Y in the word
'X interrupts Y'

d. SUBJ/AG schiebt DO auf die lange Bank
X pushes Y on the long bench
'X puts Y off'

e. SUBJ/PT möchte nicht in GEN's Haut stecken
X wants not in Y's skin be
'X does not want to be in Y's shoes'

f. SUBJ/AG legt ein gutes Wort für Y ein
X puts a good word for Y in
'X puts in a good word for Y'

Interestingly, patient arguments behave differently. They are subject to our final generalization:

(27) The Linking Properties of Idioms II

9. In idioms the usual constraints on the linking of patients are waived; patients can be linked to any NP position.

(28a, d, e) are not surprising since patients may be realized as subjects and direct objects in non-idioms. But notice the remaining examples: in (b), the non-agentive argument behaves semantically like a patient as its most natural paraphrases show, yet the patient is realized as an indirect object rather than the expected direct object. And in the final two examples the patient is realized as the object of a preposition.

(28) The Realization of Patient Arguments in Idioms

a. SUBJ/PT langweilt sich zu Tode
X bores refl to death
'X is bored to death'

b. SUBJ/AG gibt IO/PT einen Korb
X gives Y a basket
'X turns Y down, X rejects Y'

c.

SUBJ/AG	schiebt	IO/PT	die Schuld	in	die	Schuhe
X	puts	Y	the blame	into	the	shoes

'X blames Y'

d.

SUBJ/AG	wickelt	DO/PT	um	den	kleinen	Finger
X	wraps	Y	around	the	small	finger

'X twists Y round X's little finger'

e.

SUBJ/AG	wirft	DO/PT	zum	alten	Eisen
X	throws	Y	to the	old	iron

'X throws Y on the scrapheap'

f.

SUBJ/AG	läßt	kein	gutes	Haar	an	PO/PT
X	lets	no	good	hair	on	Y

'X pulls Y to pieces, X severely criticizes Y'

g.

SUBJ/EXP	hält	große	Stücke	auf	PO/PT
X	holds	great	pieces	on	Y

'X respects Y, X thinks highly of Y'

The relative freedom of the realization of the patient in idioms can also be demonstrated in English. In this language, a very productive idiomatic structure expresses the patient as the genitive of a noun phrase that bears a grammatical function to the verb. Examples are given in (29):

(29) Comparison With English: Patients Linked to Genitives

a. GEN's days are numbered.
b. GEN's eyes pop out.
c. GEN's hands are tied.
d. The cat gets GEN's tongue.
e. The world is GEN's oyster.
f. Butter would melt in GEN's mouth.

These examples are particularly striking because they show that the thematic interpretation of the genitive is strongly dependent on whether it is the argument of an idiomatic predicate or not. "GEN's X" in its non-idiomatic interpretation requires that there be some semantic connection between the referent of GEN and the referent of X. If X names a body part, then by far the most likely interpretation is that of inalienable possession, a more macabre interpretation is one of temporary control over somebody else's (severed) body part. But none of these features play any role in the interpretation of (29b, c, d, f) where the role of the genitive seems to be simply that of a canonical theme or patient.

Having so far essentially followed where the data from the German corpus have led me, maybe I can be allowed the privilege of speculation towards the end of the paper. Why might it be that patients can be realized more freely in idioms than in non-idiomatic expressions? I offer the following conjecture: according to (34b), fixed grammatical functions should be [-Human]. Since direct objects are frequently [-Human], they will often be frozen in an idiom. This presents obvious problems for those idioms which want to combine such a sentence form with an argument structure that contains an agent and a patient. The patient's usual grammatical function in such a structure is taken by the frozen noun. I suggest that the regular restrictions on the mapping of patients are relaxed to allow them to be expressed at all. This treatment of patients in idioms confirms the impression already gained from non-idiomatic predicates that this theta role doesn't have one "fixed target" in terms of mapping but that its surface realization crucially depends on which other expressions are in the sentence. Kiparsky (1987) and Bresnan and Kanerva (1989) have proposed that the patient is in principle capable of appearing both in subject and object position but that mapping an agent into the subject position has higher priority. This makes the patient more mobile. In idioms, again, the patient seems to go into whatever slot is not already occupied by some prioritized theta role of the idiom or one of the frozen expressions. This suggests that Universal Grammar in general assigns a lower priority to pair patients with a specific grammatical function than agents and perhaps other thematic roles.

References

Ackerman, F. and G. Webelhuth (in prep.) *Complex Predicates.* University of North Carolina at Chapel Hill and University of California at San Diego.

Baltin, M. (1987) "Heads and Projections." In M. Baltin and A. Kroch (Eds.) *Alternative Conceptions of Phrase Structure.* Chicago: University of Chicago Press, 1-16.

Bochner , H. (1993) *Simplicity in Generative Morphology.* Berlin: Mouton de Gruyter.

Bresnan, J. and J. M. Kanerva (1989) "Locative Inversion in Chichewa: A Case Study of Factorization in Grammar." *Linguistic Inquiry* 20.1, 1-50.

Coopmans, P. and M. Everaert (1988) "The Simplex Structure of Complex Idioms: The Morphological Status of *laten.* In M. Everaert et al. (Eds.) *Morphology and Modularity.* Dordrecht: Foris, 75-104.

Dowty, D. (1991) "Thematic Proto-Roles and Argument Selection." *Language* 67.3, 547-619.

Everaert, M. (1993) "Verbal Idioms, Subject Idioms, and Theta Theory." In *Proceedings of the Third Meeting of the Formal Linguistic Society of Mid-America*, 43-59. Distributed by Indiana University Linguistics Club.

Gestel, F. van (1989) "Idioms and X-bar Theory." In M. Everaert and E.-J. van der Linden (Eds.) *Proceedings of the First Tilburg Workshop on Idioms.* ITK Proceedings, Tilburg, 103-126.

Gestel, F. van (1992) "En-bloc Insertion." In M. Everaert et al. (Eds.) *Proceedings of the Idioms Conference.* Tilburg, ITK.

Jackendoff, R. (1975) "Morphological and Semantic Regularities in the Lexicon." *Language* 51, 639-671.

Kiparsky, P. (1987) *Morphology and Grammatical Relations.* Unpublished Manuscript, Stanford University.

Larson, R. (1988) "On the Double Object Construction." *Linguistic Inquiry* 19, 335-91.

Lupson, J.P. (1984) *Guide to German Idioms: Sprachführer zu Deutschen Idiomen.* Lincolnwood, Illinois: Passport Books.

Marantz, A. (1984) *On the Nature of Grammatical Relations.* Cambridge: MIT-Press.

Nunberg, G., I. Sag, and T. Wasow (1994) "Idioms." To appear in *Language.*

Webelhuth, G. and F. Ackerman (1994) "German Idioms: An Empirical Approach." To appear in Proceedings of FLSM V.

Weinreich, U. (1969) "Problems in the Analysis of Idioms: An Interim Report." In *Proceedings of the XIIIth International Conference of Linguistics.* Ed. by S. Hattori and K. Inoue, 102-115. The Hague: CIPL.

Preposition Selection Outside the Lexicon

STEPHEN WECHSLER
University of Texas at Austin

1. Semantically Motivated Preposition Selection

How do verbs and other predicators semantically select prepositions to head their complement PPs?[1] Some preposition selection is essentially idiosyncratic, as shown by comparing semantically similar verbs like *charge* vs. *blame* vs. *accuse: charge NP* WITH *NP, blame NP* FOR *NP, accuse NP* OF *NP*. Such verbs select their prepositions via simple lexical specifications within their complement selection features:[2]

(1) a. charge: COMPS < NP, PP[with] >
    b. blame: COMPS < NP, PP[for] >
    c. accuse: COMPS < NP, PP[of] >

---

[1]Thanks to Tony Davis, Bob Carpenter, Lee Baker, Tony Woodbury, and Larisa Zlatic for helpful comments. Author's address: wechsler@uts.cc.utexas.edu

[2]Following Pollard and Sag 1994, Ch. 9, I assume that complements are specified in the list value of a feature COMPS ('non-subject complements'). The order of the list encodes relative obliqueness of the complements.

But for other verbs the selection is semantically motivated, as with the large class of communicative act verbs which take PP's headed by *to* (to mark the intended recipient of the communicative act) and *about* (to mark the informational content of the communicative act) as in (2a); and the large class of verbs of desiring taking a PP[for] (to mark the object of desire) as in (2b):

(2) a. talk/sing/whisper/murmur to John about Bill
    b. long/yearn/hunger/hope for peace

We will focus on those cases like (2) where there is some clear semantic motivation for the choice of preposition, although I will have more to say about the idiosyncratic type below. It will be argued that preposition selection does not occur in the lexicon, which is, perhaps, a surprising conclusion. While my data comes from English, I believe these conclusions are universally applicable to adpositions, as well as to semantic case marking. In addition, the answer I will give turns out to offer a theory of one source of variable polyadicity, a theory which makes some interesting predictions.

Let us begin by asking what the lexical entry for a verb of this latter type includes when it exits the lexicon and enters the syntax. A common view holds that it looks like (3). On that view the P-selection generalizations are captured in the lexicon, perhaps by lexical redundancy rules or some other device.

(3) *sing:* COMPS < PP[to], PP[about] >

However, I argue below that this selection does not occur in the lexicon. Instead the exit form is roughly that in (4).

(4) *sing:* COMPS < PP* >

Moreover, I will posit that all verbs inherit the PP* complement specification. These 'wildcard' PPs are appended to any idiosyncratic lexical specifications. Thus the minimal information needed for the subcategorization of *sing* is shown in (5):

(5) *sing:* COMPS < >

I will argue that the apparently lexical aspect of semantically-based preposition selection is illusory. Instead, the unacceptable strings such as **John sang onto the stage* are ruled out in the syntax, or, more precisely, they are ruled out by an interaction of syntax/semantics composition rules and pragmatic constraints.

2. Zeugma and the Semantic Content of P's

It is sometimes assumed, either implicitly or explicitly, that the P heading a complement PP is a semantically empty form which functions by marking a thematic role assigned by the governing verb. We begin by showing that this is not the case for P's heading semantically selected complement PP's. On the contrary, such P's have semantic content.

There is a very general and clear property of ambiguous phrases: when a single phrase is used simultaneously as a complement of two verbs, it cannot be interpreted in two different senses, one for each verb. A *CD* is either a compact disk or a certificate of deposit, but sentence (6) clearly cannot have the meaning shown.

(6) *John can't decide whether to listen to or liquidate his CDs.
'John can't decide whether to listen to his compact disks or liquidate his certificates of deposit.'

Actually (6), with the interpretation shown, is acceptable as an instance of *zeugma*, a rhetorical figure used for comic effect. Here we will confine ourselves to non-figurative speech. We will use this as a diagnostic to test some complement PPs to see whether the preposition has semantic content.[3]

The verbs *search* and *examine* take a 'desiderative' PP[for], representing the thing which is desired; these verbs can be coordinated (7a). Similarly, *praise* and *condemn* take a for-PP representing the cause or reason for the praise or condemnation; these can be coordinated (7b). But they cannot be mixed, as shown in (7c).

(7)a. They will search and examine George for the letter.
b. They will either praise or condemn George for the letter.
c. *They will either condemn or search George for the letter.

Some further examples appear in (8) and (9).

(8)a. Somehow we must safely pile or cram the weapons into trucks.
b. Somehow we must safely transform or convert the weapons into trucks.
c. *Somehow we must safely pile or transform the weapons into trucks.

(9)a. Tommy's mother sometimes tapes or pins a note to him.
b. Tommy's mother sometimes mails or faxes a note to him.
c. *Tommy's mother sometimes mails or tapes it to him.

Crucially, there is no injunction against mixing thematic role types in this manner: in (10) Bugsy is the 'agent' of kill but the 'theme' or 'patient' of arrest.

---

[3]For our argument it makes no difference whether (6) is analyzed as right node raising or V^0-V^0 coordination.

(10) Bugsy killed someone and was arrested for murder.

Similarly, compare failed attempts at coordination like (11a), which resembles the earlier examples, in that the preposition is simultaneously used in two different senses, with relatively better examples like (11b), where the preposition appears twice, once in each sense, so there is no conflict.[4]

(11) a. ??Mikael longed and danced <u>for</u>$_{des?/ben?}$ the Princess of Muu.
b. Mikael <u>longed for</u>$_{des}$ and <u>danced for</u>$_{ben}$ the Princess of Muu.

If it is not the clash of thematic role types which is responsible for the ungrammaticality of the starred sentences, then it seems that the verbs select for particular senses of P's: *praise* and *condemn* select, not just a PP[for], but a PP[for$_{cause}$], while *search* and *examine* select a PP[for$_{desiderative}$]. Then the contrasts follow automatically from the constraint against (non-figurative) zeugma illustrated in (6). This suggests that verbs' complement specifications need even more information we thought (see (3) above). But it turns out that they need less information, as we will see shortly.

Also, it has long been observed (Gawron 1986, *inter alia*) that prepositions with very nearly the same meaning as the complement P's also head predicative and adjunct PPs, which of course have semantic content.

(12)

a. The preacher is talking about prepositions.	*complement* PP[about]
b. Today's sermon is about prepositions.	*predicative* PP[about]

This argument is weaker than the previous one, since these semantic parallels could be captured with, e.g., lexical rules, without necessarily

---

[4](11b) may involve V-P incorporation, or perhaps right node raising. As above, this does not affect our argument.

concluding that the complement P's have semantic content. But the evidence from zeugma shows that complement P's have semantic content.

3. Syntactically optional PP's

We need to distinguish between two types of syntactically optional PP: those which express semantically optional arguments and those which express semantically obligatory arguments. For example with both *complain* and *sing* the PP[to] and PP[about] are optional. But *John complained* entails (or strongly suggests) that he complained *to* someone *about* something, while *John sang* does not entail the existence of a goal or theme: it is possible to sing, just for the sake of singing, without any informational content or intended audience.

(13) Obligatory PP arguments (*complain, explain, signal, ...*)

a. John complained (to Mary) (about the heat).

b. John complained. $\models \exists\, x,y \mid$ John complained to x about y.

(14) Optional PP arguments (*sing, whistle, talk, ...*)[5]

a. John sang (to Mary).

b. John sang. $\not\models \exists\, x \mid$ John sang to x.
$\not\models \exists\, y \mid$ John sang about y.

A tempting view of the semantically optional PPs is that they are adjuncts. But they are generally assumed to be complements, because they have all the characteristic syntactic properties of complements. For example, proforms like *do so* and *do the same thing* must substitute for all complements, perhaps but not necessarily also including adjuncts (Radford 1988: 234ff). This test picks out the PP[to] and PP[about] as complements:

---

[5] The verb *talk* is included here because I assume it is possible to talk (to noone) without saying anything. Nothing crucial rests on this assumption.

(15) John sang to Mary about his homeland yesterday…

a. …and Fred did so today.

a.' …and Fred did the same thing today.

b. *…and Fred did so about his car.

b.' *…and Fred did the same thing about his car.

c. *…and Fred did so to Susan about his car.

c.' *…and Fred did the same thing to Susan about his car.

Finally, our theory must capture the well-known entailments of the following sort (see Davidson 1967):

(16) a. Xochi talked to Yo about Zeke. |= Xochi talked to Yo.

b. Xochi talked to Yo about Zeke. |= Xochi talked about Zeke.

c. Xochi talked about Zeke. |= Xochi talked.

d. Xochi talked to Yo. |= Xochi talked.

4. Analysis

As noted above, it may appear that verbs need even more information in their complement specifications than we thought because verbs select for particular senses of prepositions. But according to the present analysis, they need less information than was previously thought.

The basic approach is very straightforward. We assign appropriate semantic content to the various prepositions and other elements. General rules of compositional semantics build up the meaning of the VP from the meanings of V and its complement PPs. Once this is done, it is no longer necessary for verbs to select prepositions explicitly. The improper selections are ruled out on pragmatic grounds, because the resulting semantic combinations do not make sense. Thus *John talked to Mary* is acceptable because the meanings of *talk* and *to* are compatible in the proper way, while **John ate to Mary* is ruled out because the meanings of *eat* and *to* are incompatible.

My analysis will be in the framework of Head-Driven Phrase Structure Grammar (Pollard and Sag 1994), with situation semantics as the semantic component (Devlin 1991). In HPSG the semantic content (hereafter referred to simply as content) of a verb is a PARAMETERIZED STATE OF AFFAIRS (psoa). A psoa consists of a relation and a set of arguments. For example, (17) is the lexical sign for (one-place) *talk*. Its content is a psoa with only one participant, namely the talker.

(17)

$$\begin{bmatrix} \text{PHON} & \langle \text{talk} \rangle \\ \text{SUBJ} & \langle \text{NP}_{[1]} \rangle \\ \text{COMPS} & \langle\, \rangle \\ \text{CONTENT} & \begin{bmatrix} \textit{communicative–act–psoa} & \\ \text{REL} & \textit{talk} \\ \text{SOURCE} & [1] \end{bmatrix} \end{bmatrix}$$

This lexical sign specifies that the subject of *talk* is an NP whose INDEX (also called its PARAMETER; see presently) is token-identical to the filler of the talker (SOURCE) role.

The content of a non-predicative NP is an object containing a parameter and a set of restrictions on the anchoring of that parameter to things in the model.[6] (18) is the sign for the NP *a boy*.

(18)

$$\begin{bmatrix} \text{PHON} & \langle \text{a boy} \rangle \\ \text{CONTENT} & \begin{bmatrix} \textit{nom - obj} & \\ \text{INDEX} & [1] \\ \text{RESTRICTIONS} & \left\{ \begin{bmatrix} \textit{psoa} & \\ \text{REL} & \textit{boy} \\ \text{INSTANCE} & [1] \end{bmatrix} \right\} \end{bmatrix} \end{bmatrix}$$

---

[6]On parameters and anchors, see Devlin (1991).

Here the parameter is restricted to being anchored to a boy.

What about the content of a PP? Is it like that of an NP or a VP or perhaps something else? In most of Pollard and Sag (1994) it is assumed that a complement PP has an NP-like content, though the book briefly sketches a proposal whereby a PP denotes a psoa (Ch.9). Davis 1993 also develops the idea that the content of a PP is a psoa (some related antecedents are Gawron (1986) and Wechsler (1991)). This is the line I will pursue here, although I will suggest that unlike verbs, certain prepositions do not specify any particular RELATION within their psoas.

We will posit that every verb in the language automatically inherits a list of any number of PP complements, which are appended to the end of the verb's (minimal) COMPS list; and that the semantic CONTENT of each PP is unified with that of the verb. (17) above is the minimal lexical sign for *talk*; its minimal COMPS list is empty. (19) is the lexical sign for the verb *talk* including all the 'wildcard' PPs which it has automatically inherited by virtue of being a verb.

(19)

$$\begin{bmatrix} \text{PHON} & \langle \text{talk} \rangle \\ \text{SUBJ} & \langle \text{NP}_{[1]} \rangle \\ \text{COMPS} & \langle \text{PP:}[2]^{*} \rangle \\ \text{CONTENT} & [2]\begin{bmatrix} \textit{communicative–act–psoa} & \\ \text{REL} & \textit{talk} \\ \text{SOURCE} & [1] \end{bmatrix} \end{bmatrix}$$

This lexical entry specifies that the CONTENT of *talk* is a 1-place psoa unified with the CONTENTs of any complement PPs. The lexicon allows any PP complement, but the bad cases are ruled out by world knowledge.

Since all the action is in this world knowledge, we need to say a lot more about how to represent it. We turn to this topic next.

In HPSG all feature structures are SORTED; the sort name appears in italics at the top of the feature structure; e.g. the value of CONTENT in (19) is a feature structure of sort *communicative-act-psoa*. These sorts are organized in a hierarchy of sorts and subsorts: e.g. *communicative-act-psoa* is a subsort of *psoa*.

Let us assume that the RELATION in a psoa does not determine its valency: a psoa with the *talk* relation can be one-place, two-place, three-place, and so on.[7] However, while the relations are not sorted according to valency, I will assume that the psoas are. For example, the psoa subsort called *communicative-act-psoa* includes all communicative act psoas with at least one participant, namely a source participant simply *talking, singing, murmuring* etc.; additionally it may have other participants such as a goal or informational topic. A *monadic-comm-act-psoa* has exactly one participant, namely a source. The *comm-to-psoa* sort includes psoas like talking-to, singing-to, murmuring-to, etc. with at least a source and a goal; a *dyadic-comm-to-psoa* has source and goal and nothing else. The *comm-about-psoa* sort includes psoas like talking-about, singing-about, murmuring-about, etc.; a *dyadic-comm-about-psoa* has source and theme and nothing else. And the *comm-to-about-psoa* sort includes triadic psoas like talking-to-X-about-Y, explaining-to-X-about-Y, and so on.

These subsorts are organized in the following inheritance or subsumption hierarchy:

(20)

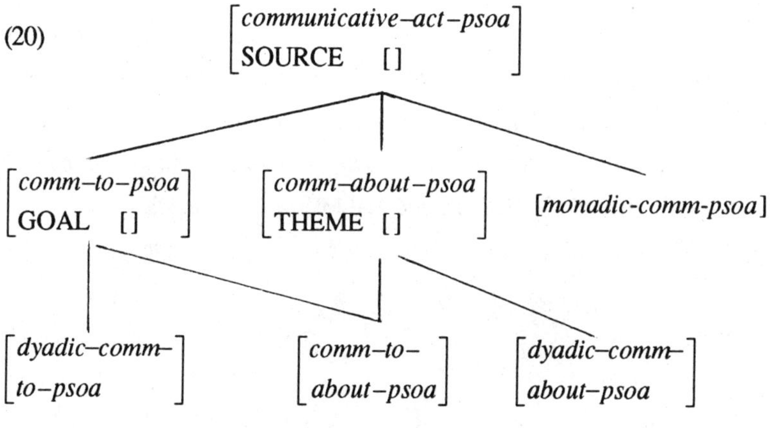

[7] Variable polyadicity of relations is not always assumed in situation semantics, but I believe it is the best way to capture our intuitions about real situations.

Each feature structure in the hierarchy inherits all the information which dominates it in the lattice. Thus every *comm-to-psoa* is also a *communicative-act-psoa*, so it has any properties of the supersort.

Note that the lexical signs for *talk* in (17) and (19) indicate that its CONTENT is a psoa of sort *communicative-act-psoa*. The lexical signs below indicate that *about* and *to* denote psoas of sort *comm-about-psoa* and *comm-to-psoa* respectively.

(21)

$$\begin{bmatrix} \text{PHON} & \langle \text{about} \rangle \\ \text{COMPS} & \langle \text{NP}_{[1]} \rangle \\ \text{CONTENT} & \begin{bmatrix} \textit{comm-about-psoa} \\ \text{THEME [1]} \end{bmatrix} \end{bmatrix}$$

(22)

$$\begin{bmatrix} \text{PHON} & \langle \text{to} \rangle \\ \text{COMPS} & \langle \text{NP}_{[1]} \rangle \\ \text{CONTENT} & \begin{bmatrix} \textit{comm-to-psoa} \\ \text{GOAL [1]} \end{bmatrix} \end{bmatrix}$$

It is part of our world knowledge, as represented by the subsumption lattice in (20), that any combination of these psoa types can be unified. It follows that each of these verbs can combine with a PP[to] or a PP[about] or both. The 'Davidsonian' entailments in (16) above also follow directly from (20).

Recall that 3-place verbs like *complain, explain,* and *signal* seem to semantically select for the GOAL and THEME of communication (see (13) above). Thus these verbs have a content of sort *comm-to-about-psoa*.

(23)

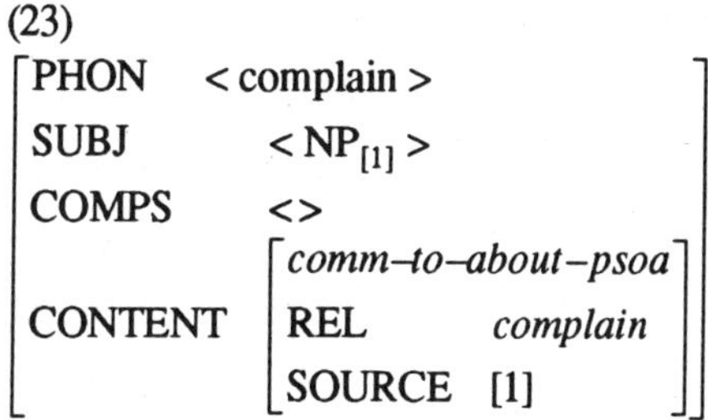

Because of its sort, the content of *complain* automatically inherits the GOAL and THEME roles. If a PP[to] or PP[about] appear in the sentence then they will fill the GOAL and THEME roles, respectively.

A more complete account must (i) prohibit one-to-many mappings from arguments to complements to rule out **John sold me his car to me* (see below on dative shift), **John talked to me to me*, and so on (cp. GB's θ-criterion; LFG's Function-Argument Biuniqueness); and (ii) provide for the interpretation of unprojected arguments (roughly, this involves existential quantification; see (13) above). The precise formulation of the needed principles will be left for future work.

5. Consequences

This account has several consequences. First, notice that this analysis automatically provides a theory of fine-grained thematic role types. The attribute names like GOAL and THEME are only labels for the argument slots within the psoa in which they occur, so they are formalizations of thematic role types in the sense that they label fine-grained equivalence classes across whatever verbs or prepositions happen to have contents of the psoa type in which the role names occur. For example, verbs of communication like *talk* can take an optional GOAL (see (20)) and the preposition *to* marks a GOAL (see (22). No further independent theory is assumed or needed to cash out the semantics of GOALs.

Consequently much of the theory of thematic role types (or argument structure, lexical decomposition, etc.) reduces to an account of the lexicosemantics of prepositions (and postpositions and semantic cases), as proposed in Wechsler (1991). While the *theory* governing these adpositions is universal, the effects naturally differ depending on the lexical resources of particular languages. Once these parochial thematic role types are accounted for in this manner, the remainder of the theory of the lexical semantics of argument structure, which is needed to account for the syntactic expression of direct arguments, turns out to be considerably more tractable than is sometimes suggested by skeptics of such theories. See Wechsler (1991) for discussion.

Secondly, this proposal for preposition selection allows us to reduce certain familiar transitivity alternations to the syntactic optionality of an NP complement. Take dative shift for example:

(24) a. John sold me his car.
b. John sold his car to me.

We need only posit that one NP of a ditransitive verb like *sell* is optional.

(25)

$$\begin{bmatrix} \text{PHON} & \langle \text{sell} \rangle \\ \text{SUBJ} & \langle \text{NP}_{[1]} \rangle \\ \text{COMPS} & \langle (\text{NP}_{[2]},)\,\text{NP}_{[3]} \rangle \\ \text{CONTENT} & \begin{bmatrix} \textit{transfer-psoa} & \\ \text{REL} & \textit{sell} \\ \text{SOURCE} & [1] \\ \text{GOAL} & [2] \\ \text{THEME} & [3] \end{bmatrix} \end{bmatrix}$$

The GOAL argument is semantically obligatory (there is no selling without a buyer). When we take the option without the optional NP, a PP[to] can express the GOAL argument: like all verbs, *sell* inherits any number of wildcard PP's (and pragmatics picks out the right ones). Thus we predict the existence of such alternations from the following basic assumption:

(26) Some complements are syntactically optional.

Given this assumption, we would need a special stipulation to explain the *absence* of dative shift. Alternations of this kind are predicted to occur as long as semantically appropriate prepositions are available in the lexicon.

Another point to mention is that we have formally delinked the verb-denoted RELations (the *talk* relation, etc.) from the psoa-sorts associated with the verbs (*communicative-act-psoa*, etc.). This formal decoupling allows a certain degree of fluidity in the classification of relations. This is probably desirable. For example, in certain discourse contexts a *communicative-act-psoa* might contain the *cough* relation, if for example coughing is understood as a signal of some sort:

(27) John coughed to the auctioneer.
(OK if coughing is a *communicative-act*)

Thirdly, notice that this proposal for preposition selection provides a theory of one type of ARGUMENT ADDITION: adding arguments by means of contentful prepositions. (Other types are applicativization, causativization, etc.) Recall that all of the 'added' (i.e. semantically optional) complement PP's lie outside the idiosyncratic lexical domain of the verb. By definition all of the added arguments are semantically optional; if we further assume that *only* the added arguments are semantically optional, then we make the following prediction:[8]

---

[8]The result in (28) is similar in spirit to the part of the GB Projection Principle that states that a lexical item cannot c-select a position unless it θ-marks the phrase filling that position. (cp. Chomsky 1981:38ff: if α subcategorizes the position β, then α θ-marks β.) Note two important differences: (i) the GB principle does not prohibit c-selection for optional roles. E.g., it would not rule out the hypothetical verb *zang* in (31b). (ii) The GB principle is an axiom, while (28) is a deduction.

(28) Prediction: Idiosyncratically subcategorized ('c-selected') complements must be semantically obligatory.

To see why this follows, recall that the minimal lexical entry for *talk* given in (17) specifies no complement PPs at all so clearly it cannot idiosyncratically select them. Instead, wildcard PPs are inherited by *talk* (see (19)), subject only to semantic and pragmatic constraints (see (20)) which do not mention particular verbs.

As an example of this prediction, consider the verbs of desiring which take PP[for]: *long for*, *yearn for*, *hope for* etc. A few of them select PP[after]: e.g. *hanker after* and *lust after*.

(29) a. John longed for(/*after) a cookie.

b. John is hankering after a cookie.

c. *hanker:* COMPS < PP[after] >

The minimal complement specification for *hanker* is given in (29c). We predict, correctly, that the 'hankered-after' role is semantically obligatory: there can be no hankering unless there is some object of hankering. Similarly, the roles expressed by the idiosyncratic PPs of *charge*, *blame*, and *accuse* (see (1) above), are correctly predicted to be semantically obligatory.

(30)a. They charged John.

$\models \exists x \mid$ they charged John with x

b. They blamed John.

$\models \exists x \mid$ they blamed John for x

c. They accused John.

$\models \exists x \mid$ they accused John of x

We predict that we will not find idiosyncratically selected PPs expressing semantically optional arguments, e.g., that we will not find a verb *to zing* which is like *sing* in having a semantically optional theme, but which expresses its theme idiosyncratically.[9]

(31) a. John sang (about Mary/*on Mary).

b. John zang (on Mary).

This follows from the present account because semantically optional roles are not specified within individual lexical entries, but instead are subject only to general pragmatic and semantic conditions.

References

Chomsky, Noam 1981. *Lectures on Government and Binding.* Dordrecht: Foris.

Davidson, Donald 1967. 'The Logical Form of Action Sentences' in Nicholas Rescher (ed.) *The Logic of Decision and Action.* Pittsburgh: University of Pittsburgh Press, 115-120.

Davis, Tony 1993. 'Linking, Inheritance, and Semantic Structures.' Handout from Stanford Linguistics Dept. Colloquium talk.

Devlin, Keith 1991. *Logic and Information.* Cambridge: Cambridge Univesity Press.

Gawron, Jean Mark 1986. 'Situations and Prepositions.' *Linguistics and Philosophy* 9, 327-382.

Pollard, Carl and Ivan Sag 1994. *Head-Driven Phrase Structure Grammar.* Chicago: U. of Chicago Press, and Stanford: CSLI Press.

Radford, Andrew 1988. *Transformational Grammar—A First Course.* Cambridge: Cambridge Univesity Press.

Wechsler, Stephen 1991. *Argument Structure and Linking.* Doctoral Dissertation, Stanford University Linguistics Department.

---

[9]Note the locution *Mandela is talking* *<u>on</u>* *freedom tonight* is not an exception: unlike the ordinary *talk*, this special use of *talk* for 'to give a talk on' has an obligatory theme (i.e. the topic of the talk).

A New Perspective on Chinese 'Ziji'

PING XUE, CARL POLLARD, & IVAN A. SAG
University of Alberta & University of Victoria, Ohio State University, & Stanford University

1. Introduction

It has been rather widely assumed that the essential properties of the Chinese reflexive pronoun *ziji* 'self' are (i) subject orientation; (ii) long-distance (LD) binding, subject to the blocking effect of an intervening subject with agreement features distinct from those of the potential antecedent; and (iii) the possibility of subcommanding antecedents (i.e., subject antecedents properly contained within a c-commander of the reflexive – see, e.g., Cole, Hermon and Sung 1990; Huang and Tang 1991; Progovac 1992). Though varying with respect to the precise nature of the mechanism connecting *ziji* and its antecedent, most current analyses attempt to account for these putative properties of *ziji* in terms of a successive-cyclic association (e.g., via movement to Agr) with each of the c-commanding subjects between *ziji* and its antecedent.

In this paper, we will point out some facts which are problematic for accounts of this kind, and propose a new analysis of *ziji* binding which accounts for the problematic facts. Central to our analysis is the idea, proposed in various forms by Baker (1994), Pollard and Sag

*This research was supported in part by the Social Sciences and Humanities Research Council of Canada (Postdoctoral Fellowship #756-92-0192). Thanks are due to Tom Hukari for valuable discussion of earlier versions of this paper, and to Steve Harlow for corrections on an earlier draft.

(1992a, 1992b, 1994), and Reinhart and Reuland (1991, 1993), that a fundamental theoretical distinction must be drawn between what we will refer to informally as syntactic reflexives and discourse reflexives. According to our analysis, the two different kinds of reflexives are subject to distinct pragmatic blocking effects. In addition, the syntactic reflexives are subject to a purely syntactic long-distance analogue of Principle A, which we will call Principle Z. However, Principle Z (as well as our version of Principle A) will not be couched in terms of the tree-configurational relation of c-command. Instead, they employ Pollard and Sag's notion of obliqueness-command (o-command), which is defined in terms of a universal hierarchy of grammatical relations.

2. Well-Known Facts and Current Analyses

Chinese *ziji* is morphologically invariant with respect to person and number (and gender is not a morphologically relevant feature in Chinese). The facts in (1)-(2) illustrate the property of *ziji* often referred to as subject orientation: its antecedent can be a subject but not a direct or oblique object:[1]

(1) Zhangsan$_i$ gei-le Lisi$_j$ yizhang ziji$_{i/*j}$ de xiangpian.
Zhangsan give-ASP Lisi one-CLA self DE picture
'Zhangsan$_i$ gave Lisi$_j$ a picture of himself$_{i/*j}$.'

(2) Zhangsan$_i$ cong Lisi$_j$ chu tingshuo Wangwu$_k$ bu xihuan
Zhangsan from Lisi place hear Wangwu not like
ziji$_{i/*j/k}$].
self
'Zhangsan$_i$ heard from Lisi$_j$ Wangwu$_k$ does not like him$_{i/*j}$/himself.'

As with a number of simplex reflexives cross-linguistically,[2] it is possible for the antecedent of *ziji* to be the subject of a higher clause. This LD property is shown in (2) above and in (3):

(3) Zhangsan$_i$ zhidao [Lisi$_j$ renwei [Wangwu$_k$ zui xihuan
Zhangsan know Lisi think Wangwu most like
ziji$_{i/j/k}$]].
self

[1]The following abbreviations are employed in the glosses throughout this paper: CL (classifier); DE (attributive particle *de*); PL (plural); ASP (aspect); FOC (focus particle *shi*); and BEI (passive marker *bei*).

[2]But not all: see Progovac (1992) for discussion of Russian *sebja*.

'Zhangsan$_i$ knows that Lisi$_j$ thinks that Wangwu$_k$ likes self$_{i/j/k}$ most.'

However, as pointed out by Tang (1989), a higher subject cannot be the antecedent of *ziji* if it or an intervening subject differs in person from the local subject of the clause containing *ziji*. This effect, which we will call unlike-person blocking, is illustrated in (4)-(5):[3]

(4) Zhangsan$_i$ zhidao [ni$_j$ renwei [Wangwu$_k$ zui xihuan
Zhangsan know you think Wangwu most like
ziji$_{*i/*j/k}$]].
self
'Zhangsan$_i$ knows that you think that Wangwu likes himself/*you/*him$_i$ most.'

(5) Zhangsan$_i$ shuo [wo$_j$ zhidao [Lisi$_k$ chang piping ziji$_{*i/*j/k}$]].
Zhangsan say I know Lisi often criticize self
'Zhangsan$_i$ said that I feel that Lisi often criticizes himself/*me/*him$_i$.'

This complex of properties – subject orientation together with the potential for LD binding subject to unlike-person blocking has been widely regarded as evidence for a successive association between *ziji* (or simplex reflexives in general) and superordinate subjects. According to many such accounts (e.g. Battistella (1989); Cole et al. (1990); Reinhart and Reuland (1991, 1993)), the simplex reflexive, which is considered to be an X^0 category devoid of inherent *phi*-features, must undergo head movement to the local I at LF, with possible successive-cyclic movement to a higher I. Because of Spec-head agreement between each I and its corresponding subject, it follows that no intervening subject can have *phi*-features distinct from those of the antecedent. According to one variant of this account, due to Progovac (1992), the successive relation is not head movement, but rather an Agr-chain; according to another (Huang and Tang 1991), the movement in question is not head movement but rather adjunction to IP.

These accounts do not all have identical consequences. For example, Huang and Tang note that subject orientation is not a consequence of their analysis, speculating – as our analysis will entail – that subject orientation and morphological simplicity of reflexives are independent

[3] Although the blocking effect is often discussed in terms of agreement features, facts cited by Battistella and Xu (1990) suggests that neither number in the case of third-person NPs nor gender is involved in blocking.

properties. As they point out, Chinese complex reflexives such as *ta-ziji* 'himself/herself', which have inherent *phi*-features and preclude LD binding, are nevertheless subject-oriented:

(6) Zhangsan$_i$ songgei Lisi$_j$ yizhang ta-ziji$_{i/*j}$ de xiangpian.
Zhangsan give Lisi one-CLA he-self DE picture
'Zhangsan$_i$ gave Lisi$_j$ a picture of himself$_{i/*j}$.'

(7) Zhangsan$_i$ gaosu Lisi$_j$ ta-ziji$_{i/*j}$ de shenshi.
Zhangsan tell Lisi he-self DE life-story
'Zhangsan$_i$ told Lisi$_j$ the story of his$_{i/*j}$ life.'

This point poses a challenge for I-to-I accounts, whether couched in terms of movement (e.g., Cole et al. 1990; Reinhart and Reuland 1991, 1993) or of chains (Progovac 1992).

Huang and Tang (1991) also point out that not all instances of *ziji* are bound by a c-commanding (or subcommanding) subject. Counterexamples include cases like (8), where the antecedent is a *psych*-verb experiencer:

(8) Ziji$_i$ de xiaohai mei de jiang de xiaoxi shi Lisi$_i$ hen
self DE child not get prize DE news make Lisi very
nanguo.
sad
'The news of his$_i$ child not getting a prize made Lisi$_i$ sad.'

An important property of *ziji* is that it refers only to animate NPs and an inanimate NP cannot be the antecedent. As observed by Tang (1989) and Huang and Tang (1991), the antecedent need not c-command *ziji* as long as (i) it is contained in an inanimate subject which does, and (ii) no c-commanding animate subject intervenes. Such subcommanding antecedents are illustrated in (9)-(12):

(9) [Zhangsan$_i$ de jiaoao]$_j$ hai-le ziji$_{i/*j}$.
Zhangsan DE pride hurt-ASP self
'Zhangsan$_i$'s pride harmed him$_i$.'

(10) [Zhangsan$_i$ neiyang zuo]$_j$ dui ziji$_{i/*j}$ buli.
Zhangsan that-way do toward self not-beneficial
'Zhangsan$_i$ acting that way didn't do him$_i$ any good.'

(11) [Zhangsan$_i$ de xin]$_j$ biaoming [Lisi$_k$ hai-le ziji$_{*i/*j/k}$].
Zhangsan DE letter indicate Lisi harm-ASP self
'Zhangsan's$_i$ letter indicates that Lisi harmed himself/*him$_i$.'

(12) [Zhangsan$_i$ de xin]$_j$ biaoming [[neiben shu]$_k$ hai-le
Zhangsan DE letter indicate that-CL book harm-ASP
ziji$_{?i/*j/*k}$].
self
'Zhangsan's$_i$ letter indicates that that book harmed him$_{?i}$.'

Though Huang and Tang (1991) point out that binding cases with c-commanding antecedents and those with subcommanding antecedents must be clearly distinguished, they have no concrete proposal to account for this distinction, other than assuming that binding cases with subcommanding antecedents fall under a suitably formulated version of Principle A. We will argue against this assumption.

3. Problematic Facts about Unlike-Person Blocking

As noted in the preceding section, it follows from I-to-I analyses of LD binding that the unlike-person blocking effect should be triggered only by intervening c-commanding subjects with *phi*-features distinct from those of the putative binder. Clearly problematic for such accounts, then, is the fact, pointed out by Huang and Tang (1991), that an intervening subcommanding NP with distinct *phi*-features can also induce blocking. This fact is illustrated by the contrast between the (a) and (b) examples in (13) and (14):

(13) a. Zhangsan$_i$ renwei Lisi$_j$ de jiaoao hai-le ziji$_{i/j}$.
Zhangsan think Lisi DE arrogance harm-ASP self
'Zhangsan$_i$ felt that Lisi's$_j$ arrogance harmed him$_{i/j}$.'

b. Zhangsan$_i$ renwei wo$_j$ de jiaoao hai-le ziji$_{*i/j}$.
Zhangsan think I DE arrogance harm-ASP self
'Zhangsan$_i$ felt that my arrogance harmed *him$_i$/me.'

(14) a. Zhangsan$_i$ renwei Lisi$_j$ neiyang zuo dui ziji$_{i/j}$ buli.
Zhangsan think Lisi that-way do toward self not-beneficial
'Zhangsan$_i$ felt that Lisi$_j$ acting that way didn't do him$_{i/j}$ any good.'

b. Zhangsan$_i$ renwei ni$_j$ neiyang zuo dui ziji$_{*i/j}$ buli.
Zhangsan think you that-way do toward self not-beneficial
'Zhangsan$_i$ felt that your acting that way didn't do him$_{*i}$/you any good.'

Observing (as noted in the preceding section) that subcommanding NPs can be antecedents of *ziji*, as can experiencer non-subject NPs, Huang and Tang contend that the blocking effect is a property of binding, rather than an effect of agreement. Specifically, Huang and Tang conclude that the set of potential LD blockers is contained in the set of potential *ziji* binders.[4]

While we are in sympathy with Huang and Tang's view that the blocking effect is not related to subject-Infl agreement, the aforementioned conclusion is untenable. For example, as noted in (1)-(2), direct or oblique objects are not potential *ziji* binders. However, examples like those in (15)-(18) show that both direct and oblique objects can induce blocking, just as subjects can:

(15) Zhangsan$_i$ gaosu wo$_j$ Lisi$_k$ hen ziji$_{*i/*j/k}$.
Zhangsan tell me Lisi hate self
'Zhangsan$_i$ told me Lisi hates *him$_i$/*me/himself.'

(16) Wo$_i$ zhidao Zhangsan$_j$ gaosu ni$_k$ Lisi$_l$ hen ziji$_{*i/*j/*k/l}$.
I know Zhangsan tell you Lisi hate self
'I know Zhangsan$_i$ told you Lisi hates *me/*him$_i$/*you/himself.'

(17) Zhangsan$_i$ dui wo$_j$ shuo Lisi$_k$ chang piping ziji$_{*i/*j/k}$.
Zhangsan to me say Lisi often criticize self
'Zhangsan$_i$ told me that Lisi often criticized *him$_i$/*me/himself.'

(18) Zhangsan$_i$ cong ni$_j$ nar tingshuo Lisi$_k$ chang piping
Zhangsan from you there hear-say Lisi often criticize
ziji$_{*i/*j/k}$.
self
'Zhangsan$_i$ heard from you that Lisi often criticized him$_{*i}$/*you/himself.'

Facts such as these also pose a serious problem for analyses based on successive I-to-I relations and Spec-Infl agreement, which, as noted above, predict that only c-commanding subjects should exhibit the blocking effect.

A further difficulty for Huang and Tang's account (and for any Agr-based analyses) is presented by examples like (19) and (20):

(19) Zhangsan$_i$ zhidao wo$_j$ de xin biaoming Lisi$_k$ hai-le
Zhangsan know I DE letter show-clear Lisi harm-ASP
ziji$_{*i/*j/k}$.
self

[4] In fact, this is entailed by most other current analyses as well.

'Zhangsan$_i$ knows that my letter makes it clear that Lisi harmed *him$_i$/*me/himself.'

(20) Zhangsan$_i$ tingshuo ni$_j$ de wenzhang jielu Lisi$_k$ hen
Zhangsan hear-say you DE article reveal Lisi hate
ziji$_{*i/*j/k}$ de taitai.
self DE wife
'Zhangsan$_i$ heard that your article revealed that Lisi$_k$ hated *your/his$_{*i/k}$ wife.'

Here, as expected on the basis of examples like (11), repeated below, the LD subcommander *ni* or *wo* is not a potential antecedent. Pretheoretically, this is because the local animate c-commanding subject *Lisi* intervenes, just as it does in (11); we will refer to this phenomenon as the animate blocking effect (for potential subcommanding antecedents).

(11) [Zhangsan$_i$ de xin]$_j$ biaoming [Lisi$_k$ hai-le ziji$_{*i/*j/k}$].
Zhangsan DE letter indicate Lisi harm-ASP self
'Zhangsan's letter indicates that Lisi harmed himself.'

What is completely unexpected from the point of view of Huang and Tang's account, however, is the fact that the LD subcommanders *wo* and *ni* in (19) and (20) respectively themselves block the superordinate c-commanding animate subject *Zhangsan* from functioning as the antecedent. Note that it is indeed the unlike-person LD subcommanding NP that triggers the blocking, not the inanimate NP containing it, for inanimate NPs are not blockers. Thus examples like (19) and (20) further counterexemplify Huang and Tang's claim that blockers of LD binding must themselves be potential *ziji*-binders. On the basis of all the facts cited so far in this section, we reject any claim that unlike-person blocking is related either to Spec-Infl agreement or to the notion of potential binder. Indeed, given the fact (noted above in footnote 3) that only distinctness of person – but not of gender or number – appears to play a role in blocking, we consider it rather implausible that any syntactic basis for this effect exists.

4. Problematic Facts about subcommand and Animate Blocking

As noted above in (11) and (12), the antecedent of *ziji* can be a subcommanding NP, subject to the animate blocking effect. In particular, the intervention of a c-commanding inanimate subject degrades acceptability only slightly, even if it contains a subcommanding animate NP (though in this case the closer animate subcommander is the preferred antecedent, other things being equal). These facts were illustrated in (12), repeated here, and (21):

(12) [Zhangsan$_i$ de xin]$_j$ biaoming [[neiben shu]$_k$ hai-le
Zhangsan DE letter indicate that-CL book harm-ASP
ziji$_{?i/*j/*k}$].
self
'Zhangsan's$_i$ letter indicates that that book harmed him$_{?i}$.'

(21) [Zhangshan$_i$ de hua]$_j$ anshi [Lisi$_k$ de xin]$_l$ zai yingshe
Zhangsan DE speech imply Lisi DE letter ASP allude-to
ziji$_{?i/*j/k/*l}$.
self
'Zhangsan's$_i$ words implied that Lisi's$_k$ letter was alluding to him$_{?i}$/himself$_k$.'

As with the unlike-person blocking effect, we consider animate blocking to be a pragmatic or discourse processing effect. To begin with, we are not aware of any independent evidence to suggest that the animate/inanimate distinction in Chinese is in any sense a syntactic one. Moreover, as the following examples show, animacy blocking is ameliorated by focusing the putative blocker with *shi*. The analogous examples with intervening c-commanding inanmimate NPs are also ameliorated by *shi* focusing, to the point of becoming fully acceptable:

(22) Zhangsan$_i$ de hua anshi shi Lisi$_j$ de xin zai
Zhangsan DE speech imply FOC Lisi DE letter ASP
yingshe ziji$_{i/j}$.
allude-to self
'Zhangsan's$_i$ words imply that it was Lisi$_i$'s letter that was alluding to him$_{i/j}$.'

(23) Zhangsan$_i$ de xin anshi shi Lisi$_j$ hai-le ziji$_{?i/j}$.
Zhangsan DE letter imply FOC Lisi harm-ASP self
'Zhangsan's$_i$ letter implies that it was Lisi who harmed him$_{?i}$/himself.'

(24) Zhangsan$_i$ de xin biaoming shi neiben shu
Zhangsan DE letter show-clear FOC that-CL book
hai-le ziji$_i$.
harm-ASP self
'Zhangsan's$_i$ letter makes it clear that it was that book that harmed him$_i$.'

For example, (22) is ambiguous; which interpretation is preferred in a given context depends not on syntax, but on what is presupposed (that someone wrote a letter alluding to Zhangsan, or that someone wrote a letter alluding to himself/herself).

There is further evidence that discourse or pragmatic considerations, not syntactic ones, figure prominently in the phenomenon of subcommanding antecedents. In the simplest subcommand examples, the antecedent is the highest subject or possessor in an inanimate subject that c-commands *ziji*, as in examples (9)-(10), repeated here, and in (25):

(9) [Zhangsan$_i$ de jiaoao]$_j$ hai-le ziji$_{i/*j}$.
Zhangsan DE pride hurt-ASP self
'Zhangsan$_i$'s pride harmed him$_i$.'

(10) [Zhangsan$_i$ neiyang zuo]$_j$ dui ziji$_{i/*j}$ buli.
Zhangsan that-way do toward self not-beneficial
'Zhangsan$_i$ acting that way didn't do him$_i$ any good.'

(25) [[Zhangsan$_i$ de] baba$_j$ de qian] bei ziji$_{*i/j}$ de pengyou
Zhangsan DE father DE money BEI self DE friend
touzou-le.
steal-ASP
'[Zhangsan's$_i$ father's]$_j$ money was stolen by his$_{*i/j}$ friend.'
(Tang's 1989 judgments)

On the basis of such examples, Tang (1989) proposed a syntactic account, whereby, in case a c-commanding subject fails to be animate, antecedency can pass to the highest subject (or possessor) contained within it. However, as noted by Wang (1990), Tang's judgments seem to reflect only preferences, which may be overridden by pragmatic factors. Thus, example (25) above can occur in discourses like the one in (26):

(26) Zhangsan$_i$ de baba de qian bei ziji$_i$ de pengyou
Zhangsan DE father DE money BEI self DE friend
touzou-le.
steal-ASP
'Zhangsan's$_i$ father's money was stolen by his$_i$ friend.'

Mama de shu ye bei ziji de pengyou touzoule.
mother DE book also BEI self DE friend steal-ASP
'(His) mother's book was also stolen by his friend.'

Ta ji-de ku qilai.
he worry cry start
'He worried so much and started crying.'

Here it is clear that *Zhangsan*, not *Zhangsan de baba*, is the antecedent, counterexemplifying Tang's claim. The second sentence of (26) is also of interest because it is another case where *ziji* need not have a c-commanding or subcommanding antecedent, even though a potential subcommanding antecedent *Mama* is available. And in example (27), there simply is no syntactic antecedent:

(27) Zhangsan$_i$ de qian he Lisi$_j$ de shu dou bei ziji$_{i\&j}$ de
Zhangsan DE money and Lisi DE book both BEI self DE
pengyou touzou-le.
friend steal-ASP
'Zhangsan's$_i$ money and Lisi's$_j$ books were both stolen by their$_{i\&j}$ friend(s).'

Instead, *ziji* has a discourse (split) antecedent, viz. the aggregate entity consisting of Zhangsan and Lisi, an entity which is not referred to by any NP but rather must be inferred from the context.

Taking stock, the facts we have examined so far can evidently be summarized as follows:

(28)
i. An antecedent of *ziji* must be animate, and can never be a (local or superordinate) direct or oblique object.[5]
ii. A c-commanding animate subject can always be the antecedent of *ziji*, subject only to the unlike-person blocking effect.[6]
iii. subcommanding antecedents cannot be accounted for as a minimal syntactic generalization of binding by c-commanding subjects (e.g. by a version of Principle A). Instead they are a special case of discourse (nonsyntactic) binding, and are subject to the completely distinct (pragmatic) animate blocking effect, which in turn can be ameliorated pragmatically.

[5]But see footnote 10.

[6]But in section 5, we exhibit some counterexamples, which our theory will explain.

Thus, it appears that instances of *ziji* are of two distinct kinds: what we will call syntactic reflexives vs. discourse reflexives. Reflexives bound by c-commanding subjects are syntactic reflexives; all others are discourse reflexives.

5. O-Command vs. C-Command

What are sometimes called the core cases of *ziji*-binding, or what we are calling the syntactic instances, are those cases where *ziji* is coindexed with a local or superordinate animate subject, as in examples (1)-(5) above. It is almost universally assumed that in such cases, the syntactically relevant relationship between *ziji* and its binder is the tree-configurational relationship of c-command. Now as Huang and Tang (1991) have pointed out, binding of *ziji* by a superordinate subject can extend into relative clauses and adverbial clauses:

(29) Zhangsan$_i$ shuo [[ruguo Lisi$_j$ piping ziji$_{i/j}$], ta jiu bu qu].
Zhangsan say if Lisi criticize self he then not go
'Zhangsan$_i$ says that if Lisi criticizes him$_i$/himself, he won't go.'

(30) Zhangsan$_i$ bu xihuan [neixie [e$_j$ piping ziji$_{i/j}$] de ren$_j$]]
Zhangsan not like those criticize self DE person
'Zhangsan$_i$ does not like those people who criticize him$_i$/themselves.'

It should be observed that in such cases, *ziji* is always contained in an object or sentential complement which is a coargument of the binder. However, it is interesting to note that, by contrast, the subject of a clause cannot always bind an instance of *ziji* which is contained in an adjunct of that clause and which is c-commanded by that subject. As shown in (31)-(32), this holds true whether the adjunct precedes or follows the clause to which it adjoins:

(31) Zhangsan shuo$_i$ [[ruguo Lisi$_j$ piping ziji$_{i/j/*k}$, [Wangwu$_k$
Zhangsan say if Lisi criticize self Wangwu
jiu bu hui qu]]].
then not will go
'Zhangsan$_i$ says that if Lisi criticizes him$_{i/*k}$/himself, Wangwu$_k$ won't go.

(32) Zhangsan$_i$ shuo [Wangwu$_j$ bu hui qu, [yinwei Lisi$_k$ mei
Zhangsan say Wangwu not will go because Lisi have-not
yaoqing ziji$_{i/*j/k}$]].
invite self

'Zhangsan$_i$ says that Wangwu$_j$ won't go because Lisi didn't invite him$_{i/*j}$/himself.'

Example (32) is particularly telling, since, out of context, the binding by *Wangwu* would appear to be pragmatically favored, and yet it is unacceptable, in spite of the fact that binding by either a higher or lower subject is wholly acceptable. Binding cases involving relative clauses provide a further interesting contrast. Consider example (33), where the reflexive occurs in a relative clause:

(33) Lisi$_i$ zhidao [Zhangsan$_j$ bu xihuan [neixie [e$_k$ piping
Lisi know Zhangsan not like those criticize
ziji$_{i/j/k}$ de ren$_k$]]]
self DE person
'Lisi$_i$ knows that Zhangsan$_j$ doesn't like those people who criticize him$_{i/j}$/themselves.'

Either the matrix subject or the subject of the clause immediately containing the relative clause, can be the antecedent of *ziji*, in contrast to examples in (31) and (32), where *ziji* occurs in an adverbial clause. The difference between relative clauses and adverbial clauses is that a relative clause is contained in a coargument of the subject, and hence an instance of *ziji* within the relative clause can take as its antecedent the subject of the immediate clause containing the relative clause. Facts such as these, which would appear to be difficult to square with c-command-based accounts, will be explained by our analysis.

6. Toward a New Analysis of *Ziji*

For English pronouns and anaphors, Pollard and Sag (1992a, 1992b, 1994) have developed an alternative to the standard binding theory of Chomsky (1986). We sketch here the essential features of that alternative theory. Of particular interest in the present connection is Principle A. First, it is assumed that the obligatory grammatical dependents of a verb (or more generally, any head) are linearly ordered by an abstract OBLIQUENESS relation as in (34); crucially, adjuncts do not participate in the obliqueness hierarchy.

(34) The Obliqueness Hierarchy:
SUBJECT $\prec$ PRIMARY OBJECT $\prec$ SECOND OBJECT $\prec$ OTHER COMPLEMENTS

Second, all non-expletive NPs in English inherently belong to one of the following referential types: ANAPHORS (reflexives and reciprocals), P-PRONOUNS (pronouns other than anaphors), and NON-PRONOUNS.

Third, the relation of o-command is defined as in (35):[7]

(35) O-Command:
X O-COMMANDS Y just in case X is a less oblique coargument of some Z that dominates Y .
In case Z = Y, X is said to LOCALLY o-command Y.

Fourth, o-binding is defined as in (36):

(36) O-Binding:
X (LOCALLY) O-BINDS Y iff X and Y are coindexed and X (locally) o-commands Y; Y is (LOCALLY) O-FREE if it is not (locally) o-bound.

With these definitions in place, Principle A is formulated as in (37):

(37) Principle A for English:
An anaphor must be locally o-bound if it has a referential (= nonexpletive) local o-commander.

As Pollard and Sag argue, this formulation of Principle A, which makes no reference to such tree-configurational notions as government and c-command, accounts for the full range of standard English anaphor binding facts, as well as a wide array of longstanding counterexamples to the standard formulation of Principle A (Chomsky 1986).

Notice that this formulation of Principle A requires an anaphor to be o-bound only if it has a referential local o-commander; otherwise the anaphor is exempt from the binding theory and is subject only to semantic, pragmatic, and processing-based constraints. Now it is clear that this principle says nothing about LD anaphors like *ziji*, nor was it intended to. To fill this lacuna, following Pollard and Sag (1992a), we propose a fourth referential type, Z-PRONOUN, together with an additional binding principle, called Principle Z, given in (38):[8]

[7] For expository purposes, we simplify slightly. The o-command relation actually holds not for constituents, but rather for the corresponding values of lexically specified valence features (See Pollard and Sag 1994). Thus, this analysis, like that of Reinhart and Reuland (1991, 1993) relates syntactic binding directly to argument structure.

[8] This formulation differs slightly from that given in Pollard and Sag (1992a).

(38) Principle Z:
Z-pronouns must be o-bound.

It should be noted that in Chinese, we must allow for the possibility that in some positions, either syntactic or discourse binding of *ziji* is possible (see examples in (13), (14) and (24)). We are now in the process of developing such an account. Provisionally, the main outlines of our current theory of *ziji* are as given in (39):

(39) Analysis of *ziji*:

i. *Ziji* is inherently animate, and ambiguous between a z-pronoun (syntactic *ziji*) and a discourse pronoun (discourse *ziji*).

ii. Syntactic *ziji* must be o-bound by a subject, subject to the pragmatic constraint of unlike-person blocking.[9]

iii. Discourse *ziji* is subject to the pragmatic constraint of animate blocking.

Now together with the putative Chinese-specific requirement that *ziji*-binders must be animate subjects, this principle already accounts for many of the facts cited above: subject orientation, LD binding, and the possibility of subcommanding antecedents. In particular, the facts in (29)-(33) that were problematic for the c-command-based accounts are predicted to the letter, since the impossible binders are precisely those that fail to o-command *ziji*.

We close by reconsidering example (32), repeated here:

(32) Zhangsan$_i$ shuo [Wangwu$_j$ bu hui qu, [yinwei Lisi$_k$ mei
Zhangsan say Wangwu not will go because Lisi have-not
yaoqing ziji$_{i/*j/k}$]].
invite self
'Zhangsan$_i$ says that Wangwu$_j$ won't go because Lisi didn't invite him$_{i/*j}$/himself$_k$.'

[9]Note that our formulation of subject orientation does not prevent *ziji* from being coindexed with an o-commanding object, as long as it is also coindexed with an o-commanding subject. Thus, examples like the following are not ruled out:

Zhangsan$_i$ yao Lisi$_j$ [PRO$_j$ xiang xuesheng jieshao ziji$_{i/j}$.]
Zhangsan ask Lisi toward student introduce self
'Zhangsan$_i$ asked Lisi to introduce him$_i$/himself to the students.'

Here PRO denotes not a constituent, but rather the value of the SUBJ feature of *jieshao*. See footnote 7.

Our account now runs as follows. First, *ziji* here can be a z-pronoun. In that case, either *Zhangsan* or *Lisi* (but not *Wangwu*) can bind it, since these are the only o-commanding subjects; as noted already, *Wangwu* only c-commands *ziji*, but does not o-command it. Second, suppose *ziji* here were a discourse pronoun. According to our theory, then, Principle Z does not apply. On purely syntactic grounds, then, there is nothing to rule out *Wangwu* as a discourse antecedent. But then, what rules it out?

The explanation, we suggest, lies with whatever pragmatic factors govern discourse binding. This suggestion is strongly supported by the following example:

(40) Wangwu$_j$ bu hui qu, [yinwei Lisi$_k$ mei yaoqing ziji$_{j/k}$.
Wangwu not will go because Lisi have-not invite self
Wangwu$_j$ won't go because Lisi$_k$ didn't invite him$_j$/himself$_k$.'

Note that this is just the sentential complement of (32), and yet *Wangwu* is now a possible antecedent. It is difficult to imagine a syntactic account of this contrast in any framework we are familiar with. Rather, it would appear that removal of the matrix context eliminates whatever pragmatic factors, say discourse prominence, logophoricity, or point of view, that disfavored *Wangwu* as the antecedent in (32).

Modulo precise accounts of the pragmatic blocking effects, this theory accounts for all the facts we have cited, including the ambiguous examples in (13), (14), and (24), since nothing prevents o-commanded *ziji* from being discourse bound. The ambiguity is an immediate consequence of the fact that *ziji* itself is ambiguous between a z-pronoun and a discourse pronoun.[10]

References

Baker, C. L. 1994. Locally free reflexives, contrast, and discourse prominence in British English. Presented at *the Annual Meeting of the Linguistic Society of America*, Boston (manuscript, University of Texas at Austin).

Battistella, E. 1989. Chinese reflexivization: A movement to INFL approach. *Linguistics* 27, 987-1012.

[10]There is ample evidence that in certain literary or British varieties, discourse-bound reflexives are permitted in positions where local syntactic binding is also an option. See Zribi-Hertz (1989), Reinhart and Reuland (1993), and Baker (1994).

Battistella, E., and Y.-H. Xu. 1990. Remarks on the reflexive in Chinese. *Linguistics* 28, 205-240.

Chomsky, N. 1986. *Knowledge of Language: Its Nature, Origin, and Use.* New York: Praeger.

Cole, P., Hermon, G., and Sung, L-M. 1990. Principles and parameters of long-distance reflexives. *Linguistic Inquiry* 21, 1-22.

Huang, C.-T. J. and Tang, C.-C, J. 1991. The local nature of the long-distance reflexive in Chinese. *Long-distance Anaphora*, ed. by J. Koster and E. Reuland, 263-282. Cambridge: Cambridge University Press.

Pollard , C. J. and Sag, I. 1992a. Binding Theory. In Byung-Soo Park, ed., *Linguistic Studies on Natural Language.* Kyunghee Language Institute Monographs, Vol. 1. Seoul: Hanshin.

Pollard , C. J. and Sag, I. 1992b. Anaphors in English and the scope of binding theory. *Linguistic Inquiry* 23, 261-303.

Pollard, C. and I. A. Sag 1994. *Head-Driven Phrase Structure Grammar.* The University of Chicago Press and CSLI Publication.

Progovac, L. 1992. Long-distance reflexives without movement. *Linguistic Inquiry* 23, 671-680.

Reinhart, T. and E. Reuland. 1991. Anaphors and logophors: An argument structure perspective. *Long-Distance Anaphors*, ed. by J. Koster and E. Reuland, 238-321. Cambridge: Cambridge University Press.

Reinhart, T. and E. Reuland. 1993. Reflexivity. *Linguistic Inquiry* 24, 657-720.

Tang, C.-C. J. 1989. Chinese reflexives. *Natural Language and Linguistic Theory* 7, 93-121.

Wang, J-H. 1990. Ziji - A Chinese long-distance anaphor. Unpublished manuscript. Carnegie Mellon University.

Zribi-Hertz, A. 1989. Anaphora binding and narrative point of view: English reflexive pronouns in sentence and discourse. *Language* 65, 695-727.

Syntax
&
Semantics

Meaning, Movement and Economy

DAVID ADGER
University of York

1. Introduction

In German, subjects of stage level predicates[1] may appear either before or after a sentential adverb (Diesing 1992: 78):

(1) weil ja doch zwei Cellisten in diesem Hotel abgestiegen sind
since indeed two cellists in this hotel stayed
'...since two (of the) cellists stayed in this hotel'

(2) weil zwei Cellisten ja doch in diesem Hotel abgestiegen sind
since two cellists indeed in this hotel stayed
'...since two of the cellists stayed in this hotel'

Assuming that the position of the sentential adverb is fixed, this means that there is an optional process that moves the object from one position to another (traditionally termed SCRAMBLING).

Such a process is at first sight problematic for the Minimalist program (Chomsky 1992) where optional operations are not countenanced. Under this program, syntactic operations are forced by morphological checking requirements. Assume that in (2) the subject has moved from a position corresponding to its position in (1). Then Minimalism predicts that (2) is well formed only if the subject has moved to check morphological features.

---

[1] I will ignore what happens with individual level predicates throughout this paper. See Kratzer (1989) for discussion.

This means that (1) and (2) contain different lexical items: (2) has a DP containing a kind of morphological feature which the DP in (1) lacks.

Is there any evidence for this position? That is, are there morphological differences between (1) and (2) which would allow us to claim that they involve a different selection of elements from the lexicon?

One might argue, given cross-linguistic evidence, that there are languages which force the subject to move to a derived position (e.g. English) and languages which deny the subject access to the derived position (perhaps Irish - see McCloskey 1993), at least at the point of SPELLOUT (S-Structure). The idea would be that English has only the type of DP that needs to raise, that German has ambiguous DPs and that Irish has the type of DP that doesn't have to raise, and therefore, given Economy, won't.[2] We could perhaps tie this down to the morphology of the D. Since we have a way of accounting for cross-linguistic variation with respect to the position of subjects in English and Irish which requires us to posit two different types of DP, it might then come as no surprise that some languages have both.

A curious empirical fact that such an explanation seems to have no way of capturing is that (1) and (2) have different felicity conditions (and in fact different truth conditions because of this). (1) is felicitous in a context where the existence of cellists is presupposed or not, while (2) is felicitous *only* when the existence of cellists is presupposed (hence the slightly different translations). This is curious because no such conditions hold on English or Irish subjects. Yet if the positional difference between (1) and (2) derives purely from a morphological difference, then we would like to explain the difference in felicity conditions in the same way. However, since we are assimilating (2) to the position of subjects in English, and (1) to the position of subjects in Irish, we would then predict that English subjects would always require their referent to be presupposed; this is not the case.

What I will do in this paper is provide an alternative analysis which does not require stipulations about the morphology and does explain the cross-linguistic variation in the correlations between position of a DP and the presuppositional status of that DP. The assumption which will drive the analysis is the rather anti-minimalist one that derivations are driven in a limited fashion by a requirement that they be meaningful. I will argue that this view is constrained enough that it does not compromise the autonomy of syntax.

---

[2] The properties of the DP rather than of the checking functional head matter because of Greed, which states that elements move only to satisfy their own morphological requirements.

2. Quantifiers and Interpretation

Lets consider in a little more depth what the difference in meaning between (1) and (2) is.

Consider the following examples from Milsark (1977):

(3) Many unicorns are in the garden
(4) There are many unicorns in the garden
(5) Most unicorns are in the garden
(6) *There are most unicorns in the garden

Milsark pointed out that in (3) there are two possible interpretations for the subject: in one interpretation the sentence states that the cardinality of the set of unicorns in the garden is fairly large (depending on the context); the other interpretation is one where a set of unicorns is assumed and the ones in the garden are a fairly large proportion of that set. We will follow Partee's (1988) terminology and call the first reading CARDINAL and the second PROPORTIONAL. Milsark termed such quantifiers WEAK QUANTIFIERS, and we can follow Reinhart (1987) and term DPs containing weak quantifiers WEAK DPS. Note that the two readings differ truth-conditionally; if there is no such thing as a unicorn, then the cardinal reading is false, whereas the proportional reading is not false, but rather truth-conditionally undefined. A peculiarity of the existential construction in English is that the proportional reading vanishes (4).

The sentence in (5) has only one (relevant) interpretation, corresponding to the proportional reading of (3). If unicorns don't exist, this sentence is not false, but rather its truth value is not specified. Milsark termed these quantifiers STRONG QUANTIFIERS, and we will speak also of STRONG DPS. Given the comment about existential constructions above, we then expect *most unicorns* to be ruled out in such a construction: as indeed it is (6).

The German data in (1) and (2) seem to be essentially the mirror image of the English data in (3) and (4). Post-copular position in an existential sentence in English gives rise to a DEFINITENESS-EFFECT, while pre-sentential adverb position in German could be said to give rise to an ANTI-DEFINITENESS EFFECT. When the subject appears to the right of the adverb, it may have either a proportional or a cardinal reading. When it appears to the left, only the proportional reading is available.
The felicity effects mentioned above follow, since the proportional reading requires that there be a set presupposed to have some proportion of.

Interestingly, although there is a class of quantifiers that head DPs which are barred from definiteness effect environments (strong quantifiers), there is no corresponding class which head DPs that are barred from anti-definiteness effect environments.[3] Strong quantifiers have only a proportional semantics, weak quantifiers have a proportional or cardinal semantics, but there is no class of 'super-weak' quantifiers which have only a cardinal semantics. Why should there be this gap?

This curious fact is explained if we assume that weak quantifiers are lexically specified as having a cardinal semantics only. The proportional reading arises when the language-user is forced to presuppose a set to which the weak DP can be related. This can happen either via inference, to make the sentence felicitous, or via syntactic information. The analysis of the German examples is that the proportional reading of the weak DP in (1) arises pragmatically, while in (2) it arises because of the syntactic position of the DP (I go into this in more detail below). I argue for this view of the semantics of weak DPs in more detail in Adger (1994a) and will assume it here.

This view entails that there is no 'gap' in the quantifiers natural language uses. Lexically there are only proportional quantifiers and cardinal ones. It is a result of the ability of language-user to presuppose a set, and to relate a linguistically defined set to that, that derives 'proportional' readings of weak DPs. One cannot 'unpresuppose' a set, so there can be no cardinal reading of strong quantifiers.

This view is rather different to that proposed by Diesing (1992), and by de Hoop (1992), who are also both concerned with cardinal and proportional readings of weak DPs. Diesing assumes that the reading of a weak DP is given entirely by its syntactic position, thus proposing a very strict mapping relationship between syntax and semantics. De Hoop argues that the readings are given by the type assignment of the DP, and that this is derived from different types of Case assigned to the DP. Although this view does not entail a strict correlation between position and interpretation, it does imply that the syntax determines the interpretation.

Under the system I have proposed (Adger 1994a), and will assume here, the syntax can underdetermine the interpretation. That is, the LF representation does not constitute the 'proposition' in all cases. Specifically, the proportional reading of an unscrambled DP in German arises via inference. However, there certainly needs to be a statement of 'mapping' between the syntax and the interpretation; the scrambled DP in (2) can only be

[3] Note that I am talking about the quantifiers here. There are classes of DPs which are barred from anti-definiteness effect envronments. Selected measure phrases are such a class. For discussion see Adger (1994c) and Adger (1994a).

interpreted as proportional, and this seems to be the result of a syntactic fact.

In Adger (1994a), I argued that a DP in the specifier of AgrP at LF was interpreted as proportional because Agr features were essentially pronominal (this idea traces back to Mahajan 1990). Scrambled DPs were scrambled into the specifier of an AgrP position, and hence were interpreted as proportional. This is empirically roughly equivalent to Diesing's claim that IP internal DPs are interpreted as proportional (which derives from her Mapping Hypothesis), or to de Hoop's claim that DPs which receive 'strong' Case are proportional (deriving from her Case to Type mapping). The differences arise in that I do not claim that the proportional reading of unscrambled DPs arises because that DP raises at LF to a position internal to IP, or is optionally assigned 'strong' rather than 'weak' Case.

It is not relevant to the point of this paper which particular version of 'mapping' is assumed, and I will remain as agnostic as possible. What is at issue is the cross-linguistic variation in the interpretative possibilities of DPs. That is, why are scrambled subjects only proportional in German, while subjects in English are ambiguous?

3. Syntax and Interpretation

There are, a priori, a number of answers one might give to this question: the fact of scrambling induces the proportional reading; the S-Structure properties of the position of the scrambled DP in German and the subject in English are different (they are different positions or they contain different features); the LF positions of the DPs in the two languages are different.

Let us make the most constraining assumption, that the phrase structure of German and English is identical. We will also assume that arguments are generated within the projection of their theta-assigning head (the Lexical Clause Hypothesis - Koopman & Sportiche 1991). Subjects in English and German then, are generated within the VP and then (possibly) move to a VP external position. The S-Structure position of the subject in English is fairly clearly external to VP, as is the position of the scrambled DP in German. The position of the unscrambled DP in German is less clear.

If we want to follow the first route, claiming that the fact of scrambling induces the proportional reading, then in order to achieve any explanatory power we must show that scrambling is characterised in such a way that it automatically derives the proportional reading. Scrambling should then be very different from subject placement in English. One possibility would be to claim that scrambled DPs are base generated and bind a resumptive null pronoun in the VP; it is then the semantics of this pronoun that leads to the proportionality of the scrambled DP.[4]

However, under such a story, it is unclear why the semantics of a scrambled DP should be different from that of a left-dislocated DP. The latter are not necessarily proportional:

(7) Many foxes, Anson thought he would be able to see.

This type of account also falls foul of the clause-bounded property of scrambling (Fanselow 1990). In addition there appear to be a number of arguments that scrambling is an A-movement process (Van den Wyngaerd 1989; Mahajan 1990; Moltmann 1991; de Hoop 1992). I refer the reader to the literature.

The other possibility, that the scrambled position in German is different in some semantically crucial respect from the subject position in English, also requires independent confirmation. De Hoop (1990) provides an analysis where the subject position in English can receive two different types of Case, correlating with the two different types of interpretation. The position to which a DP is scrambled in German would only receive the kind of Case that gives a proportional reading.[5]

Another story along the same lines is suggested by Runner (1994). He proposes, along with Adger (1994a) and Mahajan (1990), that a DP in the specifier of AgrP is interpreted in a special way (that leads to a proportional reading for weak DPs). If scrambling is movement to the specifier of an Agr projection, then this will account for why scrambled DPs are proportional. Runner sketches a proposal that Agr contains anaphoric and pronominal features, just as DPs do. The Agr involved in scrambling is pronominal, leading to the interpretational facts, while the Agr involved in English subject case assignment is non-pronominal, so there are no particular interpretational correlates.

Both of these accounts describe the facts, but neither explains why these facts should hold.

The final possibility is the one assumed by Diesing. Diesing claims that there is a strict mapping between the syntactic position of a DP and the interpretation of that DP. If a weak DP is external to VP but within IP, it is

[4]Obenauer (to appear) argues for an analysis close to that outlined here for the phenonemon of optional past participle agreement in French when an object is wh-extracted.

[5]De Hoop makes her case with Dutch, where the facts are similar. The analysis carries over unproblematically to German.

interpreted as proportional; if it is internal to VP it is interpreted as cardinal.[6] Diesing defines an algorithm (the Mapping Hypothesis) that checks the position of a DP in the tree, and assigns it the appropriate interpretation.

The position of the scrambled DP is assumed to be external to VP. Diesing therefore predicts that it is interpreted as proportional, as it is. She assumes that the DP to the right of the adverb is in its base generated in situ VP-internal position. According to her theory, it is therefore only given a cardinal reading. This is in fact not true, as we noted at the start of the paper. Under Diesing's assumptions this DP must raise at LF to get a proportional reading. However, under the assumptions about the semantics of weak DPs that I outlined above, no LF raising is necessary, providing the mapping hypothesis (in whatever form it takes) says nothing about VP internal elements. This is because a VP internal weak DP can have a proportional reading that arises simply because the language-user assumes a set which the DP can be a part of.

The more interesting case for our purposes is English. English subjects are clearly outside of VP, and yet they may have either a proportional or a cardinal reading. Diesing, to maintain her strict mapping, claims that in English the subject may lower into its original position (optionally) during the derivation from S-Structure to LF. If it lowers, then it is internal to VP at LF; the theory then predicts it is cardinal. If it does not lower, the theory predicts it is proportional.

The interesting question then becomes, why is lowering allowed in English but not in German? Essentially we can either say that the mapping algorithm applies at S-Structure in German, but at LF in English, or we can say that LF-lowering is allowed in English, but barred in German. Either way we simply state the difference. Furthermore, if we take the Minimalist conception of the grammar at all seriously, then neither option is open to us, since there is no S-Structure on which to define the algorithm, and lowering operations as such are barred.

Stepping back from the details, we have seen that in some languages weak DPs in derived positions systematically get a proportional reading (we have only looked at German subjects here; the same type of phenomenon is found for objects, and across languages as diverse as Turkish (Enç 1990), Dutch (Rullman 1989; de Hoop 1992); Hindi (Mahajan 1990); Italian (Pinto

---

[6]Diesing excludes the C system from consideration. Diesing derives the generalisation described in the text from her Mapping Hypothesis, which maps material in VP into the nuclear scope of a Heimian quantificational structure (Heim 1981; chapter 2); material from IP is mapped into the restrictive clause of this same structure.

1994); Catalan (Solà 1992) and see Adger 1994a, Runner 1993;1994 , and Meinunger 1994 for arguments that case and agreement phenomena follow similar patterns. On arguments that clitic doubling in Greek follows the same pattern, see Anagnostopoulou 1994). In other languages (English) weak DPs in derived positions can have either a cardinal or a proportional reading. We have seen three possible ways of dealing with this fact, all of which boil down to parameterising the two sets of languages with respect to whether they behave one way or the other.

In the rest of this paper I will show that this parameter derives from the fact that the languages which show the anti-definiteness effect (German etc.) have an alternative derivation to achieve the cardinal reading. In each case this derivation is cheaper than the derivation that would involve scrambling the object. The latter is therefore ruled out by principles of Economy. So in German, there is no cardinal reading for a scrambled object because the object can just be left in situ to have that reading, and it's less costly to leave something in situ than to move it. In English the object can't be left in situ (because of a morphological property of I in English) so there is no cheaper derivation to get a cardinal reading for the object. The parameterisation of the two languages follows.

The next section outlines the theoretical machinery needed to derive this result.

4. Movement and Economy

Chomsky (1991; 1992) has recently proposed that a number of grammatical principles might be reduced to principles governing the complexity of derivations and representations, where complexity is to be theoretically pinned down. For example, the principle of 'least-effort' requires that a derivation must be as 'short' as possible deriving the effects of the ECP under a relativised minimality view of the latter (Rizzi 1990). A further principle of Economy prohibits operations which are not needed to enable the derivation to successfully converge (Greed and Procrastinate are subparts of this principle, disallowing particular subtypes of operation). For my purposes, it is sufficient to propose a rather general theory of Economy, of the following sort:

(8) *Economy*:
Minimise computational operations

This principle has two immediate effects: it rules out optional operations (thus if a representation is well formed no operation may apply to that representation) and it requires operations to be computationally minimal (thus to derive the effects of relativised minimality the derivation should be as 'short' as possible, although there are empirical questions to be answered about what counts as a 'shorter' derivation).

Computational operations are copying, insertion and deletion, as in the earliest versions of transformational grammar (Chomsky 1955). I will assume that movement consists of (one or more) copying operations, followed by a deletion operation, as argued in Chomsky (1992). Note that deletion may take place at LF to satisfy the requirements of Full Interpretation (as discussed in Chomsky 1992 for reconstruction effects) or at PF (perhaps for cases of ellipsis, etc.). Deletion is of course subject to recoverability of content.

We may now reconsider LF-lowering operations in Diesing's sense to be deletion of either the topmost part of a chain, or its lower part at LF. Thus a sentence containing a weak subject of a stage level predicate will have a step in its derivation of the following form (abstracting away from irrelevant structure):

(9)[$_{IP}$ [many unicorns] [$_{VP}$ [many unicorns] arrived]]

Let us just stipulate for the moment that this is not a well-formed LF structure; the reason why it is not well formed is because, if we try to apply some version of the mapping algorithm to it, we tear it in half.[7]

However, we may freely delete up to recoverability. That is we may delete either the weak DP in the specifier of IP, or that in the specifier of VP, with no loss of thematic meaning.[8] This will result in two possible structures:

(10)a. [$_{IP}$ [many unicorns] [$_{VP}$ arrived]]
b. [$_{IP}$ [$_{VP}$ [many unicorns] arrived]]

---

[7]This is not actually quite accurate if we adopt the weaker version of the mapping that I suggested above, where the mapping algorithm says nothing about elements in VP. However, under such a view, this LF will still be ill-formed under the requirement of Effability, discussed directly below.

[8]If thematic meaning is read from LF one might wonder how a subject in the specifier of IP receives a theta-role from V when the lower half of the chain has been deleted. There are a number of technical solutions to this problem: theta-roles are assigned to the chain as a whole, so even if parts of the chain are deleted, that actual chain still receives a role; theta-roles percolate through the tree and are assigned at LF directly (using the mechanisms outlined in Higginbotham 1985); deletion leaves behind a trace which counts for theta-role transmission but not for the mapping algorithm, etc.

Note that both structures are equally economical since they both consist of exactly the same number of steps.

It is important to note that these structures are not related to the 'surface forms' that are SPELLEDOUT. (10)b. corresponds to a 'surface form' where the subject is in the specifier of IP position.

Returning now to the question of what motivates any computational operation, it is crucial to determine what precisely constitutes a well-formed representation in order to appreciate the effects of (8). Chomsky (1992) spends some effort arguing that computational operations are driven by the morphological requirements of lexical items (the theory of Checking). The idea is that a computational operation is forced to occur in order that some morphological property of a (projection of a) lexical item (or more likely two) can be satisfied. So, for example, the requirement that the subject position in English be filled, is due to the requirement that a subject check its case features. Tense assigns nominative case features, and if a subject DP is endowed with such features, it is required to move to check them - in English pre-SPELLOUT.

As well as this, I would like to propose that there is a requirement of Effability: that is computational operations are also driven by the need to express certain propositions.

This view entails that there exists a universal semantics that is given by the performance system of the mind/brain, in much the same way that there is a universal phonetics given by the acoustic/articulatory systems. (I)-Language is viewed as an independent system, the structure of which is motivated by its own formal properties. For communicative purposes it is an unnecessary but fortuitous fact that I-language may be given an interpretation by the two systems mentioned above; that is a linguistic representation may be interpreted by the acoustic/articulatory performance systems, and by the conceptual/intentional performance systems. Given this, a link between sound and meaning can be partially created (see Chomsky 1955; 1957 and for a more recent exposition of the same view 1992).

In such a system it is crucial that the universal phonetics and the universal semantics are given independently of the language. There may of course be constraints on such systems that hold across human beings (for example the constraint that closure proceeds plosivity in phonetics;[9] or that restrictive quantification is conservative (in the sense of Barwise & Cooper 1981)), but such constraints are not linguistic.

---

[9]Thanks to Richard Ogden for suggesting this possibility.

Assume then some generative system that will derive for us the possible meanings. Let us restrict ourselves to propositional meanings, perhaps singled out because of truth-conditional properties (as in Fodor 1987's system). If we define P as the set of all possible propositions[10] (abstracting away here from questions etc.) given by the conceptual-intentional system, and we define L as the set of well-formed LFs given by the computational system, then we may express Effability as:

(11) *Effability*:
For every member of P there must be a member of L

As noted before we still have LFs that are well-formed by virtue of their derivation which receive no interpretation. An example might be the case discussed above where if no deletion takes place we have the same DP in two positions with different semantic requirements. There is in essence no notion of "grammaticality", since the grammar itself gives us this part of the derivation. However, if no deletion takes place, then the expression will receive no interpretation (see Chomsky 1992 for further discussion).

5. The Analysis

Let us return to our original examples. I repeat them here for convenience:

(12) weil ja doch zwei Cellisten in diesem Hotel abgestiegen sind
since indeed two cellists in this hotel stayed
'...since two (of the) cellists stayed in this hotel'

(13) weil zwei Cellisten ja doch in diesem Hotel abgestiegen sind
since two cellists indeed in this hotel stayed
'...since two of the cellists stayed in this hotel'

Consider how the various readings arise under the theory outlined so far. The cardinal reading of (12) simply arises because weak DPs have a lexically specified cardinal semantics. Given our assumptions about the proportional readings of weak DPs, the proportional reading of (12) is not a concern of the syntax; it arises simply because we are able to make sense of this sentence if we assume a set of cellists and assume that the two mentioned in (12) are part of that set. The proportional reading of the DP in (12) arises purely through inferential processes that are of a computationally different sort to the processes that characterise syntax.

[10] I am being very loose here with the notion of proposition. I mean here a construct that involves both truth-conditional content and background information. The notion of Discourse Representation Structure defined in Kamp & Reyle (1993) approximates what I am referring to.

Turning to (13), there are really two questions to be answered: what drives scrambling, and why does the scrambled DP have only a proportional reading?

Recall that Effability requires there to be an LF for each proposition. I will assume that there are two propositions relevant here: one where the subject has a cardinal reading , and one where it has a proportional reading. Effability is partially satisfied, since (12) corresponds to an LF which will give a cardinal reading. (12) does not correspond to an LF that will give a proportional reading though, since the proportional reading of (12) arises from non-syntactic factors. But Effability requires that there has to be an *LF* which gives rise to a proportional reading. There are now two possibilities to derive such an LF: we raise the VP internal subject into IP before SPELLOUT, or after.

In English there appears to be a requirement that the subject is raised by SPELLOUT. In German, this requirement does not appear to hold. If we raise the subject in German pre-SPELLOUT , then the question is whether that raising is ruled out by a cheaper derivation. Note that we have to raise at some point to satisfy Effability, otherwise there would be no LF corresponding to the proportional reading. The question then is whether LF-raising is less costly or as costly as raising pre-SPELLOUT.

The theory of Economy given in (8) does not give an answer to this question. Chomsky (1992), however, claims that LF raising is cheaper (his principle of Procrastination). The empirical evidence for this is that raising of, for example, verbs into their dominating functional heads, is blocked in English and not in French. Chomsky assumes that this is because they are forced to raise in French, but not in English. Since they are not forced to raise in English, then why can't they raise? The answer is that it is cheaper to raise post-SPELLOUT (Procrastinate). Under the alternative presented here, nothing ever forces an English verb to raise, since there is no difference in propositional content between a sentence containing a raised verb and one containing an unraised one. Given the general thrust of Economy, an English verb will then never raise. This means that the LFs of English and French are different, but only in as much as the difference is irrelevant to interpretation. Under this view, we need no stipulation that LF-raising is cheaper. It simply doesn't take place, unless it is required to by Effability.

Given this argument, it follows that a weak subject in German can raise pre-SPELLOUT, because Effability requires there to be an LF with the proportional reading of the subject. There is no competition between raising pre and post-SPELLOUT. This is what makes scrambling in German possible. The syntactic difference between English and German is just that in German a subject can get Case either in its base position or in its derived position while in English a subject can only get case in its derived position.[11]

Let us turn now to the reading of the subject in (13). The proportional reading of the subject arises due to whatever version of the mapping algorithm we assume. Under Diesing's view, the DP is in IP and it gets a proportional reading because of where it finds itself in the quantificational structure, under de Hoop's view it is assigned 'strong' Case and is therefore interpreted as a generalised quantifier, and in the view that I have defended, the fact that it is in the specifier of AgrP means that it is interpreted as familiar to a pre-established set. The particular mechanism is irrelevant here.

In the theory I have outlined above, the LF of (13) has the weak DP in the specifier of IP. That is, the copy in the specifier of VP has been deleted. The mapping algorithm applies to that. Notice that this derivation involves two computational operations: **copy α**, and **delete α**.

(14)a. [$_{IP}$ [$_{VP}$ [two cellists] stayed]] **copy** α:
b. [$_{IP}$ [two cellists] [$_{VP}$ [two cellists] stayed]] **delete** α:
c. [$_{IP}$ [two cellists] [$_{VP}$ stayed]]

Why does this derivation not compete with the derivation that gives us the proportional reading of (12)? After all, (12) involves no movement at all and should therefore be computationally more minimal. The reason is that the proportional reading of (12) doesn't involve a derivation. It's not a matter for the syntax at all. Economy is therefore irrelevant.

Why isn't there a cardinal reading for (13)? This is really the question we have been trying to answer all along. There is certainly a derivation which would give us a cardinal reading for (13). In such a derivation we first of all **copy α** pre-spellout, and then we delete the copy that is in the specifier of IP position. This gives us a structure where the weak DP is in the specifier of VP position:

(15) a. [$_{IP}$ [$_{VP}$ [two cellists] stayed]] **copy** α:
b. [$_{IP}$ [two cellists] [$_{VP}$ [two cellists] stayed]] **delete** α:
c. [$_{IP}$ [$_{VP}$ [two cellists] stayed]]

Again, this derivation involves two steps: **copy** α and **delete** α. However, in this case there is a competing derivation. The in situ derivation of the cardinal reading of (12), which involves no steps. The cardinal reading of this DP *is* given by the syntax: it's given by the fact that we have

[11]Presumably Irish subjects only get case in their VP-internal position.

syntactically put together a weak quantifier and an NP. Economy states that computational operations should be minimised. The in situ derivation of (12) is certainly more minimal than the two step derivation to derive the cardinal reading of (13) shown in (15). This derivation (15) is therefore ruled out as a possible derivation for (13). Accordingly, (13) does not have a cardinal reading.

Contrast this with the case of English. English does not allow the option of leaving a DP in its in situ position. This is because in English DPs must receive their case in their derived position. This means that derivations corresponding to (14) and (15) in English exist for the sentence:

(16) Two cellists arrived

There is no derivation to achieve the cardinal reading which involves less steps, so a derivation like that in (15) is not ruled out in English, as it is in German. (16) is therefore predicted to have both readings, as indeed it does.

6. Conclusion

This paper has outlined an approach to explaining a cross-linguistic variation in the correlations between the positions of weak DPs and their interpretations. I have discussed very little data here (the applications to a wider range of data are discussed in Adger 1994b) preferring to sketch how the approach has considerable explanatory advantage over other approaches in the literature. Intuitively, I have argued that phenomena like scrambling are motivated because of interpretative constraints (Effability) and I have outlined a theory which explains why only certain interpretations are available for scrambling constructions. This really is just a way of making explicit the earlier intuition that scrambling is a 'stylistic' movement, where we begin to understand 'stylistic' as coming under the rubric of felicity conditions.

7. References

Adger, D. (1994a) *Functional heads and interpretation*, Ph.D, University of Edinburgh.

Adger, D. (1994b) "Economy and Interpretation: deriving the parameterisation of the Mapping Hypothesis" ms. University of York. To appear in York Working Papers in Linguistics.

Adger, D. (1994c) "On the licensing of quasi-arguments," paper presented at CONSOLE, Utrecht, 1992. In P. Ackema and M. Schoorlemmer, eds., *The Proceedings of CONSOLE 1* , Holland Academic Graphics, The Hague.

Anagnostopoulou, E. (1994) "On the representation of clitic doubling in Modern Greek" ms. Unversity of Tilburg.

Barwise, J. and R. Cooper (1981) "Generalized quantifiers and natural language," *Linguistics and Philosophy* 4, 159-219.

Chomsky, N. (1955) *The Logical Structure of Linguistic Theory*, Plenum, New York.

Chomsky, N. (1957) *Syntactic Structures*, Mouton, The Hague.

Chomsky, N. (1981) *Lectures on Government and Binding*, Foris, Dordrecht.

Chomsky, N. (1989) "Some notes on economy of derivation and representation," *MIT Working Papers in Linguistics* 10, 43-74.

Chomsky, N. (1992) "A minimalist program for linguistic theory," Occasional Papers in Linguistics, 1. MIT.

Diesing, M. (1992) *Indefinites*, MIT Press, Cambridge, Massachusetts.

Enç, M (1990) "The semantics of specificity" LI 22, 1-25.

Fanselow, G (1990) "Scrambling as NP-movement" in G. Grewendorf and W. Sternefeld, (eds.) *Scrambling and Barriers*, John Benjamins; Amsterdam.

Fodor, J. (1987) *Psychosemantics*, MIT Press, Cambridge, Massachusetts.

Heim, I. (1982) *The Semantics of Definite and Indefinite Noun Phrases*, PhD, University of Massachusetts, Amherst.

Hoop, H. d. (1992) *Case Configuration and Noun Phrase Interpretation*, PhD, University of Groningen.

Kamp, D. and U. Reyle (1993) *From Discourse to Logic*, Kluwer, Dordrecht.

Koopman, H. and D. Sportiche (1991) "The position of subjects," *Lingua* 85, 211-258.

Kratzer, A. (1989) "Stage and individual level predicates," in *Papers on Quantification*, NSF Grant Report, University of Massachusetts, Amherst.

McCloskey, J. (1993) "On the scope of verb movement in Irish," Syntax Research Centre Report, University of California, Santa Cruz.

Mahajan, A. (1990) *The A/A-bar Distinction and Movement Theory*. PhD, MIT.

Meinunger, A. (1994) " Case configuration and referentiality" ms. FAS, Berlin. To appear in the proceedings of CONSOLE II.

Milsark, G. (1977) "Towards an explanation of certain peculiarities in the existential construction in English," *Linguistic Analysis* 3, 1-30.

Moltmann, F (1991) "Scrambling in German and the specificity effect," ms. MIT.

Obenauer, H.-G. (to appear) "L'interprétation des structures *wh* et l'accord du participe passé," in H.-G. Obenauer and A. Zribi-Hertz, eds., *Structure de la Phrase et Théorie du Liage*, Presses Universitaires de Vincennes, Vincennes.

Partee, B. (1988) "Many quantifiers," paper presented at ESCOL.

Pinto, M. (1994) "Subjects in Italian: distribution and interpretation" ms. University of Utrecht.

Reinhart, T. (1987) "Specifier and operator binding," in E. J. Reuland and A. B. t. Meulen, eds., *The Representation of (In)definiteness*, MIT Press, Cambridge, 130-167.

Rizzi, L. (1990) *Relativized Minimality*, MIT Press, Cambridge, Massachusetts.

Rullman, H. (1989) "Indefinite NPs in Dutch," in *Papers on Quantification*, NSF Grant Report, University of Massachusetts, Amherst.

Runner, J. (1993) "Quantificational objects and AgrO," paper presented at SCIL V, University of Washington, Seattle. *MIT Working Papers in Linguistics 20.*

Runner, J. (1994) "A specific role for Agr" in E. Benedicto and J. Runner (eds.) *Functional Projections*, UMOP 17, GLSA, University of Massachusetts, Amherst.

Solà, J (1992) *Agreement and Subjects*, PhD, Universitat Autònoma de Barcelona.

Wyngaerd, G v.d. (1989) "Object shift as an A-movement rule," paper presented at SCIL I, MIT. *MIT Working Papers in Linguistics 11.*

Asymmetries with Decreasing QPs[1]

FILIPPO BEGHELLI
University of California, Los Angeles

DECREASING, or downward-entailing, operators are those that license inferences that go downward, from superset to subset. Clausal negation is decreasing, since *John didn't come* entails *John didn't come early* (if John is not in the set of those who came, he is also not in the smaller set of those who came early). Similarly, *N*-WORDS in English (i.e., quantifier phrases—QPs—built with *no, neither, none of the*) are decreasing, but so are non absolutely negative quantifiers like *few, fewer than **n**, less than **n***, etc.: *few/no students came* entails *few/no students came early.*

I will refer to these 'non absolutely negative' QPs as NNDS: Non-Negative, **D**ecreasing QPs; and I will often use QPs built with *few* as representative of this class, with the understanding that claims about *few* essentially extend to all other NNDS. Semantically, NNDS are distinct from the real *n*-words in English because they do not require the intersection of the head noun set and the VP set to be empty.

The first goal of this paper is to demonstrate that the licensing of NPIS (Negative Polarity Items) is more 'syntactic' than standardly thought. I will show that this licensing is sometimes sensitive to the syntactic position

[1] I am grateful to Bill Ladusaw, Tim Stowell, and Anna Szabolcsi for helpful comments and discussion of several points in this paper. Thanks also to Manuel Español-Etxeberria and Felicia Lee, and to my data consultants in the Linguistics Dept. at UCLA, especially Susan Spellmire. This work was supported in part by NSF grant SBR 9222501.

of the licenser—namely, whether the licenser is a pre- or post verbal constituent—and that in general, it interacts in non trivial ways with the complex functional structure of the clause.

The second, and more general, goal consists in showing that decreasing QPs do not undergo QR (Quantifier Raising, cf. May 1977, 1985), contra standard assumptions that say that QR is uniformly available to all QP types. The data to be reviewed in this paper, along with others in Beghelli and Stowell (1994) and other current work, support the conclusion that quantifier scope is a much more diversified phenomenon than suggested by the theory of QR. Under the assumption that QPs take scope by moving at LF, the claim is that individual varieties of QPs aim for their own specific 'target' positions, i.e., the Specifier of functional projections where their semantic/logical features are checked. The LF (scopal) order of constituents results, then, from their interaction with target functional projections which have fixed position in the clause and invariant semantic/syntactic features associated with them.

The core data discussed in this paper pertains to the distribution of decreasing QPs as licensers of certain 'strong' NPIs (Negative Polarity Items) which I will refer to as SENSITIVE NPIs. Because the syntactic properties of NNDs and *n*-words in English are not identical, I will discuss them separately, beginning with NNDs.

1 Sensitive NPIs

Sensitive NPIs include *a single thing, a damn thing, any(thing)...at all, a red cent, a word,* etc. Semantically, they are distinct from ORDINARY NPIS like *any, any of the, anything,* because they are non-referential items that resist D-linking. Syntactically, the distinction between sensitive and ordinary NPIs lies in the stricter locality of their licensing.

First, sensitive NPIs need to be clausemates with their licenser. So lack of clausemateness in (1b-c) disturbs the licensing of the sensitive NPI in (1b), but does not seem to affect the ordinary NPI in (1c)[2] :

(1) a. John said that Mary didn't hear a damn thing (that Bill said)
b. ??John didn't say that Mary heard a damn thing (that Bill said)
c. John didn't say that Mary heard any of these things

Second, the licensing of sensitive NPIs appears to fail when their licenser interacts directly with certain scopal elements like *because*-clauses

[2] I am excluding so-called Neg-Raising verbs from consideration (as matrix predicates in the examples), as with these it might be argued that the NPI becomes clausemate with matrix negation by some LF process.

or QPs built with *every*[3], while ordinary NPIs can survive this environment (cf. Johnston 1993, who elaborates on original observations in Linebarger 1987). I will illustrate this with *because*-clauses. When clausal negation cooccurs with a *because*-clause, two readings are possible: either the head proposition can be negated (NH reading in Johnston's terminology) or the adjunct proposition can be (NA reading):

(2) Marty didn't sell his bike because the gears were broken
NH: 'Marty didn't sell his bike, because the gears were broken'
NA: 'Marty did sell his bike, but not because the gears were broken'

Example (3), from Linebarger, shows that when a sensitive NPI occurs in the head clause, only the NH reading is possible:

(3) He didn't budge an inch because he was pushed
OK 'He didn't move, and this was because he was pushed' (NH)
* 'He moved some, but not because he was pushed' (NA)

However, if the sensitive NPI is substituted with an ordinary one, as in (4) —from Johnston—both NA and NH readings are again possible.

(4) Leo didn't sell any (of the) shares because the market was unstable
OK 'Leo didn't sell any of the shares, and this was because the market was unstable' (NH)
OK 'Leo sold some of the shares, but not because the market was unstable' (NA)

The NA reading of (3) seems to be ruled out because—unlike the ordinary NPI in (4)—the sensitive NPI cannot move out of the scope of negation, but needs to be licensed in the LF (immediate) scope of the licenser. I will not provide here an account of these facts; the data are included simply to establish a distinction between sensitive and ordinary NPIs.

Sensitive NPIs have a further property that distinguishes them from ordinary ones. This property has to do with the type of the licenser, and directly introduces the core data to be discussed in this paper.

---

[3] The licensing of sensitive NPIs is hindered in all contexts where a universal quantifier comes between them and their licensors:

(i) a. I didn't show every book to any student
b. I haven't shown every painting in my collection ever before
(ii) a. ?? I didn't show every book to a single student
b. ?? I didn't show every student any pictures at all / a damn thing

For other properties of sensitive NPIs, cf. fn. 7.

2 Asymmetries with NNDs

In addition to clausal negation, ordinary NPIs can be licensed by a c-commanding NND. It is immaterial whether the licensing NND is preverbal (e.g., a subject) or postverbal (e.g., an argument of the V):

(5) a. Few of the students read any of the books on the list
    b. I gave few of the students any of the books on the list

Now, sensitive NPIs can be licensed by clausal negation:

(6) a. I don't believe a single thing Mary says
    b. Prof. Smith didn't teach us a damn thing about phonology

But they are not generally licensed when c-commanded by an NND. Before discussing the relevant data, we need to recognize, and control for, an ambiguity in the use of NNDs. Sometimes NNDs have negative force: this is their 'few ... if any', or decreasing, meaning; at other times they have a non-monotone[4] meaning, paraphrasable as 'some ... , but a small number of'[5]. With the non-monotone meaning, NNDs are poor licensers for sensitive NPIs in any position. For now, let's focus exclusively on the decreasing meaning of NNDs.

In their decreasing meaning, a preverbal/postverbal asymmetry appears: a subject NND is a much better licenser than a VP-internal NND:

(7) a. At the party, few people heard a single thing Mary said
    b.?* I told few people a single thing about our plans

(8) a. Few people know a damn thing about contemporary art
    b.?* Prof. Smith can teach few people a damn thing about phonology

(9) a. These days, few people would give a red cent to charity
    b.?* These days, John would give few charities a red cent

The data in (7-9) support, then, the following claim:

(10) NNDs show a pre-/postverbal asymmetry in that only when preverbal do they license sensitive NPIs, thus patterning with clausal negation (Neg^0); but postverbal NNDs do not license sensitive NPIs.

The asymmetry in (7, 8, 9) has not, to my knowledge, been previously noticed in the literature, and is unexpected under the standard theory of NPI licensing. Although the exact conditions on the licensing of NPIs (both

---

[4] A non-monotone operator is one that neither licenses inferences that go downward nor upward. The quantifier *between one and three* illustrates: *between one and three students came early* neither entails nor is entailed by *between one and three students came.*

[5] As noted in Beghelli, Ben-Shalom, and Szabolcsi (1993), the non-negative (actually, non-monotone) meaning is forced by E-type pronouns (cf. Evans 1980):

(iii) Few senators (*if any) voted for Kennedy, and *they* are very junior

ordinary and sensitive) are in part still unclear, it is standardly assumed (since Ladusaw 1979) that NPIS are licensed when they are (i) c-commanded at S-Structure by their licenser; and (ii) in the (immediate) scope of such licenser (decreasing QPs being one type of licensers among others). When the licenser is a QP, its S-structure scope varies with its position: the whole clause for a subject, the VP for a VP-internal argument. Accordingly, it is predicted that a subject decreasing QP will license NPIS anywhere in the clause, and a VP-internal one anywhere within VP.

Straightforwardly, in (7b), (8b), and (9b) the postverbal NND both c-commands the NPI at S-Structure, and takes it in its (immediate) scope. Therefore, the standard theory predicts that licensing should take place. The fact that this is not so shows that this theory needs revision.

The data would be accounted for if we could show that subject NNDs and Neg^{o} belong together under a syntactic generalization (say, at LF); and if we could also show that VP-internal NNDs enter into a different configuration (again at LF). This is in fact what I will propose. But before doing so, we should consider two other pieces of evidence that support the existence of an asymmetry between pre- and postverbal NNDs: the relevant data pertain to: (i) the scopal interaction of NNDs with *every*, and (ii) tag questions.

It is a robust, though not widely known, fact about scope that distributive universal quantifiers like *every* do not take scope over a c-commanding clausal negation, provided no indefinite QP occurs in the clause and the intonation is neutral[6]:

(11) Jo didn't show every picture to Moe
 * 'for every picture y, Jo didn't show y to Moe' (=he showed none)
 OK 'not for every picture y, Jo showed y to Moe' (=he didn't show all)

It is striking, therefore, to observe that while a subject NND prevents inverse distributive scope of *every*, an object NND does not.

(12) a. Few students read every book
 * 'for every book y, few students read y'
 OK 'there are few students x, such that x read every book'

b. I found few mistakes in every test
 OK 'for every test y, I found few mistakes in y'

---

6 When an indefinite is present, *every* may scope out of c-commanding negation, provided the indefinite scopes out as well. This yields the scoping *every>one>not*:

(iv) John didn't show every picture of the trip to Vegas to one relative
 ?/OK 'for every picture y, there is one relative x, such that J. didn't show y to x'

An account of this 'Indefinite Intervention Effect' is presented in Beghelli-Stowell (1994).

The asymmetry is further supported by 'reversal' tags. This type of tags is well known to be sensitive to negative force at the clausal level (cf. Klima 1964): clausal negation forces the tag to be positive. But only a preverbal NND requires a positive tag. Consider:

(13) a. Few students came to the party, did / ?* didn't they ?
b. You saw few people at the party, didn't / * did you ?

3 Accounting for the Asymmetry with NNDs

The asymmetry seems to call for a more articulated account of the licensing of NPIs, at a level (such as LF) where syntactic generalizations concerning the position of the licenser with respect to the V can be stated. It also points to some basic differences between ordinary and sensitive NPIs. The question of how exactly ordinary NPIs are licensed goes beyond the scope of the present paper, however, and I will concentrate here only on the licensing of sensitive NPIs[7].

If the asymmetry needs a syntactic account, what conclusions can we draw from the facts? First, the phenomena cannot be accounted for by QR, since all QPs (including decreasing ones) would then be free to take clausal scope, whether they are pre- or postverbal. The asymmetry would be unaccountable for. As discussed more fully in Beghelli (1993) and in Beghelli and Stowell (1994), QR cannot in fact be maintained as such. Scope phenomena require a more articulated account, where different QP-types are distinguished. Some of the relevant data will be discussed at the beginning of section 5.

The fact that clausal negation always licenses sensitive NPIs suggests that perhaps only a functional head like clausal negation (=a filled Neg^{0}), and not just a QP, can be a licenser for sensitive NPIs[8]; VP-internal NNDs accordingly would fail to license because they occupy (at LF) a position lower than, and unrelated to, NegP. This is the basic intuition in the proposal that I will make. The idea is that if a VP-internal NND could reach a position at least as high as Spec,NegP, it could 'activate' Neg^{0} by a relation of agreement or just by c-commanding it. Activating Neg^{0} means

---

[7] If the gloss provided for the NA reading of example (4) is scopally accurate, this would suggest that ordinary NPIs are perhaps just indefinite QPs that occur in the scope of a decreasing operator at S-structure, but are free to take scope above it at LF. Similar views on NPIs are presented in Kadmon and Landman (1993). The suggestion made here implicitly is that their account properly applies only to ordinary (and not to sensitive) NPIs.

[8] As pointed out by Anna Szabolcsi, NNDs cannot be (by themselves) licensors of NPIs since they are bad interveners for NPI licensing. Consider:

(v) ?? I didn't show few students any films

Independent arguments for the claim that only a Neg^{0} head can license sensitive NPIs are given by Lee's (1994) analysis of *wh.. the hell* constructions. Especially relevant in this respect are Lee's observations that sensitive NPIs are licensed by (a) argument—and not adjunct—*wh...the hell*, and (b) by rhetorical Yes/No questions.

that the decreasing feature of the NND is 'passed on' to the head of NegP by a process of agreement. The negative force of a Neg^0 'activated' in this way will be comparable to that of its activator. Hence it will not be equivalent to that of clausal negation, but sufficient to license an NPI[9].

This conclusion is forced by the fact that since NNDs as subjects pattern like Neg^0 with respect to licensing of sensitive NPIs, we cannot say that NNDs are just intrinsically less able than Neg^0 to license NPIs.

But if VP-internal NNDs must sit at LF in a position lower then NegP, where exactly? We want to maintain that an object QP (including a decreasing one) takes scope over the VP, and that a subject QP takes scope over the rest of the sentence. Patterns of entailment show that this is correct from a semantic point of view.

Following Chomsky (1992), I will assume that a VP-internal NND moves (by LF) to Spec,AgrOP for Case checking. This provides a direct way to capture the semantic generalization that VP-internal NNDs take scope over VP, and I will adopt it. I will also assume that VP-internal NNDs in English do not move any higher at LF, i.e., that they don't move to, or above, Spec,NegP.

So, the reason why non-subject NNDs pattern differently than overt Neg^0 is that their negative force remains local: being in Spec,AgrOP, they take scope only over VP, and not over NegP. If we consider the asymmetry data—exx. (7) through (13)—we see that the sentences with VP-internal NNDs pattern like sentences containing constituent negation. An example of this has already been seen in (3), where it was observed that sensitive NPIs are not licensed by the NA reading, which, as pointed out by Anna Szabolcsi (p.c.) is a constituent negation reading. This is not to suggest that postverbal NNDs are structurally comparable to constituent negation: what they have in common is simply that the negation is local and unrelated to negation at the clausal level (i.e., NegP).

The core of the proposal can be encapsulated in the following claim:

(14) Assume that sensitive NPIs are directly licensed only by Neg^0, and that NNDs license only indirectly, by 'activating' Neg^0. The asymmetry derives from the fact that preverbal NNDs, being structurally higher than Neg^0, are able to 'activate' it by a process of agreement/licensing. Postverbal NNDs do not activate Neg^0 because at LF they remain lower than the position of Neg^0.

The question now is how to execute this proposal. In particular, how does the 'activation' of Neg^0 by a subject NND come about? Several options are available, and I will briefly list them below, without trying to solve the

---

9 Certainly we don't want to claim that *Few people came* is synonymous with *Few people didn't come.*

issue in a principled way (cf. Haegeman 1994 for discussion). One hypothesis is that activation of Neg^0 is brought about by the movement of a subject NND from its VP-internal base position to its Case position: we assume that a subject decreasing QP goes through Spec,NegP and can thereby activate Neg^0 by Spec-Head agreement. This is the proposal of Moritz-Valois (1993) in their account of French *personne*. To avoid improper movement, it must be also assumed that the subject Case position has 'derived' A' status, since Spec,NegP is to be considered as an A' position. As mentioned in Haegeman (1994), this treatment can in principle be extended to other case of preverbal (non-subject) NND constituents—cf. (15) below—assuming movement to preverbal position:

(15) a. On few occasions has Moe lost a single penny at Blackjack
b. Seldom has Jack (even) lifted a finger to help us

Another possibility is to consider an NND in Spec,AgrSP or in Spec,CP—as in (15)—as being in the Spec of the 'extended' projection of NegP, using Grimshaw (1991) notion of Extended Projection.

A different proposal is to extend to NNDs Haegeman (1994) treatment of preverbal *n*-words: a subject NND is in Spec-Head agreement with a covert negative head generated in $AgrS^0$, while a non-subject preposed negative constituent is co-indexed with an empty Op in Spec,NegP.

Finally, to implement the claim in (14) we could adopt a suggestion by Bill Ladusaw (p.c.), perhaps Neg^0 is activated not by Spec-Head agreement, but through c-command. We could consider Neg^0 itself as a polarity item. Neg^0 would be activated whenever a decreasing operator c-commands it, or when lexically filled by overt clausal negation (*-n't*).

I will not further elaborate on these suggestions, leaving the issue of how to precisely execute the hypothesis in (14) an open question. The trees in (16) on the next page summarize the derivation of the asymmetry in the licensing of sensitive NPIs.

One last point: so far we have accounted for the decreasing meaning of NNDs. What about the non-monotone meaning? It seems plausible to assume that with this meaning NNDs simply do not activate Neg^0.

4 Asymmetries with *n*-words in English

Having considered NNDs, let's come to *n*-words in English. At first sight, *n*-words seem to be just like NNDs, in that they show the same asymmetry found with NNDs. In subject or preverbal position, *n*-words are good licensers for sensitive NPIs; but VP-internally they are not, even when they c-command the NPI[10]:

[10] I wish to thank Bill Ladusaw for discussion of these examples.

(16) a. No one heard a single thing Mary said
b.*? I told no one a single thing about our plans

(17) a. No one knows a damn thing about phonetics in this department
b.*? Prof. Smith taught no students a damn thing about phonetics

(18) a. b.

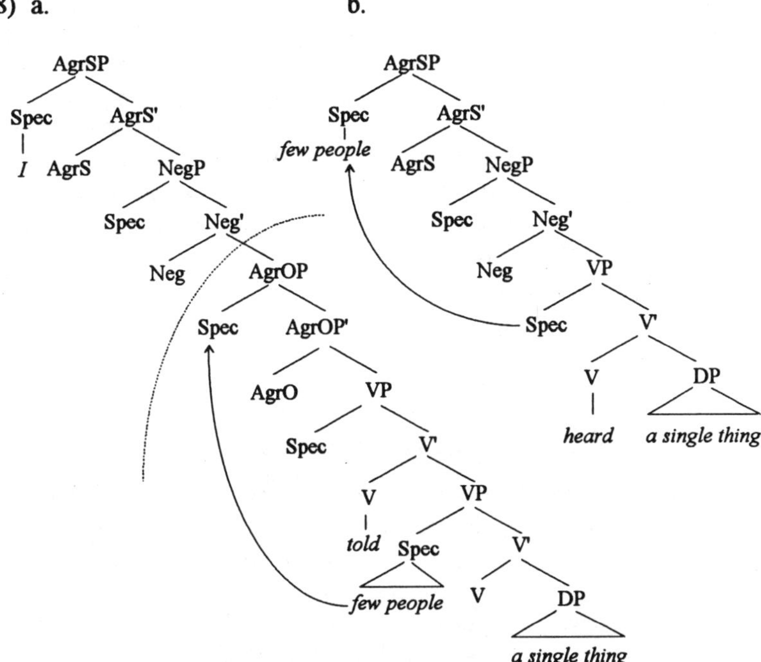

On the basis of these judgments, we could simply extend to *n*-words the account proposed for NNDs in their decreasing meaning. In fact, with *n*-words the situation is more complex and interesting, as will be shown shortly. Once other data is taken into consideration, *n*-words turn out to have quite different LF properties than NNDs.

First, there is evidence that both a preverbal and a postverbal *n*-words constitute instances of clausal negation, a conclusion that seems intuitively correct. The data comes from tag questions and *neither*-clauses, where the asymmetry between subject and non subject *n*-words disappears. Consider:

(19) a. No students came to the party, did / *didn't they ?
b. You saw no students at the party, ? did / *didn't you ?

(20) a. No professors attended John's party, and neither did Bill
b. I invited no professors to my party, and neither did Bill

The relevance of these data rests, of course, on the analysis of tag questions and *neither*-clauses. The most straightforward way to account for the data is, however, that positive tags and *neither*-clauses are conditioned by the presence of a filled Neg^{o} at LF. This invites the conclusion that postverbal *n*-words in English do activate Neg^{o} just like preverbal ones [11].

Second, the LF landing site of object *n*-words may not be that of NNDs, i.e., the Accusative Case position, or Spec,AgrOP. This becomes clear if we assume, as argued by Borer (1994), that with eventive VPs Case checking coincides with checking telic aspect. In Borer's account, AgrOP has an aspectual interpretation, and with eventive VPs it identifies with eventive Aspect Phrase, $AspP_E$ (thus directly encoding the correlation between accusative Case and telicity found in a number of languages). Unlike NNDs, that do not interfere with telic aspect, *n*-words are incompatible with telicity, whether in preverbal or postverbal position. As the contrast (21)-(22) shows, *n*-words remove the accomplishment reading of eventive predicates (at least when the temporal phrase has wide scope):

(21) a. I interviewed the students (in an hour) [accomplishment]
b. I interviewed few students (in an hour) [accomplishment]

(22) a. No one interviewed John (*in /✓for an hour) [*accompl.]
b. I interviewed no students (*in /✓for an hour) [*accompl.]

Accordingly, *n*-words must not move to Spec,$AspP_E$. The assumption that *n*-words activate Neg^{o} in both pre- and postverbal position allows us, then, to derive the known fact that telic interpretation is typically lost in the presence of negation or *n*-words. An active Neg^{o} is incompatible with telic aspect because (as argued on the basis of independent evidence in Beghelli and Stowell 1994) Neg^{o} acts as a quantifier over events, i.e. binds the event argument, effectively negating the existence of a telic event.

To summarize, the data indicate that, whether pre- or postverbal, (i) *n*-words do trigger Neg^{o}; (ii) *n*-words do not move to Spec,AgrOP at LF. We are left, now, with the problem of explaining why they support the same pre- / postverbal asymmetry found with NNDs when it comes to the licensing of sensitive NPIs.

A possible solution has been suggested by Tim Stowell (class lectures, Spring 1994), using an idea in Moritz-Valois (1993). Moritz and Valois argue that the French *n*-word *personne* ('no one') must occupy at LF the

[11] This hypothesis derives its strength from the behavior of NNDs. One could maintain, against it, that what conditions positive tags and *neither*-clauses is whether the event argument is in the scope of a decreasing operator. If a decreasing QP moves to Spec,AgrOP, that is sufficient to take scope over the event argument. This accounts for the behavior of *n*-words, but not of NNDs: we no longer explain why with postverbal NNDs the tag must be negative (and *neither*-clauses are out). If what matters is whether the event argument is in the scope of a decreasing operator, why would a preverbal NND have a different effect than an NND in Spec,AgrOP?

Spec,NegP position; in the case of postverbal *personne*, this is obtained via LF-movement. Although *personne*-movement obeys the usual island restrictions for movement, *personne* has a somewhat wider distribution than *wh*-words. An example is given in (23) below.

(23) a. Louise n'est partie avec l'ami de personne
Louise neg-is left with the friend of no one

b. * De qui$_i$ Louise est-elle partie avec l'ami t_i ?
of whom Louise is-she left with the friend

To account for this discrepancy, Moritz and Valois suggest that *personne*, as an *n*-word, has the special property that it can pass on its (negative) features to any XP it moves to the Spec of. XP is accordingly marked as negative by a process of Spec-Head agreement with X^0, and can move, as a whole, to the Spec position of the next higher XP, and so forth until the complex constituent thus formed comes to rest in Spec,NegP. This procedure, in other words, allows pied-piping of larger and larger constituents embedding *personne*. For example, the derivation of (23a) proceeds as follows:

(23a) Louise [$_{NegP}$ ↑ n'est partie [$_{PP}$ ↑ avec [$_{DP}$ ↑ l'ami de personne]]]

This idea can also be put to work to derive the asymmetry with *n*-words. Assuming that a VP-internal *n*-word moves first to Spec,VP, it will mark VP as [+negative], allowing the entire VP constituent to move (as a whole) to Spec,NegP. This will activate Neg^0; it will not, however, license a VP-internal sensitive NPI, since Neg^0 would not c-command the NPI. Hence the asymmetry in (16), (17) is derived. The tree on the next page illustrates this.

The conclusions of this section are expressed in the following claims:

(24) i. *n*-words in English do activate Neg^0 from both pre- and postverbal position;
ii. their target scope position is Spec,NegP (while in the case of NNDs it was the lower Spec,AgrOP/AspP);
iii. since movement of postverbal *n*-words to their (LF) target scope position takes place by pied-piping the constituent which contains the sensitive NPI, the sensitive NPI ends up not being c-commanded by Neg^0 and it is accordingly not licensed.

5 The scope of decreasing QPs

In the account so far, the asymmetries in the behavior of decreasing QPs have been reduced to limitations in their movement at LF: I argued that postverbal NNDs only move to Spec,AgrOP/AspP, and that postverbal *n*-words move slightly higher, to Spec,NegP. In this section, I will support this account by defending the claim that decreasing QPs do not avail themselves of QR to take clausal scope at LF.

This is shown first by the fact that decreasing QPs are generally unable to take inverse scope (i.e., take scope over a c-commanding scopal operator)—cf. Liu (1990), Beghelli (1993), Ben-Shalom (1993), Szabolcsi (1994), Beghelli and Stowell (1994). No inverse scope reading can be assigned to (26a) and (27a), for example. This contrasts sharply with (28a), where inverse scope is much more natural. The same can be seen at

(25) *? I told no one a single thing

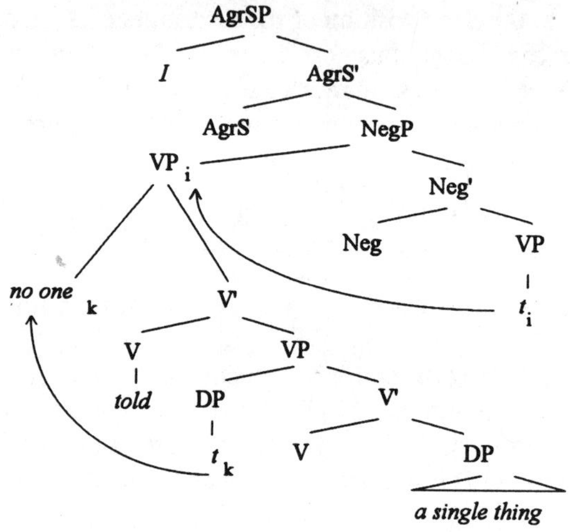

the DP-internal level, by considering inverse linking readings—cf. (26b) and (27b) vs. (28b):

(26) a. Some student read few books
?* 'for few y, y a book, a (possibly different) student read y'

b. A picture of few senators was on sale
?* 'for few y, y a senator, a picture of y was on sale'

(27) a. Some student made no mistakes on the test
* 'there are no mistakes that any student made on the test'

b. * A picture of no senator_i displeased him_i

(28) a. Some student read every book
OK 'for every y, y a book, a (possibly different) student read y'

b. A picture of every senator was on sale
OK 'for every y, y a senator, a picture of y was on sale'

Second, and more directly relevant to our point here, consider the scopal interaction of NNDs and sentential negation. Generally, NNDs (and decreasing QPs in general) do not scope over negation, while QPs built with (bare) numerals (cf. (29b)) typically can do. The contrast is illustrated below:

(29) a. John didn't see few students
OK 'John saw a large number of students'
* 'there are few students such that John didn't see them'

b. John didn't see two students
OK 'there are two students such that John didn't see them'

The claim that I want to make is that readings of decreasing QPs taking (inverse) scope over negation are only possible if this scope movement is driven by some other element associated with the QP[12].

---

[12] At the DP-internal level, cases where a decreasing QP allows an inverse scope reading are only found (i) with DPs whose determiner is *the*, and (ii) with bare plural DPs. Reasons of space prevent me from giving a full account of these cases, and I will simply indicate why they are not counterexamples to my claim. As an illustration of case (i), consider:

(vi) I saw the destruction of few cities
OK 'for few cities y, I saw y's destruction'

As the examples below show, inverse scope readings are possible with these DPs no matter what the quantifier type:

(vii) I saw the destruction of every / three / more than five cities
OK 'for every/three/more than 5 x, x a city, I saw the destruction of x'

The fact that the differences between embedded QP types cancel out with these DPs suggests that an altogether different mechanism of scope interpretation is at work in these cases. As argued by Valois 1991, with definite DPs like these, the embedded QP moves at LF to Spec,DP, thereby gaining wide scope. This accounts for the fact that definite DPs—unlike indefinite ones—allow paraphrases where the Theme argument can be expressed in the possessor/genitive position:

(viii) a. The destruction of the/a city ↔ the/a city's destruction
b. The dismissal of the/a Dean ↔ the/a Dean's dismissal
(ix) A/some picture of my girl ≠ my girl's picture

Observe also that with DPs introduced by *the*, the definiteness or indefiniteness of the complement determines that of the whole DP. 'The destruction of a city', 'the dismissal of a Dean', 'the car of a student' are indefinite DPs. In fact, the sentences below are generic:

(x) a. The car of a graduate student is usually a cheap one
b. The campus police will impound *the car of a student* if it is parked in a faculty space

Consider now case (ii). With bare plurals, it can be argued that there is no inverse scope at all. Consider:

(xi) I read descriptions of few South American cities

(xi) would seem to allow the Theme 'few South American cities' to take wide scope with respect to 'descriptions'. In fact, sentences like (xi) are not instances of inverse scope, since the

For example, inverse scope over NegP becomes (more or less marginally) possible when a decreasing operator embeds a definite DP (e.g., *few of the boys*). We can assume here that it is the definite DP that takes scope over negation at LF, pied-piping the decreasing quantifier.

(30) At the shooting gallery, I didn't hit less than five of the targets
OK 'there are less than five of the targets which I didn't hit'

For concreteness in the discussion so far, I would like to propose the following nesting of functional projections to account for the LF derivation of the scopal readings discussed in this section. For the part not argued for in this paper, the reader is referred to Beghelli and Stowell (1994):

(31)

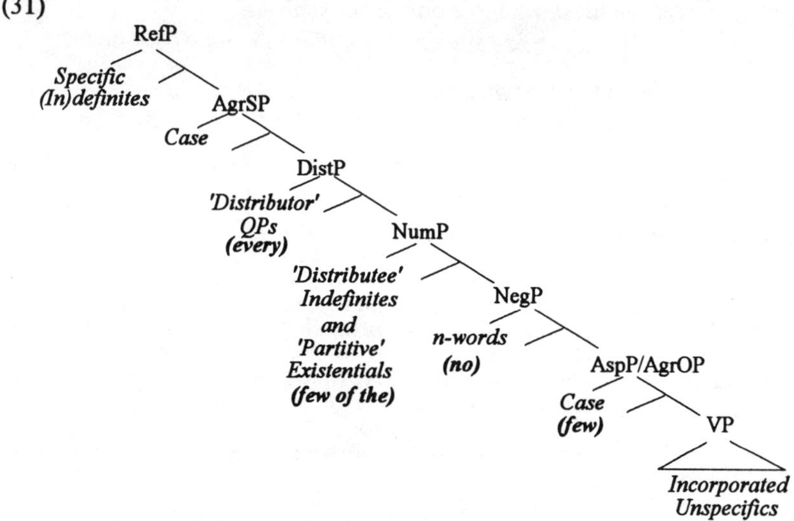

The claim is that each XP in (31) has an invariant logico-semantic specification, and that a QP will target at LF the Spec position of a particular functional XP depending on the QP′s interpretation in a given reading. For example, Num(eral)P, associated with a partitive (à la Enç) interpretation for an existential, will be accessed by *less than five of the targets* in (30), which gives it scope over negation. Being a projection

---

narrow scope quantifier does not covary with each member of the set that the wide scope quantifier talks about. There is a truth-conditional difference: an analysis of (xi) with *few South American cities* taking scope over *descriptions* would require (xi) to be true iff for each city, we find (some) descriptions of it that I read. Since *descriptions* is plural, it means at least two such descriptions. But (xi) can be true even if for each city I have read exactly one description of it.

This indicates that bare plurals, and plurals in general, embedding quantificational complements give rise to independent scope interpretations. So, the relevant reading of (xi) is that there is a sum of destructions corresponding to few cities being destroyed. That is, *descriptions* seems to be a so-called dependent plural. However independent quantification is to be represented at LF, I will assume that it does not involve scope movement of a QP over another.

where scope dependent QPs can be checked, it might also be accessed by the indefinite *some student* in (28a), under the inverse scope reading of the sentence (where books, the 'distributee', covary with individual students); whereas *every book* will move higher, to Dist(ributive)P, the projection for distributive QPs. On the other hand, if *some student* is construed as specific in (28a), it will move to Spec,RefP, taking scope over *every book. Few books* fails to take inverse scope in (26a) because it can only move to Spec,AspP, and remains lower than the scope position of *some student* in Spec,RefP (or perhaps Spec,NumP).

6 Conclusions

The data discussed in this paper support two kinds of conclusions, as anticipated in the introduction. First, the licensing of NPIS is more syntactic than standardly thought: when the licenser is a QP and the NPI is a sensitive one, licensing occurs insofar as the QP can scope over the position of Neg^{o}.

Second, contra the assumption (May 1977, 1985) that LF movement for scope is uniform across QP-types, individual varieties of QPs aim at specific target positions with invariant scope domains and semantic functions. This has been argued here limitedly to decreasing QPs.

References

Beghelli, Filippo. 1993. 'A Minimalist Approach to Quantifier Scope'. *Proceedings of NELS 23.*

Beghelli, Filippo, Dorit Ben-Shalom and Anna Szabolcsi. 1993. 'When Do Subjects and Objects Exhibit a Branching Reading?'. In Michele Hart, (ed.) *Proceedings of WCCFL XII.* CSLI, Stanford.

Beghelli, Filippo and Tim Stowell. 1994. 'The Direction of Quantifier Movement'. Manuscript, UCLA.

Ben-Shalom, Dorit. 1993. 'Object Wide Scope and Semantic Trees'. Manuscript, UCLA.

Borer, Hagit. 1993. 'The Projection of Arguments'. In Elena Benedicto and Jeff Runners (eds), *Functional Projections*. UMass. Amherst.

Chomsky, Noam. 1992. *A Minimalist Program for Linguistic Theory*. MIT Occasional Papers in Linguistics, No. 1.

Evans, Gareth. 1980. 'Pronouns'. *Linquistic Inquiry* 11, 2: 337-362.

Johnston, Michael. 1993. 'Because Clauses and Negative Polarity Licensing'. Manuscript, UCSC.

Ladusaw, William. 1979. *Polarity Sensitivity as Inherent Scope Relations.* Ph.D.Dissertation. U. of Texas.

Ladusaw, William. 1992. 'Expressing Negation'. In Chris Barker and David Dowty, eds. *Proceedings of SALT II*. Ohio State U.

Lee, Felicia. 1994. *Negative Polarity Licensing in Wh-Questions: The Case for Two Licensers*. M.A. Thesis, UCLA.

Linebarger, Marcia. 1987. 'Negative Polarity and Grammatical Representation'. *L&P* 10: 325-387.

Kadmon, Nirit and Fred Landman. 1993. 'Any'. *L&P* 16:352-422.

Klima, Edward. 1964. 'Negation in English'. In Janet Fodor and Jerrold Katz (eds), *The Structure of Language*. Prenctice Hall, Englewood Cliffs, NY.

May, Robert. 1985. *Logical Form*. MIT Press.

Moritz, Luc and Daniel Valois. 1993. 'Pied-Piping and Specifier-Head Agreement'. Manuscript, to appear in *Linguistic Inquiry*.

Scha, Remko. 1981. 'Distributive, Collective and Cumulative Quantification'. In Jeroen Groenendijk et al., eds. *Formal Methods in the Study of Language*. U. of Amsterdam.

Szabolcsi, Anna, 1994. 'Quantifiers in Pair-list Readings and the Non-uniformity of Quantification'. In *Proceedings of the Ninth Amsterdam Colloquium*. ILLC. University of Amsterdam. The Netherlands.

Valois, Daniel. 1991. *The Internal Syntax of DP*. Ph.D. Dissertation, UCLA.

Zanuttini, Raffaella. 1991. *Syntactic Properties of Sentential Negation: A Comparative Study of Romance Languages*. Ph.D. Dissertation, U. of Pennsylvania, Philadelphia.

Quantifier/Negation Construal and Negative Concord

PILAR PIÑAR
University of Arizona

1. Introduction

Recently, much discussion has focussed on the phenomenon of negative concord (henceforth NC). NC is exhibited in the Romance languages, as well as in many others, and it arises when two or more negative elements only contribute one instance of negation to the meaning of a sentence (cf. Laka 1990, Zanuttini 1991, Haegeman & Zanuttini 1991, Haegeman 1992, Ladusaw 1992 for recent discussion). Some instances of NC structures in Spanish are seen below:

1. **Nadie** dijo **nunca nada.**	2. **No** compré **nada.**
Nobody said never nothing	I didn't buy nothing
'Nobody ever said anything.'	'I didn't buy anything.'

---

*I thank Andrew Barss, Molly Diesing, Chip Gerfen, Terence Langendoen, Richard Oehrle, and Anna Szabolcsi for discussion of the issues presented here as well as for their input on this and/or on an earlier version of this paper. I also thank the audience of WCCFL XIII, and the participants of the Linguistics Department syntax reading group at the University of Arizona, to whom this paper was presented. All errors are mine.

Following Laka (1990), I will refer to negative items such as *nadie* 'nobody', *nunca* 'never', etc. as N-words. The motivation behind choosing a neutral term is that there is no consensus regarding the nature of these elements in Romance. Thus, on the one hand they behave like negative quantifiers (terms like *nobody* in English) when they are in preverbal position and not c-commanded by another instance of negation (as is the subject in (1)). On the other hand, they behave like negative polarity items (terms like *anybody* in English) when they are within the c-command domain of another negative word or negation (as are the objects in (1) and (2)).

A simple explanation that comes to mind is that there are two sets of homophonous N-words. One set would correspond to the set of negative quantifiers, and the other would consist of negative polarity items (henceforth NPIs). The problem with such an explanation is that it wrongly predicts that sentences such as (2) should be ambiguous between a NC reading and a double negative reading, and it does not account for why we do not find postverbal N-words not c-commanded by a licensing element such as negation, as can be seen by comparing (3) and (4) below:[1]

3. *Vi a **nadie**.
   #'I saw nobody.'

4. **No** vi a **nadie**.
   I didn't see nobody
   'I didn't see anybody.'

It is the behavior of N-words in postverbal contexts that has led some researchers (e.g. Bosque 1980, Laka 1990, Zanuttini 1991, Haegeman 1992, among others) to posit a unique set of N-words in NC languages. Under the assumption that there is a unique set of N-words, two obvious problems arise: the first one is to determine what the nature of N-words is; the second one is to define the relevant licensing conditions that will correctly predict the occurrence of both preverbal and postverbal N-words.

Here, I first review two of the most recent views on the issues raised by the behavior of N-words. I then present data that has not yet been incorporated into the discussion of NC and which, I argue, prove to be

---

[1]The requirement that postverbal N-words must be c-commanded by a licenser applies equally to objects, adjuncts, and postverbal subjects:

(i) *Lo vi **en ninguna parte**.
I saw him in no place
#'I saw him in no place.'

(ii) **No** lo vi **en ninguna parte**.
I didn't see him in no place
'I didn't see him anywhere.'

(iii)*Habló **nadie**.
Talked nobody
#'Nobody talked.'

(iv) **No** habló **nadie**.
Not talked nobody
'Nobody talked.'

critical both for determining the semantic content of N-words and for determining the appropriate LF representation of NC structures. Specifically, I argue that N-words are NPIs and that postverbal N-words are interpreted in situ rather than via movement at LF (contra Kayne 1981, Rizzi 1982, Jaeggli 1982, Zanuttini 1991, Haegeman 1992, among others).[2] In arguing that N-words are NPIs, I support the analysis of Laka (1990). In Laka's work, however, a movement approach to the licensing of NPIs is not falsified. In fact, Laka's analysis can be made compatible with a movement approach to NC (see, for example, Bosque 1992). Here, I present empirical evidence that argues explicitly against a movement account of negative polarity licensing in Romance. To anticipate, the data that I will discuss involve configurations in which different types of embedded quantifiers in subject position intervene between an instance of negation in a matrix clause and an N-word in the object position of the embedded clause, as in the schema in (5) below:

5. Neg...[QNP...N-word]

The configuration sketched in (5) might at first sight look like an instance of the weak island for cross-clausal, NC construal, since there is a scopal element--a potential intervener--in between the matrix negation and the embedded N-word. I will argue, however, that these configurations are never potential weak islands for NC. We will see that it is the quantifier/negation interactions across the clause boundary that determine whether the downstairs N-word will or will not be appropriately licensed.

2. Two views on negative concord and N-words

The position taken by Zanuttini (1991) and Haegeman (1992) regarding N-words in NC languages is that they are always negative quantifiers, that is, that N-words have negative force of their own, and that they undergo movement by LF. This assumption explains the behavior of Romance N-words in matrix preverbal position, where in fact they seem to have negative content. Moreover, Zanuttini (1991) and Haegeman (1992) explain the fact that postverbal N-words in Romance must be c-commanded by negation by positing that N-words are subject to the NEGATIVE CRITERION, by virtue of which by LF, N-words must move to a position in

[2]Other recent works supporting the view that Romance N-words are licensed in situ can be found in Arnáiz (1993) and Aranovich (1993).

which they can be in a Spec/head relationship with a negative head.[3] This position can very well be the Specifier of the functional projection of the Negation Phrase (NegP), which, according to Zanuttini (1991), dominates the projection of the subject Agreement Phrase in Italian, as in the schema:[4]

6. $[_{NegP}[_{Spec}][_{neg'}\text{no}][_{AgrsP}\ldots[_{TP}\ldots[_{VP}\ldots]]]]$

In this view, for a negative phrasal projection to be licensed, there must be either an overt negative head, or an overt negative operator in the [Spec NegP] position at S-Structure.[5] That explains the requirement of having either an overt negative head or another N-word c-commanding a postverbal N-word. If no overt N-word or negative head is present to license a NegP, a postverbal N-word will not have a negative projection to move to at LF in order to satisfy its morphological requirements. When more than one negative quantifier is present (as in (1) above) they all stack up at LF by adjoining to the Specifier of the licensing, negative head. They, then, undergo a process of FACTORIZATION (similar in nature to the process of quantifier absorption in Higginbotham and May 1981), yielding the effect by which a single instance of negation is contributed to the meaning of the sentence.

---

[3]Haegeman & Zanuttini (1991) discuss some data involving negative concord and scrambling in West Flemish and posit that the scrambling facts can be interpreted as movement to a Spec/head configuration with a negative head. Zanuttini (1991) and Haegeman (1992) extend the analysis of the scrambling data in West Flemish to LF configurations in the Romance languages. I am not in a position to judge whether the West Flemish scrambling data should be interpreted in the manner of Haegeman and Zanuttini. My discussion will only make reference to the Romance languages and to the consequences that Haegeman & Zanuttini's (1991), Haegeman's (1992), and Zanuttini's (1991) analyses have for negative concord in Romance.

[4]To be precise, the proposal in Haegeman (1992) is a little different from the proposal in Zanuttini (1991). Haegeman (1992) proposes that AgrP always dominates NegP (even in Italian). Negative words must be in [Spec, AgrP] at LF, and the Spec-head agreement requirement with a negative head is satisfied by movement of the negative head to Agr^o. For the purposes of the discussion here, whether negative words move to [Spec AgrP] or whether they move to [Spec NegP] is irrelevant. In any case, the basic idea in Haegeman (1992) and in Zanuttini (1991) is that N-words must be in a Spec/head relationship with a negative head by LF.

[5]Arguably, a preverbal N-word occupies [Spec NegP] (or [Spec AgrP] in Haegeman's terms). When an overt operator occupies [Spec NegP], and thus licenses a negative projection, the negative head of NegP does not need to be overt, due perhaps to the PRINCIPLE OF ECONOMY (cf. Chomsky 1991).

In contrast to Zanuttini's (1991) and Haegeman's (1992) views, Laka (1990) argues that N-words in NC languages should be analyzed as NPIs. That is, she claims that these elements are existential quantifiers equivalent to English *any*. In treating N-words as NPIs, Laka follows previous analyses by Bosque (1980), among others. The negative polarity nature of N-words would explain why, when postverbal, they must always be c-commanded by a licensor. This is because, as is discussed by Ladusaw (1979), NPIs are licensed by a c-commanding downward entailing operator such as negation.[6] A preverbal N-word is licensed, according to Laka, by an abstract negative head, which is the head of the Negation Phrase.[7] Like Zanuttini for Italian, Laka posits that the phrase hosting negation is the highest maximal projection (below CP) in languages such as Spanish and Basque.[8] In Laka's view, a preverbal N-word is simply an NPI which occupies the Specifier position of NegP, and which is licensed by the c-

---

[6]Downward and upward entailing operators correspond to monotone increasing and decreasing operators as is discussed in Barwise & Cooper (1981). Operators can be monotone increasing or decreasing depending on whether they produce upward or downward entailments for pairs such as (i) and (ii), and (i) and (iii):

(i) Every person left.
(ii) Every woman left.
(iii) Every person left early.

The entailment from (i) to (ii) is downward, since it runs from the superset of people to the subset of women. Thus, *every* is downward entailing for its first argument. (i), however, does not entail (iii). Rather, (iii) entails (i). This entailment is upward, since it runs from the subset of people who left early to the superset of people who left. *Every* is upward entailing for its second argument.

[7]This abstract negative head is actually overt in some Romance languages, as in Catalan:

(i) Ningú **no** m'ha vist.
No one not has seen me
'No one has seen me.'

[8]Laka (1990) names the maximal projection that hosts negation ΣP. ΣP is headed by negation in negative sentences, but it is headed by an affirmative head or an emphatic particle in emphatic affirmative sentences. Since in the sentences discussed here ΣP is equivalent to NegP, I will be using the latter term to refer to this projection.

commanding head of NegP.[9]

The main difference between Zanuttini's (1991) and Haegeman's (1992) views on N-words on the one hand and Laka's views on the other, then, is that whereas Zanuttini and Haegeman explicitly claim that N-words have negative content, Laka's position is that N-words do not have negative content (just like *any* in English). Although Laka (1990) does not propose an LF movement analysis to account for the licensing of NPIs, Bosque (1992) argues explicitly that the licensing of N-words (which he considers as NPIs) should be represented as LF movement to the Spec position of NegP[10]. Earlier movement analyses of what we are referring to here as N-words can be found in Kayne (1981), Rizzi (1982), Jaeggli (1982), and Longobardi (1991).[11]

There are two major issues to be clarified regarding recent discussion on N-words. One is to determine whether Zanuttini (1991) and Haegeman (1992) are correct in claiming that all N-words have negative content. The second issue is to determine whether N-words undergo movement at LF (independent of whether they have negative content). The data that I will discuss below show that: 1) N-words do not have negative content of their own, and 2) that NC is better accounted for without movement.

3. Quantifier/negation construals

It is well known that a quantifier intervening between an extracted element and its trace can create a weak island effect (cf. Szabolcsi & Zwarts 1993, Kiss 1993, Cinque 1990, Rizzi 1990, Kroch 1989, among others), as

---

[9]The fact that English does not normally allow preverbal negative polarity items would follow from the assumption that NegP is not the highest sentential projection in English. As has been pointed out (by Laka among others), English does allow preverbal NPIs providing that there is a c-commanding licensor, as in:

i) Why doesn't anybody like Fred?

[10]Note, then, that Bosque's (1992) analysis shows a close resemblance to Zanuttini's and Haegeman's analyses of N-words. The only difference between the two views lies in the semantic content of N-words (negative versus non-negative content).

[11]Kayne's (1981), Rizzi's (1982), and Jaeggli's (1982) standard analyses of negative concord posit that the lower negative term adjoins at LF to the clause containing the licensing instance of negation. They assume that N-words in Romance do not have negative content, and that they acquire it via INCORPORATION (in Klima's 1964 sense) with the licensing negative head.

illustrated by the contrast between (7) and (8):[12]

7. *How did **few people** think that you behaved?
8. How did Martha think that you behaved?

In this section, I investigate the issue of whether the scopal elements that typically create weak islands will also disrupt NC. According to Rizzi (1990), only the traces of non-referential phrases need to be licensed locally (through government rather than through binding). For this reason, it is generally the extraction of non-referential phrases that is sensitive to weak islands, since an operator intervening between the extracted phrase and its trace will disrupt local licensing of the trace by its antecedent. Given that N-words are clearly non-referential, a movement approach to NC predicts that a weak island creator that intervenes between two negative terms should disrupt the NC construal. First, consider sentences (9) and (10):

9. **No** creo [que Pedro sepa **nada**].
   I don't believe that Pedro knows nothing
   'I don't believe that Pedro knows anything.'

10.***No** creo [que **menos de dos personas** sepan **nada**].
   I don't believe that fewer than 2 people know nothing
   #'I don't believe that fewer than 2 people know anything.'

Sentence (9) illustrates the fact that NC is possible across the clause boundary. Movement approaches to NC posit that in sentences like (9) the embedded N-word moves to the higher clause in order to be construed with the licensing negation. Note, however, that (10) is uninterpretable under the NC reading; the embedded N-word *nada* is not licensed.[13] It could be argued that the intervening quantified phrase *menos de dos personas* disrupts NC construal between the two relevant negative terms. Under a movement analysis of NC, and adopting Rizzi's (1990) theory of Relativized Minimality, the effect illustrated above would, at first sight, follow. Quantifier raising of the intervening QNP subject would, arguably, block extraction of the embedded N-word. In contrast to this, an approach that treats N-words as NPIs interpreted in situ would seem to predict that *nada* in (10) above should be licensed by the c-commanding, downward entailing operator *menos de dos personas* 'fewer than two people'. Now contrast (10)

---

[12]Example (7) is from Szabolcsi & Zwarts (1993).

[13]An independent negative reading of *nada* is not possible either, since, as was illustrated in (3) and (4) above, a postverbal N-word can only be construed with the negative concord reading.

with (11) below:

11. No creo [que **más de dos personas** sepan nada].
I don't believe that more than 2 people know nothing
'I don't believe that more than 2 people know anything.'

In (11), a NC reading is possible in spite of the intervening QNP *más de dos personas*. An account along the lines of Relativized Minimality does not clearly capture the contrast between (10) and (11). By minimally changing the intervening, monotone decreasing quantifier in (10) for a monotone increasing quantifier in (11), we obtain a completely different result.

It has been claimed (cf. Szabolcsi & Zwarts 1990, 1991) that only monotone decreasing operators create weak islands.[14] If the semantic and syntactic properties of increasing and decreasing quantifiers were to be formalized in such a way as to predict that only the latter will block a government relation, the contrast between (10) and (11) could be made consistent with a movement analysis of NC. However, an approach to NC that requires construal of the lower negative term with the highest one (either via absorption, cf. Zanuttini 1991 and Haegeman 1992, or via negative incorporation, cf. Kayne 1981, Rizzi 1982, Jaeggli 1982) misses completely the interpretation of sentences such as (11). If one looks closely at the meaning of (11), it becomes apparent that the intended construal in this sentence is not between *nada* and the matrix negation (a construal that would cross over the intervening QNP subject), but rather the intended construal is that between the matrix negation and the embedded, quantified subject. In order to see this, consider the meaning of sentence (11) as paraphrased in (12):

12. No creo [que más de dos personas sepan nada].
I don't believe that more than 2 people know nothing
'I believe that **not more than two people** know anything.'

What the paraphrase in (12) reveals is that *nada* here is not construed with the matrix negation, as the classical analyses of NC would predict. Rather, what seems to be happening is that the matrix negation is associated with the intervening QNP, which, in turn, licenses the N-word in object position.[15] The construal of the matrix negation with the increasing

---

[14]But see Szabolcsi & Zwarts (1993) for counterevidence to this claim.

[15]The term ASSOCIATION here is borrowed from Jackendoff's (1972) discussion of the association of focus with negation. This type of crossclausal association seems to only be possible with Neg-raising verbs. This can be explained if, following Laka (1990), certain negated verbs subcategorize for a negative Comp in an embedded

quantified NP *más de dos personas* yields a downward entailing context that, in accordance with Ladusaw's analysis of NPI licensing, licenses *nada* as a NPI.[16]

Under the explanation sketched out above, the ungrammaticality of sentence (10), repeated here as (13), follows:

13. *No creo [que **menos de dos personas** sepan nada].
    I don't believe that fewer than 2 people know nothing
    #'I don't believe that fewer than 2 people know anything.'

The embedded QNP subject in (13) is downward entailing. Thus, construing it with the matrix negation yields an upward entailing context in which the object N-word is not licensed as an NPI. This, and not a movement-island effect, is the source of the uninterpretability of (13).

That the matrix negation actually changes the entailing properties of the embedded QNP subjects can be clearly tested. It is well known that QNPs such as *menos de dos personas* are downward entailing. As can be seen in (14) below, for example, the entailment between (a) and (b) goes from a superset (vegetables) to a subset (Brussels sprouts):[17]

14 a. Menos de dos personas comen verduras.
   'Fewer than two people eat vegetables.'
   b. Menos de dos personas comen coles de Bruselas.
   'Fewer than two people eat Brussels sprouts.'

Note, however that the entailment is reversed when the quantifier in question is embedded under matrix negation. As seen in (15), the entailment from (a) to (b) now runs from a subset (brussels sprouts) to a superset (vegetables):

---

clausal complement. This negative operator can then act as a mediator in the embedded clause for the matrix negation.

[16]I thank Anna Szabolcsi for discussion of this effect.

[17]What (14a) and (14b) show is that *menos* is downward entailing for its second argument. It should be noted that *menos* is also downward entailing for its first argument, as can be seen in:

i) Menos de dos **personas** comen verduras.
   'Fewer than 2 people eat vegetables.'
ii)Menos de dos **mujeres** comen verduras.
   'Fewer than 2 women eat vegetables.'

However, since in the examples under consideration the N-words appear within the second argument of the quantifier, what is relevant here is that the quantified phrase is downward entailing with respect to its second argument.

15 a. No creo que menos de dos personas coman coles de Bruselas.
'I don't believe that fewer than 2 people eat Brussels sprouts.'
b. No creo que menos de dos personas coman verduras.
'I don't believe that fewer than 2 people eat vegetables.'

By associating *menos de dos personas* with negation, the result is an expression with, roughly, the same properties as *al menos dos personas* 'at least two people', which is clearly upward entailing. Once this is understood, it becomes clear that in a sentence such as (13) above, the NC reading of *nada* is not possible, not because the QNP subject blocks movement of the N-word, but rather because the N-word finds itself in an upward entailing context, that is, in a context that cannot license an NPI.[18]

More examples fitting the discussed paradigm follow:[19]

16. *No creo [que pocas personas sepan nada].
I don't believe that few people know nothing
#'I don't believe that few people know anything.'

---

[18]The analysis proposed here predicts that a monoclausal structure in which *menos de dos personas* is not within the scope of negation will license an object N-word, as in:

(i) ?Menos de dos personas saben nada del asunto.
'Fewer than 2 people know anything about it.'

Although a negative polarity reading of the object N-word is clearly available in (i), the sentence sounds a little awkward to me. For reasons that I do not fully understand at this point, (i) above improves considerably if the subject QNP and the object N-word appear in different clauses:

(ii) Hay menos de dos personas [que sepan nada del asunto].
'There are fewer than 2 people who know anything about it.'

It is possible that, as is argued by Progovac (1992), NPI licensing in some cases is mediated by Comp. In any case, the availability of the negative polarity reading of *nada* above is consistent with my discussion in this section.

[19]Note that, although I am restricting my discussion to examples in which the instance of matrix negation is an overt negative head, the same effect is obtained when there is an N-word in the matrix clause as in (i) and (ii). Recall that, following Laka's analysis, the preverbal N-word in (i) and (ii) is licensed by an abstract negative head in NegP:

(i) ***Nadie** cree [que **menos de dos personas** sepan **nada**].
Nobody believes that fewer than 2 people know nothing
'Nobody believes that fewer than 2 people know anything.'

(ii) **Nadie** cree [que **más de dos personas** sepan **nada**].
Nobody believes that more than 2 people know nothing
'Nobody believes that more than 2 people know anything.'

17. No creo [que muchas personas sepan nada].
 I don't believe that many people know nothing
 'I don't believe that many people know anything.'

18. No creo [que la mayoría de las personas sepan nada].
 I don't believe that most people know nothing
 'I don't believe that most people know anything.'

(16) illustrates construal of the matrix negation with the decreasing quantified NP *pocas personas*. As predicted, the N-word in object position is not licensed, given that construal of the decreasing quantified subject with matrix negation yields an upward entailing context that can be paraphrased as 'not few people'. By contrast, in (17) and (18), the QNP in the embedded subject position is increasing. In the context of negation, *muchas personas* and *la mayoría de las personas* can license the NPI.

The data discussed in this section reveal that a movement analysis of NC is inappropriate. Specifically, raising of the lower N-word, followed by either a process of incorporation or of absorption of the concordant terms makes the wrong prediction with respect to the actual meaning of sentences such as (12), (17) and (18). Thus, if the effect of having a single contribution of negation by two negative elements (*no* and *nada*) in (17), for example, were to be derived by adjoining *nada* to the matrix clause, or by moving it into [Spec NegP] of the higher clause at LF, then the resulting interpretation would be one in which *nada* would have wider scope than the QNP *muchas personas*. That is, the resulting interpretation of (17) would be as in (19):

19. For no x, I believe that many people know x.

(19) is not the right interpretation for (17), which can be paraphrased as 'I believe that not many people know anything'.[20] As we have seen, it is the context created by the association of the matrix negation with the embedded QNP subject that determines whether an N-word in this domain will be licensed or not. Thus, moving the embedded N-word to the higher clause

---

[20]Another problem raised by the movement analysis is that of the relative scope between the N-word and the matrix verb. As Molly Diesing and Andrew Barss pointed out to me in previous discussion of these issues, if NegP is in fact the highest projection in Spanish (as has been argued by Laka 1990), then, movement of *nada* to the Spec of NegP would take the N-word out of the scope of the matrix verb. Such a result does not seem to be consistent with the actual interpretation of interclausal negative concord structures in general. The interaction of the embedded QNP and the postverbal N-word in the sentences that I discuss here highlights the scopal behavior of N-words in Romance.

and outside of the scope of the embedded QNP subject would lead us to miss the contrast between the grammatical and the ungrammatical sentences considered here. Note also that the Negative Criterion as proposed by Zanuttini (1991) and by Haegeman (1992) is flagrantly violated in example (17). Clearly, the matrix negation is not construed via Spec/head agreement with postverbal *nada*. Rather the matrix negation is construed with the QNP subject, which in turn has scope over *nada*. By the same token, the fact that the matrix negation is construed with the quantified subject, and not with the embedded N-word in the object position, shows that there is no absorption or incorporation of the concordant terms at LF.

3.1. On the non-negative nature of N-words

The discussion in section 3 makes a clear prediction as to which quantifiers will be found in the Neg...[QNP...N-word] configuration and which ones will not. So far we have seen that a downward entailing quantifier, such as *menos de dos personas* 'fewer than two people', when construed with negation, will yield an upward entailing context that will not license a c-commanded N-word. In contrast, an upward entailing quantifier, such as *más de dos personas* 'more than two people', will yield a downward entailing context when construed with negation, and will, therefore, fit perfectly well in the configuration sketched above.

Let us consider what happens when the embedded subject that intervenes between the matrix negation and the embedded N-word is another N-word, that is, an instance of what Zanuttini (1991) and Haegeman (1992) consider to be a negative quantifier (with negative content). Clearly, in the context of the behavior of the quantifiers that we have considered so far, the prediction is that, if N-words are negative quantifiers, they should yield an upward entailing context when construed with negation. A further embedded N-word should thus not be licensed in the created context. As is well known, however, an N-word embedded under negation does not yield an upward entailing context, but rather it produces a familiar NC effect, as in (20):

20. **No** creo [que **nadie** sepa **nada**].
I don't believe that nobody knows nothing
'I don't believe that anybody knows anything.'

Example (20), thus, is just a typical instance of NC. When an example such as (20) is seen in comparison to the examples considered in section 3, such as (10) and (11), it becomes apparent that N-words in NC languages do not behave the way other quantifiers do.

Of course, the theory in Zanuttini (1991) and in Haegeman (1992) is designed to deal with cases of NC just as the one illustrated in (20). In cases such as (20), they posit that both embedded N-words adjoin to the specifier of the matrix negative head at LF, and that they subsequently undergo factorization. However, recall that the claim that negative quantifiers are different from other quantifiers in that they need to raise to [Spec NegP] to satisfy the Negative Criterion has been disproved here (cf. discussion in section 3). Thus, examples such as (21) below, where the matrix negation is construed with the embedded subject and not with the embedded N-word, point out that the N-word here is not in a Spec/head relation with the licensing negation:

21. No creo [que más de dos personas sepan nada].
    I don't believe that more than 2 people know nothing
    'I don't believe that more than 2 people know anything.'

In addition to this problem, as I have already mentioned, moving the N-words to the Spec of the matrix NegP in order to comply with the Negative Criterion would produce the wrong meaning of sentences such as (21) (where the N-word has lower scope than the embedded, QNP subject). Sentence (20) above should be seen instead as an instance of multiple negative polarity licensing.

4. Conclusion

In this paper I have discussed some data involving NC structures in which a quantified subject intervenes between a matrix instance of negation and a postverbal N-word in the embedded clause (Neg...[QNP...N-word]). In these structures, the acceptability of the postverbal N-word changes as the monotonicity properties of its c-command domain are altered--due to the interaction of the QNP subject with the matrix negation. This fact in itself points out the polarity nature of N-words. In addition, the core data discussed here points to an in situ analysis of NC. An analysis of NC in terms of movement of the N-words to [Spec NegP] makes the wrong prediction with respect to the actual interpretation of the data. We saw also that the quantifier/negation interactions in the analyzed data reveal that in NC, the concordant terms are not syntactically construed via incorporation, absorption, or Spec/head agreement.

Two of the separate empirical facts demonstrated here, namely, that N-words don't move, and that they are not subject to the Negative Criterion, point to the conclusion that N-words are not negative operators, and that they are better interpreted as NPIs in situ.

5. Remaining Issues

I note here the recalcitrant behavior of the universal quantifier with respect to the licensing of N-words in its scope. As is well-known, the universal quantifier is upward entailing for its second argument. Thus, when it is embedded under a matrix negation, the result is a downward entailing environment, as can be seen in (22) (where the entailment from (a) to (b) goes from the superset of vegetables to the subset of Brussels sprouts):

22 a. No creo [que todo el mundo coma verduras].
'I don't believe that everybody eats vegetables.'
b. No creo [que todo el mundo coma coles de Bruselas].
'I don't believe that everybody eats Brussels sprouts.'

(22) shows that *todo el mundo* displays the expected behavior under negation in that its inherent entailment properties are shifted. However, my judgements indicate that the downward entailing environment that is created when the universal quantifier is embedded under negation is not sufficient to license an N-word in its scope, as in (23):

23. *No creo [que todo el mundo sepa nada].
I don't believe that everybody knows nothing
#'I don't believe that everybody knows anything.'

At present I have no explanation for the inconsistent behavior of the universal quantifier with respect to the other quantifiers that we have seen. As has been discussed by Linebarger (1987), Ladusaw's (1979) notion of downward entailment might not be a strong enough requirement for negative polarity licensing (cf. Kadmon & Landman 1993 for a recent proposal). Note that the IMMEDIATE SCOPE CONSTRAINT of Linebarger (1981, 1987) does not explain the effect in (23), given that in all the good examples considered in this paper the embedded N-word is not in the immediate scope of the matrix negation either. Crucially the embedded N-word in these good sentences appears in the licensing environment produced by the association of the matrix negation with an upward entailing quantifier. (23) should thus be just as good as, for example, (21) above.

What is important to note, however, is that the puzzling piece of data in (23) does not disprove the main argument presented in this paper, namely that NC in Romance should not be analyzed as an instance of movement to the Specifier of a negative head and that, therefore, N-words are not licensed via LF-movement. What (23) points out is that the issue of defining the specific environments in which N-words, and NPIs in general, are appropriately licensed still needs fine tuning. Thus, downward entailment might be just one of the necessary conditions for NPI licensing.

References

Aranovich, Raúl. 1993. Negative Concord and In Situ Licensing. To appear in *Proceedings of WCCFL XII*. Stanford: CSLI.

Arnáiz, Alfredo. 1993. On the parallelism between N-words and Wh-in-situ in Spanish. University of Southern California manuscript.

Barwise, Jon and Robin Cooper. 1981. Generalized Quantifiers and Natural Language. *Linguistics and Philosophy* 4.159-219.

Bosque, Ignacio. 1980. *Sobre la Negación*. Madrid: ediciones Cátedra.

Bosque, Ignacio. 1992. La negación y el PCV. *Estudios de gramática española*, número especial monográfico de la *Nueva Revista de Filología Hispánica*, México.

Chomsky, Noam. 1991. Some Notes on Economy of Derivation and Representation. *Principles and Parameters in Comparative Grammar*, ed. by R. Freidin, 417-54. Cambridge, MA: MIT Press.

Haegeman, Liliane. 1992. Negative Heads and Negative Operators: the Neg Criterion. University of Geneva manuscript.

Haegeman, Liliane and Raffaella Zanuttini. 1991. Negative Concord and the Negative Criterion. *The Linguistic Review* 8.233-251.

Higginbotham, James and Robert May. 1981. Questions, Quantifiers, and Crossing. *The Linguistic Review* 1.41-79.

Jackendoff, Ray S. 1972. *Semantic Interpretation in Generative Grammar*. Cambridge, MA: MIT Press.

Jaeggli, Osvaldo. 1982. *Topics in Romance Syntax*. Dordrecht: Foris.

Kadmon, Nirit and Fred Landman. 1993. Any. *Linguistics and Philosophy* 16.353-422.

Kayne, Richard. 1981. ECP Extensions. *Linguistic Inquiry* 12.93-133.

Kiss, Katalin. 1993. Wh-movement and Specificity. *Natural Language and Linguistic Theory* 11.85-120.

Klima, Edward S. 1964. Negation in English. *The Structure of Language*, ed. by J.A. Fodor and J.J. Katz, 246-323. Englewood Cliffs, N.J.: Prentice Hall.

Kroch, Anthony. 1989. Amount Quantification, Referentiality, and Long Wh-movement. University of Pennsylvania manuscript.

Ladusaw, William. 1979. *Polarity Sensitivity as Inherent Scope Relations*. Doctoral dissertation, University of Texas. Also published, New York: Garland Press, 1980.

Ladusaw, William. 1992. Expressing Negation. *Proceedings of the Second Conference on Semantics and Linguistic Theory*, ed. by C. Barker and D. Dowty, 237-59. Ohio State University Working Papers in Linguistics, 40. Columbus: The Ohio State University.

Laka, Mirem Itziar. 1990. *Negation in Syntax: On the Nature of Functional Categories and Projections*. Doctoral dissertation, MIT.

Linebarger, Marcia. 1981. *The Grammar of Negative Polarity*. Doctoral dissertation, MIT.

Linebarger, Marcia. 1987. Negative Polarity and Grammatical Representation. *Linguistics and Philosophy* 10.325-387.

Longobardi, Giuseppe. 1991. In Defense of the Correspondence Hypothesis: Island Effects and Parasitic Gap Constructions in Logical Form. *Logical Structure and Linguistic Structure*, ed. by C.-T. J. Huang and R. May, Dordrecht: Kluwer.

Progovac, Ljiljana. 1992. Nonnegative Polarity Licensing Must Involve Comp. *Linguistic Inquiry* 23, 2.41-47.

Rizzi, Luigi. 1982. *Issues in Italian Syntax*. Dordrecht: Foris.

Rizzi, Luigi. 1990. *Relativized Minimality*. Cambridge, MA: MIT Press.

Szabolcsi, Anna and Frans Zwarts. 1990. Semantic Properties of Composed Functions and the Distribution of Wh-phrases. *Proceedings of the Seventh Amsterdam Colloquium, Institute for language, logic, and information*, ed. by M. Stokhof and L. Torenvliet, 529-55. Amsterdam.

Szabolcsi, Anna and Frans Zwarts. 1991. *Unbounded Dependencies and Algebraic Semantics*. Lecture notes, Third European Summer School in Language, Logic, and Information. Saarbrucken.

Szabolcsi, Anna and Frans Zwarts. 1993. Weak Islands and an Algebraic Semantics for Scope Taking. *Natural Language Semantics* 2.235-284.

Zanuttini, Raffaella. 1991. *Syntactic Properties of Sentential Negation: A Comparative Study of Romance Languages*. Doctoral dissertation, University of Pennsylvania.

ppinar@ccit.arizona.edu

The Structure of Tense and the Syntax of Temporal Adverbs*

ELLEN THOMPSON
University of Maryland at College Park

1. Introduction

Recent generative analyses of the syntax of tense have identified the syntactic primitives of tense as the time points of Reichenbach (1947) (Hornstein 1977, 1981, 1990, Zagona 1988, 1990, Giorgi and Pianesi 1991, Stowell 1993). In this paper, assuming the minimalist approach (Chomsky 1993), I argue that time points are associated in a one-to-one fashion with syntactic heads. According to this view, the temporal information of a clause is represented syntactically not only by Tense Phrase (TP) but also by other phrases; I claim that these phrases are Aspect Phrase (AspP) and VP. Evidence for this proposal comes from the interpretation of temporal PP adverbs, which, depending on their adjunction site, modify different parts of the tense structure of a clause.

---

* I would like to thank the audience at WCCFL for their comments and suggestions. I would also like to thank Peggy Antonisse, Paul Gorrell, Norbert Hornstein, David Lebeaux, and David Lightfoot for discussion of this research. I am especially indebted to Jairo Nunes and Juan Uriagereka for very helpful suggestions and for their support and enthusiasm.

The paper is organized as follows: in section 2, I give a brief overview of the neo-Reichenbachian approach to tense adopted here. Section 3 presents the proposal that temporal points are linked in a one-to-one fashion with syntactic heads, the Tense Structure Mapping Condition. In section 4, I argue that the distribution of temporal adverbs gives evidence for the syntax of tense proposed in section 3. I propose that temporal adverbs adjoin to VP or to AspP, depending on their temporal interpretation. Section 5 is devoted to structural evidence for this hypothesis. I present data from constituency tests, preposition stranding facts, the position of the adverb with respect to the direct object, and scope of negation facts that support this claim. In section 6, I offer an account for why clause-initial temporal adverbs are not ambiguous in the way that clause-final adverbs are. Section 7 extends the analysis to durative time adverbs with the present perfect, which show an ambiguity which is straightforwardly accounted for within the theory developed here.

2. Framework

Within the Reichenbachian framework, tenses are composed of three TIME POINTS: the EVENT POINT, the REFERENCE POINT, and the SPEECH POINT. This system is illustrated by (1), where the Event point is the time of Mary's leaving, the Reference point is the time by which Mary's leaving takes place (in this sentence, 2:00), and the Speech point is the time at which the sentence is uttered.

(1) At 2:00, Mary had left

I assume Hornstein's (1990) neo-Reichenbachian approach to tense, according to which the structures of the basic tenses of English are as in (2), where the linear order of the Speech, Reference and Event points reflects their temporal order. If two points are separated by a line, the leftmost point is interpreted as temporally preceding the other point. If two points are separated by a comma, they are interpreted as contemporaneous.

(2)	S , R , E	present	E _ S , R	present perfect
	E , R _ S	past	E _ R _ S	past perfect
	S _ R , E	future	S _ E _ R	future perfect

3. A Syntax for Tense

Assuming that time points are the syntactic primitives of tense, the issue is how temporal points are represented structurally. I propose that the mapping between the semantic and the syntactic representation of tense is subject to the following condition:

(3) Tense Structure Mapping Condition: Time points are associated with syntactic heads in a one-to-one fashion

The tense morpheme of English, which I assume is associated with the head of TP, orders the Reference point in the tense structure with respect to the Speech point. For example, the past tense morpheme orders the Reference point before the Speech point, while the future tense morpheme orders the Reference point after the Speech point, as in (2). I thus follow Hornstein (1990) in associating the Speech point with Infl, and, in particular I claim that it is located in the head of TP.

The aspectual morpheme of English *have* orders the Event point with respect to the Reference point; the presence of *have* orders the Event point as preceding the Reference point, the absence of *have* orders the Event point as contemporaneous with the Reference point. Therefore, it is natural that the Reference point be located in the head of AspP, which I assume is positioned between TP and VP. Temporal points are thus associated with syntactic heads in the following way: the Event point is associated with V, the head of VP, the Speech point with T, the head of TP, and the Reference point with Asp, the head of AspP.[1]

4. Temporal Adverbs

Temporal adverbs have been analyzed as sentential and as verb phrase constituents. Chomsky (1965), Dresher (1976), and Hornstein and Weinberg (1981) argue that temporal adverbs are associated to S (IP), while Jackendoff (1972), Andrews (1982), Larson (1988), and Stroik (1990) claim that temporal adverbs are dominated by VP. In this section, I present evidence that, depending on the temporal interpretation, temporal adverbs are either associated to VP or to a higher functional phrase.

In order to determine the position of temporal adverbs, we must first consider what it is that these adverbs modify. Assuming that they modify tense, given the analysis of tense outlined above whereby the tense information of a clause is represented in TP, AspP and VP, there are three potential sites for temporal modifiers.

---

[1] Giorgi and Pianesi (1991) also associate temporal points with syntactic heads. However, according to their proposal, the syntactic primitives of tense are the relations between temporal points; the relation between the Speech and Reference point and the relation between the Reference and Event point, and not the temporal points themselves.

Hornstein points out that the Speech point can not be directly modified by adverbs. This is shown by the fact that (4) can not be felicitously uttered at 3:00, with the meaning *John left and it's 3:00 now.*

(4) John left at 3:00

Hornstein claims that this restriction is explained by the fact that the Speech point is deictic, and deictic elements in general can not be modified (*happy you, *empty there).

Given that the Speech point is located in the head of TP, and that it can not be directly modified, it follows that temporal adverbs are not adjoined to TP. This leaves the Reference and Event points for modification.

4.1. An Ambiguity with Temporal Adverbs

Braroe (1974) points out that certain constructions with temporal adverbs in English are ambiguous; (5) can be paraphrased as in (6a) or (6b).

(5) The secretary had eaten at 3 p.m.

(6) a. The time that the secretary actually ate was 3 p.m.
b. The secretary had already eaten by 3 p.m.

Braroe argues that this ambiguity is structural - assuming the generative semantics approach to auxiliary verbs, *have* is represented as a verb which is associated to a higher S. When the adverb adjoins to this higher S, it modifies the auxiliary verb, yielding the reading in (6b). When the adverb adjoins to the lower S, the reading in (6a) results.

Hornstein (1977) argues against Braroe's structural analysis, pointing out that the account predicts that this ambiguity should arise in all sentences containing an auxiliary, given Braroe's assumption that all auxiliary verbs hang from a higher S. However, as shown by (7), (Hornstein's (26)), this is not the case; a sentence in the progressive is not ambiguous in the way a perfective sentence is.[2]

---

[2] Temporal adverbs with simple tenses are not ambiguous:

(i) a. John left at 3:00
b. John will leave at 3:00

This is explained by the fact that in these tenses, the Reference and Event points are interpreted as contemporaneous; therefore, when one point is modified, the other is modified also (Hornstein 1990:38). As shown in (2) in the text, this is

(7) John was driving home at 3 p.m.

Another incorrect prediction that Braroe's analysis makes is that in a language such as French, where the simple past is expressed with the verb *avoir* 'to have', the same ambiguity should show up. However, this prediction is not borne out, as shown by (8), which is unambiguous in the same way that the simple past in English is unambiguous (Hornstein's (25)):

(8) La secrétaire a mangé à trois heures
the secretary had ate at three hours
'The secretary ate at 3 o'clock'

Hornstein offers an alternative to this analysis, claiming that on the reading in (6a), the adverb modifies the Event point, while on the reading in (6b), the adverb modifies the Reference point.

I adopt Hornstein's claim that this temporal ambiguity is due to modification of the Event or Reference point, and, following the intuition of Braroe, I claim that there are two different structures associated with the two different modification possibilities (Zagona 1988, Inclan 1991 and Nakajima 1991 also pursue structural analyses of this ambiguity). I propose that when the adverb modifies the Event point, it is adjoined to VP, and when it modifies the Reference point, it is adjoined to AspP.[3]

---

in contrast to the perfective tenses, which are characterized by noncontemporaneous Reference and Event points, and hence show an ambiguity depending on which point is modified.

[3] The analysis offered here for the distribution of temporal PP adverbs can be straightforwardly extended to temporal adjunct clauses, such as *when Bill left*, which could be adjoined either to VP or a higher inflectional projection (Koizumi 1991, Miyamoto 1993, Johnston 1994). Thompson (1994) argues that temporal adjunct clauses which are interpreted as simultaneous with the matrix Event are VP-adjoined, while temporal adjunct clauses which are interpreted as nonsimultaneous are adjoined to AspP.

4.2 The Overtness of Adverbial Modification

An interesting property of adverbial modification discussed by Uriagereka (1988), and attributed to Howard Lasnik, is that the modification domain of adverbs seems to be determined from the surface position of the adverb, not its LF position (see also Ladusaw 1988, Lasnik and Saito 1991).

This fact is illustrated by the Galician example in (9), discussed by Uriagereka (1988:222). In this sentence, *ónde* 'where' is interpreted as having wide scope over the clause, which is instantiated by LF movement of *ónde* to the matrix CP.

(9) pro dis que han gañar ónde os anarquistas
(you) said that will win where the anarchists
'Where did you say that the anarchists will win?'

ónde in this sentence can not be interpreted as modifying the matrix event of saying; the sentence can only ask about where the winning takes place. This is explained if the surface position of *ónde* determines its modification domain; given that it is overtly in the embedded clause, it can only modify the embedded event.

This restriction seems puzzling for a minimalist approach. Since no conditions can be placed on SPELLOUT, it is not possible to account for this generalization by claiming that the modification domain of adverbs is determined at SPELLOUT. I would like to suggest that adopting the minimalist checking theory of movement resolves this problem and explains why it is that the domain of adverbial modification seems to be determined at SPELLOUT. According to the checking theory of movement, all movement is forced by morphological checking requirements. No movement is optional, since, given two convergent derivations, the derivation with optional movement is more costly than the derivation without movement, and hence is ruled out by Economy considerations.

Applying the feature checking movement theory to adverbs, adverbs should be barred from moving, since they, plausibly, do not have any features which need to be checked. Since adverbs do not have features to check, they do not need to move, and hence, can not move. This is what gives the appearance of a SPELLOUT condition; since adverbs never move, they are interpreted at LF in the position at which they come into the structure.[4]

5. Empirical Evidence

5.1 Constituency Tests

In this section, I show that constituency test data discussed by Andrews (1982) support the claim that temporal adverbs which modify the Event point are adjoined to VP, while temporal adverbs which modify the Reference point are adjoined to AspP. VP constituency tests such as Pseudoclefting (10a), Though movement (10b), and VP fronting (10c), show that when the VP is isolated, the only reading possible for an *at phrase* temporal adverb is where the adverb modifies the Event point - in (10a - c), the leaving takes place at 6:00, not sometime before 6:00.

(10) a. What John had done was leave the store at 6:00
b. Leave the store at 6:00 though John had, Mary still didn't see him
c. John claimed that he had left the store at 6:00, and left the store at 6:00 he had

This data is predicted on the approach developed here, since in these constructions, the adverb is necessarily associated with VP, and hence is only able to modify the Event point.

5.2 Preposition Stranding

Temporal PPs allow preposition stranding, as shown in (11):

(11) a. At what time did he leave?
b. What time did he leave at?

---

[4] This reasoning does not disallow movement of adverbs in constructions such as Topicalization (i), Focus movement (ii), and WH-movement (iii). The movement of adverbs in these constructions is explained in the same way that parallel movement of other syntactic categories is explained; presumably, there are relevant features which need to be checked. Adverbs are not prohibited from having features; they just do not have intrinsic features which need to be checked.

(i) Timewise, John is really pressed right now
(ii) Only at **3:00** do I have to leave
(iii) When are you leaving?

Hornstein and Weinberg (1981) argue that PPs that are associated to VP allow preposition stranding, while PPs associated to IP do not. Given this generalization, we predict that preposition stranding with a temporal PP is only possible when the PP modifies the Event point, and not when it modifies the Reference point. The data in (12) show that this prediction is borne out; (12a) is ambiguous; it can ask for the time of the event of leaving (Event point reading), or the time by which the leaving takes place (Reference point reading). However, (12b) only asks for the time of the event of leaving, and not the time by which the event of leaving takes place.

(12) a. At what time had John left?
b. What time had John left at?

5.3 Direct Object/Adverb Asymmetries

Data involving the structural relation between the direct object and adverb give evidence for the present analysis. It has been noted in the literature (Anderson 1979, Contreras 1984, Larson 1988, Stroik 1990, Lasnik and Saito 1991) that certain adverb phrases seem to be c-commanded by their direct objects.

For example, in (13), him seems to c-command John, yielding a Condition C violation, and in (14), the quantifier phrase every crewman binds the pronoun his inside the adverb phrase. In (15), no work licenses the Negative Polarity Item at all in the adverb phrase, while in (16), the men licenses the reciprocal each other in the adverb phrase. In (17), each in direct object position seems to c-command the other within the adverbial.

(13) Condition C Effects
*Mary visited him_i during John's_i incarceration

(14) Quantifier Binding
John irritated every worker_i by criticizing his_i work

(15) Negative Polarity Item Licensing
John does no work at all quickly

(16) Reciprocal Binding
I saw the men_i somewhere near each other's_i houses

(17) Each . . . the other
I photographed each man somewhere near the other's home

Lasnik and Saito (1991) propose that this type of data can be accounted for by assuming the minimalist approach to Case, where the direct object in English moves out of VP at LF for Case-checking in Spec AgrO. Hence, at LF, the raised object asymmetrically c-commands into a VP-adjoined adverb, as shown in (18):

(18)

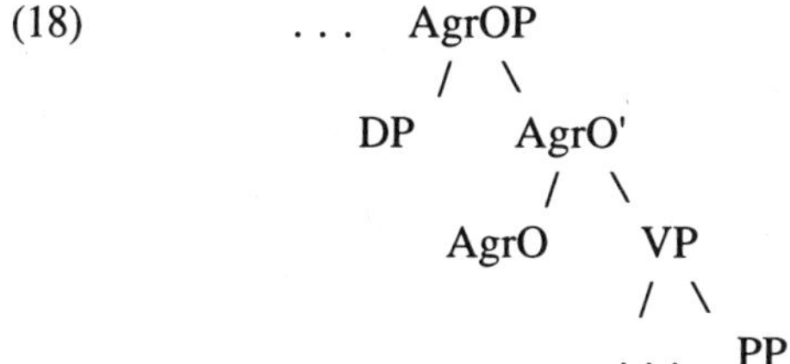

The structural analysis of temporal ambiguity offered here predicts that the direct object may be in a position at LF which c-commands into a VP-adjoined adverb, but not an AspP-adjoined adverb.

The relevant data to check this prediction is in (19)-(23), with the example in (a) and the possible readings in (b). In (19), on the reading with coreference between him and John, the only reading available for the adverb is the Reference point reading: the sentence must mean that the event of seeing takes place sometime before the time of the presentation, and cannot have the Event point reading, where the event of seeing takes place at the time of the presentation. In (20), the only reading available for the adverb on the bound reading of the pronoun is the Event point reading: the sentence must mean that the event of firing takes place at the break times, and cannot have the Reference point reading, where the event of firing takes place sometime before the break times. The same contrast is found with Negative Polarity Item Licensing, Reciprocal Binding, and Each . . . the other constructions, where the c-command effect results only on the Event point reading of the adverb, as shown in (21-23).

(19) Condition C Effects

a. Mary had seen him_i at the time that $John_i$ presented his paper

b. *Event point reading: event of seeing takes place at presentation time

Reference point reading: event of seeing takes place sometime before presentation time

(20) Quantifier Binding

a. The boss had fired every workeri at the time of hisi break

b. Event point reading: event of firing takes place at break times

*Reference point reading: event of firing takes place sometime before break times

(21) Negative Polarity Item Licensing

a. John had identified no problems at anyone's quitting time

b. Event point reading: event of identification takes place at no one's quitting time

*Reference point reading: event of identification takes place sometime before no one's quitting time

(22) Reciprocal Licensing

a. John had seen Mary and Phili at each other'si break times

b. Event point reading: event of seeing takes place at break times

*Reference point reading: event of seeing takes place sometime before break times

(23) Each . . . the other

a. I had photographed each man at the other's break time

b. Event point reading: event of photographing takes place at break times

*Reference point reading: event of photographing takes place before break times

The generalization is that the direct object c-command effect obtains only when the adverb modifies the Event point. This is predicted on the analysis pursued here, since when the adverb modifies the Event point, it is VP-adjoined, in a position which is c-commanded by the direct object. However, when the adverb modifies the Reference point, it is AspP-adjoined, in a position which is not c-commanded by the direct object.[5]

5.4 Negation

The proposal developed here of the different structural positions of temporal adverbs receives support from facts involving the scope of negation. Sentential negation seems to take scope over Event point-modifying adverbs and not over Reference point-modifying adverbs. This

---

[5] The analysis pursued here is compatible with the VP site of adverbs being VP-adjoined or VP-internal.

fact is explained by assuming that sentential negation is located between AspP and VP, and that Reference point modifying adverbs are adjoined to AspP and Event point modifying adverbs are adjoined to VP.

The fact that Event point modifying adverbs are within the scope of negation is illustrated by the possible readings of (24). On the Event point reading, where the event takes place at 3:00, negation has scope over the adverb; the reading is *It is not at 3:00 that Mary leaves the room.* The sentence cannot have the reading where the adverb takes scope over negation on the Event point reading, with the meaning *It is at 3:00 that Mary does not leave the room.*

(24) Mary hadn't left the room at 3:00

(25) Event point reading:
  a. 'It is not at 3:00 that Mary leaves the room'
  b. *'It is at 3:00 that Mary does not leave the room'

However, when the adverb modifies the Reference point, the judgments reverse; the adverb seems to be outside the scope of negation. On the Reference point reading of (24), where the event takes place sometime before 3:00, the meaning must be where the adverb is outside the scope of negation; *It is sometime before 3:00 that Mary does not leave the room*, and it cannot have the reading where the adverb is within the scope of negation; *It is not sometime before 3:00 that Mary leaves the room.*

(26) Reference point reading:
  a. 'It is sometime before 3:00 that Mary does not leave the room'
  b. *'It is not sometime before 3:00 that Mary leaves the room'

6. Clause-initial Temporal Adverbs

Clause-initial temporal adverbs in English allow only a reading where the adverb modifies the Reference point, as shown by (27), where the event of leaving takes place sometime before, and not at 3:00 (Hornstein 1990, Inclan 1991, Nakajima 1991).

(27) At 3:00, John had left the store

The analysis proposed here explains this data naturally. Assuming that clause-initial adverbs are moved (see footnote 4), this lack of ambiguity is predicted by the Shortest Movement Condition (Chomsky 1993). Movement is permitted only from AspP-adjoined position, by the following reasoning: there are two possible derivations for a sentence with a clause-initial temporal adverb; one in which the adverb has moved from VP, and one in which the adverb has moved from AspP.[6] However, the derivation in which the adverb moves from AspP-adjoined position rules out the derivation in which the adverb moves from VP-adjoined position, because the derivation with movement from AspP involves shorter movement than the derivation with movement from VP. Hence, locating the Reference point-modifying adverb as structurally higher than the Event point-modifying adverb, in combination with the Shortest Movement Condition, provides an account for the lack of ambiguity of preposed temporal adverbs.[7]

7. An Ambiguity with Durative Adverbs

This analysis can be extended naturally to durative time adverbs. It has been observed that present perfect sentences with a durative time adverb are ambiguous (Dowty 1979, Richards 1982, Mittwoch 1988, Abusch and Rooth 1990). The sentence in (28) may have what is called the EXISTENTIAL reading, where the sentence means roughly *There is a two week period in the past throughout which John is in Boston*, or what is called the UNIVERSAL or UP-TO-NOW reading, with the meaning *John is in Boston throughout the two-week period ending at the utterance time*.

---

6 These two derivations have the same array, since they share the same lexical items. However, if the comparison class of derivations is defined by derivations that have the same numeration, as in Chomsky (1994), then these derivations are not comparable. It is possible that adjuncts behave differently from arguments with respect to the numeration, different adjunction sites not resulting in different numerations. This may be related to the fact that adjuncts do not obey the Strict Cycle Condition (Chomsky 1993).

7 This account predicts that, in general, adverb preposing should disambiguate structurally ambiguous adverbs in favor of the higher attachment site reading. This is illustrated in (i), where *in the library* can modify either the matrix or the embedded event, but when the adverb is preposed, (ii), only the matrix event modification reading is possible.

(i) Mary told John to read in the library
(ii) In the library, Mary told John to read

(28) John has been in Boston for two weeks

(29) a. Existential Reading
There is a two week period in the past throughout which John is in Boston

b. Up-to-now Reading
John is in Boston throughout the two week period ending at the utterance time

The account developed here predicts this data straightforwardly. The up-to-now reading results when the adverb is interpreted as modifying the Reference point, and is therefore AspP-adjoined. Reference point modification gives the up-to-now reading since, as shown in (30), in the present perfect, the Reference point is associated with the Speech point, the time of utterance. (Following Hornstein 1990, temporal modification is represented by linking the PP to the temporal point that is modified.)

```
(30)        E _ S , R
                    |
              for two weeks
```

The existential reading results when the adverb is adjoined to VP, and hence modifies the Event point. In this configuration, the event occurs just at some point in the past, since the Event point is not linked to the Speech point in the present perfect, as shown in (31):

```
(31)        E _ S , R
            |
      for two weeks
```

Interestingly, as noted by Dowty (1979), the sentence loses the existential reading when the adverb occurs in initial position. The sentence in (32) can only mean *John has been in Boston for the last two weeks*; the up-to-now reading.

(32) For two weeks, John has been in Boston

This follows from the analysis presented here, since, as discussed in section 6, the fronted adverb must have moved from the AspP-adjoined position in order to obey the Shortest Movement Condition.

8. Conclusion

To summarize, I have argued that time points are associated in a one-to-one fashion with syntactic heads in the following way: the Event point is associated with V, the Speech point with T, and the Reference point with Asp. This led to the claim that temporal adverbs which modify the Event point are adjoined to VP, while temporal adverbs which modify the Reference point are adjoined to AspP. I discussed evidence in favor of this view from constituency tests, preposition stranding facts, and the position of these adverbs with respect to the direct object and sentential negation. I showed how this analysis, in combination with the Shortest Movement Condition, accounts for the nonambiguity of preposed temporal adverbs. The analysis was then shown to account for an ambiguity of durative time adverbs with the present perfect.

References

Abusch, Dorit and Mats Rooth. 1990. Temporal adverbs and the English perfect. *Proceedings of NELS* 21.1-15.

Andrews, Avery. 1982. A note on the constituent structure of adverbials and auxiliaries. *Linguistic Inquiry* 13.313-317.

Braroe, Eva. 1974. *The syntax and semantics of English tense markers*. Doctoral dissertation, University of Stockholm.

Chomsky, Noam. 1965. *Aspects of the theory of syntax*. Cambridge, Massachusetts: MIT Press.

Chomsky, Noam. 1993. A minimalist program for linguistic theory. *The view from building 20: essays in honor of Sylvain Bromberger*, ed. by Kenneth Hale and Samuel Keyser, 1-52. Cambridge, Massachusetts: MIT Press.

Chomsky, Noam. 1994. *Bare phrase structure*. Ms., MIT.

Contreras, Heles. 1984. A note on parasitic gaps. *Linguistic Inquiry* 15.698-701.

Dowty, David. 1979. *Word meaning and Montague grammar*. Dordrecht: D. Reidel.

Dresher, B. Elan. 1976. *The position and movement of prepositional phrases*. Ms., University of Massachusetts at Amherst.

Giorgi, Alessandra and Fabio Pianesi. 1991. Toward a syntax of temporal representations. *Probus* 3.2.1-27.

Hornstein, Norbert. 1977. Towards a theory of tense. *Linguistic Inquiry* 8.521-557.

Hornstein, Norbert. 1981. The study of meaning in natural language: three approaches to tense. *Explanation in linguistics*, ed. by Norbert Hornstein and David Lightfoot, 116-151. London and New York: Longman.

Hornstein, Norbert. 1990. *As time goes by*. Cambridge, Massachusetts: MIT Press.

Hornstein, Norbert and Amy Weinberg 1981. Case theory and preposition stranding. *Linguistic Inquiry* 12.55-91.

Inclán, Sara. 1991. Temporal adverbs and the structure of reference and event points. *Proceedings of ESCOL* 8.130-141.

Jackendoff, Ray. 1972. *Semantic interpretation in generative grammar*. Cambridge, Massachusetts: MIT Press.

Johnston, Michael. 1994. *When clauses, adverbs of quantification and focus*. Paper presented at WCCFL.

Koizumi, Masatoshi. 1991. *Syntax of adjuncts and the phrase structure of Japanese*. Master's thesis. Ohio State University.

Ladusaw, William. 1988. Adverbs, negation, and QR. *Linguistics in the morning calm 2*, ed. by The Linguistic Society of Korea, 481-488. Seoul: Hanshin Publishing Co.

Larson, Richard. 1988. On the double object construction. *Linguistic Inquiry* 19.335-391.

Lasnik, Howard and Mamoru Saito. 1991. *On the subject of infinitives*. Paper presented at the Chicago Linguistic Society conference.

Mittwoch, Anita. 1988. Aspects of English aspect: on the interpretation of perfect, progressive and durative phrases. *Linguistics and Philosophy* 11.2.

Miyamoto, Yoichi. 1993. *Temporal adverbials in Japanese*. Ms., University of Connecticut at Storrs.

Nakajima, Heizo. 1991. Transportability, scope ambiguity of adverbials and the generalized binding theory. *Journal of Linguistics* 27.337-374.

Reichenbach, Hans. 1947. *Elements of symbolic logic*. New York: The Macmillan Company.

Richards, Barry. 1982. Tense, aspect and time adverbials, part 1. *Linguistics and philosophy* 5.59-107.

Stroik, Thomas. 1990. Adverbs as V-sisters. *Linguistic Inquiry* 21.654-661.

Stowell, Timothy. 1993. *The syntax of tense*. Ms., UCLA.

Thompson, Ellen. 1994. *The syntax and semantics of temporal adjunct clauses*, to appear in *Studies in the Linguistic Sciences*, Volume 24, No. 2, Fall 1994.

Uriagereka, Juan. 1988. *On government*. Doctoral dissertation, University of Connecticut at Storrs, distributed by MITWPL, 1993.

Zagona, Karen. 1988. *Verb phrase syntax*. Dordrecht: Kluwer.

Zagona, Karen. 1990. *Times as temporal argument structure*. Paper presented at the Time in Language conference, Cambridge, Massachusetts.

Author's address:

Linguistics Department
1401 Marie Mount Hall
University of Maryland
College Park, MD 20742-7515

email: et23@umail.umd.edu

Indefinite Clauses: Some Notes on the Syntax and Semantics of Subjunctives and Infinitives*

GEORGES TSOULAS
CNRS, URA 1720 & Université Paris-8

0 Introduction

It is a long-standing observation[1] that Tense is a property relevant to the specification of extraction domains. Roughly, the multiple formulations of this observation (see fn. 1), amount to saying that extraction is much more difficult out of a tensed clause than out of a non-tensed one. Chomsky (1986a) stipulates that a tensed IP is an inherent barrier, however he notes that this stipulation is problematic conceptually as well as empirically and suggests that possibly '... the parametric variation involves not the distinction between tense vs.

---

* For comments and discussion on the material presented here I want to thank Anne Fleischman, Léa Nash, Alain Rouveret, Sarah Kennelly, Juan Uriagereka, Anne Zribi-Hertz and the audience at WCCFL XIII for their thoughtful questions and comments. Thanks also to Isabelle Viaud-Delmon for her help and support. I am of course fully responsible for all remaining errors of fact and interpretation.

1 At least since Ross (1967) (The Propositional Island Constraint). This condition has been reformulated in various ways by Chomsky (1977), (1981) (the Tensed-*S* Condition), (1986a) (In terms of barriers), Huang (1982), Manzini (1992), and others.

infinitive but the distinction between indicative vs. infinitive-subjunctive...' (p. 39). Subsequently, it has been observed that subjunctives do, in fact, demonstrate strikingly similar behaviour in a number of respects. Drawing on Chomsky's observation, I intend to investigate in this paper some properties of subjunctives and infinitives in various languages, and propose a unified treatment aiming at accounting for their behaviour. I will propose that the clausal constituents with the verb in the subjunctive or infinitive are INDEFINITES. In the first section I present evidence coming first from the extraction patterns found with subjunctives and infinitives on the one hand and indefinite DPs on the other, and, second, evidence from the semantic interpretation of the tense of subjunctive and infinitival clauses as compared to the referential status of indefinite DPs. In the second section, the implementation of the analysis and its interactions with subjunctive and infinitival morphology in different types of languages will be presented. Finally in the third section I will discuss some extensions and consequences of the theory .

1.1 Extraction Phenomena

Consider the following examples from English (1-7), French (8-16) and Modern Greek (17-23):

(1) What$_i$ did you wonder[$_{CP}$[to whom]$_j$ John gave t_i t_j] ?
(2) [To whom]$_j$ did you wonder [what$_i$ John gave t_i t_j]?
(3) What$_i$ did you wonder[$_{CP}$[to whom]$_j$ to give t_i t_j]?
(4) [To whom]$_j$ did you wonder [what$_i$ to give t_i t_j]?
(5) Who did you think that John said that Bill saw ?
(6) What did you wonder [$_{CP'}$ who [$_{VP'}$ said [$_{CP}$ that Bill [$_{VP}$ saw t]]]]?
(7) What did you wonder [$_{CP'}$ who [$_{VP'}$ decided [$_{CP}$ to [$_{VP}$ see t]]]]?
(Examples from Chomsky 1986a)
(8) * Que te demandes-tu à qui Suzy a donné ?
what$_i$ you/refl wonder to whom$_j$ Suzy gave t_i t_j
(9) * A qui te demandes-tu ce que Suzy a donné?
to whom$_i$ you/refl wonder what$_j$ that Suzy gave t_i t_j
(10) Que te demandes-tu à qui donner?
what$_i$ you/refl wonder to whom$_j$ to give t_i t_j
(11) A qui te demandes-tu quoi donner?
to whom$_i$ you/refl wonder what$_j$ to give t_i t_j
(12) Qui pensais-tu qu' Isabelle a dit que Cécile a vu?
who$_i$ did you think that Isabelle said that Cécile saw t_i
(13) * Que te demandes-tu qui a dit qu' Alex a vu?
what$_i$ you/refl wonder [who$_j$ [t_j said that Alex saw t_i]]
(14) Que te demandes-tu qui a decidé de voir ?
what$_i$ you/refl wonder [who$_j$ [t_j decided to see t_i]]
(15) Que te demandes-tu qui a voulu que Sophie voie?
what$_i$ you/refl wonder [who$_j$ [t_j wanted that Sophie see/Subj t_i]]
(16) Que te demandes-tu qui a exigé que Sophie écrive ?
what$_i$ you/refl wonder who$_j$ [t_j required that Sophie write/Subj t_i]]

(17) * Ti anarotiese se pion O Alekos oti edose?
what wonder/you to whom the Alekos that gave

(18) * Se pion anarotiese ti o Alekos oti edose?
to whom wonder/you what the Alekos that gave

(19) Ti anarotiese se pion na dosis?
what wonder/you to whom give

(20) Se pion anarotiese ti na dosis?
to whom wonder/you what give

(21) ? Pion nomizis oti o Nikos ipe oti o Kostas ide?
whom think/you that the Nikos said that the Kostas saw

(22) * Ti anarotithikes pios ipe oti o Yannis ide?
what wondered/you who said that the Yannis saw

(23) Ti anarotithikes pios apofasise na di?
what wondered/you who decided see

The above examples are fairly well known and hardly require any explanation. The interesting thing to observe here is that in French, where morphological subjunctives are to be found alongside infinitives the two pattern in the same way in that they both allow DPs to be *wh*-moved outside their clausal domain. Modern Greek is somehow the mirror image of English in that Modern Greek lacks infinitives[2]. Interestingly though, the overall pattern of the extraction is basically the same since the subjunctive in Modern Greek behaves like the infinitive in English. These data seem to lend solid empirical support to Chomsky's intuition that this type of extraction is sensitive to Mood rather than to Tense[3].

1.2 A parallel with Nominals: Extraction out of DPs

Let us now turn to a different type of data concerning extraction out of DPs. Consider the classical examples in (24-42), again from English French and Modern Greek

(24) what do you want to see a picture of

(25) what do you want to see pictures of

(26) what do you want to see some picture of

(27) * what do you want to see a given picture of

(28) * what do you want to see these pictures of

(29) (*) what do you want to see the picture(s) of

(30) De qui veux-tu voir une photo
of who want-you see one (a) picture

---

[2] If we put aside gerunds MGk has no verbal form that is not inflected for person and number agreement. For the moment I will ignore the issue of the English Subjunctive which is, at best, very marginal.

[3] It might be argued that Chomsky had in mind something akin to the traditional distinction between different Moods. Recall that traditionally the Infinitive is considered a Mood. In the analysis I am proposing here the notion of Mood does not play any significant role. Moreover I will show that the modal meaning that is commonly associated with the subjunctive is not only misleading but, more importantly, in a number of cases it yields empirically incorrect results.

(31) De qui veux-tu voir des photos
of who want you see Det/Indef/Plur pictures

(32) * De qui veux-tu voir une certaine photo
of who want-you see one(a) certain picture

(33) * De qui veux-tu voir ces photos
of what want-you see these pictures

(34) * De qui veux-tu voir la photo
of who want you see the picture

(35) ?? De qui veux-tu voir les photos
of who want you see the/Plur pictures

(36) Pianou thelis na dis mia fotografia
whose/Gen want/you COMP see one(a) picture

(37) Pianou thelis na dis fotografies
whose/Gen want/you COMP see pictures

(38) Pianou thelis na dis kamia fotografia
whose/Gen want/you COMP see any/Sing/fem picture

(39) *Pianou thelis na dis mia sigekrimeni fotografia
whose/Gen want/you COMP see one(a) certain picture

(40) * Pianou thelis na dis aftes tis fotografies
whose/Gen want/you COMP see these the/Plur pictures

(41) *Pianou thelis na dis ti fotografia
whose/Gen want/you COMP see the picture

(42) * Pianou thelis na dis tis fotografies
whose/Gen want/you COMP see the/Plur pictures

As can be seen, extraction out of an indefinite DP, a bare plural, or a weak quantifier (here *some*) is possible, whereas extraction out of a specific indefinite, a demonstrative or a definite is impossible[4]. A bit of caution is needed though when discussing this type of data. Notice that, as is the case in general, the grammaticality judgements are not absolute. What is intended is the indication of a contrast that is more or less clear cut. It would be hard to find a more commonplace remark than the fact that variation among speakers is definitely part of the linguistic reality. Thus, concerning the French examples there are a number of speakers who would accept virtually any of the starred sentences, denying the existence of any contrast whatsoever. Far more interestingly though, it seems that examples like (43), as well as one particular interpretation of (34) seem much better to virtually all speakers:

(43) De quel président veux-tu voir la photo ?
of which President want you see the picture

There are, I believe, several reasons to that. For one thing, one can say that these sentences receive a somehow 'generic' interpretation which

---

[4] These data are generally referred to as the 'Specificity Effects', see Diesing (1992), Enç (1991). I will briefly return to the, mostly terminological, question of Specificity vs. Indefiniteness.

is related more to the indefinite than to the definite interpretation[5]. Connected to the previous remark, we can suggest that what we dub here 'generic' corresponds exactly to the attributive part of the distinction referential vs. attributive uses of definite Noun Phrases (Partee (1972) assimilates Indefinites to the attributive use of definites). In Enç's (1991) framework it is with nonspecific definites that extraction is permitted, contrasting with specifics like (43a) :

(43a) * De quel président veux-tu voir la photo qui est sur la table ?
of which President want you see the picture which is on the table

Moreover, we observe that the most faithful paraphrase of (43) is (43b) and of (34), (43c):

(43b) Quel président veux-tu voir en photo ?
which President want-you see in picture
(43c) Qui veux-tu voir en photo?
who want you see in picture

It is then quite reasonable to propose that these DPs are headed by expletive determiners. I will tentatively define here expletive determiners as being 'semantically empty' or very weak. We might also add that, as far as the data considered here are concerned, this proposal seems also plausible on semantic grounds since these DPs differ from standard 'Russellian' definite descriptions in that they do not carry any uniqueness presupposition, i.e., they do not entail that *there is at most one object that is a picture (of the President)* they rather carry only an existential presupposition, hence their semantic weakness[6]. It should also be noted here that this use of the notion of 'expletive determiner ' is different from the one in Vergnaud & Zubizarreta (1992). It seems then that there is abundant evidence in favour of the claim that true definites (specifics) are the elements that block extraction and that when they don't they receive an interpretation similar to the indefinite interpretation, which is reflected in the status of the determiner that heads the DP. I will leave a more careful discussion of the issue for future research. However, it

---

5 In connection to sentences like (43) some pragmatic factors also come into play. It is generally the case that people don't know Presidents personally, thus a question like (43) is rather unlikely to be used when asking to see the picture of the President playing squash with his dog in the presence of the four bodyguards that were fired on April 12. It is rather the official, somehow prototypical presidential picture that is referred to.

6 Alain Rouveret (pc) points out that the analysis presented here may be taken as evidence for a generalisation of the use of the notion 'expletive determiner'.

should be by now clear that no real challenge is posed to the theory that I present here by the allegedly problematic judgements. Returning now to the extraction facts, the parallel between definite vs. indefinite DPs on the one hand and Indicative vs. Infinitive/subjunctive clauses on the other, is striking to say the least. The parallel seen in these contrasts seems constant enough across the different languages to require some explanation. Thus an important generalisation would be missed if the theory for these data did not also provide an explanation. Before I get into the details of the analysis I am proposing let us first turn to another aspect of the parallel in question.

1.3 Time and Event reference in Subjunctives and Infinitives

Consider the following examples :

(44) Sophie veut que les musiciens partent
Sophie wants that the musicians leave/Subj

(45) Sophie veut venir
Sophie wants to come

(46) Jenny remembered to bring the wine (Stowell (1982))

The fundamental question I would like to address concerns the relation between the two events (in the sense of Higginbotham (1985), Parsons (1990)) described by the verbs in the matrix and in the complement clause. Stowell (1982), following Bresnan (1972), suggests that the tense frame of an infinitive is an 'unrealised or possible future'. Discussing examples like (46), he admits though, that as one generally remembers things about the past, reference to the future is nothing more than a particular case of something more general. Formulated in somehow intuitive terms the relation between the two events might be spelled out as follows: the event described by the complement clause occurs at some unspecified temporal point before or after the temporal point at which the main clause's event occurs. This is roughly represented in diagram (47) (where S = Speech Time, ME = Matrix Event, and CE = Complement Event).

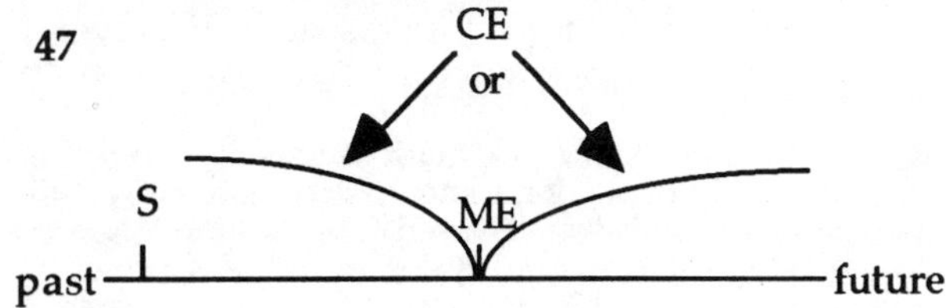

Then, according to what has just been said the temporal reference of the complement is to one of the points included in the space indicated by the curved lines. In the light of the parallel with Indefinite DPs concerning their extraction properties, it is tempting to compare the referential properties of Subjunctive/Infinitival clauses to those of indefinite DPs, consider:

(48) a. John left
b. The woman in the garden

(49) a. John decided to sing
b. A man in the garden

Just as (48b) refers to a unique, particular woman in the garden, (48a) refers, temporally, to a particular point at which the event described occurs. Correspondingly, (49b) says that there is an x such that man(x) and is_in_the_garden(x), in the same spirit (49a) says that there is an event e, which is a singing event, and there is a time t such that $e(t)$ and is_after_the_time_of_deciding(t). In somehow more formal terms this would give something similar to (50) :

(50) $\exists(e_d), \exists(e_s), \exists(t_d)\ \exists(t_s)$
$<e_d, t_d>, <e_s, t_s>\ \&\ t_d < (\text{or} \leq)\ t_s$

or, in set-theoretic terms: $t_s \in \{t_d, t_{d+1}, \ldots, t_{d+n}, \ldots\}$[7]

It becomes therefore quite clear that indefinite DPs and Subjunctive/Infinitival clauses share an important set of common properties. In order to capture their similar behaviour, it is then only reasonable to propose, that these clauses are also Indefinite constituents, which I have called *Indefinite Clauses*. In the terms of the approach just outlined, the meaning of the subjunctive mood is considered a *modal* only in a trivial sense. Traditionally the interpretation of subjunctive was thought to be related to some property like the [*irrealis*] feature postulated in various theories. Although the precise semantics of *Irrealis* is quite obscure to me, I don't believe that this is the correct way to deal with subjunctives. In terms of the [*Irrealis*] feature, whatever the precise meaning of the term, it says nothing about the temporal properties of subjunctives[8], which, as it has been shown, not only exist but are very close (maybe identical) to those of infinitives. Thus the parallel remains

---

[7] I leave aside here the question of the inclusiveness of the matrix event time into the interval of possible event times of the complement. Apparently, this depends mostly on the meaning of the matrix predicate. For example with (49a) this does not seem to be the case. Things are different with a verb like *try*.

[8] This kind of theory typically treats subjunctives as non-tensed clauses.

unaccounted for. It is also worth noting that syntactic evidence other than the one shown above argues against the claim that subjunctives are non-tensed[9]. The Case marking[10] of the subject of a subjunctive clause is a case in point: if subjunctives were tenseless it would be expected that they uniformingly involve a PRO subject, contrary to fact, French subjunctives obligatorily take an overt pronominal subject, Greek subjunctives however contain a PRO subject (on this issue see Terzi (1992)), which only strengthens the cross-linguistic parallel between subjunctives and infinitives. It also supplies an (indirect) argument for the [+Tense] status of the subjunctive, since it has long ago been established that infinitives do have temporal properties, (see Stowell (1982, 1993)). On the other hand, semantically, Temporal Indefiniteness seems to be a more appropriate tool to use in order to account for the semantic peculiarities of subjunctive clauses, mainly because they generally lack a truth value. This is quite straightforwardly captured in my theory. Since in classical possible-world semantics the truth value of propositions is evaluated at certain world-time pairs: $<w_i, t_j>$, it is then a natural consequence of my approach that indefinite clauses are unable to receive any truth value, since such a world-time pair cannot be formed[11]. It is difficult to see how a theory based on the [*irrealis*] feature could naturally arrive at the same conclusions. Moreover, the indefiniteness-based approach naturally predicts that much the same observations will hold for infinitives. A quick look at the data given in the first section and in the beginning of section 1.3 is enough to show that this is indeed the case. Bresnan's 'possible or unrealised future' is better treated as an indefinite tense, which need not be future anyway (cf. (46) and the examples in section 3.1). To my knowledge, nobody has suggested that subjunctives and infinitives should both be treated in terms of the [*irrealis*] feature or anything similar. It should be noted in passing that if it turns out to be on the right track this theory also provides an argument in favour of the propositional account of control complements as in Higginbotham (1992), among others, and against

9 Many researchers have reached the same conclusion, following somewhat different paths, for an overview of this type of work see Kempchinsky (1986), and the references cited therein.

10 It is assumed here that Nominative Case is somehow linked to the tense properties of INFL see Chomsky (1993) for an implementation of this idea within the Minimalist framework.

11 It is in this sense that we can talk about some kind of *modal* meaning of the subjunctive. The notion of *possibility* commonly used is now included in the fact that the truth of a subjunctive clause can be evaluated in those world-time pairs included in a set of entities such as defined at the end of this section.

the attributive view defended mainly by Chierchia (1984). The argument would go roughly as follows: since an infinitival complement (or a subjunctive when control effects are shown in these complements as in Modern Greek) temporally refers to a set of temporal points $t_1 \ldots t_n$, there will accordingly be a *n*-numbered set of world-time pairs: $\{ <w_x, t_1> \ldots <w_x, t_n> \}$ at which the truth value of the complement might be evaluated. It then follows that what the complement is referring to is a set of worlds (possibly a single-membered set)[12] and we know independently that the elements that refer to worlds are propositions (It is commonly assumed that the syntactic counterpart to the semantic entity *proposition* is IP) and not simple VPs, which they should have been if they were to refer to properties as Chierchia argues. More study is needed though in order to clearly spell out the force and the scope of the argument (see Tsoulas (1994b) for some discussion).

2.0 The realisation of Indefiniteness at the Clausal level.

In this section I will examine the way clausal indefiniteness is represented and some of its interactions with morphology and syntax. Since the question is about temporal indefiniteness it is natural to suppose that it is realised as a [- DEFINITE] in INFL, presumably under the T head. However, a closer inspection of the data of the different languages considered here suggests that this is not the only possibility. Modern Greek marks the subjunctive by a special complementizer *NA*[13], and has no special bound morphology for the subjunctive. On the other hand, French realises the subjunctive by special bound morphology, and has a complementizer *DE* appearing with infinitives. Finally English has the infinitival *TO* . Therefore we see that there are two possible realisation sites for clausal indefiniteness, namely C° and I (T°), yielding different results. This could *a priori* be a parametric issue in which languages would differ.

---

12 As noted, for example, in Chierchia & McConnell-Ginet (1991). The same world index x is kept in order to make it clear that it can be the same world at different times, or different worlds. The maximal situation would be a one-to-one correspondence between worlds and times. But given that possible worlds are purely theoretical constructs, it would not be unreasonable to propose that this is the actual situation, for W_x at time T_z has nothing but the name in common with W_x at time T_{z-1}. In this case, the argument given is even more forceful, but I will put aside this kind of discussion for the present paper.

13 There is an ongoing debate on whether *NA* is indeed located in Comp or somewhere under I, or as the head of a MoodP projection as in Terzi (1992) among others.

However things seem to be more complicated than that since languages like French use both options, thus distinguishing two types of indefinite clausal constituents. This situation is not really unexpected since on the one hand the quite close relation between C° and T° have been independently noticed[14], and on the other hand if the distinction Definite vs. Indefinite is to replace the distinction Finite vs. Non-finite as proposed here, then any Indefinite CP must be able to be identified as such, at least for selectional purposes, through its head C°. Notice further that, in general, the presence of a subjunctive Comp, (or a subjunctive marker) and subjunctive morphology on the verb are in complementary distribution[15]. In the light of these observations I will propose the following descriptive generalisation:

(51) **GENERALISATION**

a. [-DEFINITE] in C gives raise to (Inflected) Infinitive-type structures with particular COMPs.

b. [-DEFINITE] in I results in specific morphology, sometimes bound, French subjunctives, and sometimes not, English infinitival *to* .[16]

The obligatory presence of *Que* in French as well as in Italian and some other languages (like Albanian or Romanian) subjunctives is not problematic because *Que* is the equivalent of a proposition-introducing Complementizer (like *that*) and not a special Comp for Subjunctives. French *DE* seems at first sight more problematic since it combines with the *-r* infinitival morpheme. However, it should be noted that in the French verbal paradigm the morpheme *-r* is also encountered with the future tense and conditionals, which (cf. section 2.1) I also want to treat as (partial) indefinites. The only thing that seems to differentiate Subjunctives from infinitives in French[17] is the presence of Person-Number Agreement. What differentiates Future/Conditional from infinitives, apart from agreement is a restriction in the temporal intervals (with respect to some temporal point). At this point of this research let me only tentatively suggest that some form of agreement between C [-DEFINITE] and I, containing

---

14 Concerning purely temporal questions see Enç (1987).

15 This is at least true for the languages under consideration here.

16 It is very important to insist that this is nothing but a **descriptive** generalisation which does not aim at **explaining** anything.

17 Apart from the realisation site of the [-Definite] feature.

the morpheme *-r*, is responsible for rendering a partially indefinite element (*-r*) a true indefinite (an infinitival clause)[18].

2.1 *NA* and *THA* in Modern Greek and Indefiniteness

The status of *NA* in Modern Greek is a very controversial matter (cf. note 10). I will maintain here, that it is a complementizer (see Tsoulas (1993) for some arguments), based on the distribution of clitics and negation and its incompatibility with the lexical complementizer *OTI*. It is frequently claimed that MG patterns with the other Balkan Languages that also have a subjunctive particle realised in I. In these languages, however, the subjunctive particle is entirely compatible with a complementizer meaning *that*, which clearly is not the case in Modern Greek (cf. (52))[19]:

(52) * I Maria zitise oti na figi
The Maria asked THAT Comp leave/3rd/Sing

An explanation along the lines of a subjunctive-indicative incompatibility, in which *OTI* would be associated to the indicative, seems to me highly implausible[20]. There is nothing inherent to the subjunctive that would prevent it from being compatible with propositional COMPs, as it is generally the case cross-linguistically. A more interesting question is how to capture the difference between those two elements. This difference can be captured now if we assume that in the *NA* cases the [-DEFINITE] feature is realised in C and spelled out as the Subjunctive Complementizer NA. In the cases with *THA*, temporal indefiniteness is realised in I and spelled out as the future marker *THA*[21] (something structurally analogous to

---

18 A different path to approach this question would be to consider that the Comp *DE* is a prepositional one and therefore unable to perform the function of identifying the clause as indefinite by itself and needs to be somehow completed. This approach seems to me quite implausible however.

19 See section 2.0 for the comments on the compatibility of French *Que* with subjunctive morphology.

20 I don't intend to deny that *Oti* generally takes the indicative, this is a fact, but logically this cannot bare the subjunctive. Compare French i, ii :

(i) - Je veux que Sophie vienne
I want that Sophie come/Subjunctive

(ii) - Je dis que je connais Sophie
I say that I know/Indicative Sophie

To assume that there are two different *Que* in French seems highly implausible. Notice also that trying to approach the question solely from the point of view of the selectional properties of the embedding predicates doesn't seem very promising either. There is much more to explain here than mere lexical properties.

21 Notice that the verbal form following *NA* and *THA* is the same.

English infinitival *to*). The consequence of this analysis is that it forces us to consider the future tense on a par with subjunctives and infinitives, a very welcome result since the long-standing intuition that future tense is a modality rather than a pure tense is now captured in very natural terms[22]. Thus the meaning of the particle *THA*, and of the English modal *Will* or the French morpheme *-r-* is [-DEFINITE], [+Posterior to the Matrix Event Time][23] (in complement clauses) or [Posterior to the Speech Time] (in Root clauses)[24]. In other words it is only a partial indefiniteness since what we understand to be true clausal indefiniteness is represented by the diagram in (48), of which only the right-hand side holds for future-indefinites (cf also the remarks at the end of the previous section). We will use this notion of partial indefiniteness in section 3.1.

3.0 Extensions and Consequences

So far I have argued, on the basis of syntactic as well as semantic considerations that Clausal Constituents are marked with respect to the [± DEFINITE] like DPs and I have shown that this approach yields mostly welcome results. A very serious test for the theory proposed here would be to see if it accounts for the distribution of Clausal constituents in contexts where, a) they alternate with DPs and, b) the relevant factor governing the distribution of DPs is precisely the Definite vs. Indefinite distinction. This is indeed the case as the following examples clearly show:

(53) Il$_i$ faut [que Pierre parte]$_i$
It$_i$ is necessary [that Pierre leave/subjunctive]$_i$
(54) *Il$_i$ faut [que Pierre part]$_i$
It$_i$ is necessary [that Pierre leave/indicative]$_i$
(55) Il$_i$ faut [trouver Sophie]$_i$
It$_i$ is necessary [to find Sophie]$_i$
(56) Il$_i$ arrive [que Sophie tarde trop]$_i$
It$_i$ happens [that Sophie is-late/subjunctive a lot]$_i$
(57) * Il$_i$ arrive [que Sophie vient vite]$_i$
It$_i$ happens [that Sophie comes/indicative quickly]$_i$
Parallel to: (58) Il$_i$ arrive [plusieurs personnes]$_i$
It$_i$ arrives [a lot of people]$_i$

---

22 Although the term *modality* is, as argued before, somehow inappropriate, I continue to use it in order to indicate the real coverage of the theory proposed.
23 Or, irrelevantly, to some other reference time.
24 Roughly the same considerations also apply to French conditionals which can now be considered, along with the future 'tense' as some kind of inflected infinitives. More work is needed though in order to further clarify these intuitions.

Il$_i$ arrive [quelques personnes]$_i$
It$_i$ arrive [some people]$_i$
(59) *Il$_i$ arrive [Sophie]$_i$
It$_i$ arrives [Sophie]$_i$
(60) pro$_{expli}$ prepi [na figi o Petros]$_i$
must go(subj) the Peter
(61) * pro$_{expli}$ prepi [oti fevgi o Petros]$_i$
must that go/ind the Peter
(62) * pro$_{expli}$ prepi [oti tha fevgi o Petros]$_i$
must that FUT go the Peter

The associate in expletive-associate chains, if nominal, must always be an indefinite DP, and similarly, if clausal, needs to be what I have termed here an indefinite clause. Thus the distribution of clausal constituents in these contexts is straightforwardly explained in my theory as an instance of the *definiteness effect*.

3.1 Two Problematic Cases.

Under this theory and given the interaction noticed in the beginning of this paper with regard to the syntax of extraction, it is predicted that the following extractions should be possible, whereas it is clear that they are not:

(63) Je regrette que Paul soit venu hier soir
I regret that Paul came(subj/Past) yesterday evening
I regret that Paul came last night
(64) * Qui regrettes-tu qui soit venu hier
who regret/you that/3rd/sing is/subj come/past.part yesterday
*Who do you regret that came yesterday
(65) ??? Que regrettes-tu que Sophie ait vu
what regret/you that Sophie has/Subj seen

Upon closer consideration, far from undermining the theory, in fact, these contrasts strengthen the suggested parallel with Indefinite DPs. It is well known that factive complements have their truth presupposed[25] and on the other hand denote an individual event. In the theory presented here such data are naturally accounted for as parallel to (27), (32), (39), i.e. **Specific Indefinites**[26] The impossibility

---

[25] Note that this is a further argument against the [*irrealis*] based approaches. It is very difficult to see how something that is *unreal* could have its truth presupposed. (63)-(65) pose a very serious challenge to the *irrealis* approach.

[26] Sarah Kennelly and Anne Zribi-Hertz(pc) suggested to me that it might be a question of specificity rather than definiteness after all. Although the idea seems very appealing and despite the fact that definiteness and specificity are two very close notions(even identical under some approaches) I am, at least for the moment, reluctant to take that step mainly in order to preserve the distinction between indefinites and specific indefinites which are not really definites. Reformulating my proposal in terms of specificity would cause the loss of this very expressive and useful division.

of the extraction is then explained as an instance of the well known *specificity effects*[27]. The subject-object asymmetry (object extraction is indeed slightly better than subject extraction, according to the majority of the native speakers) remains however unexplained. Space limitations prevent us from discussing the question in any further detail. The notion of partial indefiniteness (see section 2.1), applying to the future tense, accounts for the impossibility of future indefinites in contexts like those in (53)-(62).

The second apparently problematic case comes from data like (66), (67), i.e., direct perception.

(66) I saw Keith play
(67) I heard the whales cry

It is well known that direct perception requires reduced clausal complements, crucially lacking the indefiniteness marker. This account predicts that in these cases the overt indefiniteness marker *to* must be missing because in this case the complement is not truly indefinite since it has to be strictly contemporaneous to the perception. It is therefore, an individual, unique event. Interestingly, this doesn't seem to affect extraction, a non surprising situation, since the specificity/Uniqueness operator is missing. Modern Greek provides examples in which the indefiniteness marker is present:

(68)	Ida	to	Yanni	na pleni	to	aftokinito	tou
	saw/I	the	Yanni	wash	the	car	his

The crucial property involved, is that in English a bare infinitive is used in order to express a *bare event* without any temporal specification, entering thus into the tense frame defined by the matrix. Modern Greek lacks infinitives altogether and the structure with NA is the only way of expressing a *bare event*. French uses in these cases a bare infinitive, never a subjunctive in this situation. This lends support to the analysis presented here :

(69) J'ai vu Sophie partir
I saw Sophie leave
(70) * J'ai vu Sophie que parte (or que Sophie parte)
I saw Sophie that leave/subjunctive

Clearly then, the apparent counterexamples discussed above actually further support the proposed analysis and complete the picture of the analogy between Clausal and Nominal constituents.

---

27 Presumably, it is the presence of some specificity operator, or other uniqueness predicate in the specifier of CP that is responsible for the individuation of the event described and that blocks the extraction. It is important to note that it is not a *Definiteness Operator*.

4.0 Conclusion

Summing up, in this paper, I have proposed a theory of subjunctives and infinitives in terms of the Definite vs. Indefinite distinction. Furthermore I have presented some of the evidence on the syntactic as well as on interpretive side, and pointed out at a few of the possible consequences of my proposal in connection to direct perception, factivity, and Control. The overall explanatory power of the theory of *Clausal Indefiniteness* seems quite satisfactory, though much more research is needed. A lot of questions still remain open, such as the disjoint reference effects found in subjunctives, the licensing of the subjunctive, the licensing of Negative polarity items in subjunctive clauses, and the consequences of this approach for the definition of indefiniteness and the status of indefinite elements. I believe that these questions can find satisfactory and illuminating answers within the framework defined above, some of which I address in Tsoulas (1994b), while the others I leave for future research.

REFERENCES

Bresnan, Joan. 1972. *Theory of Complementation in English Syntax.* Doctoral Dissertation, MIT.

Chierchia, Gennaro. 1984. *Topics in the Syntax and Semantics of Infinitives and Gerunds*. Doctoral Dissertation UMass. Amherst.

Chierchia, Gennaro & Sally McConnell-Ginet. 1991. *Meaning and Grammar.* Cambridge, **MIT Press.**

Chomsky, Noam. 1977. *Essays on Form and Interpretation,* **North Holland.**

Chomsky, Noam. 1981. *Lectures on Government and Binding,* , **Foris.**

Chomsky, Noam. 1986a. *Barriers,* Cambridge, **MIT Press.**

Chomsky, Noam. 1986b. *Knowledge of Language.* New York, **Praeger.**

Chomsky, Noam. 1993. *A Minimalist Program for Linguistic Theory;* in **Hale, K. & S. J. Keyser** eds.*The view from Building 20;* Cambridge, **MIT Press.**

Diesing, Molly. 1992. *Indefinites.* Cambridge, **MIT Press.**

Enç, Mürvet 1987. **Anchoring Conditions for Tense.** *Linguistic Inquiry* 18. 4. 633-657.

Enç, Mürvet 1991. **The Semantics of Specificity.** *Linguistic Inquiry* 22, 1, 1-25.

Higginbotham, James. 1985. **On Semantics**. *Linguistic Inquiry* 16. 4. 547-593.

Higginbotham, James. 1992. Reference and Control. in **Larson, R. K. et al.** eds. *Control and Grammar*. **Kluwer.** pp. 79-108.

Huang, C.-T. James. 1982. *Logical Relations in Chinese and the Theory of Grammar.* Doctoral Dissertation MIT.

Kempchinsky, Paula M. 1986. *Romance Subjunctive Clauses and Logical Form*. Doctoral Dissertation UCLA.

Manzini, Maria-Rita. 1992. *Locality. A Theory and some of its Empirical Consequences*, Cambridge. **MIT Press.**

Partee, Barbara H. 1972. **Opacity, Coreference, and Pronouns.** in **Davidson, D. & G. Harman.** eds. *Semantics of Natural Language.* Dordrecht, Reidel.

Parsons, Terence. 1990. *Events in the Semantics of English. A Study in Subatomic Semantics*, Cambridge. **MIT Press.**

Ross, John R. 1967. *Constraints on Variables in Syntax* . Doctoral Dissertation MIT.

Stowell, Timothy A. 1982. **The Tense of Infinitives.** *Linguistic Inquiry* 13. 4. 561-570.

Stowell, Timothy A. 1993. **Syntax of Tense.** Ms UCLA.

Terzi, Arhonto 1992. *PRO in Finite Clauses. A study of the Inflectional Heads of the Balkan languages*. Doctoral Dissertation, CUNY.

Tsoulas, Georges 1993. **Remarks on the structure and Interpretation of** ***NA*-clauses**, to appear in *Studies in Greek Linguistics* 14.

Tsoulas, Georges 1994a. **Subjunctives as Indefinites**; to appear in the proceedings of the *XX incontro de Grammatica Generativa*, Padova, Italy.

Tsoulas, Georges 1994b. **PRO and Control : some preliminary remarks**, to appear in. **Nash Léa & Georges Tsoulas** eds. *Paris-8 Working Papers in Linguistics.-1* .

Vergnaud, Jean-Roger & M. L. Zubizarreta. 1992. **The Definite Determiner and the Inalienable Constructions in French and in English.** *Linguistic Inquiry*, 23, 4, 595-652.

Semantics

A Deductive Account of Scope*

BOB CARPENTER
Carnegie Mellon University

1 Introduction

In this paper, we argue that the grammatical scopings of quantifiers should be treated by deductive methods. To this end, we propose a type-theoretic, categorial logic. This logic captures the broad range of allowable scopings, as well as correctly imposing constraints on impossible ones. It is particularly simple, being built out of dual introduction (proof) and elimination (use) schemes for complementation, unbounded dependencies, boolean coordination and scoping.

The second theme of this paper is an argument that a number of previously proposed grammatical operations are best seen as approximations of the logical approach. Here we consider the quantificational rules of Montague's quantifying-in and type raising, and Cooper's realization of these rules by means of storage in a phrase structure setting. Montague's rules are very similar to a sequent-based presentation of our logic, whereas Cooper's storage method appears to be an approximation of the same logic in natural deduction format. We also explicate the

*I would like to thank a number of people for helpful comments on and discussion of the ideas for this paper: Filippo Beghelli, Ariel Cohen, Robin Cooper, Dale Gerdemann, Michael Moortgat, Glyn Morrill, Dick Oehrle, Fernando Pereira, Massimo Poesio, Carl Pollard, Ivan Sag, and Ed Stabler.

logical nature of slash introduction and percolation in GPSG and HPSG. Furthermore, we will show that the non-trivial interactions between these schemes follows directly from their logical characterizations.

Unfortunately, as space here is limited, and categorial logics are not particularly familiar to most linguists, a few interesting and related topics will not be addressed in this setting. The primary omissions are island constraints on quantifiers, locality constraints on anaphora, and the syntax of interrogatives. Islands and locality are amenable to a treatment extending that given here (Morrill 1990, 1992). Furthermore, restricting our attention to English allows us to finesse difficult issues concerning word order. A deductive account of order is also possible (Hepple 1990; Moortgat and Oehrle 1994). We also do not address the semantically conditioned behavior of downward entailing quantifiers, though we believe the data in this realm to be rather controversial. We also sidestep the further complexity of plurals, which we assume to involve two levels of quantification, following Heim, Lasnik and May (1991). The integration of plurals is straightforward, though, and details can be found in Carpenter (1992, in press). Finally, we do not discuss pronominal reference and ellipsis and their interaction with quantification; these topics are discussed at length in Carpenter (in press).

We base our analysis on data drawn from English. We consider a number of standard cases of quantification, and some which seem to have been overlooked in the literature. We cover (a) standard de dicto/de re ambiguities, (b) quantifiers nested within nominal modifiers, (c) quantifiers reducing within relative clauses, control and coordination examples where sentences are incomplete, (d) quantifiers in free relatives and the possessor of possessives, (e) interactions with negation and adverbials, (f) quantifiers in the controller position of equi and raising verbs, (g) the coordination of quantifiers, their ranges, and their scopes, and (h) interactions with unbounded dependency constructions, including pied-piping of quantifiers.

We will provide not only a complete, rigorous definition of the type-theoretic categorial logic, in both sequent and natural deduction presentations, but also an English lexicon that generates all of the examples we discuss.

2 Categorial Logic

In this section, we discuss first the type-theoretic underpinnings of our syntactic and semantic formalism, and then move on to the associative categorial calculus of Lambek (1958) extended with unbounded dependency, coordination and scoping constructors.

Semantic Types and Syntactic Categories

We base our semantics on Church's (1940) simple theory of types, as applied to a higher-order logic. We base our type theory on two primitive types: the type Ind of individuals, and the type Prop of propositions. Furthermore, for every type σ and τ, we admit a functional type $\sigma \rightarrow \tau$. Semantically, we interpret elements of our individual domain in a set $\mathcal{D}_{\mathsf{Ind}}$ and our propositional domain in a set $\mathcal{D}_{\mathsf{Prop}}$.[1] The domain $\mathcal{D}_{\sigma \rightarrow \tau}$ over which terms of type $\sigma \rightarrow \tau$ are interpreted is the set of total functions from $\mathcal{D}_\sigma$ to $\mathcal{D}_\tau$.

We base our syntax on a collection of three primitive categories: the category np of noun phrases, the category n of nouns, and the category s of sentences.[2] We also adopt a limited repertoire of type constructors, whose purpose is to build complex categories. Specifically, A/B, $A\backslash B$, $A{\uparrow}B$, $A{\Uparrow}B$, and $q(A,B,C)$ are categories if A, B, and C are. Each category is assigned a type. Basic categories are assigned to the following types: s has type Prop, np type Ind, and n type Ind$\rightarrow$Prop. The types of complex categories are determined by the types of their constituents: A/B, $A\backslash B$, and $A{\uparrow}B$ each have type $\mathit{Typ}(B) \rightarrow \mathit{Typ}(A)$, $A{\Uparrow}B$ has type $(\mathit{Typ}(B) \rightarrow \mathit{Typ}(A)) \rightarrow \mathit{Typ}(A)$, and $q(A,B,C)$ type $(\mathit{Typ}(C) \rightarrow \mathit{Typ}(B)) \rightarrow \mathit{Typ}(A)$. Furthermore, we assume a boolean coordination category *coor* of type Bool$\rightarrow$Bool$\rightarrow$Bool.

Lexicon

Categorial Grammar is a purely lexical theory, basing all language-specific information in the lexicon. A lexicon provides a finite relation between linguistic expressions, syntactic categories, and semantic terms of the appropriate type. Thus a lexicon is a finite set Lex $\subseteq$ Exp $\times$ Cat $\times$ Term, where if $\langle e, A, \alpha \rangle \in$ Lex then α is a λ-term of type $\mathit{Typ}(A)$.

Logical Interpretations

In this section, we detail the logics of the constructors introduced above. The purpose of these logical calculi is to define a rewriting relation, or sequent, $\Gamma \Rightarrow A{:}\,\alpha$, where Γ is an ordered sequence of category/meaning pairs and expressions and $A{:}\,\alpha$ is a category/meaning pair.

---

[1] The particulars of our propositional interpretation are not important. We only assume here that the domain of propositions admits the standard logical operators and generalized quantifiers.

[2] For clarity in the discussion of quantification, we avoid further type refinements, such as would be necessary for dealing with distinctions such as those between number, person, case, and verb form. For a logical treatment of these cases by features interpreted as first-order terms, see Morrill (1992).

Lambek (1958) provided not only the first logical treatment of the slash constructor, but also the underlying models with respect to which such proof theories were sound and complete. Lambek interpreted categories as sets of strings, according to: e_1 should be assigned to category A/B ($A\backslash B$) if and only if every expression e_2 of category B was such that $e_1 \cdot e_2$ ($e_2 \cdot e_1$) was of category A.

The "only if" portion of the biconditional motivates the rules of use for the slash constructors, which result in the Ajdukiewicz (1935) / Bar-Hillel (1953) calculus. The converse leads to the rules of proof for the slash constructors, which together with the dual rules of use form the associative Lambek calculus. van Benthem (1983) provided the corresponding compositional semantic interpretation of these rules, based on the Curry-Howard morphism.[3]

Moortgat introduced the three remaining constructors, along with their semantic interpretations and proof rules. The category $A{\uparrow}B$ is assigned to an A with a B gap somewhere within it. Thus, Moortgat (1988) took an expression $e_1 \cdot e_2$ to belong to the category $A{\uparrow}B$ if for every e of category B, $e_1 \cdot e \cdot e_2$ belongs to A. Notice that this is only half of a proper logical relationship, as witnessed by the lack of a rule of use for $A{\uparrow}B$.[4] Moortgat (1992) introduced the category $q(A, B, C)$ for an expression that behaved locally as a C and then applied in some embedding category B to produce an A. Moortgat's (1991) previous, binary scoping constructor, $\Uparrow$, is defined by setting $A{\Uparrow}B = q(A, A, B)$; Moortgat's interpretation is based on the notion that an expression e belongs to category $q(A, B, C)$ if and only if $e_1 \cdot e \cdot e_2$ belongs to A whenever $e_1 \cdot e' \cdot e_2$ belongs to B for every e' in C. Because of the biconditional definition of q, the proof system contains both rules of use and rules of proof for q. As it is, the rule of proof is sound, but incomplete with respect to the above interpretation (Carpenter in press; Morrill in press).[5]

[3] The morphism provides two relations: the first is between implicational and conjunctive formula in intuitionistic logic with functional and product types in the λ-calculus, while the second is between intuitionistic proofs involving implication and conjunction with pure, free λ-terms. The structure preservation in the morphism is between normalization of proofs and normalization of terms. See Morrill (in press) or Carpenter (in press) for further discussion. The availability of product constructor does not enhance the power of the system, so we do not include it here.

[4] Morrill (in press) has provided an interpretation and logic for $\uparrow$ which enjoys a dual rule of use.

[5] Morrill (in press) provides a weaker interpretation of q, along with a complete logic for it in terms of gapping and infixing.

$$\frac{}{A{:}\alpha \Rightarrow A{:}\alpha}\,i \qquad \frac{\Gamma_1,\ A{:}\alpha,\ \Gamma_2 \Rightarrow B{:}\beta}{\Gamma_1,\ e,\ \Gamma_2 \Rightarrow B{:}\beta}\,l \quad [\text{if } \langle e, A, \alpha\rangle \in \mathsf{Lex}]$$

$$\frac{\Gamma \Rightarrow B{:}\beta \qquad \Delta_1,\ A{:}\alpha(\beta),\ \Delta_2 \Rightarrow C{:}\gamma}{\Delta_1,\ A/B{:}\alpha,\ \Gamma,\ \Delta_2 \Rightarrow C{:}\gamma}\,/l \qquad \frac{\Gamma,\ B{:}x \Rightarrow A{:}\alpha}{\Gamma \Rightarrow A/B{:}\,\lambda x.\alpha}\,/r$$

$$\frac{\Gamma \Rightarrow B{:}\beta \qquad \Delta_1,\ A{:}\alpha(\beta),\ \Delta_2 \Rightarrow C{:}\gamma}{\Delta_1,\ \Gamma,\ A\backslash B{:}\alpha,\ \Delta_2 \Rightarrow C{:}\gamma}\,\backslash l \qquad \frac{B{:}x,\ \Gamma \Rightarrow A{:}\alpha}{\Gamma \Rightarrow A\backslash B{:}\,\lambda x.\alpha}\,\backslash r$$

$$\frac{\Gamma_1,\ C{:}x,\ \Gamma_2 \Rightarrow B{:}\alpha}{\Gamma_1,\ q(A,B,C){:}\gamma,\ \Gamma_2 \Rightarrow A{:}\gamma(\lambda x.\alpha)}\,ql \qquad \frac{\Gamma \Rightarrow B{:}\alpha}{\Gamma \Rightarrow q(A,A,B){:}\,\lambda P.P(\alpha)}\,qr$$

$$\frac{\Gamma,\ B{:}x,\ \Gamma_2 \Rightarrow A{:}\alpha}{\Gamma_1,\ \Gamma_2 \Rightarrow A{\uparrow}B{:}\,\lambda x.\alpha}\,{\uparrow}r$$

$$\frac{\Gamma_1 \Rightarrow B{:}\beta_1 \qquad \Gamma_2 \Rightarrow B{:}\beta_2 \qquad \Delta_1,\ B{:}\,Coor(\alpha)(\beta_1)(\beta_2),\ \Delta_2 \Rightarrow A{:}\gamma}{\Delta_1,\ \Gamma_1,\ coor{:}\alpha,\ \Gamma_2,\ \Delta_2 \Rightarrow A{:}\gamma}\,cl$$

Figure 1: Categorial Calculus — Sequent Presentation

Categorial Sequent Calculus

The cut-free, sequent presentation of the logic can be found in Figure 1. The first rule is an identity that ensures $\Rightarrow$ is reflexive. The second rule allows the insertion of a lexical category. The following rules characterize the slash constructors, and come in dual pairs. The left rules, known as rules of use, $/l$ and $\backslash l$, indicate how to eliminate an occurrence of a slash from the left hand side of the rewriting relation, whereas the right rules, known as rules of proof, $/r$ and $\backslash r$, show how to eliminate an occurrence on the right. The right and left rules characterize both conditions in Lambek's interpretation of categories. Without the right rules, the logic is just that of Ajdukiewicz and Bar-Hillel. The rule for the gap constructor, $\uparrow$, follows its definition. The semantics are just that of the slash right rules. The scoping constructor left rules show how a scoping element is to be used — a placeholder with a variable semantics of category C is used to derive a B with semantics α, at which point the scope constructor applies to yield category A and semantics $\gamma(\lambda x.\alpha)$. Note that the hypothetical variable is abstracted to provide the semantics of the scope constructor, γ, a handle on the occurrence(s) of x within α. The rule of proof for q allows a B to be used as a $q(A, A, B)$, a device that is sound with respect to the definition of q, and useful, as we will see below. The coordination scheme, a fairly standard device, allows two like boolean categories to be combined, with the semantics of the boolean being distributed by $Coor$, which is defined by taking $Coor(\alpha)(\beta_1)(\beta_2)$ to be $\alpha(\beta_1)(\beta_2)$ if β_1 and β_2 are of type Bool, and $\lambda x.Coor(\alpha)(\beta_1(x))(\beta_2(x))$ otherwise.

As it stands, the rules of use for the slashes are very similar to Montague's (1970) grammar.[6] Furthermore, the rule of use for the quantifier category is nearly identical in effect to Montague's rule of quantifying in. Montague's scheme was less elegant, though, in that it relied not on the logical notion of antecedents to deductions, but rather on the insertion of dummy categories he_n, with variable semantics, and ad hoc string manipulation rules to achieve the same effect as that given more generally by our rule of use for q. Perhaps just as interesting is the fact that the rule of proof for the quantificational category is a correlate of Montague's lexical type raising scheme. Our logic illustrates the dual nature of type raising with respect to quantifying in; there are no questions, for instance, about which lexical entries should be raised, because raising is part of the logic of q.[7]

Continuing our comparison, notice that the slash rules of use are identical to the HPSG rules of subcategorization (Pollard and Sag 1994), and form the basis of Combinatory Categorial Grammar (CCG), as developed by Steedman (1985, 1988). Furthermore, the harmonic versions of Steedman's composition and type raising rules can also be generated by the combination of the left and right schemes for the slashes. Next, consider the rule for the gap constructor, $\uparrow$; it generalizes the slash introduction metarule of GPSG (Gazdar 1981), which is also employed in HPSG. Slash introduction simply admits the derived rule, $A{\uparrow}B_n \rightarrow B_1, \ldots, B_{n-1}, B_{n+1}, \ldots, B_m$, in PSG notation, from an existing rule $A \rightarrow B_1, \ldots, B_{n-1}, B_n, B_{n+1}, \ldots, B_m$. But rather than employ a notion of slash passing, the relation between an extraction site and its discharge is handled logically by hypothetical reasoning. This brings us to a typical side-condition on the rules of proof for the slashes and gap constructors, namely that the consequent sequent Γ or Γ_1, Γ_2 be non-empty. Without that constraint, an alternative method employed

[6] In fact, interest has been rekindled in defining grammars along the lines of Montague's (1970a) Universal Grammar (UG) principle in order to handle discontinuous constituency, such as that introduced by wrapping particles, idioms, certain ditransitive constructions, etc. See Morrill (in press) for a survey.

[7] This raises certain issues concerning parsing. Fortunately, the space of proofs is such that search can be limited to the finite subspace consisting only of normal proofs. This technique, originally developed by Hepple, König, and Morrill, is employed by Carpenter (1994), which includes references.

$$\frac{\begin{matrix}\vdots & \vdots\\ A/B{:}\,\alpha & B{:}\,\beta\end{matrix}}{A{:}\,\alpha(\beta)}/e \qquad \frac{\begin{matrix}\vdots & \vdots\\ B{:}\,\beta & A\backslash B{:}\,\alpha\end{matrix}}{A{:}\,\alpha(\beta)}\backslash e \qquad \frac{A{:}\,\alpha}{q(A,B,B){:}\,\lambda P.P(\alpha)}qi$$

$$\frac{\dfrac{\begin{matrix}\vdots & [A{:}\,x]^n\\ \vdots & \vdots\end{matrix}}{B{:}\,\alpha}}{B/A{:}\,\lambda x.\alpha}/i^n \qquad \frac{\dfrac{\begin{matrix}[A{:}\,x]^n & \vdots\\ \vdots & \vdots\end{matrix}}{B{:}\,\alpha}}{B\backslash A{:}\,\lambda x.\alpha}\backslash i^n \qquad \frac{\dfrac{\begin{matrix}\vdots & \begin{matrix}\vdots\\ \dfrac{q(A,B,C){:}\,\alpha}{C{:}\,x}qe^i\\ \hline \vdots\end{matrix} & \vdots\end{matrix}}{B{:}\,\beta}}{A{:}\,\alpha(\lambda x.\beta)}qe^i$$

$$\frac{e}{A{:}\,\alpha}l \quad [\text{if } \langle e,A,\alpha\rangle \in \mathsf{Lex}] \qquad \frac{\dfrac{\begin{matrix}\vdots & [A{:}\,x]^n & \vdots\\ \vdots & \vdots & \vdots\end{matrix}}{B{:}\,\alpha}}{B\uparrow A{:}\,\lambda x.\alpha}\uparrow i^n \qquad \frac{\begin{matrix}\vdots & \vdots & \vdots\\ A{:}\,\phi & co{:}\,\alpha & A{:}\,\psi\end{matrix}}{A{:}\,Coor(\alpha)(\phi)(\psi)}ce$$

Figure 2: Categorial Calculus — Natural Deduction Presentation

in HPSG and in a variant of GPSG is available, whereby the empty gap category $\epsilon \Rightarrow A\uparrow A$ is generated from the identity scheme $A \Rightarrow A$.

Categorial Natural Deduction Calculus

Lambek's logic can also be presented by natural deduction, as shown in Figure 2. Note that the antecedent derivations are ordered in this presentation, and that the ellipses notation is meant to indicate that the hypothesis occurs peripherally in both of the slash introduction schemes. A derivation $\Gamma \Rightarrow A{:}\,\alpha$ found by natural deduction can be determined by reading Γ left to right as the string of undischarged assumptions, and taking $A{:}\,\alpha$ to be the root of the derivation. The logical relation to the sequent scheme is that rules of use, corresponding to left sequent rules, are expressed here as elimination rules, and that rules of proof, matching right sequent rules, are expressed here as introduction rules. The ellipses match the use of sequences of antecedents in the sequent presentation.

The way in which hypotheses are handled here to mirror the sequent system is significant. For instance, the forward slash introduction scheme allows the derivation of an A/B if a hypothetical B can be assumed and used to derive an A. The existing material would correspond to Γ in the sequent rule, and the existing material plus hypothesis would be Γ, B, whereas the conclusion of the antecedent is represented by A, and the conclusion of the whole, discharging the assumption, is the category A/B at the root. The scope of the hypothesis B is marked by coindexing the rules, and the hypothetical nature of B indicated with brackets. Reading the quantification rules is more subtle. Here if we derive a $q(A, B, C){:}\, \alpha$, we hypothesize a $C{:}\, x$ at the same location. Then if we derive a $B{:}\, \beta$ from the assumption and the context on either side, we are able to discharge the assumption and produce $A{:}\, \alpha(\lambda x.\beta)$. It is important to notice that the dots, indicating the Γ_1 and Γ_2 of the sequent presentation, can be used only with the hypothesis $B{:}\, x$; the derivation of $B{:}\, x$, including any undischarged assumptions, is inaccessible in the derivation of $B{:}\, \beta$.

It is quite revealing that the natural deduction presentation of quantification mirrors Cooper's (1983) storage method. The point at which the quantifier is eliminated and the hypothesis made corresponds to the point in a Cooper storage derivation where the quantifier is entered into storage. It then is available at any subsequent (sentential) stage to be discharged, and to take semantic effect, which corresponds to Cooper's removing and applying an element from storage. But rather than unioning elements of stores at every stage of a derivation, the connection between assumption and discharge is logical. This not only allows much greater flexibility in some cases, especially where interaction with other logical constructors may occur, but our scheme is also more restrictive in important respects. Similarly, the natural deduction presentation of the slash rules look very similar not only to the use of empty categories in transformational theories, but to empty categories and eventual discharge of slashes in GPSG. Not surprisingly, there is also a close connection to HPSG. Furthermore, it can be shown that the polymorphic lexical entries provided by Hendriks (1987), which generalize Steedman's (1988) entries for quantifiers, are derivable consequences of our slash and quantifier logic.

3 Case Studies

In this section, we work through a number of important derivations involving quantifiers, using natural deduction. We begin, in Figure 3, with a very simple derivation, illustrating the treatment of hypotheticals, in this case to derive an unbounded dependency. The result of this derivation may serve as an argument to a relative pronoun to

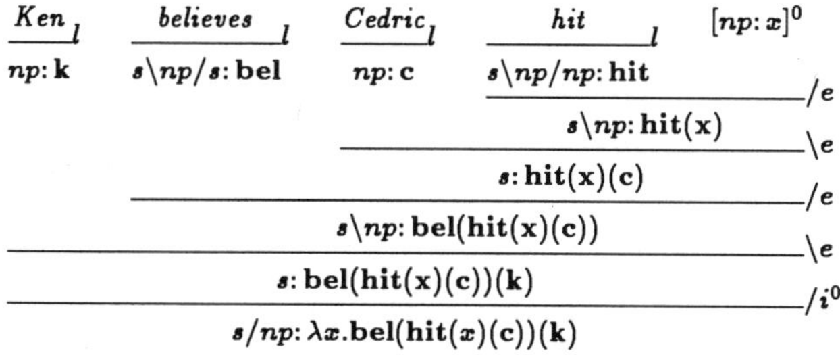

Figure 3: Slash Introduction Example

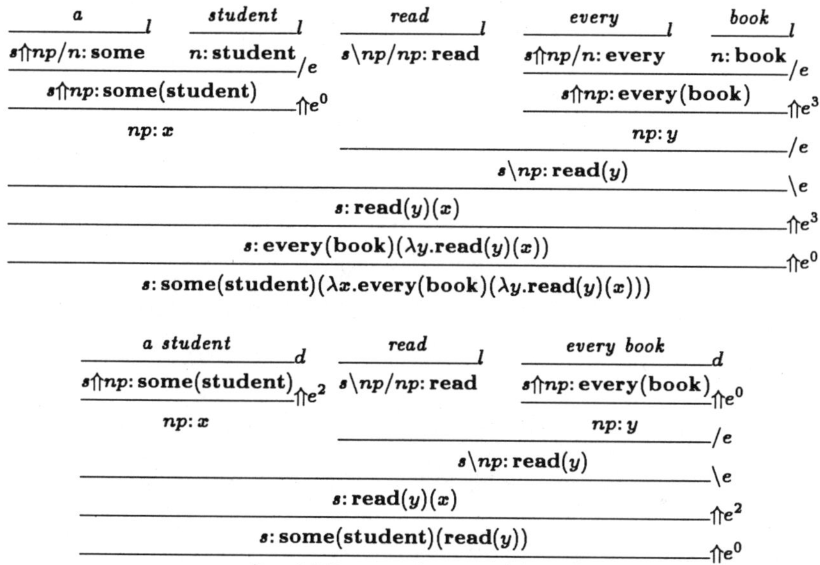

Figure 4: Quantification Example

produce a post-nominal modifier, as input to topicalization, or as a conjunct in a "non-constituent" coordination.

A case involving multiple quantifiers, with both derivations, is given in Figure 4. A case involving an intensional verb, with de dicto and de re analyses, is given in Figure 5. Note the interaction of type raising and quantifying-in in the de re analysis. The parallels to Cooper's methods should be apparent. Furthermore, we can derive the intensional lexical entry for simple transitives like *hire*, as shown in Figure 6. Dually, we

$$\dfrac{\textit{John}}{np{:}\,\mathbf{j}}\,l \qquad \dfrac{\textit{sought}}{s\backslash np/(s\Uparrow np){:}\,\mathbf{seek}}\,l \qquad \dfrac{\textit{a job}}{s\Uparrow np{:}\,\mathbf{some(job)}}\,/e$$

$$\dfrac{s\backslash np/(s\Uparrow np){:}\,\mathbf{seek} \qquad s\Uparrow np{:}\,\mathbf{some(job)}}{s\backslash np{:}\,\mathbf{seek(some(job))}}\,/e$$

$$\dfrac{np{:}\,\mathbf{j} \qquad s\backslash np{:}\,\mathbf{seek(some(job))}}{s{:}\,\mathbf{seek(some(job))(j)}}\,\backslash e$$

$$\dfrac{\textit{John}}{np{:}\,\mathbf{j}}\,l \qquad \dfrac{\textit{sought}}{s\backslash np/(s\Uparrow np){:}\,\mathbf{seek}}\,l \qquad \dfrac{\textit{a job}}{s\Uparrow np{:}\,\mathbf{some(job)}}\,d$$

$$\dfrac{s\Uparrow np{:}\,\mathbf{some(job)}}{np{:}\,x}\,\Uparrow e^0 \qquad \dfrac{np{:}\,x}{s\Uparrow np{:}\,\lambda P.P(x)}\,\Uparrow i$$

$$\dfrac{s\backslash np/(s\Uparrow np){:}\,\mathbf{seek} \qquad s\Uparrow np{:}\,\lambda P.P(x)}{s\backslash np{:}\,\mathbf{seek}(\lambda P.P(x))}\,/e$$

$$\dfrac{np{:}\,\mathbf{j} \qquad s\backslash np{:}\,\mathbf{seek}(\lambda P.P(x))}{s{:}\,\mathbf{seek}(\lambda P.P(x))(\mathbf{j})}\,\backslash e$$

$$\dfrac{s{:}\,\mathbf{seek}(\lambda P.P(x))(\mathbf{j})}{s{:}\,\mathbf{some(job)}(\lambda x.\mathbf{seek}(\lambda P.P(x))(\mathbf{j}))}\,\Uparrow e^0$$

Figure 5: De Dicto/De Re Analyses with Type Raising

$$[np{:}\,x]^4 \qquad \dfrac{\textit{hits}}{s\backslash np/np{:}\,\mathbf{hit}}\,l \qquad \dfrac{[s\Uparrow np{:}\,Q]^0}{np{:}\,y}\,\Uparrow e^5$$

$$\dfrac{s\backslash np/np{:}\,\mathbf{hit} \qquad np{:}\,y}{s\backslash np{:}\,\mathbf{hit}(y)}\,/e$$

$$\dfrac{[np{:}\,x]^4 \qquad s\backslash np{:}\,\mathbf{hit}(y)}{s{:}\,\mathbf{hit}(y)(x)}\,\backslash e$$

$$\dfrac{s{:}\,\mathbf{hit}(y)(x)}{s{:}\,Q(\lambda y.\mathbf{hit}(y)(x))}\,\Uparrow e^5$$

$$\dfrac{s{:}\,Q(\lambda y.\mathbf{hit}(y)(x))}{s\backslash np{:}\,\lambda x.Q(\lambda y.\mathbf{hit}(y)(x))}\,\backslash i^4$$

$$\dfrac{s\backslash np{:}\,\lambda x.Q(\lambda y.\mathbf{hit}(y)(x))}{s\backslash np/(s\Uparrow np){:}\,\lambda Q.\lambda x.Q(\lambda y.\mathbf{hit}(y)(x))}\,/i^0$$

Figure 6: Raising for Montagovian Lexical Entries

can lower *seek*, to yield:

$$\textit{seek} \Rightarrow s\backslash np/np{:}\ \lambda x.\mathbf{seek}(\lambda P.P(x))$$

The use of hypothetical verbal complements, and the reduction of quantifiers, allows the analyses of cases with quantifiers and missing complements, such as *likes everyone*, or *everyone likes*. These can be used as conjuncts, or as the complements to control verbs or relatives, in which case, they must allow internally scoped quantifiers (and external ones, though these are handled as usual). For instance, we have:

$$\textit{everyone likes} \Rightarrow s/np{:}\ \lambda x.\mathbf{every}(\lambda y.\mathbf{like}(y)(x)).$$

The possibility of derivations involving free variables has plagued Cooper's original proposal for storage. Consider the two valid analyses of *a picture of everyone faded*, shown in Figure 7. Here we have

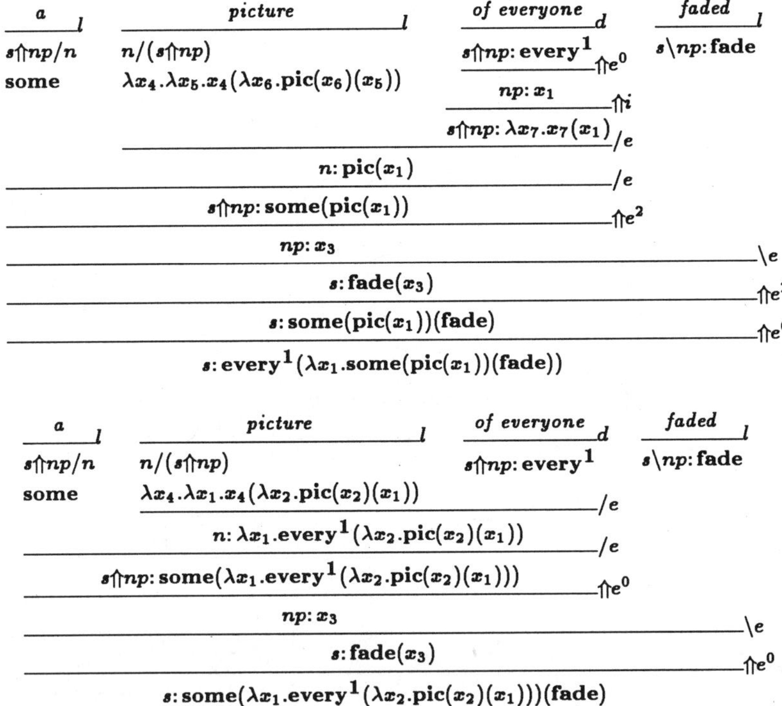

Figure 7: Analysis of *a picture of everyone faded*

followed the GPSG approach of treating the preposition *of* as a case marker, and the Montagovian approach of raising the lexical entry to deal with the embedded quantifier. Cooper's method allows *a picture of* to take wide scope over *everyone*, both at the sentential level, leaving an unbound variable, as if the quantifiers in the first derivation in Figure 7 had been eliminated in the opposite order. Under our approach, unbound variables never arise; the discharge of nested quantifiers must be nested, providing a logical basis for the nested storage devices of Keller (1988) and Gerdemann and Hinrichs (1990). The nesting in these systems represents the required order of discharge of assumptions in our framework. Also, the interaction between quantification and dependency is such that we capture the distinction between the minimal pair *everyone who John showed a picture to smiled* and *everyone who John took a picture of smiled*; the first is ambiguous, whereas in the second, the embedded quantifier must remain embedded in order for the whole derivation to be well formed, this time because of the analogous logical

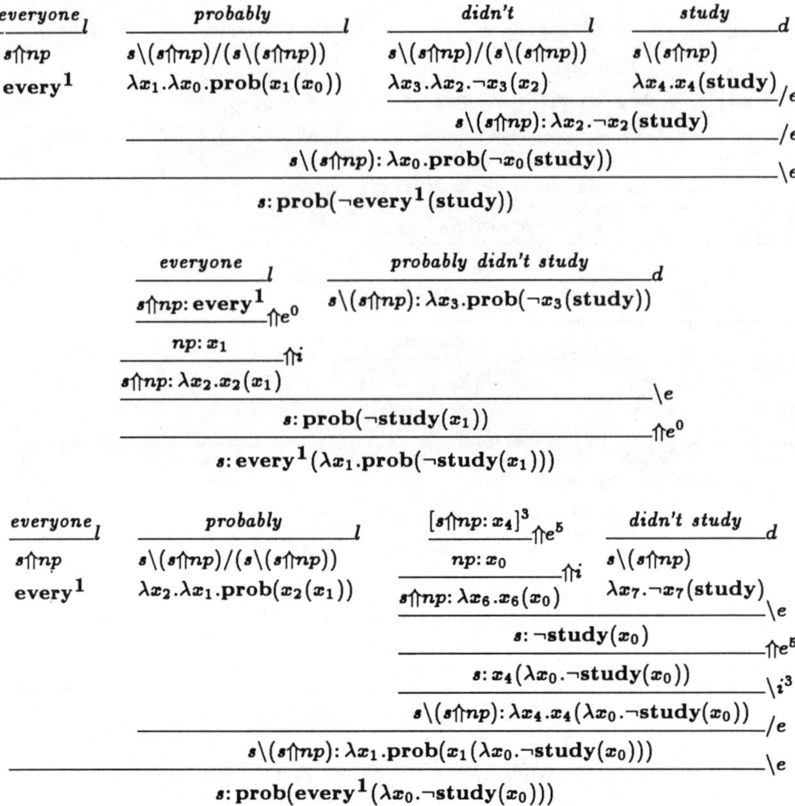

Figure 8: Analyses of Raising: *everyone probably didn't study*

structure of gap introduction.

In cases of control, which categorial grammar treats along the same lines as negation and adverbials, we see that arbitrary raising cases can be handled directly, as shown in Figure 8. Here we've used a type raised version of the intransitive verb *study*, which can be derived analogously to Figure 6. The first two analyses are just like the de dicto/de re case, only in subject position. The third, medial analysis of the quantifier involves hypothetical reasoning. Similar techniques provide readings in subject raising cases *everyone seems to like someone*, which have lexical entries just like that of adverbials and negation, and in object raising cases like *John believes everyone to like someone*, with lexical entries like $s\backslash np/(s\backslash s\Uparrow np)/s\Uparrow np$: $\lambda Q.\lambda V.\lambda x.\mathbf{bel}(V(Q))(x)$. In cases of equi control, such as *everyone promised to run*, there is no narrow

$$\dfrac{\dfrac{\dfrac{every}{s{\Uparrow}np/n\colon \mathbf{every}}\,l \qquad \dfrac{\dfrac{vegetarian}{n\colon \mathbf{veg}}\,l \quad \dfrac{and}{co\colon \wedge}\,l \quad \dfrac{socialist}{n\colon \mathbf{soc}}\,l}{n\colon \lambda x.\mathbf{veg}(x) \wedge \mathbf{soc}(x)}\,ce}{s{\Uparrow}np\colon \mathbf{every}(\lambda x.\mathbf{veg}(x) \wedge \mathbf{soc}(x))}\,/e}{}$$

$$\dfrac{\dfrac{every}{s{\Uparrow}np/n\ \ \mathbf{every}}\,l \qquad \dfrac{\dfrac{\dfrac{[s{\Uparrow}np/n\colon D]^2 \quad \dfrac{vegetarian}{n\colon \mathbf{veg}}\,l}{s{\Uparrow}np\colon D(\mathbf{veg})}\,/e}{s{\Uparrow}np\backslash(s{\Uparrow}np/n)\colon \lambda D.D(\mathbf{veg})}\,\backslash i^2 \quad \dfrac{and}{co\colon \wedge}\,l \quad \dfrac{\dfrac{[s{\Uparrow}np/n\colon E]^4 \quad \dfrac{socialist}{n\colon \mathbf{soc}}\,l}{s{\Uparrow}np\colon E(\mathbf{soc})}\,/e}{s{\Uparrow}np\backslash(s{\Uparrow}np/n)\colon \lambda E.E(\mathbf{soc})}\,\backslash i^4}{s{\Uparrow}np\backslash(s{\Uparrow}np/n)\colon \lambda F.\lambda P.F(\mathbf{veg})(P) \wedge F(\mathbf{soc})(P)}\,ce}{s{\Uparrow}np\colon \lambda P.\mathbf{every}(\mathbf{veg})(P) \wedge \mathbf{every}(\mathbf{soc})(P)}\,\backslash e$$

Figure 9: Analysis of *every vegetarian and socialist*

$$\dfrac{\dfrac{\dfrac{[s\backslash np/(s{\Uparrow}np)\colon V]^2 \quad \dfrac{a\ pen}{s{\Uparrow}np\colon \mathbf{some}(\mathbf{pen})}\,/e}{s\backslash np\colon V(\mathbf{some}(\mathbf{pen}))}\,/e}{s\backslash np\backslash(s\backslash np/(s{\Uparrow}np))\colon \lambda V.V(\mathbf{some}(\mathbf{pen}))}\,\backslash i^2 \quad \dfrac{or}{co\colon \vee}\,l \quad \dfrac{a\ pencil}{s\backslash np\backslash(s\backslash np/(s{\Uparrow}np))\ \ \lambda U.U(\mathbf{some}(\mathbf{pencil}))}\,d}{s\backslash np\backslash(s\backslash np/(s{\Uparrow}np))\colon \lambda W.\lambda x.W(\mathbf{some}(\mathbf{pen}))(x) \vee W(\mathbf{some}(\mathbf{pencil}))(x)}\,ce$$

Figure 10: Analysis of *John sought a pen or a pencil*

scope construal possible of the quantifier with respect to the promsing, and thus a simplified lexical entry $s\backslash np/(s\backslash np)\colon \lambda V.\lambda x.\mathbf{prom}(V(x))(x)$ is employed. A similar entry is required for object equi control, as found with *persuade*.

Coordination has the correct interaction with our logic. For example, consider the two derivations in Figure 9. A similar technique can be used to account for the examples discussed by Partee and Rooth (1987), such as the three way ambiguity of *John sought a pen or a pencil.* They introduced a specialized type raising operation to account for the distributive de dicto analysis, the coordinated portion of which we provide in Figure 10. We also get the proper ambiguities in simpler cases, such as *every student ran or jumped*, depending on whether or not the verb phrases are raised to take quantified arguments before being coordinated. Coordinating what have typically been called "non-constituents" is also possible, as in *every student wanted and some students had publications.* Furthermore, noun phrases, *np*, type raise to quantifiers, $s{\Uparrow}np$, and quantifiers themselves coordinate; thus deriving standard examples such as *John and every student*, and *every professor but not one student.*

Our analysis extends neatly to pied-piping, allowing the narrow construal of the the pied-piped quantifier in *a table every leg of which someone broke toppled over.* This is achieved by instantiating Morrill's (1992) pied-piping scheme:

$$which \Rightarrow q(n\backslash n/(s\uparrow A), A, np)\colon \lambda N.\lambda V.\lambda P.\lambda x.P(x) \wedge V(N(x))$$

With this category, a relative pronoun acts locally as an np, contributing to a derivation of a category A, at which point, a nominal modifier seeking a sentence with an A gap is produced. This scheme admits analyses remarkably similar to those found in GPSG and HPSG for pied-piping. Furthermore, as noted by Morrill, with $A = np$, we get the standard analysis for non-pied-piped cases, $which \Rightarrow n\backslash n/(s\uparrow np)\colon \lambda P.\lambda R.\lambda x.P(x) \wedge R(x)$, by taking the hypothetical np to be an analysis of an np by itself. The semantics is all linked together by application. Here we are interested in the case of quantifier pied-piping, where $A = s\Uparrow np$. Our logic allows the embedded *someone broke* to be analyzed as $s\uparrow(s\Uparrow np)\colon \lambda Q.\mathbf{some}(\lambda x.Q(\lambda y.\mathbf{break}(y)(x)))$, allowing the pied-piped *every leg of which* to take narrowest scope.

Our logic also handles the interesting cases of free relatives and possessives. Consider *what every kid wrote was short*, for which we derive two readings, one in which the quantifier is narrow and thus every kid wrote the same thing. Similarly, we derive two readings for *every kid's favorite toy broke*, under one of which every kid shared a favorite toy. This is achieved by assigning *what* to $np/(s\uparrow np)\colon \iota$, where ι is the description operator. We then have the option of reducing the quantifier within the argument of the free relativizer. For the possessive, we have the more complex category:

$$'s \Rightarrow np/n\backslash(s\Uparrow np)\colon \lambda Q.\lambda P.\iota(\lambda y.P(y) \wedge Q(\lambda x.\mathbf{poss}(y)(x)))$$

This allows the possessive to assign narrowest scope to a quantified possessor. Type raising, as usual, will yield the wide scope readings. Finally, consider the case of de dicto readings of embedded possessive and free relative quantifiers, as in *John sought every player's autograph* and *John wanted what every professor had.* Here we need to derive quantifiers, not just noun phrases. Under our logical interpretation of $\Uparrow$, this is unproblematic. Unfortunately, these cases also illustrate the incompleteness of the introduction schemes for q, and hence for $\Uparrow$; see Carpenter (in press) and Morrill (in press) for discussion and alternatives.

Implementation

A Prolog implementation of a complete theorem prover for the categorial logics and lexicons used to produce the derivations in this paper and in Carpenter (in press), is available via anonymous ftp at *j.gp.cs.cmu.edu* in the file */usr1/carp/ftp/nat_ded_cg_parser.tar.Z* or from the author, who can be reached at *carp@lcl.cmu.edu.*

References

Ajdukiewicz, K. 1935. Die syntaktische konnexität. *Studia Philosophica* 1, 1–27. Translated in S. McCall, ed., *Polish Logic: 1920–1939*, 207–231, Oxford: Oxford University Press.

Bar-Hillel, Y. 1953. A quasi-arithmetical notation for syntactic description. *Language* 25.

van Benthem, J. 1983. The semantics of variety in categorial grammar. Report 83-29, Simon Fraser University, Vancouver.

Carpenter, B. 1992. Plurals as further motivation for Lambek's abstraction. Presented to the *3rd Mathematics of Language Conference*, Austin.

Carpenter, B. 1994. A natural deduction theorem prover for type-theoretic categorial grammars. Carnegie Mellon Laboratory for Computational Linguistics Technical Report. Pittsburgh.

Carpenter, B. in press. *Lectures on Type Logical Semantics.* Cambridge, MA: MIT Press.

Church, A. 1940. A formulation of a simple theory of types. *Journal of Symbolic Logic* 5, 56–68.

Cooper, R. 1983. *Quantification and Syntactic Theory.* Synthese Language Library, Vol. 21, Dordrecht: Reidel.: Dordrecht.

Gazdar, G. 1980. A cross-categorial semantics for coordination. *Linguistics and Philosophy* 3, 407–410.

Gazdar, G. 1981. Unbounded dependencies and coordinate structure. *Linguistic Inquiry* 12, 155–184.

Gerdemann, D. and E. W. Hinrichs. 1990. A unification-based approach to quantifier scoping, In L. Aiello, ed., *Proceedings of the 9th European Conference on Artificial Intelligence.*

Heim, I., H. Lasnik and R. May. 1991. Distributivity and reciprocity. *Linguistic Inquiry* 22:1, 63–101.

Hendriks, H. 1987. Type change in semantics: the scope of quantification and coordination. In Klein, E. and J. van Benthem, eds., *Categories, Polymorphism and Unification*, 95–120, Centre for Cognitive Science, University of Edinburgh.

Hepple, M. 1990. *The Grammar and Processing of Order and Dependency: A Categorial Approach.* Ph.D. Thesis, Centre for Cognitive Science, University of Edinburgh.

Keller, W. R. 1988. Nested Cooper Storage: The Proper Treatment of Quantification in Ordinary Noun Phrases. In U. Reyle and C. Rohrer, eds., *Natural Language Parsing and Linguistic Theories*, 432–447. Dordrecht: Reidel.

Lambek, J. 1958. The mathematics of sentence structure. *American Mathematical Monthly* 65, 154–169.

Montague, R., 1970a. Universal grammar. *Theoria* 36:373–398.

Montague, R. 1970b. The proper treatment of quantification in ordinary English. In J. Hintikka, J. Moravcsik, and P. Suppes, eds., *Approaches to Natural Language: Proceedings of the 1970 Stanford Workshop on Grammar and Semantics* 1973, Reidel: Dordrecht.

Moortgat, M. 1988. *Categorial Investigations*. Dordrecht: Foris.

Moortgat, M. 1990. The quantification calculus: questions of axiomatization. In Deliverable R1.2.A of DYANA: Dynamic Interpretation of Natural Language. ESPRIT Basic Research Action BR3175.

Moortgat, M. 1991. Generalized quantification and discontinuous type constructors. To appear in Sijtsma and van Horck, eds., *Proceedings of the Tilburg Symposium on Discontinuous Constituency*. Berlin: De Gruyter.

Moortgat, M. and R. Oehrle. 1994. Adjacency, dependency and order In P. Dekker and M. Stokhof, eds., *Proceedings of the 9th Amsterdam Colloquium*. Dordrecht: Foris.

Morrill, G. 1990. Intensionality and boundedness. *Linguistics and Philosophy* 13, 699–726.

Morrill, G. in press. *Type Logical Grammar: Categorial Theory of Signs*. Synthese Library. Dordrecht: Kluwer.

Morrill, G. 1992. Categorial formalisation of relativisation: pied piping, islands and extraction sites. Report de Recerca LSI-92-23, Departament de Llenguatages i Sistemes Informàtics, Universitat Politècnica de Catalunya. Barcelona.

Partee, B. and M. Rooth. 1983. Generalized conjunction and type ambiguity. In Bäuerle, R., C. Schwarze, and A. von Stechow, eds., *Meaning, Use and Interpretation of Language*, de Gruyter: Berlin.

Pereira, F. 1990. Categorial semantics and scoping. *Computational Linguistics* 16:1, 1–10.

Pollard, C. J. and I. A. Sag. 1994. *Head-Driven Phrase Structure Grammar*. Chicago: University of Chicago Press.

Steedman, M. 1985. Dependency and coordination in the grammar of Dutch and English. *Language* 61, 523–568.

Steedman, M. 1988. Combinators and grammars. In Oehrle, R., E. Bach, and D. Wheeler, eds., *Categorial Grammars and Natural Language Structures*, Dordrecht: Reidel.

When-Clauses, Adverbs of quantification, and Focus

MICHAEL JOHNSTON
University of California, Santa Cruz

1. The Interaction of Adverbial Adjuncts with Adverbs of Quantification

Determination of the ways in which linguistic information such as syntactic structure and intonational focus are relevant to semantic interpretation is an important issue for linguistic semantics. The semantic interpretation of constructions with adverbial adjuncts is an interesting area of study in this regard because of the variability in their syntactic position and their intonational focus and the consequences of this variability for interpretation. In this paper, I will be concerned, in particular, with the interpretation of *when*-clause adjuncts and the consequences of syntactic structure and intonational focus for their composition with adverbs of quantification. The

---

I would like to thank William A. Ladusaw for the abundance of insight, detailed commentary, and support that he has given me throughout his supervision of the research project of which this paper is a part. I would also like to thank Donka Farkas, Sandra Chung, Cathal Doherty, Ted Fernald, Giulia Centineo, Sabine Iatridou, Chris Kennedy, Eric Potsdam, Ivan Sag, Philip Spaelti, Peter Svenonius, Kari Swingle, Daniel Flickinger, and David Adger for their help and comments and to acknowledge the support of the Linguistic Research Center at UC Santa Cruz.

results here readily generalize to a wide range of other temporal adverbial adjuncts, such as *before*-clauses and *after*-clauses, and to a wide range of other types of adverbial adjuncts including purposives and *because*-clauses. The wider application of this approach is explored in detail in Johnston 1994.

I will begin with a discussion of the different interpretations of constructions with adverbs of quantification and *when*-clause adjuncts and an outline of previous approaches to these facts. I will then go on in Section 2 to show why the range of interpretation of these constructions can not be treated as an instance of Rooth (1985)'s theory of ASSOCIATION WITH FOCUS and argue in favor of Vallduví (1990)'s proposal that intonational focus is not relevant to the determination of the truth conditions of an utterance. In Section 3, I go on to propose an account in which *when*-clauses may be base-generated adjoined to IP or VP and in which they are interpreted as descriptions of intervals. I will show how the distinction between IP and VP attachment determines whether the interval description contributed by a *when*-clause serves as part of the restriction or the nuclear scope of an adverb of quantification. These proposals are supported by facts involving clause-initial *when*-clauses, VP-deletion facts, and differences in markedness between the different possible interpretations of these constructions. In Section 4, I make a proposal which accounts for the correlation between the placement of intonational focus and the different interpretations available. Section 5 concludes and summarizes the paper.

In the interpretation of sentences with adverbs of quantification, the crucial question is how the restriction and nuclear scope of the quantifier are determined. Lewis (1975) proposed that, like *if*-clauses, the function of a *when*-clause in a quantificational sentence is to provide the restriction. The reading this gives us for example (1) is that on all occasions that Marcia is at the cafe, she writes a letter. This reading can be represented informally as the tripartite structure in (2). I will refer to this reading as the ADJUNCT RESTRICTION READING.

(1) Marcia always writes a letter when she is at the cafe.
(2) *always* {*when she is at the cafe*} Restriction
[*Marcia writes a letter*] Nuclear Scope

The assumption that the semantic function of *when*-clauses is to provide the restriction for an adverb of quantification is also made by a number of other authors, including: Partee (1984), Stump (1985), Farkas and Sugioka (1983), Farkas (1985), and Berman (1991). An immediate difficulty for all of these approaches is the availability of an alternative reading in which the head clause[1] provides the restriction and the adjunct clause provides the

[1]I will use the term HEAD CLAUSE to refer to the clause containing the main verb in the sentence. This is the clause which the adjunct is attached to.

nuclear scope. This reading of (1) means that on all occasions that Marcia writes a letter she does so when she is at the cafe. This reading can be represented informally as the tripartite structure in (3). I will refer to this reading as the HEAD RESTRICTION READING.

(3) *always* {*Marcia writes a letter*} Restriction
[*when she is at the cafe*] Nuclear Scope

Consideration of the use of (1) as an answer to the questions in (4) and (5) clarifies the two different readings. Example (1) is an appropriate answer to question (4) on the adjunct restriction reading, but not on the head restriction reading, while (1) is an appropriate answer to (5) on the head restriction reading but not on the adjunct restriction reading.

(4) What does Marcia do when she is at the cafe?
(5) When does Marcia write letters?

The adjunct restriction reading of an example like (1) can be paraphrased using *if* or *whenever* as in (6) and (7). These examples only have the adjunct restriction reading and lack the head restriction reading. The head restriction reading of (1) is a very close paraphrase of the example in (8) with *only*.

(6) Marcia always writes letters if she is at the cafe.
(7) Marcia writes letters whenever she is at the cafe.
(8) Marcia only writes letters when she is at the cafe.

In addition to only accounting for the adjunct restriction reading the previous approaches mentioned above do not address the role of syntax and focus in determining the interpretation of these constructions. Rooth (1985) proposed an account of these facts which accounts for both readings in terms of his theory of ASSOCIATION WITH FOCUS. In the next section, I will describe Rooth's account and show the problems it faces.

2. Rooth's Account in Terms of Association with Focus

Rooth (1985) observed the availability of the head and adjunct restriction readings and showed how intonational focus serves to distinguish them. Consider the examples in (9) and (10), in which capitalization represents intonational focus.

(9) John always SHAVES when he is in the shower.
(10) John always shaves when he is in the SHOwer.

Rooth claims that if *shaves* is focused as in (9) only the adjunct restriction reading is available; that is, (9) can only mean that on all occasions that John is in the shower, he shaves. If the focus is on *shower*, as in (10), only the head restriction reading is available; that is, (10) can only mean that on all occasions that John shaves, he is in the shower.

This dependence on intonational focus leads Rooth to propose that these facts should be accounted for by an extension of his theory of Association with Focus. Developing on work by Jackendoff (1972:247-254), Rooth develops an analysis of focus sensitive adverbs such as *only* and *even* in which they are necessarily semantically associated with the element in the sentence that bears intonational focus. Informally, he proposes that intonational focus sets up a second semantic value for an utterance which he calls a P-SET. The p-set is derived by abstracting over the focused element in the sentence. He proposes that, like *only* and *even*, adverbs of quantification such as *always* associate with focus, and that the p-set of an example with an adverb of quantification serves as the restriction. He extends this to account for the readings of (9) and (10) as follows. In (9), *always* is claimed to associate with a broad focus on the head clause *John shaves*. This has the effect of removing the semantic contribution of *John shaves* from the p-set for the sentence. The resulting interpretation can be represented as in (11). It requires that all intervals at which John is in the shower are intervals at which John shaves and he is in the shower.

(11) **always′[λt AT(t, in-shower′(john))]**
[λt AT(t, in-shower′(john) & AT(t,shave′(john))]
(12) **always′[λt AT(t, shaves′(john))]**
[λt AT(t, in-shower′(john) & AT(t,shave′(john))]

In (10), *always* is claimed to associate with a broad focus on the adjunct clause *he is in the shower*. This has the effect of removing the semantic contribution of *he is in the shower* from the p-set for the sentence. The resulting interpretation is represented as in (12). It requires that all intervals at which John shaves are intervals at which John shaves and he is in the shower.

Rooth's proposal that the determination of the restriction and nuclear scope in these cases is a matter of Association with Focus runs into a number of problems. First of all, there are many examples where the head restriction reading is freely available and the presence of intonational focus does not appear to be necessary. Examples (13-15) all have a freely available head restriction reading independent of the presence of focus.

(13) Sharks usually attack a human when they are hungry.
(14) Francis always submits an abstract when the deadline is very near.
(15) Marcia always goes to the store before it gets dark.

Example (13) can mean that it is usual behavior for sharks to attack people when they are hungry and not on other occasions. The strongly preferred reading of (14) is that on all occasions that Francis submits an abstract she submits it close to the deadline. A related example with a *before*-clause,

(15), is most naturally interpreted as meaning that on all occasions that Marcia goes to the store she does so before it gets dark.

Stronger arguments against the claim that this is Association with Focus can be derived from the work of Vallduví (1990). Vallduví argues that intonational focus is not relevant to the determination of the truth conditions of an utterance and that it has an information packaging function. He shows that so called FOCUS SENSITIVE operators such as *only* need not associate with focal material and demonstrates that given the appropriate context they can associate with non-focal material. Vallduví's arguments undermine Rooth's account of *only*, and this in turn undermines Rooth's extension of Association with Focus to the interpretation of quantifiers like *always*. I want to show here how given the appropriate context, Rooth's proposal regarding the correlation between the head and adjunct restriction readings and the placement of intonational focus makes the wrong predictions. Since Rooth postulates a direct connection between the appearance of intonational focus and material which does not go into the restriction, he predicts that the clause which contains focus cannot be the clause which appears in the restriction. The two particular cases are as in (16) and (17).

(16) If there is a focus in the head clause then the head restriction reading will not be available.
(17) If there is a focus in the adjunct clause then the adjunct restriction reading will not be available.

The context in (18) provides a counterexample to (16). In (18), You know that John is usually in the shower when he brushes his teeth and that there is something that he only does when he is in the shower. You do not know that that something is shaving. Examples (18a) and (18b) only have adjunct restriction readings. In this context, (18e) is a perfectly felicitous response to the question (18d). It means that shaving is something that John only does whilst in the shower and not in other places. So, even though there is an overt focus on the head clause, the head restriction reading is available.

(18) You know:(a) John is usually in the shower when he brushes his teeth.
(b) John is always in the shower when he X's.
You don't know: (c) X = shaves
The question: (d) What does John always do when he is in the shower?
In this context the following answer is felicitous:
(e) John always SHAVES when he is in the shower.

The context in (19) provides a counterexample to (17). In (19), you know that sometimes, when he is at home, John flosses. You also know that there is a situation where he always flosses. You don't know that that situation is his being at a restaurant. In this context, (19e) is a perfectly felicitous response to the question in (19d). In this context, (19e) means that on all occasions that John is at a restaurant he flosses. So, even though there is an overt focus on the adjunct clause, the adjunct restriction reading is available.

(19) You know: (a) When he is at home, John sometimes flosses.
(b) When he is at X, John always flosses.
You don't know: (c) X = a restaurant
The question: (d) When does John always floss?
In this context the following answer is felicitous:
(e) John always flosses when he is at a RESTaurant.

A further problem for Rooth's proposal is that it does not straightforwardly account for the absence of the head restriction reading in cases where the *when*-clause is clause-initial. For example, (20) can only mean that on all occasions that Mary is at the cafe, she writes a letter. It cannot mean that on all occasions that Mary writes a letter, she is at the cafe.

(20) When she is at the cafe, Mary always writes a letter.

Rooth (1985:182-183) proposes that in these cases the sentence is translated as a lambda abstraction and the quantifier fails to capture a focus in the lambda abstract. The motivation for this proposal is not clear and furthermore it will not account for VP-deletion facts discussed later in Section 3.

Another difficulty for Rooth's proposal concerns the difference in markedness between the head and adjunct restriction readings. Given an example like (21), in a context where both readings make sense, and without a clear intonational focus, informants prefer the adjunct restriction reading.

(21) Marty always shaves when he is in the shower.

Rooth's account does not explain this preference since both readings should be equally possible through Association with Focus. This difference in acceptability is expected given Lewis's proposal that *when*-clauses mark the restriction, but that proposal had no way to derive the head restriction reading.

In the next section, I propose an account which captures the availability of these readings and explains the role of focus and syntactic position in determining which is available.

3. The Factorization from Syntax to Semantics

I will first outline my proposals regarding the syntax and semantics of *when*-clauses and adverbs of quantification. I assume that *when*-clauses are descriptions of intervals. The *when*-clause *when she is at the cafe* in (1) is translated as a description of a maximal interval during which Marcia is at the cafe. I will represent the semantic contribution of this *when*-clause as in (22).

(22) **when′$_{e_1}$(at′(Marcia, the cafe, e_1))**

I am going to assume that *when* is a preposition and the *when*-clause is a PP but nothing hinges on this decision. I assume that *when*-clauses are adjuncts which are base-generated in adjoined positions within the clause. The function of a *when*-clause is to situate an eventuality with respect to the interval the described by the *when*-clause. I assume that they do not select for a particular syntactic category, but rather they select for a category which expresses an eventuality description. Given the VP-INTERNAL SUBJECT HYPOTHESIS (Kuroda 1988), all of the arguments of a predicate are saturated within VP, and therefore both VP and IP express eventuality descriptions. I propose then that both VP and IP are potential sites for the base-generation of a *when*-clause adjunct. I assume adverbs of quantification are of the category ADV and in the examples considered here they are base-generated in ADVPs adjoined to VP or I'.

Diesing (1992), building on the work of Kratzer, makes a proposal regarding the relationship between syntactic structure and semantic interpretation which she calls the MAPPING HYPOTHESIS. The Mapping Hypothesis states that in order to determine the interpretation of a sentence with an adverb of quantification, from the syntactic level of logical form, the contents of VP are mapped into the nuclear scope and the rest of IP is mapped into the restriction. Diesing supports this proposal with a range of facts involving NP interpretation in English and German. The insight that I want to draw out from Diesing's proposal is the connection of IP material and the restriction and VP material and the nuclear scope. I am not going to be concerned with NP interpretation here. I believe though that these connections are also relevant to the interpretation of adjuncts. I propose that in the interpretation of quantificational structure with temporal adverbial adjuncts, if the adjunct is adjoined to IP, it is mapped into the restriction, and if it is adjoined to VP, it is mapped into the nuclear scope. I will refer to this as ADJUNCT FACTORIZATION as defined in (23).

(23) Adjunct Factorization:
(i) Adjuncts adjoined to IP are mapped into the restriction.
(ii) Adjuncts adjoined to VP are mapped into the nuclear scope.

It does not make any difference to this analysis whether this factorization takes place at surface structure or logical form. I will assume for the purposes of this paper that the factorization takes place at logical form[2].

Given this proposal, the adjunct restriction reading will arise if the *when*-clause is IP-adjoined. Example (24) will have the structure in (25) when the *when*-clause is IP-adjoined.

(24) Marcia always writes a letter when she is at the cafe.

(25)

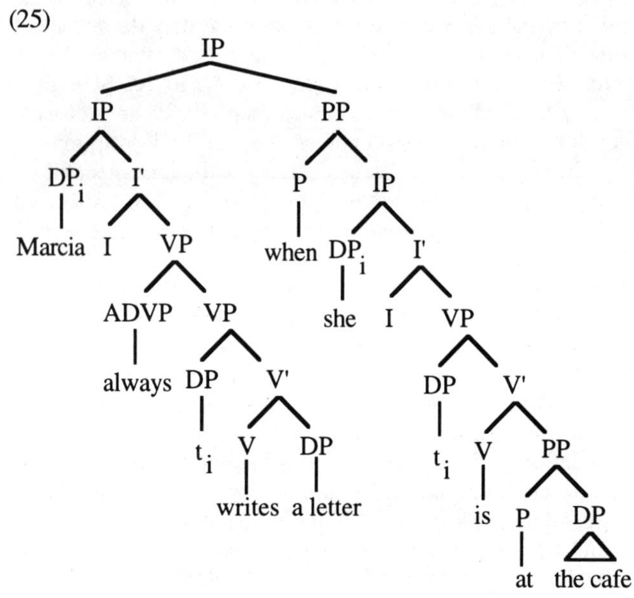

In this position the semantic contribution of the *when*-clause will be mapped into the restriction of the adverb of quantification. The resulting interpretation for (25) can be represented as in (26).

(26) **always′** **{when′$_{e_1}$(at′(Marcia, the cafe, e_1))}**
[write′(Marcia, a letter, e_2)]

The contribution of the *when*-clause is a description of an interval which corresponds to a maximal eventuality of Marcia being at the cafe. This

---

[2]If the analysis proposed here was coupled with an account of DP interpretation that did not require movement the result would be compatible with the assumption that semantic interpretation is read from surface structure.

serves as the restriction on the adverb of quantification. The set of objects being quantified over are maximal intervals of Marcia being at the cafe. The head clause provides the nuclear scope. It is a description of an eventuality of Marcia writing a letter. The interpretation represented by (26) is that for all intervals which correspond to maximal eventualities of Marcia being at the cafe, there exists an eventuality of Marcia writing a letter which is included within that interval. The truth conditions of these constructions are explored and explicated in more detail in Johnston 1994.

I propose that the head restriction readings result from VP-adjunction of the *when*-clause. In addition to the structure in (25), example (24) could also have the structure in (27).

(27)

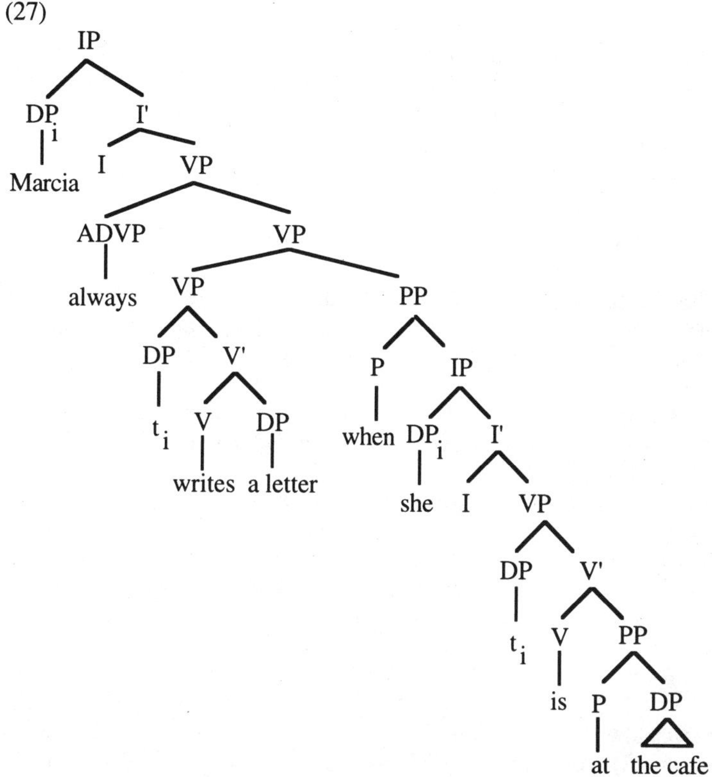

Given the factorization that I have proposed, both the head clause and the *when*-clause will be mapped into the nuclear scope of the quantifier. I assume that the *when*-clause composes with the head clause. The resulting semantic representation is the same as that which I propose is assigned to episodic uses of *when*-clauses, which are those which report a single instance of an eventuality. They involve an existential quantification in which the adjunct clause serves as the restriction and the head clause serves as the nuclear scope, as in (28).

(28) ∃ **{when'$_{e_1}$(at'(Marcia, the cafe, e_1))}**
[write'(Marcia, a letter, e_2)]

The interpretation this represents is like that for the example above with *always*, except that the quantifier only requires that there be one interval of Marcia being at the cafe during which she writes a letter. This representation of the composition of the *when*-clause and the head clause is mapped into the nuclear scope of *always*, resulting in the representation in (29).

(29) **always'{} [∃{when'$_{e_1}$(at'(Marcia, the cafe, e_1))}**
[write'(Marcia, a letter, e_2)]]

As it stands, this quantificational structure is not licit because there is nothing in the restriction and an adverbial quantifier must necessarily quantify over something. One formulation of this necessity is the ban on vacuous quantification proposed by Kratzer (1989), given in (30).

(30) Prohibition against vacuous quantification
For every quantifier Q, there must be a variable x such that Q binds an occurrence of x in both its restrictive clause and its nuclear scope.

In the terms employed here, there has to be something in the restriction which provides a set for the quantifier range over and the nuclear scope must be a suitable test for the members of that set.

It is of course possible for an adverbial quantifier like *always* to have a restriction derived from context. For example, (31) has an interpretation which is that in all relevant intervals it is the case that Francesca goes running. This can be represented as in (32). The symbol **C** here is intended to represent a contextual restriction function that gives you the appropriate intervals from context. The condition in the nuclear scope is that each of those intervals contain an eventuality of Francesca going running.

(31) Francesca always goes running.
(32) **always'{C}[goes running'(Francesca, e_1)]**

An interesting property of *when*-clause constructions is that they cannot have a restriction which is solely determined from context. Example (24) cannot mean that in all intervals that are relevant Marcia writes a letter and she is at the cafe. Either the *when*-clause or the head clause must provide the restriction on *always*. I propose that general contextual restriction readings require the eventuality in the nuclear scope to be situated in time and for that time to be unspecified. Since *when*-clauses provide the time at which an eventuality takes place, examples with *when*-clauses cannot have a restriction which is solely determined from context, a general contextual restriction reading. Given that this sort of reading is not available, the question which remains is how the head restriction reading arises.

I propose that *always* may bind the eventuality variable in the head clause eventuality description. The representation is as in (33).

(33) **always'$_{e_2}${}[∃{when'$_{e_1}$(at'(Marcia, the cafe, e_1))}**
[write'(Marcia, a letter, e_2)]]

I propose that when a quantifier binds an eventuality variable the resulting quantificational structure is interpreted as if the eventuality description which the eventuality variable is an argument of were in the restriction. This means that the representation in (33) is interpreted the same as the representation in (34).

(34) **always'$_{e_2}${write'(Marcia, a letter, e_2)}**
[∃{when'$_{e_1}$(at'(Marcia, the cafe, e_1))}
[write'(Marcia, a letter, e_2)]]

The interpretation this represents is as follows. The restriction of **always'** is a description of an eventuality of Marcia writing a letter. The nuclear scope is a quantificational statement. It states that there exists an interval of Marcia being at the cafe and that the eventuality of Marcia writing a letter is contained within that interval. The resulting interpretation is that for all eventualities of Marcia writing a letter there exists an interval of Marcia being at the cafe which contains that eventuality.

This process of eventuality variable binding also provides an account of several other phenomena in which the syntactic structure does not provide a restriction for an adverb of quantification. It also accounts for the interpretation of constructions with adverbs of quantification and embedded WH-clauses discussed by Berman (1991), and it is involved in the composition of adverbs of quantification with *because*-clauses and purpose clauses. These further applications are discussed in Johnston (1994).

So then, the picture we have is that there are two ways in which the restriction and nuclear scope are determined in these constructions. In both cases there is a factorization from surface structure to semantic representation. If the *when*-clause is IP-adjoined, this factorization determines the content of both the restriction and nuclear scope and the resulting reading is an adjunct restriction reading. If the *when*-clause is VP-adjoined, the head clause and the *when*-clause compose and form the nuclear scope, but the restriction is left undetermined. In this case the restriction is determined not through factorization from the syntax but through the process of interpretation of the quantificational structure. The quantifier *always* binds the eventuality variable in the head clause eventuality description and that eventuality description serves as the restriction. The resulting reading is the head restriction reading.

This proposal is supported by a number of different pieces of evidence. First, it explains the absence of a head restriction reading for clause-initial *when*-clauses, as in example (35).

(35) When she is at the cafe, Marcia always writes a letter.

(36)

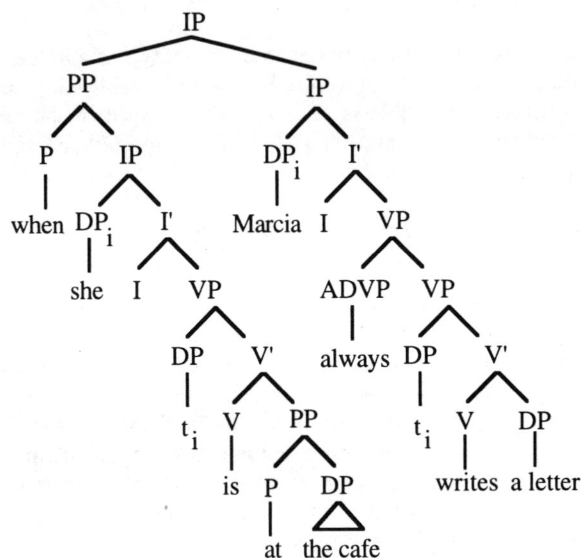

In this position the *when*-clause can only be adjoined to IP and not to VP, as shown in (36). In the factorization from syntax to semantics, the semantic content of the *when*-clause will necessarily be mapped into the restriction of *always*. A clause-final *when*-clause, on the other hand, can be adjoined to either IP or VP, as in (25) and (27), and therefore is either mapped into the restriction or the nuclear scope.

Further support for the connection between IP attachment and the adjunct restriction reading comes from examples involving VP-deletion.

(37) Lions always attack a human when they are hungry.
(38) Lions always attack a human when they are hungry and tigers always do __ when they are scared.

An example like (37) has both head and adjunct restriction readings. The adjunct restriction reading is that on all occasions that you have a hungry lion it attacks a human. The head restriction reading is that on all occasions that a lion attacks a human it is hungry. In (38), however, in which the main VP in the second conjunct has undergone deletion, both conjuncts can only have an adjunct restriction reading. Sag (1976) argues that the target of VP-deletion must be the sister of an AUX. In the framework here this amounts to requiring that the sister of I be what is deleted, or alternatively that VP-deletion can only delete maximal VPs. If the *when*-clause is VP-adjoined, the structure of the second conjunct of (38) would be as in (39).

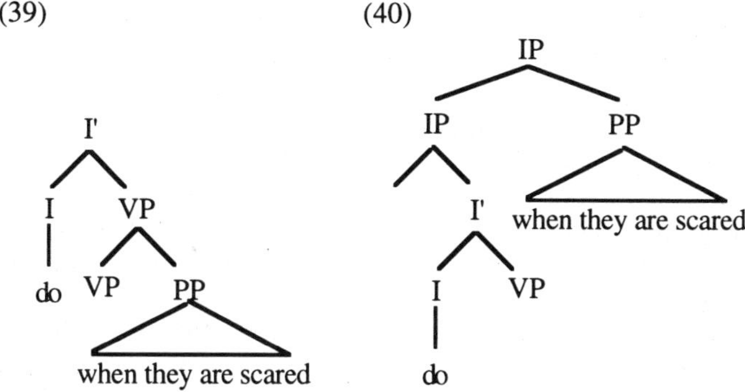

If this was the structure in the second conjunct, VP-deletion could not apply to the lower VP because it is not a sister of I. On the other hand if the *when*-clause is IP-adjoined, the structure in the second conjunct of (38) would be as in (40). In this case the VP could be deleted because it is the sister of I. These facts show that if the VP is deleted the stranded *when*-clause must be IP-adjoined. Since the *when*-clause can only be IP-adjoined, we expect there to only be an adjunct restriction reading for (38), as is the case.

The proposal I have made is also supported by the relative markedness of the head restriction reading compared to the adjunct restriction reading. Given a case where the *when*-clause could be IP or VP adjoined, if it is IP-adjoined the determination of the restriction and nuclear scope will fall out from the factorization from syntax to semantic representation. This results in the adjunct restriction reading. If the adjunct is VP-adjoined the determination of the restriction does not fall out from the factorization, the quantifier has to bind the eventuality variable in the head clause eventuality description, and because of this binding the structure is interpreted as if the head clause were in restriction. It is reasonable to assume that the adjunct restriction reading would be preferred since it does not require this further complication of interpretation.

This account is also supported by the discussion in Section 2, since it is not dependent on the presence of intonational focus to determine the head and adjunct restriction readings. However, there is a strong correlation between the placement of intonational focus and the availability of these readings which needs to be explained. This is the topic of the next section.

4. The Correlation of Focus with the Head and Adjunct Restriction Readings

I have proposed that there is no direct reference to the presence of intonational focus in the composition of *when*-clauses with adverbs of quantification. Although, as I showed earlier, intonational focus does not necessarily indicate the nature of the quantificational structure, there is still a strong correlation between the placement of focus and the availability of head and adjunct restriction readings. If there is a focus on the head clause, as in (41), the adjunct restriction reading is preferred. If there is a focus on the adjunct clause, as in (42), the head restriction reading is preferred.

(41) John always SHAVES when he is in the shower.
(42) John always shaves when he is in the SHOwer.

In order to understand this correlation we need to consider the relationship between quantificational structure and information structure. Vallduví (1990) makes a distinction between focus and ground which corresponds roughly to the distinction between what is PRESUMED and what is AT ISSUE. The part of an utterance which is at issue is the part which is the point of the speaker telling the utterance to the hearer. The presumed part is material which the hearer considers to be uncontroversial but not necessarily familiar. For all quantificational operators, the restriction is assumed to be non-empty; that is, there is at least one thing which meets the description in the restriction. The object described by the restriction is what is being talked about. In this sense the restriction is presumed while the operator and the nuclear scope are what is at issue. I propose that the unmarked case is for quantificational structure to match up to information structure as in (43).

(43)	{Restriction}	|	OP [Nuclear scope]
	Ground =	|	Focus =
	Presumed	|	At Issue

What I am claiming is that there is a strong tendency for the operator and nuclear scope to be at issue while the restriction is presumed. In a neutral context, (41) prefers an adjunct restriction reading because the head clause is focused and therefore at issue. If the head clause was mapped into the restriction the tendency for the restriction to be presumed material would be broken. In (42) since the adjunct clause is focused the sentence will be least marked if the adjunct clause goes into the nuclear scope rather than the restriction. This is the case on the head restriction reading, so that reading is preferred in that case.

5. Conclusion

I have shown here how the determination of the head and adjunct restriction readings of constructions with adverbial quantifiers and *when*-clause adjuncts is independent of the placement of intonational focus but is dependent on the syntactic position of the adjuncts. The account I have developed captures the dependence of the two readings on syntactic structure. I proposed that *when*-clauses can be base-generated adjoined to either IP or VP. As a result of a general process of factorization of the clause into restriction and nuclear scope, IP adjoined *when*-clauses become part of the restriction, resulting in the adjunct restriction reading. Given the proposal that *when*-clauses are descriptions of intervals, the quantification on the adjunct restriction reading is over intervals. VP-adjoined *when*-clauses are factored into the nuclear scope where they compose with the eventuality description expressed by the VP. In those cases, the quantifier binds the eventuality variable in the eventuality description expressed by the VP and the structure is interpreted as if that eventuality description were in the restriction. This results in the head restriction reading. On this reading, the restriction contains an eventuality description and the quantification is over eventualities. This account is supported by the absence of head restriction readings for clause-initial *when*-clauses, VP-deletion facts, and the relative markedness of the head restriction reading. The correlation between the placement of intonational focus and the availability of these readings is the result of a general tendency for the restriction to be part of the ground, while the quantifier and nuclear scope are part of the focus.

The discussion in this paper concentrates on the interaction of *when*-clauses with the adverb of quantification *always*. The constructions addressed here are representative examples of a much larger phenomenon regarding the composition of adverbs of quantification and adverbial adjuncts, and the analysis developed here extends readily to a wide range of other data. The account extends to other quantificational adverbs such as *usually* and *sometimes*. It also accounts for the interaction of adverbs of quantification with other temporal adverbials such as *before*-clauses, *after*-clauses, and temporal phrases like *on Thursday* and *between 3 O'clock and 5 O'clock*. In Johnston (1994), more detailed explanation of the semantic interpretation of *when* is given and semantic interpretations for *before*-clauses and *after*-clauses are proposed.

DeSwart (1991:183-258) makes a proposal regarding the composition of temporal adverbial clauses with adverbs of quantification which accounts for the availability of both head and adjunct restriction readings. In Johnston (1994), facts involving the role of the aspectual class of the head clause in determining the availability of the head restriction reading are addressed. DeSwart's proposals do not account for these aspect facts. Furthermore they do not explain the role of syntactic structure and focus in the interpretation of these constructions. The account I have proposed succeeds in accounting for these aspect facts. Discussion of these issues, more detailed explanation of the proposed truth conditions, and further applications of the process of eventuality variable binding are to be found in Johnston (1994).

References

Berman, Steve R. 1991. *On the Semantics and Logical Form of WH-clauses*. Doctoral dissertation, University of Massachusetts at Amherst.

Diesing, Molly. 1992. *Indefinites*. Cambridge, Massachusetts: MIT Press.

Farkas, Donka F. 1985. *Intensional Descriptions and the Romance Subjunctive Mood.* New York: Garland Publishers.

Farkas, Donka F. and Yoko Sugioka. 1983. *Restrictive If/When-clauses*. Linguistics and Philosophy 6.225-258.

Heinämäki, Orvokki. 1978. *Semantics of English Temporal Connectives*. Bloomington: Indiana University Linguistics Club.

Jackendoff, Ray. 1972. *Semantic Interpretation in Generative Grammar*. Cambridge, Massachusetts: MIT Press.

Johnston, Michael. 1994. *The Syntax and Semantics of Adverbial Adjuncts*. Doctoral dissertation, University of California at Santa Cruz.

Kratzer, Angelika. 1989. *Stage-level and Individual-level predicates*. (ms.)

Kuroda, S. Y. 1988. *Whether We Agree or Not: A Comparative Syntax of English and Japanese*. Linguisticae Investigationes 12.1-47.

Lewis, David. 1975. *Adverbs of Quantification. Formal Semantics of Natural Language*, ed. by Edward L. Keenan, 3-15. Cambridge, England: Cambridge University Press.

Partee, Barbara. 1984. *Nominal and Temporal Anaphora*. Linguistics and Philosophy 7.243-286.

Rooth, Mats. 1985. *Association with Focus*. Doctoral dissertation, University of Massachusetts at Amherst.

Sag, Ivan. 1976. *A Note on Verb Phrase Deletion*. Linguistic Inquiry 7.664-671.

Stump, Gregory T. 1985. *The Semantic Variability Of Absolute Constructions*. Dordrecht: Kluwer Academic Publishers.

de Swart, Henriëtte. 1991. *Adverbs of Quantification: A Generalized Quantifier Approach*. Doctoral dissertation, Rijksuniversiteit Groningen.

Vallduví, Enric. 1990. *The Informational Component*. Doctoral dissertation, University of Pennsylvania.

Exhaustivity, The Scalar Principle, and Focus Semantics

YAE-SHEIK LEE
University of Texas at Austin

0. Introduction

In recent work on the semantics of question-answer pairs, much attention has been paid to the following phenomenon:

(1) Q: Who solved the problem?
A: John.

The answer in (1) is likely to mean that *only John solved the problem*, the so-called exhaustive interpretation. Groenendijk and Stokhof (1983 & 1992, hereafter, G&S) convincingly argue that such an interpretation obligatorily occurs on the answer terms. This means that they treat exhaustivity as a semantic phenomenon. My goal in this paper is to explain exhaustivity in terms of focus and to show that it is a pragmatic phenomenon.

1. Previous Analyses

G&S propose the following exhaustivity operator, which is obligatorily applied to answer terms to get the right interpretation.

---

* I would like to thank Manfred Krifka for his comments. I also benefited from the Monday Colloquim of the Dept. of Linguistics of the University of Texas at Austin. Of course, all of the remaining errors are mine.

(2) $\underline{exh} = \lambda\wp\lambda P\,[\,\wp(P)\ \&\ \neg\exists P'[\,\wp(P')\ \&\ P\neq P'\ \&\ P'\subset P]\,]$

Notice that the exhaustivity operator filters out the smallest sets among a set of sets. Let us assume that the exhaustive interpretation is semantic, and see how the above operator is supposed to work. For this purpose, the following small model is supposed.

(3) Example: M=< E, F>: E is Discourse Domain. F is the denotation function. E={a,b,c,d}, F(girl) ={a,b,c}, and F(boy)= {d}.

(4) Q: Who came to the party?
A: (I don't know precisely, but)
a. at most two girls (came to the party.)
b. at least two girls (came to the party.)
c. no girls (came to the party.)

If we exhaustivize the denotation of the answers of (4), we will get the following sets in (5).

(5) a.$\underline{exh}$ $(\{X \mid \#(X\cap \text{girl}) \leq 2\})=\{\{\varnothing\}\}$
b.$\underline{exh}$ $(\{X \mid \#(X\cap\text{girl}) \geq 2\})=\{\{a,b\},\{b,c\},\{a,c\}\}$
c.$\underline{exh}$ $(\{X \mid \#(X\cap\text{girl})) =0\})=\{\{\varnothing\}\}$

The above exhaustivization leads to the following problems: First, the exhaustivized denotations of *at most two girls* and *no girls* are equivalent with that of *nobody*. Monotone decreasing quantifiers don't submit to this operation appropriately. I call this problem the 'empty set' problem. Second, the exhaustivized denotation of *at least two girls* is equivalent with the meaning of *only two girls*. I call this the 'minimalization' problem.

To remedy this shortcoming, von Stechow and Zimmermann (1984) and von Stechow (1990) propose to classify terms into two groups, as follows:

(6) 'a term T might be regarded as positive if it implies that at least something in its quantificational domain has the property to which T is applied; T is negative if something in T's domain must not have that property'

Based on the above classification, von Stechow (1990:77) gives two definitions for the exhaustivity operator[1].

---

1 von Stechow takes the meaning of *only* minus the presuppositional meaning of *only* as equal to that of exhaustiveness.

(7) *Only* $(Q)(P)$ is true
iff $\sim\exists P' [\, Q(P') \,\&\, P \neq P' \,\&\, \forall x [\, P'(x) \rightarrow P(x) \,]]$,
if Q is a positive quantifier
$\sim\exists P' [\, Q(P') \,\&\, P \neq P' \,\&\, \forall x [\, P(x) \rightarrow P'(x) \,]]$,
if Q is a negative quantifier.

Even if we admit that the above definition of exhaustivity can solve the 'empty set' problem for the 'negative' terms, the problem with *at most* or *at least N* based terms still remains unsolved since they are not 'negative' terms according to von Stechow.

G&S themselves were aware of these problems and tried to overcome them in plural logic. They introduce the notions of 'group'[2] individuals, of collectiveness, distributiveness, and others. To see whether we can really solve the above mentioned problems or at least avoid them with the help of the plural logic, I introduce a plural logic as follows;

(8) $M = \langle E, \oplus, \perp, F \rangle$, where E is a structured discourse domain. $\oplus$ is the sum operator. $\perp$ is the bottom element of the structure. F is denotation function for basic expressions.

With the help of the sum operation, we can define the part-relation of (9)-a. In turn, 'atomicity' is defined in terms of the part-relation. Similarly the other notions can be defined as follows:

(9) a. part-relation, $\leq_p$: $x \leq_p y$ iff $x \oplus y = y$
b. Atomicity, ATOM: ATOM (x) iff $\forall z [\, z \leq_p x \rightarrow z = x \,]$
c. Identity, =: $x=y$ iff $\forall z [\, z \leq_p x \leftrightarrow z \leq_p y \,]$

(10) A predicate P is collective iff $\forall x \, [\, P(x) \rightarrow \neg$ ATOM $(x) \,]$

(11) $\text{DISTR} =_{def} \lambda P \lambda s \forall x [\, x \leq_p s \rightarrow P(x)]$, (where the variable P is ranging over predicates, s is over sums of individuals.)

Assuming some plural logic similar to the above one, G&S represent terms two ways:

---

2 This paper doesn't deal with group individuals since an appropriate treatment of them might be possible by extending the structure assumed above with theories in the literature (e.g., Barker 1992). The distinction between group and sum individuals is important in the semantics of plurals because even if a group individual and a sum individual happen to be extensionally equivalent, the former has its own right and differs from the latter. (For more about the distinction see Link 1984, Landman 1989, Barker 1992, etc.)

(12) a. Collective readings
at most/least two girls: $\lambda P \exists G$ [$G \in M(N)$ & $G \in$ girl & $G \in P$],
where M(N) stands for a modified number.
For here, *at least two* $= \{ G \mid \exists G' \in 2 [G \supseteq G'] \}$, and
at most two $= \{ G \mid \exists G' \in 2 [G' \supseteq G] \}$. (Notice that 2 means the set of sum entities whose atomic entities are two.)
b. Distributive readings
at most two girls $= \lambda X [\forall G [G \in X \rightarrow \#(G \cap \text{girl}) \leq 2]$
at least two girls $= \lambda X [\forall G [G \in X \rightarrow \#(G \cap \text{girl}) \geq 2]$

Their main reason for representing terms in two ways seems to be just to avoid the 'empty set' problem. They argue that any term answer whatsoever should have the 'collective' reading, and then the result of the application of the exhaustivity operator in (2) to a collectivized denotation of an answer term leads to a right reading. If a 'distributive' reading is required, the 'decollectivization' operation[3] should be applied on the exhaustivized denotation of an answer term. For example, if the predicate *walk* in a question like *who walks?* really requires a 'distributive' reading, and *at most two girls* is an answer to the question, then first the exhaustivization is applied to the denotation of *at most two girls,* because it is used as an answer, and then the 'decollectivization' is applied to the exhaustivized collective reading of *at most two girls.* Such a three-step operation, 'collectivizing-exhaustivizing-decollectivizing' the denotation of an answer term, is ad hoc and causes new problems. Let us see why this is so.

It is ad hoc since they take all answer terms to have the 'collective' reading only to avoid the 'empty set' problem without presenting any other independent reasons. Seemingly the redundant operation, 'decollectivization' follows from the ad hoc operation, 'collectivization'.

(13) the exhaustivized collective reading:
a. exh(at most two girls) $= \{\{a\},\{b\},\{c\},\{a \oplus b\},\{a \oplus c\}, \{b \oplus c\}\}$
b. exh(at least two girls) $= \{\{a,b\},\{b,c\},\{a,c\},\{a \oplus b\},\{a \oplus c\}, \{b \oplus c\},\{a \oplus b \oplus c\}\}$
c. exh(no girls)=0}) = {??}

Why does the three-step operation lead to new problems? The sets in (13a-c) are the result of the application of the exhaustivity operator to the collectivized denotation of *at least two girls, at most two girls* and *no girls.* Problems are that 'collectivization' is not really a collectivization: (13a-b) contain sets consisting of atomic individuals. For example, {a,b}, {a,c},

[3] G&S say that 'decollectivization' consists of adding to each set of groups (or each element of the exhaustivized denotaion of 'collective' reading of a plural term) the group which is their union with all subgroups of that union. Unfortunately it is unclear what group we should add to each element of the exhaustivized denotation of a plural term.

{b,c}, {a}, etc. It is unclear what the 'decollectivization' will do to the exhaustivized collective denotation of a term. Will it dissolve a sum individual into its atomic parts? For instance, {a⊕b} changes into {a,b}. Partly this operation reverses the effect of exhaustivity since the set, whose sum individual is dissolved into atomic individuals, will have its subset(s). For *at least N* based terms, to get the desired reading, we have to choose the maximal sum individual or the largest set from the exhaustivized denotation of them. Otherwise, the reading of *only N CN* will be likely to occur. Obviously, this is not the intended reading of an *at least N* based term answer. To make it worse, by representing the collective reading of a term with the existential quantifier, G&S totally rule out room for the case that the empty set is really required as in (14). I think that one way out is to make use of the bottom element {⊥} since it doesn't stand in a subset relation with other non bottom elements of the structured discourse domain. But this is a technical trick rather than a real solution.

(14) Q: what are the solutions to this equation?
A: (I don't know, but there are) at most two solutions.

In conclusion, regardless of whether or not we make use of some plural logic, the way G&S deals with exhaustivity doesn't work appropriately. In other words, the exhaustivity operation of G&S can no longer be maintained as a semantic operation.

2. Exhaustivity as a Pragmatic Phenomenon

Among previous analyses, Kadmon (1987) accounts for the ambiguity of the 'exactly' reading and 'at least' reading in *N CNs* in terms of scalar implicature. She argues that the 'exactly' reading of the following answer is pragmatic but the 'at least' reading is semantic. I think that her account is on the right track.

First, let us introduce the notion of scalar implicatures to see how these implicatures work to trigger the 'exactly' reading or the effect of exhaustivity on *N CNs*. Scalar implicatures are a special species of conversational implicatures (Grice 1975), due to the 'quantity' maxim and 'quality' maxim and based on quantitative scales, which are arranged in an order by the degree of informativeness or semantic strength. (15) shows typical examples of such scales.

(15) a. <all, most, many, some, few>
ex.) *I met all of the boys* entails *I met some of boys.*
b. <....5, 4, 3, 2, 1>
ex.) *I have five chairs* entails *I have four chairs* .
c <love, like>
ex.) *I love her* entails *I like her* .

All the scales of (15) are linearly ordered. That is, they are transitive. It is desireable to generalize these linear ordered scales to include non-linear ordered scales, since it would allow us to account for more cases of implicatures[4]. Such a generalization is presented in (16). I call this a 'Pragmatic Scale'.

(16)[5] <u>Pragmatic Scale</u> : $\leq$ is a pragmatic scale for R (predicate) iff for all x, y in the domain of $\leq$, if R(x) and $x \leq y$, then R(y).

From the above Pragmatic Scale, the following inference pattern can be derived since we assume that a speaker is always maximally informative. Here we use the term 'Scalar Principle' to refer to such inference patterns.

(17) <u>Scalar Principle:</u>
If 'R(x)' is uttered as the most informative from a set of alternatives R(y), R(z),..., then we can conclude that $\forall y,x\ [\ y \leq x\ \&\ y \neq x \rightarrow \neg R(y)]$, otherwise R(y) would have been uttered, with $y \leq x$.

We can account for how the reading of *exactly four (kids)* can be obtained from *Lief has four kids* as follows: The word *four* belongs to the scale <...,5, 4, 3, 2, 1>, and *five (kids)* would be false, while *three (kids)* is less informative that *four (kids)* according to the above 'Scalar Principle'. Hence we obtain the reading of *exactly four*.

(18) Q: How many people came to the party ?
A: a. At least twenty.
b. Twenty.

Can we get the 'exactly' or 'only' reading in terms of Kadmon (1987) from the answer a. above? The answer is *yes* and *no*. I will explain why it is so below.

---

4 Typical examples of nonlinear scales described in(16) are those introduced by negative polarity items. For more on such scales, see Krifka (1991).

5 This pragmatic scale can be easily turned into informativity scale. I developed such an informativity scale in Lee (1994:101) as follows:

$X \leq_I Y$ (Y is as much as or more informative than X), where X and Y belong to a set of same sort and are properties of t-based type, e.g., <s, <e,t>>, iff either

a. $\forall w',x,y\ [X(x)(w')\ \&\ Y(y)(w')\ \&\ x \leq_{p,w'} y \rightarrow [\{w' \mid [\![Y(y)(w')]\!] = 1\} \subseteq \{w' \mid [\![X(x)(w')]\!] = 1\}]]$, or

b. $\forall w, X, Y\ [\ Y(w) \subseteq X(w) \rightarrow \{w \mid [\![\exists y\ [\ Y(y)(w)\ ]]\!] = 1\} \subseteq \{w \mid [\![\exists x\ [X(x)(w)]]\!] = 1\}]$

3. Focus and Assertions

I will follow the common assumptions of current focus theories given in (19).

(19) Common assumptions of focus theories:
a. Focus is a feature assigned to a syntactic node of a sentence.
b. Focus (feature) is associated with a focus-sensitive operators such as *even* or *only*. The operator c-commands its focus.
c. Focus is marked by sentence accent (or by special syntactic construction such cleft-sentence in English, or by a specially designated position as in Hungarian, or by focus plus particles as in Korean and Japanese.)
c. Semantically the focus marking partitions the sentence into two parts: The part in focus and the rest, commonly called the 'background'.

Particularly, following Jacobs (1984) and Krifka (1992), I assume that every focused constituent is bound by the nearest focus-sensitive operator(s): For a 'free' focus, by an illocutionary operator. In addition, following Rooth (1985 & 1991), I adopt the idea that a focus feature introduces a set of alternatives to the focused constituent. For a representational format, I will adopt the 'Focus-Background Semantics' of von Stechow and Jacobs.

The connection between focus and exhaustivity has been pointed out before. Horn (1981:131) observes that 'If (20a) is uttered against the background assumption (or pragmatic presupposition that someone kissed Mary. (20b) is automatically inferred from (20a).'

(20) a. John kissed Mary.
b. John (and only John) kissed Mary,
among those under discussion, it was John who kissed Mary.

Similarly Kuno (1973:63) overtly points out the role of focal stress with regard to 'exhaustive listing' in his terms in Japanese as in (21)

(21) a.[$_F$John]-ga Mary-ni okane-o yatta
-Nom -Dat money-Acc gave
It was John who gave the money to Mary.'
b. John-ga [$_F$Mary]-ni okane-o yatta
'It was to Mary that John gave the money.'
c.John-ga Mary-ni [$_F$okane]-o yatta
'It is the money that John gave to Mary.'
d. *John-ga mainiti [$_F$gakkoo]-ni iku
every day school-to go
'It is to school that John and only John goes every day.'

Similarly to G&S, Szabolcsi (1981:520) argues that 'exhaustive listing' in (22a) is taken as the prominent semantic characteristic of focus.

(22)
a. [$_F$Herom lany] latta Peter.
' Only three girls saw Peter.'
b. [$_T$Heron lany] nem latta Peter.
' Three girls, didn't see Peter.'

As the following example shows, the exaustivity effect is readily cancelable. I believe that it is the case in Hungarian, too. The semantic part of the meaning of *only* cannot be canceled. In that sense I don't agree with her view on the exhaustivity effect as semantic.

(23) a. Three girls saw Peter. Indeed, five girls did.
b. *Only three girls saw Peter. Indeed, five girls did.

Reviewing what we have seen so far, we can reach the conclusion that focal stress provides information on which item(s) the speaker is asserting[6]. In terms of Rooth (1985), all the focuses involved in the data above are 'free' focus. I assume that focus-sensitive assertional operators bind them since all the sentences in which the focuses occur are declarative, and contain nothing especially disagreeable with the assertional illocutionary force. I define the focus-sensitive assertional operator as follows:

(24) ASSERT (<B,F>): B(F) is asserted with the following felicitous conditions:
a. $B(F) \cap C = C'$ & $C \neq C'$ & $C' \neq \{\varnothing\}$, where C is a common ground.
b. For every F', $F' \in ALT_C(F)$, the speaker has good reasons not to assert B(F'):
For some F's $B(F') \cap C = \{\varnothing\}$, in other words , B(F') is false, for some F's if $B(F') \cap C = C'$ & $C \neq C'$ & $C' \neq \{\varnothing\}$, it is less informative than B(F), and for some F's the speaker doesn't have appropriate information on whether B(F') is true or not.

---

6 Similarly, Rooth (1991) accounts for the difference in the scalar implicature of the following sentences based on the difference of the location of focus.
a. Well, I [$_F$ passed]. b. Well, [$_F$ I] passed.
(The context of the above two utterances as an answer is that 'my roommates Steve and Paul, and I took a quiz in a class, and the other guy asked the speaker how it went.) He gives the following set as an alternative set of [$_F$ passed] { ace (m), pass (m)}. As the alternative set of [$_F$ I], { pass (s), pass(m), pass(p), pass(s⊕p), pass(s ⊕m), pass(m⊕p), pass(s⊕p⊕m) }. Thus a. means that the speaker only passed, but not aced.

(The notion of 'common ground' is due to Stalnaker 1979 and $ALT_C(F)$ means the set of contextually salient alternatives to the meaning of the focused constituent. See Roberts 1991, von Stechow and Zimmermann 1984, and others for the problem of establishing the contextually salient alternative sets.) If the assertional operator applies to the Horn's example, the result will be as follows:

(25) [$_F$John] kissd Mary.
a. Background: λ x [x kissed Mary]
b. Focus: John
c. ASSERT (< λ x [x kissed Mary], John>)
d. Result of computing c: John kissed Mary but no other people among the contextually salient alternatives.

The result of the application of the ASSERT in (24) leads to the effect of exhaustivity on the subject *John*. What if ASSERT is applied to a different constituent? In other words, what will happen if it is applied to a non-focused constituent?

(26) Q: Why do you think Mary is so healthy?
A: She drinks milk a lot.

If the operator ASSERT is applied to the constituent *milk* in the above answer, we will come up with something odd. In short, the result will be that *she drinks only milk a lot* is the reason that she is so healthy. In this case the focus domain is sentential. The contextually salient alternatives are propositions which are relevant with the explanation of why Mary is so healthy. Such an alternative set would be like λp [p is the reason that Mary is so healthy]. Similarily if the operator ASSERT is applied to such a background and focus, the result will be that *she drinks milk a lot* is only the contextually salient reason that Mary is so healthy.

Interestingly, Kadmon (1987:74) observes that the 'exactly' reading is less likely for (27a), than (27b), 'at least not if a strong stress falls on *sexy*.'

(27) a. Leif is sexy.
b. Three professors are sexy.

The reason for Kadmon's observation of the difference between the two sentences in (27) can be attributed to the different degrees of difficulty of establishing alternative sets to the focuses. It is much easier to think of the alternative set of [$_F$Three] than that of [$_F$Leif] because for [$_F$Leif], all filter-terms[7] should be considered as possible candidates for an element of the

---

7 By the filter-terms, I mean terms that denote a set of set $\{X | X \supseteq P\}$. Thus the universal quantifiers and proper names belong to the filter-terms. If the focused

contextually salient alternative set, while for [$_F$Three], we can easily come up with the scale <..., 5, 4,3,2,1>.

4. Types of Focus and Exhaustive Assertion

As mentioned above, von Stechow and Zimmermann (1984), and von Stechow (1990) argue that, for the effect of exhaustivity on 'negative' terms, we have to select the largest set satisfying the term in question. On the 'mixed list' terms, the effect of exhaustivity is not present because their closure operation cannot be done on such terms. I think that their view on these two terms is partly right because of the following reasons.

(28) Q: Who called for me today ?
  A: a. Not Bert.
    b. Anna but not Bert.

The answers in (28) have two interpretations each: For answer a, the first interpretation is *except Bert, everybody in the discourse domain called the questioner*, the second is *Bert didn't call the questioner but the answerer doesn't commit himself to whether the others called the questioner or not.* Similarly, for answer b we get the following interpretations: The first is *only Anna called the questioner and only Bert did not.* That means that the contextually salient discourse domain is {Anna, Bert}. The second interpretation is among the indivisuals of the alternative set, the answerer chooses to contrast two people, *Anna* and *Bert* without mentioning the other people. I think that answer (a) is a marked answer while (b) sounds overly informative unless the questioner has shown a special interest in Bert's calling. Arguably, a contrastive focus is involved in the second interpretation of each answer in (28). Such a contrastive focus can be bound by a different illocutionary operator from the assertional one. I assume that there is an implicit contrastive focus operator involved in such utterances as the answers in (28). In short, with such a contrastive focus operator involved in an utterance, the speaker contrasts the focused constituent against a background with other alternatives but reserves his judgment about the truth of them against the background. I propose the following definition of contrastive focus.

(29) CONTR (< B, F>): $\Leftrightarrow$ B(F) & $\forall$F' [F'$\in$ ALT$_C$ (F) & F $\neq$F' & *Poss* ($\neg$B(F'))], where *Poss* is the possibility modal operator.

One thing to note is that an overt focus sensitive operator can influence the meaning of covert illocutionary operator. For example, Fauconnier (1975: 364) observes that most of the superatives can be modified by *even* with no

constituent is a filter-term, then its alternatives should also be filter-terms, according to a proposal by Krifka (1993:275).

change in meaning as in (*Even*) *the faintest noise bothers him.* The focus-sensitive operator *even* can be taken as an exponent of an illocutionary operator. This means that the meaning of the illocutionary operator is relativized to or modifyed by the meaning of *even.* (For this, see Jackendoff 1972, and Krifka 1992.)

Similarly, we can relativize ASSERT of (24) into ASSERT_{exh} with regard to the exhaustivity as seen in (30).

(30)[8] $\text{ASSERT}_{exh}(\langle B, F\rangle){:}\Leftrightarrow B(F)\&\forall F'[F'\in ALT_C\,(F)\&$
$[\neg \mathit{Ness}\,(B(F)\rightarrow B(F'))] \rightarrow \neg B(F')]$, where *Ness* is the necessity modal operator.

To get the first intrerpretation of the answer a. in (28), it should be analyzed in terms of (30). (31) shows this roughly.

(31)[9]
a. ASSERT_{exh} [$_F$ Not Bert]
b. Background:$\lambda Q\,[\,Q(P)\,]$, P= *called me* , and Q is of type $\langle\langle e,t\rangle,t\rangle$.
c. Focus: Not Bert: $\lambda P\,[\,\neg P(b)\,]$
d.$\text{ASSERT}_{exh}\,(\langle \lambda Q\,[\,Q(P)\,], \lambda P\,[\,\neg P(b)\,]\rangle)$
e.Result of computing of d:
$\neg P(b)\ \&\forall\, F'\ [F'\in ALT_C\,(\lambda P\,[\,\neg P(b)\,])\ \&$
$\neg \mathit{Ness}\ \ [\neg P(b)\rightarrow B(F')]\rightarrow \neg B(F')]$

The result means that Bert didn't called the questioner but the other people belonging to the alternative set called the questioner. This meaning arises for the following reasons: P stands for *called me* and $ALT_C(\lambda P\,[\,\neg P(b)\,])$ is $\{\lambda P\,[\,\neg P(x)\,] \mid x \in A\,\}$,where A is the domain of discourse in question. Additionally, for every F' different from $\lambda P\,[\neg P(b)]$, $[\,\neg B(F')]$ which in turn means $\neg\ \neg\ P\,(f')$. Here f' stands for a generator of F'.

For the second interpretation of the answer a. in (28), it should be analyzed in terms of the operator CONTR as in (32).

(32) a. [$_F$Not Bert]
b. Background: $\lambda Q\,[\,Q(P')\,]$, P'= *called me*, and Q is of type $\langle\langle e,t\rangle,t\rangle$.
c.Focus : Not Bert: $\lambda P\,[\,\neg P(b)\,]$
d.$\text{CONTR}\,(\langle\lambda Q\,[\,Q(P')\,], \lambda P\,[\,\neg P(b)\,]\rangle){:}\Leftrightarrow\neg\ P'(b)\ \&$

---

8 $[\neg \mathit{Ness}\,(B(F)\rightarrow B(F'))] \rightarrow \neg B(F')$ means that the meaning of any alternatives against the background that is not entailed by that of the focused constituent doesn't hold. This means that B(F) is the most informative.

9 In this case, the contextually salient alternatives might be the 'negative' terms because the answerer is talking about people who didn't call the questioner.

$\forall F' [F' \in ALT_C (\lambda P [\neg P(b)]) \,\&\, \lambda P [\neg P(b)] \neq F' \,\&\, Poss (\neg F'(P'))]$

e. Result of computing d. : Bert didn't called the questioner but possibly all the contextually salient alternative(s) to Bert who called the questioner.

The above result shows that the effect of exhaustivity is absent because of the involvement of the contrastive focus operator. In short, if the focus of $ASSERT_{exh}$ is involved in *not Bert*, we get what von Stechow argues for the 'closure' of negative terms. A contrastive focus involved in negative terms, there is no 'closure' or exhaustiveness.

We can give the same analysis for answer b *Anna but not Bert*. First is the case where two foci of $ASSERT_{exh}$ operator are involved, falling on *Anna* and *not Bert*. I will not go into a detailed analysis of this case since it involves merely a second computation as in (31). The result will be that *only Anna called the questioner and only Bert didn't*. As mentioned above, this means that the contextually salient set is {Anna, Bert}. Hence such an answer is eligible for the question *Who called me but who didn't*. The other case is that two contrastive foci fall on the two terms. We cannot get the effect of exhaustivity in the latter as follows:

(33) a.CONTR ($[_F$Anna]) but CONTR ($[_F$ not Bert])

b. Background:$\lambda Q [Q(P)]$, P stans for *called me* .

c. Foci: $[_F$Anna] : $\lambda P [P(a)]$, $[_F$ not Bert]: $\lambda P [\neg P(b)]$

d. CONTR ($<\lambda Q[Q(P)], \lambda P[P(a)>$), CONTR ($<\lambda Q[Q(P)], \lambda P[\neg P(a)>$)

The computation of d is the same as (32).

e. Result of computing: Among contextually salient alternatives, Anna called the questioner but possibly all the other people didn't. In addition, Bert didn't call the questioner but possibly the other people called the questioner.

The above result means that the answerer commits himself only to Anna and Bert. In other words, he contrasts Anna's calling with Bert's not calling but he leaves the other persons unspecified with regard to the property of calling to the questioner. Finally we come up with non-exhaustiveness effect.

5. *At least / most N CN* and Exhaustivity

We can account for the exhaustivity of *at least N* or *at most N* based terms in the same way as in the data above. That is, *at least/most* can fill the same function as that of other focus-sensitive particles like *even* or *only*. These two particles cannot be an exponent of the assertional illocutionary operator since, unlike *even*, a focus can fall on the particles themselves. Another possibility is that they are part of a term. Actually G&S argue that exhaustivity is present only on such a form as [[at least/most two] girls], where *at least/most* are modifiers of the number *two*, which in turn modifies the common noun *girls*, while if the particles modify the term *two girls*, then the effect of exhaustivity is absent. Such presence and absence of the effect of exhaustivity can be accounted for within the framework of this paper.

For the absence of the effect of exhaustivity, let's assume that a focus falls on the word *two*.[10] We can give the following analyses: I propose the following interpretaitions for the two particles as a focus operator.

(34) a.. **at least** (<B, F>): $\Leftrightarrow$
$\lambda P\ [\ \exists F'\ [F' \in ALT_C\ (F)\ \&\ F' \leq F\ \&\ B(F')(P)\ ]\ ]$

b. **at most** (<B, F>) :$\Leftrightarrow$
$\lambda P\ [\ B(F)(P) \vee \neg\exists F'\ [F' \in ALT_C\ (F)\ \&\ F' \leq F\ \&\ B(F')(P)\ ]\ ]$
(Notice that $\leq$ is a pragmatic scale. E.g., $3 \leq 2$)

(35) [**at least** [$_F$ two]] girls]
a. Background : $\lambda N.N$ (girls), N is of the same type as that of the focus.
b. Focus : 2, 2 stands for $\lambda P'\ \lambda Q\ \exists x\ [\ P'(x)\ \& Q(x)\ \&\ |x| = 2]$
c. **at least** (< $\lambda N.N$ (girls), 2>)
d. Result of computing c: $\lambda P[\ \exists F'\ [F' \in ALT_C\ (2)\ \&\ F' \leq 2\ \&$
$\exists x\ [\ P(x)\ \&\ girls(x)\ \&\ |x| = F']\ ]]$

If P is *came to the party* , (35d) means that the number of girls who came to the party is two or more than that. This is exactly what we want to get from *At least two girls came to the party.*

For the presence of the effect of exhaustivity, if an assertional focus falls on the term *at least two girls* which is the result of the application of the particle *at least* to the focused constituent *two* as in (35), we can think of the following structure and analysis.

(36) ASSERT [$_F$ [**at least** [$_F$ two]] girls]
a. Background : $\lambda T\ T\ (P)$, P=.*came to the party*
b. Focus : **at least** two girls: $\lambda P'[\ \exists F'\ [F' \in ALT_C\ (2)\ \&\ F' \leq 2\ \&$
$\exists x\ [\ P'(x)\ \&\ girls(x)\ \&\ |x| = F']\ ]]$ (= [1], for short)
c. ASSERT ($\lambda T\ T\ (P)$, [1] >)
d. Result of computing of c: The speaker asserts
$\exists F'\ [\ F' \in ALT_C\ (2)\ \&\ F' \leq 2\ \&\ \exists x\ [\ P(x)\ \&\ girls(x)\ \&\ |x| = F'\ ]\ ]$

---

10 Particles like *at least* , *at most,* and *exactly* can be associated with number words as the following example shows:
a. ?? Exactly male persons came.
b. Exactly three male persons came.
In such a sense it is plausible to assume that in the presence of such particles, focus, if any, falls on a number word.

but for other alternatives $F' \in \{T \mid T = \lambda P \exists x [P(x) \& girl(x) \& |x| \geq n \& n \in \mathbf{N} \}$, where **N** is the set of natual numbers., B(F')s are not asserted because of the following reasons: Some are less infromative than B(F). Some are false based on speaker's information, and so forth.

According to the result of computing the meaning of (36), the speaker only asserts as true $\exists F' [F' \in ALT_C (2) \& F' \leq 2 \& \exists x [P(x) \& girls(x) \& |x| = F']]$, which corresponds to *at least two girls* (*came to the party*). The other *at least N girls* are not asserted for whatever reasons. For example, *at least one girl* is not asserted because it is entailed by, and less informative than, *at least two girls*. As for such terms as *at least four/ five/ six /... girls*, they are not asserted probably because the speaker thinks that they might be false. Finally we can get the effect of exhaustivity. However, obviously it is not what G&S think of as exhaustivity.

The absence and presence of exhaustivity on *at most N* based terms can be accounted for much like the case of *at least N* based terms. First, for the absence of the effect of exhuastivity, let's assume as in (35) that the particle *at most* is a focus-sensitive particle and a focus falls on the number word *two* which is in turn bound by *at most*.

(37) [**at most** [$_F$ three]] girls]
a. Background : $\lambda N.N$ (girls)(P), N is of the same type as that of the focus. P= *came to the party* .
b. Focus : 3, short for $\lambda P' \lambda Q \exists x [P'(x) \& Q(x) \& |x| = 3]$
c. **at most** (< $\lambda N.N$ (girls), 3 >)
d. Result of computing c : $\exists x [P(x) \& girls(x) \& |x| = 3] \vee \neg \exists F' [F' \in ALT_C (3) \& F' \leq 3 \& \exists x [P(x) \& girls(x) \& |x| = F']]]$

(37d) means that the number of girls who came to the party is equal to or less than three. The effect of exhaustivity is absent on *at most N CN* due to the second disjunct of (37d), which doesn't rule out cases that *only one/ two girl(s) came to the party*.

For the presence of the effect of exhaustivity, let's assume that an assertional focus falls on *at most three girls*, which is the result of computing of (37), and the focus is associated with the operator ASSERT as in ASSERT [$_F$ [**at most** [$_F$ three]] girls]. The steps of computing the meaning of ASSERT [$_F$ [**at most** [$_F$ three]] girls] are virtually identical to those in (36); therefore I will not discuss them here. The result of the meaning computation is shown in (38).

(38) a. ASSERT [$_F$ [**at most** [$_F$ three]] girls]
d. Result of computing of a: The speaker asserts $\exists x [P(x) \& girls(x) \& |x| = 3] \vee \neg \exists F' [F' \in ALT_C (3) \& F' \leq 3 \& \exists x [P(x) \& girls(x) \& |x| = F']]]$. But for other alternatives F',

F'$\in$ {T | T= λ P $\exists$x [P(x) & girl(x) & |x| $\leq$ n & n $\in$ **N**), where **N** is the set of natural numbers., (e.g., 1, 2, 4,...), B(F')s are not asserted because of the following reasons: Some are less infromative than B(F). Some are false based on speaker's information, and so forth.

Accordingly, the speaker only asserts *at most three girls came to the party.* The speaker doesn't assert *at most one/two girls* (*came to the party*) because they are less informative than *at most three girls came to the party.* While *at most four/ five... girls came to the party* are not asserted probably because they are false according to the speaker's information. Finally we can get the effect of exhaustivity. (For more precise compositional derivations of sentences which contain focused constituents and focus-sensitive operators, see Krifka 1992.)

6. Concluding Remarks

In this paper, we have reached the following conclusions: exhaustivity presupposes an alternative set to be compared. This can explain why the constituent in focus is associated with exhaustivity. The account of exhaustivity based on focus, the alternative set, and 'Scalar Principles' is not concerned with which category exhaustivity is associated with (cf. G&S's exh operator can only apply to terms). In addition, the domain of exhaustivity can be fixed with the help of the contextually salient set introduced by focus (cf. in G&S, nothing is mentioned about a way of restricting the domain of exhaustivity). Specifically, *at least / most N* based terms resist the operation of exhaustivity seen in G&S. Nevertheless, the effect of exhaustivity in terms of the ordinary assertional illocutionary force exists even on them. In short, the candidates for the exhaustivity satisfy the requirements that a focused constituent whose focus is bound by the ASSERT_{exh} operator, and the alternatives can be arranged in an order of a 'Pragmatic Scale'. Thus, the effect of exhaustivity is a pragmatic phenomenon, and 'Scalar Principle' and focus are the main sources of exhaustivity.

References

Barker, C. 1992. Group terms in English: representing group as atoms. *Journal of Semantics 9.* 69-93.

Fauconnier, G. 1975. Pragmatic Scales and Logical Structure. *LI 4.* 353-375.

Grice, H.P. 1975. Logic and Conversation . In *Syntax and semantics 3: Speech Act.*, ed. by Cole & Morgan, 41-58. New York:Academic press.

Groenendijk, J. and M. Stokhof. 1983. On the semantics of questions and the pragmatics of answers. ms., University of Amsterdam.

Groenendijk, J. and M. Stokhof. 1992. A Note on Interrogatives and Advers of Quantification, 99-124. In *the proceedings of SALT II*. The Ohio State University, Columbus, Ohio.

Horn, L.R. 1972. *On the semantic properties of Logical Operators in English*. Doctoral Dissertation, UCLA.

Horn, L. R. 1981. Exhaustiveness and the Semantics of Clefts. *NELS 11*. 125-142.

Jacobs, J. 1984. Funktionale Satzperspektive und IllokutionssemantikLinguistische *Berichte 91*. 25-28.

Kadmon, N. 1987. *On unique and non-unique reference and asymmetric quantification*, Diss. Univ. of Massachusetts, Amherst.

Krifka, M. 1991. Some Remarks on Polarity Items. MS. University of Texas at Austin.

Krifka, M. 1992. A compositional semantics for multiple focus constructions. In *Informationsstruktur und Grammatik* , ed. by J. Jacobs, 17-53. (Linguistische Berichte, sonderheft 4).

Krifka, M. 1993. Focus and Presupposition in Dynamic Interpretation. In *Journal of Semantics 10*. 269-300.

Kuno, S. 1973. The Structure of the Japanese Language. Cambridge:The MIT Press.

Landman, F. 1989. Groups I & II. *Linguistics and Philosophy 12*. 559-605 & 723-44.

Lee, Y-S. 1994. Negative Plarity Items and the Semantics of the Particles *-to* and *-na* in Korean. *Kansas Working Papers in Linguistics Vol. 19*, the University of Kansas, Lawrence, Kansas. 89-123.

Link, G. 1984. Plurals. To appear in *Handbook of Semantics*, ed. by A. von Stechow &D. Wunderlich.

Roberts, C. 1991. Domain Restriction in Dynamic Semantics. MS., The Ohio State University.

Rooth, M.E. 1985. *Association with focus*. Doctoral Dissertaion, Univ. of Massachusetts, Amherst.

Rooth, M.E. 1991. A theory of focus interpretation. In *Natural Language Semantics I*. 75-116.

Stalnaker, R. 1979. Assertion. In *Syntax and Semantics*, ed. by Peter Cole, 315-332. New York: Academic Press.

Stechow, A. von. 1990. Focusing and backgrounding operators. In *Discourse Particles, Pragmatics and Beyond*, 37-84. Amsterdam:John Benjamins.

Stechow, A. von. & T. E. Zimmermann. 1984. Term answers and contextual change. In *Linguistics 22*. 3-40.

Szabolcsi, A. 1981. The semantics of topic-focus articulation. In *Formal Methods in the study of language.*,ed. by Groenendijk et al , 513-541. Amsterdam: Mathematical Centre.

The Syntactic Representation of Degree and Quantity: Perspectives from Japanese and Child English*

WILLIAM SNYDER, KENNETH WEXLER, & DOLON DAS
Massachusetts Institute of Technology

I. Introduction

Converging evidence from child language acquistion and cross-linguistic variation has the potential to provide important insights into the structure of Universal Grammar and the nature of language-specific knowledge. This paper examines the syntactic representation of degree and quantity in the English of children up to five years of age, and demonstrates that a variety of striking differences between adult and child English are paralleled by differences between (adult) English and Japanese. The proposed explanation is that children initially hypothesize a determiner system that is impoverished relative to that of adult English, and that in key respects resembles the 'impoverished' determiner system of adult Japanese (cf. Fukui 1986).

* The authors are especially grateful to T. Aikawa and S. Miyagawa for their extensive comments and assistance at many stages of this research. We should also like to thank S. Avrutin, K. Broihier, S. Carey, S. Crain, I. Heim, H. Hoji, N. Hyams, W. Ladusaw, A. Marantz, D. Pesetsky, D. Poeppel, R. Thornton, and the audience at WCCFL XIII for numerous comments and helpful suggestions. All errors remain our own. The authors are grateful to the staff and pupils at Another Place to Grow, in Arlington MA, for their kind cooperation. Snyder was supported by an NSF Fellowship in linguistics, an NSF Research Traineeship in linguistics and cognitive science, and the McDonnell-Pew Center for Cognitive Neuroscience at MIT.

Specifically, we take the adult English representation of degree in APs, and quantity in plural NPs, to be mediated by a null Deg^o or plural D^o, respectively, as argued by Abney (1987).[1] We take these types of D^o to be absent from the inventory of determiners in both Japanese and child English, as suggested to us by Tom Roeper (p.c.). This gap in the determiner system has the character of a *parametric* property, in the sense that it has widespread syntactic consquences in Japanese and child English.[2]

We thus find that English-style 'subcomparatives', involving quantification over a degree- or quantity-type variable associated with an AP or plural NP, are disallowed in both Japanese and child English (§2). This pattern is not found with 'subequatives' in Japanese or child English, where we argue that the correct meaning is obtained through 'parallel distribution', rather than quantification over degree or quantity (§3). Our account directly explains the impossibility of overt degree phrases with adjectives in both Japanese and child English (§ 4), as well as the apparent Left Branch Constraint violations found with degree questions in child English (Hoekstra, Koster, & Roeper 1992) and Japanese (§ 5). Further supporting evidence comes from the optionality of plural marking on plural NPs both in Japanese (e.g. Miyagawa 1989) and (in specific environments) in child English (Cazden 1968) (§ 6).

2. Subcomparatives

English comparative constructions have been studied extensively in the syntax and semantics literature (e.g. Bresnan 1972, Cresswell 1976, Chomsky 1977, Pinkham 1982, Heim 1985, Grimshaw

---

1 We will henceforth refer to both Deg^o and plural D^o as types of determiners (D^o). Modifying the proposals of Abney slightly, we will take a measure phrase in adult English to be the SPEC of a DP headed by Deg^o, and a bare numeral modifier to be the SPEC of a DP headed by a null plural D^o.

2 Preliminary investigations suggest that the pattern we will report for Japanese and child English may be replicated, more or less exactly, in French, Russian, and Mandarin Chinese. If borne out by further research, the findings for French will be especially interesting, in that the determiner system of French is not systematically 'impoverished' in any sense, but may nonetheless differ from that of English along parametric lines.

1987, Corver 1990, Ishii 1991, Moltmann 1993, among many others), but major issues raised by this work have not been addressed in previous studies of children's acquisition of comparatives. In this section we present and discuss the results of a study of children's comprehension of three types of English comparatives: Comparative deletion (1), subdeletion (2), and so-called 'subdeletion with ellipsis' (3).[3]

(1) 'Comparative Deletion'
John reads more books than Mary reads.

(2) 'Subdeletion'
John reads more books than Mary reads magazines.

(3) (So-called) 'Subdeletion with Ellipsis'
John reads more books than magazines.

We began the present project by using Crain & McKee's (1985) Truth Value Judgement Task to examine preschool children's comprehension of comparative sentences as in (1-3). Two versions of this study were run in the course of an academic year. The first study included eight children (4;1 - 5;1 ; Mean Age 4;7), and the second included twelve children (4;2 - 5;4 ; Mean Age 4;9).

In contrast to earlier studies on children's comprehension of comparatives, our materials were designed so that a strategy of interpreting the comparative as a superlative, or a simple strategy of always guessing 'yes', would yield at best 'chance' performance (50% correct). Also in contrast to earlier studies, our comprehension task never depended on correct interpretation of pronouns, and our materials satisfied Crain & McKee's pragmatic condition of 'plausible denial'.

The first study examined comprehension of comparative deletion, subcomparatives, and subdeletion-with-ellipsis. The first study also checked for evidence of a 'more = most' strategy,

---

3 While (3) has often been treated as an elliptical form of, 'John reads more books than he reads magazines,' and while we shall adopt the term 'subdeletion with ellipsis' for (3), we use this terminology with the understanding that the acquisitional evidence, at least, casts some doubt on such an analysis, at least in children's English.

differences between noun versus adjective comparsion, and differences between comparisons on mass versus count nouns.[4] The second study examined deletion and subdeletion in both comparatives and equatives. (Equatives will be discussed in § 3.)

	PERCENTAGES CORRECT		
	Adult-like Children	Other Children	
Comparative Deletion	100%	88%	
Subdeletion	100%	18%	($p < .001$)
Subdeletion With Ellipsis	100%	76%	
Mass	100%	57%	(Not Significant)
Count	100%	60%	
Noun	100%	54%	(Not Significant)
Adjective	100%	67%	

Table 1. Results of first study of children's comprehension of comparatives.

Our results were consistent with a largely forgotten observation made by Townsend (1975) and by Townsend and Erb (1976): A sizable percentage of four-to-six year olds exhibit a fairly specific comprehension deficit for subcomparatives. We found, in particular,

4 Differences between noun and adjective comparison were, however, tested only with (full) comparative deletion. Other types of comparatives were evaluated exclusively with NPs. Work by Townsend & Erb (1976) indicates that our findings for NP subcomparatives also hold for AP subcomparatives.

that full subcomparatives constrasted sharply with both comparative deletion and so-called subdeletion-with-ellipsis. In the first version of the study, six of eight children exhibited specific and marked difficulty with subcomparatives, while the remaining two performed as adults. These findings are summarized in Table 1. Performance of each child was consistent across noun and adjective comparisons, as indicated at the bottom of the table.

Three of the six children exhibiting difficulty in subcomparatives also appeared to be using a 'superlative-like' interpretation of *more* and *-er*. Yet, this was not literally a 'superlative' interpretaion, because the children were still sensitive to the first NP in the *than*-phrase. ('John has more silver than gold/Mary.') We will suggest an explanation for this finding below.

Thus far we have demonstrated that English-speaking children as old as four and five years of age often exhibit a specific comprehension deficit for subcomparatives as in (2), but perform at near-adult levels on (full) comparative deletion as in (1), as well as on so-called 'subdeletion with ellipsis' as in (3). These findings are summarized in (4).

(4) Child English (Comprehension):

Comparative Deletion	-	OK
Subdeletion	-	Impaired
Subdeletion with Ellipsis	-	OK

We observe that this pattern bears a striking resemblance to a point of cross-linguistic variation in adult languages: Japanese differs from English in that subcomparatives, insofar as they are possible at all, are *far* more restricted than in English (6). Yet, comparative deletion (5) and subdeletion-with-ellipsis (7) are fully grammatical.

(5) Comparative Deletion
John-wa [Mary-ga (*hon-o) yomu yori-(mo)] hon-o takusan yomu
John-top Mary-nom book-acc read than book-acc many reads
`John reads more books than Mary reads (*books).'

(6) Subcomparative (Ungrammatical)

a. * John-wa [Mary-ga zasshi-o yomu yori-(mo)] hon-o takusan yomu
John-top Mary-nom book-acc read than magazine-acc many reads
`John reads more books than Mary reads magazines' (NP)

b. * Heya-ga hiroi yori doa (-no-hoo)-ga ookii
window-nom wide than door (-gen direction)-nom is-big
`The door is bigger than the window is wide' (AP)

(7) (So-called) Subdeletion with ellipsis
John-wa zasshi-yori hon-o takusan yomimasu
`John reads more books than magazines.'

Our informants reject both (6a), a subcomparative involving two plural NPs, and (6b), a subcomparative involving two APs. As we shall discuss below, there does exist some variability in the judgements of Japanese NP subcomparatives, as in (6a), but to our knowledge Japanese speakers consistently reject AP subcomparatives as in (6b), and for all Japanese speakers NP subcomparatives, if possible at all, are a highly restricted option, as discussed by Ishii (1991).

Notice that *yori* `than' can take a full clausal complement in Japanese comparative deletion, as illustrated in (5). Also, as noted by Kikuchi (1989), the gap in the *yori*-clause of (5) is obligatory, in contrast to the marked but grammatically possible English subcomparative, 'John reads more books than Mary reads books'. The main Japanese facts are schematically represented in (8), directly parallelling the pattern in (4).

(8) Japanese:

Comparative Deletion	-	OK
Subdeletion	-	Ungrammatical
Subdeletion with Ellipsis	-	OK

The leading idea of this paper is that in both Japanese and child English, expressions denoting quantity or degree can never serve as syntactic arguments within an AP or plural NP. We will now briefly examine two types of analysis that have been proposed for English subcomparatives, and we will point out that both types of analysis crucially depend on the presence of syntactic positions corresponding to degree or quantity. Our conclusion will be that a difficulty in syntactically licensing variables (such as the trace of a null operator) ranging over degree or quantity, can account for the observed restrictions on subcomparatives in Japanese and child English.

Two broad types of analysis for English subcomparatives have been advanced in the literature. Both types of analysis, in order to provide the full range of English subcomparatives, depend crucially on the availability of a syntactic argument position, denoting degree or quantity, within the DP. Bresnan (1972) argued that in a subcomparative such as (2) (repeated as 2′ below), there is a covert quantification over possible numbers of magazines (denoted in 2′ by the phonologically null expression `x-many').

(2′) John reads more books than Mary reads (x-many) magazines.

Thus, the truth conditions for (2′) are (roughly) that John reads more than x books, where x is the number of magazines that Mary reads.

Cresswell (1976) formalized Bresnan's analysis in terms of the semantic type 'degree/quantity'; x in (2′) is then taken as ranging over this special semantic type. Chomsky (1977) suggested (albeit with some hesitation) that the x in (2′) should be identified with the trace of a null *wh*-operator. A now fairly standard approach to subcomparatives involves extraction of a null operator from a degree/quantity position in the plural DP (*magazines* in 2′) up to the head of the *than*-phrase. Lambda-abstraction causes the *than*-phrase to be interpreted as a predicate over quantities (<Q,t>): 'Lambda x: Mary reads x-many magazines'. Similarly, *more* can be taken as a generalized quantifier that undergoes LF extraction, and creates the lambda-abstract, 'Lambda x: John reads x-many books'. Following the analysis of (Bresnan 1972), the *than*-phrase is taken as an extraposed argument of *more*. At LF the comparative morpheme takes two arguments of type <Q,t>. The sentence is then true if and only if the (maximum) quantity x_1 such that John reads x_1 books, is greater than the (maximum) quantity x_2 such that Mary reads x_2 magazines.

Crucially, the standard approach to subcomparatives in terms of null operator movement assumes that the operator originates in a syntactic position inside the DP, and leaves behind a variable that ranges over quantities (for an NP) or degrees (for an AP). That the operator should be able to extract from the DP without violating the Left Branch Constraint is a bit surprising, and has often been taken as an argument against this approach to subcomparatives (e.g. in Grimshaw 1987), but a variety of technical solutions to this problem are available. One might, for example, argue that LBC effects are exclusively a PF phenomenon, tied to cliticization of a (null or overt) determiner onto its specifier; LBC effects would then not be expected in LF movement operations.

A second, slightly different approach to English subcomparatives has been suggested by Ishii (1991). This approach is motivated by the results of a variety of tests for *wh*-movement (see Pinkam 1982, Grimshaw 1987, Corver 1990), suggesting that English subcomparatives do not (necessarily) involve movement of a *wh*-operator denoting degree or quantity.

The main idea of Ishii's approach, as we interpret it, is to allow an abstract comparison operator to unselectively bind two lower positions, one in the matrix clause and one in the *than*-clause. Following a suggestion of Pinkam (1982), Ishii argues that there are two types of *more* in English: A quantificational form of *more*, as in standard accounts of comparative deletion, and also a non-quantificational form that marks a variable position. The abstract comparison operator MORE unselectively binds a non-quantificational instance of *more* and a gap parallel to *more*. The cases of 'multiple subcomparison' discussed by Corver (1990) can be readily handled by the unselective binding approach, if more than one abstract comparison operator is present, as in (9).

(9) a. Santa Claus gave more girls more dolls than he gave boys trucks. (Corver 1990)

b. S.C. gave more girls dolls than he gave boys trucks, and S.C. gave more dolls to girls than he gave trucks to boys. (von Stechow 1984)

c. MORE(1,2) MORE(3,4) S.C. gave more(1) girls more(3) dolls than he gave e(2) boys e(4) trucks

In our view, to obtain the correct semantic interpretation in the unselective binding approach to subcomparatives, the two positions bound by the abstract comparison operator must both denote expressions of degree or quantity. The unselective binding approach will then be ruled out in (full) comparative deletion, because the gap in the *than*-clause denotes an individual rather than a degree or quantity. Thus, an analysis with movement of *wh*-operators will be forced in comparative deletion, as indicated by the standard diagnostics for *wh*-movement (Chomsky 1977).

Ishii discusses a number of possibilities for comparative deletion with quantification over semantic types other than degree or quantity, notably quantification over event variables. Such possibilities can create the illusion of subcomparison, and very plausibly account for the highly restricted cases of 'subcomparison' allowed by some Japanese speakers (e.g. 6a). Yet, as noted by Ishii, quantification over frequency (i.e. events), for example, cannot account for the full range of English subcomparatives, because in English we do not find the types of aspectual restrictions expected on an event-quantification account. Moreover, to obtain the reading for (9a) paraphrased in (9b), an approach in terms of event quantification fails, and reference to quantity-type variables seems to be crucial.[5]

Thus, in both major approaches to subcomparison with which we are familiar, existence of the full range of subcomparatives found in English depends on the availability of quantity- and degree-type arguments within DP. We conclude that the difficulties with subcomparison observed in Japanese and adult English could be due to a lack of the determiners needed to license degree- and quantity-type arguments with APs and plural NPs. In § 4-6 we shall provide evidence that various predictions of this hypothesis are borne out. First, however, we shall examine an apparent counterexample to the hypothesis.

3. Subequatives

The second of our comprehension studies on four-to-five year olds was designed again to test the contrast between full deletion and subdeletion in comparatives. In addition, the second study examined

---

5 Ishii (1991:146-152) applies an event-quantification approach to (9a), but contrary to his discussion he obtains a semantic interpretation that is distinct from (9b) and not in fact possible for English speakers.

whether the same contrast between full deletion and subdeletion would be found with *equatives* (10a,b).

(10) a. John has as many books as Mary has
b. John has as many books as Mary has magazines

The results of the second study, in brief, were that the contrast between full deletion and subdeletion in comparatives was replicated, but there was no such contrast in equatives, and in fact children on average performed better on subdeletion than on full deletion with equatives. Five of twelve children were 'at chance' on *comparative* subdeletion (i.e., they received approximately the score predicted for random guessing), and there was a statistically significant contrast between deletion and subdeletion in comparatives. Yet, there was no statistically significant contrast between deletion versus subdeletion in *equatives*, and all twelve children were well above chance on *equative* subdeletion.

We propose that the contrast between subequatives and subcomparatives is due to the possibility of giving subequatives, but not subcomparatives, an interpretation in terms of 'parallel distribution'. For example, (10b) can be paraphrased as in (11).

(11) For each magazine that Mary has, John has a book.

We will leave open the details of how the interpretation in (11) is obtained compositionally. (One possibility, along the lines of Ishii's approach to subcomparison, would be that a null distributive operator unselectively binds both the NP marked by `as many' in the matrix clause, and the corresponding NP in the *as*-clause.)

Strikingly, the same contrast between subcomparatives and subequatives found in child English is also found in adult Japanese. Thus, even our informants who reject subcomparison in (6a) accept (12).

(12) Equative subdeletion in Japanese
John-wa [Mary-ga hon-o motte-iru hodo] zasshi-o motte-inai
John-top Mary-nom book-acc have as-many-as magazine-acc
have-not
`John doesn't have as many magazines as Mary has books.'

(For our informants, Japanese *hodo* 'as many as' is most acceptable as a negative polarity item, hence the negation in 12.) Thus, whatever the correct account for the contrast between subcomparatives and subequatives in child English, the parallel we claim between child English and adult Japanese holds for subcomparatives and subequatives. We tentatively suggest that an approach in terms of parallel distribution be extended to (12), at least for the Japanese speakers who reject (6a). If this approach is borne out in further research, it may turn out that subequatives are 'the exception that proves the rule'. We now turn to a variety of observations confirming predictions of our hypothesis that the determiner systems in Japanese and child English do not license degree- or quantity-type arguments.

4. Degree-phrases with Adjectives

A direct prediction of our hypothesis is that overt expressions of degree in APs should be impossible in both Japanese and child English. For example, pre-adjectival degree modifiers as in `two meters tall' should be ungrammatical. The prediction is clearly confirmed for Japanese, where our informants categorically reject (13a), requiring instead a circumlocution such as (13b).[6]

(13) a. * John-wa sei-ga ni meetoru takai
John-top height-nom two meters tall-is
`John is two meters tall.'

b. John-wa sei-ga ni meetoru da
John-top height-nom two meters is
`John's height is two meters'

We so far have only preliminary evidence about the availability of degree-phrases in APs in child English, but this evidence is consistent with the prediction. Snyder & Das (in preparation) have examined transcripts of spontaneous production for (7) English-

---

6 Interestingly, some of our informants allow (13a) on the reading, 'John is two meters taller (than someone understood from the discourse)'. This suggests to us that Japanese may form comparatives with a null comparative morpheme that, unlike simple APs, can take a degree-type argument. This observation thus supports an approach in which the restrictions observed in Japanese are tied to the determiner system proper, rather than being a global (but language-specific) property of Japanese argument structure.

speaking children (mean age of last transcript: 5;0). They find that only two of the seven children use degree-modifiers in APs productively by the end of their transcripts. For the two children who do acquire the relevant degree-modifiers, the ages of first clear use are 4;5 (`ten feet tall') and 3;9 (`four years old'). Thus, a majority of the children examined are not producing degree expressions in APs even at ages in the four-to-six range, precisely as predicted by our hypothesis.

5. *Wh*-questions of Degree and Quantity

Another immediate prediction of our hypothesis is that *wh*-questions of degree and quantity should function differently in Japanese and child English than they do in adult English. This is because in adult English such questions involve generation of a *wh*-expression (*how* or *how many*) in a degree- or quantity-position (presumably SPEC) within the DP.

Again, this prediction appears to be borne out, in that *wh*-questions of degree in Japanese and in child English (in contrast to adult English) are not subject to the Left Branch Constraint. Japanese exhibits LBC effects with possessors, for example, in (15) (contrast 14). Yet, no such LBC effect is found in the *wh*-question of degree in (16).

(14) John-ga dare-no hon-o yonda-no
John-nom who-gen book-acc read-interrog
`Whose book did John read?'

(15) ?* Dare-no John-ga hon-o yonda-no
who-gen John-nom book-acc read-interrog
`Whose book did John read?'

(16) Dono gurai ie-ga ookii-no?
to-what extent house-nom big-is-interrog
`How big is the house?'

Very similar LBC violations have been reported by Hoekstra, Koster, and Roeper (1992) for child English and child Dutch, in a study of children in the age-range of four-to-six years. For example, English-speaking children in this age-range often allow (17a) to have both the adult interpretation in (17b), and a non-adult interpretation as in (17c) (in apparent violation of the LBC).

(17) a. How did John paint the cup yellow?
b. `By what means did John paint the cup yellow?'
c. `How yellow did John paint the cup?'
(Hoekstra, Koster, & Roeper, 1992)

Although we will not attempt a detailed account of the semantics of degree questions in Japanese and child English, we suggest an approach in terms of a discourse relation, rather than syntactic binding, between the *wh*-word and a semantic degree argument in the predicate. As discussed by Cresswell (1976), even in English the semantic degree-argument of a gradable predicate can be supplied through the discourse as well as in the syntax. For example, when we say that John is tall, the discourse determines whether we mean `tall for a three-year-old' or 'tall for a basketball player'. As suggested in the gloss of (16), we take the Japanese equivalent of `how' to be interpreted more literally as, `to what extent'; that is, as an adverbial element related through the *discourse* to the semantic degree-position in the predicate.[7]

6. The Syntactic Representation of Number

Still another prediction of our approach is that bare numeral modifiers, which we take to be licensed in adult English by a null plural determiner, will be either absent or different in nature in Japanese and child English. Again, the prediction appears to be borne out. As is well-known, Japanese numerals with plural NPs take the form of numeral classifiers, rather than prenominal modifiers of the English type. For example, in (18), the English phrase, 'three people',

---

7 A similar approach can be applied to the semantics of comparative deletion and subdeletion-with-ellipsis in Japanese and child English. The idea would be that in comparative deletion, for example, `Mary reads more books than John buys' would be interpreted along the lines of, `The number of books that Mary reads is greater than (the number associated with) what John buys'. Here we assume operator movement from direct object position in the *than*-clause, and a discourse-mediated process by which the individual-type variable is understood as a quantity-type variable. (The quantity-type argument in the *matrix* clause might come from a null comparative element, but there would be no way of introducing a quantity-type variable in a DP within the *than*-clause; subcomparison would thus be disallowed.) Another approach would be to interpret this example along the lines of, `Relative to what John buys, Mary reads a lot of books.' Here the *than*-clause would be interpreted as a type of free relative, and related through the discourse to the semantic quantity-argument of an implicit quantifier (`a lot of').

corresponds to the Japanese phrase, 'hito-o san-nin', where *san-nin* is interpreted along the lines of, 'a set of three', and has been argued by Miyagawa (1989) to stand in a predication relation to the NP *hito* `person(s)'.

(18) Mary-wa hito-(tati)-o san-nin miru
Mary-top person-(PL)-acc 3-CL see
`Mary sees three person(s)'

As discussed by Miyagawa (1989), Greenberg (1972) has observed that numeral classifier systems (with optional plural marking) and prenominal number modifiers (with obligatory plural marking) stand in complementary distribution to one another across the world's languages. A language may have one, or neither, but not both. (Notice that plural-marking is strictly optional in Japanese, as illustrated in 18.) In light of the present discussion, this generalization may again be related to parametric variation in the way degree and quantity expressions are syntactically realized within the NP/DP system.

Cazden (1968) has also examined the use of plural marking in the longitudinal transcripts of spontaneously produced English from three children studied by Brown (1973). Cazden reports that all three children mastered the obligatoriness of plural marking in nouns preceded by a numeral fairly early. Yet, with semantically plural NPs not preceded by a numeral or 'plural' quantifier, the children were still using plural marking only about half the time at the end of their transcripts (ages 4;1, 2;3, 3;6). In all of the cases reported, plural marking was obligatory in adult English. These findings suggest to us that children treat bare numeral modifiers, not as specifiers of a null plural D^o, but rather as plural determiners in their own right. Semantically plural NPs in adult English always occur with a null D^o that forces overt plural marking on the N^o. The children, it would seem, either use bare NPs or assume a null D^o that imposes no morphological requirements on the N^o.

7. Conclusions

In this paper we have demonstrated a striking parallelism between Japanese and child English in the syntactic representation of degree- and quantity-type arguments. We have argued that in adult

English the syntactic representation of degree and quantity is mediated by null determiners that are plausibly absent from the D^0 inventories of Japanese and child English. This hypothesis is supported by evidence from subcomparatives, *wh*-questions of degree, degree phrases with APs, bare numeral modifiers with NPs, and plural marking on semantically plural NPs.

Our findings support Cresswell's contention that degree- and quantity-type arguments are semantically and syntactically distinct from individual-type arguments. Moreover, if the differences we have observed between adult English versus Japanese and child English are all plausibly derived from a small difference in the determiner system of these languages, then this result lends support to the view that parametric variation (and thus language-specific syntactic knowledge) should be understood in terms of the lexically encoded properties of functional categories (cf. Borer 1984; Pica 1987; Chomsky 1991, 1993; Hyams 1994). Such a view contrasts with the widely held `switchbox' model of parameters. Thus, we believe that parallel research in comparative syntax and child language acquisition holds the potential to provide important insights into both Universal Grammar and language-specific syntactic knowledge.

References

Abney, Steven Paul. 1987. *The English noun phrase in its sentential aspect*. Doctoral dissertation, MIT.

Borer, Hagit. 1984. *Parametric syntax: Case studies in Semitic and Romance languages*. Dordrecht: Foris.

Bresnan, Joan. 1972. Theory of complementation in English syntax. Doctoral dissertation, MIT. (New York: Garland, 1979.)

Cazden, Courtney. 1968. The acquisition of noun and verb inflections. *Child Development* 39.433-448.

Chomsky, Noam. 1977. On *wh*-movement. *Formal Syntax*, ed. by Peter Culicover, Thomas Wasow, and Adrian Akmajian. New York: Academic Press.

Chomsky, Noam. 1991. Some notes on economy of derivation and representation. *Principles and parameters in comparative grammar,* ed. by Robert Freidin. Canbridge, MA: MIT Press.

Chomsky, Noam. 1993. A minimalist program for linguistic theory. *The view from Building 20: Essays in honor of Sylvain Bromberger*, ed. by Ken Hale and Samuel Jay Keyser, 1-52. Cambridge, MA: MIT Press.

Corver, Norbert. 1990. *The syntax of left branch extractions.* Doctoral dissertaion, Tilburg University.

Crain, Stephen, and Cecile McKee. 1985. Acquisition of structural restrictions on anaphora. *Proceedings of NELS* 16. Amherst, MA: GLSA.

Cresswell, Max J. 1976. The semantics of degree. *Montague Grammar*, ed. by Barbara Partee, 261-292. New York: Academic Press.

Fukui, Naoki. 1986. *A theory of category projection and its applications.* Doctoral dissertation, MIT.

Greenberg, Joseph. 1972. Numeral classifiers and substantival number: Problems in the genesis of a linguistic type. *Working Papers on Language Universals* 9.1-39.

Grimshaw, Jane. 1987. Subdeletion. *Linguistic Inquiry* 18.659-669.

Heim, Irene. 1985. Notes on comparatives and related matters. UT-Austin ms.

Hoekstra, Teun, Charlotte Koster, and Tom Roeper. 1992. Left-branch violations in child grammar. Paper presented at the 17th Annual Boston University Conference on Language Development.

Hyams, Nina. 1994. The underspecification of functional categories in early grammar. Paper presented at the Great Britain Child Language Seminar, Bangor, Wales, 27-29 March 1994.

Ishii, Yasuo. 1991. *Operators and empty categories in Japanese.* Doctoral dissertation, University of Connecticut.

Kikuchi, A. 1989. Comparative deletion in Japanese. Yamagata University ms.

Miyagawa, Shigeru. 1989. *Structure and case marking in Japanese.* Syntax and semantics vol. 22. San Diego: Academic Press.

Moltmann, Friederike. 1993. *Coordination and comparatives.* Doctoral disseration, MIT.

Pinkham, Jesse. 1982. *The formation of comparative clauses in French and English.* Bloomington, IN: Indiana University Linguistics Club.

Snyder, William & Dolon Das. In preparation. The syntactic representation of degree and number in children's English: Evidence for delayed parametric learning. Cambridge, MA: MIT ms.

Townsend, David J. 1974. Children's comprehension of comparative forms. *Journal of Experimental Child Psychology* 18.293-303.

Townsend, David J. and M. Erb. 1975. Children's strategies for interpreting complex comparative questions. *Journal of Child Language* 2.271-277.

Von Stechow, Arnim. 1984. Comparing semantic theories of comparison. *Journal of Semantics* 3.1-79.

Comparative Progressives and Bare Plural Subjects

KARINA WILKINSON
Ben Gurion University/Cornell University

In this paper, I will present an analysis of bare plural subjects of progressive sentences. I am interested in accounting for the data in (1) and (2).

1) Dogs are barking
2) Californians are exercising more (these days)

In (1), the bare plural subject of the progressive sentence has only an existential interpretation, and in (2), a progressive sentence that also contains an adverbial comparative, the bare plural gets only a generic interpretation. Carlson (1977) first observed the behavior of bare plurals in sentences such as (2), calling them comparative progressives. The contrast in (1) and (2) is problematic for recent theories of bare plural subjects such as Diesing's (1992) and Kratzer's (1989), assuming following Carlson that progressivized VPs are stage-level. Kratzer and Diesing predict both interpretations for bare plural subjects of stage-level predicates, the generic or the existential, but not all progressive sentences have both interpretations.

Another property of comparatives that I discuss is the the possibility of progressivizing certain stative verbs in the presence of an adverbial comparative. *Resemble* normally doesn't occur in the progressive:

3) *John is resembling his father,

but (4) is ok. Sentence (4) is taken from Zucchi (1993), who attributes the observation to Leech (1971).

4) John is resembling his father more and more

Notice that in this construction a bare plural subject gets only a generic interpretation.

5) Boys are resembling their fathers more and more

First, to account for (2), I discuss the tendency of quantified NPs to take scope over the comparative operator and argue that on a theory such as Diesing's, the generic interpretation of the bare plural in (2) is expected. Then, I present two ways of capturing the existential only reading of the bare plural in (1), one pragmatic and the other structural. Finally, I offer an account of the generic only reading of *boys* in (5) and consider some implications for Zucchi's analysis of aspect shift.

1. Generic Bare Plurals in Comparative Progressives

In this section, I want to explain how the presence of the comparative triggers the generic interpretation of the bare plural even in progressive sentences. I treat the comparative as a sentential operator which in (2) makes a comparison to an implicit past time interval. I will show that the comparative gets narrower scope than a quantified NP in subject position (cf. Larson, 1988).

First, I assume a syntactic approach such as the one proposed in Bresnan (1973) where the comparative forms a degree phrase with the *than*-clause, which contains an empty operator, as in (6). To interpret the sentence, the degree phrase is given scope, as in (7). Then the AP, *tall* to degree d_i is copied where it is missing in the *than*-clause in (8).

6) a. Felix is taller than Max is

b.

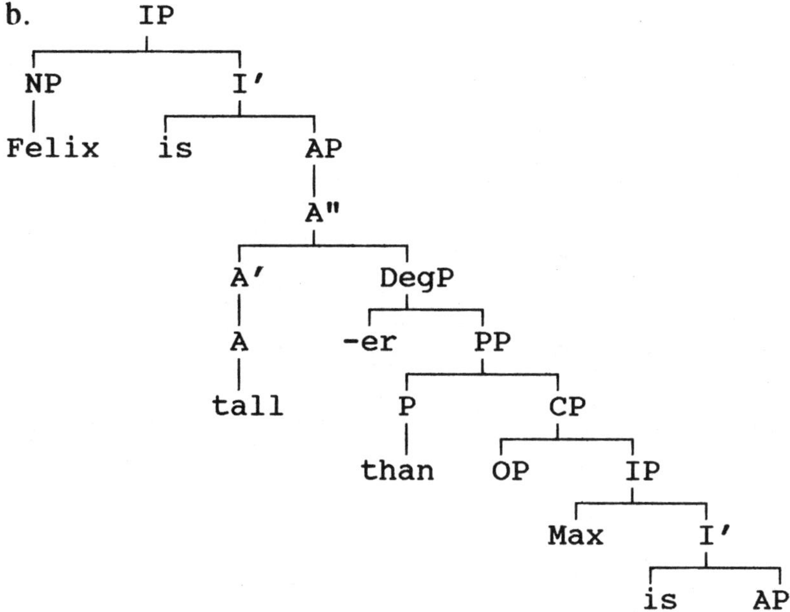

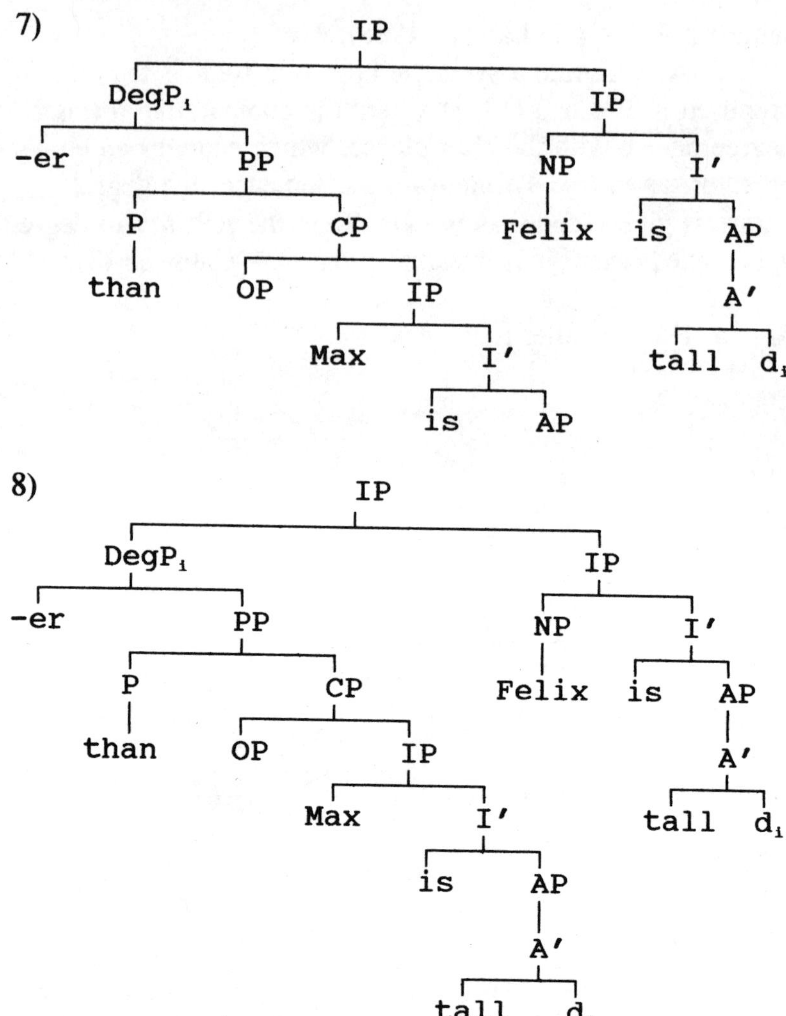

The *-er* introduces existential quantification over the degree predicate given by the matrix clause and compares it with the degree given by the *than*-clause. The empty operator is understood as a definite descriptor over degrees. So, (8) is translated as in (9).

9) ∃ d'[Felix is d'-tall & d' > the d [Max is d-tall]]

(9) says there is a degree, d' such that Felix is tall to degree d' and d' is greater than the degree d to which Max is tall. I assume that "x is d'-tall" expresses x's exact height, though this is not necessary.

Quantified NPs in a comparative take wide scope with respect to the degree phrase (this is also argued in, eg. Larson (1988)). If the subject has wide scope with respect to the comparative operator, we get the right interpretation as in (10').

10) Everyone is taller than Max
10') ∀x ∃d'[x is d'-tall & d' > the d [Max is d-tall]]

If the subject has narrow scope as in (11), then depending on the assumptions we make about the semantics of degrees, we may get a funny interpretation. For example, with our assumption that "x is d'-tall" expresses x's exact height, (11) entails that everyone has the same height.

11) ∃ d'[d' > the d [Max is d-tall] & ∀x (x is d'-tall)]

The problem is worse when the subject is *no one* (see also von Stechow, 1984). (12) is translated as in (12').

12) No one is taller than Max
12') not(∃y (person (y) & ∃d'[d' > the d [Max is d-tall]
& y is d'-tall]))

The translation in (13) is wrong, where *no one* is given narrow scope with respect to the comparative, since (13) is trivially true, as long as there are other things besides people that can be measured for height. There will be many degrees of tallness that do not reflect anyone's height.

13) ∃d'[d' > the d [Max is d-tall] & not(∃y person(y) &
(y is d'-tall)

It should be clear then that a quantified subject gets wide scope with respect to the comparative operator.

Similarly, a quantified NP in the *than*-clause must take scope over the comparative, as has been observed by Hoeksema (1983) (for NP comparatives), Heim (1985), Larson (1988).

14) Todd exercised more than everyone else did

14') $\forall y\ \exists d'$[d' > the d [y exercised d-much] & Todd exercised d'-much]

15) $\exists d'$[d' > the d [$\forall y$ (y exercised d-much)] & Todd exercised d'-much]

(15), with narrow scope for *everyone*, presupposes that everyone has the same height.

In general, the interpretation is straightforward if the quantifier has wide scope. So, whatever it is about the comparative that forces the wide scope reading for quantifiers will do so also in the case of bare plural subjects as in (16).

16) Californians are running more

16') GEN californian(x) [$\exists$d[d > the d' [x used to run d'-much] & x is running d-much]]

It follows on Diesing's mapping hypothesis that bare plural subjects get a generic interpretation. They adjoin to IP, outside the scope of *-er* at LF. Scoping the bare plural results in the generic interpretation, since material from such an adjoined position will be mapped to the restrictor of a generic operator. Thus we get the representation in (16'), not (17).

17) a. $\exists$d [d > the d' [GEN californian(x) [x used to run d'-much]] & GEN californian(x) [x is running d-much]]

b. $\exists$d [$\exists$Y (californian(Y) & Y are running d-much) & d > the d'[$\exists$X (calif(X) & X used to run d'-much)]]

If we try to give the bare plural a narrow scope existential reading, we end up with a translation as in (17b). If (17b) were the translation, then we predict that (16) would be true if a few exercise fanatics run alot more than they used to, but the majority of Californians run less.

I have been assuming that the bare plural is interpreted distributively. The representation in (17b) allows also a collective interpretation, but, in general, plurals are not interpreted collectively under the scope of the comparative, even for predicates that allow a collective interpretation. A sentence, such as *Dogs weigh more than cats*, does not involve a comparison between some total weight a group of dogs has and the total weight of some group of cats. A more complete discussion of collective readings is outside the scope of this paper.

We have seen that the generic interpretation of the bare plural subject of (2) follows from the behavior of quantified noun phrases in comparative sentences and Diesing's mapping hypothesis.

2. Existential bare plurals in progressives

In this section I offer two accounts of (1), one I will call pragmatic and the other structural. The pragmatic account follows a suggestion of Diesing's for certain stage-level predicates that allow only an existential interpretation of a bare plural subject The structural account relies on Chierchia's (1992) mapping hypothesis.

A number of researchers (e.g. Landman (1992)) have analyzed the progressive as a relation between an event and sets of events denoted by the VP, $\lambda x.\lambda e.PROG(e, VP(x))$. Kratzer argues that stage-level predicates have an event argument which is external, so progressives count as stage-level, which is consistent with Carlson's classification of them. Kratzer also argues that since the external argument of a stage-level predicate is the event argument, the subject of a stage-level predicate is internal to the VP. According to Diesing, a bare plural subject that is in SPEC of IP at S-structure and has a trace in the VP may be mapped either into a restrictive clause of an unselective quantifier or generic operator or it may lower to the VP-internal position, in which case it is mapped into the nuclear scope where it is bound by existential closure.

18) Mapping Hypothesis (Diesing, 1992:15)
Material from VP is mapped into the nuclear scope.
Material from IP is mapped into a restrictive clause

But, as I have said, this makes the wrong prediction for progressive sentences, since it allows both a generic interpretation and an existential interpretation for bare plural subjects of sentences like (1), which only have an existential interpretation.

Diesing herself suggests as an explanation for why we get only the existential reading with progressives, "The progressive aspect is an indicator of the stage-level Infl..., which selects stage-level predicates." (Diesing 1992:44). But it is not clear how this solves the problem, since stage-level predicates that allow a generic interpretation also have a stage-level Infl.

19) $[_{IP}$ Firemen$_i$ $[_{I'}$ $[_{stage\ Infl}$ be $]$ $[_{VP}$ t_i $[_{V'}$ V available $]]]]$

The existential reading is allowed for (19) by the possibility of reconstructing the NP *firemen* into the VP, and the generic interpretation arises if the NP is left in its SPEC of IP position. As I understand her, there is no change in the type of Infl to get the generic interpretation.

There is another line that Diesing could take. To see

that, let us consider Vlach's (1993) arguments that progressives are locative statives. I will propose that the behavior of bare plural subjects supports his claim.

One of Vlach's main argument that progressives are locative statives, comes from their behavior with *when*-clauses. If the matrix clause contains a non-stative verb, a *when*-clause is interpreted as occuring just before the matrix.

20) a. Mary left when John arrived
    b. Mary ran when John arrived

In (20a) and (20b), the arriving takes place immediately before the leaving and the running. If there is a locative stative predicate in the matrix, e.g. *be at work* in (21a), the time of matrix clause must be simultaneous with the *when* clause:

21) a. Betsy was at work when Allen sold the car.
    b. Mary was working when Allen arrived

Vlach notes that when the matrix clause is in the progressive, e.g. *was working* in (21b), the working is also understood as simultaneous with the arrival.[1]

What I want to point out is that there is further support for his claim in the behavior of bare plural subjects, which with locative statives also get only an existential interpretation, as in (22).

---

[1] Vlach also finds a difference between a non-locative stative, such as *Betsy was angry*, and locative statives. With a predicate like *be angry*, a *when*-clause is understood as causing the anger.

Vlach also notes that progressives were historically locative statives. In earlier stages of English, the progressive was preceded by a preposition, *at* or *on*, later reduced to *a* as in *John was ahunting*.

22) Dogs are on the lawn

One could extend the pragmatic solution that Diesing gives for locative sentences to progressive sentences. Diesing discusses embedded locative sentences in Dutch. She accounts for the ungrammaticality of bare plural subjects in constructions such as (23) pragmatically. As has been discussed by Reuland (1988) and Rullman (1989) among others, in Dutch (or certain dialects of Dutch) bare plural subjects in locative sentences are not allowed without the particle *er*. When they do occur with the particle, they only have an existential interpretation.

23) a. *Fred denkt dat koeien op het dak liggen
Fred thinks that cows on the roof lie
b. *Gen_x [x is a cow] x is on the roof

Diesing generates a structure as in (23b), but she states, "this generic interpretation is pragmatically incompatible with the locative predicate *on the roof*, leading to the judgment of ungrammaticality" (Diesing, 1992:82). But, it is not clear why we want a pragmatic solution for just these cases and a syntactic solution elsewhere in the analysis of the stage/individual contrast.

An alternative to Diesing's theory is offered in recent work by Chierchia. He argues that there is an implicit generic operator that may be the specifier of an Aspect Phrase. Chierchia suggests that the head of the Aspect Phrase is a habitual morpheme that carries an agreement feature requiring the presence of the GEN operator in its SPEC:

24) S-str: $[_{\text{AspP}}$ GEN $[_{\text{Asp'}}$ $[_{\text{Asp}}$ Hab $]$ VP $]]$.

Chierchia presents a mapping hypothesis slightly different from Diesing's. He argues that at LF, an adverb of quantification, including the generic operator, is sister to the IP, VP or small clause that constitutes the nuclear scope of the adverb. "Adverbs of quantification select their scope via LF adjunction" (Chierchia, 1992:23). So in addition to the type of structures that Diesing allows, Chierchia allows structures as in (25) to (27), where what precedes the adverb is interpreted as being in the restrictor of the quantifier and what follows it, in some cases an IP, is interpreted as the nuclear scope.

25) LF: $[_{IP}$ NP ... ADV IP]
restrictor nuclear scope

26) a. A bird flies
a.' $[_{IP}$ a bird$_i$ [GEN $[_{VP}$ t_i flies]]]
a." $GEN_{x,s}$ [bird(x) & C(x,s)][fly(x,s)]

27) a. A computer routes a modern plane
a.' $[_{IP}$ a plane GEN $[_{IP}$ a computer routes t_i]
a." $Most_y$, plane(y), $\exists$x [computer(x) & route(x,y)

The LFs in (26a') and (27a') correspond to the (a) sentences, which are interpreted as in (26a") and (27a"), respectively. In contrast, for Diesing, only the VP is mapped to the nuclear scope, which forces her to use a reconstruction rule for those bare plural subjects such as in *a computer* in (27a) which is mapped to the nuclear scope and has an existential reading.

Since PROG is also an aspectual operator, it too is found in the SPEC of the aspect phrase. To account for the fact that *dogs* in (1) has only the existential interpretation, we need to say, in addition to Chierchia's claim that GEN is in SPEC of AspP, that PROG and GEN are in complementary distribution in the SPEC of AspP. This accounts for why there is no generic interpretation of bare plural subjects of sentences such as (1). A bare plural subject of a progressive sentence will only have an existential interpretation, since the occurrence of the GEN operator in Spec of AspP is blocked by the presence of the PROG operator.

However, since GEN can also be adjoined to IP, movement of the bare plural subject by QR to adjoin to the left of GEN must be blocked, otherwise we could derive a generic interpretation for the bare plural in (1). Perhaps, this movement could be blocked since nothing is forcing it.[2]

The account of (2) given in section 1 can also be made compatible with this account of (1) by assuming that an NP that has undergone QR must be mapped into a restrictor.[3]

3. *More and more* and bare plural subjects

In this section, I begin to explore the question of how to get a generic interpretation of the bare plural in (5), since bare plural subjects of progressive sentences normally have an existential interpretation, and the iterated *more and more*, as I will show, is not amenable to an analysis like that given in section 1 for the simple comparative, *more*.

---

[2] If NPs do not move unless they have to, then we lose certain ambiguities that arise with stage-level predicates that are not locative or progressive. The ambiguity of bare plural subjects of these predicates can be derived since the GEN operator may occur in either the SPEC of AspP or be adjoined to IP. The former case yields the generic interpretation and the latter the existential. What is unexplained, however, are ill-behaved objects, eg. in (27a). Bare plurals in object position are expected to only have an existential interpretation, contrary to fact. I do not have an account of the behavior of the object NPs.

[3] I may have to return to the pragmatic account for (1), depending on whether sentences, such as (i) and (ii) can be analyzed as covert comparatives or not. I leave this for future research.
i) Californians are exercising these days
ii) After relief aid, people are eating bread again
Thanks to Anita Mittwoch for pointing (ii) out to me.

First notice that *more and more* differs in its ability to take a *than* phrase.

28) *Sue is exercising more and more than Bill (is)

(28) shows that *more and more* does not undergo the same kind of reconstruction as was discussed in section 1.

Second, consider Zucchi's truth conditions for (4) paraphrased in (29). I refer the reader to Zucchi's paper for discussion of the use of precision states in the analysis of the comparative.

29) An event of John's resembling his father more and more is an event which is the sum of (at least) two subevents e' and e" occurring at successive times such that e' and e" are events of John's resembling his father for some precision states s and s', and e' is more a resembling of John to his father than e". (Zucchi 1993:33)

Note that the times at which the subevents occur, say t' and t" are contained in the time, t, at which the event occurs.

The simple comparative and the iterated one differ in this respect. Consider (30) containing the simple comparative. It compares a future time to the present.

30) Sue will be exercising more next year
31) John will be walking more and more

In contrast, (31) compares subevents of an event occuring at a future time interval, where the times of the subevents are contained in the future time, suggesting that the scope of *more and more* is narrower than Tense. Thus, it is possible that the scope of *more and more* is narrower than the subject NP and does not force the subject to undergo QR.

So, if *more and more* does not force *boys* in (5) to take wide scope as was suggested for the comparatives in section

1, how does *boys* in (5) get a generic reading? I suspect that the the generic reading arises because *more and more* involves implicit generic quantification.

Zucchi suggests that (4) is made true by the existence of at least two subevents of John's resembling his father, **each** (sequential) pair of which reflects an increase in the amount of resembling.[4] Even when we make the universal quantifier overt as in (32), I do not think the sentence is false, because on a few days there is no increase.[5]

32) Sue is running more and more each day

I would like to suggest that the implicit universal in *more and more* is instead a generic operator. The truth conditions look like what Carlson has suggested for his G operator, e.g. "if Bill smokes, then there have to be two or more occasions on which Bill is (actually) smoking" (Carlson 1977:275b), and like Carlson's G operator, it is (part of) a VP adverb, rather than a sentential operator as discussed, e.g. in Wilkinson (1991). From the covert presence of the generic operator in the meaning of *more and more*, we derive the generic reading of *boys* in (5).

However, such an analysis depends on giving *more and more* scope outside PROG, otherwise the bare plural may incorrectly get an existential interpretation. Thus, we lose Zucchi's explanation of why PROG can apply to a predicate containing the stative verb, *resemble*. Zucchi (1993) following Dowty (1979) argues that the progressive only

---

[4] Since when there are only two subevents the truth conditions are similar to the truth conditions of the simple comparative *more*, I think there should be at least three subevents, representing two increases in the amount of resembling.

[5] This does not seem to be the same kind of contextual restriction as we normally find with universals. In (32), it is not that I consider only a certain set of relevant days.

occurs with interval predicates, roughly, those predicates that are true at an interval without being true at every moment within the interval. He shows that for a stative verb, P, such as *resemble*, for all x and I, if *P(x)* is true at I, then *P(x)* is true at any moment in I, and thus statives are non-interval predicates. If we apply *more and more* to such a predicate, we get an interval predicate which may progressivize.

However, if I am right about the implicit generic quantification of *more and more*, and the result of applying *more and more* to a predicate is what Dowty calls a "generic predicate," then PROG does not apply to *more and more* (P). Dowty's account of the progressive extends to generic predicates, since generic sentences, if true of an interval, are true of every moment in the interval, preventing them from occurring under PROG.

So, if PROG applies directly to *resemble his father*, the predicate must undergo "aspect shift," which I will assume is the normal shift that statives undergo in the progressive, that is, they become inchoative.[6] *More and more*, then operates on the progressivized predicate.

Space limitations prevent me from doing justice to the problems raised in this section, and further implications for Zucchi's analysis are left for future research.

In conclusion,[*] I have tried to show that a correct theory of the interpretation of bare plural subjects in English must include a treatment of aspect and operators such as the comparative.

---

[6] Perhaps that is what is being marked overtly by *get* in sentences such as *It is getting hotter and hotter*.

[*] This paper was presented at the Israeli Theoretical Linguistics Association Tenth Annual Conference. Thanks to Roger Schwarzschild, Fred Landman, Anita Mittwoch, Tova Rapoport, Susan Rothstein, and Nomi Shir for comments.

References

Bresnan, J. 1973. Syntax of the Comparative Clause Construction in English. LI 4.275-343.

Carlson, G. 1977. Reference to Kinds in English. PhD. dissertation. UMass.

Chierchia, G. 1992. Individual Level Predicates as Inherent Generics. manuscript. Cornell University.

Diesing, M. 1992. *Indefinites*. Cambridge, Massachusetts: MIT Press.

Dowty, D. 1979. *Word Meaning and Montague Grammar*. Dordrecht: Reidel.

Heim, I. 1985. Notes on Comparatives and Related Matters. manuscript. UTexas.

Hoeksema, J. 1983. Negative Polarity and the Comparative. NLLT, 1.403-434.

Kratzer, A. 1989. Stage and Individual Level Predicates. manuscript. UMass.

Landman, F. 1991. The Progressive. Natural Language Semantics, 1.1-32.

Larson, R. 1988. Scope and Comparatives. Linguistics and Philosophy 11.1-26.

Leech, G. 1971. *Meaning and the English Verb*. London: Longman.

Reuland, E. 1988. Indefinite Subjects. Proceedings of NELS 18, 375-394. GLSA

Rullman, H. 1989. Indefinite Subjects in Dutch. manuscript. UMass

von Stechow, A. 1984. Comparing Semantic Theories of Comparison. Journal of Semantics.

Vlach, F. 1993. Temporal Adverbs, Tenses, and the Perfect. Linguistics and Philosophy 16.231-284.

Wilkinson, K. 1991. Studies in the Semantics of Generic Noun Phrases. PhD. dissertation. UMass, Amherst.

Zucchi, A. 1993. Aspect Shift. manuscript. U of Illinois, Champaign-Urbana.

Index